HISTORICAL DIALOGUE ANALYSIS

Pragmatics & Beyond New Series

Editor:
Andreas H. Jucker
(Justus Liebig University, Giessen)

Associate Editors:
Jacob L. Mey
(Odense University)

Herman Parret
(Belgian National Science Foundation, Universities of Louvain and Antwerp)

Jef Verschueren
(Belgian National Science Foundation, University of Antwerp)

Editorial Address:
Justus Liebig University Giessen, English Department
Otto-Behaghel-Strasse 10, D-35394 Giessen, Germany
e-mail: andreas.jucker@anglistik.uni-giessen.de

Editorial Board:
Shoshana Blum-Kulka (*Hebrew University of Jerusalem*)
Chris Butler (*University College of Ripon and York*)
Jean Caron (*Université de Poitiers*); Robyn Carston (*University College London*)
Bruce Fraser (*Boston University*); John Heritage (*University of California at Los Angeles*)
David Holdcroft (*University of Leeds*); Sachiko Ide (*Japan Women's University*)
Catherine Kerbrat-Orecchioni (*University of Lyon 2*)
Claudia de Lemos (*University of Campinas, Brasil*); Marina Sbisà (*University of Trieste*)
Emanuel Schegloff (*University of California at Los Angeles*)
Paul O. Takahara (*Kobe City University of Foreign Studies*)
Sandra Thompson (*University of California at Santa Barbara*)
Teun A. Van Dijk (*University of Amsterdam*); Richard Watts (*University of Bern*)

66
Andreas H. Jucker, Gerd Fritz and Franz Lebsanft (eds)
Historical Dialogue Analysis

HISTORICAL DIALOGUE ANALYSIS

Edited by

ANDREAS H. JUCKER
Justus Liebig University, Giessen

GERD FRITZ
Justus Liebig University, Giessen

FRANZ LEBSANFT
Ruhr University, Bochum

JOHN BENJAMINS PUBLISHING COMPANY
AMSTERDAM/PHILADELPHIA

The paper used in this publication meets the minimum requirements of American National Standard for Information Sciences — Permanence of Paper for Printed Library Materials, ANSI Z39.48-1984.

Library of Congress Cataloging-in-Publication Data

Historical dialogue analysis / edited by Andreas H. Jucker, Gerd Fritz, Franz Lebsanft.
   p.   cm. -- (Pragmatics & beyond, ISSN 0922-842X ; new ser. 66)
  Includes bibliographical references and index.
  1. Dialogue analysis. I. Jucker, Andreas H. II. Fritz, Gerd, 1943- . III. Lebsanft, Franz. IV. Series.
P95.455.H57   1999
401'.41--dc21   99-31509
ISBN 90 272 5080 4 (Eur.) / 1 55619 944 9 (US) (alk. paper)   CIP

© 1999 – John Benjamins B.V.
No part of this book may be reproduced in any form, by print, photoprint, microfilm, or any other means, without written permission from the publisher.

John Benjamins Publishing Co. • P.O.Box 75577 • 1070 AN Amsterdam • The Netherlands
John Benjamins North America • P.O.Box 27519 • Philadelphia PA 19118-0519 • USA

Contents

Preface	vii
Historical Dialogue Analysis: Roots and Traditions in the Study of the Romance Languages, German and English *Andreas H. Jucker, Gerd Fritz, and Franz Lebsanft*	1
Ritual Levelling: The Balance between the Eristic and the Contractual Motive in Hostile Verbal Encounters in Medieval Romance and Early Modern Drama *Marcel M. H. Bax*	35
The Pragmatic Form of Religious Controversies around 1600: A Case Study in the Osiander vs. Scherer & Rosenbusch Controversy *Thomas Gloning*	81
The Use of Dialogue in Early German Pamphlets: On the Constitution of Public Involvement in the Reuchlin-Pfefferkorn Controversy *Johannes Schwitalla*	111
The Polite Answer in Pre-modern German Conversation Culture *Manfred Beetz*	139
Minnegespräche: Die galante Konversation in der frühen deutschen Lyrik *Hannes Kästner*	167
On the Fringes of Interaction: The Dawn-Song as a "Linguistic Routine" of Parting *Thomas Honegger*	189
Refugiate in a strange countrey: Learning English through Dialogues in the 16th Century *Richard J. Watts*	215
Dialogues in Late Medieval and Early Modern English Medical Writing *Irma Taavitsainen*	243

A Late Medieval French Bargain Dialogue (*Pathelin* II), Or: Further Remarks on the History of Dialogue Forms
    Franz Lebsanft   269

Modifying Pragmatic Force: Hedges in Early Modern English Dialogues
    Jonathan Culpeper and Merja Kytö   293

So he says to her, he says, "Well," he says ...: Multiple Dialogue Introducers from a Historical Perspective
    Anne Herlyn   313

Que fais, Adam?: Questions and Seduction in the *Jeu d'Adam*
    Angela Schrott   331

Dialoge im Rechtsprotokoll: Ein Wetzlarer Erbstreit a. 1309 und die Entstehung einer neuen Textsorte
    Hans Ramge   371

Court Records and Cartoons: Reflections of Spontaneous Dialogue in Early Romance Texts
    Peter Koch   399

Dialogue and Violence: The Inca Atahualpa meets Fray Vicente de Valverde (Cajamarca, Peru, 16 November, 1532)
    Wulf Oesterreicher   431

Index   465

Preface

The papers of this volume took their origin in a conference that we organized at the conference center of the Justus Liebig University in Rauischholzhausen from March 12 to 15, 1997. It had been our aim for that conference to bring together the most eminent scholars specializing in historical dialogue analysis in German, English and the Romance languages. At the same time we wanted to keep the conference small enough to avoid parallel sessions and to guarantee a maximum of interaction between the participants. By all accounts the conference turned out to be a success, and we, as conference organizers and editors of this volume, hope that something of the stimulating atmosphere of the conference has carried over into the papers that are included in this volume.

The present volume is more than just the proceedings of the Rauischholzhausen conference. All the papers have been carefully refereed and revised before they were included in this volume. The languages of the conference were English and German. For this volume the papers by Johannes Schwitalla, Manfred Beetz, Peter Koch and Wulf Oesterreicher were translated by Rosemary Bock, Andreas H. Jucker and Sabine Prechter. The papers by Hannes Kästner and Hans Ramge appear in German with English abstracts.

Translation is never an easy exercise, but in these cases we were faced with differences that often went beyond the mere linguistic problems. Researchers from the fields of English, German and Romance studies not only publish in different languages, but according to different academic traditions. They have different ways of expressing themselves, they have their own academic rhetoric, and it is this aspect which is most difficult to translate. In many cases we have opted for a conservative translation strategy that retains some of the rhetoric flavour of the original.

We wish to express our gratitude to several institutions which made both the conference at Rauischholzhausen and this volume possible. In particular we thank the German Science Foundation (*DFG*), which very generously provided travel grants for some of the participants, and to the *Giessener Hochschulgesellschaft* of Justus Liebig University, which provided funds for the organisation of the conference. Our thanks also go to Sabine Prechter for a lot of practical help at the conference and for compiling the index of this volume and Julia Erbe, Britta Hoops, Karin Thönes and Simone Roth for their editorial assistance that included everything from layouting, formatting and proofreading to the checking and double-checking of references, and to Jacob Mey, whose meticulous reading of the entire manuscript saved us from a great number of embarrassing typos and other blunders.

Finally, of course, we want to thank the conference participants and the contributors to this volume for their stimulating contributions and for their cooperation and patience in the production process of this book.

Historical Dialogue Analysis
Roots and Traditions in the Study of the Romance Languages, German and English

Andreas H. Jucker
Justus Liebig University, Giessen

Gerd Fritz
Justus Liebig University, Giessen

Franz Lebsanft
Ruhr University, Bochum

1. Introduction

In essence all language use is dialogic, whether it is written or spoken, whether it is spontaneous or formal. Speakers or writers use language to communicate with some actual, potential or merely fictional addressee or addressees. It is this dialogic nature of language that dialogue analysis is interested in. In a somewhat more restricted sense, dialogue analysis deals with particular forms of dialogue, such as a teacher-student interaction, a dinner table conversation or an interaction during a service encounter.

Until recently dialogue studies were for several reasons restricted to modern languages. Dialogue was considered to be mainly a spoken phenomenon for which no direct evidence was available except for the very immediate past. This meant that dialogue analysts did not concern themselves with any historical data. Similarly, historical linguists did not concern themselves to any great extent with dialogues or the dialogic nature of language. This situation has changed. Historical dialogue analysis has become a legitimate branch of linguistic inquiry, but it is still a very young discipline and it may therefore be presumptuous to talk about the roots and traditions of such a discipline.

However, the current interest in studying dialogic aspects of language from a historical perspective has different sources in older research paradigms, and it is the aim of this introductory chapter to outline the most important of these traditions.

The papers in the present volume use data from the Romance languages, German and English. These three philologies have notably different histories as far as their precursors of historical dialogue analysis are concerned. This paper will therefore try to outline these three traditions in turn and show how they have led to the research in historical dialogue analysis that is currently carried out in these fields and that appears in the papers of this volume.

The fact that scholars working on different languages use different methodologies and ask different research questions even if they are all interested in the dialogic nature of language may be an indication that there has not been sufficient communication between these research traditions. It was the explicit aim of the conference at which earlier versions of the papers in this volume were presented and it is the explicit aim of this volume to counterbalance this situation. There is a great potential for cross-fertilization between the different research traditions. If this volume manages to make scholars aware – or more aware – of what is going on in neighboring fields, it has achieved one of its most important aims.

2. Romance linguistics: The history of spoken language and dialogue analysis

Within the area of Romance linguistics there is no well established discipline called "historical dialogue analysis", with a proved methodology and a well-defined field of research. At this time, there only exist some pioneer studies that can be understood as the first steps in an almost entirely unexplored territory. However, concern with the study of historic dialogues has been prepared by research in neighbouring domains and in different countries with distinct academic backgrounds. In Romance studies, interest in historical dialogue analysis springs from research on the history of spoken language and from the application of modern dialogue analysis to historical data. In our brief survey of the roots and traditions of historical dialogue analysis in Romance linguistics we will start with the research on spoken language, then sketch a rough outline of modern dialogue analysis and finally turn to historical dialogue analysis (a short review of the situation in Romance corpus linguistics is given in Gleßgen/Lebsanft 1997: 4ff.).

2.1. Research on Spoken Language

At the very beginning of historical linguistics, the founders of the discipline, notably Jacob Grimm, showed a great interest in the study of spoken language, which they considered as being the genuine object of the new science (Christmann 1978). Especially Romance philology was inconceivable without the notion of "vulgar Latin", i.e. spoken Latin. Friedrich Diez described the opposition between classical and vulgar Latin in a way that clearly anticipates the concept of diglossia (Ferguson 1959, cf. the bibliography of Fernández 1993, and the history of the term, documented since 1885, Fernández 1995). In fact, Diez (^{5}1882: 1f.) tells us that "popular Latin" *(Volkslatein)* is the "lower variety" of one and the same language, characterized by a more negligent pronunciation, an inclination towards the dissolution of grammatical forms, the frequent use of expressions avoided by (good) writers and, finally, peculiar forms of expressions and constructions. In a diachronic perspective, spoken Latin turned out to be a sort of proto-romance; from a synchronic viewpoint, within the heterogeneous diasystem of a language, it proved to be a substandard variant (cf. Herman 1996: 50f.).

Hence, the general framework of historical Romance linguistics tried to explain the history of successful Romance languages as a long process of language elaboration or cultivation. It showed how initially oral languages conquered the realm of literacy (cf. below). Much later, Helmut Lüdtke (1978) explained in a seminal article the passage from Latin to the vernacular languages as the abandonment of a diglossic situation, where the lower Romance variants took over the scriptural functions of the higher Latin variant. Therefore, most of the historians of individual Romance languages were paradoxically turned away from the study of spoken language. Instead they repeatedly related a sort of "success story" under the general heading "From Spoken Latin to Written French, Italian, Spanish", etc. (for a recent example, cf. the excellent history of French, Lodge 1993). In sum, diachronic research focused on the written language (cf. Ayres-Bennett 1996: 4).

However, interest in the spoken language kept alive in the growing domain of synchronic research, beginning with the neogrammarians, and in close contact with the discipline of applied linguistics, especially the teaching of language (Christmann 1976, Hausmann [ed.] 1983: 2ff.). In the first third of the 20th century, diatopic and diastratic spoken variants, geographical and social dialects, became a favorite topic of Romance linguistics. Investigations initially concentrated on structural "deviations" from the written standard language (Bauche 1920, Frei 1929). But then researchers began to take an interest in the problem of verbal interaction too, based on the so-called "colloquial language", i.e. the language used in everyday talk and situations (Italian: Spitzer 1922, Latin: Hofmann 1926, Beinhauer 1930; cf. Held 1992). A new and solid ground for the study of spoken and written language was prepared by the late Ludwig Söll. His *Gesprochenes und geschriebenes Französisch* ("Spoken and written French", Söll 1974) constitutes a landmark in Romance linguistic studies (cf. Hausmann 1975, Söll ^{3}1985), which unfortunately has gained very little attention outside the discipline. Söll's second chapter, "Basic Notions" (1974: 11-43), introduced the important twofold distinction between *code phonique* and *code graphique* on the one side, and *code parlé* and *code écrit* on the other side. The first dichotomy concerns the medial, phonic or graphic realization of a message, the second dichotomy the conceptualization of language, the circumstances and linguistic means by which a speaker conveys his message. Of course, spontaneous oral language is primarily realized in the phonic medium, whereas planned written language is normally delivered in the graphic medium. Nevertheless, oral texts can be reproduced graphically, and written texts (as this introduction) may be read to a listener.

In the same chapter, the author discusses the relations between the conceptualization of language and other domains of linguistic organization. Fundamental to our purpose is the strong affinity between orality and dialogue. Following Abercrombie (1963), Söll (1974: 24ff., 37ff.) shows not only that dialogue is the "basic category" of spoken language, but outlines also a "typology" of orality, i.e. an elementary draft of textual genres or forms of dialogue (normal face-to-face talk, telephone conversation, TV conversation, etc.) on the basis of some basic features (actuality, proximity, immediacy, directness, reciprocity). The subsequent chapters explore first "general" features of orality and then specific traits of spoken French. Important, from the viewpoint of dialogue analysis, is the ample examination (Söll 1974: 132ff.) of the so-called "sequence-signals" (Fries 1952: 248ff.) or "*Gliederungssignale*" (Gülich 1970), i.e. pause fillers and discourse markers that help to arrange turns and turn-taking (cf. subsequently also Schiffrin 1987 and Jucker/Ziv 1998).

Very soon, the enormous gap between contemporary spoken and written French, described by Söll (1974), led to a growing interest in the history of spoken French. Obviously, the synchronic facts required a diachronic explanation. The polemic debate, which concentrated on the archaism or modernism of modern spoken French (cf. the survey by Hausmann 1992), was certainly premature, but provoked increasingly penetrating studies on the subject (cf. also the review article of Holtus/Schweickard 1991).

Helmut Stimm (1980) published three important contributions to the Congress of the German Romanicists at Saarbrücken which illustrate very well the issues that dominated the current discussions at that moment (Ernst 1980, Hausmann 1980, Schmitt 1980). Obviously, the main concern was the data problem. Ernst lists types of possible sources (authentic material, pragmatic and fictional texts, mainly teaching books, direct speech in drama and novel), while Schmitt and Hausmann evaluate the significance of early textbooks and drama for the reconstruction of spoken French. Ernst (1980: 4) announced a new, partial edition of the famous *Journal d'Héroard*, the diary of the personal physician to the later Louis XIII, who recorded as meticulously as possible each and every utterance of the little dauphin. This important edition was published five years later, preceded by a dense introduction to the spoken language of the highborn child. However, Ernst's excellent description concentrates on phonetico-phonological, morphological, syntactical and lexical phenomena (Ernst 1985; cf. Ernst 1989). Since that time, it seems that this important pattern of diachronic research will keep within the limits of the examination of "non-conventional" structural features of French (Ernst 1995).

The diachronic study of spoken French took for granted the supposition that oral elements could be found in written texts only as quotations; more recently, scholars assume that the written records of earlier periods of a language reflect orality in a more general manner. Fleischman (1990: 21f.) holds that "Old French is very much a spoken language, the communicative instrument of a fundamentally oral culture, adapted – sometimes better, sometimes worse – to writing". Selig (1997: 215-218), using the theoretical framework by Koch and Oesterreicher (1990; cf. below), proposes to interpret this statement as the characterization of medieval French as an "unelaborated" language. Medieval documents in their totality would then reflect the activity of spontaneous verbal interaction more than modern texts do. This assumption rejoins, then, the general conceptions about the history of languages, but focuses not so much on the achievements in the conquest of literacy as on its deficiencies. Outside French studies, investigation of early modern Spanish texts written by so-called *semicultos* has shown the fruitfulness of the approach (Oesterreicher 1994).

Koch and Oesterreicher (1990: 5-17), two of the contributors to the present volume, have very successfully proposed to modify and develop some of Ludwig Söll's basic concepts. In general terms, they accept the idea of a twofold classification of linguistic data from the viewpoint of orality and literacy. They insist however – much more than Söll (1974: 17f.) did – on an important difference between the two dichotomies. While the medial opposition "phonic vs. graphic" is a clear-cut dichotomy, the terms of the conceptual opposition "spoken vs. written" represent only the two poles of a large scale.

Koch and Oesterreicher (1990: 8-12) suggest replacing the traditional designations "spoken/written language" by "language of immediacy" (*Nähesprache*) and "language of distance" (*Distanzsprache*). Depending on extra-linguistic conditions, the speaker chooses appropriate linguistic procedures in order to formulate his or her utterance. The more speakers formulate their message under the extra-linguistic conditions of immediacy (private domain, familiarity, emotions, etc.), the more they will use the tools of spoken language. And on the other hand, the more speakers formulate their messages under the conditions of distance (public domain, formality, lack of emotions, etc.), the more they will choose the devices of written language.

Secondly, Koch and Oesterreicher (1990: 6-8) reformulated within the framework of Coseriu's language theory the difference between general and language-specific elements of orality. The typical traits of orality/literacy belong to different levels of linguistic structure; oral features may well be universals or peculiar to a certain language. Most of the dialogic elements of orality are universals, as discourse markers, turn-taking signals, phatic signals, hesitation phenomena, etc. Others, as for instance the omission of the negative particle (*[ne] ... pas*), the omission of the impersonal subject pronoun (*[il] faut*), the loss of the *passé simple*, etc., only belong to French. Within the diasystem of a language, they believe that oral and written language constitute a specific type of variation.

Thus, Koch and Oesterreicher develop a general model which allows to account not only for spoken and written French, but for different languages. Furthermore, they integrate the perspectives of traditional, structural research on spoken language, and of dialogue analysis (cf. below, 2.2), though this latter approach is certainly not their major concern. Finally, they offer a comprehensive view of both the synchronic and diachronic aspect of language (Koch/Oesterreicher 1990: 127-238). In fact, the specificity of oral French (Italian, Spanish, etc.) elements implies their having a history.

2.2. Contemporary French Dialogue Analysis: Subjectivity in Language

Although Hosch ([1895-1897]/1983) is an early and valid attempt to describe French discourse markers within the pattern of Adolf Tobler's today nearly forgotten "syntactical lexicology" (cf. however below, 2.3), Gülich (1970) is legitimately considered a turning point in Modern French studies. In a move out of the paradigm of textlinguistics, the comprehensive description of markers on the basis of an oral corpus opened the doors to the investigation of dialogues in authentic settings. However, the new focus of concern did not lead to a particular methodology of dialogue analysis, but rather integrated the ethnomethodological approach filtered by German studies in this field. As a result, modern dialogue analysis became a well-established discipline with a substantial presence at national and international conferences (Gülich/Kotschi 1985, Dausendschön-Gay/Gülich/Krafft 1991, Hilty 1993).

Parallel developments of linguistic paradigms can be found in France. The starting-point, however, is slightly different, in so far as dialogue analysis in the French style derives from Émile Benveniste's (1966-1974) original concept of subjectivity in language. Antoine Meillet's prize pupil coined the term of "enunciation" (énonciation), subsequently developed by Kerbrat-Orecchioni (1970: 32) as the linguistic means by which the producer of a speech act marks his presence in an utterance (cf. recently also Nølke 1993). Parallel to a flowering structural (cf. especially François 1974) and pragmatical (Ducrot 1972, 1973) investigation of spoken French, Kerbrat-Orecchioni (3 vols.: I ^{3}1998, II ^{2}1994, III ^{2}1998; cf. also Cosnier/Kerbrat-Orecchioni 1987) proposed to analyze dialogues as "verbal interactions", incorporating, thus, the findings above all of Erving Goffman, but also of ethnomethodology, and the ethnography of communication. Kerbrat-Orecchioni set directions for later studies as can be seen from many French contributions to the Paris Congress of the International Association for Dialogue Analysis (Piétri 1997).

In a different context, Eddy Roulet formed the Geneva school of dialogue analysis, which offers a highly elaborated methodology, based on a refined terminology. This methodology includes a somewhat scholastic "standard model", a "formal standard model", and a "revised standard model" (Moeschler 1994). A recent "summa", however, seems to be more open to discussion (Moeschler/Reboul 1996; cf. also Hilty 1993).

2.3. Historical Dialogue Analysis

When, in the early eighties, Franz Lebsanft proposed to present a paper about Old French greeting formulae at a colloquium on dialogue analysis, he was rejected with the argument that this topic was "a bit peripheral" to the discussions of that moment. Even today, diachronic investigations on dialogues are quite marginal in Romance Linguistics. The application of the methodology of modern dialogue analysis to historical data is obviously still in its infancy.

Paradoxically, when in the seventies the controversy about speech act theory led to the beginnings of dialogue analysis, an important paper already dealt with the problem of the historicity of speech acts (Schlieben-Lange/Weydt 1979). Furthermore, Schlieben-Lange (1979) presented a brilliant analysis of the central and indeed sophisticated dialogue in the Old Provençal romance *Flamenca,* using the framework of Gricean conversational principles. This paper was later integrated in a methodological essay on a pragmatic history of speaking (Schlieben-Lange 1983). However, with the noteworthy though somewhat critical exception of Christmann (1986: 14-18), it did not find a great response in the scientific community.

In nearly the same vein, and with explicit reference to Schlieben-Lange (1983), Lebsanft (1988: 144-306) analyzed openings and closings in Old French dialogues, thus showing "the power of greeting" in medieval interaction (cf., alluding to a Hasidic tale, Lebsanft 1988: 270). Kristol (1992) qualifying this monograph as forerunner, examined discourse markers in Late Medieval textbooks, which had already been taken into consideration by Ernst (1980) and Schmitt (1980). Finally, in his important 1987 "habilitation thesis" (Holtus/Schweickard 1991: 551f.) Radtke gave a first synthesis of historical dialogue analysis in Romance studies. Unfortunately he up-dated only the bibliography for the subsequent publication of his book in 1994, so that his findings took advantage of neither Lebsanft (1988) nor Kristol (1992). However, Radtke (1994) remains the first major attempt to integrate the history of dialogue forms into a history of spoken French. Language change is viewed as a change of linguistic techniques in everyday practice.

In France, diachronic research in our domain has not emerged from modern dialogue analysis. Nevertheless, an important current of syntactical investigation can be related to the interest in the history of dialogues. Parallel to modern dialogue analysis, the concept of subjectivity has been used to examine the traces of enunciation in Old French texts. Cerquiglini's *Parole médiévale* (1981) was certainly not an (*a priori* impossible) description of medieval everyday talk (cf. also Lebsanft 1985), but it proposed to tackle the problem as the "representation" of discourse "inscribed" in a narrative text.

An indisputable philological masterpiece is Cerquiglini's analysis of Old French *mar* as a sentential adverb marking the distance of the speaker to the propositional content of his or her utterance (Cerquiglini 1981: 128-245, Cerquiglini 1976). Cerquiglini set directions for further research, being at the centre of a group of investigators of related phenomena, for instance the Old French connector *si* (Marchello-Nizia 1985; cf. Blumenthal 1980a, who is also the author of a monograph of Modern French sentential adverbs, 1980b).

The contributions of Romanicists to this volume show the wide range of objects and methods in this field of historical dialogue analysis. On the basis of Italian and Spanish documentary sources, Peter Koch and Wulf Oesterreicher deal primarily with different aspects of the data problem, while Angela Schrott and Franz Lebsanft examine dialogue structures and dialogue sequences in Old and Middle French literary texts.

Peter Koch aims at describing the situation in which dialogic language of immediacy (cf. above, 2.1.) pervades the graphic medium during the Italian Middle Ages. He makes clear that authentic, documentary orality, i.e. various types of testimonies, depends on a juridical frame, while fictional, mimetical orality (the *iscrizione di San Clemente*) is related to a religious, propagandistic context. In both cases, the participants in the dialogues are shown to be emotional, dissonant or even hostile. Wulf Oesterreicher deals with the echoes that an alleged "real" historic "conversation" has found in historiographic documents. He shows that the "dialogue", previous to the massacre of the Indios, between the Inca Atahualpa and Fray Vicente de Valverde at Cajamarca, Peru, on 16 November 1532 never took place. The hostile meeting between the Inca and the Spanish conquerors has to be understood in the light of the cynical procedure of the *requirimiento*, a formal legal act by which the colonists justified the brutal submission and conversion of the Indios.

Angela Schrott analyzes different types of interrogative acts – as loaded interrogative acts, rhetorical questions, echo questions, and focusing interrogative acts – in the Old French *Jeu d'Adam*. She explains in which manner in this play questions are related to the concept of *curiositas*: The Devil – Diabolus – instigates Adam to ask questions, in order to awaken his desire of knowledge (*cupiditas scientiae*) and thus turn him away from God. Finally, Franz Lebsanft examines the bargain scene of the Middle French farce *Pathelin* with the intention of discussing some of the problems of historical dialogue analysis raised by Fritz (1997). In the diachronic study of dialogue forms, he argues, the object of change should be carefully identified. Thus in the case of sales talk, it is the things a dialogue form helps to talk about which change rather than the verbal interaction itself. Nevertheless, the knowledge about things influences the way in which verbal strategies are accomplished. Therefore, a diachronic analysis needs both a historic knowledge and a knowledge of verbal interaction in order to reconstruct earlier dialogue forms. In the case of the farce it is juridical and didactic texts, i.e. custumals and teaching books, which help us to reconstruct the verbal interaction in its extralinguistic context.

3. German Studies: From the history of spoken German to the evolution of dialogue forms

In the field of German Studies historical dialogue analysis mainly springs from four sources:

3.1. Literary studies

In studies on the history of German literature we find a wealth of observations on the presentation of dialogue in literary texts of earlier periods. Work on the function of dialogue in literary texts goes back to the 19th century and is represented by Heusler's studies on dialogue in Germanic epic poetry (Heusler 1902) and, more recently, by studies like Kästner (1978) on medieval didactic dialogues. As literary authors have to draw on their knowledge of naturally occurring dialogue – apart from using literary traditions – when rendering dialogue in their works, literary presentations of dialogue are a possible, if not an unproblematic source for the history of dialogue forms (cf. Betten 1994). Therefore literary studies of the function of dialogue in literary works provide useful information on various aspects of historical dialogue forms and can therefore be considered forerunners of historical dialogue analysis.

3.2. The history of spoken German

The history of spoken German received growing attention from the 1960s onwards (e.g. Sandig 1973). Relevant studies deal with the grammar of spoken German in the Middle Ages and Early Modern German (e.g. elliptical sentences, extraposition), with the use of formulaic greetings and protestations, and with the form of questions and answers etc. (cf. Sonderegger 1990). Results of this work, which relies on the reconstruction of traces and reflections of spoken language in written texts, have been collected in handbook articles on historical linguistics (e.g. Grosse 1985, Sonderegger 1985). Early work in what we could term "proto-pragmatics" includes studies of forms of address (e.g. Ehrismann 1901/1904, Metcalf 1938) and of the use of swearwords and insults (cf. Lepp 1908, Maas 1952). In the latter field, more recent research makes use of methods of modern pragmatics (e.g. Lötscher 1981). From 1980 onwards, we find analyses of the history of the use of modal particles, discourse particles, and interjections which are also influenced by recent developments in pragmatics (cf. Burger 1980, Henne 1980, Weydt 1983, Hentschel 1986, Burkhardt 1994). One of the recurrent topics in this tradition of research is the question of how characteristics of spoken dialogue can be methodically reconstructed from written sources (cf. Henne 1980: 90f.). Not surprisingly, this question also arose on several occasions in the discussions of our workshop (cf. the papers by Culpeper & Kytö, Herlyn, Koch, and Ramge).

3.3. The history of rhetoric

The history of rhetoric has been a particularly fruitful field of research during the last twenty years (cf. Braungart 1988, Fauser 1991). One of the central topics of this line of research concerns conversational principles, especially politeness principles, and their application in different historical periods, e.g. from the 17th to the 19th century (cf. Beetz 1990 and the contribution of Beetz to this volume). One of the interesting aspects of this line of research is the fact that authors not only describe conversational practices at a certain point in history but also try to track historical developments and their causes, e.g. the decline of the 18th century culture of polite conversation in the course of the 19th century.

3.4. The historical extension of speech act theory and the theory of language games

The lively discussion of speech act theory in German linguistics during the 1970s also sparked off attempts to extend speech act theory to the history of language use. Early contributions to this type of research mainly describe individual types of speech acts as represented in medieval texts (aggressive speech acts in v. Polenz 1981, declarations of love in Schwarz 1984). Other studies considered sequences of speech acts and dialogue genres and in so doing contributed to historical dialogue analysis in a strict sense. The types of dialogue sequences analyzed include medieval quarrelling sequences (Weigand 1988), 16th century polemics (Schwitalla 1986), medieval ritual challenges (Bax 1991), and patterns of accusations and reactions to accusations in medieval legal procedure (Fritz/Muckenhaupt 1981) and in 15th century private life (Fritz 1995: 474ff.).

A very useful concept for dialogue analysis, which is applied by some of the latter authors, is Wittgenstein's concept of language game. The basic idea embodied in the Wittgensteinian picture of language use is that linguistic acts are normally not isolated acts – like in Searle's theory – but that they are embedded in contexts of linguistic and practical action. It is worth noting that Wittgenstein himself in his *Philosophical Investigations* conceived of language games as social institutions which are subject to historical change: "And this multiplicity is not something fixed, given once for all; but new types of language, new language-games, as we may say, come into existence, and others become obsolete and get forgotten" (Wittgenstein 1958: § 23).

Drawing on the Wittgensteinian idea of language games, Fritz (1994, 1995) developed a program for historical dialogue analysis which focuses on the organizing principles of dialogue forms or genres (patterns of local and global sequencing, communicative strategies, turn-taking principles, topic structure, conversation principles, utterance forms – including lexical material) and the interaction of these organizing principles. Any one of these organizing principles may be subject to change in history, and – due to their interaction – this may in turn influence other aspects of the dialogue form.

Historical changes in topics often correlate with lexical changes. Adherence to the principle of brevity during a certain period may favor the use of elliptical forms of utterance in certain types of dialogue, whereas in a later period the principle of brevity might be subordinated to the principle of explicitness, which in turn may lead to a preference for complex utterance forms. If the mode of application of the principle of politeness changes, traditional politeness markers may become obsolete. New forms of dialogue will emerge in institutional contexts (formal planning dialogues in committees, different types of oral examinations etc.) and may spread from one type of situation to the other. This program aims at an evolutionary history of dialogue forms on a par with the evolutionary history of institutions (cf. Toulmin 1972) and the well-established evolutionary history of linguistic forms (e.g. historical syntax, historical semantics). Recent work on the history of forms of controversy from the 16th to the 18th century aims to put this program into practice. Thomas Gloning's contribution to this volume is part of this line of work in progress.

A few remarks on the papers from the Germanist field included in this volume will be in order. Ramge documents an early example of a new genre of texts in 14th century Germany, i.e. legal protocols which contain reports of dialogues pertaining to the legal case at hand. He gives strong arguments for the view that the production of reported speech in this genre is not so much guided by the principle of authenticity but by the principle of legal relevance. It is the legally relevant traits of the reported dialogues on which the protocol focuses. Bax deals with two types of ritual dialogue presented in Dutch late medieval romances and in early 16th century drama. The first type is a chivalrous challenging ritual, the second a kind of verbal duel between *sinnekens*, allegorical figures of a diabolic nature who are bent on harming the virtuous principal character(s) of the plays. Both dialogue types are shown to be versions of a contract-by-conflict procedure, viz. they both have – at least in part – the function of securing common ground for an activity which is to follow, a chivalrous fight or a joint attack on the protagonist of the drama. Schwitalla analyzes the structure of an early 16th century controversy and the strategies applied by both participants in the controversy, including the use of dialogical elements in their writings. He shows the remarkable armory of polemical moves available to the controversialists, both verbal and pictorial. In his paper "The pragmatic form of religious controversies around 1600" Gloning provides an interesting object of comparison from the end of the 16th century. He reconstructs basic structures of controversies of the counter-reformation period, including typical sequences of moves, polemical strategies and communication principles. Generally speaking, there is much continuity in the dialogue form of controversy throughout the 16th century.

In sharp contrast to the theme of antagonistic talk in the articles mentioned so far, Kästner deals with the rules of courtly love-talk as presented in medieval poetry (cf. also the paper by Honegger). He analyzes various dialogical exchanges and also the explicit reflections on maxims of courteous conversation which are to be found in poetry, narrative and didactic literature. Finally, Beetz discusses second moves in polite dialogue around 1700, e.g. return compliments, polite refusals and apologies. As sources he uses a large number of contemporary books on etiquette. This article contributes both to our historical knowledge of politeness rules and to an understanding of historical types of initiating acts like compliments. Beetz also describes some historical changes to prescribed reply behavior from the 16th to the 18th century.

4. English studies: Pragmaticization and computerization of English historical linguistics

Historical dialogue analysis in English has not yet emerged as a coherent field, and it is doubtful whether it ever will, but there are clearly some influences that have shaped the historical study of dialogues in English. In recent years, both historical English linguistics and pragmatics, the parent field of dialogue analysis, have changed in ways which made a fruitful interaction between the fields possible. It may be useful to view the recent interest in historical dialogue analysis in English historical linguistics as a result of, on the one hand, the pragmaticization and, on the other hand, the computerization and corpus-orientation of English historical linguistics. These two driving forces shall be reviewed in turn.

4.1. The pragmaticization of English historical linguistics

In English historical linguistics there is a growing awareness of the context dependent nature of language and therefore also of language change. Histories of the English language are now regularly written with a much more social focus than in earlier decades. Knowles (1997) is a good example of a history of English which traces changes in the English language in their social and cultural context. Such a more context sensitive approach to language change must necessarily lead to a greater awareness of the dialogic nature of language and the types of dialogue in which language is used.

In the more restricted field of historical dialogue analysis, one can distinguish research efforts that deal with dialogic elements and their development in the history of English and research efforts that deal with specific dialogic genres in the history of English. In a pioneering book, Finkenstaedt (1963) studied the use of the pronominal address terms *you* and *thou* in the history of English. In Old English only one form was used to address a single addressee, i.e. *þu*. In Middle English and in Early Modern English two forms, *you* and *thou*, competed, while in Modern English the distinction has disappeared again from everyday usage. *You* is the normal form, while *thou* is restricted to religious and some poetic and dialectal context. Twenty years later, Breuer (1983) analyzed address terms, including the use of title and address formulae, in Shakespeare's work. He argues that social rank and power, age, and sex are important factors in the selection of these forms.

The publication of Brown and Levinson's politeness theory in 1978 (republished as Brown & Levinson 1987) turned out to be important not just for pragmatics in general but also for the field of English historical dialogue analysis. They argue that every rational human being has face wants and that conversational interactants use a variety of strategies to maintain and enhance each other's face wants. They also propose that power, distance and the ranked extremity of a face-threatening act are the universal determinants of politeness levels. Brown and Gilman (1989), for instance, subjected Brown and Levinson's politeness theory to a test on Shakespeare's use of Early Modern English in *Hamlet*, *King Lear*, *Macbeth* and *Othello*. Hope (1994) continues this line of research. He analyzes Early Modern English pronoun usage (*thou* and *you*) in depositions made to the Durham ecclesiastical court in the northeast of England in the 1560s, and in particular from actual conversations recounted within the depositions. Kopytko (1993, 1995) criticizes Brown and Levinson's approach and argues that deterministic, predictive models of politeness are inadequate. They must be replaced by theories based on an indeterministic, non-categorical, non-essentialist and non-modular view of pragmatics. These points are developed in an analysis of the interactional style in four tragedies and four comedies by William Shakespeare. Forms of address in letter salutations are the subject of a study by Nevalainen and Raumolin-Brunberg (1995). Their data covers a period of two hundred and sixty years (1420-1680) from Late Middle English to Early Modern English.

Several studies deal with politeness issues beyond address terms. Klein (1994), for instance, investigates the development of linguistic thinking as it related to politeness in the late seventeenth and early eighteenth centuries. Sell (1994) advocates a diachronic approach to politeness and argues that literary texts provide relevant evidence, not only because the texts portray the speech and behavior of characters in the story but also in the way the literary writers address prospective readers.

The historical study of discourse markers began in the early 1990s with papers by Laurel Brinton (1990a, 1990b, 1995). In 1996 she published updated versions of these papers together with substantial new research as a book (1996). She studies a variety of pragmatic markers such as *gan*, *bifel*, *hwæt*, *anon* and *gelamp* in Old and/or Middle English. In a recent paper (1998) she discusses the origins of the Modern English discourse marker *only*. From the middle of the 1990s several other important papers appeared on English discourse markers. Fludernik (1995), for instance, studies the development of narrative discourse markers (in particular *tho*) in Middle English. Taavitsainen (1995) gives an outline of the use of interjections (such as *ah*, *alas*, *benedicite*, *eh*, and *fie*) in Early Modern English and discusses their use with special reference to text types. Blake (1996) studies the discourse markers *why* and *what* in Shakespeare's *Henry VI Part 3*, *The Two Gentlemen of Verona*, and *Othello*. Jucker (1997) studies the discourse marker *well* diachronically from Old English to Modern English. Fischer (1998) discusses the development of the discourse marker *marry*, and Kryk-Kastovsky (1998) analyzes a range of discourse markers in Early Modern English court hearings.

The systematic analysis of particular speech acts in the history of English has only just started. Leslie Arnovick has presented two case studies of speech acts. In a 1994 paper she argues that promises made in the Old English of Anglo-Saxon England differ substantially from those heard in Present-Day English of North America (Arnovick 1994). In another paper, she analyzes the speech event of the agonistic insult in English, which has its roots both in the heroic "flyting" of the Anglo-Saxon warrior and in the competitive "sounding" of the African-American youth (Arnovick 1995).

Danet and Bogoch (1994) draw on ideas from sociolinguistics, discourse analysis and speech act theory in order to analyze the language of sixty-two

Anglo-Saxon wills in Old English, where they show the transition to the use of writing for legal purposes in the Middle Ages. Taavitsainen (1997a) assesses the field of secondary interjections, especially oaths and swearing, in the Late Middle English period, where secondary interjections are understood as exclamatory words that can also be used as other parts of speech.

Besides the approaches reviewed above which try to account for specific dialogic features in the history of English, there are also studies which try to provide a more comprehensive dialogic analysis of historical sources. Specimens of written language, as for instance books, are seen as dialogic contributions in their own right. They have senders with communicative intentions and audiences to whom they are addressed and whom they try to influence in certain ways. Watts (1995), for instance, analyzes the sociocultural and pragmatic context of English grammar writing from the late sixteenth to the late eighteenth century by studying a sample of sixteen grammars of English. He focuses in particular on the prefatory texts of these grammars (approbation of censor, title page, dedication to a patron or to a reader/user, comments on the work by third persons, and preface). The analysis reveals the intended addressees of the texts and their writer-reader relationships, and it contextualizes these grammars within the world of publishing in the seventeenth and eighteenth centuries, the world of patronage and even the world of marketing.

Moreover, both literary and non-literary texts contain fictional representations of dialogues. Such representations are no longer shunned as unreliable sources. They may not tell us directly how people communicated in Middle English or Early Modern English, but it is interesting in itself to study how Middle English or Early Modern English authors chose to represent dialogues. Rudanko (1993), for example, provides a comprehensive discourse analytical study of several Shakespeare plays. He examines exchanges introduced by questions and requests in *Othello*, drawing on the concepts of the adjacency pair, Grice's cooperative principle and speech act theory. He also applies a Searlean variety of speech act theory to *Coriolanus*, and Brown and Levinson's politeness theory to *Timon of Athens*. Bergner (1998) lists a range of dialogic features in Middle English mystery plays talking both of their communicative intention and their overall pragmatic orientation.

4.2. Computerization and sociohistorical corpus studies in English historical linguistics

In recent years English historical linguistics has witnessed a radical computerization of its research tools in the form of computer readable diachronic corpora, easily accessible text retrieval software, and computerized historical dictionaries. These research tools have changed the field of English historical linguistics far more substantially than German or Romance historical linguistics. It made it possible to apply the methods of modern sociolinguistics to historical data. But these approaches focused on morphological, syntactic and lexical problems. Initially they did not encourage the field of historical dialogue analysis. It is only in the last few years that some trends have become discernible to combine the newly available computer tools with a systematic historical analysis of dialogue features and dialogues.

With the publication of the diachronic part of the Helsinki Corpus of English texts in October 1991 a computer readable stratified corpus of English texts ranging from about 800 to 1710 became available (see in particular Kytö 1991 and Rissanen *et al* 1993). This corpus comprises texts from a wide range of literary and non-literary sources, and is arranged into the traditional sections of the history of English, that is to say Old English (800 to 1150), Middle English (1150 to 1500) and Early Modern English (1500 to 1710). Each period is subdivided into three or four subperiods. The entire corpus comprises over 1.5 million words. The compilers of the corpus at the University of Helsinki had four general aims in their selection of texts for the corpus: 1. They aimed at a representative coverage of all the periods the corpus was intended to cover. 2. They paid attention to the regional variation so that it included samples from all regions to be covered by the corpus. 3. They made sure that the authors of the texts represented both male and female writers, and that different age groups, social levels and educational backgrounds were included. 4. The texts were selected to represent a wide range of genres or text types (see Kytö and Rissanen 1993: 7).

At the same time new and user-friendly text-retrieval programs were developed and became widely accessible, for instance WordCruncher, Tact, Micro OCP, MicroConcord and more recently Word Smith. With these tools it became possible to study historical developments in the English language from the angle of diachronic variation. The methods of modern sociolinguistic variability studies could now be applied more systematically and more comprehensively to historical data taking into account also discourse and textual features. Early results of research on the Helsinki Corpus of English Texts was published in several volumes by Matti Rissanen and his research team (Rissanen et al 1992; Rissanen et al 1993; and more recently Rissanen et al 1997a, 1997b).

Moreover, in 1992 the second edition of the *Oxford English Dictionary* became available on CD-ROM. With this research tool searches in the vast treasure of the *Oxford English Dictionary* are no longer restricted to the alphabetical access of individual headwords. It is possible to search, for instance, for entries with a particular etymology, entries first attested in a particular year, entries with an illustrative quotation by a particular author, or for any combination of these search criteria.

The computerization of English historical linguistics has had an enormous impact on the field because these tools made it possible to ask entirely new questions. However, all these research tools favor the analysis of decontextualized elements that are electronically searchable and they turned out to be most useful for studies of morphology, syntax and lexis (see Kytö and Rissanen 1993: 1, and the collective volumes by Rissanen and his research team mentioned above).

In recent years, however, the computer has also asserted its place as a research tool for English historical dialogue analysis. Some of the studies mentioned in the previous section rely heavily on electronic corpora such as the Helsinki corpus or the *OED* on CD-ROM to retrieve specific dialogic elements, most notably discourse markers. Taavitsainen (1995), who analyzes the use of interjections, uses data from the Early Modern English section of the Helsinki Corpus. Jucker (1997) in his study of the development of *well* uses data from the *OED* on CD-ROM, the Helsinki Corpus and from computer readable corpora of the works by Chaucer and Shakespeare. And Fischer (1998) also uses the *OED* on CD-ROM for his study of the discourse marker *marry*.

The Helsinki Corpus also proved invaluable for the study of genres and subgenres and their development (Taavitsainen 1993, 1997b, 1997c). In her 1993 paper, she analyzes genres and text types in the Late Middle English sections of the Helsinki Corpus on the basis of a large number of linguistic – mainly lexical – features, which she subjects to a multidimensional factor analysis. Her 1997 paper deals with the Early Modern English sections of the Helsinki Corpus, but it is noteworthy that in this investigation she focuses specifically on discursive properties such as exclamations, swearing, direct questions and pragmatic particles, which had received no or only incidental attention in the earlier study.

The Helsinki Corpus influenced English historical dialogue analysis also in more indirect ways in that it initiated the development of several more specific satellite corpora. Some of these are aimed specifically at the study of dialogue or dialogue features. Terttu Nevalainen and Helena Raumolin-Brunberg compiled the Corpus of Early English Correspondence (cf. Nevalainen & Raumolin-Brunberg 1994, 1995, 1996a, 1996b). It consists of personal letters totaling about 2.4 million words and covers the Late Middle English and the

Early Middle English period (1420-1680). The language of these private letters is claimed to relate closely to the spoken idiom of the time (Nevalainen & Raumolin-Brunberg 1996b). In the first instance this corpus is intended to provide more focused data for sociohistorical variation studies, but it also turned out to be useful for more dialogically oriented work, as for instance in the study of address terms (see Nevalainen & Raumolin-Brunberg 1995, Raumolin-Brunberg 1996).

Jonathan Culpeper and Merja Kytö are developing an historical corpus with a very specific application to historical dialogue analysis (see their paper in this volume). Their Corpus of Early English Dialogue covering the period from 1550 to 1750 will consist of naturally occurring speech that was recorded verbatim or nearly so, such as courtroom proceedings, witness depositions and "eye-witness" accounts, and constructed imaginary speech such as play texts and dialogues in prose fiction. The ultimate aim is a corpus of about 1.2 million words.

Thus it appears that the computerization of English historical linguistics which initially may have diverted researchers from the analysis of dialogues and dialogic elements is now starting to have a positive impact on historical dialogue analysis. It is to be hoped that the increased sophistication of the computer tools and the growing experience of the historical linguists will further enhance English historical dialogue analysis.

There are five papers in the present volume that deal primarily with English language data (Herlyn, Honegger, Watts, Taavitsainen and Culpeper & Kytö). They represent both the pragmaticization and the computerization of English historical linguistics reviewed above. Anne Herlyn focuses her attention on the development of what she calls multiple dialogue introducers of the form *So he says to her, he says, "well," he says ...* , in which direct reported speech is introduced by two or more verbs of saying. In Present-Day English the construction is more or less restricted to oral communication, while in Middle English narratives it was quite common. Thomas Honegger's paper is devoted to literary representations of the verbal interactions that take place between lovers when one of them has to leave on the approaching morning, so-called dawn songs. He analyzes such songs in the writings of Chaucer and Shakespeare. He assesses them both as a literary genre with roots in French, Provençal and Middle High German and as (fictional) representation of spoken interaction in which the interactants aim at reducing the face-threat inherent in the parting of two lovers.

Watts and Taavitsainen both investigate didactic dialogues. Richard Watts' data are dialogues in English-language teaching books of the 16th century. He analyzes these texts in the socio-cultural context of 16th-century London with its French-speaking and Spanish-speaking immigrant communities who depended on such teaching aids. Irma Taavitsainen assesses didactic dialogues and dialogic elements in Late Medieval and Early Modern English medical writing. Instruction in scientific handbooks was often given in the form of fictional conversations between a master and a pupil, which to a certain extent may reflect natural speech. Her paper is a good example of the combination of the pragmaticization and the computerization of English historical linguistics mentioned above. Her findings are based on a computer readable database of Early English medical writing that consists of medical treatises originally published between 1375 and 1750. In her analysis she uses both the traditional tool of close textual study of selected passages and the more recent tool of computerized lexical searches for elements with dialogic potential such as "question", "answer", "ask", "tell" and personal pronouns.

Jonathan Culpeper and Merja Kytö's corpus of Early Modern English dialogues has been mentioned above. In their paper in this volume they analyze hedges occurring in their corpus in an attempt to provide at least a partial answer to the question of what spoken conversation of the past was like.

5. Outlook and conclusion

In this paper we have tried to give a brief outline of the research traditions in the fields of Romance, German and English linguistics that have been instrumental in the present interest in historical dialogue analysis. It has become apparent that so far – in spite of several points of interaction – the fields have developed largely independently of each other. What is very encouraging at this time is that there are now signs of convergence between the different traditions, which can also be seen in the contributions to this volume. Not only do we find recurring topics in contributions from the different traditions (aspects of conflict talk, legal dialogues, religious dialogues, and teaching dialogues), but there are also various cross-references on theoretical matters.

The papers of this volume are arranged thematically. The first three papers are devoted to hostile interactions. Bax analyzes hostile verbal encounters between Medieval knights; Gloning religious controversies in Germany around 1600, and Schwitalla public controversies fought out with the help of pamphlets. The papers by Beetz and Kästner deal with the avoidance of controversies, i.e. with politeness in Early German conversations. The next four papers deal with different forms of dialogues. Honegger analyzes the literary genre of the dawn song as a "linguistic routine" of parting. Watts and Taavitsainen both investigate teaching dialogues, Watts in 16th century English-language teaching books and Taavitsainen in Early English medical writing. Lebsanft assesses a fictional form of a Late Medieval French bargaining dialogue. The next group of four papers deals with specific dialogic elements. Culpeper and Kytö investigate hedges in a corpus of Early Modern English dialogues. Herlyn traces the development of multiple dialogue introducers. Schrott analyzes interrogative acts in an Old French play. And Koch assesses the reflexes of spontaneous dialogues in Early Romance texts. The final two papers concern themselves with very specific dialogues. Ramge provides a close analysis of the record of an actual early 14th century legal dispute, while Oesterreicher deals with an allegedly real conversation recorded in an historiographic document which turns out to be largely fictional.

Thus the papers of this volume give a survey of the approaches in the young discipline of historical dialogue analysis, and they bring up a wide range of issues which will be of continuing relevance, as for instance: an awareness of the problem of historical sources, the feeling for hermeneutical problems, the interest in actual utterance forms, the knowledge of classical traditions of speech and the practice of modern methods for the description of dialogue, to mention just a few.

References

Abercrombie, David
    1963   Conversation and Spoken Prose. *English Language Teaching* 18, 10-16.
Arnovick, Leslie K.
    1994   The expanding discourse of promises in Present-Day English: A case study in historical pragmatics. *Folia Linguistica Historica* 15.1-2, 175-191.
    1995   Sounding and flyting the English agonistic insult: Writing pragmatic history in a cross-cultural context. In: Mava Jo Powell (ed.). *The Twenty-First LACUS Forum 1994*. Chapel Hill, N.C.: The Linguistic Association of Canada and the United States, 600-619.
Ayres-Bennett, Wendy
    1996   *A History of the French Language Through Texts*. London: Routledge.
Bauche, Henri
    1920   *Le langage populaire. Grammaire, syntaxe et dictionaire du français tel qu'on le parle dans le peuple avec tous les termes d'argot usuels*. Paris: Payot ([5]1951).

Bax, Marcel M. H.
 1991 Historische Pragmatik: Eine Herausforderung für die Zukunft. In: Dietrich Busse (ed.). *Diachrone Semantik und Pragmatik. Untersuchungen zur Erklärung und Beschreibung des Sprachwandels.* Tübingen: Niemeyer, 197-215.

Beetz, Manfred
 1990 *Frühmoderne Höflichkeit. Komplimentierkunst und Gesellschaftsrituale im altdeutschen Sprachraum.* Stuttgart: Metzler.

Beinhauer, Werner
 1930 *Spanische Umgangssprache.* Bonn: Dümmler (^{2}1950; Spanish Translation Madrid: Gredos ^{3}1978).

Benveniste, Émile
 1966-1974 *Problèmes de linguistique générale.* 2 vols. Paris: Gallimard.

Bergner, Heinz
 1998 Dialogue in Medieval drama. In: Raimund Borgmeier, Herbert Grabes and Andreas H. Jucker (eds.). *Anglistentag 1997 Giessen. Proceedings.* Trier: Wissenschaftlicher Verlag, 75-83.

Betten, Anne
 1994 Analyse literarischer Dialoge. In: Gerd Fritz and Franz Hundsnurscher (eds.). *Handbuch der Dialoganalyse.* Tübingen: Niemeyer, 519-544.

Blake, N. F.
 1996 *Essays on Shakespeare's Language.* 1st Series. Misterton: The Language Press.

Blumenthal, Peter
 1980a Über 'gemütliches si' in mittelalterlichen Erzählungen. In: Hans Dieter Bork, Artur Greive, and Dieter Woll (eds.). *Romanica Europaea et americana. Festschrift für Harri Meier.* Bonn: Bouvier, 55-67.
 1980b *La syntaxe du message. Application au français moderne.* Tübingen: Niemeyer.

Braungart, Georg
 1988 *Hofberedsamkeit. Studien zur Praxis höfisch-politischer Rede im Deutschen Territorialabsolutismus.* Tübingen: Niemeyer.

Breuer, Horst
 1983 Titel und Anreden bei Shakespeare und in der Shakespearezeit. *Anglia* 101, 49-77.

Brinton, Laurel J.
 1990a The development of discourse markers in English. In: Jacek Fisiak (ed.). *Historical Linguistics and Philology.* (Trends in Linguistics, Studies and Monographs 46). Berlin: Mouton de Gruyter, 45-71.

1990b The stylistic function of ME *gan* reconsidered. In: Sylvia M. Adamson, Vivien Law, Nigel Vincent, and Susan Wright (eds.). *Papers from the 5th International Conference on English Historical Linguistics.* (Current Issues in Linguistic Theory 65). Amsterdam: Benjamins, 31-53.

1995 Pragmatic markers in a diachronic perspective. In: Jocelyn Ahlers, Leela Bilmes, Joshua S. Guenter, Barbara A. Kaiser, and Ju Namkung (eds.). *Proceedings of the Twenty-First Annual Meeting of the Berkeley Linguistics Society, February 17-20, General Session and Parasession on Historical Issues in Sociolinguistics / Social Issues in Historical Linguistics.* Berkley: Berkley Linguistics Society, 377-388.

1996 *Pragmatic Markers in English. Grammaticalization and Discourse Functions.* Berlin: Mouton de Gruyter.

1998 *The flowers are lovely; only, they have no scent.*: The evolution of a pragmatic marker in English. In: Raimund Borgmeier, Herbert Grabes and Andreas H. Jucker (eds.). *Anglistentag 1997 Giessen. Proceedings.* Trier: Wissenschaftlicher Verlag, 9-33.

Brown, Roger, and Albert Gilman

1989 Politeness theory and Shakespeare's four major tragedies. *Language in Society* 18.2, 159-212.

Brown, Penelope, and Stephen C. Levinson

1987 *Politeness. Some Universals in Language Usage.* (Studies in Interactional Sociolinguistics 4). Cambridge: Cambridge University Press.

Burger, Harald

1980 Interjektionen. In: Horst Sitta (ed.). *Ansätze zu einer pragmatischen Sprachgeschichte.* Tübingen: Niemeyer, 53-70.

Burkhardt, Armin

1994 Abtönungspartikeln im Deutschen. Bedeutung und Genese. *Zeitschrift für germanistische Linguistik* 22, 129-151.

Cerquiglini, Bernard

1976 Un phénomène d'énonciation: a.fr. *mar. Romania* 97, 23-62.

1981 *La parole médiévale, Discours, syntaxe, texte.* Paris: Seuil.

Christmann, Hans Helmut

1976 Sprachwissenschaft und Sprachlehre: Zu ihrem Verhältnis im 18., 19. und 20. Jahrhundert. *Die Neueren Sprachen* 75, 423-437.

1978 Gesprochene Sprache von heute oder alte Sprachstufen als 'wahrer' Gegenstand der Linguistik? Zur historischen Sprachwissenschaft des 19. Jahrhunderts und ihrer 'Überwindung'. *Zeitschrift für romanische Philologie* 94, 549-562.

1986   Sprachwissenschaft im Dienst der Mediävistik – Sprachwissenschaft als Mediävistik. In: Joerg O. Fichte and Bernhard Schimmelpfennig (eds.). *Zusammenhänge, Einflüsse, Wirkungen. Kongreßakten zum ersten Symposium des Mediävistenverbandes in Tübingen*. Berlin/New York: de Gruyter, 1-26.

Cosnier, Jacques, and Catherine Kerbrat-Orecchioni
1987   *Décrire la conversation. Linguistique et sémiologie*. Lyon: PUL.

Danet, Brenda, and Bryna Bogoch
1994   Orality, literacy, and performativity in Anglo-Saxon wills. In: John Gibbons (ed.). *Language and the Law*. London: Longman, 100-135.

Dausendschön-Gay, Ulrich u.a. (Hgg.)
1991   *Linguistische Interaktionsanalysen: Beiträge zum 20. Romanistentag 1987*. Tübingen: Niemeyer.

Diez, Friedrich
⁵1882   *Grammatik der romanischen Sprachen*. 3 vols. Bonn: Eduard Weber.

Ducrot, Oswald
1972   *Dire et ne pas dire*. Paris: Hermann
1973   *La preuve et le dire*. Paris: Mame.

Ehrismann, Gustav
1901/1904   Duzen und Ihrzen im Mittelalter. *Zeitschrift für deutsche Wortforschung* 1 (1901) 117-149; 2 (1902) 118-159; 4 (1903) 210-248; 5 (1903/04) 127-220.

Ernst, Gerhard
1980   Prolegomena zu einer Geschichte des gesprochenen Französisch. In: Helmut Stimm (Hrsg.). *Zur Geschichte des gesprochenen Französisch und zur Sprachlenkung im Gegenwartsfranzösischen. Beiträge des Saarbrücker Romanistentages 1979*. Wiesbaden: Steiner, 1-14.

1985   *Gesprochenes Französisch zu Beginn des 17. Jahrhunderts. Direkte Rede in Jean Héroards "Histoire particulière de Louis XIII" (1605-1610)*. Tübingen: Niemeyer.

1989   Le langage du prince. In: Madeleine Foisil (ed.). *Journal de Jean Héroard*. 2 vols. Paris: Fayard, 189-214.

1995   Zur Herausgabe autobiographischer Non-Standardtexte des 17. (und 18.) Jahrhunderts: für wen? wozu? wie? In: Guido Mensching and Karl-Heinz Röntgen (eds.). *Studien zu romanischen Fachtexten aus Mittelalter und früher Neuzeit*. Hildesheim: Olms, 45-62.

Fauser, Markus
1991   *Das Gespräch im 18. Jahrhundert. Rhetorik und Geselligkeit in Deutschland*. Stuttgart: M&P. Verlag für Wissenschaft und Forschung.

Ferguson, Charles
1959 Diglossia. *Word* 15, 325-340.
Fernández, Mauro
1993 *Diglossia: A Comprehensive Bibliography, 1960-1990.* Amsterdam: Benjamins.
1995 Los orígenes del término *diglosia.* Historia de una historia mal contada. *Historiographia Linguistica* 22, 163-195.
Finkenstaedt, Thomas
1963 You *and* thou*: Studien zur Anrede im Englischen.* Berlin: De Gruyter.
Fischer, Andreas
1998 *Marry.* From religious invocation to discourse marker. In: Raimund Borgmeier, Herbert Grabes and Andreas H. Jucker (eds.). *Anglistentag 1997 Giessen. Proceedings.* Trier: Wissenschaftlicher Verlag, 35-46.
Fleischman, Suzanne
1990 Philology, linguistics, and the discourse of the medieval text. *Speculum* 65, 19-37.
Fludernik, Monika
1995 Middle English *þo* and other narrative discourse markers. In: Andreas H. Jucker (ed.). *Historical Pragmatics. Pragmatic Developments in the History of English.* Amsterdam: Benjamins, 359-392.
François, Denise
1974 *Français parlé. Analyse des unités phoniques et significatives d'un corpus recueilli dans la région parisienne.* 2 vols. Paris: SELAF.
Frei, Henri
1929 *La grammaire des fautes. Introduction à la linguistique fonctionnelle.* Paris: Geuthner (Reprinted Genève: Slatkine, 1971).
Fries, Charles C.
1952 *The Structure of English.* New York: Harcourt, Bruce & World.
Fries, Udo
1998 Dialogue in instructional texts. In: Raimund Borgmeier, Herbert Grabes, and Andreas H. Jucker (eds.). *Anglistentag 1997 Giessen. Proceedings.* Trier: Wissenschaftlicher Verlag, 85-96.
Fritz, Gerd
1994 Geschichte von Dialogformen. In: Gerd Fritz and Franz Hundsnurscher (eds.). *Handbuch der Dialoganalyse.* Tübingen Niemeyer, 545-559.
1995 Topics in the history of dialogue forms. In: Andreas H. Jucker (ed.). *Historical Pragmatics. Pragmatic Developments in the History of English.* Amsterdam/Philadelphia: Benjamins, 469-498.

1997 Remarks on the history of dialogue forms. In: Etienne Pietri (ed.). *Dialogue Analysis V. Proceedings of the 5th Conference Paris 1994*. Tübingen: Niemeyer, 47-55.

Fritz, Gerd, and Manfred Muckenhaupt
1981 Beweisen – Kommunikationsformen und ihre Geschichte. In: Gerd Fritz and Manfred Muckenhaupt. *Kommunikation und Grammatik*. Tübingen: Narr, 196-207.

Gleßgen, Martin-Dietrich, and Franz Lebsanft
1997 Von alter und neuer Philologie. Oder: Neuer Streit über Prinzipien und Praxis der Textedition. In: Martin-Dietrich Gleßgen and Franz Lebsanft (eds.). *Alte und neue Philologie*. Tübingen: Niemeyer, 1-14.

Grosse, Siegfried
1985 Reflexe gesprochener Sprache im Mittelhochdeutschen. In: Werner Besch, Oskar Reichmann, and Stefan Sonderegger (eds.). *Sprachgeschichte. Ein Handbuch der Geschichte der deutschen Sprache und ihrer Erforschung*. Vol 2. Berlin/New York: De Gruyter, 1186-1191.

Gülich, Elisabeth
1970 *Makrosyntax der Gliederungssignale im gesprochenen Französisch*. München: Fink.

Gülich, Elisabeth, and Thomas Kotschi (eds.)
1985 *Grammatik, Konversation, Interaktion. Beiträge zum Romanistentag 1983*. Tübingen: Niemeyer.

Hausmann, Franz Josef
1975 Gesprochenes und geschriebenes Französisch. *Romanistisches Jahrbuch* 26, 19-45.

1980 Zur Rekonstruktion des um 1730 gesprochenen Französisch. In: Helmut Stimm (ed.). *Zur Geschichte des gesprochenen Französisch und zur Sprachlenkung im Gegenwartsfranzösischen. Beiträge des Saarbrücker Romanistentages 1979*. Wiesbaden: Steiner, 33-46.

1992 L'âge du français parlé actuel: bilan d'une controverse allemande. In: Groupe d'Étude en Histoire de la Langue Française (ed.). *Grammaire des fautes et français non conventionnel*. (Actes du IVe Colloque [...]). Paris: ENS, 355-362.

Hausmann, Franz Josef (ed.)
1983 *Die französische Sprache von heute*. Darmstadt: Wissenschaftliche Buchgesellschaft.

Held, Gudrun
    1992   Aspekte des Zusammenhangs zwischen Höflichkeit und Sprache in der vorpragmatischen Sprachwissenschaft. *Zeitschrift für romanische Philologie* 108, 1-34.

Henne, Helmut
    1980   Probleme einer historischen Gesprächsanalyse. Zur Rekonstruktion gesprochener Sprache im 18. Jahrhundert. In: Horst Sitta (ed.). *Ansätze zu einer pragmatischen Sprachgeschichte. Zürcher Kolloquium 1978.* Tübingen: Niemeyer, 89-102.

Hentschel, Elke
    1986   Funktion und Geschichte deutscher Partikeln. *Ja, doch, halt* und *eben*. Tübingen: Niemeyer.

Herman, Joseph
    1996   Varietäten des Lateins. In: Günter Holtus, Michael Metzeltin and Christian Schmitt (eds.). *Lexikon der romanistischen Linguistik*. Vol. II/1. Tübingen: Niemeyer, 44-61.

Heusler, Andreas
    1902   Der Dialog in der altgermanischen erzählenden Dichtung. *Zeitschrift für deutsches Altertum* 46, 189-284.

Hilty, Gerold (ed.)
    1993   *Actes du XXe Congrès International de Linguistique et Philologie Romanes*, vol. 2: Section II, Analyse de la conversation, Section III, La fragmentation linguistique de la Romania. Tübingen/Basel: Francke.

Hofmann, Johann Baptist
    1926   *Lateinische Umgangssprache*. Heidelberg: Winter (^{4}1978).

Holtus, Günter, and Wolfgang Schweickard
    1991   Zum Stand der Erforschung der historischen Dimension gesprochener Sprache in der Romania. *Zeitschrift für romanische Philologie* 107, 547-574.

Hope, Jonathan
    1994   The use of *thou* and *you* in Early Modern spoken English: Evidence from depositions in the Durham ecclesiastical court records. In: Dieter Kastovsky (ed.). *Studies in Early Modern English*. Berlin: Mouton de Gruyter, 141-152.

Hosch, Siegfried
    1983   Französische Flickwörter. Ein Beitrag zur französischen Lexikographie. In: Franz Josef Hausmann (ed.). *Die französische Sprache von heute*. Darmstadt: Wissenschaftliche Buchgesellschaft, 37-69 (Originally 1895-1897).

Jucker, Andreas H.
    1997   The discourse marker *well* in the history of English. *English Language and Linguistics* 1.1, 91-110.

Jucker, Andreas H. (ed.)
- 1995 *Historical Pragmatics. Pragmatic Developments in the History of English.* (Pragmatics & Beyond New Series 35). Amsterdam/Philadelphia: John Benjamins.

Jucker, Andreas H., and Yael Ziv (eds.)
- 1998 *Discourse Markers. Descriptions and Theory.* Amsterdam/Philadelphia: Benjamins.

Kästner, Hannes
- 1978 *Mittelalterliche Lehrgespräche. Textlinguistische Analyse. Studien zur poetischen Funktion und pädagogischen Intention.* Berlin: Erich Schmidt.

Kerbrat-Orecchioni, Catherine
- 1994-1998 *Les interactions verbales.* 3 vols. Paris: Colin (I, ^{3}1998, II ^{2}1994, III ^{2}1998).

Klein, Lawrence
- 1994 "Politeness" as linguistic ideology in late seventeenth- and eighteenth-century England. In: Dieter Stein and Ingrid Tieken-Boon van Ostade (eds.). *Towards a Standard English 1600-1800.* (Topics in English Linguistics 12). Berlin: Mouton de Gruyter, 31-50.

Knowles, Gerry
- 1997 *A Cultural History of the English Language.* London: Arnold.

Koch, Peter, and Wulf Oesterreicher
- 1990 *Gesprochene Sprache in der Romania: Französisch, Italienisch, Spanisch.* Tübingen: Niemeyer.

Kopytko, Roman
- 1993 *Polite Discourse in Shakespeare's English.* Poznań: Wydawnictwo Naukowe Uniwersytetu im. Adam Mickiewicza w Poznaniu.
- 1995 Linguistic politeness strategies in Shakespeare's plays. In: Andreas H. Jucker (ed.). *Historical Pragmatics. Pragmatic Developments in the History of English.* (Pragmatics & Beyond New Series 35). Amsterdam/ Philadelphia: Benjamins, 515-540.

Kristol, Andres Max
- 1992 Que dea! Mettes le chapron, paillard, com tu parles a prodome! La représentation de l'oralité dans les *Manières de langage* du XIVe/XVe siècle. *Romanistisches Jahrbuch* 43, 35-64.

Kryk-Kastovsky, Barbara
- 1998 Pragmatic particles in Early Modern English Tracts. In: Raimund Borgmeier, Herbert Grabes, and Andreas H. Jucker (eds.). *Anglistentag 1997 Giessen. Proceedings.* Trier: Wissenschaftlicher Verlag, 47-56.

Kytö, Merja
  1991   *Manual to the Diachronic Part of The Helsinki Corpus of English Texts. Coding Conventions and Lists of Source Texts.* Helsinki: Department of English, University of Helsinki.

Kytö, Merja, and Matti Rissanen
  1993   General introduction. In: Matti Rissanen, Merja Kytö and Minna Palander-Collin (eds.). *Early English in the Computer Age. Explorations through the Helsinki Corpus.* Berlin/New York: Mouton de Gruyter, 1-17.

Lebsanft, Franz
  1985   Review of Bernard Cerquiglini 1981. *Zeitschrift für romanische Philologie* 101, 526-527.
  1988   *Studien zu einer Linguistik des Grußes. Sprache und Funktion der altfranzösischen Grußformeln.* Tübingen: Niemeyer.

Lepp, Friedrich
  1908   *Schlagwörter des Reformationszeitalters.* Leipzig: Heinsius.

Lodge, R. Anthony
  1993   *French, from Dialect to Standard.* London/New York: Routledge (French Translation 1997: *Le français. Histoire d'un dialecte.* Paris: Fayard).

Lötscher, Andreas
  1981   Zur Sprachgeschichte des Fluchens und Beschimpfens im Schweizerdeutschen. *Zeitschrift für Dialektologie und Linguistik* 48, 145-160.

Lüdtke, Helmut
  1978   Die Entstehung romanischer Schriftsprachen. In: Reinhold Kontzi (ed.). *Zur Entstehung der romanischen Sprachen.* Darmstadt: Wissenschaftliche Buchgesellschaft, 386-409 (Originally 1964).

Maas, Herbert
  1952   Das Nürnberger Scheltwort. *Mitteilungen der Vereins für Geschichte der Stadt Nürnberg* 43, 361-483.

Marchello-Nizia, Christiane
  1985   *Dire le vrai: l'adverbe "si" en ancien français. Essai de linguistique historique.* Genève: Droz.

Metcalf, George F.
  1938   *Forms of Address in German (1500-1800).* St. Louis MO: Washington University Studies.

Moeschler, Jacques
  1994   Das Genfer Modell der Gesprächsanalyse. In: Gerd Fritz and Franz Hundsnurscher (eds.). *Handbuch der Dialoganalyse.* Tübingen: Niemeyer, 67-94.

Moeschler, Jacques, and Anne Reboul
  1996   *Dictionnaire encyclopédique de pragmatique.* Paris: Seuil.
Nevalainen, Terttu, and Helena Raumolin-Brunberg
  1994   Sociolinguistics and language history: The Helsinki Corpus of Early English Correspondence. *Hermes, Journal of Linguistics* 13, 135-143.
  1995   Constraints on politeness: The pragmatics of address formulae in Early English correspondence. In: Andreas H. Jucker (ed.). *Historical Pragmatics. Pragmatic Developments in the History of English.* Amsterdam/ Philadelphia: Benjamins, 541-601.
  1996a   *Sociolinguistics and Language History. Studies based on the Corpus of Early English Correspondence.* Amsterdam: Rodopi.
  1996b   The corpus of Early English correspondence. In: Terttu Nevalainen and Helena Raumolin-Brunberg (eds.). *Sociolinguistics and Language History. Studies based on the Corpus of Early English Correspondence.* Amsterdam: Rodopi, 39-54.
Nølke, Henning
  1993   *Le regard du locuteur. Pour une linguistique des traces d'énonciation.* Paris: Kimé.
Oesterreicher, Wulf
  1994   El español en textos escritos por semicultos. Competencia escrita de impronta oral en la historiografía indiana. In: Jens Lüdtke (ed.). *Normas del español americano en el siglo XVI.* Frankfurt am Main: Vervuert, 155-190.
Pietri, Etienne (ed.)
  1997   *Dialoganalyse V. Referate der 5. Arbeitstagung. Paris 1994.* (Beiträge zur Dialogforschung 15). Tübingen: Max Niemeyer.
Polenz, Peter von
  1981   Der Ausdruck von Sprachhandlungen in poetischen Dialogen des deutschen Mittelalters. *Zeitschrift für germanistische Linguistik* 9, 249-273.
Radtke, Edgar
  1994   *Gesprochenes Französisch und Sprachgeschichte. Zur Rekonstruktion der Gesprächskonstitution in Dialogen französischer Sprachlehrbücher.* Tübingen: Niemeyer.
Raumolin-Brunberg, Helena
  1996   Forms of address in early English correspondence. In: Terttu Nevalainen and Helena Raumolin-Brunberg (eds.). *Sociolinguistics and Language History. Studies based on the Corpus of Early English Correspondence.* Amsterdam: Rodopi, 167-181.

Rissanen, Matti, Ossi Ihalainen, Terttu Nevalainen, and Irma Taavitsainen (eds.)
- 1992 *History of Englishes. New Methods and Interpretations in Historical Linguistics.* Berlin: Mouton de Gruyter.

Rissanen, Matti, Merja Kytö, and Kirsi Heikkonen (eds.)
- 1997a *English in Transition. Corpus-based Studies in Linguistic Variation and Genre Styles.* Berlin: Mouton de Gruyter.
- 1997b *Grammaticalization at Work. Studies of Long-term Developments in English.* Berlin: Mouton de Gruyter.

Rissanen, Matti, Merja Kytö, and Minna Palander-Collin (eds.)
- 1993 *Early English in the Computer Age. Explorations through the Helsinki Corpus.* (Topics in English Linguistics 11). Berlin: Mouton de Gruyter.

Rudanko, Juhani
- 1993 *Pragmatic Approaches to Shakespeare. Essays on* Othello, Coriolanus *and* Timon of Athens. Lanham: University Press of America.

Sandig, Barbara
- 1973 Zur historischen Kontinuität normativ diskriminierter syntaktischer Muster in spontaner Sprechsprache. *Deutsche Sprache* 1, 37-57.

Schiffrin, Deborah
- 1987 *Discourse Markers.* New York: Cambridge University Press.

Schlieben-Lange, Brigitte
- 1979 Ai las - Que planhs? Ein Versuch zur historischen Gesprächsanalyse am Flamenca-Roman. *Romanistische Zeitschrift für Literaturgeschichte* 3, 1-30.
- 1983 *Traditionen des Sprechens. Elemente einer pragmatischen Sprachgeschichtsschreibung.* Stuttgart: Kohlhammer.

Schlieben-Lange, Brigitte, and Harald Weydt
- 1979 Streitgespräch zur Historizität von Sprechakten. *Linguistische Berichte* 60, 65-78.

Schmitt, Christian
- 1980 Gesprochenes Französisch um 1600. In: Helmut Stimm (ed.). *Zur Geschichte des gesprochenen Französisch und zur Sprachlenkung im Gegenwartsfranzösischen.* Wiesbaden: Steiner, 15-32.

Schwarz, Alexander
- 1984 *Sprechaktgeschichte. Studien zu den Liebeserklärungen in mittelalterlichen und modernen Tristan-Dichtungen.* Göppingen: Kümmerle.

Schwitalla, Johannes
- 1986 Martin Luthers argumentative Polemik: mündlich und schriftlich. In: Franz Josef Worstbrock and Helmut Koopmann (eds.). *Kontroversen, alte und neue. Bd. 2: Formen und Formgeschichte des Streitens. Der Literaturstreit.* Tübingen: Niemeyer, 41-54.

Selig, Maria
 1997 "Mündlichkeit" in mittelalterlichen Texten. In: Martin-Dietrich Gleßgen and Franz Lebsanft (eds.). *Alte und neue Philologie*. Tübingen: Niemeyer, 201-221.

Sell, Roger D.
 1994 Postdisciplinary philology: Culturally relativistic pragmatics. In: Francisco Fernández, Miguel Fuster, Juan José Calvo (eds.). *English Historical Linguistics 1992. Papers from the Seventh International Conference on English Historical Linguistics Valencia, 22-26 September 1992*. Amsterdam/ Philadelphia: Benjamins, 29-36

Söll, Ludwig
 1974 *Gesprochenes und geschriebenes Französisch*. Berlin: Erich Schmidt (^{3}1985: edition revised and amplified by Franz Josef Hausmann).

Sonderegger, Stefan
 1985 Reflexe gesprochener Sprache im Althochdeutschen. In: Werner Besch, Oskar Reichmann, and Stefan Sonderegger (eds.). *Sprachgeschichte. Ein Handbuch der Geschichte der deutschen Sprache und ihrer Erforschung.* Vol 2. Berlin/New York: De Gruyter, 1060-1068.
 1990 Syntaktische Strukturen gesprochener Sprache im älteren Deutsch. In: Anne Betten (ed.). *Neuere Forschungen zur historischen Syntax des Deutschen.* Tübingen: Niemeyer, 310-323.

Spitzer, Leo
 1922 *Italienische Umgangssprache*. Bonn/Leipzig: Schroeder.

Stimm, Helmut (ed.)
 1980 *Zur Geschichte des gesprochenen Französisch und zur Sprachlenkung im Gegenwartsfranzösischen. Beiträge des Saarbrücker Romanistentages 1979.* Wiesbaden: Steiner.

Taavitsainen, Irma
 1993 Genre/subgenre styles in Late Middle English. In: Matti Rissanen, Merja Kytö, and Minna Palander-Collin (eds.). *Early English in the Computer Age. Explorations through the Helsinki Corpus.* (Topics in English Linguistics 11). Berlin: Mouton de Gruyter, 171-200.
 1995 Interjections in Early Modern English: From imitation of spoken to conventions of written language. In: Andreas H. Jucker (ed.). *Historical Pragmatics. Pragmatic Developments in the History of English.* Amsterdam/ Philadelphia: Benjamins, 439-465.
 1997a *By Saint Tanne*: Pious oaths or swearing in Middle English? An assessment of genres. In: Raymond Hickey and Stanislaw Puppel (eds.). *Language*

        History and Linguistics Modelling. A Festschrift for Jacek Fisiak on his 60th Birthday. Berlin: Mouton de Gruyter, 815-826.
1997b   Genre conventions: Personal affect in fiction and non-fiction in Early Modern English. In: Matti Rissanen, Merja Kytö, and Kirsi Heikkonen (eds.). *English in Transition. Corpus-based Studies in Linguistic Variation and Genre Styles.* Berlin: Mouton de Gruyter, 185-266.
1997c   Genres and text types in Medieval and Renaissance English. *Poetica* 47, 49-62.

Toulmin, Stephen
1972   *Human Understanding. The Collective Use and Evolution of Concepts.* Princeton NJ: Princeton University Press.

Watts, Richard J.
1995   Justifying grammars: A socio-pragmatic foray into the discourse community of Early English grammarians. In: Andreas H. Jucker (ed.). *Historical Pragmatics. Pragmatic Developments in the History of English.* Amsterdam/Philadelphia: Benjamins, 145-185.

Weigand, Edda
1988   Historische Sprachpragmatik am Beispiel: Gesprächsstrukturen im Nibelungenlied. *Zeitschrift für deutsches Altertum und deutsche Literatur* 117, 159-173.

Weydt, Harald
1983   Semantische Konvergenz. Zur Geschichte von *sowieso, eh* und *ohnehin*. Ein Beitrag zum Bedeutungswandel von Partikeln. In: Harald Weydt (ed.). *Partikeln und Interaktion.* Tübingen: Niemeyer, 172-187.

Wittgenstein, Ludwig
1958   *Philosophical Investigations.* Translated by G.E.M. Anscombe. 2nd ed. Oxford: Blackwell.

Ritual Levelling
The Balance between the Eristic and the Contractual Motive in Hostile Verbal Encounters in Medieval Romance and Early Modern Drama

Marcel M. H. Bax
University of Groningen

> Forms are fictions of the human soul,
> unless it be allowable to call the laws of action Forms.
> Francis Bacon, *Novum Organon* (1620),
> Book The First, par. 51

1. Introduction

In this article, I am concerned with two historical dialogue forms that are paradoxical in character, namely, the challenging ritual performed by chivalrous knights in order to join battle, and the preparatory dialogue of fiendish imps who aspire to join forces to try and undo a human being. As I intend to show, both (literary) dialogic genres – the former occurring in mediaeval narrative and the latter in early modern drama – build upon the discrepancy between animosity and collaboration. While the verbal interaction proceeds in a hostile manner, its overall objective is nonetheless to contract for concerted action – hence, the notion of a "paradox". How in Middle Dutch romances of chivalry and sixteenth-century rhetorical stage-plays of the Low Countries antagonistic verbal behaviour functions as a ritual means to create a contractual framework, is the central theme of this study.

2. Ritual conflict and contract formation in mediaeval romance

In chivalric romances, first and foremost those of the late-mediaeval period (thirteenth and fourteenth centuries), physical encounters between knights are usually preceded by an argumentative verbal exchange that ostensibly supplies the motive for jousting. Historical-pragmatic analyses of such exchanges have disclosed the thoroughly conventional nature of the hostile interaction prior to single combat. The investigation of linguistic communication in bygone eras is possible because of the evolved theoretical perspectives, the improved research methods, and the cumulative findings and insights of pragmatics, the fertile field of language study that is devoted to the detailed examination of how verbal behaviour is organised as meaningful social (inter)action, and has "experienced something of a renaissance after the sixties and seventies, which were dominated by Chomskyan linguistics" (Jucker 1995: ix).

Although I have treated this subject with a certain amount of detail elsewhere (cf. Bax 1981 and 1991), I assume that for the sake of my argument it is worthwhile that I first elucidate the invariant basic pattern of speech actions that typifies such verbal encounters; subsequently, I shall be in a position to argue that knights follow this verbal procedure solely for the purpose of "enacting" a controversy that must be dealt with in mortal combat, and to explain the (socio-)historical backgrounds to this behavioural mode.

2.1. Close encounters of the antagonistic kind

Precombat dialogues in mediaeval romance have a characteristic interactional structure. When two knights happen to meet, one inquires after the other's name, his parentage, his destination, or some other private matter. Since this request is put in a coercive manner, the addressee refuses to render the information. Quite the reverse, apparently feeling slighted by the compelling nature of the request, the addressee challenges the initial speaker to a duel in order to settle the matter by force. The latter accepts the challenge, and the knights commence to fight.

For an example, I shall instance, and comment on, one such encounter occurring in the renowned Middle Dutch Carolingian epic *Karel ende Elegast* ('Charlemagne and Elegast,' ll. 358-381). Late one night, the emperor Karel is summoned by *een heilich engel* 'a holy angel' to go stealing. Although he is ill at ease because of its astounding nature, Karel resolves to comply with the divine assignment. After he has managed, with help from above, to leave the castle unobserved, the willy-nilly robber-knight finds himself riding through the forest in full panoply, albeit that the imperial shield is covered over in order to remain incognito. In the wood, he comes across a knight clad in a black coat of mail. They pass each other in silence, but then Elegast, the black-armoured knight, calls out:

1   Ridder ontbeyt!
     Waer na ist dat ghi rijt?
     Ic wil weten wat ghi soect
     Ende iaecht ende roect,
5   Eer ghi mi ontrijt van hier.
     Al waerdi noch so fier
     Ende so diere uwer tale,
     Berechtes mi so doedi wale.
     Ic wil weten wie ghi sijt,
10   Ende waer ghi vaert op deze tijt,
     Ende hoe dat v vader hiet.
     En machs v verlaten niet.

   [Stand ho, you knight!/ Whither is it that you ride?/ I wish to know what you have in mind/ and what you are up to/ before you ride away and escape me./ No matter how dignified you are,/ or how self-important your speech,/ enlighten me on that matter, then you do right./ I want to know who you are,/ and where you are bound for,/ and what your father's name is./ (*If otherwise,*) you are not allowed to proceed on your way.]

In reply, Karel rebukes his interrogator.

     Ghi vraget mi so menich dinc,
     En wistu hoe berechten.
15   Ic hebbe lieuer dat wi vechten,
     Dan ic v seide bi bedwanghe,
     So haddic gheleeft veel te langhen,
     Dat mi een man dwinghen soude
     Van dinghen die ic niet en woude
20   Berechten, ten ware mi lief.
     Coemter mi goet af of miskief,
     Wy sullen desen strijt nv scheyden
     Ende becorten tusschen ons beyden.

   [You enquire after so many things/ that I would not possibly know how to respond./ I prefer that we fight,/ rather than answer you under coercion,/ for I would have lived far too long,/ if anyone could compel me into disclosing things/ about which I do not wish to give any information./ For good or ill,/ we shall fight it out now among ourselves.]

After Karel has clarified his position, both knights get ready for the fray.

>   Si worpen omme met deser dinc
> 25 Haer orssen sterc ende snel
>   (...)
>   Manlic vingen si ten swaerde
>   Als die vechtens begaerde
>
> [At once, they turned their mounts,/ steeds both strong and speedy,/ (...)/ Stoutheartedly, they drew the sword,/ like braves who hunger after a gallant fight.]

Intertextual research has established that such verbal exchanges build on the dialogue model shown in Figure 1, representing the overall sequential structure of the verbal encounter in terms of its constitutive speech actions. Although it contains certain optional elements, and allows for a degree of structural variation, most notably amplifications of the kernel format (cf. Bax 1981), the three-turn model is prototypical (See Fig. 1).

1	First knight:	a *Request* (*for Information* or *for Action*)
		b *Threat*
2	Second knight:	a *Refusal* (*with* or *without Account*)
		b *Challenge*
3	First knight:	a *Acceptance* (*verbal* and/or *non-verbal*)

Figure 1: The Sequential Structure of the Challenging Ritual

As regards the Karel-Elegast dialogue, we note that Elegast essentially performs two verbal actions. In 2-4 and 8-11 he "requests information", whereas in 5, 6-7, and, in particular, 12 Elegast "threatens" his interlocutor by alluding to an act of violence in case of an unfavourable reply. Manifestly, Karel is not overwhelmed by Elegast's awe-inspiring deportment. As his rejoinder evidences, he thinks fit to withstand his opponent. In 13-14 he sneeringly "declines" to give the requested information, and in 16-19 he circumstantially "accounts" for this refusal. What his account reveals is that Karel feels humiliated by the impelling nature of Elegast's request, that his pride is injured. That Karel's honour is at stake can also be inferred from his act of challenging Elegast to (potentially lethal) combat (15, 21-22). As can be gathered from the non-verbal sequel – both he and his opponent turn their horses and withdraw in order to create sufficient space for striking into a gallop

(l. 24 ff.) – Elegast accepts Karel's challenge. Let me note in passing that the third interactional "move" of accepting a challenge is often realised verbally.

At this point, it is apposite to raise the question what "motivates" the alleged pattern of verbal actions, what considerations or circumstances underlie, and can explain, this interactional practice. A significant thing to record, then, is that the initiating move invariably consists of a request put in a compulsive manner. The first knight makes it clear that a non-compliant reaction will be met with serious repercussions. Given this threat of punishment, the request partakes of the characteristics of the speech action of commanding. According to Searle (1969: 66-67), a command, or order, marks a special form of directive speech act, in that it is essentially an attempt by the speaker to make the hearer do something (or desist from doing something) by virtue of his authority over the hearer. As a result, the speech act of giving an order can only be taken seriously if the speaker is factually in a position to somehow "chastise" the hearer in case of his being defiant. In other words, the speaker's authority, exemplified by his ability to take punitive measures, is one of the pragmatic (preparatory) conditions of the directive speech act at issue.

This condition appears to be eminently relevant. If a speaker forthrightly gives the hearer an order, he apparently presupposes that he has authority over the hearer, and, consequently, that he (believes that he), if necessary, is capable of executing retributive actions. This presupposition is the very crux of the mediaeval challenging procedure. While Knight-the-First tries to coerce Knight-the-Second into supplying information, he clearly makes manifest his conviction that he is in a position to render retaliatory actions. In effect, Knight-the-First's compulsory request can be perceived as an act of "proclaiming dominance". Now this can definitely explain Knight-the-Second's rejection. If the Second acted upon the order of the First, he would thereby implicitly concede to the First's claim to pre-eminence. That, however, is the very last thing any knight would do. As Karel's reaction proves, a self-esteeming knight does not accede to duress. Being bound in honour to reject his opponent's claim to precedence, Knight-the-Second responds with an action that "mirrors" the presumptuous behaviour of the initial speaker: he challenges him. It goes without saying that such an act reveals that the challenger is not at all awed by the other's putting on airs, and that he does not give in to the claim to dominance entailed by that behavioural mode. As a result, his honour remains unblemished.

Within this perspective, the speech actions that make up the challenging procedure must primarily be understood as efforts at "context definition". Via an impelling request, Knight-the-First delineates the social context as one in which he is superior to his interlocutor. But then the latter, by his non-compliant reaction and his subsequent challenge, also defines his position. As indicated, these verbal actions are sure (indexical) signs of his belief that he is in no respect inferior to his opponent.

At this juncture, we may well widen the scope of the considerations, and situate the speech event under discussion within its cultural-historical context. Given the formidable, widely-attested honour cult existent in the age of chivalry (cf. Huizinga 1990: ch. 2; Verbruggen 1997), one is prone to rule out beforehand the prospect of any knight responding, when faced with effrontery, in an affable or yielding manner. For each and every knight, it was mandatory to be without fear or reproach or, in keeping with the premises of what cultural anthropologists call a "shame culture" (as opposed to "guilt cultures", cf. Peristiany 1966; Elias 1983), to be recognised as such in the relevant public domains. In the chivalrous society, the protection of one's honour is the leading principle. Thus, a knight would rather engage in potentially deadly warfare than disgrace himself by ignominiously meeting high-handed demands.

2.2. Seeking and hiding information as a "language-game"

Now that I have described, and up to a point explained, the speech-actional characteristics of the late-mediaeval challenging procedure, I need to stress the altogether ritual character of the speech activity. What I take this concept to mean is largely on a par with the perceptive view on rituality advanced by William Labov in his acclaimed study of Afro-American "sounding" practices (1972). Although sounds tend to be highly offensive from the perspective of literal meaning, such slights are not (meant to be) heard as sincerely intended insults. Labov has cogently shown that, given a culture-bound set of interpretation rules and normative assumptions, an exchange of feigned, hence "ritual", insults establishes a verbal match between rivals who put to the test their ability of outclassing the opponent as regards (ingenious) slanging. I employ the term "ritual" henceforward in like manner, in order to indicate that the functional meaning of an utterance that forms part of the challenging procedure is not on a level with its *prima facie* (pragmatical) meaning drawing on conventional felicity conditions and propositional content (cf. Austin 1962; Searle 1969).

In my focal material – a corpus of seven Middle Dutch romances of chivalry, each one including numerous trials of arms and their oral "preambles" (cf. Bax 1981) – there is one example that quite convincingly illustrates the "would-be", *ergo* ritual, character of knightly requests for information. The encounter I refer to occurs in an Arthurian adventure called *Die Wrake van Ragisel* ('The Avenging of Ragisel,' l. 2977 ff.). Two knights of the Round Table, Lanceloet and Ydier, have a chance meeting. Lanceloet, who is exceedingly ill-tempered at the time because of the outcome of a chastity test involving a magic cloak that has incriminated his secret beloved, Queen Guinevere (cf. Bax 1981), wants to joust with Ydier. Lanceloet's belligerence is directly motivated by the fact that Ydier happens to be escorting a gentlewoman who is wearing a mantle:

> Ende om dat dese vrouwe nu
> Enen mantel droech oec mede,
> Soe wildi nu al hier ter stede
> Jegen Ydire vechten.
>
> [And because this damsel/ also wore a cloak,/ he (= *Lanceloet*) wanted to duel with Ydier there and then.]

Of special interest is how Lanceloet manages to arrange combat. *Met haesten ende met gewoude* 'promptly and forcibly', as the narrator relates,

> (Lanceloet) wilde weten daer ter steden
> Wanen dat her Ydier quam,
> Want Lanceloet was utermaten gram
> Vanden mantele.
>
> [(Lanceloet) wanted to know without any delay/ where Sir Ydier came from,/ because Lanceloet was in a towering rage/ because of the cloak.]

It will be perceived that the text establishes a tight connexion between what Lanceloet actually says and what he intends by his utterance. For Lanceloet – and presumably any knight – making a coercively styled request for information is a means to provoke a fight. That such an inquiry is indeed a suitable means to that end is witnessed by Ydier's immediate response.

> (..) wat eest, wildi mi dwingen
> Te berechtene van enegen dingen
> Dies ic niet berechten wille?
> Ic soude eer vechten lude en stille,
> Eer ic u berechte een word
> Met bedwange.
>
> [Now what! do you want to compel me/ to give information about matters/ about which I have no wish to tell you?/ I'd rather fight with you,/ than give you one piece of information/ under compulsion.]

Although the intention to find out something seems to be the illocutionary point, in Searle's (1969) sense, of Lanceloet's request, the *Ragisel* episode evidences that the purpose of receiving information is not truly at issue. At issue is an attempt at putting down and insulting the interlocutor with a view to the latter's disobliging reaction, and, consequently, the provocation of "conflict". In *Karel ende Elegast*, too, the combat motive lies at the root of Elegast's query. Directly antecedent to his verbal initiative, Elegast entertains these malevolent ideas (ll. 347-353):

> Biden heere die mi ghewrochte,
> Hine ontrijt mi te nacht.
> Ic sel proeuen sine cracht
> Ic willen spreken ende kennen.
> Hy mach sulc sijn ic sel winnen
> Sijn ors ende dat hi heuet an
> Ende doen met lachter keeren dan.
> [By the Lord Who has created me,/ he (= *Karel*) will not escape me tonight./ I shall try his strength/ I shall speak to him and get to know him./ Whoever he may be, I shall gain/ his horse and all that he is wearing (= *Karel's costly coat of armour*)/ and make him withdraw in disgrace.]

Elegast's musings immediately inspire a practical course of action. He quickly turns his horse, catches up with the emperor, and then begins to grill him (l. 355 ff., *supra*). As we have seen, Karel feels mortified by Elegast's insolent behaviour, and finally they join issue.

It is material to my argument to maintain that, just like the controversy between Lanceloet and Ydier or similar cavalier altercations (cf. Bax 1995), the contention that motivates armed confrontation is merely a ritual conflict. In each case, the conflict is, contrary to its face-value, not genuinely about eliciting or withholding information, but about superior status. This, then, is how I conceive of this speech activity type. Given *a priori* intentions to engage in physical battle, chivalrous knights follow a prearranged and largely standardised verbal procedure in order to stage, or enact, a disagreement about precedence that must be dealt with in mortal combat. Since the subsequent utterances are only fully explicable in relation to this overall meaning structure of the speech activity, the ritual procedure bears comparison with a "language-game" as envisaged by the later Wittgenstein (1953: xi-xii; 1958: 81; see also Levinson 1983: 227, 280-281).

The concept of a "language-game" calls our attention to several salient general properties of the challenging procedure; in the next sections, I shall elaborate these vital points. In the first place, the concept indicates that the ritual designates a social institution of sorts, with structural properties, objectives, behavioural constraints, and practical consequences characterised by societal, or "public", recognition. Within the game-theoretical perspective, the ritual encounter represents a category of social activity that is typified by a limited set of constitutive rules; on that account, each instance of this particular language-game can be described in terms of rule-governed conduct. By the same principle, the notion of a game implies that the ritual is conditioned by the competence of the participants; they must know how to play the game, and they are only capable of playing it by bringing this (cultural) knowledge into practice.

As concerns the structural make-up of such actual performances, the concept of a game emphasises the relevance of an adjoining notion, that of the "interactional move" (cf. Jacobs and Jackson 1982). Like any game, the ritual procedure as a whole can be regarded, and should be analysed, as a temporally developed progression of moves and counter-moves. Thus stressing the underlying dynamics of the interaction order – *i.e.* the "dialectic" coupling of verbal actions and their co-ordinated sequels – the concept of a language-game underscores the idea that the ritual entails the element of (competitive) collaboration. While the participants jointly execute the ritual procedure by going through a co-ordinated series of structurally coupled initiating and responding moves, each interactional move controls the nature, and predetermines the effective power, of the competitor's supplementary action.

2.3. *The challenging ritual as a multilayered speech encounter*

Speaking of language-games, one is inclined to make reference to comparable concepts as well, such as "speech events" or "frames". Anthropological linguistic approaches, like the ethnography of speaking (Hymes 1972), or linguistically-informed sociological theories, like frame analysis (Goffman 1974), appear to be more specific and explicit, and theoretically more fully developed, than language-game philosophy; also, they have been put to the test empirically on a fairly large scale. (For the field of the ethnography of speaking, see Saville-Troike 1989 and Foley 1997; for frame analysis, see Tannen 1993, especially the Introduction, and Collins 1988). Therefore, if one strives for a deeper understanding of the mediaeval challenging ritual, it is perhaps well-advised to turn to such paradigms in order to delve into its general characteristics as elucidated by game theory.

Frame analysis, in particular, seems to offer excellent prospects to scrutinise and clarify the structural and functional dimensions of the ritual. As for the verbal actions performed within the course of the ritual, I shall argue that the utterances primarily function as cues for what Erving Goffman has called "keying".

In the sections above, I have tried to ascertain that the challenging ritual is a "stratified" interactional phenomenon. On the *prima facie* level, the verbal exchange amounts to a dispute of sorts, yet on closer inspection this strife is but a pretence. It is under the pretext of conflict that the interlocutors take up arms. Pivoting upon systematic modifications of the interpretation of social events, frame analysis may well be an appropriate method to distinguish, disentangle, and separate the diverse meaning levels of the ritual. In particular, utilising Goffman's technique of "bracketing" – a convenient methodology to dissect the multiple nature of social realities – is presumably most rewarding. When we put between brackets, and thus isolate, the concurrent events taking place in ritual challenging, we acquire a formally transparent representation of the ritual's interpretational prerequisites. As I see it, this is the complex interpretation structure of the challenging ritual:

[[[antagonistic behaviour][1] *ritual conflict*][2] **CONTRACT FORMATION**][3]

Figure 2: The Interpretation Structure of the Challenging Ritual

Figure 2 exhibits that there are three different things "going on" simultaneously in ritual challenging. In the first place, the verbal intercourse can be perceived as such. Goffman introduces the notion of a "primary frame" to refer to the unprejudiced observation and interpretation of events as they present, or seem to present, themselves. As regards primary frames, Goffman distinguishes between natural and social frames. Both natural and social events can be appreciated at face-value. We may make the observation that it is raining outside (a natural event), or that several individuals are waiting for the bus to arrive (a social event), without venturing at the eventual deeper meaning(s) of what we behold. Within the social primary frame of the knightly encounter, an entirely intelligible exchange of linguistic messages transpires. At the level of directly observable behaviour, we discern two participants engaged in conversation; there is a harsh tone to the discussion, seemingly the result of the contentious fashion in which one of the speakers makes a request for information. The general impression of the interchange within the primary frame is that the participants fall out over ungracious style, and finally have such an argument that they come to blows. On this interpretation, the encounter is completely meaningful in its own right – so meaningful indeed that literary scholarship has failed to appreciate the wholly symbolic nature, as conceived by Geertz (1973), of this battle-provoking agonistic verbal procedure (cf. Bax 1984).

As argued with particular reference to the *Ragisel* episode, there is more to the mediaeval speech encounter than meets the eye. From the onset, the friction about impudence is "staged", since haughty conduct is but a mutually recognised device to invite a trial of arms. Thus considered, the subsequent utterances eventuating in the (social) primary frame make up a secondary frame, one of ritual conflict. This "transformation" partakes of the characteristics of what Goffman calls a "make-believe" key, in that the participants play the role of authentic quarrellers, only to bring about the anticipated, and mutually desired, effect of the simulated controversy. According to Goffman (1974: 45 ff.), in order for tranformations to qualify as "keyings" several conditions must be satisfied. If we relate these (three) general conditions to the historical speech activity on hand, we may eventually gain access to a (not just temporally) remote "world of significance" (cf. Foley 1997: 17). As a first condition, Goffman asserts that

> (..) a systematic transformation is involved across materials already meaningful in accordance with a schema of interpretation (Goffman 1974: 45).

As I have established, the secondary frame of ritual conflict builds completely upon a primary frame that is already meaningful in itself. Goffman then explains the second requirement.

> Participants in the activity are meant to know and openly acknowledge that a systematic alteration is involved, one that will radically reconstitute what it is for them that is going on (Goffman 1974: 45).

That for at least one participant an insolent request for information amounts to the effort of drastically modifying the character of the speech event, is abundantly clear in the *Ragisel* episode. Given its motivational context, we cannot but presume that Lanceloet is fully aware that his request functions as a means to transform the context into a hostile encounter necessitating battle. Although Ydier's reply conforms with the interpretation that an alteration is involved, it cannot be weighed as conclusive evidence. Since his unyielding response is altogether comprehensible within the primary interaction frame, it does not necessarily imply his awareness that he is ritually challenged. There is another case, however, that portrays an addressee fully in the know of the "policy" of the transformation ritual. It involves an incident in the *Roman van Moriaen* ('The Romance of Blackamoor,' ll. 445-464), where Moriaen addresses Lanceloet as follows.

> Bericht mi, ridder, bi uwer trouwen,
> Anders maget u wel berouwen,
> Die beste warheit die gi wet
> Dat ic u sal vragen ende nine let

[Tell me, knight, upon your honour,/ or otherwise you will regret it,/ the truth as you best know it (= *as faithfully as you can*),/ that I am going to ask you, and do not fail to respond.]

Lanceloet reacts thus:

> Ic ware mi liuer doet,
> Dan mi een ridder dwingen soude
> Van dies ic doen nine woude.

[I'd rather be dead,/ than let a knight force me/ into doing something against my will.]

The follow-up of the verbal exchange is a clash. The interaction certainly has a familiar ring. Yet there are two things that mark the speciality of this case. The first is that Moriaen does not raise any question at all; he merely announces a request. He nevertheless ritualises the interaction by hinting at retributions. The other thing to emphasise is that Moriaen is a juvenile knight who came from abroad in search of his unknown father. On his way to the Holy Land, this obscure retainer of King Arthur's had begotten him on a dark-skinned princess – hence, the youngster's name, Blackamoor. In quest of his father, the black wanderer chances on Lanceloet and his companion Walewein. He sincerely intends to inquire after his father's whereabouts. But being an outsider from the chivalrous community in almost every respect, young Blackamoor formulates his query in a rather hapless fashion. Unapprehensive of its repercussions, or so it seems, he sturdily impersonates the demeanour of authentic knights. As becomes manifest only after the fight, it was more or less "by accident" that he defied Lanceloet. For the sake of guidance, Walewein, the paragon of idealistic chivalry, reproves Moriaen afterwards.

> (..)   Hets onsede
> Dat gi pleget ende doet mede.
> Gi sijt hier af nu ontweget:
> Haddi hoveschlike gevreget
> Daer u die sin toe hadde gedragen,
> Die riddere hads u gewagen
> Ende hads u bericht geerne.

[(..) Impudent and uncustomary/ is what you do and the way you behave (= *adopting a lofty tone with Lanceloet*)./ As to that, you're totally off course:/ if you had inquired in a courteous manner/ after what you desired to know,/ (*then*) the knight would have told you/ and would have given you the information gladly.]

This, then, is how I fathom the gist of the episode. Because he is unaware of the actual interpretation norms of the chivalric warrior caste, the interaction has only primary frame value for the "barbaric" youngster. For Moriaen, verbal dealings between gallant peers seem to require the display of role-inherent, but ultimately non-committal, rigour. Lanceloet, on the other hand, appreciates his interlocutor's solicitation for what it normally is, at least according to the "heroic standard", i.e., the customary understanding among the members of his social grouping: for the initiation of the challenging procedure. Hence his "conventional" reaction. It can be inferred from Walewein's critique that Lanceloet's taking up the gauntlet, be it thrown down deliberately or not, is the only worthy option.

Let me note in passing that there are other arguments in favour of the contention that in ritual challenging the participants adhere to the make-believe interpretation. As regards inquiries after the opponent's name, we must assume that such a request is oftentimes superfluous, because the addressee's identity can be gathered from his heraldic charge. It may well be that if the addressee bears a shield that reveals his identity, or if the participants already know each other (as is the case, for example, in the Lanceloet-Ydier encounter where, strikingly enough, the request for information pertains to something different than the opponent's name), the challenger selects another opening move, like a request for action or a (ritual) accusation (cf. Bax 1981).

Another point worthy of mention is that the provision of information is rarely an issue in the aftermath of the physical trial. If the addressee loses, it is rare for the initiator to insist on an answer. This is in full agreement with the idea that in ritual challenging the (Searlean) sincerity condition of normal requests is suspended – or that the (Gricean) quality maxim is violated – and, *ipso facto*, that the fight is only apparently inspired by the conflict in the primary frame.

In the above, I used the term "cue", thereby intentionally referring to Goffman's third requirement applying to keyings. He purports that

> (..) cues will be available for establishing when the transformation is to begin and when it is to end, namely, brackets in time, within which and to which the transformation is to be restricted (Goffman 1974: 45).

From the perspective of on-going interaction, cues are the very devices by which the participants initiate, affirm, sustain, and terminate the non-primary meaning level(s) of their interchange. It will be obvious that, given certain contextual conditions, I regard an interactional opening move embodying a compelling request for information (or for action) as a cue for the creation of a context of ritual conflict. Furthermore, the interaction is so rigidly prestructured (compare Figure 1), that each and every subsequent action must be considered as an endorsement or reaffirmation of its ritual nature.

The view that following the rules is tantamount to playing the game can be validated by numerous examples of distinct, but not altogether dissimilar, forms of ritualised verbal duelling: ancient forms, like the heroic flytings in the Homeric tradition (cf. Parks 1990), the Old Norse duelling genres of the *senna* and the *mannjafnaðr* (cf. Bax and Padmos 1983), or the verbal contests in the Old English *Beowulf* (cf. Clover 1980; Parks 1990); but also contemporary varieties, like the Afro-American sounding matches (cf. Labov 1972; Garner, 1983), or the Near-East verbal duelling rhymes (cf. Dundes *et al.* 1972). What these verbal competition genres have in common is that the "laws of the game" that regulate the interaction also have the import of defining actual practices. To the extent that the contenders adhere to the generic norms, their interchange can be perceived as an instance of the genre, whereas departures from the rules immediately result in the annulment of the ritual activity (cf. Labov 1972: 332-334; Kochman 1983).

As concerns the multiple, or "stratiform", meaning structure of the challenging ritual, there is one final point to attend to. I venture that by virtue of the make-believe character of the encounter the verbal procedure also amounts to the fabrication of a third key, namely, the extremely significant framework of contract formation, in that the overall functional import of the verbal procedure is the realisation of a mutually agreed outcome that allows for a trial of knightly prowess. If this view is accurate, the precombat request-for-information sequence has a threefold meaning structure (compare Figure 2).

1. Within the primary frame, an antagonistic encounter takes place. At this level of meaning, we are dealing with an argument of sorts, in which "biographical information" is the bone of contention.

2. Within the superordinate frame of make-believe, the series of subsequent hostile actions reiterates a conventional pattern of verbal behaviour. While the obligatory speech actions mark the emergence and the escalation of conflict, this conflict is only a matter of pretence, since the acts of requesting and refusing information violate the sincerity condition. At this secondary level of meaning, we deal with speech activities of a thoroughly symbolic nature.

3. Within the tertiary frame, both participants further the achievement of the projected outcome of their interaction, *viz.*, physical combat. Since the precombat manoeuvre of action and reaction is a (rule-governed) collaborative enterprise, the interaction qualifies as a co-operative undertaking. At this supreme level of meaning, we are dealing with a complex, and indirect, form of contract formation: By their readiness to fill the predestined parts of verbal contenders, and by playing these parts

according to the rules of the genre, both opponents make manifest their eagerness to contract for an imminent (non-verbal) course of action entailing a trial of arms (cf. Parks 1990: 42 ff.).

2.4. The literary challenging ritual as a mimetic representation of reality

It follows from the foregoing considerations that the discerned levels of meaning of the literary speech event are closely interrelated. It is obvious that the ritual conflict taking place in the secondary frame builds upon the violation of the sincerity condition of the initial request made within the primary frame. On the assumption that this request is "playful", it functions as a cue for the higher-ranking interpretation that the requestor is in fact challenging his opponent. Consequently, the addressee's refusal to provide the information speaks of his readiness to engage in battle: By countering his opponent's claim to dominance – for that is what his denial amounts to – the addressee demonstrates that he does not eschew warfare.

When viewed in this light, the subsequent acts of requesting and withholding information are symbolic actions bearing indirect pragmatic meanings. Contrary to their ostensible illocutionary force, they ultimately function as a challenge by Knight-the-First and its acceptance by Knight-the-Second, respectively. As such, these indirectly realised (primarily commissive) speech acts neatly reflect the explicitly formulated challenge subsequently performed by Knight-the-Second, and its unambiguous (verbal or non-verbal) acceptance by Knight-the-First (compare Figure 1). According to this interpretation, the mediaeval challenging ritual has a delicately balanced actional structure (cf. Bax, 1983). As Figure 3 shows, the verbal procedure guarantees that both adversaries prove equally strong as regards their boldness and their use of forceful language: Each contender challenges the other (the First indirectly and the Second directly), and each contender accepts his opponent's challenge (the First directly and the Second indirectly).

Given the inevitable, or – to put it even more strongly – predetermined, outcome of the verbal encounter, a trial of arms is necessary to settle the conflict about precedence. The ritual thus fulfils its practical function of "projecting" a military showdown. Exploiting the opposition between rivalry and co-operation, the level-headed challenging ritual exhibits "the classic flyting dialectic" (Parks 1990: 137) of contract negotiation through agonistic behaviour.

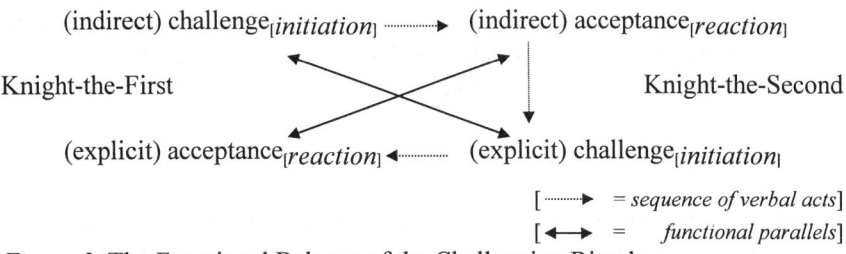

[⋯▶ = *sequence of verbal acts*]
[◀▶ = *functional parallels*]

Figure 3: The Functional Balance of the Challenging Ritual

But the complex contract-by-conflict process seems to serve at least two other practical goals as well. One notable property is that the ritual procedure allows for the selection of relevant opponents. My focal texts clearly manifest that the bipartite challenging ritual is exclusively performed on a "members only" basis – that is, by contestants belonging to the chivalrous in-group. Whereas knights who wish to joust with one another are prone to apply the ritual challenging procedure, they never do so when they engage in violent action directed at lesser, ungenteel opponents. Also, inferiors, like uncivilised robber knights, combative commoners, or pugnacious villains, never approach their opponents in a manner that stands comparison with the sophisticated indirect challenging procedure. Their policy is either to attack right away, or to openly threat and intimidate the adversary.

The *Roman van den Riddere metter Mouwen* 'The Romance of the Knight with the Sleeve' offers several examples of such direct confrontations. First, I quote a passage that instances an assault without further preface (ll. 1943-1954). In this episode, the Knight with the Sleeve attends a tournament. For reasons that need not concern us here, he is dressed up like a monk; he nevertheless rides a splendid horse. A bunch of daredevils armed with cudgels emerge from the crowd and get at him, aspiring to steal his costly mount.

> Doe quamen hem die colvenaren
> Ende waenden winnen sijn goede paert,
> Dat sijn gewichte van selvere was waerd.
> Si waenden den moenc scire afsteken,
> Dies hem sere sal willen wreken.
> Daer sloech een an hem die hant:
> Die colve hi hem scire ontprant,
> Die eyken was ende groet genoech,
> Dat was sere wel sijn gevoech.
> Hi ginc daer slaen onder hoep,

Sine cochten nie so diren coep:
Hi sloechse, dat si ter eerden lagen.

[Then the club-men confronted him;/ they thought they could gain his good horse/ that was worth its weight in silver./ They believed they could easily hurl the monk from the saddle/ (but) the latter will take revenge./ One attacked him then:/ forthwith, he (= *the Knight with the Sleeve*) forced his bludgeon out of his hand,/ it was made of oak and big enough./ This was very much to his (= *the Knight's*) liking./ He assailed the whole pack,/ they never struck such a bad bargain:/ he hit them until they lay (*dead*) on the ground.]

The other example of unceremonial provocation, exposing the abundant display of non-ritual verbal intimidation, stems from the same Middle Dutch narrative. It involves the encounter of the Knight with the Sleeve with a "tyrant" who oppresses the realm he has usurped (ll. 1653-1694). This sinister character, who avers to live by theft, addresses the Knight in a right-down ungentlemanlike fashion. To wit:

"Vasseel, ic sal u volgen naer!
Gine sult mi niet ontriden,
Gine selt jegen mi eer striden."
(..)
"Vaste," seit hi, "beet hier te voet.
Geeft op wapine ende paerd,
Al waerd vif hondert marc waerd.
Sidi spire, ic doe u hangen,
Sidi bode, ic doe u vangen,
Ende sidi riddere van aventuren,
Sone mogedi vor mi niet geduren:
Ic neme alden ridderen dleven.
(..)
Mi ontfoer noit man, sonder blijf,
Hine verloes sine ere oft sijn lijf.
Dit sijn mine seden, secgic u.
Geeft u op, dat radic nu."

["Knave, I shall pursue you!/ You will not escape me,/ first you will fight with me."/ (..)/ "Be quick," said he, "get off your horse./ Yield to me your weapons and your warsteed,/ even if it costs fivehundred marks./ If you are a spy, I shall have you lynched,/ if you are an envoy, I shall have you captured,/ and if you are a questing knight,/ you will be no match for me:/ I take the life of each and every gallant./ (..)/ No man has ever escaped me, with no exception,/ he either lost his honour or his life./ This is my custom, I assure you./ Surrender, that is what I recommend now."]

Although this specimen exhibits several verbal activities that echo speech actions which suit the ritual procedure (especially, the tyrant's challenge, and the way he menaces the Knight by boasting over his former feats), it must be noted that the resemblance is only superficial. It is, of course, self-evident that threats, insults, challenges, and cautions to surrender as such belong to the battlefield repertory. More importantly, the usurper's acts do not conform to the sequential pattern of the ritual (compare Figure 1). All in all, the tyrant's brutal approach is a far cry from the formalised enactment of controversy. For one thing, he *really* wants to rob the Knight of his horse and armour. In other words, his requests (for action) do not function as cues for a make-believe key, whereas Lanceloet, at the time of his encounter with Ydier, does not really wish to know where the latter happens to come from; what Lanceloet really intends is to contract for a test of martial prowess. As regards the non-ritual nature of the tyrant's verbal way of acting, we see that the Knight with the Sleeve reacts in a similar vein (ll. 1688-1692). He insults his interlocutor by using a foul term of abuse (while invectives are outside the scope of the ritual conflict), and gives a threatening back-answer. Subsequently (but in full disagreement with the rules of the ritual), the tyrant once again challenges the Knight, and they begin to fight (l. 1695 ff.).

"Opgeven, quade hont!
Ja, en benic noch gesont,"
Seide die riddere metter mouwen,
"Ic sal u noch heden doen berouwen,
Dat gi mi comen sijt dus naer."
Die tyrant antwerde hem daer:
"Nu weerd u dan, dat radic u."
Si reden te gadere beide nu
So sere dat haer speren braken.
Men horetse harde verre craken.
(*et cetera*)

["(Should I) relinquish, you wicked mongrel!/ Indeed so, if I were crack-brained,"/ said the Knight with the Sleeve,/ "This very day I shall make you regret/ that you have thus infringed upon me."/ The tyrant replied to him then:/ "Defend yourself now, that is my counsel."/ They hurled themselves upon each other/ so fiercely that their lances broke/ From faraway one could hear them crack.]

As he undid the greedy club-men, so the Knight with the Sleeve slays the tyrant. It is for certain that chivalrous knights could gain credit by the elimination of unruly riff-raff, or by the overpowering of felonious potentates. But what truly reaps glory and enhances prestige is gaining victory over a fellow-member of the distinguished warrior guild. At this junction, it is important to note that the *Moriaen* incident and comparable episodes clearly indicate that it is only they who seem to know, or are apt to apply, the rules of the ritual challenging game. I therefore surmise that, next to arranging combat, the practical function of the ritual is that it serves as an identification means. By acting and reacting according to the rules of the genre, both participants disclose that they belong to the elite category of high-principled military men. Thus, by "playing the game" they mutually bespeak their special significance as contenders.

Now this is the main reason that I am tempted to advance the far-reaching hypothesis that the alleged speech convention goes far beyond a literary motif. In light of its practical qualities – *viz.*, (1) the potential of establishing a trial of arms (2) between relevant opponents – we can go as far as to postulate that the ritual precombat dialogue suited, and in fact fully answered, particular realistic needs. One historical development that may be put forward in this connexion is the down-fall of the official tournament in the thirteenth century. Of old, tournaments, originally perilous events involving grave injuries and casualties, had been among the principal contexts for knights to gain honour and establish a reputation. Yet the persistent strictures of the Church against the sinful influences of tournaments – which, in addition to inciting combatants to commit the mortal sin of homicide, were supposed to inspire ungodly vanity, and rouse impious sentiments like wrath, envy, and greed – eventually resulted in a ban on tournaments. In turn, this prohibition led to an ever-swelling number of unofficial, unauthorised jousts, because the chivalrous community was loath to give up this opportunity for reaping glory (cf. Barker 1987).

Meanwhile, another factor also contributed to the decline of the attraction of the institution of tilt-yard jousting, *viz.*, technical innovations aimed at the increase of bodily safety (cf. Niedner 1881; Schultz 1889). It is very likely that, from the viewpoint of the dauntless, these substantial improvements derogated from the splendour of battle. Furthermore, the production costs of these "modern" armour-suits were such that eventually only the truly high and mighty were wealthy enough to purchase such commodities. Consequently, only grand lords and gentlemen of great substance were factually in a position to organise tourneys. At such events, knights competed in battle outfits supplied, for the time being, by the organiser; instead of winning the spoils of war (*i.e.*, the horse and armour of the losing party), they had to content themselves with a prize or some mark of honour.

As Barker (1987) has argued, both historical developments furthered the rise and the spread of "unorchestrated" trials of arms. During the late-mediaeval era, a great many errant knights, roving the lands alone or travelling as a group – their minds invariably set on glorious exploits – pitted their strength against the known and unknown knights they came across. Unlike the tournament at the time of its deterioration into "an innocent form of sport" (van Winter 1965: 98), these encounters more often than not amounted to combat *à outrance*, to a life-and-death struggle. It was on victories won in such an honourable fashion that a knight could honestly pride himself.

Returning to the presumption that the challenging ritual rendered in literary texts depicts a real-life tradition, I feel I ought to stress how well this procedure accords with the facts of history. One thing requiring emphasis is that the interactional structure of the ritual is such that it inevitably effects in the balanced condition of "symmetrical" verbal performance (compare Figure 3); that this undecisive outcome requires that the participants ensuingly engage in physical combat exemplifies the functional relevance of the ritual procedure under real-life conditions.

The practical significance of the challenging ritual can even be strengthened more if we assume, as I think we have sufficient reason to, that the multifarious contract-by-conflict procedure also functioned as a membership categorisation device of sorts (cf. Sacks 1972), and accordingly served as a means to assess the relevance, in the context of the courtly honour cult, of potential adversaries. As I have just advanced, the practice of unarranged jousting seems to have been rather wide-spread during the period of the waning of the Middle Ages. Recently, quite a lot of historical evidence in support of this contention has become available. On the basis of his research on the non-fictional (Middle Dutch) discourse genre of the *ererede* (*literally*: 'laudatory speech'), designating ideology-abiding eulogies by kings-of-arms, or heralds, that revere the honourable exploits of knights, van Anrooij (1990) has pointed out that, especially during the fourteenth century, knights habitually undertook long journeys. As he contends, the illustrious figure of the *chevalier errant* – for a long time deemed a romanticised character – is not a literary motif at all. In point of fact, knights used to travel far and wide, often choosing the borderlands of the Christian world (Lithuania, Prussia, Cyprus, Rhodes, North Africa, the Holy Land) for their destination. Such tours offered a plentitude of opportunities for "unrestrained" valorous action, including single combat of the hazardous, hence supremely prestigious, variety. Since a heraldic *ererede* in many respects comprises the biography of a knight, it is the choice medium to relate and laud his heroic deeds, and to sing the praise of his chivalrous excellence. The real-life phenomenon of chronicling knightly exploits fits in well with another wide-spread literary motif. In chivalric romances, we repeatedly find that the knight who has lost the duel is sent to the royal court in order to report how he was vanquished, and how magnanimously he was treated by the victor.

Now this brings me to a third practical quality of the challenging ritual as a social institution. Although my conclusions are as yet not final, I am inclined to believe that the ritual procedure has defining import as regards the nature of the physical violence that is allowed in chivalrous combat. As several contributions to the volume on the anthropology of violence edited by Riches (1986) attest, assumptions about the use, or the manner of use, of force and about the extent to which violence is permitted are in a large measure of a societal nature. For obvious reasons, cultural communities are liable to develop norms that surround and regulate violent action, although these normative premises may be of a rather implicit character. Encultured individuals who are in the know of the cultural code concerning corporeal atrocity have all kinds of notions pertaining to aggressive behaviour: when outrage is appropriate, allowed, or even mandatory; what kind of violence may or ought to be practised; towards whom an act of violence may or may not be directed; and so on.

It seems to me that the overall impact of the joint performance of the challenging ritual is not only that the contenders give evidence of their group identity and enter into a contract for combat, but also that they contract for the actual fashion in which the battle will be fought, namely, according to the chivalrous ideal of what we may tentatively call "fair play". First, it must be noted that this combat code exclusively applies to duels between peers in the form of a joust. Knights also used to engage in warfare in the sense of military actions against an opposing army (cf. Verbruggen 1997), but this warfare was of a completely different nature than chivalrous jousting. Parenthetically, the political need of a mounted military force is originally the very *raison d'être* of knighthood (cf. van Winter 1965: 105-106).

As concerns the chivalrous combat code, several characteristics come to mind. From my readings through mediaeval epic, I gather that jousts usually begin with the two contenders retreating in opposite directions in order to hurtle together in a preliminary charge with couched lances; this action is repeated until one of the contenders is hurled from the saddle. It should be remarked that the combatants must refrain from "tricks" like, for instance, stabbing the other in the back with a dagger that the deceiver has kept hidden under his shield. In modern Dutch, there is an idiom reminiscent of such-like malpractices, namely, *Hij voert iets in zijn schild*, which can be rendered in English as 'He is up to no good'. Literally understood, though, the expression means 'He carries something (dangerous) under his shield'.

Although his position on horseback is advantageous, the knight who has managed to remain in the saddle also dismounts. Sword in hand, the contenders recommence their fight; this clash lasts for as long as it takes for one contender to fell his opponent, or until one party gives up. Normative assumptions apply again to the aftermath of the fight: the victor must not mutilate his victim, be he dead or alive; if the loser has survived the incident, and has proven to be a praiseworthy enough opponent, his life should be spared; if he is slain, the victor should see that he gets a decent burial; if he is gravely wounded, the winner should see that the sufferer is properly taken care of. As the verbal phase of the encounter is severely rule-governed, its physical sequence is likewise strictly regulated.

As for the professed injunct against mutilation – a cruel practice with a time-honoured tradition (cf. Segal 1971) – I would like to note, as an aside, one deviant case that may be of interest. It concerns a trial of arms between the meritorious Knight with the Sleeve and Keye, who in (the later) Arthurian literature represents the very essence of unchivalry and cowardice. Early in his exemplary chivalric career, the Knight with the Sleeve has been grossly insulted by Keye's remark that he would rather make a good farm-hand than an estimable knight (compare *Roman van den Riddere metter Mouwen*, ll. 202-214). When they meet later on, the Knight gives Keye a firm dressing down under the full gaze of his peers (*o.c.*, l. 1584 ff.). During the precombat exchange, the Knight comes back to his enemy's previous insult.

"Her Keye, bi Gode, ic segt u,
Gi hebt mi versproken nu ende echt,
Mochtics mi wreken, ic hadde recht.
Gine ontgaet mi heden, ic segt u twi:
Ic sal u doden, oft gi mi."

["Sir Keye, by God, I tell you this:/ You have defamed me now and before,/ if I could take revenge, I would have every right to it./ You will not escape me today, I tell you twice:/ I shall kill you or you me."]

Then the fight begins.

Si quamen te gader met haren speren;
Die riddere staken in der weren
Dore halsberch, ende dor curie
Ende dorre die borste. – "Ic lie! Ic lie!,"

Ritual Levelling 57

Riep her Keye met haesten groet,
Dor die vrese vander doet.
Ende alse die riddere trecte weder
Sijn spere, viel her Keye ter neder.
Die riddere beette doe ter eerde
Ende minctene sere met sinen swerde.

[They hurled together with their lances;/ defending himself, the Knight thrust him (= *Keye*)/ through his armour-suit and his leather jerkin/ and in the breast. – "I surrender! I surrender!,"/ Sir Keye cried at once,/ because of his fear of death./ And when the Knight pulled back/ his lance, Sir Keye fell down./ *The Knight dismounted then/ and maimed him brutally with his sword.*]

As to this corporal abuse, the narrator candidly comments *Nu heeft hi, dat hem behiet* 'Now he [= *Keye*] gets what he deserves'. That maiming one's victim is allowed under special circumstances (like the utterance of a particularly hateful insult or the demonstration of excessive poltroonery), and is then not necessarily detrimental to one's reputation, is confirmed by the Court's "official reaction" (l. 1625 ff.).

Ende alsment te hove comen sach,
Wisten si wel van Keys mesvalle.
Si warens te hove blide alle.
Doen quam daer saen die niemare,
Dat Keye sere gewont ware.
Hi was der coninginnen oem,
Nochtan nam sijs crancken goem:
Dat quam bi sire quader tongen.
"Ic wilde, hem sine ogen utsprongen,"
Sprac Jenevre, die coninginne,
"Dine tirst brachte hier inne.
Laet den dorper licgen daer,
Hi heves dicke verdient, vorwaer."
Nochtan haeldemene dor die scame,
Om dat hi hadde ridders name.
Men vordene gewont toter doet
In die borch te Carmeloet.

[And when at the court they saw it coming (= *Keye's horse returning to the castle without its rider*),/ they fully understood what ill-fate had befallen Keye./ At the court, everybody rejoiced over that./ Soon followed the news/ that he was seriously hurt./ He was the queen's brother-in-law,/ but she nonetheless did not care a snap:/ that was because of his sharp tongue./ "I wish the eyes would spring out,"/ spoke Jenevre, the queen,/ "of the very one who first brought him in here./ Let the yokel lie there,/ it serves him absolutely right."/ They picked him up, yet, because they were ashamed/ because he was, after all, a knight./ Fatally injured, he was brought/ to the castle of Carmeloet (= *Camelot*).]

It appears to me that the practical qualities of the challenging ritual that I have elucidated are well in accord with specific real-life requirements. By following this procedure, knights make sure (1) that they can engage in battle, (2) that they contend with a fitting opponent, and (3) that they fight according to the fair-play norms of the chivalrous community. All this goes far to substantiate the feasibility of the fact that the ritual speech convention rendered in mediaeval narrative represents an authentic tradition of language use. Thus far, however, genuinely conclusive evidence is lacking that the literary ritual is in truth a mimetic represention; the term "mimetic" is used here in the sense of Auerbach's (1953), and designates the concept of a firm correspondence between textual and extra-textual particulars. Although it can be argued, as I have tried to show, that the challenging procedure in principle marks out a highly "realistic" mode of behaviour, there exists, as far as I know, no source that unambiguously testifies to its factual occurrence. Therefore, all evidence is circumstantial.

I am fully aware of the danger of utilising fictional texts as sources of information about reality. Of course, it would be absurd to maintain that literature at all times, and in all cultures, conforms exactly to reality. But is there really so much more logic, to paraphrase Otto Jespersen's felicitous expression (1922: 397-398), in the opposite extreme, which denies any kind of mimetic rapport between literary documents and the actual cultural contexts from which they have emerged? I certainly don't think so. Elsewhere – and also in connexion with the chivalrous challenging ritual – I have treated the strained relations between literary fiction and reality in some detail (cf. Bax 1981 and 1991), referring, among other things, to the attested analogy of the representation of judicial combats, or "ordeals", in historical chronicles and literary texts (cf. Pfeffer 1885; van Caenegem 1967; Bloch 1974). Furthermore, I have tried to ascertain that in mediaeval epic the alteration of, or the deviation from, reality tends to affect the overall moral message, or *sen*, rather than the *matière*, that is, narrative content matter as such (cf. Owen 1968: 121-124). Be that as it may, we must reckon with the possibilty that the claim that the literary ritual captures a real-life custom can never be proven.

But then the more or less "positivist" standpoint that its factual existence ought to be corroborated is not on a par with mediaeval conceptions of truth and falsity. It is an established fact of historical science that ostensibly trustworthy written documents from the Middle Ages, such as chronicles, annals, and records of travels – that reiterate the veracity of the accounts they offer – are characterised by what modern scholarship inclines to regard as a curious, if not bizarre, mixture of solid *facta* and amazing *ficta* (cf. Tilmans 1989 and 1992). In effect, recent developments in the philosophy of history, inspired above all by the seminal work of Hayden White on historical representation, have furthered radical scepticism as regards the *veritas topos*, the truth-claim that since Aristotle's theoretical reflections on history has become a distinctive feature of the historiographic genres. It appears that in former ages the mutual "pragmatic understanding" (Searle 1979) between the historical writer and his audience differed considerably from the presuppositions related to such a bond today, and that we should distinguish, for instance when dealing with mediaeval texts, between epistemic truth and renderings that meet the criterion of "mimetic reliability".

What a mediaeval audience required, or so it seems, is that works of art and learning have sufficient "openness" to the world as they know and experience it. Even if not truly authentic, mimetically reliable texts, both historical and fictional, comply with the body of beliefs, norms, preoccupations, and preferences that make up a culture's "climate of opinion" (cf. Becker 1932), and agree with the rhetorical principles and representation or "emplotment" modes that characterise the concerned genres (cf. White 1987; Rigney 1990). It goes indeed without saying that the mediaeval "world of significance" (to quote Foley again) is in nearly every respect vastly different from the world as we perceive it. To the degree that I can probe the mind of the aristocracy – *casu quo*, the primarily intended audience of chivalrous romances, consisting of sovereigns, vassals, paladins, knights, and other representatives of the elite – I believe that what Coleridge once aptly called "a willing suspension of disbelief" is not involved. Even when it concerns the attitude of contemporary audiences towards literary motifs that from the viewpoint of modern Western society are unequivocal fabrications, like fairy-tale themes, miraculous phenomena, magical events, cases of enchantment, *et cetera*, we may take it for granted that such matters were not apprehended as fictional in our sense of the word.

Two of many possible examples can serve to illustrate this point. In *Karel ende Elegast* (l. 733 ff.), it is related how Karel and Elegast, who by now have resolved to join forces in a criminal activity, burgle the mansion of one of the emperor's peers. After they have dug a hole in the wall surrounding the abode, Elegast sneaks in to size up the situation. It then emerges that Elegast, whose name is usually understood as "Friend of the Elves", has a truly remarkable proficiency (ll. 804-811):

> Hi trac een cruyt vut eenen vate
> Ende deet binnen sinen monde
> Die sulc een hadde hi verstonde
> Wat hanen crayen ende honden bilen
> Doen verstont hi ter wilen
> An enen hane an enen hont
> Ende seide dat die coninc stont
> Buten den houe in haer latijn

[He took a herb out of a holder/ and put it into this mouth./ Whoever possessed such (*a means*) could understand/ what cocks crowed and dogs bayed./ He then learned/ from a cock (*and*) a dog,/ who said so in their latin (= *language*), that the king (= *Karel*) was/ standing outside the court.]

When Elegast reports to his ally what he has discovered, Karel, who is averse from exposing his identity, feigns utter disbelief. But then Elegast urges him to find out for himself (ll. 836-840):

> Nv hoort sprac elegast
> Hi stac den coninc inden mont
> Een cruyt dat daer voor hem stont
> Ende seyde nv suldi verstaen
> So ic te voren hebbe ghedaen

["Hear now," spoke Elegast./ He put into the king's mouth/ a herb growing right in front of him/ and said "Now you shall hear/ what I have heard before".]

Now Karel also overhears the cock's and the hound's communications. How he subsequently copes with his trying position is of no interest here. My point is that we have to assume that for the contemporary audience the concept of a magic herb is by no means unrealistic or mistaken, but mimetically "sound". The same holds for the marvellous charm we encounter in an episode of *Ridder metter Mouwen* (l. 870 ff.). The Knight with the Sleeve has fought against Sir Amelant, the guardian of *Twout sonder genade* 'The Unmerciful Forest'. Both warriors are severely injured. Amelant summons his servant, the dreadful dwarf Felloen, who has supernatural powers, and charges him to heal them (ll. 1010-1015).

> Een vingerlijn hadde Felloen
> Daer met seindi die wonden doen.
> Daer was een steen in gewracht.

Die steen hadde sulke cracht:
Al hadde een man doetwont gewesen,
Seindine daermet, hi ware genesen.

[A wee ring had Felloen./ With that he blessed the wounds then./ It was adorned with a gem./ Such was the power of this stone:/ even if a man were fatally wounded,/ if he blessed him with it, he was instantly recovered.]

Taking into consideration, then, that it is as good as certain that for contemporary audiences even such quaint story-elements represented credible enough accounts, I posit that the far more down-to-earth challenging procedure rendered in romance must have had a very close resemblance to an actual routine. If it were essentially at variance with what could be observed, and indeed experienced, on a regular basis, it would have been downright anomalous, whereas aberrations concerning content matter *per se* are not specifically to the mediaeval taste. It is scarcely imaginable that the literary challenging procedure modelling a verbal practice that was highly occurrent in the real world, was nevertheless seriously deviant from that actual method. All things considered, it seems warranted to hypothesise – although the strong confirmatory data upon which this assumption will stand or fall is as yet unavailable – that the narrative transformation ritual, with its conventional opening moves and restricted set of stock-responses, bears upon, and is firmly rooted in, reality.

To bring this section to a close, I would like to elaborate on this theoretical speculation, and slightly complicate the picture. Siding with the commanding thinker Merlin Donald, who only recently proclaimed that "historically, the proscription of speculation in science has been unproductive" (1993: 1), I put forth that we cannot preclude the possibility that it is the literary challenging convention that has acted upon actual (pre)combat customs.

First of all, it is not inconceivable that the literary ritual served as an exemplary model of sorts. In his essay on the influence of Arthurian romance on factual events, expressly those of a festive character, Loomis (1959) describes how, from the beginning of the thirteenth century, fictional characters, narrative episodes, and literary occurrences (including the passage of arms) were "mimicried". There is no compelling reason to discard out of hand the presumption that such-like re-enactments, or imitative "reproductions", exceeded the bounds of festal or sportive contexts. True enough, we cannot rule out the possibility that knights fashioned the verbal phase of their contentious encounters after an outstanding literary role-pattern.

But a contiguous conjecture is just as intriguing, namely, that the ritual method embodied in celebrated narrative texts actually strengthened and propagated an already established oral practice. If this tentative proposition is not erroneous, then we have a significant historical example of the intricate interplay of literacy and orality as distinct communicative modes.

Whether or not the literary language-game of "ritual levelling" – *viz.*, the illuminated method of reciprocal verbal abasement that is so devised that the participants eventually draw level, and, consequently, must get level with each other – functioned as, or reinforced, a practical action model, is by no means certain. The mere thought, however, that either of these, or some scenario similar in kind, is indeed the case puts a different complexion upon the vexed question concerning the interdependencies and the mutual influences of life and art.

3. The contract-by-conflict procedure in rhetorical stage-plays

In order to explain ritual conflict as a means to forge a contractual framework, I now turn to another example of artificial verbal intercourse, *viz.* a peculiar (literary) speech convention exemplified by dramatic art. During the early-sixteenth century, the stages, boards, scenes, and theatres in the Netherlands featured – and apparently they were unique in this – grotesque characters that must have been fully outside the common run, namely, *sinnekens*. *Sinnekens* are allegorical *dramatis personae* – the word form *sinneken* is the diminutive of *sin(ne)*, 'sense', 'symbol'. As emblematical characters, *sinnekens* are symbolic of destructive human weaknesses (like the leaning to sensual pleasure or idleness), and potentially damaging psychological dispositions (like jealousy, conceit, or unfaithfulness). Hence, *sinnekens* have "telling" names, like *Schijn van Heligheyt* 'Hypocrisy', *Jalours Ghepeyns* 'Spiteful Regard', *Tversteent Hertte* 'Heart-of-Stone', or *Vleyschelijcke Sin* 'Carnal Lust'.

Sinnekens, who are either male or female, are diabolic figures, limbs of the Devil. In the transitional epoch from the Middle Ages to the Renaissance, they were the heirs to the earlier wide-spread tradition of devil-belief and "witchmania" to which, in addition to historical sources, the extensive corpus of mediaeval miracle plays and mysteries bears witness. That *sinnekens* achieved great popularity, if that is the word, with playwrights and the play going public, although their horrifying impact on contemporary audiences should not be underestimated, can be inferred from their appearance in approximately one hundred and fifty of the two hundred-odd rhetorical stage-plays that have come down to us from the early-sixteenth century (cf. Hummelen 1958: 28). The presumption, by the way, that *sinnekens* were apprehended as absolutely hideous characters is not inconsistent with the fact that their eerie dialogues can occasionally be facetious; it seems a patent truism that making fun of it is one way of coping with the macabre.

As regards their on-stage performance, *sinnekens* always act in pairs, and join forces to try and deceive, and ultimately undo, the upright but wavering principal character(s) of the play. Like *Vreese voor Schande* 'Fear of Disgrace' avows, *Wy bedrieghen de gantse werelt te gadere* 'We beguile the whole world'. Sometimes *sinnekens* perform their devilish duties as hidden persuaders, but more often than not they engage in verbal interaction with their prey. In each case, they are after one thing only: the victim's descent into hell. Compare the equivocal raillery of the female *sinnekens Natuerlijcke Begheerte* 'Sensual Desire' and *Quaet Ingheven* 'Evil Inspiration' in *Gevallen en weer opstaande Mensch* 'The Man Who Fell but was Again Resurrected', ll. 261-265.

NB: Wij crijghen hem tavent al in ons coyken.
QI: Vorwaer, ghij sijt een dobbel proyken,
    Ghij bringt wel menighe in uw stalleken.
NB: Pronct hoe hi wille, hij moet in 't valleken
    Noch tavent wesen als een gevanghen man.

[(SD:) As soon as this evening, we shall trap him in our cage/ (EI:) For certain, you are quite a light-o'-love,/ you lure many a man into your love-nest./ (SD:) He may strut along as he likes, but eventually he must enter into the pit/ this very night, he will be wrenched.]

Given the heinous character of *sinnekens*, we should not make light of the alleged cage, love-nest, and pit. Since *sinnekens* are fiendish creatures, accomplices of the Prince of Darkness, they are determined to lead their victims to their fatal doom. In *Tspel van den Ontrouwen Rentmeester* ('The Play of the Unjust Steward', ll. 40-43), the *sinnekens Tversteent Hertte* and *Ontrouwen Dienst* 'Unfaithful Service' thus sound the praises of each other's wrong-doings:

TH: En duer u is ons Meester, Lucifer, dick gloriënde;
    Menighen ghy doet metten brande vernielen.
OD: Men soudse niet cunnen getellen, alle die siele
    Die ghy met u, Versteent Herrte, hebt bracht tondere.

[(HoS:) And it is because of you that our Lord, Lucifer, is ofttimes triumphant;/ many a one you have destroyed by the fires (*of hell*)./ (US:) One is incapable of counting all the souls/ that you, Heart-of-Stone, have brought down with you (= *to hell*).]

Although *sinnekens* are prone to work together, their collaboration is invariably hampered by the fact that these perfidious figures, each one being evil through-and-through, profoundly distrust each other. This "unproductive" attitude becomes manifest in the course of the preparatory dialogue that precedes the actual attempt to entice the victim; literary scholarship has termed this bilateral "aside" the *scene apart* (cf. Hummelen 1958).

On the grounds of a comparative pragmatic analysis of six specimens of the *scene apart*, I conclude that the interactants overcome their aloofness by performing a rather eccentric identification ritual. Throughout the verbal exchange that the *scene apart* encompasses, *sinnekens* mockingly abuse and level at each other. Compare, for instance, how the interaction proceeds in the *scene apart* of the rhetorical history-piece *Joseph* (ll. 94-99); the antagonists are *Quaet Ingheven* 'Evil Inspiration' and *Nijdigh Herte* 'Angry Heart'.

QI: Deur u, Nijdigh Herte, wert Daniel ook gesonden
    Om te werden verslonden inden leeuwencuijl.
NH: Houdt, zegh ick, u backhuijs!
QI: Swijcht oock, ghij uuijl,
    En hout uwen muijl: we en derren ons vuijl
    Voor elck een niet int openbaer brengen.

[(EI:) It was by your accomplishment, Angry Heart, that Daniel was sent/ to be devoured in the lion's den./ (AH:) Keep your mouth shut, I say!/ (EI:) Be silent too, you silly clod,/ and shut up: there is no need for us/ to wash our dirty linen in public.]

Such fickle arguments flare up instantly, but are brought to a conclusion just as easily, as is evidenced by *Ontrouwen Rentmeester* (ll. 52-56). After a bout of verbal sparring, *Ontrouwen Dienst* and *Tversteent Hertte* agree that rivalry is now not at issue.

OD: Ou, waerom spraeckt ghy my toe soe vileynlyck
    Daer wy gemeynlyck syn en vry in eenen spele?
TH: Wy en dueghen, certeyn, bey niet veele;
    Dus, bons pays, laet sulcx doch staken.
OD: Je suis content, neve

[(US:) Ouch, why do you speak to me in such a vilifying fashion/ while we are unanimous and much of a muchness in our game?/ (HoS:) We undeniably are a bad lot;/ so let us make peace and give up jumping on each other./ (US:) I am appeased, cousin.]

Even though such insulting sequences and squabbles seem contentious enough, the verbal skirmishes between *sinnekens* – that unlike the precombat hostilities between jousting knights are not of a heroic, or martial, nature – appear on second thoughts to be ritual in character, since offence is not sincerely intended (cf. Bax and Vuijk 1990). As is the case with the mediaeval challenging procedure, so the antagonistic verbal behaviour of *sinnekens* solely functions as a device to contract for combined action. The verbal procedure that constitutes the make-believe key of ritual discord is a means to the end of ascertaining that between the interlocutors there is enough common ground to proceed together with the dupery of the protagonist.

3.1. Ritual contract formation in sinneken *dialogues*

How the contract-by-conflict model applies to the *sinneken* dialogue will primarily be illustrated on the grounds of the *scene apart* in *De Spiegel der Minnen* ('The Mirror of Love', l. 145 ff.). Although this example portrays two *sinnekens* who are relatively restrained as regards verbal abuse, it is one of the most elaborated *scenes apart* occurring in the corpus of published rhetorical stage-plays. (For the larger part these texts have not yet been edited.) When expedient, I shall draw into the exposition examples from the other plays I have studied.

The *scene apart* in *De Spiegel der Minnen*, the appraised "*spel van sinne*", or morality, written by the Brussels rhetorician Colijn van Rijssele, presumably before 1530, concerns a precursory dialogue between the female *sinnekens Begheerte van Hoocheden* 'Craving for Eminence' and *Vreese voor Schanden* 'Fear of Disgrace', who conspire against a young needle-woman of low birth, one Katherina Sheermertens. What they want to accomplish is that she falls in love with a man of high station. Because the love-affair will indubitably be thwarted by the distinction of rank, the meddlesomeness of family-members, and slander in the community, the *sinnekens* presume that Katherina will become susceptible to their infernal prompts.

Beforehand, I have partitioned the conversation between "Eminence" and "Disgrace", as I shall henceforth call them, into four sections; as we shall see in due course, each of these exchanges serves a specific (sub)goal.

3.2. Round One: The projection of joint action

The first round functions as a summons-answer sequence (Schegloff 1972): Eminence's request for action – *i.e.* Disgrace is urged to pay attention to something – opens up the conversation, while Disgrace shows by her rejoinder that she is willing to engage in verbal intercourse.

Eminence 1:   Kijct, broerken, kijckt!
Disgrace 1:   Wat wil ick kijcken?
Eminence 2:   Ick weet waert strijct.
Disgrace 2:   Soo latet blijcken,
              Wy moeten doen ons offerhande.

> [(E1:) Look, little brother, look!/ (D1:) Why (or where) should I look?/ (E2:) I know where something (*of interest*) is going on./ (D2:) (*If so,*) then show me,/ (*for*) we must make our sacrifice (= *we must render our services to Lucifer*)].

Yet there is more to Disgrace's reaction, and to this discourse stretch as a whole, than appears. Just like practically every speech act, a request for action has a limited set of continuation options (cf. Franck 1979): the addressee can either comply with the request, or refuse to carry it out. And then there is this third continuation option. In preparation of his final (non)compliant reaction, the addressee may raise questions pertaining to the particulars of the initial request; in the case of such an "explorative" reaction, the addressee "puts off" the request, as Labov and Fanshel have called it (1977: 87).

Putting off Eminence's request is what D1 clearly amounts to. Before she commits herself, Disgrace wants to obtain more information. What she desires to know is for what reason she should pay attention, or at what she should look – the text is ambiguous in this respect, but given Eminence's reaction (E2), I favour the first reading. In E2, Eminence stresses the significance of her request. She alleges to be in the know of something that is relevant to *sinnekens*, and thus re-enforces her original request. On this interpretation, E2 marks the interactional perspective of common concern. Whereas requests for action predominantly presuppose that the requester is the availing party, Eminence's request is apparently made with a view to what is beneficial for *both* of them. Disgrace responds in a likewise fashion, acknowledging that it is about time that *they* should come into action on behalf of their mutual master. But D2 contains an additional piece of information as well, *Soo latet blijcken* 'Then show me'. In saying something to the effect of "If indeed you know about something that may be profitable to us, then make out your case," Disgrace puts off Eminence's request again. She challenges her interlocutor to back up her claim.

It is my contention that by twice putting off Eminence's request Disgrace puts in a proviso as concerns combined action. As her reservation implies, she may eventually join in with Eminence, but her availability is as yet conditioned. Now what would be the ordinary follow-up, given Disgrace's wariness? One might expect an account by Eminence to underscore her idea that Katherina Sheermertens is a likely victim to enticing. Such an explanation might have set Disgrace's qualm at rest. Yet Eminence's actual reaction amounts to something completely different. "I am Craving for Eminence," says she, whereupon Disgrace also introduces herself, as if this continuation is quite unremarkable (compare E3-D3, *infra*).

Given its blatantly marked character, the continuation E3-D3 probably indicates that the sequential structure E1-D2 constitutes an entire "functional block", a complete discourse unit with specific interactional goals. As we have seen, this discourse unit opens up the conversation (cf. Schegloff 1972). D2, in particular, demonstrates that Disgrace is willing to engage in verbal interaction with Eminence. But opening up the conversation is not the only motive of this interactional phase. If I am not mistaken, it also contains a cue to the nature of the dialogue, in that Eminence uses a membership term (cf. Sacks 1972). Notwithstanding her femininity (compare E4-D4), she calls the addressee *broerken* 'brother'. Similar (affected) intimate forms of address occurring in the *scene apart* can be found in *Ontrouwen Rentmeester* (namely, *neve, nichte* = male and female cousin, respectively) and in *De Wellustige Mensch* 'The Decent Man' (*maetgen* = matey, partner). Another example is *mijn alderliefste maech* 'my dearly beloved relative'. In the opening sequence of *Gevallen en weer opstaande Mensch*, the *sinnekens* call each other by their names; but in the second round they nonetheless present themselves to each other (compare the corresponding passage in *Spiegel der Minnen, in casu* E3-D3).

In all the texts I have studied, *sinnekens* make use of this particular membershipping device, supposingly in order to impart that they recognise each other as devotees of *Rex Mundi*, as fellows of the villainous order of soul-snatchers. If so, this property of the initiating exchange of the *scene apart* is a first clue as to the ritual nature of the speech event. Membershipping makes manifest the intention to contract for joint action at the expense of a particular individual.

What this collaborative enterprise will virtually amount to is an issue that the *sinnekens* eventually deal with in the fourth and final round. The preceding exchanges are meant to verify if the conditions applying to concerted action are satisfied. As Disgrace's reservation evidences, *sinnekens* need to know where they are with each other, especially because they have good reasons to distrust each other. In the preliminary sequence in *Ontrouwen Rentmeester* (ll. 8-12), suspicion is straightforwardly blazoned:

TH: Wat schuylter, nichte?
OD: Al gaet dat ick weve.
TH: Ick schatte een lueghen dichte.
OD: Ten is, by bey myn tuyten.
TH: Eest anders, ghy cryges verwyt

[(HoS:) What's up, cousin?/ (US:) All that I undertake works out splendidly./ (HoS:) That I deem an outrageous lie./ (US:) 'Tis not, I swear on both my braids./ (HoS:) If it turns out to be different, then I shall settle with you.]

The second and third round serve to warrant that co-operation is indeed possible and desirable. In the course of the second exchange, the associates-to-be reveal, or reaffirm, to each other their vile character, whereas the third exchange bears out that the *sinnekens* are equally ill-disposed towards the victimised party.

3.3. Round Two: Offensive behaviour as an identification device

It follows from what I said about the structure and the function of the opening exchange of the *scene apart* in *De Spiegel der Minnen* that E3-D3 is only apparently incoherent. On the assumption, then, that the goal of the preliminary exchange, *viz.* the tentative prospect of collaboration, is reached, I propose that the second round of the speech event furthers the allayment of suspicions.

Eminence 3: Ick ben begheerte van hoocheden.
Disgrace 3:   Ende ick vreese voor schande,
    Die alle reyn maechdekens versimpelt.
Eminence 4: Ons namen zijn vrouwelijck.
Disgrace 4:   Daerom zijn wy ghewimpelt,
    Al waren wy Venus quackernellekens,
    Verstadijt, nichte?
Eminence 5:   Wy zijn twee ghesellekens
    Beneden thooft, alsomen sien mach.
Disgrace 5: Tis wonder wat duer ons beyden gescien mach.
    Begeerte van hoocheden mach wonder coken.
Eminence 6: By u heeft menich den hals ghebroken
    Om het radt van fortuyne op te rechtene.
Disgrace 6: Dat en staet ons hier niet te beslechtene,
    Hoe hoogher gheclommen, hoe swaerder val.

Eminence 7: Sulck waent, hij mist.
Disgrace 7: Daer hebdijt al,
Wy bedrieghen de gantse werelt te gadere.
Eminence 8: Leo is ons beyder vadere,
Ondancx den ghenen diet benijen.
Disgrace 8: Wy porren natuere tot hovaerdijen,
Dies de arme catijvighe lijdt veel smertens.

[(E3:) I am Craving for Eminence./ (D3:) And I am Fear of Disgrace,/ who keeps all chaste maidens demure./ (E4:) Our names are female./ (D4:) That's why we wear ribbons (*on which their names are written*),/ as though we were lasses in Venus's suite (= *prostitutes*),/ do you get my meaning, cousin?/ (E5:) We are two (*identical*) companions,/ from the head downwards, as can be observed (= *by the audience*; *the likely meaning of this utterance is that they wear the same kind of costume*)./ (D5:) It is miraculous what we can both achieve (*or*: what we can achieve together)./ Craving for Eminence can accomplish real wonders./ (E6:) Through you, many a man has broken his neck/ who tried to turn the wheel of fortune (*into a better position*)./ (D6:) There is no reason to vie about that:/ the higher up, the greater the fall./ (E7:) Many a man entertains illusions that come to nothing./ (D7:) That's the patent truth,/ (*for*) we beguile the whole world./ (E8:) (*the idol*) Leo fathered both of us,/ in spite of the fact that for many this is a matter for regret./ (D8:) We encourage the (*human*) soul towards haughtiness.]

When we note what goes on during this interchange, we perceive that for the most part Eminence and Disgrace render information about each other and their collective exploits. All this seems a serious violation of Grice's maxim of relevance (Grice 1975), for what is the point of supplying information that is already shared? Literary scholars have ordained that these divulges of the records of service of *sinnekens* are exclusively audience-oriented (see, e.g., Hummelen 1958: 95 ff.). It goes indeed without saying that such revelations are an excellent means to inform the public about the wicked nature of the personages concerned. But contending that informing the audience is its sole function is equivalent to claiming that in the fictional world in which *sinnekens* manifest themselves the meaning of the exchange is next to nil, and, consequently, to failing to appreciate the role of the exchange as a ritual identification device.

Adopting the view that within the context of the (theatrical) encounter as such the performed speech acts must somehow be meaningful in their own right, I maintain that by referring to shared knowledge about their notorious wrong-doings – which only goes to show that they are quite well-matched – Eminence and Disgrace (re)assure each other of their viciousness. As such, the mutual allegations and imputations only ostensibly conform to the motif of conflict that according to literary scholarship governs the interaction (cf. Hummelen 1958: 99). Albeit in a paradoxical fashion, the (self-)accusations make for co-operation. For each participant, the series of "ritual insults" proves that they are both utter scoundrels up to the hilt.

In support of the view that in the *sinneken* dialogue insolent remarks do not count as truly-meant insults, I should add that there seems to exist a kind of standard inventory of infamous offences, frequently pertaining to Biblical events. As Wim Hummelen, whose studies encompass the larger part of the unpublished *sinneken* plays, concludes (1958: 93), various *sinnekens* are held responsible for one and the same catastrophic event. Which *sinneken* is "accused" of having caused a particular incident, like Daniel's descent into the lion's cage, varies with the circumstances. As for the incrimination of *sinnekens* in the context of the *scene apart*, one gets the impression that the mere association of a participant with some unscrupulous act is more important than whether he or she really was the culprit or no. In other words, such "symbolic" insinuations are of a ritual character. In their context of utterance, these charges and quasi-reproaches primarily have classificatory import.

The same holds for indictments that, from the referential perspective, are vague in the extreme, like the "prototypical" arraignments in *De Wellustige Mensch*, ll. 34-36.

Quaet Gelove:	Ghij maecht temptatije.
Vleyschelijce Sin:	En ghij murmeratije
Quaet Gelove:	Deur u compt blamatije
Vleyschelijce Sin:	Ghij sticht alteratije,
	Swerrels natije hout ghij in erruere.

[(Evil Faith:) You concoct temptation./ (Carnal Lust:) And you induce rebelliousness (*against God*)./ (EF:) You inspire calumny./ (CL:) You cause confusion,/ all the nations of the world you keep in great turmoil.]

3.4. Round Three: Rating the dupe

As already mentioned, the third round of the interchange serves to find out if the sisters-in-arms, who by now have certified that they are hand in glove as regards playing a dirty trick on a person, have similar views about the intended victim. In *De Spiegel der Minnen*, Eminence has picked out the young seamstress Katherina. During the third exchange, she and Disgrace review and criticise her character, considering which disposition suggests a convenient point of contact for an attempt at persuasion. It is Katherina's – in itself not dishonourable – ambition to better herself that seemingly offers excellent prospects.

Eminence 9:   Dat blijct wel aen Katherina Sheermertens,
               Diemen met hovaerdijen inden sack schiet.
Disgrace 9:   Daer en is nochtans eenen vogel int dac niet,
               Om eenighe hoogeyt te verwervene.
Eminence 10:   Niemant en gave haer een stroo op tstervene,
               Al steltse haer selven in grooter pruesheden.
Disgrace 10:   Sy gaet stinkende van orgueilleusheden.
Eminence 11:   Sy climt nae eere
Disgrace 11:   Sy haet vileynichheyt.
Eminence 12:   Sy verwaent haer te seere,
Disgrace 12:   Dat doet haer reynicheyt.
Eminence 13:   Sy vreest die cleynicheyt,
               Daer nijders reyn hertekens mede verstrangen.

[(E9:) A case in point is K.S./, who can be fooled and snatched because of her haughtiness./ (D9:) There is however not a bird on the roof/ that aspires after highness (*to the degree that K.S. does*)./ (E10:) No one will raise a finger to help her in the hour of her death,/ even though she thinks pretty much of herself./ (D10:) She is a very proud miss indeed./ (E11:) She yearns for honour./ (D11:) She loathes all baseness./ (E12:) She is too conceited./ (D12:) That's because of her candour./ (E13:) She abhors the pettiness/ that backbiters oppress virtuous hearts with.]

Since the satanic walk of life is typified by the radical *Umwertung aller Werte*, it is not surprising that *sinnekens* scorn all human virtues and righteous aspirations. Such is their hatred of God and His "retinue" that in *De Wellustige Mensch* (l. 22 ff.) *Quaet Gelove* and *Vleyschelijcke Sin* dare even ridicule, especially by adopting a deriding tone, the Grace of God, who is represented here as a celestial creature:

QG: Kijckt, wie staet achter hem?
VS: Tis de gratij goods.
      Tdunckt mij wadt sodts die volcht hem altijt naer.
      (..)
QG: Sij staet op hem en siet wel also blauwelijck,
      Oock swijcht sij flauwelijck, sij mach, seg ik,
      Gestoort sijn.

[(Evil Faith:) Look, who is standing behind him? (= *the Decent Man*)/ (Carnal Lust:) It is God's Grace./ I think it is rather preposterous, she follows him wherever he may go./

(..)/ (EF:) She's standing near him, and looks a bit pale in the face (= *bowled over*),/ peevishly, she keeps silent too, she might well be, I daresay,/ out of temper.]

In connexion with my focal text, *De Spiegel der Minnen*, it should be observed that the statement of Eminence that initiates the third round (E9) not only links on to what Disgrace says in conclusion of the second phase of the dialogue (D8), but also harks back to Disgrace's second put-off in the first round, *Soo latet blijcken* (D2, 'let it on then'). What Eminence relates about Katherina can be seen as an effort at backing up her earlier claim that she knows *waert strijct* (E2, 'where something of interest is going on').

When viewed in this light, this *sinneken* dialogue is anything but a loosely structured affair. If we accept that the *scene apart* embodies a verbal ritual encompassing four more or less autonomous, but tightly interrelated, functional units, then the conversation as a whole is, contrary to first glance impressions, not a random collection of sneers, insults, vaunts, and rashly-planned intrigues, but a well-structured and coherently organised form of verbal communication. While the first round serves to lay the foundation of a joint venture, it is the second and third rounds that must annul slumbering reservations, and establish whether the association commends itself as a "workable relationship".

3.5. Round Four: Heading for concerted action

As is the case also in the other stage-plays I have studied, the fourth round of the *scene apart* in *De Spiegel der Minnen* is devoted to a resolution upon a collaborative course of action, *verwaentheyt bringhen ten spele* 'to bring vanity into play'. In this instance, it involves an ardently made, but not particularly detailed, plan.

Disgrace 13: Wy sullen haer die blauwe heucke om hangen.
Eminence 14: Wy sullen verwaentheyt bringhen ten spele,
　　　　　　　Tot datmen tmutsken heeft onder de kele.

[(D13:) We shall put the blue cape over her shoulders (= *we shall delude her*)./ (E14:) We shall contrive that vanity comes into play,/ until her bonnet is right under her chin (= *until she is completely in love* (*with a man of high degree*)).]

This characterisation also applies to the action plan that the *sinnekens* in *Gevallen en weer opstaande Mensch* draw up (ll. 261-265, *supra*), and to its structural equal in *Ontrouwen Rentmeester* (ll. 70-75):

TH: Nichte, uwen dienst moetty hem te kinnen geven,
　　Aen my en sal vrylyck niet gebreken.

OD: Sulcx werdt van my terstont bedreven,
    Ick salt tvier blasen, maer neve...
TH: ... En ick salt vrylyck wel ontsteecken
OD: Aldus sout te werck gaen, greve.

> [(HoS:) You must show him your eagerness to oblige, cousin,/ it surely won't be for my want of trying (*if we don't succeed*)./ (US:) I shall do it right away,/ I shall blow the coals, but cousin.../(HoS:) ... and I shall positively kindle it (= *the fire* (*of his passion*))/ (US:) That's the line to work upon, guv'nor (*literally*: count).]

In *De Wellustige Mensch*, however, the course of action is relatively well thought-out (ll. 37-41):

QG: ghaen wij seg ick deurre,
      Den mensche veurre in sijn ontmoetenisse.
VS: Doet ghij dan twoort.
QG: Biet ghij hem groetenisse;
      Met een versoetenisse sijn hoocheijt vercleert.

> [(EF:) let us commence, I counsel,/ by striking up the man's acquaintance./ (CL:) You take the floor then./ (EF:) You salute him;/ bring his grandeur into prominence by a bit of sweet talk.]

When the fourth round is completed, the *sinnekens* proceed to business, and make contact with their victim. How they in fact try to work the victim's destruction is outside the scope of this contribution. However, as concerns these attempts to ruin a personage, I conclude that the assault is well-prepared. Although the execution of the second and third exchanges may seem a rather roundabout way to get started, these rounds are indispensable, in that they allow for surmounting difficulties. In that connexion, I ought to stress, once again, that *sinnekens* have the very best of reasons to doubt one another, because they do not scruple, if circumstances allow, to dupe each other too. When *Nijdigh Herte* levels at *Quaet Ingheven* "*waer ghij meucht, sult liever quaet dan goet geven*" (*Joseph*, l. 87: 'whenever you see the opportunity, you'd rather do evil than good'), her observation is presumably remarkably well to the point.

It can hardly be accidental that in every *scene apart* I have analysed the *sinneken* who is summoned puts in, by putting off the initial request, a proviso as to his or her readiness to co-operate with the *sinneken* who appeals for help. In *De Spiegel der Minnen*, Disgrace indicates that the enterprise Eminence alludes to commends itself to her, but also that it takes more to secure her assistance. But then the subsequent exchanges only go to show that both shrews are odious miscreants who are united in their loathing of Katherina.

Apparently, this very outcome of the interaction is satisfactory enough, because in the fourth exchange they concerted measures.

In *Tspel van den Ontrouwen Rentmeester* (ll. 16-17), *Tversteent Hertte* also stipulates a condition: *Ist al profyt, soe sal ick met jolyt/ my lieffelyck by u paren* 'If it is a matter of profit, then I shall gladly/ (and) lovingly join hands with you'. This contingent agreement is followed by a round of ritual accusations, and a lengthy deliberation about the contemplated victim. Whatever the *profit* of duping him may be remains fully implicit. Obviously, the second and third round are sufficient to quench Heart-of-Stone's objections.

The same pattern applies to *Joseph* (l. 66 ff.). *Roet vast u koten* 'Get started', Evil Inspiration rouses Angry Heart, *Wilt ghij anders niet troten, want ick sonder respijt zaen/ Wil naer Sichem* 'if you want to be on the move, for I am going right now/ to Sichem'. Angry Heart is not immediately convinced that he should join in with Evil Inspiration, for he replies: *Soudt ghij er om proffijt gaen,/ Ick neem met u den strijdt aen int soet int zeure* 'If you would go there because of the benefits,/ then I shall unite with you, and stand by you through thick and thin'. What gains there may be remain nevertheless unexplained in the following discourse units.

Another example is *Gevallen en weer opstaande Mensch*. Evil Inspiration – who, incidentally, also appears in the *Joseph* play – summons Sensual Desire: *Wij moeten te weghe in corte spatie* 'We must get going very soon'. *Wat esser nieuws?* 'What's the news?', Desire begs to know. But then again intelligence is scant. She is told no more than that *Wij crijghen den palinck vleus metten steerte/ Het comt te wensche recht naer ons natie* 'Soon we shall catch the eel right by its tail,/ as if to order, it is coming to our territory (= *hell*) straightaway'. Conspicuously, this is sufficient to obliterate Desire's misgivings. All she says is: *Zo eest genuechlijck* 'That's enough', 'That will do'.

In conclusion, I submit that my analysis of the *scene apart* of rhetorical stage-plays allows for the thesis that the verbal interaction of *sinnekens* is not loosely structured, nor that it is exclusively, or even for the most part, audience-oriented. What happens in the course of this enigmatic colloquy is predominantly relevant for the participants themselves, since the dialogue embodies a ritual procedure aimed at contract formation.

As regards the overall make-up of the ritual, I should like to emphasise that the speech activities, particularly those that constitute the first two rounds, entail the element of contention, albeit that the eristic motive is of a different character, and definitely less prominent, than the stylised enmities that constitute the mediaeval challenging ritual. I conclude nonetheless that the ritual contract-by-conflict procedure – that, as Parks (1990) has pointed out, comprises an ancient, and universally spread, behavioural pattern – also underlies, at any rate in part, the relatively novel dialogic genre of the dramatic *scene apart*. It is of paramount significance, for that matter, that the *sinneken* ritual partakes of all the interpretational exigences that the model in Figure 2 epitomises (for particulars, see Bax 1998).

Contrary to what I have attempted with regard to the mediaeval challenging ritual, I refrain from arguing that the ritual procedure employed by *sinnekens* exemplifies a mimetic genre of literary language use. Although it would seem that (relevant aspects of) this fictional dialogue type can be traced back to factual flyting traditions, the arcane speech event designated by the demonic *scene apart* cannot be envisaged, for what I take are obvious reasons, as a truthful depiction of what goes on in the natural world. This does not amount to the claim, though, that the *scene apart* was not intended as a veritable account of authentic proceedings in the transcendental nether regions. In the eye of the early-modern beholder, this gripping other-worldly plotting scene may well have presented a convincing picture of what time and again befalls, very much to the detriment of mortal souls, in Lucifer's shrouded sovereignty.

Sources of quoted text fragments

De Spiegel der Minnen (1913). In: M.W. Immink (ed.). *De Spiegel der Minnen door Colijn van Rijssele*. Utrecht [s.n.]

De Wellustige Mensch (1950). In: C. Kruyskamp (ed.). *Dichten en Spelen van Jan van den Berge*. 's-Gravenhage: Nijhoff.

Die Wrake van Ragisel (1963). Onderzoekingen over de Middelnederlandse bewerking (..) [door] W.P. Gerritsen. Assen: Van Gorcum.

Gevallen en weer opstaande Mensch (1893). In: J. Broeckaert (ed.). *Rederijkersgedichten*. Gent: Siffer.

Joseph, een historiaalspel van Jeronimus van der Voort (?) (1975). Een tekstuitgave, ingeleid en van aantekeningen voorzien door G.R.W. Dibbets en W.M.H. Hummelen. In *Jaarboek (1973-1974) van de Koninklijke Soevereine Hoofdkamer van Retorica "De Fonteine" te Gent*. Gent [s.n.].

Karel ende Elegast (1969). Diplomatische uitgave van de Middelnederlandse teksten en de tekst uit de Karlmeinet-compilatie, bezorgd door A.M. Duinhoven. Zwolle: Tjeenk Willink.

Moriaen (1970). Opnieuw uitgegeven en geannoteerd door H. Paardekooper-van Buuren en M. Gysseling. Zutphen: Tjeenk Willink.

Roman van den Riddere metter Mouwen (1914). Opnieuw naar het Hs. uitgegeven (..) door Dr. Bertha M. van der Stempel. Leiden: Brill.

Tspel van den Ontrouwen Rentmeester (1899). In: *De Roode Roos*. Zinnespelen en andere Toneelstukken der zestiende eeuw, voor het eerst naar het Hasseltse handschrift uitgegeven door Osc. van den Daele en Fr. van Veerdeghem. Bergen [s.n.].

References

Auerbach, Erich
    1953   *Mimesis*. New York: Doubleday.
Austin, J.L.
    1962   *How to Do Things with Words*. Oxford: Oxford University Press.
Barker, Juliet R.V.
    1987   *The Tournament in England. 1100-1400*. Woodbridge: The Boydell Press.
Bax, Marcel
    1981   Rules for ritual challenges: A speech convention among medieval knights. *Journal of Pragmatics* 5: 423-444.
    1983   Die lebendige Dimension toter Sprachen. Zur pragmatischen Analyse von Sprachgebrauch in historischen Kontexten. *Zeitschrift für germanistische Linguistik* 11: 1-21.
Bax, Marcel M.H.
    1984   Conversatie-analyse als filologisch instrument. De tweegesprekken in het Oudhoogduitse *Hildebrandlied* en het Middelnederlandse *Van den ouden Hillebrant*. In: J.J.Th.M. Tersteeg and P.E.L. Verkuyl (eds.). *Ic ga daer ic hebbe te doene*. Groningen: Wolters-Noordhoff, 15-44.
    1991   Historische Pragmatik: Eine Herausforderung für die Zukunft. Diachrone Untersuchungen zu pragmatischen Aspekten ritueller Herausforderungen in Texten mittelalterlicher Literatur. In: Dietrich Busse (ed.). *Diachrone Semantik und Pragmatik. Untersuchungen zur Erklärung und Beschreibung des Sprachwandels*. Tübingen: Niemeyer, 197-215.
    1995   *Een spiegel van de geest. Over taal, communicatie en cognitie*. Groningen: Martinus Nijhoff.
    1998   Ritual discord and the contractual framework. An essay on a paradoxical framing device of the Early Modern Theatre and its foundation in oral tradition and mimetic culture. [Ms.].
Bax, Marcel, and Tineke Padmos
    1983   Two types of verbal dueling in Old Icelandic: the interactional structure of the *senna* and the *mannjafnaðr* in *Hárbarðsljóð*. *Scandinavian Studies* 55: 149-174.

Bax, Marcel, and Wim Vuijk
  1990   Wy porren natuere tot hovaerdijen. Taalhandelingsconventies van sinnekens in het zestiende-eeuwse rederijkerstoneel. *Tijdschrift voor Nederlandse Taal- en Letterkunde* 106: 15-39.
Becker, C.L.
  1932   *The Heavenly City of the Eighteenth-Century Philosophers*. New Haven, Conn.: Yale University Press.
Bloch, R. Howard
  1974   From Grail Quest to Inquest: the death of King Arthur and the birth of France. *Modern Language Review* 69: 40-55.
Clover, Carol J.
  1980   The Germanic context of the Unferth episode. *Speculum* 55: 444-468.
Collins, Randall
  1988   Theoretical continuities in Goffman's work. In: Paul Drew and Anthony Wootton (eds.). *Erving Goffman. Exploring the Interaction Order*. Cambridge: Polity Press, 41-63.
Donald, Merlin
  1993   *Origins of the Modern Mind. Three Stages in the Evolution of Culture and Cognition*. Cambridge, MA and London: Harvard University Press.
Dundes, Alan, Jerry W. Leach and Bora Özkök
  1972   The strategy of Turkish boys' verbal dueling rhymes. In: John J. Gumperz and Dell Hymes (eds.): 130-160.
Elias, Norbert
  1983   *The Court Society*. Oxford: Blackwell.
Foley, William A.
  1997   *Anthropological Linguistics*. Oxford: Blackwell.
Franck, Dorothea
  1979   Speech act and conversational move. *Journal of Pragmatics* 3: 461-466.
Garner, Thurmon
  1983   Playing the dozens: folklore as strategies for living. *Quarterly Journal of Speech* 69: 47-57.
Geertz, Clifford
  1973   *The Interpretation of Cultures*. New York: Basic Books.
Goffman, Erving
  1974   *Frame Analysis. An Essay on the Organization of Experience*. New York: Harper and Row.
Grice, H. Paul
  1975   Logic and conversation. In: Peter Cole and Jerry L. Morgan (eds.). *Syntax and Semantics, Vol. 3: Speech Acts*. New York: Academic Press, 41-58.

Gumperz, John J., and Dell Hymes (eds.)
  1972   *Directions in Sociolinguistics*. New York: Holt, Reinhart and Winston.
Huizinga, Johan
  1990   *The Waning of the Middle Ages. A Study of the Forms of Life, Thought, and Art in France and the Netherlands in the Fourteenth and Fifteenth Centuries*. Harmondsworth: Penguin.
Hummelen, W.M.H.
  1958   *De sinnekens in het rederijkersdrama*. Groningen [Doctoral dissertation, University of Groningen].
Hymes, Dell
  1972   Models of the interaction of language and social life. In: John J. Gumperz and Dell Hymes (eds.), 35-71.
Jacobs, Sally, and Scott Jackson
  1982   Conversational argument: a discourse analytic approach. In: J. Robert Cox and Charles A. Willard (eds.). *Advances in Argumention Theory and Research*. Carbondale: Southern Illinois University Press, 205-237.
Jespersen, Otto
  1922   *Language. Its Nature, Development and Origin*. London: Allen and Unwin.
Jucker, Andreas H. (ed.)
  1995   *Historical Pragmatics*. Amsterdam and Philadelphia: Benjamins.
Kochman, Thomas
  1983   The boundary between play and non-play in black verbal dueling. *Language in Society* 12: 329-337.
Labov, William
  1972   Rules for ritual insults. In: W. Labov. *Language in the Inner City. Studies in the Black English Vernacular*. Philadelphia: University of Pennsylvania Press, 297-353.
Labov, William, and David Fanshel
  1977   *Therapeutic Discourse. Psychotherapy as Conversation*. New York: Academic Press.
Levinson, Stephen C.
  1983   *Pragmatics*. Cambridge: Cambridge University Press.
Loomis, Roger S.
  1959   Arthurian influence on sport and spectacle. In: Roger S. Loomis (ed.). *Arthurian Literature in the Middle Ages. A Collaborative History*. Oxford: Clarendon Press, 553-559.
Niedner, Felix
  1881   *Das deutsche Turnier im XII. und XIII. Jahrhundert*. Berlin [s.n.].

Owen, D.D.R.
  1968   *The Evolution of the Grail Legend.* Edinburgh and London: Oliver and Boyd.
Parks, Ward
  1990   *Verbal Dueling in Heroic Narrative. The Homeric and Old English Traditions.* Princeton: Princeton University Press.
Peristiany, J.G. (ed.)
  1966   *Honour and Shame. The Values of Mediterranean Society.* London: Weidenfeld and Nicolson.
Pfeffer, M.
  1885   Die Formalitäten des gottesgerichtlichen Zweikampfs in der altfranzösischen Epik. *Zeitschrift für Romanische Philologie* IX: 1-74.
Riches, David (ed.)
  1986   *The Anthropology of Violence.* Oxford: Blackwell.
Rigney, Ann
  1990   *The Rhetoric of Historical Representation.* Cambridge: Cambridge University Press.
Sacks, Harvey
  1972   On the analyzability of stories by children. In: John J. Gumperz and Dell Hymes (eds.): 325-345.
Saville-Troike, Muriel
  1989   *The Ethnography of Communication.* Oxford: Blackwell.
Schegloff, Emanuel
  1972   Sequencing in conversational openings. In John J. Gumperz and Dell Hymes (eds.): 346-380.
Schultz, A.
  1889   *Das höfische Leben zur Zeit der Minnesinger.* Leipzig [s.n.].
Searle, John R.
  1969   *Speech Acts. An Essay in the Philosophy of Language.* Cambridge: Cambridge University Press.
  1979   *Expression and Meaning. Studies in the Theory of Speech Acts.* Cambridge: Cambridge University Press.
Segal, Charles P.
  1971   *The Theme of the Mutilation of the Corpse in the Iliad.* Leiden: Brill.
Tannen, Deborah (ed.)
  1993   *Framing in Discourse.* New York and Oxford: Oxford University Press.
Tilmans, Karin
  1989   'Autentijk ende warachtig'. Stedenstichtingen in de Hollandse geschiedschrijving: van Beke tot Aurelius. *Holland. Regionaal-historisch tijdschrift* 21: 68-87.

1992   *Historiography and Humanism in Holland in the Age of Erasmus: Aurelius and the Divisiekroniek of 1517.* Nieuwkoop: De Graaf.

van Anrooij, Wim
1990   *Spiegel van ridderschap: heraut Gelre en zijn ereredes.* Amsterdam: Prometheus.

van Caenegem, R.C.
1967   *De instellingen van de middeleeuwen. Geschiedenis van de westerse staatsinstellingen van de Ve tot de XVe eeuw.* Gent: Wetenschappelijke Uitgeverij.

van Winter, J.M.
1965   *Ridderschap. Ideaal en werkelijkheid.* Bussum: Van Dishoeck.

Verbruggen, J.F.
1997   *The Art of Warfare in Western Europe during the Middle Ages.* Woodbridge: The Boydell Press.

White, Hayden
1987   *The Content of the Form: Narrative Discourse and Historical Representation.* Baltimore: Johns Hopkins University Press.

Wittgenstein, Ludwig
1953   *Philosophical Investigations.* New York: Macmillan.
1958   *The Blue and Brown Books.* Oxford: Blackwell.

The Pragmatic Form of Religious Controversies around 1600
A Case Study in the Osiander vs. Scherer & Rosenbusch Controversy

Thomas Gloning
Justus Liebig University, Giessen

1. Introduction

The aim of this paper is to analyze the structure of typical controversies around 1600 from a pragmatical point of view. The paper has three parts. First, I shall briefly describe some outlines of the Osiander vs. Scherer and Rosenbusch controversy. Second, I shall make a few methodological remarks about (my view of) pragmatic form and historical pragmatics. In the third part, I shall describe major linguistic and pragmatic aspects of the Osiander vs. Scherer & Rosenbusch controversy. This case study is also a contribution to a more global picture of controversies as an important form of communication in 16th- and 17th-century Europe. In addition to the quotations from the Early New High German texts in the left column I have given short English paraphrases in the right column for those not familiar with Early New High German. These short paraphrases are not exact translations, but I hope they will be helpful and facilitate comprehension or at least give an idea of what "happens" in the left column.

2. Osiander vs. Scherer & Rosenbusch 1585-89

In 1587, the Jesuit Georg Scherer published his *Triumph Der Warheit/ wider Lucam Osiandrum* 'Triumph of truth against Lucas Osiander', a pamphlet of some 150 pages. After a preface, specially dedicated to Duke William of Bavaria, he speaks to the general reader:

GVnstiger lieber Leser/ es ist wahr vnd recht geredt/ daß nichts mächtiger vnnd stärcker vnderm Himmel sey/ weder die liebe Warheit/ (...). Also hat sie auch jüngstlich wider Lucam Osiander/ im Streit vber der Jesuiter Vnschuld/ wegen der bezichtigten Blůtdurstigen Anschlägen vnd Practicken die *Victoriam* erobert/ vnd das Sigkräntzlein redlich vnd auffrecht gewunnen vnd heimgetragen. Dagegen aber ist dem Osiander sein vnwahrhaffte Goschen dermassen zerklopffet vnd zerblewet worden/ dz er nun mehr kaum einem Menschen/ geschweigen einem Doctori gleich sihet. Solches wirdt der Christliche Leser auß den nachuolgenden Capiteln ohn allen weitgesůchten Vmbschweiff/ fein kurtz vnd rund verstehen vnd abnemmen.[1]	Dear reader! Nothing is more powerful or stronger than truth. (...) Most recently truth has gained the victory against Lucas Osiander in a quarrel about the Jesuits' innocence or their alleged bloody plans and practices. Lucas Osiander's untrue and malicious tongue has been beaten in such a way, that he does not look like a human being any more, let alone a doctor. This is what you can read clearly in the following chapters.

The body of Scherer's pamphlet has 159 pages, in which Scherer either answers the points Lucas Osiander made or makes his own points for the purpose of defense or counterattack. Lucas Osiander was then a Protestant preacher at the court of the Duke of Württemberg in Stuttgart. In 1585 he published a pamphlet, in which he severely attacked the Jesuits: *Warnung Vor der Jesuiter blutdurstigen Anschlägen vnnd bösen Practicken* 'Warning of the Jesuits' bloody plans and malicious practices'. In this text, he accused the Jesuits of working towards extinction of the protestant religion by way of influence on the sovereigns. The Jesuits Georg Scherer (Vienna) and Christoph Rosenbusch (Ingolstadt) countered this attack. This was the beginning of a violent controversy that lasted from 1585 to 1589. Both parties wrote several pamphlets, all of them fairly long. Here are some abbreviated titles:

1585	*Osiander, Warnung Vor der Jesuiter blutdurstigen Anschlägen*	Warning of the Jesuits' bloody plans
1586	*Rosenbusch, Antwort vnd Ehrerrettung auff die verbottne Schmachschrifft Lucae Osiandri*	Vindication of honour, as an answer to the pamphlet of Lucas Osiander

1586	Scherer, Rettung der Jesuiter Unschuld wider die Giftspinnen Lucam Osiander	Defense of the Jesuits' innocence against the calumniator (the venomous spider) Lucas Osiander
1586	Osiander, Verantwortung wider die zwo Gifftspinnen Georgen Scherern vnd Christophorum Rosenbusch	Reply to the two calumniators (the venomous spiders) Georg Scherer and Christoph Rosenbusch
1587	Osiander, Abfertigung der vermeindten Replic Christophori Rosenbusches	Rejection of Christoph Rosenbusch's supposed reply
1587	Scherer, Triumph Der Warheit/ wider Lucam Osiandrum	Triumph of Truth against Lucas Osiander
1587	Osiander, Bericht: Vom Faßnacht Triumph/ Georgij Scherers	Account of Georg Scherer's triumph of Carnival
1588	Scherer, Fortsetzung Deß Triumphs der Warheit/ wider Lucam Osiandrum	The Triumph of Truth against Lucas Osiander, continued
1589	Osiander, Endtliche Abfertigung Der beider Jesuiter/ Christoffen Rosenbuschen/ vnd Georgen Scherers	Final rejection of the two Jesuits Christoph Rosenbusch and Georg Scherer

Controversies of this kind and style were all-pervasive at that time. The controversy Osiander contra Rosenbusch & Scherer was just one of a bulk of religious quarrels that also had important political implications. Within twenty years, Osiander, for example, was engaged in eight controversies published in German and several others published in Latin. A controversialist of this kind had to write several hundred pages a year, which were either published or delivered as sermons or both.

The question of religion and of its political organization was one of the most important issues at that time. As a consequence, controversies as a form of communication were of central importance.

3. Forms of communication and the "communicative budget" in historical pragmatics

Each period has a sort of "communicative budget".[2] First, there are communicative problems to be solved and tasks to be performed.

Communicative problems or tasks are, for example, transmission of information, coordination of action, settlement of differences, fixing of prices etc. Second, there are communicative acts. These acts are a means of solving problems or of performing tasks. Bargaining, for example, is a means of fixing prices, if prices are not otherwise defined. Controversies are a family of forms of communication that serve to clarify differing points of view and to settle differing claims. Single communicative acts and complex forms of communication are more or less conventionalized in that they are organized according to type, so that we can speak of types of linguistic acts and of forms of communication. Third, groups and their members may differ in respect of their linguistic practice. One method of applying historical pragmatics is to describe the communicative budget of a period. To describe (parts of) a communicative budget means to describe forms of communication, their organization and their "sense" (function, task) and how they were socially used by different groups.

The following are some major aspects of the communicative budget and of forms of communication in a period:
- What communicative problems or tasks are there?
- What communicative acts/forms of communication are there?
- Which communicative act serves to solve which problem?
- Which group(s) use different communicative acts?

One of the basic units of a communicative budget is a linguistic act or a more complex form of communication. To describe a linguistic act or a form of communication, it is crucial to describe the problem it is supposed to solve. There are, moreover, several other aspects of organization which deserve our attention. The product of their interaction is a specific pragmatic form of a certain type of communicative activity.

- the purpose, typically or conventionally achieved by performing an act of type X;
- the consequences, typically or conventionally connected with an act of type X;
- the way of performing an act of type X by means of performing an act of a more primitive kind (level-generation);
- the sequential organization of moves (local and global);
- the linguistic means and expressions for performing an act that are typical of different languages or different periods of languages (e.g. vocabulary, organization of text);
- topical and thematic aspects;

- the constellation of speakers (or writers) with respect to their knowledge, their communicative roles and rights;
- the communicative principles that apply universally or with respect to certain forms of communication;
- the connection with other forms of communication and the embedding of a form of communication in the Wittgensteinian *Lebensform*.

These are some aspects that may prove useful in describing historical forms of communication and their change. In the following chapters, some of these aspects will be used as organizing principles.

4. Religious controversies with pamphlets

Controversies are a multiform family of different forms of communication. Communications of this type mainly serve to settle differences or to clarify opposite views. In the following chapter I shall analyze a certain historical variety of this type of communication, i.e. controversies about religious matters with pamphlets written around 1600. I will rely mainly on texts from the Osiander vs. Scherer & Rosenbusch controversy.

4.1. A "monks' squabble" or public debate?

Around 1600, numerous pamphlets with religious topics were published. The information from the bibliographies (e.g. Sommervogel 1890-1932) indicates that these controversies were widespread and presumably of great public interest. These facts suggest the following view:

(i) Controversies and the use of pamphlets were not merely internal squabbles among theologians. They were public debates that had great influence on political life and on public opinion.

This view contrasts with the one held by several historians:

(ii) Religious pamphlets contain just verbal squabbles; they are only the quarrels between fanatic theologians. Today they are deservedly forgotten (Krebs 1890: 10 and 164; Leube 1935).

There are at least three valid arguments against the view expressed in (ii):
The first argument in favour of (i) is the publication of these pamphlets in the German language. There are many pamphlets in German, and such texts formed an important part of the stock of printers and publishers like Sartorius in Ingolstadt or Gruppenbach in Tübingen. Usually, in 1600 internal

theological disputes and discussions were conducted in Latin. Theological texts meant for other theologians were written in Latin. If a theologian used the German language for his publication or if a discussion was conducted in German, the purpose was to reach a wider audience. In addition, many a sovereign had only a poor command of Latin. There are also examples of a twofold strategy of publication. One version of the pamphlet was published in Latin with all the learned apparatus whereas another version was published in German without or with only a reduced set of references. Thus, the use of German is a strong indicator that the purpose of these controversies was to reach a wider audience.

The second argument in favour of (i) is the role that polemic activities had in daily life and in the "communicative biography" of theologians like Osiander in those days. Several theologians spent much of their time writing contributions to ongoing controversies or preparing polemical sermons. This applies especially to the important figures in controversies like Georg Scherer or Lucas Osiander. They were the flagships of their parties and had to write copiously. Lucas Osiander once accuses an opponent of dishonestly using only two pages from his writings. Then he proudly tells his readers that at the age of 62 years he has written somewhat more than two pages, namely "fünfftausent vnd zweintzig Blätter"[3] (5020 folios or 10040 pages).

A third argument in favour of (i) is to be seen in the consequences of one's actions in controversies. Depending on one's view, an active participation in a controversy could have serious consequences like the loss of one's profession or even expulsion (e.g. Samuel Huber in a controversy with Lucas Osiander). Probably, no one would have taken these risks for mere internal quarrels with colleagues who could be assumed to be unconvincible anyway.

All these arguments, especially the first one, indicate that controversies were an important part of public communication and not mere "squabbles among monks". It is, however, not easy to specify to what extent different recipients read these controversies, because evidence pertaining to ordinary people (e.g. in diaries or letters) is rare and hard to find.

4.2. Opponents, pairs, parties and the audience

Today's TV-debates are not controversies between opponents trying to find the truth, and neither were the quarrels with pamphlets around 1600. The basic relationship of the participants of these quarrels can be described as follows:

(i) Controversies with pamphlets were quarrels for an audience, for the laymen and for the sovereigns.

(ii) The participants did not act only on behalf of their own convictions and beliefs, they were also representing a party. In some cases they were even the "communicative flagships" of their party.
(iii) Many authors did not participate in just one controversy, they were engaged in several at a time. The opponents formed a changing net of pairs with changing states of opposition or confederation.

A religious controversy with its political aspects was a quarrel between two persons who had their personal convictions and beliefs and who had personal honour and a reputation to gain, to sustain or to lose.

Some well-known authors of pamphlets were, for example, Georg Scherer, Lucas Osiander, Conrad Vetter, Jacob and Philipp Heilbrunner, Samuel Huber or Christoph Rosenbusch. These authors were engaged in a number of controversies that were conducted by pairs of opponents. An author was possibly engaged in several controversies at a time, and he could have several opponents and allies. These states of opposition and coalition formed changing networks. To give an example, around 1590, Georg Scherer not only wrote pamphlets against Osiander, but also against several other theologians. One of these opponents was Samuel Huber. At first, Huber was closely allied to Osiander, but later on he came into conflict with most of the Protestant theologians, and finally Huber exchanged pamphlets not only with the Jesuit Scherer or some Calvinists, but also with Osiander, his former confederate. Some of these authors wrote and published voluminous pamphlets. One of Scherer's pamphlets, for example ran to 500 printed pages. Conrad Vetter, one of the notorious pamphleteers among the Jesuits, wrote or translated some 150 booklets or books in the 30 years of his active life (each about 80 to 150 printed pages in most cases). The text of many a pamphlet was based at least in part on a sermon, but, on the other hand, not many polemic sermons were actually printed. So, much of the time of a 16th-century theologian was dedicated to controversy, either in the form of sermons, pamphlets or in other forms, e.g. in disputations.[4]

Authors like Scherer or Osiander did not write their pamphlets as private persons. They had an important role as "communicative flagships" for certain religious parties. Thus, they did not write to defend their personal views and beliefs but to propose and defend the views of their parties. The main parties in the 16th and 17th centuries were Catholics and non-Catholics. But there were also many controversies among the non-Catholic groups (e.g. *Evangelische, Reformierte, Lutheraner, Calvinisten, Schwenckfeldianer* and others). The fights among these groups were often as acrimonious as those against the Catholics, the "papists". Among the Catholics, there were also internal quarrels. For example, the newly founded order of the Jesuits had powerful opponents within the group of the Catholics, and these anti-Jesuit Catholics were quoted by a Protestant like Osiander in his pamphlets against the Jesuits.

The authors of pamphlets use a typical vocabulary for the reference to groups. The use of words from this vocabulary seems to be clearly divided into in-group and out-group expressions. Some of these expressions could be used to characterize an opponent or his views as most objectionable, disreputable or infamous. It sufficed to call him a "Calvinist" or his views "Calvinism".

The parties can be characterized not only by common views but also by association with a local community. Ruth Kastner (1982) has shown in her study on the reformation jubilee of 1617 that the Strasbourg theologians had published several works for this jubilee and that the Molsheim Jesuits immediately "answered" to this form of publicity. This was the beginning of a controversy that lasted several years. Such a controversy reminds one of a soccer game with the theologians of each city as teams.

But the most important point is the fact that these controversies are quarrels produced for an audience, mainly for laymen (*der einfältige pöfel*) and for the sovereigns (*die Potentaten*). As a consequence, we cannot reasonably assume that an author like Scherer had any hope of "convincing" an opponent like Osiander with a pamphlet or in any other way, nor could Osiander hope to convince his opponent.

4.3. Global organization of pamphlets and textual elements

The pamphlets used in religious controversies could have up to 500 printed pages, but the average seems to have been around 70 printed pages, ranging from about 50 to 150 printed pages in most cases.

Pamphlets normally comprise a title, a preface, the body of the text which was organized into "points" or "articles", and a final part with a summary, a conclusion or a pious wish.

The titles of the pamphlets are in many cases quite detailed and extensive. The parts of a title can have different functions. First, an element of a title can give a topical orientation for the reader. Second, an element of a title can contain a reference to an opponent and/or a certain pamphlet, to which the actual pamphlet is a reply. Third, many authors of pamphlets use the titlepage to proclaim their own victory and the ruin of the opponent. Thus, the titlepage is a sort of a verbal pose of triumph. Here are some examples:

The Pragmatic Form of Religious Controversies around 1600 89

Endtliche Abfertigung Der beider Jesuiter/ Christoffen Rosenbuschen/ vnd Georgen Scherers.	Final defeat of the two Jesuits Christoph Rosenbusch and Georg Scherer [Own victory + Reference to opponents]
Bericht An alle fromme Christen/ welche die Warheit lieben: Warumb die beide rasende Barfüsser Mönch/ Georg Eckhart vnd Michel Anisius/ keiner Antwort werth seien.	Account to all pious Christians who love the truth, why the two raving monks G. Eckhart and M. Anisius don't deserve a (full-blown) answer. [Reference to opponents + characteristics of the own pamphlet]
Gründtlicher Bericht. Auff Doctor Samuel Hubers Lästerschrift (deren Titul/ Notwendige entdeckung/ rc.) in deren er D. Lucas Osiandern (...) mit Gewalt will zu einem Caluinisten machen.	Thorough account against Dr. S. Huber's calumny (with the title *Notwendige entdeckung* etc.), in which he groundlessly wants to make a Calvinist of Dr. L. Osiander. [Reference to opponent and to a certain pamphlet + topical orientation]

In its *preface*, a pamphlet is often dedicated to a sovereign or some other person of influence. In those days, the sovereigns had the right to take decisions in religious matters. Thus, theologians did what they could to influence their sovereigns. On the other hand, the sovereigns used the *vota* and counsels of their theologians as a basis for religious and political decisions. In many cases, the sovereigns supervised the religious quarrels. They gave permission to print pamphlets and they organized disputations, which were, at least in some cases, meant as an attempt to find an agreement (the socalled *Religionsgespräche*, e.g. 1603 in Regensburg). Thus, the dedication of a pamphlet to a sovereign was an important religious and political move.

The body of the text of a pamphlet is typically arranged into different points or articles. A point typically consists of two components: the rendering or quotation of the opponents view and the retort. There is a wide range of forms of how such a point can be organized: on the one hand, there are whole chapters on one point, which are themselves internally structured, on the other hand, there are just short theses or statements in which a certain view is defended or contrasted with an opponent's view. The following text from Osiander's *Faßnacht Triumph* is an example of a less complex "point". It contains a quotation from the writing of Scherer, followed by Osiander's retort. In the margin, there is a topical characterization of the point at stake (an English paraphrase follows the German text).

"Ferner schreibt der Scherer also: Was *locum de hæ-* "*reticis comburendis* (den Puncten/ ob man die Ketzer ver= "brennen soll) betrifft/ *in Enchiridio locorum communium* "*Doctoris Ioannis Eccij*: laß ich alles beim Geistlichen vnd "Keiserlichen Recht verbleiben/ vnnd sage mit *Augustino/* "daß alle zeitliche Straffen für die halßstarrige Ketzer vil zu "wenig vnd zugering sein. Dann was ist es? die Ketzer wer= "den am Leib gestrafft/ dagegen tödten sie die armen See= "len/ für welche Christus gestorben: klagen/ sie müssen den "zeitlichen todt leiden/ vnnd dagegen verursachen sie bey vi= "len den ewigen todt. Hie hastu/ Christlicher Leser/ deinen bescheid vom Scherer/ daß man die halsstarrigen Ketzer verbrennen/ vnd jnen das zeitlich leben nemen soll. Wil= tu wissen/ wer die Ketzer seien? so frag den Scherer/ so würdt er sagen: Die Lutherische Buben/ die nicht wöllen das Tridentische *Concilium* annemen/ die seind halßstarri= ge Ketzer/ die soll man hinrichten/ wie man jhr halt kan mächtig werden. Dannoch wöllen die Jesuiter nicht blut= girige Leut sein? (Osiander, *Faßnacht Triumph,* 1587: 14f.)

Scherer will/ daß man die Luthe-rische Ketzer ver-brennen soll

Furthermore, Scherer writes: "Concerning the question whether heretics should be burned or not, I accept the decisions in both laws, and I say with Saint Augustine that no corporal punishment is enough for hard-nosed heretics. Because heretics are responsible for the *death of the soul* of many persons." – Here is what Scherer says about hard-nosed heretics: that one should kill them. Do you want to know who the heretics are? Ask Scherer and he would say: The Lutheran criminals, who do not want to accept the Tridentinum, they are hard-nosed heretics. One should kill them, wherever one can get hold of them. – In spite of these views, the Jesuits claim not to be bloodthirsty people.

Scherer demands that the Lutheran heretics be burned

An example of a contrastive exposition of short and disputed theses can be found in Osiander's defense against Samuel Huber, who had blamed Osiander for crypto-Calvinism. After having replied to Huber's different points in some detail, Osiander closes his defense with a contrastive account of the views he was blamed for and those he really held. This account consists of short theses or short renderings of positions from his own writings.[5]

The division of a pamphlet into different points is the basis for an ordered dispute. When Osiander, in the course of the controversy, did not keep to

Scherer's order of the articles at stake, Scherer pointed out the difference and continued to follow his own organization: *daß ich in disem Tractätlein bey meiner vorigen Abtheilung vnd Capiteln bleibe* 'that in this treatise I shall keep my previous arrangement and organization into chapters or articles,' *Fortsetzung des Triumphs* (1588: 1).

The division into different articles or points was also the basis for an examination, whether the reply was complete or at least comprehensive. As will be shown later, the communicative principle of giving a comprehensive reply competed with the principle of brevity and the principle of immediate reply. But whenever a reply was said to be incomplete or not comprehensive, the division into articles or points was the basis for such a complaint. In his *Fortsetzung des Triumphs* 'Triumph of Truth, continued' for example, Scherer repeats a whole range of points to which Osiander had not replied. Scherer does not mention that Osiander followed a different principle, the principle of selecting the most important points. Nevertheless, Scherer comments on every repetition of a point without reply with a phrase like:

| Was sagt Osiander dazů? Nichts/ Er verbeisset vnd verschlücket auch disen Brocken.[6] | What does Osiander say to this point? Nothing. He has no reply to this hard problem. |

The division of disputes or quarrels into articles or points is an old pattern. It can be found in the university *disputationes* as well as in different forms of legal disputes. Around 1600, this form of organization was customary in quite different communicative domains. In the statutes of the *Reichskammergericht* of 1566, for example, it was ordained that all legal documents and pleadings be organized into articles or points to avoid any unnecessary loss of time.

The function of the final part is to bring the reader back from the often very subtle and sometimes long discussions of the different points to a more global view. This can be done by pointing out once more some major points or by formulating a result of the discussion, e.g. one's own victory and the ruin of the opponent. The final parts often contain pious wishes. The following example is a final passage with two parts. In the first part, the result of the controversy and of the discussion in the present pamphlet is given, whereas the second part contains a pious wish:

| Derhalben/ dieweil der Scherer (welcher auff seinem Faßnacht Triumphwagen mit prächtigen worten auffgezogen) so vbel in seiner Schrifft bestanden/ daß er sich vnd seine Jesuiter/ jhres blutdürstigen gemüts halben/ nicht weiß gebrennt/ oder rein gemacht: Doctor Luthern | The pamphlet of Scherer (who boarded his triumphal car with boasting words) did not bear close examination. He did not succeed in defending himself and his Jesuits in respect of their |

aber/ vnnd andere Euangelische Predicanten keiner Auffrhur vberwisen: aber vil vnnöttigs gewäsch/ das nicht zur Hauptsach dienlich/ eingeführt: vnnd in den Articuln (vnsere Christliche Religion betreffend) bestanden ist/ wie Butter an der Sonnen: so ist jm zurahten/ daß er geschwind mit seinem Triumphwagen außreisse/ ehe dann die jungen Knaben mit kot zu jm werffen/ vnd jm seinen Triumphwagen vnsauber anstreichen.

Der Allmächtig ewig Gott vnd Vatter vnsers HErrn Jhesu Christi wölle die Ehre seines eingebornen lieben Sons retten/ vnnd durch seinen heiligen Geist/ der vnwissenden Leut Hertzen erleuchten/ daß sie zur erkanntnus der seligmachenden Warheit kommen: Der wölle auch der Jesuiter anschläge (als des Achitophels) zur Narrheit/ vnd sie in jren Listen vnnd Gottlosen fürnemen/ zuschanden machen/ sein Christliche Kirchen aber in fried vnd rhue/ bey seinem heiligen Wort erhalten/ AMEN.[7]

bloodthirsty plans, nor could he prove that Dr. Luther and other Protestants were rebels. Instead, he brought many points to the fore that do not belong to the matter at all. In discussing the articles of our Christian religion, his arguments melted like butter in the sun. Thus, I should like to give him the advice to turn around his triumphal car, before the young boys throw mud upon him and paint his car brown with mud.

Almighty God, please save the honour of your Son and lead the unknowing to the truth. May the plans of the Jesuits fail and may your Christian Church remain in peace and without disturbance.

4.4. Threads of controversy and dialogical connections

A controversy with pamphlets usually consists of the publication of two or more texts that are connected in a more or less explicit way. The texts are connected at least in two different ways, and there are at least two levels of connectedness:

(i) the level of the whole pamphlet and its reference to one or more other pamphlet(s);
(ii) the internal organization of a pamphlet and the reference of certain parts of the text to the respective parts of the opponent's text. A crucial feature is the division into "points", "questions" or "articles" that are directed at the counterparts in the opponent's text.

To give an example, the author of the pamphlet *Jesuiter Latein* (1607) says in his preface to which text he is referring and how his own text will be divided into "questions", which his opponent put forward:

CHristlicher Leser: Es hat ohnlangst einer auß dem Päpstischen Hauffen/ der sich Herman Joseman nennet/ ein liederlich Patent in Teutschen Reymen/ vnter dem seltzamen Tittel deß Prædicanten Lateins, dem gemeinen Mann hiemit das Maul auffzusperren/ in Druck außgesprenget: Darinn er jhm drey Fragen kurtzumb will beantwortet haben (...). Belangt demnach die erste Frag dahin. Ob der Papst der Antichrist sey? (...).[8]

Christian reader. Recently, one of the papists, who calls himself Herman Joseman, has published a nasty pamphlet with the strange title 'The Latin of the predicants' with the aim of influencing laymen. In this pamphlet, he puts forward three questions. (...) The first question is, whether or not the Pope is the Antichrist. (...)

In this passage, it is first made clear to which pamphlet the author refers, and then the mode of division and a rough survey of the points at stake are mentioned. In the following text these points or "questions" are treated step by step and in a polemical fashion. In many pamphlets such references to the opponent's text and the way it is thematically organized are given in the title or at the very beginning of the text.

With a pamphlet one could open a controversy or one could react to a polemical contribution of an opponent in an ongoing controversy. There are examples that an opponent did not or not completely accept the opening of a controversy. The case of someone not answering at all seems to be rare. If an opponent or the content of a pamphlet was not assumed to be worth an answer, at least a few short remarks were published, stating that one was not going to enter the controversy and why. But, as a rule, when a controversy was opened, it could take several "moves" and sometimes several years until it was ended. The controversy of Osiander against the Jesuits, represented by Scherer and Rosenbusch, is not an untypical example.

The principle of division into "points" or "articles" is an important device for making transparent the internal connection of textual elements in a pamphlet. In addition, there are various linguistic means of textual organization, e.g. linguistic means of enumeration (*erstlich* 'first'; *zum andern* 'second' etc.) or linguistic means of topical organization, which serve to characterize different sub-topics (e.g. *Belangend den Punkt von XY ...*, 'concerning XY, ...').

4.5. Aims and intentions

Lucas Osiander says more than once that he could have made better use of his time than to exchange pamphlets with opponents he detested (*Lotterbuben*). Similar complaints are made by other authors. Thus, the writers engaged in controversies must have had good reasons to write and publish a great number of pamphlets anyway. Although our authors in most cases did not comment on their aims and intentions, there is a whole range of possibilities we have to discuss.

(i)   Defending one's personal honour

First, there is the possible aim to publicly defend one's own personal honour in cases where an opponent did not attack a group or party, but an individual person. Personal attacks often had their history. For example, Jakob Andreae reports in his autobiography that his successful appearances at religious disputations were a provocation for his opponents to calumniate and defame him as a person and to attack his personal honour. In his autobiography he expressly contradicts his opponents, who said in a personal attack that he, Andreae, was ashamed of his descent. Thus, it was possible and not unusual in controversies of that time to attack an opponent personally. In these cases, above all, a reply can be seen as a necessary defense of one's personal honour. The lack of a reply would have been regarded as a sign of weakness that could have been used in further pamphlets.

(ii)   Defending the honour of one's own group

In most cases, the authors of pamphlets do not only act on behalf of themselves, but on behalf of a certain group or party, whose honour they have to defend. The reason for such an aim is that most attacks in religious controversies of that time are not directed against authors as persons, but against parties or against authors representing parties. For instance, the aspect of a defense of honour (*Ehrerrettung*) is mentioned already in the title of Rosenbuschs reply to Osiander, whose pamphlet is said to be defamatory (*ehrnrürig*):

| Antwort vnd Ehrerrettung auff die Ehrn-rürig (...) Schmachschrifft Lucae Osiandri, die er intituliert/ Warnung Vor der Jesuiter Blutdurstigen Anschlägen vnd bösen Practicken. | Reply and defense of honour against the defamatory (...) pamphlet by Lucas Osiander with the title 'Warning of the Jesuit's bloodthirsty plans and evil machinations'. |

Thus, the Jesuits took the accusations of Osiander to be defamatory, and an aim of their replies was to defend the honour of their party against such accusations.

(iii) Finding the truth/settling disputes – the problem of hard-nosed opponents

It is extremely doubtful that opponents around 1600 expected to find the truth or to settle disputed matters by way of exchanging pamphlets. In the course of their controversy, both Osiander and Scherer refuse to believe that the opponent could be convinced. Both see the respective opponent falling prey to the devil. They continue the controversy because they see the laymen in danger. Thus, it seems that the different points of view of the opponents were unchangeable and that they were fully aware of this.

A passage in a text by Conrad Vetter, directed against Jakob Andreae, shows that he took the incompatibility of positions as given. The possiblity of a settlement is mentioned only in an ironical way:

Jn summa/ lieber Schmidl/ wann jhr Predicanten werd anfahen vns Jesuiter auff eweren Cantzlen zuloben/ so lasts vns wissen/ alßdann soll es Wurst wider Wurst heissen.[9]	To sum up, dear Schmidl [i.e. Andreae], if you and the predicants will begin to praise us, the Jesuits, in the pulpit, then let us know: then we will praise you in return.

(iv) Publishing one's opinions and claims – influence on public opinion

Obviously, the pamphleteers did not expect to convince their opponents. Rather they hoped to gain influence on the laiety and the sovereigns by their pamphlets. The controversy and the opponent seem to have been just an occasion to write down and to publish one's own opinions and claims. Furthermore, they were an opportunity to publish these opinions and claims together with refutations, proofs, arguments and so on.

The points at stake were not just theological positions and sophistries, which are burried today in the handbooks of dogmatic history. We also find claims that had or could have had important political consequences. An important goal of pamphlets was to introduce such claims, to put forth arguments in favour of them and to prepare public opinion for a political realization or enforcement. An example is the claim to prohibit the Jesuits in Poland and expel them from the country. This claim is introduced and argued for in the *Wichtig vnd hochnötig Bedencken/ Welcher gestalt der Jesuiter blutdürstigen anschlägen vnd Practicken zu begegnen seyn möge* (1610; 'Important and highly necessary opinion how one could face the Jesuits' bloodthirsty plans and perfidies').

Thus, it was an important global goal of pamphlets to take influence on public opinion. As mentioned above, the sovereigns and the laiety had to be convinced of one's opinions; in addition, the pamphleteers had to win their support for the realization of their claims. Especially the sovereigns were addressed, because they played a crucial role in matters of religious politics.

(v) Influencing the public appearance of one's own group

For many a religous group it was important to improve its public appearance. This was especially true of the order of the Jesuits, which was disputed since the days of its foundation in 1541. The Jesuits had to defend themselves not only against the Protestants, but also against certain groups among the Catholics. To influence the public appearance and the public assessment of a group, a pamphleteer could, for example, disparage the opponent or the founder of the opponent's group; on the other hand, he had to defend himself and the founder of his own group against similar attacks by the opponent. Such a defense and counter-defamation is the main goal of a pamphlet against the Jesuits with the following title:

Der Keusche Pabst. Das ist/ Helle vnd Augenscheinliche Beweisung/ daß die Jesuwider/ an weiland D. Martin Luther/ der Keuschheit halber nichts zu tadlen/ sondern vielmehr sich selbs vnd die jhrigen straffen vnd reformirn solten. Dem Jesuwiderischen vnnd Pistorianischen gifftigem Gespött/ vom Keuschen Luther/ entgegen gesetzt. Philippus Heilbrunner D. Getruckt zu Laugingen bey Leonhart Reinmichels Wittib. ANNO M.DC.	The chaste Pope. That is: a clear demonstration that the *Jesuwider* [those against Jesus; a pun on *Jesuiter*] have no reason to criticize D. Martin Luther in respect of chastity; on the contrary they should criticize and reform themselves and all the other Catholics. Against the venomous calumniations about the chaste Luther by the *Jesuwider* and by Pistorius. Philippus Heilbrunner D. Printed in Lauingen at Leonhard Reinmichel's widow's. Anno 1600.

4.6. The repertoire of linguistic acts

The repertoire of linguistic acts in the pamphlets under study is exceedingly rich, as are the possibilities of connecting and sequencing those acts in greater units. In order to give an idea of the organization of the relevant "cosmos" of linguistic acts, I shall begin with some basic moves and their possible sequences. Then, I shall enrich the basic system by further moves and types of units.

A speaker or writer can open a controversy mainly by using moves of the following types:
(i)   asserting one or more (controversial) point(s);
(ii) making one or more demands or claims (that are controversial);

The Pragmatic Form of Religious Controversies around 1600   97

(iii)   reproaching, blaming, calumniating someone;
(iv)   giving backing for the moves of type (i) – (iii).
These types of moves are closely connected to different aims and points at stake, viz. to the question of what is true or what is the proper conviction to have, to the question what to do and how to act in a certain situation, and to the aim of disparaging the opponent in public.

A speaker or writer wishing to reply can choose his moves among the range of specific reactions to the moves of type (i) – (iii). He can reply either to all the moves of the opening or only to a relevant selection.

An example: reproaches

In the pamphlets under study, reproaches are mainly aimed at "wrong" views (i.e., views, that were generally regarded as heretical) or abominable actions and habits like alcoholism, the habitual faking of quotations or immoral affairs. Here is an example:

Vnnd da schon bißweilen auff den Dörffern ein Ernst gebraucht/ vnd die Pfaffen Köchin abgeschafft werden/ so giebt man den Pfaffen nur vrsach/ daß sie andere Weiber vnnd Töchter zu Huren machen.[10]	And sometimes, when a serious reform in the villages is sought by abolishing the clergymen's female cooks, the only consequence is that the priests fornicate with other women and daughters and thus make them whores.

There were many ways of providing backing to an accusation in advance. These possibilities were as manifold as the reactions to a defense in reply to a reproach. In fact, these backings can be regarded as reactions to anticipated forms of defense in reply to a reproach. To give just one example: When claiming that the opponent holds a blameworthy view one may back up this claim by quoting a passage from the work of the opponent and – if necessary – give the passage a suitable interpretation. Note that the sequential organization of such moves may change (reproach followed by quotation as backing; quotation followed by reproach as conclusion).

Among the reactions in reply to a reproach are the following moves, sequences of moves or communicative strategies:
(i)   One can deny what has been reproached. For example, in a pamphlet of defense against Huber, Osiander denied that he was a Crypto-Calvinist as Huber had claimed. Scherer, in a similar situation, not only states that the claim of his opponent is a lie, but even makes a more general statement. He thus combines a defensive move with a counterattack:

"die Predicanten liegen vnnd triegen/ sie sehen nu in die Stern/ oder in die Bibel."[11]

The predicants all lie and cheat, whether they look to the stars or into the Bible.

(ii) One can demand relevant backing for a reproach, e.g. a proof:

Probier Vtzinger probier/ Bist du dann jetzt nicht daheimb? (*probieren* 'beweisen').

Give proof, Utzinger. Give proof. Why don't you give proof? Are you not at home now?

(iii) One can deny that the opponent is entitled to make a certain reproach, for example, in the case where the same reproach would be true of the opponent himself or of some members of his party.

(iv) One can make a counter-reproach. Georg Scherer used a strategy that combined (iii) and (iv) in a rejoinder to the reproach that the Jesuits were seeking to destroy the peace of religion in a bloodthirsty way. He said that Luther had goaded on the peasants to revolt and had encouraged them to kill the papists. Therefore, the adherents and disciples of Luther were not entitled to accuse anybody of bloodthirsty plans or actions (in *Triumph der Warheit*).

Among the standard reactions in reply to reproaches[12] three types of move are used only seldom or not at all: (v) defending the point of view, action or habit in question; (vi) denying that there is any substance to the attack; (vii) denying that there is or was an alternative to what has been reproached. – The reason for avoiding these moves seems to be that in making one of these moves one incurs the commitment that one does in fact hold the objectionable view or that one has in fact performed the objectionable action. This commitment may turn out to be unfavourable in the course of the controversy.

Personal assaults, polemics and calumniations

The pamphlets written in the years around 1600 are full of personal assaults, personal polemics and all kinds of insults and calumniations against opponents and their work.

Among the main types of moves are insults and offences. The linguistic means for such moves comprise abusive words and invectives, e.g. words used to express contempt like *Papist* or to express disapproval of points of view like *Wirbelgeist* 'wayward spirit', *Jrrgeist* 'lunatic'. The latter and a few other invectives refer to abilities, habits and attitudes of an opponent, e.g. *SchalcksNarr* 'fool' or *Lotterbube* 'immoral person'. Next to invectives, adjectives could be used (*ein auffgeblasner/ rhumrähtiger Jesuiter*[13]), defamatory predications (e.g. that someone had not a sufficient command of foreign languages) or disparaging attributes (e.g. *sampt zweien langen Ohren/ stultitiæ & arrogantiæ*[14]). Furthermore, puns and distortion of words with the name of the opponent were widely used. All these means served to personally assault the opponent.

In addition, the pamphleteers used familiar forms of address like *lieber Osiander* 'dear Osiander' that lacked the usual expression of respect, where something like *würdiger vnd hochgelerter Herr* 'most worthy and learned gentleman' would have been appropriate. These forms of address are meant to make the opponent ridiculous or to signal the writer's superiority. Diminutives are used with the same intention and the same effect in pamphlets.

An important type of move is the depreciation of persons, texts or textual elements. Osiander, for example, follows the principle of brevity and conciseness and therefore characterizes and critizises some arguments of his opponent, Scherer, as too lengthy and verbose (*mit langem gewäsch*[15]). On the other hand, Scherer censures the lack of solidity of Osianders text in the following:

| Lieber was soll man disem deinem Büchlein für ein Zahn außbrechen? wie du dich dann rhümest/ daß jhm die Jesuiter noch kein Zahn sollen außgebrochen haben/ ist doch kein Zahn/ oder jchtes starckes verhanden? sonder alles weich/ teigig/ wurmbstichig vnd faul (*Triumph* 84). | Dear friend, is there any tooth to extract from your booklet? You said that up to now the Jesuits did not succeed in extracting a single tooth from your book. The reason is: there is no tooth or any other firm structure. Everything in the book is flabby, pasty, worm-eaten and rotten. |

The following form of communicative disparagement is not very frequent, but noteworthy. Both Scherer and Osiander complain to the respective superior of the opponent about the opponent's incompetence and "nullity". Osiander states in his *Faßnacht Triumph* that Scherer does not write as a private person, but that his opinions were approved by his superiors. One page later, he complains to the said superiors, asking why they allow such incompetent writers to publish their texts:

Vnnd ist dis wol zumercken/ daß der Scherer disen seinen Triumph mit vorwissen vnnd approbation seiner andern Jesuiter (die höher seind dann er) geschriben hat. Dann dise wort stehn am end seines Büchlins: *Cum facultate superiorum.* Das ist/ diß Büchlin sey geschriben/ mit bewilligung vnd gutheissen seiner Obersten (18).	Note that Scherer published his *Triumph* with the prior knowledge and the approbation of his superiors. The words *cum facultate superiorum* at the end of the booklet mean that the text was published with the permission and the approval of his superiors.
Vnnd eben in denen jhren schrifften/ darinn sie sich entschulgen möllen/ [= wöllen] machen sie die sachen noch böser. Dann was sie zuuor gemahlet vnnd versificiert/ das sagen sie jetzt mit lauttern worten/ nemlich/ daß jhr will vnnd begeren sey/ daß die Päpstische Potentaten/ das Euangelion mit dem Schwerdt verfolgen vnnd außreutten sollen. Darumb mich in der warheit wundert/ warumb die Päpstische zugeben/ daß solche lose vnd tolle Leut/ (als der Scherer vnnd Rosenbusch sein) in den Truck/ in so wichtigen sachen/ ettwas schreiben/ die doch nichts können/ dann übel ärger machen? Wann die Papisten nicht verstendigere vnnd gelehrtere fürsichtigere Scribenten haben/ dann den Scherer vnd Rosenbusch/ so muß gewißlich ein grosse leutterung bey jhnen sein. Dann wann man solche Narren will vber Eier setzen/ werden sie nichts guts außbrüten (19).	But in the texts in which they aim to defend themselves they make everything worse. What was only depicted before, they now say clearly: that they wish that the Catholic sovereigns should extirpate the Lutherans. I cannot but wonder why the Catholic superiors give permission for such wanton and crazy people as Scherer and Rosenbusch to publish something in such important matters, people who are incompetent and are only able to make bad things worse. If the Papists do not have writers who are more competent, more learned and more careful than Scherer and Rosenbusch, it is surely because of a lack of staff. You may give such fools any task, they won't hatch anything good.

The same type of move can be found in one of the earlier writings of Scherer, who complained about the *Hofprediger* 'court preacher' Osiander and his writings to the Duke of Württemberg:

Jch Scherer antworte dem Osiander auff dise Jntzicht kurtz vnd rund/ daß nemblich er Osiander/ oder wer solches für glaubwürdig außgibt/ nicht ein einfacher/ sonder sibenfacher ehrloser Bůb sey vnd bleibe/ so lang vnd souil er dises auff die Jesuiter nicht	In reply to Osiander's accusations, I say that Osiander or anybody else who repeats these accusations, is an infamous scoundrel, as long as he gives no proof for his accusations. I believe that you are totally misled,

wahr machet. Jch glaub es reiten dich Osiander mehr dann tausent Teufel/ daß du also ohn allen Beweiß/ vnd ohn alle Proba/ mit so schrecklichen Aufflagen vnd Bezichtigungen die Vnschuldigen antastest. Wann ich dein Fürst wäre/ Osiander/ so wolte ich dich zur Proba vnd Beweiß halten/ oder zum Teufel weck jagen/ vnd sagen/ trolle dich/ du bist mit deinem Liegen/ Lästern vnd Calumnieren meinem Hoff kein Zierd/ sonder ein Schand/ schreib was du verantworten kanst/ oder stecke dein Feder ein/ vnd halte das Maul (*Triumph* 107).

Osiander, to accuse and charge the innocent in such a horrible way. If I were the Duke of Württemberg, your superior, I would demand a proof for the accusations or else send you to the devil and say: "Get off, you are not an honourable member of my court with your lies and your calumnies, but a disgrace to it. Write what you can prove, or shut up."

Communicative stratagems and strategies

Some types of moves can be seen as communicative stratagems or as strategies that were closely connected to the intended effect of the pamphlet. Of these moves and strategies I should like to highlight only two.

(i) A first stratagem consists in making explicit certain consequences of views or actions, especially for the sovereigns. It seems to be a peculiar strategy of Scherer's to make explicit or to impute such consequences to the writings of his opponent that are in some way dangerous or prejudicial to his sovereigns. Such a strategy fits the abovementioned global strategy to win the sovereigns for one's plans and convictions.

(ii) A second stratagem could be labelled "self-ascription of victory *lite pendente*". It is widely used on both sides of the controversy. This type of move runs as follows: A writer proclaims his victory prematurely in a pamphlet long before the controversy is over, declaring his opponent to be well and truly beaten, or at least exhausted. The passage quoted at the beginning of this paper[16] is a first example of this stratagem, another one is the following passage from the same pamphlet:

Du armer Osiander/ wie jage ich dich von einem Winckel zů dem andern/ vnd von einer ellenden Distinction zur andern? Du zauffest ein weil hindersich/ ein weil fürsich/ springst jetzt auff die recht/ bald auff die lincke Seiten/ woltest gern meine Straich versetzen/ aber du můst mir herhalten/ vnd Haar lassen/ da hilfft nichts darfür (*Triumph* 64).

Poor Osiander, how I chase you back and forth, from one distinction to the other. You would like to defend yourself, but you are unable to do so successfully, and so you have to suffer defeat, there is no other choice.

On the other hand, Osiander declares himself the victor. He writes several times that Scherer had an accident with his triumphal car, that Scherer was bogged down in the mud etc. Thus, it seems that we have here a kind of self-ascription of a winner's diploma, conferred on both sides while the conquest is still going on. Closely connected with this type of move is the declaration of the opponent's end.[17]

4.7. Principles of communication in controversies

The principles which the opponents follow or enforce in controversies play a major role in the choice of types of actions and in the outcome of a controversy. Such principles do not form a universal or previously fixed set. They are negotiated by the participants, they are introduced and justified, and the adherence to these principles can be claimed by an opponent. Another important point is the fact that principles can be mutually incompatible. There seem to be four major principles which are used in controversies around 1600:

(i) the principle of comprehensive reply;
(ii) the principle of brevity;
(iii) the principle of fast and immediate reaction;
(iv) the principle of thematic rigour or of thematic restriction.

The principle of comprehensive reply can be formulated in the following way:

(i) Each and every point that an author made in a pamphlet and that is given the opponent as a task (*auffgegeben*) has to be dealt with sufficiently in the opponent's counter-pamphlet.

This principle is introduced by Conrad Vetter in his *Heilbrunnischer Trumpff* (1604), when he claims that every point has to be discussed and that it is not acceptable to discuss just a choice of major points. Such a principle of comprehensive reply is also found in the earlier writings of Vetter: *damit nichts vnuerantwortet bleibe* 'no point should be without reply'.[18]

The principle of comprehensive reply becomes apparent in the organization of pamphlets, where usually every point of an opponent's text is discussed, often in the same order as in the opponent's pamphlet. But even more instructive are the complaints which are voiced when an opponent did not follow the principle, or the explicit demand that an opponent should follow the principle. Thus, the principle serves as the basis for an author to point out omissions and deficiencies in his opponent's text. It is also used to interpret omissions as a sign of weakness of the opponent or even as a partial victory on the side of the author.[19]

The principle of brevity and the principle of immediate answer are incompatible with or at least compete with the principle of comprehensive reply. In order to discuss every point of a pamphlet, an opponent has to produce a long text and, consequently, he will generally need a longer production time.

The principle of brevity is formulated in (ii):

(ii) A reply should be as short as possible. Therefore it is acceptable or even necessary to discuss only major points from the opponent's pamphlet.

The principle of brevity is introduced several times by Osiander. He gives different reasons for this principle. First, he mentions the reading habits and reading preferences of his readers, who are assumed to dislike long texts (*vmb geliebter kürtze willen*[20]). Second, the author does not have enough time. Osiander says that he has to do other work that is more important than quarrelling with the Jesuits, who, in his eyes, are *Lotterbuben* and do not deserve a fully fledged answer. The principle of brevity is used by Osiander to justify his omission of certain points made by his opponents. Nevertheless, his opponents put down these omissions as a success.

The principle of immediate answer is formulated in (iii):

(iii) Every reply by a "strong" author has to be fast and immediate. Delay must be seen as a sign of weakness.

Such a principle can be extracted from a passage by Gretser and Vetter, who take a certain production time of the opponents as a case of delay and as a sign of weakness.

haben die Augspurgische Predicanten jhnen zimlich der weil gelassen/ biß sie die Häfelen zusam getragen/ vnnd (da schier jederman an jhnen verzweifelt) endtlich nach vierzehen gantzer Monaten ...[21]	It took the Augspurg predicants a long time to get their act together. Finally, after 14 long months, when almost nobody had any hope left for them to reply at all, they came up with an answer.

And Osiander says about Scherers *Triumph der Warheit*:

[Vor seinem Triumphwagen sind] ettliche grawe Müllerpferdt (des vnuerstandts vnnd vnwissenheit) gespannen. Welches villeicht die vrsach gewesen/ dz diser Triumphwagen ettwas später ankommen.[22]	His triumphal car is drawn by some grey, lame horses – the horses of stupidity and ignorance. Maybe these horses are the reason why his car arrived rather late.

Thus, a typical use of the principle of immediate answer is to interpret a somewhat belated reply as a sign of weakness. This move can be found also in later controversies, e.g. in the 19th century.[23]

A further example of the use of communicative principles in controversies is the principle of thematic rigour or of thematic restriction:

(iv) In a pamphlet, one should only address points that have already been introduced into the controversy.

Such a principle is the basis of a complaint by Osiander: He claims that his opponent Scherer has strategically introduced a lot of points that do not belong to the topic of the controversy.

Darneben mischet er auch (vber seine gewohnliche vilfeltige Frecharts vnd Schalcksnarrenbossen) ettliche sachen ein/ die doch zu obgemeltem Hauptstritt nicht gehörig: allein daß er Bletter fülle/ vnd man gedencken soll/ er hab geantwortet.[24]	Furthermore, in addition to his usual fooleries, he brings in several points that have nothing to do with the abovementioned main argument. He does so just to fill the paper and to make the reader believe this to be a sufficient reply.

The principle of thematic rigour is just one aspect in a whole field of moves and principles that are related to the negotiation of the *status quaestionis*, i.e. the problem of defining the topic of the controversy.[25] Furthermore, the quotation shows this principle to be related to the principle of comprehensive reply. Obviously, a voluminous pamphlet was more likely to be considered a fully fledged answer than a small one, even if the voluminous one did contain many off-topic points.

These were some examples of how communicative principles are introduced in a controversy, how they can be used for strategic purposes, and how they can be incompatible or interrelated.

5. Further perspectives

So far, I have taken religious controversies (i) as an important element of the "communicative budget" of the time around 1600, and (ii) as a complex linguistic activity with a specific pragmatic form. The main aspects of the pragmatic form of controversies I dealt with were: the status of controversies in public life around 1600 (section 3.1), the participants, their typical constellation and roles (3.2), the global organization of controversies and the typical textual elements of pamphlets (3.3), the dialogical connectedness of

The Pragmatic Form of Religious Controversies around 1600   105

pamphlets (3.4), the aims and intentions of the participants (3.5), the repertoire of linguistic acts and some relevant linguistic means (3.6), and, finally, the use of communicative principles for strategic purposes (3.7).

There is a long road ahead of us. Other religious controversies need to be treated from the angle of historical dialogue analysis. Other linguistic and pragmatic aspects which could not be examined here merit serious observation. The controversy under study and those of other types and time frames call for comparison, as do the results already at our disposal.[26] Let us hope there will one day be a multi-volume history of controversies, of their pragmatic forms, and of their implications for the history of ideas and their public influence. The topic is important enough.

Notes

1 Scherer, *Triumph* (1587: 1f.).
2 German *kommunikativer Haushalt*; see (Luckmann) 1997.
3 Osiander, *Gründtlicher Bericht. Auff Doctor Samuel Hubers Lästerschrifft* (1596: 23).
4 There were not only the officially arranged, public disputations (e.g. the Regensburg *Religionsgespräche*), but also more or less private disputations. Scultetus, the preacher at the court in Heidelberg, reports an episode from one of his travels. By chance he finds himself lodged in the same inn with a clergyman of an opposing party. Both agree to hold a disputation in the evening and in the night. Of course, Scultetus claims to be the winner in this disputation (see his autobiography).
5 Osiander, *Samuel Hubers Lästerschrift* (1596: 43ff.).
6 Scherer, *Fortsetzung des Triumphs*, p. 32. See also Scherer (1588: 60). Here, Scherer enumerates some questions that Osiander did not answer.
7 Osiander, *Faßnacht Triumph* (1587: 58f.).
8 *Jesuiter Latein* (1607: 3).
9 *Antwort Conradi Vetters* (1589: 10).
10 Heilbrunner, *Der Keusche Pabst*, 1600, B1a.
11 Scherer, *Vtzinger* (1589: 15).
12 See for example Austin's "A plea for excuses"; Fritz and Hundsnurscher (1975).
13 Osiander, *Faßnacht Triumph* (1587: 3). – 'An arrogant and boasting Jesuit'.
14 Osiander, *Faßnacht Triumph* (1587: 4). – 'with two long ears of stupidness and arrogance'.
15 Osiander, *Faßnacht Triumph* (1587: 19).
16 "GVnstiger lieber Leser/ es ist wahr vnd recht geredt/ daß nichts mächtiger vnnd stärcker vnderm Himmel sey/ weder die liebe Warheit/ (...). Also hat sie auch jüngstlich wider Lucam Osiander/ im Streit vber der Jesuiter Vnschuld/ wegen der bezichtigten Blůt-durstigen Anschlägen vnd Practicken die *Victoriam* erobert/ vnd das Sigkräntzlein redlich

vnd auffrecht gewunnen vnd heimgetragen. Dagegen aber ist dem Osiander sein vnwahrhaffte Goschen dermassen zerklopffet vnd zerblewet worden/ dz er nun mehr kaum einem Menschen/ geschweigen einem Doctori gleich sihet. Solches wirdt der Christliche Leser auß den nachuolgenden Capiteln ohn allen weitgesûchten Vmbschweiff/ fein kurtz vnd rund verstehen vnd abnemmen." – For a translation see the first quotation in section 1.

17 Similar moves can still be found nowadays in the verbal duels that are arranged as forms of advertising before important boxing matches.

18 *Antwort Conradi Vetters* (1589: 3).

19 E.g. C. Vetter, *Heilbrunnischer Trumpff* (1604: 9f.).

20 Osiander, *Faßnacht Triumph* (1587: 45).

21 Gretser, J., und C. Vetter, *Widerholung/ Der Augspurgischen Predicanten/ wegen der Cambilhonischen Relation/ mit Macht vberhand nemmenden Furien/ vnd erbärmlichen Tobsucht (...). Durch Iacobvm Gretservm, vnd Conradvm Vetter (...).* Ingolstadt (Angermayer, Hertzroy) 1612, 2f.

22 Osiander, *Faßnacht Triumph* (1587: 3).

23 Görres (1958), Bd. 15, 323.10ff.

24 Osiander, *Faßnacht Triumph* (1587: 6).

25 See e.g. Dascal 1990: section 3; 1995a: 109 (4.3.) and 111 (4.6.).

26 See e.g. the work by Dascal mentioned in the references.

Sources

Andreae, Jacob
    1991   *Leben des Jacob Andreae, Doktor der Theologie, von ihm selbst mit großer Treue und Aufrichtigkeit beschrieben, bis auf das Jahr Christi 1562*. Lateinisch und deutsch. Hg. und mit einer Einleitung von Hermann Ehmer. Stuttgart: Calwer Verlag.

Görres, Joseph
    1958   *Gesammelte Schriften. Band 15: Geistesgeschichtliche und politische Schriften der Münchner Zeit (1828-1838)*. Hg. von Ernst Deuerlein. Köln: Verlag J.P. Bachem.

Gretser, Jacob, und Conrad Vetter
    1612   *Widerholung/ Der Augspurgischen Predicanten/ wegen der Cambilhonischen Relation/ mit Macht vberhand nemmenden Furien/ vnd erbärmlichen Tobsucht (...). Durch Iacobvm Gretservm, vnd Conradvm Vetter (...).* Ingolstadt: Angermayer, Hertzroy.

Heilbrunner, Ph.
    1600   *Der Keusche Pabst. Das ist/ Helle vnd Augenscheinliche Beweisung/ daß die Jesuwider/ an weiland D. Martin Luther/ der Keuschheit halber nichts zu*

The Pragmatic Form of Religious Controversies around 1600   107

        tadlen/ sondern vielmehr sich selbs vnd die jhrigen straffen vnd reformirn solten. Dem Jesuwiderischen vnnd Pistorianischen gifftigem Gespött/ vom Keuschen Luther/ entgegen gesetzt. Lauingen (Leonhart Reinmichels Witwe).

Huber, Samuel

    1596   *Notwendige Entdeckung/ Wie D: Lucas Osiander in seiner Predigt von der GnadenWahl/ die verzweyffelte Caluinische Lere versteckt (...).* O.O.

Jesuiter Latein.

    1607   *Jesuiter Latein. Das ist: Antwort auff drey Fragen/ den Evangelischen/ von genannten Catholischen auffgeben/ so gleichwol jederzeit gründtlich Beantwortet werden: (...) Gestelt durch Christianum Christmannum Christlingensem. Gedruckt im Jahr/ 1607.*

Osiander, Lucas

    1585   *Warnung Vor der Jesuiter blutdurstigen Anschlägen vnnd bösen Practicken.* Tübingen: Gruppenbach.

    1587   *Bericht: Vom Faßnacht Triumph/ Georgij Scherers/ eines Jesuiters.* Tübingen: Gruppenbach.

    1589   *Endtliche Abfertigung Der beider Jesuiter/ Christoffen Rosenbuschen/ vnd Georgen Scherers.* Tübingen: Gruppenbach.

    1591   *Widerlegung Der Bekandtnus Caspar Schwenckfelds/ welche Anno 1547. getruckt worden.* Tübingen: Gruppenbach.

    1592   *Bericht An alle fromme Christen/ welche die Warheit lieben: Warumb die beide rasende Barfüsser Mönch/ Georg Eckhart vnd Michel Anisius/ keiner Antwort werth seien.* Tübingen: Gruppenbach.

    1593   *Badkromet/ auß dem Wildbad/ Doctoris Lucæ Osiandris, für ettliche Papisten/ welche von jhm außgeben/ daß er (...) zum Papsthumb gefallen sey.* Tübingen: Gruppenbach.

    1596   *Gründtlicher Bericht. Auff Doctor Samuel Hubers Lästerschrifft (deren Titul/ Notwendige entdeckung/ rc.) in deren er D. Lucas Osiandern (...) mit Gewalt will zu einem Caluinisten machen.* Tübingen: Gruppenbach.

Rosenbusch, Christoph

    1586   *Antwort vnd Ehrerrettung auff die Ehrnrürig (...) Schmachschrifft Lucae Osiandri, die er intituliert/ Warnung Vor der Jesuiter Blutdurstigen Anschlägen vnd bösen Practicken.* Ingolstadt: Sartorius.

Scherer, Georg

    1586   *Rettung der Jesuiter Vnschuld wider die Gifftspinnen Lucam Osiander.* Ingolstadt: Sartorius.

    1587   *Triumph Der Warheit/ wider Lucam Osiandrum.* Ingolstadt: Sartorius.

1588   *Fortsetzung Deß Triumphs der Warheit/ wider Lucam Osiandrum.* Ingolstadt: Sartorius.

1589   *Georg Scherers Antwort/ auff die zwey vnuerschämpte vnd Ehrenschmähende Famos/ Schandt vnd Lästercharten/ M. Alexanders Vtzingers eines Predicanten zuo Schmalkalden: Newlich wider (...) alle Catholische Francken (...) außgeworffen.* Ingolstadt: Satorius.

Scultetus, Abraham

1966   *Die Selbstbiographie des Heidelberger Theologen und Hofpredigers Abraham Scultetus (1566-1624).* Neu hg. und erläutert von Gustav Adolf Benrath. Karlsruhe: Verlag evangelischer Presseverband Karlsruhe (Baden).

Sohn, Georg

1615/1988   *Eine schöne Rede (...) Vom Vrsprung der alten löblichen Vniversitet Heydelberg/ vnd was sich bey derselben denckwürdig zugetragen. Gehalten im Jahr 1587 (...).* Heidelberg 1615. Nachdruck mit einem Nachwort von Reinhard Düchting. Heidelberg: Winter, 1988.

Vetter, Conrad (Pseud.: Conrad Andreae)

1589   *Antwort Conradi Vetters/ der Societet Iesv: Auff Jacob Schmidels nechst vberschickt Sendschreiben/ Vnd darinn in öffentlichen Truck außgegoßne/ vngegründte Klagen.* Ingolstadt: Sartorius.

1604   *Heilbrunnischer Trumpff. Das ist/ Gründtliche Erklärung/ wie die zwen Predicanten Lip vnd Jacob Heilbrunner (...) am Hag hinab zudeichen gedrungen worden.* Ingolstadt: Andreas Angermeyer.

Wichtig vnd hochnötig Bedencken

1610   *Wichtig vnd hochnötig Bedencken/ Welcher gestalt der Jesuiter blutdürstigen anschlägen vnd Practicken zu begegnen seyn möge. Sampt einer Relation Von der Jesuiter geheimsten sachen/ auch (...) von dem Triumph vnd Siegzeichen der Jesuiter zu Paris.* (o.O. 1610). Hg. von Hans Ludwig Held. München/Leipzig 1912: Hans Sachs-Verlag.

References

Austin, John L.

1956/57   A plea for excuses. *Proceedings of the Aristotelian Society* 57, 1-30.

Barner, Wilfried

1977   Streitschriften und Theater der Jesuiten als rhetorische Medien. In: Martin Bircher und Eberhard Mannack (Hg.). *Deutsche Barockliteratur und europäische Kultur.* Hamburg: Hauswedell, 242-243.

The Pragmatic Form of Religious Controversies around 1600 109

Cremaschi, Sergio, and Marcelo Dascal
 forthcoming Persuasion and argument in the Malthus-Ricardo correspondence. *Research in the History of Economic Theory and Method* 16.
Dascal, Marcelo
 1989 Controversies as quasi-dialogues. In: Edda Weigand und Franz Hundsnurscher (eds.). *Dialoganalyse II*. Band 1. Tübingen: Niemeyer, 147-159.
 1990 The controversy about ideas and the ideas about controversy. In: Fernando Gil (ed.). *Controvérsias Científicas e Filosóficas*. Lissabon: Editorial Fragmentos, 61-100.
 1995a Observations sur la dynamique des controverses. *Cahiers de Linguistique Française* 17, 99-121.
 1995b Epistemología, controversias y pragmática. *Isegoría* 12, 8-43.
 1995c Strategies of dispute and ethics. "Du tort" and "La place d'autruy". In: *Leibniz und Europa. VI. Internationaler Leibniz-Kongreß*. Hannover: Gottfried-Wilhelm-Leibniz-Gesellschaft. Vorträge II. Teil. Hannover 1995, 108-115.
 1997 Epistemology, controversies, and pragmatics. Ms.
 1998 Types of polemics and types of polemical moves. In: Dialoganalyse VI. Referate der 6. Arbeitstagung, Prag 1996. Hg. von Světla Čmejrková, Jana Hoffmannová, Olga Müllerová und Jindra Světlá. Teil 1. Tübingen: Niemeyer.
 forthcoming The balance of reason. In: Daniel Vanderveken (ed.). *Language, Thought, and Reason*. Oxford: Oxford University Press.
Fritz, Gerd
 1994 Geschichte von Dialogformen. In: Gerd Fritz und Franz Hundsnurscher (Hg.). *Handbuch der Dialoganalyse*. Tübingen: Niemeyer, 545-562.
 1995 Topics in the history of dialogue forms. In: Andreas H. Jucker (ed.). *Historical Pragmatics*. Amsterdam/Philadelphia: Benjamins, 469-498.
Fritz, Gerd, und Franz Hundsnurscher
 1975 Sprechaktsequenzen. Überlegungen zur Vorwurf/Rechtfertigungs-Interaktion. *Deutschunterricht* 27, 81-103.
Gloning, Thomas
 1993 Sprachreflexive Textstellen als Quellen für die Geschichte von Kommunikationsformen. In: Heinrich Löffler (ed.). *Dialoganalyse IV. Referate der 4. Arbeitstagung, Basel 1992*. Teil 1. Tübingen: Niemeyer, 207-217.
 1998 Das sprachliche Wirken der Jesuiten in der frühen Neuzeit. In: Hans-Gert Roloff (ed.). *Editionsdesiderate zur Frühen Neuzeit. Zweiter Teil*. (Chloe, Beiheft zum Daphnis 25). Amsterdam: Editions Rodopi B.V., 739-762.

Kastner, Ruth
    1982   *Geistlicher Raufhandel, Form und Funktion der illustrierten Flugblätter zum Reformationsjubiläum 1617 in ihrem historischen und publizistischen Kontext.* Frankfurt a.M./Bern: Lang.

Krebs, Richard
    1890   *Die politische Publizistik der Jesuiten und ihrer Gegner in den letzten Jahrzehnten vor Ausbruch des Dreißigjährigen Krieges.* Halle a.d. Saale: Max Niemeyer.

Leube, Hans
    1935   *Der Jesuitenorden und die Anfänge nationaler Kultur in Frankreich.* Tübingen: J.C.B. Mohr – Paul Siebeck.

Luckmann, Thomas
    1997   Allgemeine Überlegungen zu kommunikativen Gattungen. In: Barbara Frank, Thomas Haye und Doris Tophinke (Hg.). *Gattungen mittelalterlicher Schriftlichkeit.* Tübingen: Narr, 11-17.

Naumann, Victor (Pseud.: Pilatus)
    1905   Die antijesuitische Literatur von der Gründung des Ordens bis auf unsere Zeit. In: Ders.: *Der Jesuitismus.* Regensburg: Manz, 351-540.

Schwitalla, Johannes
    1983   *Deutsche Flugschriften 1460-1525. Textsortengeschichtliche Studien.* Tübingen: Niemeyer.
    1986   Martin Luthers argumentative Polemik: mündlich und schriftlich. In: Franz Josef Worstbrock und Helmut Koopmann (Hg.). *Kontroversen, alte und neue.* Band 2. Tübingen: Niemeyer, 41-54.

Sommervogel, Carlos (éd.)
    1890-1932   *Bibliothèque de la Compagnie de Jésus.* Nouvelle édition. 12 vols. Bruxelles/Paris: Schepens.

Werner, K.
    1861-67   *Geschichte der apologetischen und polemischen Literatur der christlichen Theologie.* Fünf Bände. Nachdruck Osnabrück: Zeller (1966).

The Use of Dialogue in Early German Pamphlets
On the Constitution of Public Involvement in the Reuchlin-Pfefferkorn Controversy

Johannes Schwitalla
Bavarian Julius Maximilians University, Würzburg

1. Introduction

In the short period between 1518 and 1525, the new medium of the pamphlet led to the rapid constitution of a public forum hitherto unknown in Germany. Not only did a great number of academics and the clergy take active part in this debate, but a considerable sector of the general public also participated at a receptive level. The points to be treated here will include the consideration of how this public involvement came about. The number of pamphlets published between 1501 and 1530 is estimated at about 10,000, but figures up to the year 1517 are negligible (see Fig. 1).

Seldom has there been such sudden public involvement in Germany affecting the whole German population as the result of just one new medium.[1] The special feature of the pamphlet (to a lesser extent also the leaflet; cf. Schilling 1990: 157ff.) is that — under relatively free production conditions — texts can be written which refer to each other dialogically, representing the development of a discussion. In contrast with modern dialogical media (telephone, internet), it constitutes public debate.

We can follow the increase in public discussion step by step from Luther's "95 Theses" onwards. The pattern is always the same. A text is written, distributed and reprinted by others. Counter-arguments then appear to which the original author replies and others become involved. Within two months, Luther's "95 Theses" are printed three times in German and posted on walls in Latin. In the space of one and a half years (November 1517 to May 1519) 17 texts appear.[2]

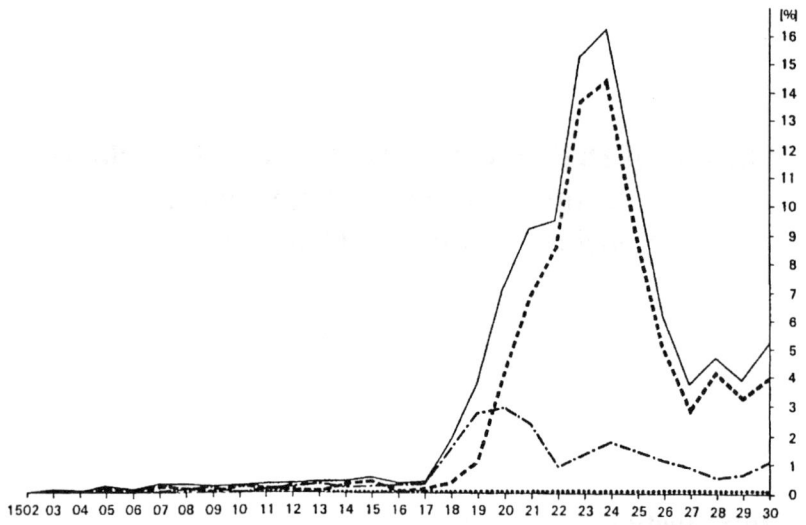

Figure 1: Pamphlet production in Germany from 1502 to 1530 according to Köhler (1986: 266)

——— total amount	3016 =	100.00%	
---------- High-German pamphlets	2373 =	78.68%	⎫
.... Low-German pamphlets	14 =	0.46%	⎬ (79.14%)
–·–·–·– Latin pamphlets	629 =	20.85%	⎭

Note: Low-German pamphlets are under-represented in this selection. A better distribution is to be found in the *Herzog August Bibliothek*, Wolfenbüttel, where they amount to 3.33%.

2. Summary of the Reuchlin–Pfefferkorn controversy

From 1507 to 1509, Johannes Pfefferkorn, who had been converted from Judaism to Christianity, wrote four anti–semitic pamphlets, appearing both in German and Latin. In 1510 he had a pamphlet ("Zu Lob und Ehre ...") and a leaflet printed on the occasion of the Augsburg *Reichstag*.[3] All these texts are anti-semitic invectives in which Pfefferkorn reduces the Jews to religious, social and economic stereotypes of a negative kind and incites the ruling classes to deprive the Jews of their Hebrew books, ban them from money-lending, force them to attend sermons with a view to Christian conversion, drive them out or have them carry out menial tasks:

sy musten alle verworffne arbait thun/ als die gassen sauber halten oder dye Camin keren deßgelichn die scheussheuser fegen und huns dreck klauben etc. ("Judenfeind" 1590: 11a)
[They should do base work such as cleaning the streets or sweeping chimneys, likewise sweeping the shithouses and cleaning up dogs' mess etc.]

The novel aspect of these texts is that a layman, of his own volition, even if he does have the support of some theologians, has taken up a matter of public interest and tried to use the new medium of the pamphlet to gain political influence. He throws himself into publishing one text after another in German and in Latin so as not to miss any reader out. In his "Vortrag" (C 3a) of 1509 (Martin 1994: 113f.) and the "Klag über alle Klag" (H 5a) of 1521, he even exhorts subjects to ask their lords to act against the Jews.

Pfefferkorn's writings contain mixed text-types; they consist of narrative and argumentative text parts, of translations and renderings of Hebrew texts, of reprints of official writings, lists, bills etc. To attract sales of the prints they are provided with wood-engravings, partly with Christian motifs (Mary with her mantle spread over the Pope and princes, the Crucifixion), but even at an early stage with anti-semitic illustrations (title pages of the "Judenspiegel" and the "Lob und Ehre", Fig. 2).

Figure 2: Wood-engraving of the title page of "Zu Lob und Ehre" 1509: a crippled Jew walking on crutches and wearing the Jewish ring

Pfefferkorn is fully aware of the journalistic impact of his texts: they range between 8 and 24 sheets only (in order to shorten the "Verlengerung des lesens" 'length of reading', "Judenfeind" 9b).[4] As early as in his first pamphlet ("Judenspiegel" 1507), Pfefferkorn demonstrates that he masters various genre styles. It opens with a very long, complex sentence of 240 words in the style of officialdom without any anacolutha. But most of the text is written like a sermon with its stylistic features of oral communication. Pfefferkorn writes freely in short, paratactic sentences which are easy to understand, displaying a rhetorical perfection altogether Lutheresque (cf. Martin 1994: 390f.). Pfefferkorn makes use of idioms, interjections and other forms of spoken language, vivid illustrations and comparisons drawn from everyday life; he makes up scenes and characters (the devil's speech to the Jewish community in Frankfurt in the "Beschirmung") — such are the linguistic and textual devices with which pamphlets in the Reformation are to be successful. Narratives (anti-semitic tales of horror) have a strong, suggestive power. Pfefferkorn, who believes he has been called by God ("Lob und Ehre" C 1b), frequently and proudly uses light metaphors in his own publications which are commonly applied to book-printing:

> hab ich solche artickel welche lang/ zeit verborgen nun offentlich [...] an tag gebracht vnd zu teüstz gesetzt ("Judenfeind" 10b).
> [I have brought such articles, which were long hidden, out into the open daylight and put them into German.]

The anti-semite, Pfefferkorn, is probably the first author in Germany without university education to make systematic use of the "pamphlet" medium for his propaganda and to be (initially) very successful. He addresses his readership; he depicts himself as a persecuted, sick man calling out for sympathy; he puts his hope in his readership for assistance in persecuting the Jews:

> vmb willen aller Christen mensen welche das lesen oder hören lesen/ sollichs zu hertzen fassen ... ("Judenfeind": 11a)
> [For the sake of all Christian people who read or hear this read, may they be moved in their hearts ...]

Pfefferkorn's pamphlets brought him success and he even managed to win over the sister of Emperor Maximilian I for his anti-semitic campaign. In 1510 the Emperor ordered Johannes Reuchlin, by then already a famous lawyer, to write a legal assessment on the question of whether the Jews should be deprived of their books. Reuchlin was not in agreement (October 1510). When Pfefferkorn saw the handwritten assessment, he was furious. His pamphlet entitled "Handspiegel" appeared at the Frankfurt Easter Mass in 1511, introducing a

The Use of Dialogue in Early German Pamphlets   115

new character to the polemic. From now on the argument is of a personal nature. The parties involved write pamphlets in quick succession to defend themselves against their opponents' insults, to attempt to weaken their arguments, shower them in accusations, and put themselves in a good light. It is the first large–scale journalistic controversy to be carried out in the German language and to meet with a large response.[5]

To Reuchlin's mind the appropriate forum would have been the court (designated by the Emperor) of the Bishop of Augsburg. Since, however, no hearing had been arranged, and, on the other hand, the next Frankfurt Mass was about to take place, he decided to defend his honour before an anonymous audience (*vor fremden leütten die mich nit kennen* 'in front of people who do not know me') by printing the "Augenspiegel":

> muß ich mich selber artzneyen vnd hailn [...] daz ich nit also für ainen leichtuertigen man gehalten werde/ wie mich der taufft iud inn nechst verschiner [in der letzten] meß offenlich verunglimpfft hat (Aug. A 4a).
> [I have to cure and heal myself so that I will not be considered an irresponsible man as the baptised Jew publicly insulted me at the last mass.]

The most important points in the development of the controversy are as follows (Schwitalla 1983: 256f.; Martin 1994: 163ff.):

1. Pfefferkorn's "Handspiegel" (= Han.), 1511
2. the direct reply to this: Reuchlin's "Augenspiegel" (= Aug.), autumn Mass 1511
3. in reply: Pfefferkorn's "Brandspiegel" (= Bra.), at the end of 1512 and his "Sturmglock" (= Stu.), 1514
4. the satirical collection of letters "Epistolae obscurorum virorum" (= EOV), 1515 and Ulrich Hutten's extremely aggressive "Geschichte und Bekenntnis des getauften Juden Johannes Pfefferkorn" 'History and confession of the baptised Jew Johannes Pfefferkorn'
5. in answer to both of these: Pfefferkorn's "Streitbüchlein" (= Str.) and "Beschirmung" 1516.

The EOV shift the controversy from a polemic–factual level to a literary–satirical one, where Pfefferkorn and his allies in the circle of Dominicans at the university of Cologne are out of their depth. Pfefferkorn's solemn argumentation in the "Streitbüchlein" completely misses the point of the ironic modality of this text. The majority of intellectuals who are critical of the Church support Reuchlin. They are successful with the Emperor and the Pope. At least Reuchlin's life is saved.[6] In the following analysis I will describe some dialogue features of the pamphlet controversy.

3. Establishment of the text reference

When Pfefferkorn refers in his "Handspiegel" to Reuchlin's hand-written legal assessment, he speaks of the "Schreiben" 'piece of writing', the "Ratschlag" 'advice' of Doctor Reuchlin. If, however, he makes reference to a printed article, such as Reuchlin's "Deutsch Missive, warum die Juden solange im Elend sind" of 1505, he cites the title of the book and the position of the quotation:

> Vnnd namen oder dichter des selbigen büchlins Heisset Doctor Johannes Reuchlin. *Warumb die Jüdenn so lang imm Ellend seindt.* etc. Dar uß hab ich *in dem hindersten bladt* dise nochfolgende Wort gezogen. (The quotation then follows, Han. A 4a.)
>
> [And the name or author of the same book is called Doctor Johannes Reuchlin, *Why the Jews have so long languished in exile*, etc., from the last sheet of which I have quoted the following words.]

In the "Streitbüchlein", Pfefferkorn quotes the sheet number when he refers to the "Augenspiegel" (in addition to alphabetical ordering, the "Augenspiegel" also had pagination throughout with Roman numerals from I to XLI):

> Die ander vnwarhait. *an dem iij. blat uff der ander seytten.* seynes Oughenspyghels. vnder den andern worten schreibt er also. das ich hab mandat erlangt ... (Str. D 3b).
>
> [The other lie, on sheet 3 on the other side of his "Augenspiegel", together with the other words he writes: that I have received a decree ...]

If a text has its own system of numbering, it may be adopted, e.g. the numbering of the letters in the EOV:

> Welch artickelen der Obscurorum von Item zu Item laudent also.
> ¶ Item in der ij. Episteln Obscurorum werden die Doctores der heylger schryfften den juden geleicht vnd wurt verspot sant Peter mit seynen schlusseln.
> ¶ Item in der .v. vnd vj. Episteln. wurt verspott der heylig geist ... (Str. D 1b).
>
> [The articles of the Obscurorum, the items being:
> Item: in the second Epistola Obscurorum: the doctors of Holy Writ are likened to the Jews and St Peter is scorned with his keys.
> Item: in epistles 5 and 6 the Holy Spirit is scorned...]

They also refer to the sheet numbers of their own printed work (e.g. Reuchlin in the "Klare Verständnis" A 4 on sheet X in the "Augenspiegel"). Thus a catalogue of references of familiar, "current" texts is created, indicating the passage an author is referring to. The reader is able to form his or her own opinion by looking up the texts. By exploiting such a method of citation, the author gives himself the air of objectivity.

4. Dialogue in monologue

Linguistic–textual forms of the controversy in its content are citation and "reply" in the sense of a counter–argument. This is a traditional method of academic argumentation. In his tracts before the "Augenspiegel", Pfefferkorn uses the well–known figure of procatalepsis:

> Nun möcht yemant sprechen so die Juden nun allenthalben vernemen daz yn yre bücher genomen söllen werden. sie die haimlich abhendig machen vnd verstqsen Antwurt Pfefferkorn... ("Zu Lob und Ehre", B6a)
> [Now someone might say, if the Jews perceive everywhere that their books are to be taken away from them, they will secretly remove and hide them, answer Pfefferkorn...]

> möcht ymant sprechen ... Den selben gib ich antwurt mit zwayen redlichen ursachen... ("Judenfeind", 10b).
> [someone might say ..., I will give him an answer with two honest reasons...]

Anticipated dialogue is also used to back up the author's own claims. When addressing the readers of his "Vortrag" (D 1a), Pfefferkorn provides them with arguments against the powers that be who are unwilling to persecute the Jews, giving the wording of objections and counter-arguments. Reinforcement of the author's own theses against the opponent's arguments is a procedure for which a text genre of its own was later invented in dialogue pamphlets of the Reformation.

After Reuchlin's legal assessment, dialogue becomes increasingly prominent. Pfefferkorn now has an individual opponent. Let us consider the first argument in the whole controversy, namely Pfefferkorn's refutation in the "Handspiegel" of various opinions expressed by Reuchlin:

Citation:

Der selbig Reüchlin schreibt vil von den jüdischen Talmudischen büchernn/ die er vß mangel nit vmb zwey gelt [Gulden?] bekommen haben moge Deßhalb Er darin keinen verstandt vnd nye gelesen hab
[This same Reuchlin writes much about the Jewish Talmudic books which he had not been able to acquire for two guilders [?] owing to the lack of them. Therefore he had never understood or read them.]

Reply:

Die wort wil ich nit widerfechten/ es mag auch woll ware sein
[I do not want to dispute these words, it may well be true.]

Citation:

Aber an einem andern ort schreibt er. Wann man einen jüden vß den propheten nit vberwinden mag/ das Cristus der ware messias ist/ als dann wil er die jüden vß jren Talmudischen bücher weisen.
[But elsewhere he writes: If one cannot convince a Jew with the words of the prophets that Christ is the true Messiah, then he wants to prove it to them in their Talmudic books.]

Reply:

Do strafft sich Reüchlin abermals selber/ so er vor dem schreibt Er hab darinnen keinen verstandt noch nyt gelesen. Demnach so mogen die rede vnd aber rede by eyn nit steen. (Han. C 1a)
[Reuchlin reprimands himself as he wrote beforehand that he had never read or understood them. Therefore, his words and contradicting words cannot be true together.]

Counter–arguments are often listed and numbered and receive their own metacommunicative announcement in the structure of the text:

will ich ains nach dem andern in sonderhait von item zu item fürnemmen also ("Klare Verständnis", A 4b).
[I will deal with one item after the other in detail, namely:]

so volgent hernach mer dann vier vnd dreissig vnwarheiten oder lüginen/ Nemlich also. (Aug. H 4b).
[there then follow more than thirty-four untruths or lies, namely:]

¶ Vort in das Dritte theyl zu greyffen der menchuoltigen offenbarn vnwarheit vnd ertzloegen Johan Reuchlyn [...]

· The Use of Dialogue in Early German Pamphlets 119

Meyn antwortt dar gegen vnd warhafftig entschuldigung meyner eer [...] (Str. D 3a).
[¶ To take the word in the third part of the many obvious untruths and lies by Johann Reuchlin.
My answer to this and true defence of my honour [...]]

The general structure of counter–argumentation is in two or three parts: two parts for citation and the author's own counter–opinion, and three parts if a conclusion and an address to the readership or even to the opponent are included:

O Reuchlin wie gedars du solche freueliche. verfloechte. ketzerische Wort gedencken. Ich geschweig zu schryben. [...] deßhalben so mach dein mutter in dem grab wol waffen schreyen. das sy einen solchen wyderspennigen vnd vngetruwen son zu der welt gebracht hat. (Str. C 4a)
[O Reuchlin, how dare you consider such wicked, cursed, heretical words, let alone write them. Therefore your mother may well cry alarm from the grave for having brought such a rebellious and unfaithful son into the world.]

In those passages where Pfefferkorn addresses Reuchlin, he has Reuchlin use direct speech; for example, Reuchlin should have warned him with these words:

Pfefferkorn [...] du hast ein vngeschickten handel. vnd thust den juden vnrecht. (Str. C 2a).
[Pfefferkorn [...] your lawsuit is hopeless and you do the Jews an injustice.]

The use of dialogue extends to three–part sequences of questions, answers and refutations, which, of course, support the author's position:

[Pfefferkorn:]
Reuchlin. hie will der teufel die kertz halten [= Sprichwort]. Darauff so frag ich dich/ Hastu es den Juden geglaubt. Wiltu mir zu antwort geben/
[Reuchlin:]
Pfefferkorn wie fragstu so nerrisch. hett ichs nit glaubt. so hett ichs dem Keyser nit thüren schreiben.
[Pfefferkorn:]
Reuchlin ich sag dir du hast unrecht glaubt. und hast dem Keyser ein lugen zü geschrieben. ("Klag" C 2a)

[Pfefferkorn:]
[Reuchlin, Here the devil wants to hold the candle [= saying]. Upon which I ask you: Did you believe the Jews? If you want to answer]
[Reuchlin:]
[Pfefferkorn, what a foolish thing to ask me! If I had not believed them, I would not have dared write so to the Emperor.]
[Pfefferkorn:]
[Reuchlin, I tell you, you have been wrong in what you believed and you have written the Emperor a lie.]

The direct speech used approaches spoken language (apocope, elision, short clauses).

The two opponents also invent dialogues. In his legal assessment, Reuchlin has a dumb *biffel oder esel* 'buffalo or ass', make a ridiculous speech to the Emperor, with arguments similar to Pfefferkorn's. The Emperor gives a negative, dismissive reply: *ich merck vnd sich das du nichtz inn der selben kunst gerlernet hast* (Aug. D 3b) 'I notice and see that you have not learnt anything in the art'.

Pfefferkorn imagines the court hearing of a Jew who is quoted in direct speech and agrees with Pfefferkorn. The satirical form of language perhaps mimics the Jewish manner of speaking (*verkr<u>ei</u>gt* 'got', *geschr<u>ei</u>ben* 'written', *m<u>i</u>r* = wir 'we', *s<u>ie</u>ne* = seine 'his'; Han. E 4a/b). In the "Brandspiegel" and the "Klag", he places Reuchlin at the centre of a fictional court hearing, his answers proving that Pfefferkorn is right.

Pfefferkorn and Reuchlin sometimes both refer to each other without making explicit mention of the opponent's opinion. Reuchlin compared Pfefferkorn indirectly with an ass in his legal assessment (*Was solt die kaißerlich maiestat ainem sollichen biffel oder esel zu antwurt geben* Aug D 3b 'What should his imperial majesty say in reply to such a buffalo or ass?'). Pfefferkorn returns this comparison with an ass in the "Handspiegel", claiming that Reuchlin understood Hebrew *gleich wie eyn Esel den mann ylendig die stegen oder trappen vfftreiben wil* (A 3b) 'just like an ass that one tries hastily to drive up the steps'). Reuchlin makes use of this image once again in the "Augenspiegel" (explaining the difference between the lexical meaning and the intended reference of a word):

> Als ob ich zu ainem schuler sagte. Asinus ascendit gradus/ mach mir das zu teutsch. So sprech der schuler also/ der Pfefferkorn laufft die stegen vff/ das wer nit recht geteutst/ sunder dis were sein rechtes teutsch/ der esel stygt die staffeln vff/ wie wol der schuler möcht by ainem esel den Pfefferkorn verston/ (Aug. J 1a/b).

[As if I said to a pupil: "Asinus ascendit gradus": translate into German. So the pupil would say "Pfefferkorn goes up the steps". That would not be a proper translation into German. The right German would be "The ass goes up the steps", although the pupil might well take it that Pfefferkorn is meant by an "ass".] [7]

This is one of the few ironic passages written by the opponents which provide their readers with amusement.

Such elements of dialogue break up the text structure of the monologue into a to–and–fro, obviously still very much controlled by the author. Another dialogue feature is that there are whole passages, at least in Pfefferkorn's writing, which are directed at Reuchlin and in which Reuchlin is constantly addressed (Stu. B 2b - B 4b; "Klag").[8]

Similarity between the opposing texts exists right down to individual phrasing so that nothing might be conceded to the other side, e.g. stereotyped phrases such as the following:

Reuchlin:

Vnnd wa sollichs [Pfefferkorns Verunglimpfung] [...] also vngestrafft hin gieng/ würde es leicht ainen yngang vnd nachuolgung geberen. (Aug. A 1a; cf. K 6b).
[And if such [Pfefferkorn's disparagement] [...] passed without punishment, it would easily produce acceptance and imitation.]

Pfefferkorn:

Vnnd wo mann solches vbels. vngestrofft hin gen het lassen so ist es zu vermuten, das in kurtzen Jahren groß irrung. vnd ergernuß. in der heiligen kirchen dar vß erwachsen wer worden. (Stu. A 2b; Bra. D 3b).
[And if such evil had been left unpunished, it may be supposed that in but a few years erroneous and troublesome ways would have arisen in the Holy Church.]

In this argument, Pfefferkorn copies the enumeration of social groups that Reuchlin had initiated:

das ain yeder so dem andern widerwertig were [...] all frum erber vnschuldig vnd vnversprochen biderb leüt mans vnnd frawen personen auch iunckfrawen/ vnnd yeden hoch oder niders stands mit der vnwarhait hinderrucks [...] moecht schenden vnd lestern (Aug. A 1a).
[so that any person who was hostile to any other person [...] could dishonour and slander behind their backs any pious, honourable, innocent, respectable people who do not even stand accused, be it men, women or maidens and anyone of high or low standing.]

Pfefferkorn:

So solt sich weder Bapst nach keyser. weder Furst noch her. weder geystlich noch weltlich. weder Ritter noch knecht seiner eren [...] nit sycher wyssen zu huetten.
[Neither Pope nor Emperor, neither prince nor lord, neither sacred nor secular, neither knight nor vassal, should be unable to defend securely his honour.]

5. Indication of contradictions in pamphlets by the same author

Book printing makes it possible to compare one author's texts with each other in order to detect contradictions. Pfefferkorn never tires of reproaching Reuchlin with the opinion disseminated in his little "tütsch missive, warumb die Juden so lang im ellend sind", 'German letter, why the Jews have so long languished in exile' published in 1505 about the present blasphemy by the Jews:

> formals hat er dem Edelman obgemelt geclagt [...] wie die juden teglichen pucher wyder vns christen schreiben. vnd ein sunderliche freudt dar jnnen haben. Vnd ytzund ist er ym selbst in seinez Ratslag entgegen. vnd spricht wyder sein eygen mondt. (Str. C 3a/b)
> [he previously complained to the nobleman [...] of how the Jews wrote books against us Christians daily and took great pleasure in so doing. And now he is opposed to himself in his own advice and speaks against his own words.]

Reuchlin tries to refute the accusation of self-contradiction by explaining that he had written about different Hebrew books in the "Missive" and in the "Ratschlag" 'Advice' ("Klare Verständnis" C 1b-2a). On the other hand, both opponents refer to their own writings sometimes quite specifically with exact sheet numbers: *da ich am fünfften blat .C. schreib nemlich also ...* (Aug. J 3a) 'since I wrote on the fifth sheet, C, namely ...'. The pamphlets produced in the course of the controversy form a corpus of texts to which reference can be made for the purpose of attack and defence.

6. Increasing dominance of the relationship aspect

6.1. Defence of honour

Viewed later from the angle of the Reformation period, it is striking how often the opponents claim they have to defend their honour. The double expression "Ehre und Glimpf" 'honour and repute', is frequently used by both. A good reputation in society is of importance in urban and academic circles, too, and is enough to justify the publication of a written response. They mutually accuse each other of having insulted their honour:

Reuchlin:

> alles mir zu schmach/ schandenn/ verachtung vnnd vnere (Aug. A 4a).
> [everything to bring shame, ignominy, contempt and dishonour on me]

Pfefferkorn:

> an meiner Ere vnd glymph zu nachteil (Han. A 2b); hat er mich [...] aen alle vrsach. vnuerwart meiner eren wyder Got ere vnd recht [...] jemerlich verraten (Str. C 2a).
> [to the disadvantage of my honour and repute; without any cause and disregarding my honour he has betrayed me unexpectedly against God, honour and right.]

Both assure the reader that their writings were composed for moral, Christian and legal reasons and in order to defend their own honour, but not to pour scorn on the opponent:

Reuchlin:

> daz sag ich nieman zu schmach/ sunder allain zu meiner entschuldigung (Aug. J 2a).
> [I say this not to scorn anybody but only to free myself of guilt.]

Pfefferkorn:

> wil ich das püechlyn ynen zu smaich ader [w]rach yres vnrechten an meyner person nyt gemacht [...] haben (Str., A 1b; cf. Stu. B 4b: denoch nit vß haß. oder nid. oder zu schmach. oder zu rauch [Rache] seines vnrechten).
> [I pledge that I did not write the book to revile anyone or to avenge myself for the wrong done to my person (Str. A 1b; cf. Stu. B 4b: but not out of hate or envy or to revile or for revenge for his wrong-doing).]

6.2. Attacks of a similar vein

A typical feature of bitter conflicts is that the opponents accuse each other of the same misdeeds. The accusations in this case are as follows:

6.2.1. Material interest

Reuchlin: By selling his pamphlets, Pfefferkorn has *mer guldin auß mir geloeßt/ wan Judas pfennig vß vnserm herre got* (Aug. H 4b) [eked more guilders out of me than Judas pennies out of Our Lord]:

Pfefferkorn accuses Reuchlin of being bribed by the Jews and of receiving payment for his legal assessment:

> Darumb er dan vileycht eyn dausent Ducaten vur seyn arbeitsloen entfangen mach haben (Str. C 1a).
> [He may well have received a thousand ducats as his wage.]

He claims that the "Augenspiegel" had been bought by far more Jews than Christians because the Jews used it to support their arguments against the *kleinmutigen ode symplen cristen* (Bra. A 2b) 'timid or simple-minded Christian'.

6.2.2. The opponent accused of provoking the controversy

Reuchlin, at the beginning of the "Augenspiegel":

> All vnd yeglich [...] Bitt ich Johannes Reüchlin [...] disen nachfolgenden/ hinderrücklingen/ vnwarhafftigen vßgegossen handel ains getaufften iuden (got wollt cristenlich bestetigt) so sich Pfefferkorn nempt wider und gegen mir gantz vermessenlich meinenthalb on all vervrsachen vnd wider got eer vnd recht durch ain offen getrucktes schmachbüchlin vnd lasterschrift daz er nent handtspiegel geübt vnd menigklichen in nechst verruckter Franckfurter vasten meßß eröffnet [...] zu erachten/ wie ainen gamainen gifftigen landtschaden (Aug. A 1a).
> [I, Johannes Reuchlin, ask all and everybody to consider as mean and poisonous damage the following, insidious, untrue case brought against me by a baptized Jew (I hope to God it is certified as christianly done) who calls himself Pfefferkorn, totally outrageous, without any reason, against God, honour and right, produced by a printed slanderous and offensive pamphlet, which he calls "Handspiegel" and published for everybody during the last Mass at Frankfurt.]

Pfefferkorn in his reply:

The Use of Dialogue in Early German Pamphlets 125

ich hab das genant puechlein [= "Handspiegel"] nit wider yn/ sonder wyder die juden vßgeen lossen. Ich hab auch den tzanck tzwischen ym vnd myr nit erweckt/ sunder er ist der haderman (Bra. A 3a).
[I did not intend to publish the afore mentioned book [= "Handspiegel"] against him, but against the Jews. Nor did I start the quarrel between him and me, but he is the troublemaker.]

6.2.3. Assurance of their own goodwill, deception by the opponent

Reuchlin recounts in the "Augenspiegel" how he helped Pfefferkorn upon their first meeting, how he pointed out defects in the legal phrasing of his decree and even wrote down *dieselben stuck vff ain zedelin ab ainem bappier gerissen/ dar durch er nit gedecht ich woelt inn vffsetzlich vom gemelttem kaiserlichen mandat abzeston [...] über reden* (A 1bf.) 'the same things on a piece of paper so he would not think that I deliberately intended to persuade him to abandon the afore mentioned imperial decree'; how stunned he was when he saw his own arguments, which still had the status of a confidential document, published in the "Handspiegel".

The same line of argumentation is to be found in Pfefferkorn: he himself had suggested Reuchlin as an expert for the legal assessment; he had travelled to see Reuchlin to win him over in his fight against the Jews; Reuchlin had given him a friendly reception; Pfefferkorn had believed he had found a loyal attorney in Reuchlin, who then surprisingly betrayed him *in guttem glauben so uncristenlich* (Str. B 1b) 'in good faith in such an unchristian fashion'.

6.2.4. The opponent accused of breaching confidence

Reuchlin reproaches Pfefferkorn with quoting without permission from his legal assessment which was sealed and had been delivered by a messenger sworn to secrecy. Pfefferkorn accuses Reuchlin of having breached the secrecy and loyalty of a lawyer:

hab ich [...] alle meyn hall [Hehl?] vnd heymlichkeit [...] vurgedragen vnd in beychtes weiß zu behalten ghegeben. des hatt er myr eyn zü sagung [...] gegeben ein getrewer aduocat. vnd guot gonder [Gönner] zü seyn [...] so hat er mich zu rugg schalckhafftiger verraden. dan judas vnsern lieben herre got (Str. A 2b; cf.: hat er sich zu meynen Feynden gekert, C 1b).
[I talked about all my secrets and asked him to conceal them as a priest treats a confession. He promised me he would be a faithful lawyer and a good patron. Nevertheless he betrayed me more wickedly than Judas did our dear Lord (Str. A2b; cf.: he has turned to my enemies, C 1b).]

Accusations in a pamphlet prompt the accused party to put up some kind of defence. For this reason, long passages are now given to self-defence rather than to the issue of Jewish books. Relationship communication outweighs the actual altercation.

Pfefferkorn defends himself in his "Streitbüchlein" (E 4a–Ga) against the following accusations: of being the false *Pfaffe Rapp* 'priest called Rapp' (a swindler) or his brother; of having been a *Fleischhauer* 'butcher' in Dachau and of having stolen; of being a dishonest Jew who had to flee from Nuremberg; of being a tempter of Christians and a precursor of the Anti-Christ. Each time, Pfefferkorn prints official documents in his favour (from civil, royal and archbishop's offices; culminating in the highest authority, the decree of the Emperor). This gives the text the flavour of a personal vindication with the aid of documents of an authoritative nature.

With hindsight, there is a striking stubbornness and acidity to the attacks and their prompt replies. Reuchlin's zeal is carried to such lengths that he takes literally Pfefferkorn's imagery of Reuchlin's having given him donkey's ears and attempts to refute the accusation of ever having written about donkey's ears. It is not until this moment that he is capable of an ironic touch:

> Da leße man meinen ratschlag durch vnd durch/ so findt man an kainem ort von esels oren geredt/ dan man mag wol ainen esel finden der kain or hat/ vnnd ist dannocht ain esel (Aug. K 5b).
>
> [Read my "advice" thoroughly and one will find no mention of an ass's ears. One may well find an ass which has no ears and it is nevertheless still an ass.]

6.3. Mutual accusations of incompetence

Both opponents accuse each other of incompetence with regard to the Hebrew language. Reuchlin's knowledge of Hebrew is said to be as good as an attempt at driving an ass up steps ("Handspiegel") and Pfefferkorn is reputed to be able merely to recite by heart as a nun recites the psalter (Aug. J 4a). In the "Streitbüchlein", Pfefferkorn adheres to his (erroneous) claim that Reuchlin was unable to read any unvocalised Hebrew texts, or any words without their Latin translation, or even to write a simple letter in Hebrew (Str. E 3b).

It was embarrassing to Pfefferkorn that he had not studied and could not understand any Latin. It was therefore easy for Reuchlin to rub it in by saying Pfefferkorn ought to translate his German texts into Latin. Switching to Latin, either only in part of a pamphlet (with the academic text type, the disputatio, in the "Augenspiegel") or as a complete text ("Defensio", EOV) was also always an attempt at excluding the opponent on a social level.[9] Likewise the Cologne theologians are excluded from the community of humanists when they are told they know nothing about Holy Writ or about Latin authors ("Defensio" I 3b; cf. Geiger 1871, 275).

In their attacks on each other, both opponents are led to pride themselves. Reuchlin: Nobody before him had ever *regulirt* 'systematised' the Hebrew language in a book in such a way *daz sie moecht von dem latinischen gefaßt vnd empfangen werden* (Aug. J 3b) 'that it may be comprehended and received by the Latin'; he had read more Hebrew books than Pfefferkorn who could not understand them, anyway (Aug. K 1b). Pfefferkorn defends himself in the face of the accusation of being unlearned (Str. E 3-4) by arguing in the same fashion as Reuchlin: before his times *keyner [habe] so clair vnd verstendich gedan* (Str. E 3a) 'noone had pointed out as clearly and prudently' as he the failure to recognise the Messiah, the evil, unfaithfulness and blasphemy by the Jews.

6.4. Personal attacks

Both in the pamphlets of the pre-Reformation and of the Reformation period itself, the increasing use of material derived from private circumstances, which has absolutely nothing to do with the object of their dispute, is particularly striking. Reuchlin spreads the rumour about Pfefferkorn offering his "Handspiegel" for sale at the Frankfurt autumn mass in 1510 *durch sein weib inn offem grempelkraum yderman faill gebotten* (Aug. A 4a) 'by his wife to everyone amongst all the other junk at the fair'. Several times he insinuates that his *bellula mulier* 'beautiful wife' is in contact with the Cologne Dominicans (Geiger 1871: 277). This is a topic that the EOV treat with relish (13th epistle).

6.5. Increasing aggression in word and illustration

The greater the number of pamphlets, the worse the aggressive tone of the controversy. Comparisons with animals are part and parcel of the polemic. Reuchlin, speaking of Pfefferkorn's pamphlets as "ducks' quacking" (Aug. C 1b, cf. Brod 1965, 216, *Entengeschnatter*); he calls the Cologne Dominicans 'sheep', 'goats', 'sows', 'pigs', 'more inhuman than wild animals, not unlike horses and mules' ("Defensio" D 2b, C 4a; cf. Geiger 1871, 276); Pfefferkorn is a *bestia venenata* 'poisonous beast'("Defensio" A 4b). The language in the "Defensio" is altogether more abrasive and acidic than in the German texts.

Pfefferkorn depicts a graphic scene when he compares Reuchlin with a wolf that has fallen into a pit and keeps scratching at the sides, thereby throwing more and more earth (= lies) into his eyes (Str. D 1a).

There are further linguistic forms of defamation:

1. Enumeration:
   Bolwerck des Teuffels. Ein müntzmeister der boeßheit. eyn dichter der mennichfeldiger lügen. eyn lesterer der heyliger kyrchen. eyn felscher der Gotlichen schrifft. ein totslager der selen. ein uncristenlich Patron vnd advocat der treülosen jüden. (Str. G 1b; cf. A 2a).
   [Bulwark of the devil, a mint-master of evil, an inventor of manifold lies, a blasphemer of the Holy Church, a forger of God's Word, a murderer of souls, an unchristian patron and advocate of the faithless Jews.]
   Enumeration of this kind is typical of the rhetorical artistic form of the Latin invective. It is a component part of the rhetorical exercises practised by budding authors (e.g. Ulrich von Hutten's invective against Duke Ulrich of Württemberg).

2. Similes
   Comparisons with a chicken thief (Str. ibid.), with the devil besmeared with faeces (Klag F 4a).

3. Pfefferkorn threatens torture and death: in Reuchlin's case one ought to *die jüdisch zung auß reyssen* (Str. C 1b) 'tear out his Jewish tongue', *blyxs [Blitz] vnd das hellisch fuyr* 'lightning and the fires of hell', ought to burn him *in [in den] abgrunt der hellen* (Str. C 4b) 'in the depths of hell'.

4. Associations with the devil and heretics:
   Pfefferkorn's ethnic stereotype of the Jews' similarity with the devil is turned by Reuchlin against Pfefferkorn himself: He says he is not surprised at Pfefferkorn's many lies since the devil is a father of lies, and if the Jews have a satanic nature, as Pfefferkorn claims, then Pfefferkorn himself must also have been *von tüwfelscher natur empfangen vnd geboren/ vnd [het] tüwfelschs milch gesogen* (Aug. K 6a) 'conceived and born of a devilish nature and suckled on devil's milk'. Here, Reuchlin adopts the common negative stereotype of Jews being liars and applies it to Pfefferkorn whom he constantly calls *taufft Jud* 'baptized Jew'.
   Pfefferkorn, too, shows little delicacy in comparing his opponent with the devil and heresy: *So ist im die deufelisch hoffart. vnd yppigkeit. in das hertz geschlagen* (Str. A 2b) 'Satanic arrogance and haughtiness are driven into his heart'; in the hour of bitter death, Reuchlinists would then see whom they had served (D 3a; cf. D 4a); the writings of Reuchlin and his followers came about by *einblasung des hofertigsten teufel Lucifer* (Stu. B 2a) 'insinuation by the haughtiest devil, Lucifer'; the

"Augenspiegel" and its adherents were *mit heymlicher ketzerey vmbfangen* (Str. G 2b) 'embraced with secret heresy'. There are examples of hyperbole: the "Augenspiegel" and the EOV are *schedelicher vnd ergerlicher dan alle ketzer der welt oder falsche propheten* (G 3a) 'more dangerous than all the heretics in the world or false prophets'. The judges at the court of heresy *werden in mit seinem ketzerischen buch. zu dem fuwr weisen* (Stu. B 2a) 'will send him to the flames with his heretical book'.

5. Names:
Pfefferkorn, writing in the "Klag" (C 2a), says: *Reuchlin [...] soll mir doctor löffel oder Doctor duppen [Betrüger] heyssen* 'Reuchlin should be called Dr Spoon[10] or Dr Cheat' and calls him *Löffelholtz, Saulöffel* and *Rechuchlin*. Polemic name alterations are very common in the early Reformation period (e.g. Luther on Cochlaeus: *Koch-, Rotzlöffel*).

Illustrations, too, become more and more aggressive (Fig. 3).

Figure 3: Pfefferkorn pushes Reuchlin over, the latter with a split tongue. Title page to the "Streitbüchlein"

In the "Streitbüchlein" (C 3b), allusion is made to Reuchlin's contradictions between the "Missive" and the "Augenspiegel" by the depiction of Reuchlin as a two-tongued liar. The text tells us that this false tongue should be ripped out along with one of the two spoons which are in a pot. Reuchlin is pointing two fingers at a Hebrew book. The Jews behind him are blind.

The wood-engraving entitled "Triumphus Capnionis" of 1518 (Fig. 4),[11] part of the pamphlet of the same name, Pfefferkorn is shown as a condemned criminal, his arms and legs bound, lying on the ground and being mistreated by henchmen. The dog licking up his own vomit is probably an allusion to 2 Peter 2.22 (*canis reversus ad suum vomitum*).

Figure 4: Detail from "Triumphus Capnionis"

The increase in insulting words, verbal aggression and crude expression culminates in Pfefferkorn's "Klag über alle Klag" of 1521 in which he lends words and illustration to a flight of fancy about Reuchlin's execution as a criminal (Fig. 5).[12]

Then as now, public interest in quarrels played an important role in the popularity of an issue. In 1541, Johannes Eck complained, also in an anti-semitic writing, that readers did not despise ignominious books. If nobody read them, they would have no chance of being printed.

The Use of Dialogue in Early German Pamphlets   131

So nun aber das schmähen vnd laster gschrifften/ so gmain seind worden bey den Newen Euangeli jn teutschen land// also vor nie von welt her: das machen die zu hoerer/ die gern haben/ das man jhn die ohren krawen: dann wa die hoerer nit verbittert wären/ vnnd [nit] ain wolgefallen hetten an schmähen vnd schänden/ wurden die klaffer selbs ihr maul zuhalten (Eck, "Eins Judenbüchleins Verlegung" A 4a).

[Defamatory and abusive writings have become so common in the case of the New Protestants in Germany as never before in the world: that is the fault of the listeners who like to have their ears tickled: for if the listeners were not bitter and did not find pleasure in dishonour and abuse, the yappers would shut their own traps.]

Figure 5: Reuchlin quartered, "Klag" H 4b

7. Dialogical structures of public discussion created by printed works

From the perspective of media history, the pamphlets of the Reuchlin-Pfefferkorn conflict produced public discussion for the first time in Germany in which any literate person was invited to take a decision. An increasing number of social communication circles became involved in the case. Texts originally hand–written were then printed:

1. The imperial chancellery releases decrees as single-sheet prints (Maximilian I's decrees appeared in printed form from 1489 onwards). All these decrees are included in the pamphlets and are thus spread further. More and more of the ruling class pronounce their judgment: royalty (King Francis I of France, King Charles of Spain, Elector Frederick of Saxony etc.), politicians in imperial chancelleries (Cuspinian in Vienna) and of the territories (Spalatin in Wittenberg), city councils (Frankfurt, Cologne, Worms), the towns of the Swabian Federation.

   A new feature are open letters[13] to the Emperor: Reuchlin's "Defensio" (with Maximilian addressed throughout). Communication within the political world brings Reuchlin great success. His appeal to the Pope (1514) to abandon proceedings in Rome which had been reopened in Cologne is supported by the Emperor, several Electors, princes, bishops, abbots and 53 Swabian towns.

2. Within church institutions, communication is initially handwritten: Reuchlin appeals to the Pope (September 1513); the Pope delegates the case to the Bishops of Worms and Speyer. The verdict of the delegated jurists leading to Reuchlin's acquittal (March 1514) is finally printed as posters and *an allen orten vnnd enden in dem Romischen reich vffgeschlagen* (Stu. B 1a) 'displayed everywhere in the Roman empire'.

3. The Latin assessments provided by the five universities (Cologne, Mainz, Erfurt, Louvain, Paris) on Reuchlin's "Augenspiegel" are at first written by hand and dispatched. They are then printed partly individually ("Articuli") and partly together, and their contents appear in German in Pfefferkorn's pamphlets ("Sturmglock", "Beschirmung"). Pfefferkorn also publishes part of the handwritten correspondence between Reuchlin and the theological faculty of Cologne ("Beschirmung"; Martin 1994, 316).

4. The humanists' letters initially written by hand are later printed together in one publication ("Clarorum virorum epistolae hebraice graece et latine ad Jo. Reuchlinum", with Erasmus in first position; altogether 43 authors' names). The humanists keep to Latin (EOV), but before Ulrich von Hutten translates his Latin dialogues against Duke Ulrich of

The Use of Dialogue in Early German Pamphlets 133

Württemberg ("Phalarismos") and the Roman Church ("Dialogi") into German, he has a German text against Pfefferkorn printed.

5. To a lesser extent there are also events with an oral proclamation, such as the spectacular heresy trial in Mainz. Here a messenger reads out to the people the German decree of the archbishop in which the trial is adjourned. This is greeted with jubilation. Reuchlin turns this into a satirical report.

The fundamental feature of the constitution of a far-reaching public forum was, however, the use of dialogue in pamphlets directed at an individual or several specific opponents. This was true of the Reuchlin-Pfefferkorn debate and also of the numerous feuds in the early Reformation period. This applied not only to the issues under discussion, but to personal attributes, which were treated with increasing venom (Kästner/Schütz 1998).

Notes

1 Production figures of leaflets and pamphlets may well have risen sharply in times of revolution and war (30 Years' War, the Mainz Republic 1792/93, 1848), but they never achieved the high numbers produced between 1518 and 1525. Subsequent new media are either not opinion-forming and agitatory (periodicals in the 17th century), are restricted to a social class and a town or a region (the moral weekly journals in the first half of the 18th century in Zurich, Hamburg, Leipzig etc. primarily for academics and the upper class) or are split into different ideological directions (the press in the 19th century). It is not until 1933 that a new medium, the radio, is exploited by the National Socialists to form the public opinion of a whole people, but this time to the exclusion of any opposition (for example, as early as February 1933 in the lead-up to the Reichstag elections on 5th March).

2 Two other examples from the Reformation period: When Luther wrote a pamphlet entitled "De captivitate Babylonica ecclesiae" on the sacraments, the text was printed five times in the same year in the German-speaking world and was printed four times the following year in neighbouring countries. Provoked by the reply by King Henry VIII, in the next six years 23 pamphlets with 75 issues were produced (Flood 1996: 26ff.). In the dispute over the territories belonging to the Duchy of Wolfenbüttel-Brunswick from 1540, there were more than 120 pamphlets (Edwards 1983: 146ff.).

3 Latest representation of the events in Martin (1994: 138ff.).

4 Only the "Streitbüchlein" (28 sheets), the "Beschirmung" (56 sheets) and the "Klag über alle Klag" (34 sheets) are longer. The time required for reading (out) a publication consisting of 10 sheets is about one hour.

5   Polemics published and printed before then were written in Latin, such as the sensational controversy between Jakob Locher ("Comparatio mulae ad Musam" 1506) and Jakob Wimpfeling ("Contra turpem libellum Philomusi defensio theologiae" 1510).
6   As opposed to the two reformatory Augustine monks from Amersfoort who were burned by Jakob von Hochstraten in 1521, the same inquisitor who charged Reuchlin.
7   Reuchlin receives a late reply to this distinction between literal and figurative meaning in 1521 in Pfefferkorn's "Klag über alle Klag" (D 1a/b): *klicksteyn [Klickerkugel] ist kein verreter nach der teutschen Grammatica. dennoch wenn man eynen eyn klicksteyn heyßt so meynt man dich mit 'Klickstein* [marble] is no traitor according to German grammar, but if one calls someone a *Klickstein*, you are meant'. Reuchlin's simile of the reader wanting to read the Bible only with the traditional commentaries being like someone who did not have *vil überigs/ als da sich ainer im winter mit hosen deckt* (Aug. D 6b) 'much more than someone who covers himself in winter with trousers' is taken up by Pfefferkorn and used to jeer at Reuchlin: *du bist der hosen decker. [...] und wen du hest alle die hosen. so du al dein tag zerrissen hast und die dein vatter geflickt hatt [...] den nocht magstu dein schand nit zudeckenn* (Stu. B 3b) 'You are the trouser-coverer, and if you have all the trousers you have ever torn in your life and which your father has patched, you still cannot cover your shame'. (Similar images of scant clothing are used by Luther against the fanatics of Karlstadt and against the Papists.)
8   The use of dialogue in writing such as address, question-answer (dubitatio), invented citation, and procatalepsis, are rhetorical devices used in sermons and in academic literature since the Middle Ages. From the point of view of the media history of the pamphlet, a sudden change in quality took place when complete texts criticising the Church or society were written in dialogue form, first of all in Latin (also subsequent to the Reuchlin-Pfefferkorn controversy: the "Hochstratus ovans" in 1520 and the "Conciliabolum Theologistarum" in 1521; Hutten's Latin dialogues against Ulrich von Württemberg and the Roman Church from 1516/17; Erasmus' "Colloquia familiaria" in 1518), then in German in tremendously increasing numbers. Estimates run at about one hundred dialogue texts.
9   At the beginning of the "Klare Verständnis in Deutsch" (A 2a), Reuchlin justifies writing his text in German by pointing out that only *ain schlechter [schlichter] gemain man* 'a simple, common man' and those who *nit latin verston ... die unvolkummen[en] und die klainmütigen* 'do not understand Latin ... the imperfect and the timid ones' might be offended by his remarks to whom he now wishes to explain the Latin passages of the "Augenspiegel" in German.
10 The German word *Löffel*, 'spoon', also denotes a fool; hence the various references in the text and illustrations to spoons.
11 *Capnio (kapnos* 'smoke') is the Greek translation of Reuchlins name: *Räuchlein* 'little smoke'. A triumphal procession of true theology and a mockery of false theology (one theologian is picking up the excrement of an ass) were already contrasted by Jakob Locher

The Use of Dialogue in Early German Pamphlets   135

in his "Comparatio sterilis mulae ad Musam" in wood-engravings in 1506 (Heidloff 1975: 259, 269). A dialogical reception is developed in illustrations, too: Pfefferkorn has Reuchlin fall out of the triumphal coach in the "Klag über alle Klag" (H 2a) in which he was represented by Hutten.

12 This is similar in vein to Luther's "Abbildung des Papsttums" of 1545 in which the Pope and the Cardinals are shown hanged as criminals. Pfefferkorn often depicted himself as the victor and Reuchlin as conquered in wood-engravings ("Streitbüchlein", "Klag über alle Klag").

13 Since the letters are printed addressed to the Emperor, they receive a primary and a secondary addressee, the latter being perhaps of greater importance than the former (Wolf 1996: 365).

Sources and abbreviations

Microfiches:
Köhler, Hans-Joachim, Hildegard Hebenstreit-Wilfert and Christoph Weismann (eds.)
    1978ff.   Flugschriften des frühen 16. Jahrhunderts. *Microfiche Serien.* Zug, Switzerland.
Köhler, Hans-Joachim
    1996   *Bibliographie der Flugschriften des 16. Jahrhunderts. Teil I. Das frühe 16. Jahrhundert (1501-1530).* Tübingen.

Pfefferkorn (standardized titles):

1507   *Der Juden-Spiegel.* Nürnberg, lat. Köln, Speyer 1507 [Ex. UB Freiburg].

1508   *Ich heiß ein Büchlein der Juden Beicht.* Augsburg, Nürnberg, Köln [Köhler 3704, 3705]; lat. Nürnberg 1508.

1509   *Ich bin ein Büchlein, "Der Juden Feind" ist mein Name.* Augsburg [Köhler 3703]; lat. Köln 1509.

1509   *In diesem Büchlein findet ihr einen Vortrag, wie die Juden ihre Ostern halten.* Köln, Augsburg [Köhler 3707, 3708]; lat. Köln 1509.

1510   *Zu Lob und Ehr dem Fürsten Maximilian, Römischen Kaiser.* Köln, Augsburg [Köhler 3711, 3719], lat. Köln. = Lob.

1510   *Allen und jeglichen, Geistlichen und Weltlichen ...* Augsburg. In: Eduard Böcking: Ulrichi Hutteni Opera. Suppl. Bd. II, 73f. Nachdruck Osnabrück 1966.

1511   *Handspiegel wider die Juden und jüdischen talmudischen Schriften.* Mainz [Köhler 3701] = Han.

1512   *Abzutreiben und auszulöschen eines ungegründeten Lasterbüchleins mit Namen Augenspiegel [...] dies Büchlein genannt Brandspiegel.* [Köhler 3700] Köln. = Bra.

1514	*Sturm über und wider die treulosen Juden.* Köln [Köhler 3718] = Stu.
1516	*Streitbüchlein für die Wahrheit, fechtend wider den falschen Bruder Doktor Johannes Reuchlin.* Köln [Köhler 3717] = Str.
1516	*Beschirmung Johannes Pfefferkorns.* Köln, lat. Köln 1516.
1521	*Eine mitleidige Klag über alle Klag an unsern Kaiser gegen Johann Reuchlin.* Köln [Köhler 3713] = Klag.

Johannes Reuchlin:

1505	*Deutsch Missive, warum die Juden so lange im Elend sind.* Pforzheim [Köhler 3873].
1511	*Doctor Johannes Reuchlins wahrhafte Entschuldigung. Augenspiegel.* Tübingen. Faksimileausgabe. Josef Benzing (ed.). München 1961. [Köhler 3874] = Aug.
1512	*Eine klare Verständnis in Deutsch.* Tübingen. [Ex. UB Freiburg]
1513/1514	*Defensio Joannis Reuchlin contra calumniatores suos Colonienses.* Tübingen [Köhler 3871, 3872].

References

Brod, Max
    1965   *Johannes Reuchlin und sein Kampf.* Stuttgart: Kohlhammer.

Edwards, Mark U.
    1983   *Luther's Last Battles. Politics and Polemics, 1531-46.* Leiden: E. J. Brill.

Flood, John F.
    1996   Heinrich VIII. und Martin Luther. Ein europäischer Streit und dessen Niederschlag in Literatur und Publizistik. In: Kurt Gärtner u.a. (ed.). *Spannungen und Konflikte menschlichen Zusammenlebens in der deutschen Literatur des Mittelalters.* Bristoler Colloquium 1993. Tübingen: Max Niemeyer, 3-32.

Geiger, Ludwig
    1871   *Johann Reuchlin. Sein Leben und seine Werke.* Leipzig: Duncker & Humblot. Reprinted 1964. Nieuwkoop: de Graaf.

Heidloff, Günter
    1975   *Untersuchungen zu Leben und Werk des Humanisten Jakob Locher Philomusus.* Diss. phil. Freiburg/Br.

Kästner, Hannes and Eva Schütz
    1998   Gottesbote oder Lügenprophet? Bemerkungen zur Genese und den Entwicklungstendenzen der konträren Lutherbilder in der Frühzeit der Reformation. In: André Schnyder et al. (eds.). *"Ist mir getroumet mîn leben?" Festschrift Karl Ernst Geith.* Göppingen: Kümmerle, 49-66.

Köhler, Hans-Joachim
    1986   Erste Schritte zu einem Meinungsprofil der frühen Reformationszeit. In: Volker Press and Dieter Stievermann (eds.). *Martin Luther. Probleme seiner Zeit.* Stuttgart: Klett-Cotta, 244-281.

Martin, Ellen
    1994   *Die deutschen Schriften des Johannes Pfefferkorn. Zum Problem des Judenhasses und der Intoleranz in der Zeit der Vorreformation.* Göppingen: Kümmerle.

Schilling, Michael
    1990   *Bildpublizistik der frühen Neuzeit. Aufgaben und Leistungen des illustrierten Flugblatts in Deutschland bis um 1700.* Tübingen: Max Niemeyer.

Schwitalla, Johannes
    1983   *Deutsche Flugschriften 1460-1525.* Tübingen: Max Niemeyer.

Wolf, Norbert Richard
    1996   Sprache über Konflikte vs. Sprache in Konflikten. Linguistische Überlegungen zum Medienwandel. In: *Spannungen und Konflikte menschlichen Zusammenlebens in der deutschen Literatur des Mittelalters.* Ed. Kurt Gärtner u.a. Tübingen: Max Niemeyer, 359-370.

The Polite Answer in Pre-modern German Conversation Culture

Manfred Beetz
Martin Luther University, Halle-Wittenberg

1. Introduction

Since Brown and Levinson's study "Universals in language usage: Politeness phenomena", a host of international papers describing intracultural and intercultural polite behaviour have been published.[1] The disparity in the empirical results has induced more recent assessments to be rather sceptical towards postulations of universality of behaviour. The correlation between indirectness and politeness has been called into question, as has also the dominant role of politeness strategies which are seen to be less decisive than the situation adequacy and conformity to norms displayed by polite behaviour. There has been criticism of Goffman's face metaphor, as used by Brown and Levinson, in that it abstracts too rashly from macro-sociological determinants. There has also been criticism of the postulated differentiation between positive and negative face-threats and finally of the illusion of a quantification of degrees of politeness.[2] All in all, current research appears to be tending towards a relativising description of polite behaviour which is specific to culture, class and gender as well as bound by time and situation. Criticism of Brown and Levinson's model of verbal politeness strategies may well be justified, but on the other hand a more convincing description model of comparable elaboration has to this day still to emerge. Alternative definitions of politeness, describing it as behaviour appropriate to the social and situational context, state conditions which are necessary to its definition but which still fail to be sufficient (Meier 1992: 29 f., Meier 1995a: 351 f.). More recent definitions are to my mind often too unspecific. They do not take account of the distinction between customary and polite behaviour or between propriety and politeness. The definition of politeness put forward by Adegbija as a property associated with a communicative situation by virtue of which a person speaks or behaves in a way that is socially and culturally acceptable and pleasant to the hearer

would, for example, include as an act of politeness a challenge to a duel from the point of view of the person who provoked it by an intended insult (Adegbija 1989: 58). Also, Meier's explanation of impoliteness as non-compliance with socially acceptable behaviour smacks of the historical status of discussion in the 18th century and its differentiation between *honestum*, *justum* and *decorum* (Meier 1992: 30). In polite intercourse, at least one interaction partner is the recipient of the politeness. The sole aim of propriety on the other hand is to serve the speaker's own self-respect. Other people function merely as potential witnesses. As early as 1706, the baroque author, Amthor, and later Jhering, discussed the difference between the antonyms *unanständig* 'improper' and *unhöflich* 'impolite', pointing out that an improper act did not necessarily require interaction with (at least) one partner and that the domain of propriety, to a far greater extent than that of polite behaviour, was governed by moral norms (Amthor 1706: 89; Jhering 1905: 281 ff., 379; Beetz 1990: 144). Similarly, in the 18th century Johann Georg Feder recognised that propriety rules relate to behaviour towards oneself whereas rules on politeness always concern the treatment of others (cf. Machwirth 1970: 44).

For linguists specialising in present-day language, it is certainly not easy to tackle problems concerning historical linguistics and culture as, for example, Ehlich has done in his study on the historicity of politeness (Ehlich 1991; English translation in Watts *et al.* 1992). The complexity of politeness rituals embedded in history and culture, however, demands such considerations. Modern and historical books on etiquette should, therefore, be an important source in linguistic studies on politeness rules of today.

Early-modern books on propriety, conversation and complimenting offer a code of behaviour for verbal and non-verbal exchange of politeness. From the 16th to the 18th century, on which we are concentrating here, educated readers of the middle and upper estates[3] in the Old German empire were expected to find guidance for their speech acts from the explicit rules and sample texts provided by these books. The techniques suggested and examples of dialogue not only give us a picture of the social ethics of that time, but, notwithstanding obvious historical breaks in civilisation and new orientations, uncover the preliminary stages leading to our ritualistic interaction behaviour today.

The purpose of socio-ethical norms of behaviour is to deal with the routine of recurrent situations of interaction. They adjust the obligation by the speaker and the listener. The resulting pattern of co-operatively developed behaviour demonstrates social harmony between the partners even if there are conflicts of interest or an obvious social gulf. If, in the manner of Janney and Arndt (1992), we consider behaviour directed by the politeness code to be ritualised and routine, we suggest reserving the term "tact" for the aspect of consideration which Ehlich calls "going beyond what is socially expected" (Janney and Arndt 1992: 21-24; Ehlich 1991: 5). Tact can, in the sense of 17th century politeness theory, set limits to intended offers of politeness. Christian Weise gives examples of expressions of respect which in certain circumstances may give rise to embarrassment rather than pleasure.

> "Mancher soll mit spatzieren fahren/ und er ist gleich mit dem heimlichen Leiden behafftet/ daß er kein Geld hat" (Weise 1693: I, p. 73).
> [Someone may be expected to join others on a pleasure trip, and he is at once daunted by the secret mishap of having no money.]

A tactful person shows consideration in this particular situation. Tactful behaviour comprises at least six conditions:

1. an appropriate assessment of a situation
2. a knowledge of the partner's vulnerable points
3. a willingness to assume a protective role
4. an anticipation of the partner's individual interests
5. sensitivity to the development of the partner's interests dependent on the situation during the course of the interaction
6. a knowledge of how others interpret one's own acts and how one should interpret theirs.

The function of image protection is essential to tact. It helps the partner to save face or restore his/her image (Goffman 1975: 112). John Locke defined tact as consideration which aimed at showing no disdain or neglect towards the other in the interaction (Locke 1693/1823: Vol. IX, § 143, p. 134). Goffman sees tactless behaviour as threatening the self-image projected by the other or a group (Goffman 1976: 190). A person of tact avoids embarrassing situations and topics, and ignores face-threatening *faux pas* committed by the other. Although the delicacy of tact may also express itself in the non-verbal and paralinguistic modulation of messages, in contrast to the rules of politeness it heeds prohibitions and taboos (Beetz 1988: 19 ff.; Janney and Arndt 1992: 23; Jhering 1968: 80-84). As opposed to Janney and Arndt, I would not agree that the difference between social politeness and tact is that the former offers ritualised and routine rules of behaviour whereas tact is exclusively concerned with face-work and regulates interpersonal relationships (Janney and Arndt

1992: 24). These two aspects are not mutually exclusive. Goffman has given sufficient proof of the significance of face-work in the case of interaction rituals, too, by referring to the effusiveness of greetings, hesitation in farewells or the refusal of a salutation. The criterium is rather that there is a whole arsenal of concrete rules available for polite behaviour whereas there is none for "conscious variations" of tact (Adorno 1982: 38; Jhering 1905: 282). At the most there are just some general principles, the application of which depends on each individual case and implies a new exercise in individualising politeness every time.

2. Structure and basis of pre-modern answer-compliments

The term *compliment* as used in the Old German empire indicates its French origin in its spelling, pronunciation and above all in its meaning. It does not only signify a compliment as we understand the word today, but is a far more comprehensive term embracing oral, written and even non-verbal interaction rituals for everyday and ceremonious communication situations. For example, we may list here greetings and farewells, congratulations and condolence, requests and thanks, all forms of initiating and maintaining contact such as introducing oneself and others, regards, recommendations, invitations, announcements, invitations to dance, good wishes, promises, offers of service, presentations, apologies; even "reprimand *compliments*" are not considered to be a contradiction in terms (Beetz 1990: 14-21, 109-115).

Answers in interaction rituals are not independent discourse units. As responding acts they complete the initiating act in speech-act pairs and sequences. They may close a dual sequence as a communicative unit or give rise to longer sequences and conversations. One of the undisputed contract conditions of polite communication is the duty to answer, which may take place in written form, orally or non-verbally depending on the medium of communication chosen (Wächtler 1722: 18; Rohr 1730: 323 f.). If no reply is given, it will be interpreted as a dismissive reaction and a termination of polite intercourse. Silence or even bewilderment over a *compliment* are reactions which are shunned in central European polite discourse.[4] Just as inadmissible – unless a rebuke is intentional – is a change of subject initiated by the hearer without any reference to what s/he has just heard (von Rohr 1730: 152; Beetz 1997: 575 f.). The replier is expected to demonstrate a command of the situation linked with role distance while realizing the fictional character of the polite expression.

The Polite Answer in Pre-modern Conversation Culture   143

The structure of the initiating act, too, indicates close dialogue grounding. It is uttered with the knowledge and expectation of a responding act. A circular motivation structure is thus the basis of the social exchange of interaction rituals: the *compliment* made by A is the reason for B's answer, and because B's reply is usually anticipated by A, A utters the *compliment* in the first place. Interaction rituals display elements of phatic communion (Beetz 1990: 138 ff.). Therefore the relationship level essentially determines the propositional content of the utterances. To couch this in more concrete terms, speaker-oriented utterances are always formulated to anticipate the addressee's reaction while addressee-oriented utterances are phrased to include the speaker's attitude.

The main aim of politeness is to create conditions for social harmony in interaction (Beetz 1997: 564 ff.). This is achieved by the following:

1. ritual adoption of the other's interests and putting aside one's own, while simultaneously balancing out image rights to which both partners are entitled
2. heeding the congruence principle within the hierarchical framework of the Old European estate system
3. maintaining the theatre conventions tacitly accepted by the protagonists.

The politeness strategies of the speaker's ritual self-degradation and of the partner's enhancement bear no serious risk to image because both interactants know it is their duty to exchange compliments: *lauda ut lauderis* (Greflinger 1675: 25 ff.). The play-acting in this complimenting technique sets off a correction process in interaction rituals to restore the original status of the interlocutors in the sense of "social justice". Nietzsche's vitalistic reinterpretation of a quotation from the Bible puts the real intention in a nutshell: "Luke 18, 14, improved: he that humbleth himself wants to be exalted." (Nietzsche 1878/1979: 500). Acknowledgement of the partner and of the self is in no way of mutual hindrance. On the contrary, the speaker's compliment is repaid, if not verbally, then at least through the social appreciation – familiar to all participants – of polished behaviour (Hunold 1715: 78). The money metaphor applied by Werkhofer to polite exchange characterises first and foremost bourgeois manners, but this cost-benefit calculation is not unfamiliar to the courtly baroque age: the speaker is seeking goods or information and calculates the politeness expenditure required.[5]

A general rule of polite intercourse prescribes a tendency to surpass the partner in politeness and indeed to have the last word (Wächtler 1722: 18). The inevitable result are lengthy exchange sequences which reflect a socially refined process of mastering a situation. The *Neu A la modisch* ...

Complementir-Buch of 1695 demonstrates by means of ten changes in turn-taking the measures required *Sich anzubiethen / seinem Freund Gesellschaft zu leisten* 'to offer to keep one's friend company' (anon. 1695: 8 f.). Potential face threats must be formulated in several stages and are to be played down by the conversation partner. Similarly complicated procedures were expected for the introduction of a friend to a company including young women in the baroque period, and even into the first third of the 18th century in the case of visiting *compliments* or chance encounters.[6]

Compliments and minimizing responses may well make up the total content of discourse on the level of phatic communion – in particular in *galant* conversation – so that the conversation comprises purely a *höffliche(n) wort=streit* 'polite battle of words' (Kemmerich 1711: 1084). Contemporary meta-communicative comments describe this striving for courtesy quite rightly in eristic metaphors as *Wettkampf* 'competition', *Überwindung* 'vanquishing' and *Sich-Überbieten* 'outdoing each other'. The politeness champion is the successful loser who subordinates himself the most convincingly (Bary 1668: 309 ff.).

The principle of congruence claims recognition in the framework of conversation in company, face-to-face communication or in written correspondence. It demands of socially equal actors a mirror-image of their behaviour or complementary behaviour. From the point of view of content it concerns the scope of conversational topics, their perspectives, and the adoption of the viewpoints and interests of the other. The aim here is cognitive and affective homogeneity. Letters of reply according to baroque etiquette were expected to correspond to the disposition of the letter received and the style and expression were to be adapted to the situation and state of mind of the correspondent.[7] An adequate execution of the reply concerning details is, however, guided by pragmatic constellations of status. If someone of the same or higher rank has written to ask us for certain things, *muß man auf alle und jede Puncte richtig und ordentlich antworten* 'one must answer each and every point correctly and properly' (Wertheim 1711/1746: 74). A close imitation of the letter to be answered demonstrates not only respect for and compliance with the addressee, but the meticulous attention to detail also signals an interweaving of interests. In oral communication, variants are possible depending on the context and the acccentuation of utterances: the speaker takes into account the whole *compliment* or touches on only certain points. Neutral multi-purpose formulations such as *obéissant serviteur* 'obedient servant' are only recommendable with reservation. Such a stereotype *durch welches man nichts bejahet noch verneinet* 'by which nothing is affirmed or negated' is only useful if escape routes are to be kept open thanks to the ambiguity of the routine phrase. It is not suitable if a distinct reply *compliment* is called for (Rohr 1730: 167). The phrasing must include an acknowledgement of the content and an effort towards careful elaboration.

Social inequality of the interlocutors alters the requirements expected in urbane dialogue. Generally the length of a reply corresponds to the initiating *compliment* in line with the norm of congruence. A short *compliment* is followed by a short answer, a long one by an answer of similar length. This is the rule for interactants of a similar social standing. If, however, there is social distinction, von Rohr would recommend a longer reply from the inferior partner. High-ranking gentlemen are allowed to give a short answer to a long *compliment* uttered by an inferior (Rohr 1730: 166). In contrast with premodern conversation, the length of speech passages in oral or written dialogue situations should be proportional to the respect expected of the *compliment*-payer. In convivial company, indeed, the opposite is true. The participant with the highest status and prestige is entitled to the longest speaking time (cf. Beetz 1997: 14). Apart from status decorum, gender decorum pays a considerable part in speech distribution. Greater restrictions are imposed on women than on men in this respect. Ethical norms, which were subjected to certain changes in the course of history between the 16th and the 18th century – we shall refer to these in the third section – may also include the refusal to communicate with the partner of the opposite sex.

Pretend agreements belong to the conventions mutually recognised by combatants fighting for the politeness victory. Books on etiquette make it quite clear that interactants are perfectly aware of their "shadow-fencing" and the theatrical nature of role-play (Beetz 1990: 147 ff.). Although, for example in dyadic communication, both partners expect alternating and cooperative acts, the exchange character of certain interaction rituals must not be overdone. Reducing addressee enhancement and self-degradation to mere mock-fighting would then be disruptive and the actors would be stripped of their indispensable theatrical masks (Lochner 1730: 393). Meta-conventions ensure that certain conventions are treated as if they were non-existent. Declarations pointing to superfluousness when gifts are received or apologies are accepted, deny conventions in order to shed the right light on the undeservedness of the present or the voluntary nature of the act (Lochner 1730: 409). Upon receiving a gift, the bridegroom uses a concessive expression to distance himself from any expectation of entitlement: the binding gratitude to the guest for the wedding present is expressed not without verbalised scruples: *ob es wohl billig nicht annehmen solte, so will doch darunter Dero Befehl nicht zuwieder leben (...)* 'although I am not worthy to accept this gift, I do not wish to ignore your command'.[8] A qualification of this kind is necessary so as to defuse a threatening conflict of norms between unthinking acceptance, which would usurp a face-threatening entitlement, and offence-giving refusal or vain coyness. The conventional declaration of superfluousness is therefore by no means superfluous at the relationship level. It functions as a stabiliser of good relations and restores harmony if there is an imbalance. In the case of gifts, the contrast paraded by such a declaration between the unworthiness of the receiver and the exquisite value of the gift puts the generosity of the donor in the right light. A declaration of superfluousness as a reaction to an apology is also not to be interpreted literally but is a face-saving form of acceptance. It ratifies image-repair or categorises a potential face-threat as being of no consequence.

3. Reply strategies in genres

3.1. On the typology of replies

While a distinction is made according to the communication medium between non-verbal and verbal reply *compliments*, and the latter in turn are subdivided into oral and written categories, it is important to observe that polite reactions do not necessarily abide by the actual medium used in the initiation of the interaction. Just as verbal reply *compliments* (such as an expression of gratitude) may be considered as an adequate answer to non-verbal acts – e.g. nodding to let someone go ahead – speech acts such as requests or exhortations often merely require non-verbal reactions. Teachers of etiquette in the early 18th century recommend a *reverence* (i.e. a deep bow) or simply a gallant bow to replace a huge flow of words (Hallbauer 1736: 597). If a patron offers a favour, Hunold recommends rising from one's seat and bowing; this *gibt so wenigen Worten mehr Nachdruck, als weitläufftige Complimenten* 'gives more emphasis to few words than effusive *compliments*' (Hunold 1710/1730: 24). Above all, a polite refusal of an offer, not to be confused with an intended rejection in polite words, often consists of a deep bow or reverence without any utterance. The rejection of favours in the behaviour code of the age of *galanterie* belongs to a ritual which is differentiated according to the social constellation. If someone of higher social standing offers us a seat at the theatre, we must refuse the first offer but may accept the second; whereas we may sit down next to our peers upon the first offer (anon. 1715 *Thorheit und Klugheit*: 156). If a minister insists on our taking a seat, it would be a serious *faux pas* to comply immediately. The offer must be refused twice with all due respect in the form of a deep bow accompanied by no speech and not accepted until the third invitation (Neukirch 1726: 450). In the symbol-semantics of etiquette, there is apparently a shift – with social differentiation – from the quantity to the quality of utterance intentions. The refusal of favours tests whether the offer is non-binding or is truly intentional. In the case cited, refusal demonstrates that socially equalising familiarity is considered to be an exception and may be accepted by the inferior partner only upon his superior's insistence.

A typology of verbal sequence patterns can follow Ferguson's and Coulmas' distinction between echo answers and complementary replies (Ferguson 1976: 143; Coulmas 1981a: 109 f.).

In the case of echo answers, which, for example, occur in greetings, farewells, greetings in passing and wishes on feast-days and holy days, the initial formulation and the reactive forms are virtually congruous, whereas complementary answers are a reaction triggered and prescribed by the initial form and the interaction framework. The striking aspect of complementary sequences is that the very same reaction is expected for different speech-act types, e.g. thanks after congratulations, condolence, invitation or some other offer. The act of thanking honours the sympathy and esteem shown by the partner. The phrasing used for the ready granting of a demand (*Anwerbungskompliment*), of a request or the acceptance of an apology is also more or less identical: Any face-threat the interlocutor may fear is negated or declared void in each case.

Coulmas rightly distinguishes between New Year's wishes and congratulations by means of the symmetry criterium for the usage of modern-day speech. The former calls for a symmetrical pattern owing to the occasion shared by both partners whereas congratulations as a rule give rise to an asymmetrical pattern (Coulmas 1981a: 150). Historical dialogue analysis has given rise to a relativisation of both assumptions with regard to previous centuries. In the 18th century there is still a clear differentiation concerning New Year's wishes depending on the status and dependence of the interactants. The initiative is taken by inferiors and dependents: The child speaks to the parents and servants to their masters, whereupon the addressees return the wishes. More important still is the propositional and illocutionary asymmetry of New Year's wishes. Inferiors are bound to swear a vow of allegiance at the beginning of a new year: Servants promise to fulfill their duty, be diligent and obedient and beg for the goodwill of their masters for the coming year, who in their reply are not sparing with their admonitions to be good (anon. 1714/1727 *Manier zu Reden bey Gebuhrt, Hochzeiten und Absterben*: 154 f.). In a similar vein, children wish their parents a happy new year and proceed to ask for goodwill and care and promise obedience and love, as illustrated by a 26-line sample text (anon. 1714/1727: 146). From the point of view of mentality, there is historical evidence that patterns not only of symmetry but also of asymmetry may be treated as variables. What is today considered to be an example of asymmetry, such as wedding congratulations, called for symmetrical role assumption in the reply around 1700. The bridegroom returns the wedding congratulations expressed by a bachelor saying that he for his part would be extremely glad to hear soon of the happy news *daß Monsieur in Erwehlung einer geliebten Braut mir behertzt nachgefolget* 'that Monsieur has joyfully followed me in the choice of a beloved bride' (Bohse 1700: 200). Birthday congratulations are treated similarly. Here again, the sample answer returns the compliment: May the Almighty likewise grant Monsieur many long years (Bohse 1700: 201). Politeness strategies in replies offer another opportunity for typologisation.

3.2. Politeness strategies in answers

The basic politeness principles of adopting the interests of others and putting aside one's own determine the following strategies in answer *compliments*:

- addressee enhancement in counter-*compliments*
- minimisation of one's own achievements
- reference shift effected by praise
- the redefinition or refutation of appreciative words through self-condemnation[9]

The prohibition of self-praise, which goes back into antiquity, serves the purpose of preserving social harmony. If it were lifted, it would lead to rivalry à la Hobbes of each man unto his own. Disparagement of one's own achievements or values is, for example, required in reply to congratulations on professional success or to thanks for a gift (Richter 1662: 133 f). If a well-wisher extols the virtues of someone upon his promotion, the latter may – according to Lochner – *ganz kurz sich vor das gütige Urtheil bedanken und wünschen, desjenigen so man noch nicht ist würdig zu werden* 'briefly express thanks for the kind appreciation and hope to become worthy of it' (Lochner 1730: 154). The speaker declines to accept the achievement or quality recognised by the partner as a *fait accompli* and at the same time pledges to strive for its attainment. He thus balances out the ritual high esteem with his modesty, simultaneously showing recognition of socially accepted ethical standards. This minimisation is not seldom linked to a counter-*compliment* or a redefinition of a voluntary favour as a matter of duty. Here is an example of a

The Polite Answer in Pre-modern Conversation Culture   149

reply *compliment* in the context of the expression of gratitude for a gift, i.e. the third turn in the interaction sequence gift – thanks – reply to thanks:

> Daß meine Schuldigkeit, die ich durch ein geringes praesent am heutigen Tage erwiesen/ ihnen einige Freude verursachet/ hat mich sonderlich vergnüget/ und wiewohl ich bekenne/ daß es etwas bessers hätte seyn sollen/ so legen doch Mademoiselle aus einer ungemeinen Güte durch die einer schlechten Sache geschenckte estim ihr den ermanglenden Werth bey (...) (Bohse 1692: 492).
> [That my indebtedness, to which I today attested by token of this small gift, should have caused you some joy is of great pleasure to me, and though I admit it should have been something better, Mademoiselle has made up the worth of this inadequate thing by bestowing her esteem upon it from an uncommon goodness (...)]

We ascribe praise of our merits to the speaker's cleverness and flattery, whereby he truly does deserve our debt of recognition (anon. 1695: 23; Kemmerich 1711: 1085 f.). In the same way, Lochner urges us to put our own good deed or service rendered in a lower category in reply to thanks (Lochner 1730: 404). Minimisation and reference shifts as balancing techniques in polite discourse can be traced back to antiquity. Seneca recommends being silent about one's own good deeds. Should someone else mention them in our presence, one should admit that the addressee deserved far greater gifts than those he received (Seneca 1914: II, 11, 3, p. 28). Plutarch recommends a reference shift: The recipient of praise should ascribe his achievements to luck or to the gods (Plutarch 1838: 1680). Transferring praise to other causes is also advised by Althusius in the Humanist tradition (Althusius 1601: 36). Likewise, in the *galant* era the reply to congratulations contains a reference shift, which indeed bears no small measure of truth in the days of courtly absolutism: the man promoted owes his lucky position not to his minor qualities, but to the favour of his benefactors (Bohse 1700: 968 f.) Counter-*compliments* are presented *with* and *without* self-degradation. Barth makes reference to the former:

> Die ganze Kunst bestehet darinnen, daß man des andern Reden Stück=weise und ordentlich, entweder, wenn darinnen unsere Qualitäten und Geschicklichkeiten gerühmet werden, wiederlege, und solches vielmehr, indem man es von sich ablehnet, auf den andern applicire (...) (Barth 1728: 128)
> [The whole art consists either in refuting the other's speech in part and properly when it praises our qualities and abilities, and, by declining it, applying it to the other (...)]

Counter-*compliments* with self-degradation argue that 'It is not I that possess quality A, but you', or 'Quality A ascribed to me exists purely because of your quality B and I am not or only to a small degree worthy of it'.

The adoption of interests in polite interaction is manifested above all in face-saving and image repair. An example of face-saving is the expression of reservations upon receipt of an invitation for fear of the impoliteness caused by imposing oneself again ('Ethophilus' 1728: 123 f.). Expression of respect and signals maintaining distance are a matter of course within a social structure in which class distinction defines almost insuperable bounds of conduct, not only during initial contact, but also in the case of opening gambits between acquaintances (Beetz 1991: 32 ff.). The following quotes the first five of a total of eleven dialogue sequences recommended for visiting a friend around 1700:

Sich anzubiethen/ seinem Freund Gesellschaft zu leisten.
Alexander und Christian.

(1) A. Mein Herr/ ich wolte euch gerne meine Gesellschafft anbieten/ wann ich wüste/ daß sie euch angenehm wäre/ und euch keine Ungelegenheit brächte.

(2) C. nichts weniger mein Herr/ es wäre mir eine grosse Ehr/ und tausendmahl mehr als ich werth bin/ dann die Gesellschafft derjenigen/ die euch gleich sind/ kan nicht mißfallen/ noch denen die Ehr und Tugend lieben/ Ungelegenheit machen.

(3) A. Mein Herr/ wann meine Gesellschafft euch könte einige Erquickung bringen/ wolte ich sie euch von gutem Hertzen anbiethen/ aber ich fürchte/ euch zu beunruhigen.

(4) C. Ach mein Herr/ ihr würdet zu viel Mühe nehmen/ und ich verdiene es nicht/ und wäre mir leyd/ euch sie zu verursachen.

(5) A. Vergebet mir mein Herr/ das ist keine Mühe/ im Gegentheil wolte ich gern das Glück haben/ allezeit in eurer Gesellschafft zu seyn/ wo es geschehen könte/ und werde jederzeit die Zeit für sehr wohl angelegt halten/ die ich da zu werde anwenden. (...) (anon. 1695: 8 f.).

[Offering one's company to a friend
Alexander and Christian.

(1) A. Sir, I would greatly wish to offer you my company if I knew that it were pleasing to you and would cause you no inconvenience.

(2) C. Nothing would please me more, Sir; it would be a great honour to me and a thousand times more than of which I am worthy, for the company of those who are similar to you can neither displease nor be of inconvenience to those who love honour and virtue.

(3) A. Sir, if my company might provide you with some ease, I would offer it with my whole heart, but I fear I may disturb you.

(4) C. Dear Sir, you would be taking too much trouble which I do not deserve and I would be sorry to be the cause.
(5) A. Forgive me, Sir, it is no trouble; on the contrary, I would that I might have the fortune of being in your company at all times wherever possible, and I shall always consider the time well invested which I shall take for this purpose. (...)]
The simple question *Am I disturbing you?* must be repeatedly varied and refuted in formulations expressing anxiety. Conditional clauses sound out whether the situation permits a visit and offer Christian, the addressee, room for decision. A repetition of the precautionary measure in (3) tests whether the counter-*compliment* in (2) contains a polite or seriously intended invitation to stay. Counter-*compliments* work with the erosion of the speaker's own qualities (*einige Erquickung* 'some ease' in (3)), hyperbolic enhancements of the partner (*tausendmahl mehr* 'a thousand times more' in (2)) and re-interpretations: A's wish for company is presented as an imposition in (4). Re-interpretations are the order of the day in polite discourse: *Sagt jener, er wolle sich ein Viertelstündlein zu einem Gespräch außbitten etc. So sagen wir: Wir erwarten zu jeder Stund seine Befehle.* (*Thorheit und Klugheit* 1715: 85). 'The other says he wishes to ask for but a quarter of an hour for a conversation. Then we say: We await his commands at any hour.' A wish is turned into a command. The face threat, which appears to be reduced to a minimum by the diminutive form of a short interval of time, is countered with the unrealistic exaggeration that one is constantly at the other's service (*jederzeit* 'at all times' in (5)). An acute face threat is inevitable if an outright refusal is given. This is why it must be extremely carefully formulated so as to protect the addressee's image. He who is not able to grant a request for money laments nothing more than his inability in this instance to serve. The would-be creditor asks the credit-seeker to give him the opportunity on another occasion to prove his willingness to comply (Hunold 1710/1730: 470). He names good reasons which now hinder his ability to serve and stresses that turning down the request in no way constitutes a rejection of the petitioner himself (Lochner 1730: 396). If justified requests are to be rejected, the politeness code requires valid arguments, such as circumstances beyond one's control or situational constraints. As *rationes a necessario* reasons are acceptable according to this pattern of argumentation: 'One would if one could', or 'although one could, one may not' (Weise 1693: 228). Should the revelation of the true motives behind a refusal be likely to cause offence, measures granting protection of the addressee should be taken (Weise 1693: 60 f.). Even flimsy reasons are preferable to blunt refusals as they demonstrate a cooperative attempt at mutual face-saving.

The duties of verbal politeness cannot simply be categorised as indirectness strategies as Brown and Levinson suggest. Recent research on explicitness rules and the duty to provide an explanation in face-threatening acts has stressed this on several occasions.[10] In face-to-face interaction, 'heartfelt' regret for the unfortunate rejection of a request calls for a polished theatrical performance involving both prosody and body-language. The emphasis and intonation used in the expression of regret signal full understanding of the petitioner's distress and are meant to prevent a threatening deterioration of the relationship. Converse behaviour is prescribed as early as Seneca if a request is granted: One should listen kindly to the petitioner and even interrupt him cheerily in order to accommodate him and to curtail the request phase which humiliates him. One should scold him for not asking sooner (Seneca 1914: II, 3, 2 f., p. 22 f.). Lochner considers the granting of a request to contain gratitude for the trust received, assurance of loyalty and the natural, joyful compliance with the request; any trouble this may cause is to be played down. A concrete example of a reply reads as follows:

> Sie haben nicht Ursach sich zu entschuldigen/ ich statte ihnen vielmehr Dank ab/ daß sie mir Gelegenheit zeigen ihnen zu dienen/ wie wol dieses etwas geringes/ und werde ich mir jederzeit eine grose Freude daraus machen, ihnen auch in wichtigen Angelegenheiten etwas angenehmes erweisen zu können (Lochner 1730: 395 f.)
>
> [You have no reason to apologise; it is rather for me to thank you for the opportunity you have given me to be of service to you, though it be so small, and it will at all times be a great pleasure for me to be in a position to be your servant in important matters also.]

Strategies of image repair or a minimisation of a threat particularly come to the fore in apologies. Three hundred years before Florian Coulmas, Kaspar Stieler and Christian Weise distinguish between anticipatory and *ex post* apologies. Stieler calls the former "pre-apologies" (*preoccupationes*), Weise differentiates between *remedia praecaventia* and *remedia corrigentia*.[11] Apologies *ex ante* intend to defuse a face-threat to the addressee, whereas apologies *ex post* try to repair one's own (and possibly the other's) image. The alter-culprit is split into someone who has damaged his own (and maybe someone else's) image by a certain act, and into another person who distances himself from this act. In image repair-work, there is harmonious cooperation in accordance with the behaviour code between the one to apologise and the one who accepts the apology. When addressed, one *perdoniret, ob auch schon nicht im Herzen, doch äuserlich* 'pardons, even if not yet in one's heart, but at least on the surface' by firstly minimising the mistake, secondly granting the sinner absolution and thirdly giving the assurance *daß man keinen Verdruß darüber habe und ihm weiterhin treu ergeben bleibe* 'that one bears no grudge and will continue to remain his loyal servant'. At the end the apology is rejected for being superfluous (Lochner 1730: 409). A reply to an apology varies, of course, like the apology itself, depending on the degree to which moral and legal norms have been violated or on the purely prophylactic nature of a polite apology made to ward off any potential upset. An example of a written apology *ex post* and its acceptance in the age of *galanterie* is furnished by Bohse: *Entschuldigungs-Schreiben eines Frauenzimmers/ die sich nicht hat wollen sprechen lassen* 'Letter of apology from a lady who refused an audience.' The reason for her refusal was that she wished to save her reputation since a ladyfriend was present who might have thought ill of the gentleman's visit. The passage quoted below is from the letter written by the rejected gentleman in reply to the lady's apology:

> Mademoiselle.
> Sie haben nicht nöthig/ sich so höfflich zu entschuldigen/ weil ich mich allezeit verbunden halte/ dero respect meiner Vergnügung vorzuziehen: Und da ich heute die Ehre haben soll/ ihnen auffzuwarten/ ersetzet schon selbiges die gestrige Verseumniß. (Bohse 1692: 360 f.)
> [Mademoiselle,
> You have no need to apologise so politely as it is at all times my obligation to give preference to your respect rather than to my pleasure: And since I am today to have the honour of being received by you, this replaces yesterday's loss.]

The superfluousness declaration is considered to be the normal reaction in the case of low-scale face threats.[12] The claim that an apology is not necessary is contrafactual. In the politeness code, apologies that have been declared superfluous by the addressee are considered to be accepted by him/her. In the fictional worlds of polite convention, a role is also played by apologies for *etwan (!) begangene Fehler* 'any mistakes that may have been committed' when guests are bidden farewell ('Ethophilus' 1728: 201 f.). The host and the guest are left with an image of perfect harmony which will remain with them long after their separation.

Leave-taking gives the most impressive display of the theatrical aspect of politeness rituals. Drawing the process out ensures that interaction does not come to an abrupt end or allow any hint of mutual relief, but rather portrays the farewell as being a painful and gradual separation (van Gennep 1909/1960: 36; Laver 1981: 303). The host usually does not accept the guest's first farewell *compliment* ('Ethophilus' 1728: 201 f.). He must maintain the fiction of an attachment far closer than is really the case and protest that the presence of the guest cannot be long enough. This theatrical performance of bathing each other in illusions implies a duty to make utterances which are not necessarily congruous with the truth. The various stages of bidding a bride and groom farewell at their wedding must follow a certain convention:

(1) The wedding guest expresses thanks for the lavish hospitality and the wish to be able to reciprocate soon.

(2) On the first day of the wedding celebrations, the bridegroom answers: *Es ist mir leid, daß nicht länger die Ehre haben sollen (!) Ihrer angenehmen Gegenwart zugeniessen (!), da es doch nicht späte, und wenn es seyn kan, will gantz ergebenst bitten noch ein halb Stündgen uns beyzuwohnen.*
[I regret that I am no longer to have the honour of enjoying your pleasant company, for it is not late, and if it is possible, I would most humbly beg you to stay with us another half an hour.]

(3) The guest replies: *Sie verzeihen mir, es ist in der That schon späte, ich habe mich so schon über die Zeit aufgehalten, bitte also gar sehr, mich vorjetzo zu beuhrlauben (!).*
[Forgive me, it is indeed already late and as it is I have overstayed my welcome, so I beg you to grant me leave now.]

(4) Now the bridegroom interjects: *Wenn den vorjetzo so glücklich nicht seyn soll, so will eine angenehme Ruhe angewünschet und zugleich nochmahls gebeten haben, uns Morgen mit Dero angenehmer Gesellschaft wieder zu erfreuen.*
[If my wish is unfortunately to be denied, I bid you goodnight and would again request the pleasure of your charming company tomorrow.]

(5) *Das letzte Complement des Gastes.*
Ich werde Dero Befehl folgen, und mich Morgen wieder einfinden, inzwischen aber wünsche wohl zu ruhen ('Ethophilus' 1728: 124 ff.)
[The guest's final *compliment*:
I shall obey your command and be present again tomorrow, but in the meantime I wish you goodnight.]

Although the bridegroom would no doubt prefer to be in the company of his bride rather than of the guests after such a long celebration, as a token of consideration and respect he must ask them to tarry even longer. In so doing, he assumes the role of an endearing tempter and tries to persuade them at least to stay for another *halb Stündgen* 'half an hour' (2). This makes his attempt more convincing and frees him of the suspicion of a conventional lie. The contrasting approaches to the time in (2) and (3) are striking. Their relativity is dictated by situation roles. Politeness clocks show different times to guests and hosts. In view of the unevenly spread load of hospitality, it is only the guest who may refer to the lateness of the hour as an external obligation which will put an end to the need for never-ending company. The *vorjetzo* or immediacy

The Polite Answer in Pre-modern Conversation Culture 155

of the separation confirmed by both guest and host stresses that this is an exceptional case and the anticipation of meeting again on the morrow conjures up a utopia of constant attachment.

4. On historical changes to prescribed reply behaviour

Apart from a few notable exceptions, which include Ehlich's study and papers on the history of the form of address, there is a lack of linguistic research into the diachrony of polite language. The graveness of this deficit becomes evident through distinct processes of change to which even underlying norms of conduct are subject. The duty to reply is an example of these changes. If we compare its development from the 16th to the 18th century – leaving regional varieties aside – we will find, apart from the social differentiation of an obligation, noticeable historical shifts in accentuation. At the end of the 16th century Antonio de Guevara emphasises *wie es eine grosse Vnhöfligkeit seye/ auff eines andern schreiben nicht Beantworten wöllen* 'what great impoliteness it is to refrain from answering a letter'. Whoever makes the effort to write deserves a reply.

> Einem grössern beantworten ist eine genöttigte sach/ einem gleichen stants beantworten/ ist eines freyen Will/ aber dem wenigern beantworten/ ist ein lauter tugent (de Guevara 1598/1600: I, S. 37)
> [Replying to one's superior is imperative, to one's equal is of one's free will, but replying to one's inferior is pure virtue.]

Various degrees of obligation are dictated by the status constellation. It is, however, striking that there is an appeal to a moral sense of duty to reply even to inferior addressees. In the Humanist tradition, the Aristotelian teaching on friendship evidently comes into play here: a letter, which embodies a gift to the recipient, maintains the friendship thanks to its philophronesis and counts as 'half a dialogue'. This ethical-humanistic perspective of correspondence disappears in the 17th century with the rise of absolutism in the Old German empire, albeit with territorial differences. Kaspar Stieler notes:

> Grosse Herren antworten den Privatpersonen nicht/ oder gar selten auf Lobesbriefe/ Glückwüntschungen/ Trostschreiben/ Dedicationes, Geschenk Uberreichungs=schreiben (...). Es sey denn zuweilen durch einen ihrer Bedienten/ schrift= oder mündlich. Ein anders ist es gegen ihres gleichen (...). (Stieler 1680 (*Der Politische Brief-Verfasser*): 923).
> [High lords do not or only seldom reply to private persons for letters of praise, congratulations, condolence, dedications, those accompanying gifts (...), unless

now and again through one of their servants in written or spoken form. It is a different matter in the case of their peers (...).]

The answer would have to include thanks each time on their part which, on the basis of the political status of great lords, could lead to a confusion between fictional polite submission and an obligation for reasons of political interests. The reality of the power differential requires symbolic expression.

As far as the expression of interaction rituals is concerned, replies in the baroque period, as already observed in *compliments*, show a tendency to exaggerate the speaker's submission and the addressee's enhancement, whereas more moderate protestations of respect were the case in the preceding Humanist period and in the later *galant* epoch and, in particular, the Age of Enlightenment (cf. Beetz 1990: 259). The strategy of the apology, as Erasmus suggests, does not, for example, indulge in exaggerated self-degradation, but one admits one's manifest blame and asks for forgiveness. One then attempts to tone down one's misdemeanour, promises to improve and emphasises the goodness of the patron (Erasmus 1521/1971: 537 f.). In the 17th century, by contrast, the increasing show of respect is a sign of the the individual's growing dependence on the favour of patrons and superiors in the age of courtly absolutism. Loredano presents the following sample text as an answer to an *Ermahnungs=Schreiben*, a 'letter of admonition':

> Ich demüthige mich vor den liebreichen Ermahnungen E. Exc. mit solcher Ehrerbietung/ die eines solchen Hertzen/ welches die Gunst zu ehren/ und die Gutthaten zu erkennen weiß/ eigen ist. Ich wolte/ daß seine Gütigkeit/ die sich also sehr umb meine Sachen bemühet/ mich ferner mit seinem Befehl ehretete (!). In deren Vollziehung ich zu erkennen geben würde/ daß ich nicht weniger von seinen Beredungen überwunden/ als seiner grossen Gutthätigkeit verpflichtet sey. E. Exc. empfange diese geringe Erklärung zum Zeugnüß meines Gehorsams/ mit welchem ich zu allen Zeiten bekennen werde/ daß ich sey/ etc. (Loredano 1670: 305).
>
> [I humble myself before the kindly admonitions of your Excellency with such respect which belongs to a heart that honours favour and appreciates the good deeds. I would that his goodness, which has taken such pains on my behalf, may continue to honour me with his commands. In the performance of these latter I would like to show that I am not only vanquished by his words but am obliged by his benefaction. May your Excellency accept this small declaration as a testimony of my obedience with which I shall at all times proclaim that I am, etc.]

It is the speaker's duty to show deep gratitude to the patron for his intervention in affairs that were not his own and for his face-threatening complaints. As

The Polite Answer in Pre-modern Conversation Culture   157

early as the *galant* period, letters of apology show signs of self-respect despite the admission of one's fault:

Entschuldigungs=Compliment an einen Patron wegen Trunckenheit.

Ich habe gestern einen solchen Exceß begangen/ daß ich deswegen recht beschämet bin/ und nicht weiß/ wie ich mich gegen meinen Patron genugsam entschuldigen sol. Doch ich wurde von dem starcken Weine über vermuthen übereilet/ weil ich dergleichen sonsten nicht gewohnet/ auch die Gesellschafft mich ein wenig zu viel nöthigte. Bitte dannenhero gantz unterdienstlich/ die begangenen Grobheiten gütigst zu verzeihen/ und wegen dieses Fehlers keine Ungunst auff mich legen: Hinführo werde mich also in acht zu nehmen (...) wissen (Bohse 1700: 279).

[Compliment of apology to a patron on account of drunkenness

I yesterday indulged in such an excess that I am quite ashamed of the same and do not know how I am to apologise to my patron adequately. However, I was surprised by the strong wine beyond my estimation because I am not accustomed to such and the company encouraged me a little too much. I therefore ask you most humbly to be so kind as to forgive my coarse behaviour and not cast disfavour upon me. Henceforth I shall know to be on my guard (...).]

After the perturbation shown initially, which makes use of the rhetorical topos of incapacity, the ashamed transgressor soon turns to the strategy of justifying his irresponsible conduct by diminishing the degree of his responsibility. The transparent reasons for exoneration – he is unaccustomed to the level of alcohol in wine and the company encouraged him to raise his glass – are an indication of the mentality of the times which still retained a baroque estimation of drunkenness: drunkenness in itself did not call for an apology but was more likely to be regarded as extenuating circumstances for unseemly behaviour (cf. Bohse 1700: 1311; also Bohse 1692: 106). It was not until the *Moralische Wochenschriften*, the moral weeklies in the Age of Enlightenment, that the bourgeois ideal of moderation in the consumption of wine was to be propagated (Martens 1971: 268 ff.). In the period of *galanterie*, verbalised regret and requests for leniency after alcohol abuse were by and large not as excessive as might have been expected in view of the serious face-threat upon losing control of one's behaviour.

Judging from a corpus of about 130 early-modern texts on etiquette, the style of replies reflects a transition from the complicated, syntactically convoluted *compliments* of the baroque period to plainer and more moderate expressions in the 18th century (Beetz 1990: 280 ff.). Owing to the dominance of the level of relationships in all areas of interaction, long *compliments* were not considered to be a waste of time in the 17th century. On the contrary, the civilisation status, way of life and rhetorical skill documented by them served as a political tool to private success. In the 18th century, the French influence caused polite discourse to become more relaxed and free (Bellegarde 1698/1708: 354 f.). Bourgeois norms of economy and ethics gained more profile in the Old German empire. For example, time-budgeting pruned the number and length of baroque *compliments*, and efficiency caused more importance to be placed on the propositional content of an utterance and its instrumental function than on the ritualisation of the image aspect on the relationship level. The feeling of dependence on the favour of individuals began to give way to dependence on society at large in the modern period owing to an increase in economic interweaving. In the 18th century, ethical maxims of honesty and naturalness tempered down baroque precepts of effusiveness, relaxed and slimmed down the stiff ceremony of conduct and introduced a process at the end of which the restriction of polite forms is considered a genuine form of politeness.

Reply conduct recommended to women underwent different changes between the 15th and the end of the 17th century. There was great rivalry between the various images of the ideal woman – all created by men – in this cultural period. Eyb's *Spiegel der sitten* (1474) considers chastity to be the highest honour for a woman (Eyb 1474/1511: CXXIX). In line with this hierarchy of values and with the authority of the Church Fathers, she is warned to observe reticence, discipline, decency and modesty:

> Die red der junckfrauen sol weiß wol bedacht mässig vn seltzam sein/ nit mit hübschn worten sunder mit scham getziert (!) (Eyb 1474/1511: CXXX).
> [The speech of women should be prudent, well-considered, moderate and rare, adorned not with pretty words but with modesty.]

In a similar fashion, Barbaro admonishes women to be silent and make only sparing contributions to the conversation in company in the 15th century (Ruhmer 1915: 33). Along these lines, in the 16th century Vives dictates that particularly young women should consider nun-like chastity followed by modesty as the most important virtues (Vives 1523/1881: 216-222, 237-243). Although this Humanist author is one of the first to plead for education for women, he emphasises a standard of behaviour that society demands of women which is far stricter compared with the decorum expected of men. The female standard is virtually impossible to fulfill: If a young woman speaks little, she is considered uneducated, if she speaks too much, then she is thought to be too free. If she listens to a man in a kindly fashion, she will be suspected of granting favours too willingly; if she goes as far as to bestow a smile, this will be interpreted as an erotic signal (Vives 1523/1881: 250 ff.; Bömer 1904: 350). Moscherosch continues this repressive tradition in the Upper-Rhine area: *Zucht vnd Schamhafftigkeit* 'discipline and modesty' are again impressed upon the young woman as the most important virtues. She should lead a quiet, withdrawn life according to Jesus Sirach: *Nimmer reden, sie werde denn gefragt. vnnd doch so kurtz antworten, als sie immer kan* 'Never speak unless she is asked to do so, and then give the shortest reply she can' (Moscherosch 1643/1893: 66 f.).

The reason for the diverging ethical norms is to be found in the complementary social role distribution for the sexes: The male sphere is public in the professional and working world outside the home, whereas a woman's domain is the hearth, home and family, and the rigid moral code is apparently supposed to protect and maintain the institution.

Whereas in Moscherosch's *Väterliches Testament* axioms are still to be found of the tenor *Eine Jungfraw soll nicht viel wort machen: dann sie soll nicht viel wissen* 'A maiden should not speak many words, for she should not know much' (Moscherosch 1643/1893: 66), Harsdörffer pursues a different line of tradition when he pleads for women's education in the higher classes and more active participation for educated women in cultural life. The first volume of his *Frauenzimmer Gesprächspiele* already contains praise of female sense, which an administrator of purse strings and educator of children requires, as he later explains (Harsdörffer 1641-49/1968 f.: I, 47 f.; VIII, 77). Harsdörffer's pleading for the cultivated, educated woman harks back to Castiglione's *Libro del cortegiano* which is the earliest Humanist document to present in practice and theory the constructive role in society of the noble lady by means of courtly conversation (Harsdörffer III, Pref. (16 f.); Loos 1955: 196 f.). Yet, despite his postulation of equality for women in participation in education and the arts, the Italian Renaissance author does not give up the socio-ethical differentiation between the roles of the sexes. In company, women must remember that men may show signs of affection with less danger. In other words, a woman must not take any vows of love a man may utter at their face value, but interpret them as a joke and gallantry: 'she will belittle her merits and ascribe the praise he speaks to her to his politeness' (Castiglione 1528/1960: 302-304).

Harsdörffer, too, still adheres in *Der Teutsche Secretarius*, his 'art of secretariat', to the rigid rules of gender-specific decorum.[13] A lady's written reply to a gentleman's "offers of service" must be clarity itself. She should inform him *daß dieses Orts der Gebrauch nicht ist/ die Jungfrauen mit vielen Grußbrieflein zu besuchen* 'that here it is not the custom to address maidens with many letters of greeting'. Respectable girls ought to avoid any appearance of evil. The writer urges the man to refrain from further correspondence, otherwise she would have to send his letters *unerbrochen zu rucke* 'back unopened' or commit them to the flames (Harsdörffer 1656: I, part 5, p. 375). Greflinger's *Complimentir-Büchlein* in the middle of the 17th century contains similar rebuffs (cf. Beetz 1990: 317). Half a century later, in the *galant* era, extreme precaution was still being prescibed in the German-speaking area for letters initiating contact. They were to include apologies and terms of respect since the very hint of wishing to make contact was a face threat ('boldness') requiring toning down. After an initial refusal by the lady as dictated by duty, success is not achieved until after another attempt by the gentleman, and thus the interaction dance begins (Bohse 1692: 4 ff.). In France, the *Précieux* in the 17th century had already entrusted ladies with the refinement of culture who were later to become queens of the *salons*.[14] With a respectful cultural delay of about three decades, *galant* authors in Germany also confer on women the leading role in the delicate matter of taste and politeness. Benjamin Neukirch can recommend to young gentlemen *keine bessere(n) lehrmeisterinnen in der galanterie, als die damen* 'no better teachers of *galanterie* than ladies'. Johann Ulrich von König likewise favours women as the better judges of propriety and taste (Neukirch 1695/1727: 585; von König 1727/1765: 431). Goethe has the occidental tradition of polite culture in mind when the princess instructs the poet on the aesthetic utopia of the golden age, as she sees it, in a dialogue in *Tasso* (II, 1):

> Willst du genau erfahren was sich ziemt;
> So frage nur bei edlen Frauen an (Goethe 1990: 453).
> [If you wish to learn what is befitting;
> Then enquire only from noble women.]

Notes

1 Brown and Levinson (1987). More recent research is to be found in: Fraser (1990), Kasper (1990), Held (1992), Meier (1992), Meier (1995a), Meier (1995b)
2 Fraser (1990: 231 ff.); Kasper (1990: 195 ff.); Werkhofer (1992), in Watts *et al.* (1992: 158, 162, 176, 192); Meier (1992: 25, 29 f).
3 European hierarchical society was divided into estates (aristocracy, clergy, commoners) defined by birth or profession and on which certain special rights and duties were conferred. Each estate was distinguished by its own culture.
4 Hallbauer (1736: 604). According to Coulmas, silence is not necessarily considered to be impolite in Finland and Japan, cf. Coulmas (1981a: 181).

5 Werkhofer (1992: 170). Cf. the section "Ökonomisch profitable Höflichkeit" in: Beetz (1990: 191 ff).
6 Sommer (1664: 48-52). Feyerabend recommends ten turns for encounters on the street, eight for visiting compliments. Feyerabend (1729: 212 ff).
7 Stieler (1673/74: 9); Stieler (1680: 174) (printing error '274'); Weise (1691): I, p. 190, Weise (1707): 497 ff.
8 Ethophilus' (1728): 137. A young woman gives similar assurances in a sample letter *wegen übersendete(!) Messe* to the effect that the present really was not necessary and that something much smaller would have pleased her, too. Bohse (1692): 490.
9 Pomerantz distinguishes judgement shifts from reference shifts. Cf. Pomerantz (1978): 93 ff., 106.
10 Schulze (1985): 229; Held (1989): 424; Beetz (1990): 166 ff., 229 ff.; Held (1992): 180; Meier (1992): 25.
11 Coulmas (1981b): 73; Stieler (1680): 396; Weise (1693): 17.
12 Fraser (1981): 265; Coulmas (1981a): 77.
13 Harsdörffer (1659/1971): II, p. 571 f.: *Die Weiber sollen zu Hause bleiben.* 'Women should stay at home'. They should appear bashful, demure and modest.
14 Magendie (1925): I, p. 88 ff., 143. Chalesne: L'homme de qualité (...). Amsterdam (1671): p. 197: *Ce n'est qu'en frequentant des Dames, que nous acquerons cet air du monde, et cette politesse que nul conseil, ny aucune lecture ne peuvent donner* (cited in Strosetzki 1981: 203).

References

Adegbija, E.
    1989   A comparative study of politeness phenomena in Nigerian English, Yoruba and Ogori. *Multilingua* 8(1), 57-80.
Adorno, Theodor W.
    1982   *Minima Moralia.* Frankfurt/M.: Suhrkamp.
Althusius, Johannes
    1601   *Civilis conversationis Libri Duo (...).* Hanoviae.
Amthor, Christoph Heinrich
    1706   *Einleitung Zur Sitten-Lehre.* Kiel.
Anonymous
    1695   *Neu A la modisch Nach itziger gebräuchlichen Arth eingerichtetes Complementir-, Frisier- Trenchier- und Kunst-Buch.* Hamburg.
Anonymous
    1714/1727   *Manier zu Reden bey Gebuhrt, Hochzeiten und Absterben (...).* Leipzig.

Anonymous
- 1715 *Lebhaffte Abbildungen und Grundrisse Der Thorheit und Klugheit (...).* Frankfurt/M., Leipzig.

Barth, Johann Christian
- 1728 *Die Galante Ethica (...).* Dresden, Leipzig.

Bary, René
- 1668 *Der Hoff-Geist Oder Anweisung zu Höfflichen Conversationen (...).* Frankfurt/M.

Beetz, Manfred
- 1988 Der gute Ton. Normen der Soziabilität in der Sprecherziehung der Anstands- und Rhetoriktradition. In: Norbert Gutenberg (ed.). *Kann man Kommunikation lehren?* (Sprache und Sprechen 19). Frankfurt/M.: Scriptor, 19-32.
- 1990 *Frühmoderne Höflichkeit. Komplimentierkunst und Gesellschaftsrituale im altdeutschen Sprachraum.* Stuttgart: Metzler.
- 1991 Soziale Kontaktaufnahme. Ein Kapitel aus der Rhetorik des Alltags in der frühen Neuzeit. *Rhetorik* 10, 30-44.
- 1997 Leitlinien und Regeln der Höflichkeit in Konversationen. In: Wolfgang Adam (ed.). *Geselligkeit und Gesellschaft im Barockzeitalter,* Vol. 2. Wiesbaden: Harrassowitz, 563-579.

Bellegarde, Jean-Baptiste Morvan de
- 1698/1708 *Betrachtungen über die Artigkeit derer Sitten (...).* Leipzig.

Bömer, Aloys
- 1904 *Anstand und Etikette nach den Theorien der Humanisten. Neue Jahrbücher für das klassische Altertum, Geschichte und deutsche Literatur und für Pädagogik* 14, 223-285, 320-390.

Bohse, August (Talander)
- 1692 *Des Galanten Frauenzimmers Secretariat-Kunst (...).* Leipzig.
- 1700 *Talanders neuerläuterte Teutsche Rede-Kunst und Briefverfassung (...).* Leipzig.

Brown, Penelope, and Stephen C. Levinson
- 1987 *Politeness. Some Universals in Language Usage.* (Studies in International Sociolinguistics 4). Cambridge: Cambridge University Press.

Castiglione, Baldesar
- 1528/1960 *Das Buch vom Hofmann (1528).* Übers. Fritz Baumgart. Bremen 1960.

Coulmas, Florian
- 1981a *Routine im Gespräch. Zur pragmatischen Fundierung der Idiomatik.* Wiesbaden: Athenaion.

1981b Poison to Your Soul. In: Florian Coulmas (ed.). *Conversational Routine. Explorations in Standardized Communication Situations and Prepatterned Speech.* The Hague: Mouton de Gruyter, 69-91.

Ehlich, Konrad
1991 *Die Geschichtlichkeit der Höflichkeit.* Dortmund: University of Dortmund. (engl. version in Richard J. Watts, Sachiko Ide, Konrad Ehlich (eds.). (1992) *Politeness in Language.* Berlin, New York: Mouton de Gruyter, 71-107.

Erasmus, Desiderius
1521/1971 *De conscribendis epistolis.* In: Desiderius Erasmus (ed.). *Opera omnia.* (1971) Amsterdam I, 2.

'Ethophilus' (Pseud.)
1728 *Neues und wohleingerichtetes Complimentir- Und Sitten-Buch (...).* Nordhausen.

Eyb, Albrecht von
1474/1511 *Spiegel der sitten (...).* Augsburg.

Ferguson, Charles A.
1976 The structure and use of politeness formulas. *Language in Society* 5, 137-151.

Feyerabend, Georg Heinrich
1729 *Der Allzeit fertige Complimentist (...).* Rothenburg.

Fraser, Bruce
1981 On Apologizing. In: Florian Coulmas (ed.). *Conversational Routine. Explorations in Standardized Communication Situations and Prepatterned Speech.* The Hague: Mouton de Gruyter, 259-271.
1990 Perspectives on Politeness. *Journal of Pragmatics* 14, 219-236.

Goethe, Johann Wolfgang
1985 ff. *Sämtliche Werke nach Epochen seines Schaffens.* Münchner Ausgabe. München: Hanser.

Goffman, Erving
1975 *Interaktionsrituale. Über Verhalten in direkter Kommunikation.* Frankfurt/M.: Suhrkamp.
1976 *Wir alle spielen Theater. Die Selbstdarstellung im Alltag.* München: Piper.

Greflinger, Georg
1675 *Ethica Complementoria Das ist: Complementir-Büchlein (...).* Amsterdam.

Guevara, Antonius de
1598/1600 *Guldene Sendtschreiben (...).* Trans. A. Albertinus, 2 Vols. München.

Hallbauer, Friedrich Andreas
1736 *Anweisung Zur Verbesserten Teutschen Oratorie (...).* Jena.

Harsdörffer, Georg Philipp
1641-49/1968/69 *Frauenzimmer Gesprächspiele.* 8 Teile. In: Irmgard Böttcher (ed.). Tübingen: Niemeyer.
1656-59/1971 *Der Teutsche Secretarius.* 2 Teile. Neudruck Hildesheim, New York.

Held, Gudrun
1989 Beziehungsarbeit und Konversationsanalyse am Beispiel eines Bittgesprächs. *Folia Linguistica* 23 (3-4), 405-431.
1992 Politeness in linguistic research. In Richard J. Watts, Sachiko Ide, and Konrad Ehlich (eds.). *Politeness in Language.* Berlin, New York: Mouton de Gruyter, 131-153.

Hunold, Christian Friedrich (Menantes)
1710/1730 *Die Manier Höflich und wohl zu Reden und Leben* (...). Hamburg.

Hunold, Christian Friedrich (Menantes)
1715 *Die Beste Manier in Honnéter Conversation (...).* Hamburg.

Janney, Richard W., and Horst Arndt
1992 Intracultural tact versus intercultural tact. In: Richard J. Watts, Sachiko Ide, and Konrad Ehlich (eds.). *Politeness in Language.* Berlin, New York: Mouton de Gruyter, 21-41.

Jhering, Rudolph von
1905 *Der Zweck im Recht* Vol. 2. Leipzig: Breitkopf und Härtel.
1968 Der Takt. *Nachrichten der Akademie der Wissenschaften in Göttingen* I. *Philosophisch-Historische Klasse.* 1968(4), 75-97.

Kasper, Gabriele
1990 Linguistic politeness: current research issues. *Journal of Pragmatics* 14, 193-218.

Kemmerich, Dieterich Hermann
1711 *Neu-eröffnete Academie Der Wissenschafften (...). Conduite.* Leipzig.

König, Johann Ulrich von
1727/1765 Untersuchung von dem Guten Geschmack in der Dicht- und Rede-Kunst. In: *Des Freyherrn von Canitz Gedichte.* Berlin, 372-476.

Laver, John
1981 Linguistic routines and politeness in greeting and parting. In: Florian Coulmas (ed.). *Conversational Routine. Explorations in Standardized Communication Situations and Prepatterned Speech.* The Hague: Mouton de Gruyter, 289-304.

Lochner, Johann Hieronymus
1730 *Kunst zu reden in gemeinem Umgang (...).* Nürnberg.

Locke, John
1693/1823 Some Thoughts concerning Education. In: *The Works of John Locke.* 10 Vol., Vol. IX. London.

Loos, Erich
  1955 *Baldassare Castigliones "Libro del cortegiano"*. Frankfurt: Klostermann.
Loredano, Gian Francesco
  1670 *Italiänischer Secretarius in drey Theil (...)*. Franckfurt.
Machwirth, Eckart
  1970 *Höflichkeit. Geschichte, Inhalt, Bedeutung*. Diss. Saarbrücken. Trier.
Magendie, Maurice
  1925 *La Politesse Mondaine et les théories de l'honnêteté, en France, au XVIIe siècle, de 1600 à 1660*. 2 Vol. Paris: F. Alcan.
Martens, Wolfgang
  1971 *Die Botschaft der Tugend. Die Aufklärung im Spiegel der deutschen Moralischen Wochenschriften*. Stuttgart: Metzler.
Meier, Ardit J.
  1992 Brown and Levinson's legacy of politeness. *Views. Vienna English Working Papers* 1(1), 15-35.
  1995a Defining politeness. Universality in appropriateness. *Language Sciences* 17(4), 345-356.
  1995b Passages of politeness. *Journal of Pragmatics* 24, 381-392.
Moscherosch, Johann Michael
  1643/1893 *Insomnis Cura Parentum*, Straßburg, Halle.
Neukirch, Benjamin
  1695/1727 *Anweisung zu Teutschen Briefen*. Leipzig.
Neukirch, Johann George
  1726 *Politisch-Moralische Maximen in der Conversation (...)*. Braunschweig.
Nietzsche, Friedrich
  1878/1979 *Menschliches, Allzumenschliches*. In *Werke* Vol. 1. Frankfurt, Berlin: Ullstein.
Plutarch
  1838 *Plutarch's Werke. Moralische Schriften*. Trans. J.C.F. Bähr. Vol. 32. Stuttgart: Metzler.
Pomerantz, Anita
  1978 Compliment responses: notes on the co-operation of multiple constraints. In: Jim Schenkein (ed.). *Studies in the Organization of Conversational Interaction*. New York: Academic Press, 79-112.
Richter, Daniel
  1662 *Thesaurus oratorius novus (...)*. Nürnberg.
Rohr, Bernhard von
  1730 *Einleitung zur Ceremoniel-Wissenschafft Der Privat-Personen (...)*. Berlin: Rüdiger.

Ruhmer, Wilhelm
    1915   *Pädagogische Theorien über Frauenbildung im Zeitalter der Renaissance (...)*. Diss. Bonn.
Schulze, Rainer
    1985   *Höflichkeit im Englischen*. Tübingen: Narr.
Seneca, Lucius Annaeus
    1914   *De beneficiis libri* VII. In: Carolus Hosius (ed.). *L. Annaei Senecae opera quae supersunt*, Vol. I, Fasc. II. Leipzig: Teubner.
Sommer, Albertus
    1664   *Vermehrte und verbesserte Ein Hundert Teutsche Conversations-Gespräche (...)*. Hamburg.
Stieler, Kaspar
    1673/74   *Teutsche Sekretariat-Kunst (...)*. 4 Vol. Nürnberg.
    1680   *Der Allzeitfertige Secretarius (...)*. Nürnberg.
Strosetzki, Christoph
    1981   Moralistik und gesellschaftliche Norm. In: Peter Brockmeier and Hermann H. Wetzel (eds.). *Französische Literatur in Einzeldarstellungen* Vol. 1. Stuttgart: Metzler, 177-223.
van Gennep, Arnold
    1909/1960 *The Rites of Passage*. Chicago: University of Chicago Press.
Vives, Johann Ludwig
    1523/1881 Die Erziehung der Christin. In: Johann Ludwig Vives (ed.). *Ausgewählte pädagogische Schriften*. Leipzig.
Wächtler, Johann Christian
    1722   *Commodes Manual, Oder Hand-Buch (...)*. Leipzig.
Watts, Richard J., Sachiko Ide, and Konrad Ehlich (eds.)
    1992   *Politeness in Language*. Berlin, New York: Mouton de Gruyter.
Weise, Christian
    1691   *Curiöse Gedancken Von Deutschen Brieffen (...)*. 2 Vols. Dresden.
    1693   *Politische Nachricht von Sorgfältigen Briefen (...)*. 2 Vol. Dresden, Leipzig.
    1707   *Oratorisches Systema (...)*. Leipzig.
Werkhofer, Konrad T.
    1992   Traditional and modern views: the social constitution and the power of politeness. In: Richard J. Watts, Sachiko Ide, and Konrad Ehlich (eds.). *Politeness in Language*. Berlin, New York: Mouton de Gruyter, 155-199.
Wertheim, Heinrich Volck von
    1711/1746 *Auf neue Manier abgefaßter und allzeit fertiger Brief-Steller (...)*. Chemnitz.

Minnegespräche
Die galante Konversation in der frühen deutschen Lyrik

Hannes Kästner
Albert Ludwigs University, Freiburg

Abstract

The hypothesis that the Minnesang may be used as a text source for the reconstruction of courtly speech is verified as follows: First of all, regulations and recommendations befitting men and women in their use of the language of love are drawn from the didactic literature, and the rules of spoken interaction inherent in them are examined. It will then be shown that conversational songs (turn-taking, dialogue songs) are indeed exemplary in presenting a model conduct of speech for the subject of love and condemn any gender-specific infringements of the rules. Finally, reflexion on the intention of rules of gallant conversation in some love songs shows that Minnesingers give expression to the ideal of courtly speech.

> er minnet iemer deste baz
> swer von minnen etewaz
> hoeret singen oder lesen
> (Konrad von Würzburg,
> Herzmaere, 19-21)

> mesura es de gen parlar,
> e cortesia es d'amar
> (Marcabru)

Es ist eine erstaunliche Tatsache, daß der literarische Kult der Minne, der die mittelhochdeutsche Literatur seit den siebziger Jahren des 12. Jahrhunderts so entscheidend prägte, keinen Niederschlag in außerpoetischen, d.h. realhistorischen Quellen gefunden hat. Das gilt in besonderer Weise für den Minnesang, über dessen Einbindung in die höfische Lebenswelt seiner Entstehungszeit wir so gut wie nichts wissen. Dieser Mangel an Informationen hat zu der "unaufgelösten Divergenz der Minnesangdeutungen" (Eisbrenner 1995: 89) geführt, mit der sich jeder konfrontiert sieht, der sich mit dem Thema beschäftigt. Die unterschiedlichen Auffassungen über den Sitz im Leben der Minnelieder besetzen eine Skala, deren erster Extrempunkt von einer Interpretationsmethode markiert wird, die von postulierten Übereinstimmungen der Textaussagen mit der Gefühls- und Erlebniswelt der Autoren, ihren schichtenspezifischen Lebenslagen und -einstellungen etc. ausgeht. Der entgegengesetzte Pol wird von Forschern vertreten, die betonen, daß "keine der Aussagen in den Liedern ... von der außerliterarischen Realität her aufgefaßt und gedeutet werden" (Eisbrenner 1995: 89) darf, weil die Texte, "alle Aspekte, die der höfischen Wirklichkeit wichtig waren, bewußt ausgeschlossen" (Eisbrenner 1995: 91) hätten, und auch der Minnesang *un monde poétique clos* – so Pierre Bec über die Troubadourlyrik – darstelle. Wie die Übersichten zur Forschungsgeschichte des Minnesangs in neueren Arbeiten eindrucksvoll belegen, pendeln die Meinungen für den richtigen methodischen Zugriff unaufhörlich zwischen diesen Extrempunkten hin und her und sind in gewisser Weise für die gesamte mediävistische Forschungsgeschichte repräsentativ (vgl. Willms 1990: 1-8; Eisbrenner 1995: 7-98).

Ich möchte diese Diskussion hier nicht nochmals ausbreiten, sondern formuliere statt dessen meinen eigenen Standpunkt, der mein methodisches Vorgehen rechtfertigen soll. Die Basis meiner theoretischen Plattform ruht auf zwei Pfeilern, deren einer rein hypothetischen Charakter hat. Es ist dies die Vermutung, daß angesichts der Quantität und Qualität der Minnelieder, des sichtbaren Aufwands an praktizierter Kunstfertigkeit und des teilweise spürbaren Ernstes dieser Dichtung, diese in jedem Falle eine Aussage oder eine Bedeutung für die sie produzierenden und rezipierenden Menschen gehabt haben muß (Schnell 1985: 108-115). Ich unterstelle den Autoren also, daß sie neben dem *delectare* auch das *prodesse* ihrer Dichtung nicht vernachlässigt haben, was übrigens gänzlich unmittelalterlich gewesen wäre und nebenbei durch Selbstaussagen der Dichter gestützt werden kann (Willms 1990: 223). Meinen zweiten Grundpfeiler bilden die Aussagen über den erzieherischen Charakter der Minne in der zeitgenössischen Lehrdichtung. Didaktische Texte, wie Hofzuchten, Anstands- und Minnelehren repräsentieren natürlich ebenfalls in keiner Weise die höfische Realität; sie entstanden jedoch in der eindeutigen Absicht, auf das Verhalten der höfischen Gesellschaft, die auch das Publikum der öffentlich vorgetragenen Minnelieder ist, normierend und bessernd einzuwirken. Hier werden in direkter Anweisung, verbunden mit Ratschlag,

Warnung oder Verbot auch Regeln und Verhaltensmuster für Mann und Frau bei der Liebesbegegnung formuliert, einer ebenso existenziellen wie spannungsvollen Geschlechterbegegnung, deren verschiedene Möglichkeiten und Ergebnisse ja gerade der Minnesang variantenreich vorführt.

Aus beiden Prämissen haben einige Forscher schon sehr früh die Schlußfolgerung abgeleitet, daß die Minnelieder u.a. auch in der Absicht komponiert worden seien, die Zuhörer auf unterhaltsame Weise mit einer angemessenen Verbalisierung von Liebesgefühlen vertraut zu machen (Kraus 1930: 5). Dieses Imitationsangebot gelte vor allem für den Mann, der sich am Verhaltensmuster des männlichen Rollen-Ichs im Werbungslied, in der Mannesstrophe des Wechsels oder im männlichen Part des Dialoglieds orientieren könne, um "seinen Gefühlen und Wünschen in poetisch schönen Wendungen Ausdruck zu geben und auf geziemende, höfisch akzeptable Weise zu werben" (Willms 1990: 221). Die *vox feminae* in den Frauenstrophen des Minnesangs fand hingegen erst in den letzten Jahren größere Beachtung, wobei das Hauptaugenmerk der Frage galt, wie die Frau als ein vom männlichen Sänger sprechend gemachtes Subjekt in die verschiedenen lyrischen Liebeskonzeptionen eingebunden wird, und welche Einstellungen (Erhörung, Zaudern, Abwehr etc.) gegenüber dem werbenden Mann in den unterschiedlichen Liedgattungen thematisiert werden (Plummer 1981). Noch weniger als bei der Männerrolle hat man bei der weiblichen Kunstfigur untersucht, inwieweit direkt oder indirekt Regeln eines angemessenen höfischen Sprechens der Partnerrede zugrunde liegen, d.h. mit anderen Worten, welche positiven oder negativen Qualifizierungen sprachlichen Handelns im Hinblick auf eine mögliche Übernahme von "Formulierungsmustern" aus der Frauenstrophe in die galante Konversationspraxis vorauszusetzen sind (Willms 1990: 231).

Nun ist einzuräumen, daß im Bereich der deutschen Literatur im Gegensatz etwa zur Romania keine Texte existieren, in denen das Regelwerk einer galanten Konversation für beide Geschlechter vollständig ausgebreitet wird. In der deutschen didaktischen Literatur stehen die Minnelehren nicht im Mittelpunkt des Erziehungsprogramms; wenn aber die Geschlechterbeziehung dort zur Sprache kommt, dann finden sich stets auch Anweisungen über die Strategien der verbalen Annäherung an die Geliebte für den Mann und Direktiven für das angemessene reaktive Redeverhalten der umworbenen Frau. Nimmt man diese rudimentären Hinweise als erste Versuche, auch in der deutschen Adelswelt der Stauferzeit eine galante Konversationskunst nach französischem Vorbild zu etablieren, in deren Zentrum die Minne steht, dann könnten – so meine Hypothese – in vielen Minneliedern, vornehmlich solchen, die dialogisch inszeniert sind, Reflexe einer theorieorientierten Regulierung der vorbildlichen Liebesrede sichtbar werden. Zwar darf man im Deutschen sicher nicht von einem Kanon ausgehen, da die Gebote und Verbote nur unvollständig ausformuliert und unsystematisch vorgetragen werden; man kann aber sicher diese Ansätze zu einer Sprachregelung nach dem Vorbild der provenzalischen und französischen Minnetheoretiker als wesentlichen Bestandteil des *cortezia/courtoisie*-Ideals betrachten. Und vielleicht ist es kein Zufall, daß die erste deutsche Minnelehre, *Der heimliche Bote* (um 1170), die zu einem Zeitpunkt entsteht, als die deutsche Lyrik sich dem romanischen Einfluß öffnet, dem werbenden Mann die kunstvolle Rede empfiehlt, die Andreas Capellanus als dritten und entscheidenden unter fünf Wegen einstuft, auf denen die Liebe einer Frau errungen werden könne.[1]

Bevor ich nun einige zentrale Anweisungen und Regeln für das Redeverhalten und die -techniken der Partner bei der Minne-Konversation aus der deutschen Lehrdichtung[2] vorführe, um sie dann auf ihre Relevanz für den Minnesang zu überprüfen, gilt es vorher noch, zwei möglichen Einwänden gegen einen solchen methodischen Ansatz für die Minnesang-Interpretation vorzugreifen:

(1) Ich bin mir durchaus im klaren darüber, daß es sich bei den Minneliedern um Dichtung in musikalischer Fassung handelt. Selbst dort, wo der Minnesänger ein direktes Gespräch zwischen Mann und Frau nachbildet, im Wechsel, Dialoglied oder im Tagelied[3], haben wir natürlich immer eine der Praxis enthobene Konversation vor uns, bei der das ästhetische Moment dominiert. Ich sehe das aber für meine Fragestellung als Vorteil an, denn im Rahmen des poetischen Spiels sind die Grenzen der Liebesrede in einem Ausmaß strapazierbar und in viele Richtungen hin expandierbar, wie das in realer, alltäglicher Rede niemals möglich wäre. Dies gilt für die Partnerrede über erotische und sexuelle Inhalte ebenso wie für verwerfliche Arten der Liebeswerbung und die dadurch provozierten Folgen.

(2) Da es im Unterschied etwa zu den Anweisungen in altprovenzalischen Lehrgedichten (*Ensenhamen*), das Publikum möge sich Vorbilder und Anregungen für die eigene gefällige Rede (*gen parlar*) und die gelungene Unterhaltung (*solatz*) aus der höfischen Liebeslyrik nehmen,[4] im Deutschen nicht gibt, müssen wir im Minnesang selbst nach Belegen suchen, in denen die Sänger ihr vorbildliches Sprechen als für andere übernehmbar darstellen. Und in der Tat gibt es einige Aussagen, die selbst dann noch auf diese Übernahmemöglichkeit schöner Redeweisen und Komplimente hinweisen, wenn sie innerhalb des eigentlichen Argumentationsgefüges der Liedstrophe eigentlich einen anderen Aussage-

zweck verfolgen. So meint etwa der Minnesänger Reinmar in gespielter Resignation:

Sît mich mîn sprechen nû niht kan gehelfen noch gescheiden von der swaere mîn, Sô wolte ich, daz ein ander man die mîne rede hete zuo der saelde sîn (...)	Da mir mein Sprechen nun nicht helfen noch mich von meinem Leid befreien kann, so wünschte ich, daß ein anderer Mann über meine Sprache zu seinem Glück verfügte (...)

(*Reinmar* VII,5,1-4, Übs. n. Schweikle)

Denn bei Reinmars *guote(r) rede* handelt es sich nach seiner eigenen Einschätzung, die er in einem anderen Lied äußert, um wohlgesetze Worte,

(...) die besten, die ie man gesprach (XXV, 5,4).[5]	die besten, die man jemals äußerte.

Um meine Hypothese von den Reflexen einer galanten Konversationskunst im Minnesang zu überprüfen, gehe ich nun folgendermaßen vor: Ich stelle getrennt nach Geschlechtern einige Forderungen und Empfehlungen zur Liebesrede aus der didaktischen Literatur um 1200 zusammen und frage nach den ihnen inhärenten Regeln über sprachliche Interaktion. Anhand von Liedbeispielen aus der Sammlung *Des Minnesangs Frühling*, die Texte vom Beginn der deutschen Lyrik um die Mitte des 12. Jahrhunderts bis zu Walther von der Vogelweide umfaßt, möchte ich dann exemplarisch demonstrieren, daß diese Regeln in vielen Liedern zur Anwendung gelangen, bzw. daß über sie reflektiert wird. Dies wäre übrigens nicht nur an Gesprächsliedern wie Wechsel und Dialoglied zu zeigen, auf die ich hier ausführlicher eingehen will, sondern auch in vielen anderen Männer- oder Frauenliedern, die keinen direkten Dialog nachbilden, aber dennoch die Ansprache an den Geschlechtspartner als Verständigungsrahmen voraussetzen. Wenden wir uns zunächst dem Mann zu: Welches Redeverhalten beim Thema Liebe wird ihm, wenn er das Prädikat *courtois/hövesch* für sich beanspruchen will, gegenüber dem weiblichen Geschlecht empfohlen? Was wird ihm andererseits als unhöfisches Sprechen untersagt?

In der ältesten deutschen Minnelehre werden dem *wol minnende[n] man* neben tugendhaftem Handeln und demütigem Dienst für die Dame auch *schone antwurte vnd gute gruze wise (rede) vnd suze* bei seiner Werbung empfohlen, *wan ze guten minnen horet (list)*.[6] Elegante Antworten und angemessene Anrede umschreiben die galante Kunst (mhd. *list*!) der Liebesrede des Mannes, deren wesentlicher Bestandteil dann aber die kluge und einschmeichelnde Werbungsrede ist. Gemeint ist zweifellos die auch in den Minneliedern immer wieder vorgetragene Empfehlung für den werbenden Mann, er möge *wol sprechen den wîben*.[7] In den Minneliedern konkretisiert sich diese Forderung einmal im Frauenpreis, der laudativen Rede, die sich auf äußere Schönheit und innere Tugend der Frau konzentriert und die wichtigste Werbungsstrategie im klassischen Minnesang darstellt. Ihre Techniken entstammen zum Teil der Panegyrik, einer Spezialdisziplin der Rhetorik, und wurden in diesem Rahmen schon ausführlich analysiert (Willms 1990: 88ff.; Eisbrenner 1995: 116ff.; Hübner 1996). Neben dem praktizierten Frauenpreis wird die laudative Rede in den Liedern noch häufig unter zwei weiteren Aspekten thematisiert: Einmal ist es die Selbststilisierung des Sängers zu einem männlichen Ich, das "die für den Minnesang konstitutive Kunst des *wol sprechens* oder *wol redens*" (Stevens 1983: 181) in besonderer Weise beherrscht. Zum anderen reflektiert das Rollen-Ich in einer Art Metadiskurs manchmal darüber, wie, mit welchem Ziel und mit welchen möglichen Ergebnissen der Frauenpreis von ihm eingesetzt wird (Eikelmann 1996: 31ff.). Selbstbewußt verkündet z.B. Walther von der Vogelweide:

Ich han ir sô wol gesprochen,	Ich habe so gut über sie geredet,
daz si maneger in der welte lobet	daß sie nun viele in der höfischen Gesell-
(L 40, 19f.)	schaft loben.

Dem *wol sprechen* steht übrigens das *übel reden* oder *schelten* gegenüber, das als grober Verstoß gegen die *courtoisie/hövescheit* gewertet und selbst bei Abweisung der Werbung durch die Frau nicht gestattet wird. Reinmar stellt fest:

Sprach in anders ieman danne wol,	Sprach von ihnen einer anders als gut,
daz was ein schult, die ich nie verkôs	das war ein Vergehen, das ich nie verzieh!
(XIII 1,3f.)	

Und an anderer Stelle:

Bezzer ist ein herzesêr,	Besser ist ein Herzeleid,
danne ich von wîbe misserede	als daß ich schlecht von Frauen rede.
(XX 2,5f.)	

Ich fasse diesen ersten und wichtigsten Punkt für die männliche Liebesrede zusammen: Willms hat sicher recht, wenn sie das vorbildliche *sprechen wider diu wîp*, das in didaktischen, lyrischen und auch epischen Texten immer wieder dem Mann empfohlen wird, für den Minnesang "am ehesten als Kunst des Komplimentemachens übersetzen würde. Es dürfte dem allgemeinen *wol sprechen* eine intimere, erotischere Komponente beigefügt haben. Gelegentlich wird es zu den erlaubten Lügen gezählt" (Willms 1990: 153). Darauf wird noch zurückzukommen sein. Fragen wir uns weiter, welche negativen Verhaltens- und Redeweisen die Ermahnung *hüete dich, daz du mit frowen zühtelich schallest* im Blick hat. Im *Deutschen Cato*, aus dem dieses Zitat stammt, wird auf die Problematik der gesuchten Nähe zum weiblichen Partner als eine Voraussetzung für die als notwendig empfohlene Heimlichkeit bei der Liebesrede eingegangen. Wenn eine Frau die Erlaubnis zur Annäherung für ein vertrauliches Gespräch gewährt hat, dann, so heißt es in einer späteren deutschen Übersetzung der lateinischen *Disticha Catonis*, der verbreitetsten Lehrschrift des Mittelalters:

bis gemant und sitz ir niht ûf ir gewant	sei ermahnt: setze dich ihr nicht auf ihr Kleid,
ouch niht ze nâch, daz rât ich dir,	komme ihr nicht zu nahe, das rate ich dir,
wiltu iht reden heimlich zir;	wenn du etwas heimlich mit ihr besprechen willst,
begrîf sie mit den armen niht,	fasse sie nicht an,
swaz dir ze reden mit ir geschicht.	worüber auch immer ihr euch unterhaltet.

(*Deutscher Cato*, S. 132, V.143-148)

Hier wird in drastischer Direktheit ein Fehlverhalten beim intimen Liebesgespräch verurteilt, das eine weitere grundlegende Konstituente der männlichen Werbung im Minnesang darstellt: die Verletzung der Distanzregel.[8] Die Wahrung einer gewissen Distanz gilt aber bis heute als Teil des Höflichkeitsprinzips bei der Gesprächsführung. In der Konversationsanalyse erscheint diese Distanz als Teil des "Interaktionsmanagements", welches das Glücken der Sprechakte, unabhängig vom Thema, sichert. Distanz bedeutet in diesem Sinne, daß man dem Gesprächspartner einen Persönlichkeitsraum zugesteht (nach Goffman könnte man auch vom eigenen Territorium sprechen), in den ohne Erlaubnis des Besitzers einzudringen, ihm also zu nahe zu treten, einen groben Verstoß gegen die Höflichkeit bedeutet. Dorothea Franck hat solche Territoriumsabgrenzungen auch für sprachliche Handlungen untersucht und dabei gezeigt, daß Rücksicht auf den anderen nicht nur den Anspruch des anderen auf Respekt, Unversehrtheit, Selbstbestimmung etc. gerecht zu werden bedeutet, sondern daß es auch variable Territoriumsgrenzen bei speziellen Themen gibt (wie z.B. in unserem Fall beim Gespräch mit dem Thema Liebe zwischen Mann und Frau), die zwar während des Gesprächs erst ausgehandelt, aber, einmal festgelegt, ohne Gesichtsverlust nicht überschritten werden können (Franck 1980: 162ff.). Als besonders unhöflich wird deshalb eine männliche Werbungsrede bewertet, die den weiblichen Gesprächspartner unvermittelt durch eindeutige Anträge zum intimen Kontakt überrascht, und ihn so in seinem Selbstwertgefühl verletzt und gleichzeitig in den Augen der anderen Gruppenmitglieder herabsetzt. Die Reaktion der umworbenen Frau kann dann nur Abbruch der Kommunikation heißen. Diesen verbalen Regelverstoß beim Minnegespräch hat Heinrich von Veldeke in einer Großform des Wechsels (Liedwechsel) (MF 56,1 u. 57,10) thematisiert. Das Rollen-Ich der Mannesstrophe bedauert darin, daß es wegen seiner *tumbheit* und *al ze hôhe gernde(r) minne* die Huld der schönsten und besten Dame verloren habe. Den Grund gibt die 4. Strophe an:

Daz übel wort sî verwâten,	Das böse Wort sei verwünscht,
daz ich nie kunde verlâten,	das ich nicht konnte unterdrücken,
3 dô mich betroug mîn tumber wân.	3 als mich mein törichter Wahn betrog.
Der ich was gernde ûz der mâten,	Die ich über die Maßen begehrte,
5 ich bat si in der caritâten,	5 ich bat sie um der Barmherzigkeit willen,
daz si mich mües al umbevân.	daß sie mich fest umfangen möge.
7 sô vil het ich niht getân,	7 So viel hatte ich nicht geleistet,
daz si ein wenic ûz der strâten	daß sie ein wenig neben der Straße
9 durch mich zu unrehte wolte stân.	9 meinetwegen schuldhaft stehen wollte.
(MF 57,1; Übs. n. Schweikle)	

Die Frauenstrophen bekräftigten die Selbstvorwürfe des Mannes, jegliche Distanz aufgehoben und die Grenze zur unerlaubten Intimität durch ein *übel wort* voreilig überschritten zu haben; erläutert wird ebenso die darauf folgende Veränderung in der Partnerbeziehung. Die umworbene Frau hatte dem Mann zunächst ihre Zuneigung geschenkt, weil sie glaubte "daz er hovesch wâre". Nun aber habe er von ihr "al ze ungefüeger minne" begehrt. Eine Zusatzstrophe in Hs. A erläutert dieses falsche verbale Werbungsverhalten genauer und kennzeichnet es als *dorperlîch*, dem begrifflichen Gegenpol zu *hövesch*:

Ez kam von tumbes herzen râte,	Es kam vom Rat eines törichten Herzens,
ez sal ze tumpheit ouch ergân.	es wird zur Torheit auch ausschlagen.
3 ich warnete in alze spâte,	3 Ich warnte ihn allzu spät,
daz he hete missetân.	daß er falsch gehandelt habe.
5 wie mohte ich dat für guot entstân,	5 Wie konnte ich das für gut hinnehmen,
dat he mîn dorperlîche bâte,	daß er mich tölpelhaft bat,
7 dat he mich muoste al umbevân.	7 daß er mich fest umfangen müsse.
(MF 57,26; Übs. n. Schweikle)	

Und am Schluß fordert die Frau den Mann auf, daraus zu lernen:

daz er sîn spil niht wol beschiet,	daß der sein Spiel nicht gut anlegte,
er brichet ê daz erz gewinne.	der es zerstört, ehe er es gewinnt.
(MF 58,9f.)	

Gerade die Metapher des kommunikativen Spiels, die hier erscheint, verweist auf die Regelgebundenheit der Interaktion in Sachen Liebe, Regeln, welche nicht die Sache selbst betreffen – die Frau war ja anfangs kooperationsbereit, als sie glaubte, er würde sich an den höfischen Komment der Werbung halten –, sondern die Art des sprachlichen Miteinander-Umgehens.

Anzumerken bleibt noch, daß die Grundforderung des Einhalts der Distanz zwischen Mann und Frau im höfischen Verhaltenskodex nicht auf den sprachlichen Sektor beschränkt ist, sondern den Gesamtkomplex der Praxis höfisch-höflichen Umgangs der Geschlechter miteinander betrifft. So resultiert daraus u.a. die auch im Minnesang so häufig thematisierte Institution der *huote*, der für die Frau bestellten Aufpasser und Anstandsdamen, als Garanten der vom Mann einzuhaltenden Distanz gegenüber der schwächeren Frau. Wie notwendig diese Einrichtung, die gleichzeitig Überwachung und Schutz für die Frau war, in einer von Männern dominierten Lebenswelt gewesen sein mag, kann die im oben zitierten *Cato*-Text gezeigte, plump-aggressive Annäherung des Mannes an die Frau verdeutlichen.

Betrachten wir unter den weiteren Anweisungen zum Sprachverhalten des Mannes bei der Werbung noch eine letzte: es geht hier um das Rühmen. Der *ruom* bezieht sich zunächst auf das Selbstlob, eine seit der Antike und dann ebenso im Christentum als Laster verurteilte Haltung. Thomasin von Zerklaere, ein italienischer Kleriker, der in den Jahren 1215/16 die erste umfassende praktische Lebens- und Verhaltenslehre für den deutschen Adel schreibt, kann in seinem Kapitel über die Minne deshalb die Frauen vor solchen Männern mit den Worten warnen:

(...)	(...)
und wizzet, daz ein boesewicht	Wißt, daß ein böser Mensch
sich harte wol geruomen tar,	sich überaus stark zu rühmen untersteht,
daz gehoeret ze boesheite gar.	das gehört zur Lasterhaftigkeit.

(*Thomasin von Zerclaere, Der welsche Gast*, V.1632 ff.)

Ein prahlerischer Mann wird kaum das rechte Verhalten eines vorbildlich Liebenden an den Tag legen, das in der Haltung des Dienens für die Frau besteht und auf der sprachlichen Ebene sich nicht im Selbstlob, sondern im Frauenlob und in der Bitte um Erhörung niederschlägt; gerade das demütige

Bitten des Mannes wird in den theoretischen Lehren wie in den Liedern als die von den Frauen erwünschte Haltung ausgegeben. So findet sich die Sentenz des Spruchdichters Freidank: *Verzîhen ist der wîbe site, / doch ist in liep, daz man si bite (Fridankes Bescheidenheit*, 100, 24 f.) im Minnelied bei Reinmar wieder: *In ist liep, daz man si staeteclîche bite, und tuot in doch so wol, daz sî versagent.* (XX 3,1 f.) Gänzlich gegen die Regeln der höfisch-galanten Konversation verstößt aber das Selbstlob der Männer, *die sich von wîben rüement anders danne in wol an stê* (Heinrich Teschler 3,16 f. zitiert nach Willms 1990: 325). Konkret gemeint ist das öffentliche Renommieren des Mannes mit seinen weiblichen Eroberungen, das der Kleriker Heinrich von Melk geradezu als typische Gesprächshandlung bei Männerzusammenkünften beschreibt:

swa sich div reiterschaft gesamnet,	Wo immer sich die Ritter versammeln,
da hebet sich ir wechsel sage,	brüsten sie sich,
wie manige der vnt der behuret habe.	mit wie vielen sie herumgehurt hätten.
ir laster mvgen si nicht versweigen,	Ihre Schande können sie nicht für sich behalten
ir ruom ist niwan von den weiben.	sie tun sich nur mit Weibergeschichten groß.
swer sich inden ruom nicht enmachet,	Wer bei der Prahlerei nicht mithält,
der dunchet sich verswachet	fühlt sich zurückgesetzt
vnder andern seinen geleichen.	unter seinen Standesgenossen.

(*Heinrich von Melk, Von des todes gehugde*, V.354-361)

Es handelt sich dabei aus der Sicht der Frau nicht nur um einen Vertrauensbruch, sondern vor dem Hintergrund des Verlustes ihres guten Leumunds und ihrer Ehre um eine Bedrohung ihrer sozialen Existenz. Walther von der Vogelweide fragt deshalb in einem Lied ganz zu recht:

waz touc zer welte ein ruemic man?	Was taugt in der höfischen Welt ein prahlerischer Mann?
wê den selben die sô manegen schoenen lîp	Wehe denen, die so viele schöne Frauen
habent ze boesen maeren brâht.	in Verruf gebracht haben ...
ir sult si mîden, guotiu wîp. (...)	Ihr sollt sie meiden, edle Frauen.
(L. 41,16 ff.)	

Und Dietmar von Aist hat dieses ungalante Verhalten des Mannes zusammen mit der abweisenden Reaktion der Dame in einem erweiterten Wechsel dargestellt (MF 40,19) und so zu einem "Beispiel pikanter Gesellschaftspoesie" (Schweikle, *Mittelhochdeutsche Minnelyrik I* 1993: 407) geformt. Der werbende Mann gibt vor, die *huote* ebenso überwunden zu haben wie die Unnahbarkeit der umworbenen Frau. Er macht seine Eroberung in der Absicht öffentlich, die Partnerin unter Druck zu setzen:

si ist sô vaste niht behuot,	Sie ist so fest nicht behütet, -
5 iedoch sô dunket si mich guot,	5 jedoch gerade so dünkt sie mich gut, -
des bringe ich si wol inne,	das bringe ich ihnen wohl zur Kenntnis,
7 ez wære an mîner frouwen ein slac.	7 es wäre für meine Dame ein Schlag:
si sol gedenken, ob si tœrschen ie bî mir gelac.	Sie soll daran denken, ob sie nicht jemals leichtsinnig bei mir lag!
(MF 40,30; Übs. n. Schweikle)	

Die Frau entrüstet sich über "diese rüde Pointe, ... verwahrt sich gegen das hämische Triumphieren" (Schweikle 1993: 406) und weist die kompromittierende Behauptung zurück, indem sie ihr einen ambiguosen Sinn verleiht:

Waz wîzet mir der beste man.	Was wirft mir der beste Mann vor!
Ich habe ime leides niht getân.	Ich habe ihm kein Leid getan.
3 er fröit sich âne schulde.	3 Er freut sich ohne Grund.
Daz er in hât von mir geseit,	Was er ihnen von mir gesagt hat,
5 daz ist mir hiute und iemer leit.	5 das ist mir heute und immer leid.
er verliuset mîne hulde.	Er verliert meine Huld.
7 mir wirret niht sîn bœser kîp.	7 Mich verwirrt sein böses Zanken nicht:
waz half, daz er tœrschen bî mir lac,	Was half es, daß er leichtsinnig bei mir lag,
jô enwart ich nie sîn wîp.	wahrhaftig ich wurde nie seine Frau!
(MF 40,35; Übs. n. Schweikle)	

Die Situation der Frau, die in dieser Frauenstrophe skizziert wird, ist nun genau diejenige, die von den Frauen am meisten gefürchtet wird, und vor der in den Minnelehren am intensivsten gewarnt wird: Der Mann kann mit *lop* und *süezen worten*, mit Frauenpreis, Komplimenten und Schmeicheleien die Frau zum *bîligen* überreden; anstatt die Vertraulichkeit und Heimlichkeit zu wahren, wie sie z.B. in der dritten dialogischen Liedart, dem Tagelied, inszeniert wird, kann er aber ebenso vom galanten Verehrer zum taktlosen, unritterlichen Galan mutieren. Sein Fehlverhalten liegt dabei nicht im Ansprechen der Tabu-Zone der praktizierten Sexualität – das kommt in den Liedern öfter vor,[9] sondern im Öffentlichmachen des errungenen Erfolgs. Resultat ist für die Frau dann Scham und Schande, die, so zeigen es die Minnelehren und die Frauenstrophen des Minnesangs unisono, unbedingt vermieden werden müssen.[10] Die Anweisungen zum Sprachverhalten der Frau beim Gespräch mit dem Thema Liebe kreisen denn auch alle mehr oder weniger um diesen zentralen Problempunkt: Woran kann die Dame erkennen, daß das *wol sprechen* des werbenden Mannes, respektive sein Frauenpreis aufrichtig gemeint ist? Ist die *copiosa sermonis facundia* des Mannes, die bei Andreas Capellanus zu den Liebesgründen gehört, Ausdruck echter Liebesempfindung, oder handelt es sich um *spaehe rede*[11] 'kunstvolle, feine Wendungen', mit denen die Frau überredet werden soll? Besteht die galante Konversation auf Seiten des Mannes zum größten Teil aus Komplimenten und damit aus Lügen? Stimmt der Spruch *swer minne pfligt der liuget ouch* und *lüge ist der minne site* (*Friedrich von Sonnenburg* 46, 6 ff.)? Nun haben Untersuchungen zum Höflichkeitsdiskurs in der Neuzeit (Beetz 1990: 135) wie zur Linguistik der Lüge (Hundsnurscher 1994: 110) gleichermaßen darauf hingewiesen, daß Komplimente und Höflichkeitsfloskeln zu den harmlosen Lügen zu zählen sind, weil die auf Schädigung des Adressaten ausgerichtete Täuschungsintention entfällt. Da bei Höflichkeitsritualen die Aufhebung der Aufrichtigkeitsbedingung Usus ist, können faktisch nur diejenigen getäuscht werden, welche die Spielregeln des höflich-galanten Gesprächs nicht kennen oder die Situation falsch einschätzen. Diese Meinung über die moralische Unbedenklichkeit galanter Rede scheint man schon im Mittelalter geteilt zu haben, denn ein Sänger versichert: *doch seite mir ein wiser predegaere, / daz hübische lüge niht groziu sünde waere*. (Rumslant von Schwaben 1,11 f.). Dennoch wird sowohl in der didaktischen Literatur wie im Minnesang und hier speziell bei den Dialogliedern das *loben* und *wol sprechen* des Mannes zunehmend stärker mit dem Lügenverdacht der Frau konfrontiert. In dem Lehrgespräch zwischen Mutter und Tochter in der *Winsbeckin* benennt erstere die Gefahr und warnt:

wer weiz nû, wâ die stæten sint?	Wer weiß jetzt, wo die zuverlässigen Männer sind?
Vil missewendic sint die man,	Die Männer sind sehr tadelnswert,
si tragent helekäppel an.	sie tragen Tarnkappen.
Zu guoten wîben süeziu wort	Die meisten vermögen anständigen Frauen gute
diu meiste menge sprechen kann,	Komplimente zu machen, doch meistens nicht ohn
doch mêrenthalp niht âne schaden.	Nachteile.
(Str. 17,3-8)	

Die Tochter beruhigt ihre Mutter mit der Versicherung:

mich vâhet niht ir wehselsite.	Ihre Unbeständigkeit nimmt mich nicht gefangen.
Mîn stætez herze ich wol erbite,	Ich bitte mein beständiges Herz, daß es mich
daz ez mich vride vor ir untât.	vor ihrem schlechten (Rede-)Verhalten schützt.
Ich vürhte niht ir spæhen snite:	Ich fürchte ihre verschlagenen Reden nicht:
die suln mich vinden in der aht,	sie werden mich so aufmerksam finden, daß mich
daz mich iht triege ir lôsiu rede.	ihre schmeichlerische Rede nicht betrügen kann.
(Str.18,4-9)	

Die Minnesänger des 13. Jahrhunderts legen der Frau im Minnegespräch diesen Vorwurf der betrügerischen Rede direkt in den Mund:

Minnegespräche

ir waenet lîhte toeren mich, ir sint ein lügenaere. (...)	ihr glaubt, mich auf leichte Weise zu betrügen, ihr seid ein Lügner. (...)
si sprach: 'daz ist rehte erlogen: / ir hânt enunt her dâ mite vil manic wîp betrogen'.	sie sagte: 'das ist gewiß gelogen: ihr habt bisher damit sehr viele Frauen betrogen'.
(Ulrich von Winterstetten, XI 2,2f. u. 5,9f.), oder:	
ich hân gesworn daz ich vor lôser manne tucke mich behüete.	ich habe geschworen, daß ich mich vor der Arglist heuchlerischer Männer hüte.
(Ulrich von Singenberg, 5, 24)	

Im Dialoglied des 13. Jahrhunderts geben solche Äußerungen oft den Grund der Ablehnung männlicher Werbung durch die Frau an; die daraus folgende Weigerung, das Liebesgespräch fortzusetzen, bringt den werbenden Mann nun ebenfalls in eine schwierige Lage. Walther von der Vogelweide hat das Problem – wie so oft – auf den Punkt gebracht. Er könne sich seiner Dame deshalb nicht als ehrlicher Liebhaber präsentieren *sît man valscher minne mit so süezen worten gert, / daz ein wîp niht wizzen mac / wer si meine.* Deshalb verflucht er denjenigen, *der diu wîp von êrst betrouc, / der hât beide an mannen und an wîben misse varn* (L 14,25 f. u. 30 f.). Eine unmittelbare Folge ist, daß nun die Topik der Wahrheitsbeteuerungen in der männlichen Werbungsrede wichtig wird und neben der Betonung der *triuwe* und der *staete* des Dienstes in den Liedern einen bevorzugten Platz einnimmt.

Besonders Thomasin von Zerklaere, dem wir ein ausführliches Kapitel Minnelehre in deutscher Sprache verdanken, hat diese Problematik von allen Seiten beleuchtet. Er referiert in seinem *Welschen Gast* aus einem von ihm früher verfaßten Buch in romanischer Sprache (es ist verloren) Anleitungen für eine Dame, die sich vor *valschen minnern* schützen möchte. Mit Blick auf die galante Konversation, *schoene rede* (840), heißt es auch bei ihm, daß die Frau zu allererst die Fähigkeit zur *discretio* entwickeln muß, so daß sie in der Lage ist, personen- und situationsadäquat zu reagieren.

ein vrouwe sol haben die sinne, swer mit ir ret von minne, si sol halt haben den muot, swaz man ret übel ode guot,	Eine Dame soll folgende Fähigkeiten haben: Sie soll entschlossen sein, jedem der mit ihr über Minne redet – was auch immer man Schlechtes oder Gutes spricht –, auf der Stelle zu antworten,

daz si antwurte zuo der vrist	je nachdem wie der Mann einzuschätzen ist und wie
dar nâch unde der man ist	er geworben hat; handelt sie so, dann ist die
und dar nâch und er habe gegert,	Dame und der Mann zufriedengestellt.
sô ist diu vrouwe und er gewert.	
(828-836)	

Thomasin erklärt später auch, warum die Dame ein Sensorium für die Beurteilung der männlichen Liebesrede entwickeln sollte. Der *arge, valsche* Mann (1482) wirbt nämlich bevorzugt bei Frauen, die leicht durch Bitten und Flehen zu beeindrucken sind; hat er leichtes Spiel und schnellen Erfolg, dann wird er das publik machen und seine Partnerin in Verruf bringen (1483-1493). Deshalb ist es wichtig, daß die Frau einen tugendhaften, aufrichtigen Verehrer unter ihren Standesgenossen (1591) findet, der kein *rumaere* (1599) ist. Heinrich von Morungen rühmt deshalb unter den besonderen Vorzügen seiner Dame, daß sie nur vorbildliche Gesprächspartner hat:

Dîne redegesellen	Deine Gesprächspartner besitzen
die sint, swie wir wellen,	– ganz wie wir es wünschen –
guoter worte und guoter site.	die richtige Redeweise und höfischen Anstand.
Dâ bist dû getiuret mite	Der Umgang mit ihnen erhöht dein Ansehen.
(MF 146,23ff.)	

Bei den Ratschlägen zur Frauenrede in der didaktischen Literatur fällt im übrigen auf, daß sie häufig im Zusammenhang mit Anweisungen zur Affektzügelung[12] vorgetragen und an das tugendhafte Handeln gekoppelt werden.

Swâ ein vrouwe reht tuot,	Wo auch immer eine Frau richtig handelt:
ist ir gebaerde niht guot	sind ihre Gebärden und ihre
und ist ouch niht ir rede schône,	Redeweise nicht vorbildlich, dann
ir guot getât ist âne krône,	fehlt ihrer guten Tat der krönende Schmuck.
wan schoene gebaerde und rede guot	Denn anmutige Gebärden und angemessene
die kroenent daz ein vrouwe tuot.	Redeweise schmückt das, was eine Frau tut.
Ich sagiu daz ir guot getât	Ich sage euch, daß ihre gute Tat auch nicht
mac ouch nimmer wesen stât,	Bestand haben kann, wenn sie sich
kann si niht gebären wol	nicht gut zu benehmen weiß und das
und reden daz si reden sol.	spricht, was ihr zu sprechen gebührt.
(*Thomasin, Welscher Gast* 199-208)	

Ganz ähnlich belehrt in der *Winsbeckin* die Mutter ihre Tochter:

den êre gerndan soltû geben	Diejenigen, die nach Ehre streben, denen
ze rehte dînen werden gruoz	sollst du zu recht deinen freundlichen Gruß zukommen
(...)	lassen. (...)

schiuz wilder blicke niht ze vil	Blicke nicht zu forsch umher,
da lôse merker	dort wo hinterhältige Aufpasser
bî dir sîn. (...)	in deiner Nähe sind. (...)
Sint wîsiu wort den werken bî,	Begleiten vernünftige Reden die Taten, so ist
sô ensint die sinne niht betrogen:	die Gesinnung aufrichtig: wenn die Reden
sint aber si guoter werke vrî,	aber nicht von gutem Handeln begleitet werden,
sô sint diu wîsen wort gelogen.	dann sind kluge Reden erlogen.
(Str.5,5-10 und 9,1-4)	

Und die Tochter stimmt zu:

Sint mîniu wort wîs âne werc,	Folgen meinen klugen Worten keine Taten,
des lobe ich niht: ez ist enwiht.	das lobe ich nicht: das ist ohne Wert.
(...)	(...)
lêre mich nâch êren leben,	Lehre mich nach dem Gebot der Ehre
gebâren unde sprechen eben,	zu leben, mich angemessen zu verhalten und
daz ich den wîsen wol	zu sprechen, auf daß ich den Verständigen gut
behage (Str.10,1-2 und 12,4-6)	gefalle.

Die *guote rede* wird von einzelnen Autoren noch näher bestimmt. So soll z.B. die höfisch erzogene Frau nicht *baltlîche* (d.h. nicht kühn und unbedacht) sprechen; sie soll sich vor *vrîen worten* 'offenherziger Rede' und vor dem Schelten hüten.[13] Erwünscht sind *senfte sprüche* und *minneclîchiu wort* (weitere Belege bei Willms 1990: 23 u. 273f.) Den Eindruck, den eine angenehme und angemessene Frauenrede auf den liebenden Mann haben kann, beschreibt wiederum Heinrich von Morungen in topischer Weise.

Swenne ich sie hoere sprechen,	Immer, wenn ich sie reden höre,
sô ist mir alse wol,	tut mir das so gut,
daz ich gesitze	daß ich gänzlich ohne Verstand
vil gar âne witze	(berauscht) dasitze,
non weiz, war ich sol.	und nicht weiß, wohin ich soll.
(MF 141, 32ff.)	

Schließlich greife ich unter den Anweisungen zum Gesprächsverhalten der Frau nur noch einen besonders interessanten, weil zeittypischen Aspekt heraus: Thomasin empfiehlt der höfisch gebildeten Dame, sie möge im Gespräch mit dem Mann den Eindruck vermeiden, sie gebe den Ton an, indem sie mit ihren geistigen und sprachlichen Fähigkeiten brilliert und so den Eindruck erwecken könnte, daß sie den Mann dominieren wolle. Im Gegensatz zum *hövischen* Mann, der seine Fähigkeiten und Geschicklichkeiten gerade auch im galanten Dialog demonstrativ entfalten soll, empfiehlt sich für die Frau das gegensätzliche Verhalten, denn *einvalt stêt den vrouwen wol* (849). Wir werden nicht fehlgehen, diese Empfehlung nicht nur als Ausfluß der patriarchalischen Gesellschaftsordnung zu interpretieren, sondern sie auch als geschickte Strategie weiblicher Selbstdarstellung[14] und Anweisung zur Konfliktvermeidung anzusehen, die der vorgeblich einfältigen Frau viele Möglichkeiten der Abwehr und des Rückzugs bei aggressiver männlicher Werbung eröffnet.

Fast alle bisher zusammengetragenen Gebote und Verbote für die Liebesrede von Mann und Frau, die auf die Existenz einer regelgeleiteten galanten Konversation zumindest in der Vorstellung von Lehrdichtern und Minnesängern schließen lassen, kann man in dem wohl bekanntesten Dialoglied aus *Minnesangs Frühling* aufdecken. In diesem Lied von Albrecht von Johansdorf (MF 93, 12),[15] einem galanten Zwiegespräch zwischen werbendem Sänger und seiner Dame in sieben Strophen, sind die Gesprächsanteile je Strophe (mit Ausnahme von Strophe 1, die mit einer epischen Situationsbeschreibung beginnt) im Vers-Verhältnis 2/2/1/1 symmetrisch auf Frau und Mann verteilt. Vor der Gesprächseröffnung erzählt der Mann in der ersten Strophe, daß er die verehrte Frau *âne huote* (I,1), d.h. ohne Aufsicht angetroffen habe, was bedeutet, daß sich eine ebenso außergewöhnliche wie günstige Gelegenheit für ein Gespräch mit dem Thema Liebe ergibt. Die Frau, die im gesamten Dialog bevorrechtigte Sprecherin ist, verlangt denn auch umgehend Auskunft vom Mann über den Grund dieser ungewöhnlichen Annäherung (Aufhebung der Distanzschranke). Der Metadiskurs über die Sprechsituation zwingt den Mann in der zweiten Strophe zum Eingeständnis seines Beweggrundes: Er klagt über Liebeskummer. Die Frau reagiert in der Gegenrede mit Abwehr: Der Mann handle ungebührlich und unbedacht (*ir tumper*, II,3), wenn er seine Liebesklage zum Gesprächsthema mache. Auf seine Versicherung hin, er sei außerstande, anders zu handeln, weist sie ihn spielerisch-ironisch ab. Das dialogische Spiel mit Rede und Gegenrede wiederholt sich in der dritten Strophe, in der am Ende die Frau etwas von ihrer Haltung entschiedener Abweisung abrückt. Der Mann reagiert darauf in der vierten Strophe sofort mit dem üblichen Mittel der Werbung im Minnesang, dem Schönheitspreis (*iuwer schoene* IV,1). Die Frau bezeichnet dies als galante Schmeichelei (*iuwer süezen doene* IV,3), deren Ziel es sei, ihre Standhaftigkeit zu erschüttern. Gäbe sie nach, dann würde das sein Ansehen (*êre*) steigern, ihr aber bliebe der Spott (IV,6). Auf sein erneutes Bitten und seine Liebesversicherung in der fünften Strophe reagiert sie mit ironischer Abwehr seiner praktizierten Kunst des Komplimentemachens (*wortel boln* V,4). Worauf er, – vielleicht verunsichert – fragt, ob sie seine galante Rede für schlecht halte (*dunket iu mîn rede niht guot?*, V,5)? Die Antwort ist zweideutig und deutet die Lösung, die in diesem Konflikt in der letzten Strophe angeboten wird, schon an. Die Dame gibt dem unerschütterlich werbenden

Mann schließlich doch ein Lohnversprechen; freilich nicht im Sinne der Erfüllung seines Liebesbegehrens, sondern durch die Verschiebung des Lohns für seinen Minnedienst auf die unverfängliche, ideelle Ebene der *werdekeit* und des *hohen muots* (VII,6). Mit diesem geschickten Ausweichmanöver, mit dem die Frau dem auf körperlichen Lohn fixierten Mann die spirituelle Seite der Frauenverehrung in Erinnerung ruft, erhält sich die Dame ihren Verehrer wie ihren guten Ruf gleichermaßen. Zwei Minnesänger des 13. Jahrhunderts, Ulrich von Singenberg (Lied 5) und Ulrich von Winterstetten (Lied XI) haben die hier aufgezeigte Thematik in eigenen Dialogliedern erneut durchgespielt und die Kontroverse über die Zulässigkeit galanter Werbung und ihre Zurückweisung als lügenhafte Schmeichelei noch verschärft.

Im ersten Drittel des 13. Jahrhunderts erscheint schließlich das Bildthema *Conversation galante* auch "im Kontext des ikonographischen Standardrepertoires der Minnedarstellungen in der Buchmalerei und Elfenbeinschnitzerei" (Müller 1996: 105), zuerst in Frankreich, dann auch in Deutschland. Angeregt werden diese Dialogbilder besonders durch Illustrationen der Minnegespräche in der Epik, einem Textbereich, der in dieser Untersuchung ausgespart wurde, aber als weiterer Beleg für regelgeleitetes Sprechverhalten im Minnegespräch herangezogen werden könnte.[16]

Anmerkungen

1 Andreas Capellanus, De amore, ed. Trojel 1964, lib I, Cap. VI, 14 u. 195 ff.
2 Außer dem *Heimlichen Boten* werden die *Winsbeckischen Gedichte*, der *Deutsche Cato*, vor allem aber Teile aus dem ersten Buch von *Thomasins von Zerklaere, Welschen Gast* berücksichtigt.
3 Dialogisches Sprechen ist in den drei Liedarten in unterschiedlicher Weise konkretisiert. Beim Wechsel orientiert sich der Sprecher zwar an seinem Partner und oft auch an der Partnerrede, diese wird aber von Mann und Frau monologisch und in der 3. Person dargeboten. Die dadurch bewirkte Distanziertheit des Sprechens macht den Hauptunterschied zum Dialoglied aus. Vgl. dazu Scholz (1989). Zum Partnerverhältnis und zur Sprechsituation im hier aus Raumgründen nicht analysierten Tagelied vgl. Einleitung und Kommentar der Tagelieder-Ausgabe von Backes 1992.
4 Städtler (1989: 77). Die Verfasserin zeigt darüber hinaus, "daß in der altprovenzalischen Didaxe für adlige Frauen die wohlgesetzte Rede bereits in der ersten Hälfte des 12. Jahrhunderts einen zentralen Platz einnimmt", und "eine gelungene Unterhaltung ... der erste Schritt auf dem Weg zu einem Liebesverhältnis" ist.
5 Vgl. ebenso Lied XII, Str.1 u. 2 in der Ausgabe Schweikle (1986) und die Verse L 53,31-34 und L 41,25-28 von Walther von der Vogelweide. Reinmar formuliert übrigens auch die

Gegenposition, wenn er etwa eine ihm in der galanten Gesprächskunst überlegenen Konkurrenten beneidet: *Ich weiz manigen guoten man,/an dem ich nîde, daz sie in sô gerne siht,/durch daz er wol sprechen kann.* 'Ich kenne manchen höfisch-gebildeten Mann, den ich darum beneide, daß sie ihn wegen seiner galanten Gesprächskunst gerne erblickt'. (Lied L II 4,1-3 in *Des Minnesangs Frühling* 1988, S. 387)

6 *Der heimliche Bote.* 1920, S. 30-32, V.17 u. 26. Mhd. *list* bedeutet hier ebenso Klugheit wie Kunstfertigkeit in der Werbungsrede.

7 Vgl. die zahlreichen Belege aus Lyrik und Epik bei Willms 1990: 152ff.

8 "Der weitaus größte Teil aller Lieder aus *Minnesangs Frühling*, in denen die Haltung der Frau überhaupt deutlich wird, ist also gekennzeichnet durch die *eine* Gemeinsamkeit: den Einhalt der Distanz zwischen dem Mann und der Frau." (Willms 1990: 231)

9 Die Bitte um Lohn wird besonders im Kontext der Gattungen wie Pastourelle, Tagelied, Mädchen- oder Erntelied auch als Aufforderung zum Koitus verstanden. Vgl. Zeyen (1996).

10 Im berühmten Lindenlied Walthers von der Vogelweide sagt die Frau: *Daz er bî mir laege, /wesse ez iemen /(nu enwelle got!), so schamt ich mich.* (L 40,10f.)

11 Bei Reinmar äußert die Frau über den Sänger, der wie *keiner sprach sô wol ... von wîben,* daß dennoch *sîn spaehe rede in sol lützel wider mich vervâhen* (MF 187,22f. u. 24f.).

12 Zur Regulierung von Gestik und Mimik beim Reden vgl. z.B. folgende Anweisungen: *Kein juncfrowe sol /zeigen mit den henden niht, /ob ir ze reden iht geschiht. / sie sol ir ougen unde ir houbet / stille haben, daz geloubet.* 'Keine junge adlige Dame soll mit den Händen gestikulieren, wenn sie redet. Sie soll ihre Augen und ihren Kopf still halten, glaubt mir das'. (*Deutscher Cato*, S. 134, V. 206-210). Elias (1969) ging von solchen Beispielen aus, um zu zeigen, wie eng die Entstehung der Troubadour- und Minnelyrik mit der Entwicklung courtoiser Umgangsformen verknüpft ist. Im Kapitel "Zur Soziogenese des Minnesangs und der courtoisen Umgangsformen" (II, 88-122) geht es ihm weniger um die neue Art des Gesprächsverhaltens zwischen Mann und Frau als vielmehr um den allgemeinen zivilisatorischen Aspekt des Minnesangs. Das ist deshalb erstaunlich, weil er sich selbst die Frage stellt: "Warum veränderte sich die Art, in der sich die Menschen auszudrücken suchten?" (112); es dann aber dabei beläßt, für den Minnesang die "Fragerichtung" angegeben zu haben (113). Über die Normen des Sprechverhaltens, die Disziplinierung des Sprechens und Elias' Zivilisationstheorie vgl. Bogner (1997: 47-54).

13 *Ein frowe sol niht frevellih / schallen, daz stât fröwlich* 'Eine Dame soll nicht ausgelassen schreien, lärmen oder prahlen; das zu vermeiden, entspricht weiblichem Verhalten'. (*Deutscher Cato*, S. 135, V. 221/22).

14 Am Rande sei hier erwähnt, daß in den Anweisungen für die moderne Frau zur richtigen, erfolgreichen Partnersuche ähnliche Regeln empfohlen werden. Vgl. Fein/Schneider (1995: 19).

Minnegespräche   185

15 Abdruck des Liedes mit Übersetzung bei Schweikle (1993: 343-345). Text und Interpretation, der ich mich allerdings nicht anschließen kann, auch bei Willms (1990: 21-25).

16 Die Gesprächstypen sind in der Epik teilweise anders zu differenzieren als in der Lyrik, grundsätzlich lassen sich aber auch hier die oben aufgezeigten Gebote und Verbote für das Redeverhalten von Mann und Frau nachweisen.

Quellen und Textausgaben

Capellanus, Andreas
    1964   *De amore: libri tres*. Rec. Emil Trojel (ed.). München: Eidos.
Der Deutsche Cato
    1852   hg. von Friedrich Zarncke. Leipzig: Wigand.
Deutsche Liederdichter des 13. Jahrhunderts
    1952   hg. von Carl von Kraus. Bd.1. Tübingen. 2. Aufl. durchges. v. Gisela Kornrumpf. Tübingen 1978: Niemeyer.
Fridankes Bescheidenheit
    1872   hg. v. Heinrich Ernst Bezzenberger. Halle: Verlag d. Buchhandlung des Waisenhauses.
Friedrich von Sonnenburg, Sprüche
    1879   hg. von Achim Masser. (Altdeutsche Textbibliothek 86). Tübingen: Niemeyer.
Der heimliche Bote
    1909   In: Heinrich Meyer-Benfey (Hg.). *Mittelhochdeutsche Übungsstücke*. Halle/S.: Niemeyer, 30-32.
Heinrich von Melk, Von des todes gehugde. Mahnrede über den Tod.
    1994   Mittelhochdeutsch/Neuhochdeutsch. Hg. von Thomas Bein u.a. Stuttgart: Reclam.
Des Minnesangs Frühling
    1988   unter Benutzung der Ausgaben von Karl Lachmann und Moriz Haupt, Friedrich Vogt und Carl von Kraus bearbeitet von Hugo Moser und Helmut Tervooren. Bd. 1, Texte, 38. Aufl. Stuttgart: Hirzel.
Mittelhochdeutsche Minnelyrik I. Frühe Minnelyrik. Texte und Übertragungen, Einführung und Kommentar
    1993   hg. von Günter Schweikle. Stuttgart. Weimar: Metzler.
Reinmar. Lieder. Nach der Weingartner Liederhandschrift (B).
    1986   Mittelhochdeutsch/Neuhochdeutsch. Hg. von Günter Schweikle. Stuttgart: Reclam.

Die Schweizer Minnesänger
1990   nach d. Ausg. v. Karl Bartsch neu bearb. u. hg. v. Max Schiendorfer, Bd. 1: Texte, Tübingen: Niemeyer.

Tagelieder des deutschen Mittelalters
1992   Mittelhochdeutsch/Neuhochdeutsch. Hg. v. Martina Backes, Stuttgart: Reclam.

Thomasin von Zerklaere, Der welsche Gast
1852   hg. v. Heinrich Rückert. Quedlinburg/Leipzig. Nachdruck Berlin 1965: de Gruyter.

Die Gedichte Walthers von der Vogelweide
1965   hg. von Karl Lachmann. 13., aufgrund der 10. v. Carl von Kraus bearbeiteten Ausg. neu hg. v. Hugo Kuhn. Berlin: de Gruyter.

Winsbeckische Gedichte nebst Tirol und Fridebrant
1962   hg. von Albert Leitzmann, 3. Aufl. v. Ingo Reiffenstein (Altdeutsche Textbibliothek 9) Tübingen: Niemeyer.

Forschungsliteratur

Beetz, Manfred
1990   *Frühmoderne Höflichkeit. Komplimentierkunst und Gesellschaftsrituale im altdeutschen Sprachraum*. Stuttgart: Metzler.

Bogner, Ralf Georg
1997   *Die Bezähmung der Zunge. Literatur und Disziplinierung der Alltagskommunikation in der frühen Neuzeit*. (Frühe Neuzeit 31). Tübingen: Niemeyer.

Brown, Penelope und Stephen Levinson
1987   *Politeness. Some Universals in Language Usage*. (Studies in Interactional Sociolinguistics 4). Cambridge: University Press.

Eikelmann, Manfred
1996   wie sprach sie dô? war umbe redte ich dô niht mê? Zu Form und Sinngehalt narrativer Elemente in der Minnekanzone. In: Michael Schilling und Peter Strohschneider (Hg.). *Wechselspiele. Kommunikationsformen und Gattungsinterferenzen mittelhochdeutscher Lyrik*. (Germanisch-romanische Monatsschrift, Beiheft 13). Heidelberg: Winter, 19-42.

Eisbrenner, Axel
1995   *Minne, diu der werlde ir vröude mêret. Untersuchungen zum Handlungsaufbau und zur Rollengestaltung in ausgewählten Werbungsliedern aus 'Des Minnesangs Frühling'*. (Helfant Studien 10). Stuttgart: Helfant Edition.

Elias, Norbert
   1969   Über den Prozess der Zivilisation. Soziogenetische und psychogenetische Untersuchungen. Zweiter Band. Zweite Aufl. Bern, München: Francke.
Fein, Ellen and Sherrie Schneider
   1995   The Rules. Time-tested Secrets for Capturing the Heart of Mr. Right. London: Thorsons.
Franck, Dorothea
   1980   Grammatik und Konversation. (Monographien Linguistik und Kommunikationswissenschaft 46). Kronberg: Scriptor.
Hübner, Gert
   1996   Frauenpreis. Studien zur Funktion der laudativen Rede in der mittelhochdeutschen Minnekanzone. 2 Bde (Saecula Spiritalia 34/35). Baden-Baden: Koerner.
Hundsnurscher, Franz
   1994   Lügen – auch eine Form sprachlichen Handelns. In: D. V. Halwachs, Chr. Penzinger, I. Stütz (Hg.). Sprache, Onomatopöie, Rhetorik, Namen, Idiomatik, Grammatik. Festschrift für K. Sornig (Grazer Linguistische Monographien 11). Graz: Institut für Sprachwissenschaft der Universität Graz, 97-113.
Kasten, Ingrid
   1989   Das Dialoglied bei Walther von der Vogelweide. In: J. D. Müller und Franz Josef Worstbrock (Hg.), Walther von der Vogelweide, Hamburger Kolloquium 1988, Stuttgart: Hirzel, 81-93.
Kraus, Carl von
   1930   Unsere älteste Lyrik. München: Oldenbourg.
Montandon, Alain (Hg.)
   1991   Über die deutsche Höflichkeit. Entwicklung der Kommunikationsvorstellungen in den Schriften über Umgangsformen in den deutschsprachigen Ländern. Bern/Berlin: Lang.
Müller, Markus
   1996   Minnebilder. Französische Minnedarstellungen des 13. und 14. Jahrhunderts. (Pictura et poesis 7). Köln: Böhlau.
Plummer, John F. (ed.)
   1981   Vox feminae: Studies in Medieval Woman's Song. (Studies in Medieval Culture 15). Kalamazoo: Medieval Institute Publications.
Schnell, Rüdiger
   1985   Causa amoris. Liebeskonzeption und Liebesdarstellung in der mittelalterlichen Literatur. (Bibliotheca Germanica 27). Bern/München: Francke.

Scholz, Manfred Günter
  1989   Zu Stil und Typologie des mittelhochdeutschen Wechsels. *Jahrbuch für Internationale Germanistik* 21: 60-92.
Städtler, Katharina
  1989   Schule der Frauen. Altprovenzalische Liebeslehren, Lehrgedichte und Konversationsregeln für Mädchen und Frauen: Vorstufen einer weiblichen Ästhetik des Mittelalters? In: Wolfgang Haubrichs (Hg.). *Konzepte der Liebe im Mittelalter, Zeitschrift für Literaturwissenschaft und Linguistik* 19: 75-91.
Stevens, Adrian
  1983   Dîn wol redender munt: Reinmar der Alte als Minnesänger. In: Helmut Birkhan (Hg.). *Minnesang in Österreich* (Wiener Arbeiten zur germanistischen Altertumskunde und Philologie 24) Wien: Halosar 176-196.
Watts, Richard, Sachiko Ide und Konrad Ehlich (eds.)
  1992   *Politeness in Language. Studies in its History, Theory and Practice.* Berlin/New York: Mouton de Gruyter.
Willms, Eva
  1990   *Liebesleid und Sangeslust. Untersuchungen zur deutschen Liebeslyrik des späten 12. und frühen 13. Jahrhunderts.* (Münchner Texte und Untersuchungen zur deutschen Literatur des Mittelalters 94) München/Zürich: Artemis.
Zeyen, Stefan
  1996   *Daz tet der liebe dorn. Erotische Metaphorik in der deutschsprachigen Lyrik des 12. – 14. Jahrhunderts.* (Item mediävistische Studien 5). Essen: Item.

On the Fringes of Interaction
The Dawn-Song as a "Linguistic Routine" of Parting

Thomas Honegger
University of Zurich

1. Introduction

The often difficult and emotionally painful act of taking leave of a beloved person has been the subject of many a poem. In the context of medieval courtly love poetry, this very theme gave rise to a lyrical genre of its own in the 12th century: the alba, aubade or dawn song. The genre enjoyed its greatest popularity not in its "homelands" (i.e. southern and, later, northern France), but in the neighbouring German-speaking countries. We possess over a hundred Middle High German "tageliet", while there are hardly more than a dozen Old Provençal and Old French dawn songs extant.[1] English dawn song poems are even rarer, though the French-speaking nobility of England was most likely familiar with the French and Provençal ones. However, we have very little concrete evidence of this. Apart from a few allusive lines in Middle English poetry, no traces of English dawn songs, let alone entire poems, dating from before the late fourteenth century have survived.[2] It must, therefore, remain an open question whether any Middle English dawn song lyrics were composed and then lost, or whether the genre remained productive only in French and was received in England in this form. In any case, Chaucer (c. 1340-1400) is the first courtly poet writing in the English vernacular whom we know to have made significant use of the dawn song tradition. Yet, he did not compose independent dawn song poems but, like his successors, incorporated dawn song sequences into his longer works.[3] Both dawn song passages to be discussed in this paper, i.e. the one by Chaucer from *Troilus and Criseyde* (III, 1415-1533) and the one by Shakespeare from *Romeo and Juliet* (III, v, 1-59), differ conspicuously in this repect from their Old French, Provençal and Middle High German counterparts. Continental dawn songs primarily constitute a sub-genre of the (courtly) love lyric tradition and are, as a rule, "stand-alone" poems; i.e., they do not refer to a preceding or following text. They are not concerned with the individualizing characterization of knight and lady, but focus exclusively on the presentation of a "typical" situation, namely the parting of the lovers at dawn. Chaucer's and Shakespeare's passages, however, are intimately linked to the overall action of the poem and play, respectively, and to the characterization of their protagonists. The significant feature of these two dawn song passages, which separates them from the normal dawn song lyric, is that, because they occur within the framework of a larger literary work, they can be treated in the same way as any other passage of dialogue, i.e. they are, as literary depictions of a routine of parting, susceptible of conversational analysis.

The influence of the (continental?) dawn song tradition on Chaucer, and also on Shakespeare, is difficult to establish. Chaucer's source text, Boccaccio's *Il Filostrato*, already contains a passage that could be classified as a dawn song (*Il Filostrato*, canto III), which Chaucer then expanded and altered. Shakespeare's source, Brooke's *Romeus and Juliet*, by contrast, features no such model, so that the presentation, and elaboration, of the given situation (parting at dawn) as a dawn song must be seen as Shakespeare's original contribution.

Shakespeare is also innovative in making use of the dawn song for the parting of the newly-wed husband and wife (Romeo and Juliet), since, so far, the dawn song genre has been used predominantly in the context of adulterous, or at least illicit relationships. Shakespeare, therefore, provides an example of those changes that affected the genre with the decline of courtly culture and the rise of the middle class. In the course of this development, dawn songs did not remain limited to the context of courtly love, but were adapted to the new cultural environment.[4] Thus, the most frequent reason for the separation of the two courtly lovers, which is the danger of their being discovered by the jealous husband (the *gilos* in the Old Provençal dawn songs), is no longer valid and must be replaced by new ones. Non-courtly lovers, including modern ones, often see themselves forced to separate owing to more trivial circumstances, e.g. the constraints imposed by the need to earn one's living. This discrepancy between the demands of a bourgeois society and the ideals of "courtly love" finds explicit expression in John Donne's (1573-1631) "dawn song poem" *Break of Day* (Smith 1973: 45-46):

[woman speaking]
[...]
Must businesse thee from hence remove?
Oh, that's the worst disease of love,
The poor, the foul, the false, love can
Admit, but not the busied man.
He which hath business, and makes love, doth do
Such wrong, as when a maryed man doth woo.

Yet, even when no business matter drives modern man from the embrace of his beloved, there is a definite lack of common "savoir faire" in matters of amorous goodbyes. Modern books of etiquette may give fairly direct and helpful advice in matters amorous (e.g. Leisi and Leisi 1992: 146-151 and Sucher 1996: 128f., 194, 251). However, more often than not they omit leavetaking as the last stage of a nightly love-encounter. Similarly, movies and novels circumnavigate the problem by letting the man "slink away" in the early morning while the woman is still sound asleep. Of course, it depends on the socio-cultural system whether or not one has some sort of routinized speech behaviour available for a specific situation;[5] medieval western courtly culture obviously had some routinized speech behaviour for the recurrent situation of "taking leave after a night of love" (at least in literary works).[6] Our modern culture, however, seems to do without such a consciously cultivated routine - both in literature and reality.

Thus, it is not surprising that one finds lovers who, after a night of passion and having missed the opportunity to "slink away", know no better than to read their newspaper over a lovingly prepared breakfast, as Tannen (1990: 85) reports.

The lack of such a generally accepted modern "routine of parting" contrasts negatively with the situation in medieval times. There, dawn songs not only perform an important function within the context of courtly love, but they also meet, to a high degree, the demands made on the closing phase of an interaction. Ideally, such a closing phase: " [...] assuages potential feelings of rejection. [...] [Its] chief function [...] seems to be to announce a continuing provisional consensus for future interactions" (Laver 1975: 232-233). And this is exactly what dawn songs do: they re-establish the "normal" social interactional mode by signalling the end of the physical love interaction and by leading back to the more distanced and hierarchically structured courtly love setting.

In the following discussion, I will first present the basic structure of the dawn song and then go on to analyse its function within the framework of courtly love; finally, I will discuss two early dialogic English dawn song passages (by Chaucer and Shakespeare) and, taking the lovers' dialogues as (literary) representations of conversations, examine how they are affected by the selection of this form.

2. The Structure of Medieval Dawn Songs

The dawn song, in contrast to the poems of the *hôhe minne*, celebrates the (physical) fulfilment of the love-relationship between lady and knightly lover. Though most such poems present only the situation towards the end of the night, we do have a few lyrics that provide us with the entire interaction.[7] This starts with the secretive meeting of the lovers at dusk,[8] the joys of the night spent together, described mostly in retrospect as part of the dawn song, and the final stage of separation at dawn in the dawn song proper. The following depiction illustrates the situation.

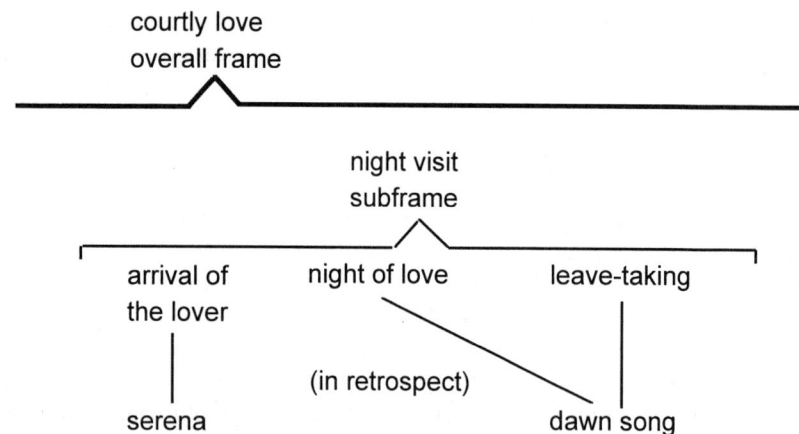

In terms of conversational analysis, we can classify the entire nocturnal love interaction, within the overall frame of courtly love, as the "night visit subframe". The dawn song, then, is an "activity type"[9] found towards the end of the night visit sequence. It typically consists of the lament of one of the lovers about the watchman's announcement of dawn or of a reproachful address to the sun, on how quickly the night has passed and, if the male lover is speaking, that he is loath to leave the beloved lady. The lady may join in with this lament and express her regret at the impending separation. The two lovers successfully try to forget the separation at hand by once more dedicating themselves to love, or they reassure each other of their love by other means and put off the moment of leave-taking for as long as possible. The leave-taking itself, then, often goes hand-in-hand with a reference to the acute danger to the lady's reputation and to the knightly lover's life – usually expressed by the person not directly affected. Furthermore, we often find references to future meetings and exchanges of farewells. A simplified listing of the typical dawn song features might look as follows:[10]

I   one of the lovers wakes up
II   reference is made to signs which herald the coming of dawn and thus implicitly refer to the lover's impending departure
III   the lovers lament the impending departure of the man
IV   they give verbal or nonverbal (kisses, embrace, lovemaking) mutual reassurance of love
V   reference is made to the impending danger either to the lady's reputation or to her lover's life
VI   reference is made to future meetings
VII   they exchange farewells
VIII   the knightly lover departs

The exact number and sequence of these features may vary, but this rough scheme will prove sufficient for our purpose. The important point is that dawn songs usually depict the emotionally most highly charged and most dangerous phase of the night visit. The two lovers are subject to mounting pressure from the outside world. They may counter this pressure for a while, yet finally have to yield to the demands of safety and break up their intimate union. Dawn songs help them to handle this situation.

3.   The Function of Dawn Songs

What, then, is the specific function of the dawn song within the context of courtly love? In order to answer this question, a few words about "courtly love interaction" in general are necessary. The model courtly lady of the early Provençal lyrics is the silent, unattainable "domna". The poet venerates her from a distance. She is the object of the poet's endeavours in matters of courtly love and, for social as well as poetical reasons, she has to remain unattainable.[11] Thus, the prototypical "courtly love" scenario usually does without much interaction between the two main protagonists, and the venerated lady rarely appears as a personality (cf. Dodd 1913: 8). Not so in the dawn song. As Sigal (1996: x) points out, the alba poets introduced two important new elements. First, they gave a voice to the hitherto mute and passive lady; second, they stressed the equality of the two lovers (Sigal 1996: 94, 101 and 105). This means that, even though the alba lady occupies a hierarchically higher position than her lover, they find themselves on an equal level "*as a result* [...] of their sexual union" (Sigal 1996: 101). The coming of dawn is, therefore, not only an unwelcome intrusion of the outer world into the private world of the lovers, but it also puts an end to the suspension of hierarchical inequality. The privacy of the night has allowed them to shut out the outer world for the time being, to ignore differences in status and rank, and to indulge in an amorous equality which cannot be transferred to everyday reality. The coming of day puts an end to this mode of interaction and forces them to re-enter the superordinate, hierarchically structured system of courtly love, in which the relationship between lady and knightly lover (vassal) mirrors the feudal relation between lord and vassal. It must be stressed that the lovers' intimacy does not affect their "official courtly relationship". The problem they see themselves confronted with at the end of the night is that of re-establishing their former identities as "courtly lovers", i.e. lady and "vassal". In this context, the dawn song assumes the function of a "rite of passage" which facilitates the transition from the equality of the night of love back to the hierarchical structure of courtly society. The woman again becomes the superior courtly lady, and the man again the faithful courtly servant. Thus, dawn songs function as analeptic rites, i.e. they are used "to emphasize the resumption of identities appropriate to the broader social macrocosm outside and largely independent of the encounter and its events" (Laver 1975: 235).

Are there, linguistically speaking, reasons to consider dawns songs as literary representations of "routines"? Of course, dawn songs are more elaborate, longer and far less formalized than, for example, routines such as greetings and farewells. Yet, they contain enough repetitive elements to allow us to see them as typified speech behaviour – and thus meet, at least to some degree, the criterion of "form". More important, however, is the fact that they share important functional characteristics with routines.[12] Thus, Coulmas' (1981: 12) general statement that routines "have a function in sustaining orderliness in conversation and in securing a smooth flow of interaction" is equally valid for dawn songs in particular.

The other point which Sigal mentions, namely that the formerly silent courtly lady is given a voice of her own by the alba poet, is worth a brief comment. It may not seem to be a remarkable achievement to have a female speaker. However, to let the idealized lady of the courtly love lyrics open her beautiful mouth to address her lover involves no small risks. Not unlike the silent-movie stars who did well as long as their voices were not heard, the silent and remote courtly lady could hardly do anything wrong, as long as she kept her red lips sealed. Her silence, as well as her remoteness, did nothing to contradict or correct the admirer's wishful projections. Therefore, to present the formerly unattainable lady not only in close intimacy with her lover, but also to let her speak her mind, is a somewhat risky undertaking, risky in so far as one of the most popular misogynistic prejudices against women was – and perhaps still is – that "women talk too much" (cf. Bloch 1991: 15 and 54). Thus, the poet has to be careful to keep the distance from "the loud but lowly pastourelle shepherdess" (Sigal 1996: 13).

A certain formalization of what, when and to whom the lady speaks minimizes this risk.[13] First, the poet refrains from reporting the amorous inanities which all lovers are liable to utter during a night of passion. Secondly, the time when the lady is shown speaking is during the transitional phase from erotic intimacy to courtly distance. And thirdly, she addresses a *courtly* and *knightly* lover, and not just any man.

4. The Dawn Song Passage in Chaucer's *Troilus and Criseyde* (III, 1415-1533)

After these preliminary remarks, let us now turn to our first English example of a dawn song, namely the passage found in Chaucer's *Troilus and Criseyde* (Book III, 1415-1533; all references are to *The Riverside Chaucer*). This is one of the very few dawn songs extant in early English literature and, though no model dawn song, it meets most of the requirements of its genre and will thus give us an idea of how this literary form may function as a routine of parting within the larger context of a courtly epic. I have annotated the text with marginal glosses that refer to the list of typical dawn song features mentioned above and point out the crucial passages.

Troilus and Criseyde have spent their first night together at Pandarus' house, and the narrator introduces the last phase of their nocturnal interaction by mentioning the traditional signs of day (cockcrow, rising of the planet Venus and other stars):[14]

But whan the cok, comune astrologer,	1415	feature II
But when the cock, astronomer-in-general to the world,		
Gan on his brest to bete and after crowe,		
Began to beat his breast and then to crow,		

And Lucyfer, the dayes messager,
And Lucifer, the messenger of day,
Gan for to rise and out hire bemes throwe,
Began to rise and spread abroad his beams,
And estward roos – to hym that koude it knowe –
And in the east were rising, for such as were informed,
Fortuna Major, *that anoon Criseyde,*   1420
The stars together called Fortuna Major, then Criseyde,
With herte soor, to Troilus thus seyde:
with sore heart spoke thus to Troilus:

Since the two lovers have not wasted the precious hours of the night with sleep, they are still awake when the cock as well as the stars announce the end of the night and the impending break of day. Criseyde initiates the final sequence of their nocturnal interaction by addressing Troilus with three rather intimate forms (l. 1422):[15]

[Criseyde]
"Myn hertes lif, my trist, al my plesaunce,
"Life of my heart, my trusted one, all my joy,
That I was born, allas, what me is wo,   feature III
It grieves me now that I was ever born,
That day of us moot make disseveraunce!
Since day must part us!
For tyme it is to ryse and hennes go,   1425
It is time to rise and go away,
Or ellis I am lost for evere mo!   feature V
Or I am lost forever!
[...]

She begins directly with lamenting the impending departure of her lover and skilfully sets the stage for the ensuing dialogue in the first five lines of her turn (ll. 1422-1426). What she says is this: 'Troilus, I love you (l. 1422); I am very sad that we have to part (ll. 1423-24); it is time for you to go (l. 1425); if you don't leave, you jeopardize my reputation' (l. 1426).

It is important not only how she says this, but also in what sequence. Her very first utterance (l. 1422) is aimed at leaving no doubt as to her feelings towards Troilus (affective level), thus making it clear that the following statements must not be seen as containing emotional metamessages. This is a typical instance of "giving positive face" before going on with a potential FTA

The Dawn-Song as a "Linguistic Routine" of Parting   197

('you have to go'). The next line (l. 1423) continues the line of argument by stressing the displeasure which the necessary and unavoidable (since imposed from outside; cf. l. 1424[16]) departure of her lover causes her. She furnishes the "explanation" for their separation in the next line (l. 1426). However, Criseyde's explanation is not as convincing as the usual danger to the lady and her lover in the form of the jealous husband. Criseyde is a widow, and the one most likely to disturb their nightly meeting, Pandarus, is actually the mastermind of the love affair between Troilus and his niece Criseyde – and is thus already in the know. Thus, Criseyde remains quite vague about the nature of the danger which forces them to separate and counts on the persuasive quality of the dawn song convention to patch over any flaws in her line of argumentation. Her choice of the "dawn song activity type" successfully predetermines the ensuing interaction. The following lines (ll. 1427-1442), with the conventional motif of "cursing of night for passing too quickly", help to further establish the "dawn song activity type".

[Criseyde]
O nyght, allas, why nyltow over us hove   feature III
Ah, night, why will you not brood over us
As longe as whan Almena lay by Jove?
As long as when Alcmena lay with Jupiter?

"O blake nyght, as folk in bokes rede,
"Ah, black night whom, as people read in books,
That shapen art by God this world to hide   1430
God designed to hide this world
At certeyn tymes wyth thi derke wede,
At certain times in your dark garment,
That under that men myghte in reste abide,
That beneath it men might be at rest,
Wel oughten bestes pleyne and folk the chide,
Well may the beasts complain and people chide you,
That there as day wyth labour wolde us breste,
That as day must come to afflict us with labour,
That thow thus fleest, and deynest us nought reste.   1435
That you fly thus and will not let us rest.

"Thow doost, allas, to shortly thyn office,
"You do, alas, too briefly, your office,

Thow rakle nyght! Ther God, maker of kynde,
You hurrying night! May God, the author of nature,

The, for thyn haste and thyn unkynde vice,
For your haste and your unnatural vice,

So faste ay to oure hemysperie bynde
So firmly bind you to our hemisphere

That nevere more under the ground thow wynde!　　　　1440
That you may never again wheel underground!

For now, for thow so hiest out of Troie,
For now, so fast you hie away from Troy,

Have I forgon thus hastili my joie!"
I have already lost my happiness!"

Criseyde first chides Night for depriving people in general, and themselves in particular, of their rest (cf. *reste* in lines 1432 and 1435). The passage is highly conventional, not only in its theme, but also because she does not "personalize" her lament by applying the stock elements to her individual situation. It is only towards the very end of her turn (l. 1442) that she gives us and Troilus a glimpse of her personal feelings.

Troilus, then, model knight that he is, obediently takes up (also in Austin's meaning of the term) his lady's lead and follows suit with a lamentation of his own.

This Troilus, that with tho wordes felte,
Troilus, feeling with these words,

As thoughte hym tho, for piëtous distresse
As thought him then, for pitiful hardship

The blody teris from his herte melte,　　　　1445
That the bloody tears were melting from his heart,

As he that nevere yet swich hevynesse,
As one who never such an anguish

Assayed hadde, out of so gret gladnesse,
Had tasted out of so great a joy,

Gan therwithal Criseyde, his lady deere,
Began Criseyde, his beloved lady,

In armes streyne, and seyde in this manere:　　　　feature IV
To strain in his arms, and said thus:

The Dawn-Song as a "Linguistic Routine" of Parting   199

[Troilus]
"O cruel day, accusour of the joie   1450   feature III
"Ah, cruel day, discloser of the joy

That nyght and love han stole and faste iwryen,
That night and love have stolen and concealed,

Acorsed be thi comyng into Troye,
May you be cursed for coming into Troy,

For every bore hath oon of thi bryghte yën!
For every chink has one of your bright eyes!

Envyous day, what list the so to spien?
Jealous day, why does it please you to spy?

What hastow lost? Why sekestow this place?   1455
What have you lost? Why do you search this place?

Ther God thi light so quenche, for his grace!
May God, in his grace, put out your light!

"Allas, what have thise loveris the agylt,
"Alas, what have these lovers done to offend you,

Dispitous day? Thyn be the peyne of helle!
Spiteful day? The pains of hell be yours,

For many a lovere hastow slayn, and wilt;   feature V
For you have slaughtered many a lover and will again;

Thy pourynge in wol nowher lat hem dwelle.   1460
Your pouring in will leave them nowhere to go.

What profrestow thi light here for to selle?
Why do you offer here to peddle your light?

Go selle it hem that smale selys grave;
Go peddle it to engravers cutting their tiny seals;

We wol the nought; us nedeth no day have."
We do not want you, we need no daylight."

And ek the sonne, Titan, gan he chide,
And the sun, Tithonus, he chided too,

And seyde, "O fool, wel may men the dispise,   1465
And said, "Ah, fool, people may well despise you,

That hast the dawyng al nyght by thi syde,
Who have Dawn at your side all night

And suffrest hire so soone up fro the rise
And let her rise from you so early
For to disese loveris in this wyse.
To discomfort lovers in this way.
What, holde youre bed ther, thow, and ek thi Morwe!
What, keep your bed there, you and your Morning!
I bidde God, so yeve yow bothe sorwe!" 1470
I beseech God to grieve you both!

On the whole, Troilus complies with the "dawn song activity type" given by his lady. Yet, in contrast to Criseyde, who cursed Night for leaving too early, Troilus accuses Day (and the Sun) of coming into Troy too soon (ll. 1450-1470). Apart from imparting a sense of passing time, this complementary selection of the objects of anger by the two lovers may already hint at their future disunion and separation. Troilus, then, by personifying Day, has "him" take the place of the "gilos" or "merkære". Furthermore, he shows understanding for Criseyde's fears of being discovered, by alluding to the dangers threatening lovers in a rather general and conventional way (l. 1459). His own despair at their imminent parting finds its expression in a sequence that mirrors Criseyde's. Thus, his lines 1450-1470 correspond to Criseyde's lament in lines 1427-1442; and Troilus' speech in lines 1472-1484, among other things, takes up themes alluded to in Criseyde's turn (lines 1422-1426). Since it is he who has to perform the more active and thus potentially greater FTAs of getting up and leaving, he has to mitigate his actions. The following passage illustrates his technique:

Therwith ful soore he [Troilus] syghte, and thus he seyde:
Then bitterly he sighed, and said:
"My lady right, and of my wele or wo
"My lady, of my happiness or pain
The welle and roote, O goodly myn Criseyde,
The root and wellspring, my excellent Criseyde,
And shal I rise, allas, and shal I so? feature III
Must I rise, alas, must I indeed?
Now fele I that myn herte moot a-two, 1475
I feel now that my heart must break in two.
For how sholde I my lif an houre save,
How can I keep my life a single hour,
Syn that with yow is al the lif ich have?
Since all the life I have is but with you?

"What shal I don? For, certes, I not how,
"What shall I do? For truly, I do not know how,
Ne whan, allas, I shal the tyme see   feature VI
Nor when, alas, shall I see the time
That in this plit I may ben eft with yow;   1480
That I may be with you this way again;
And of my lif, God woot how that shal be,
And God knows what my life will be,
Syn that desir right now so streyneth me
Since longing constrains me even now
That I am ded anon, but I retourne.
So that I shall die unless I can return.
How sholde I longe, allas, fro yow sojourne?   feature III
How can I live apart from you for long?

"But natheles, myn owen lady bright,   1485
"Nevertheless, my very own excellent lady,
Were it so that I wiste outrely
If I could know for certain
That I, youre humble servant and youre knyght,
That I, your humble servant and your knight,
Were in youre herte iset so fermely   feature IV
Were settled in your heart as firmly
As ye in myn – the which thyng, trewely,
As you are in mine, a thing that would, in all truth,
Me levere were than thise worldes tweyne –   1490
Be dearer to me than both these kingdoms,
Yet sholde I bet enduren al my peyne."
I could better bear all that I suffer."

First, he re-establishes and stresses the hierarchical structure of the courtly love relationship, a move made necessary after the equalizing intimacy of the night. He does this by calling Criseyde *my lady right* (l. 1472) and *myn owen lady bright* (l. 1485) and by using the deferential and thus "distancing" polite pronoun *ye* (l. 1477, l. 1480, l. 1484, etc.). Furthermore, he refers to himself as *youre humble servant and youre knyght* (l. 1487). Yet, at the same time, he also calls her *myn Criseyde* (l. 1473), thus counterbalancing the somewhat distanced and formal forms of address. In this way, Troilus manages to signal both hierarchical subjection (as a *courtly* lover) and emotional closeness (as a lover).

Second, nearly all his subsequent utterances (up to line 1484) that touch upon the subject of parting are formulated as questions (twice in l. 1474 and once in l. 1478) – a negative politeness tool which helps to preserve the addressee's freedom of action.[17] This double strategy allows Troilus to indirectly pass on the greater part of the responsibility for his leave-taking to Criseyde.

Next, Troilus introduces two new features which advance their interaction. First, he mentions the possibility of future meetings (l. 1479ff.). Second, he asks for, and gives, a reassurance of love (l. 1485ff.), which he does with a great deal of "hedging".

From line 1488 onwards, then, Troilus and Criseyde explicitly reassure each other of their love.

To that Criseyde answerde right anon,		
To this Criseyde answered immediately		
And with a sik she seyde, "O herte deere,		feature IV
And with a sigh she said: "Indeed, dear heart,		continued
The game, ywys, so ferforth now is gon		
The game has gone so far		
That first shal Phebus fallen fro his speere,	1495	
That Phoebus shall first tumble from his sphere		
And everich egle ben the dowves feere,		
And every eagle mate with doves,		
And everich roche out of his place sterte,		
And every rock be torn from place,		
Er Troilus oute of Criseydes herte.		
Rather than Troilus from the heart of Criseyde.		
"Ye ben so depe in-with myn herte grave,		change to 'ye'
"You are engraved so deeply in my heart,		
That, though I wolde it torne out of my thought,	1500	
That though I wished to efface you from my thoughts,		
As wisly verray God my soule save,		
So truly God save my soul,		
To dyen in the peyne, I koude nought.		
(Not for the fear) to die under torture, I could not do so.		
And, for the love of God that us hath wrought,		
For the love of God who made us,		

The Dawn-Song as a "Linguistic Routine" of Parting   203

Lat in youre brayn non other fantasie
Let your brain allow no other fancy
So crepe that it cause me to dye!   1505
To creep in, lest it should make me die!

"And that ye me wolde han as faste in mynde
"And that you will keep me in your mind as fast
As I have yow, that wolde I yow biseche;
As I keep you, for this I beseech you;
And if I wiste sothly that to fynde,
If I were sure of that,
God myghte nought a poynt my joies eche.
God could not eke my joy out by a point.
But herte myn, withouten more speche   1510
My heart, without more words,
Beth to me trewe, or ellis were it routhe,   change back
Be true to me, or else it were a pity,   to 'thou'
For I am thyn, by God and by my trouthe!
For I am yours, by God and by my faith!

"Beth glad, forthy, and lyve in sikernesse!
"And so be glad, and live in confidence!
Thus seyde I nevere er this, ne shal to mo;
I have never spoken thus, and never shall;
And if to yow it were a gret gladnesse   1515   change to 'ye'
If it would be to you a great delight
To torne ayeyn soone after that ye go,
To come back soon again after you go,
As fayn wolde I as ye that it were so,
I too am just as anxious that it should happen,
As wisly God myn herte brynge at reste!"
As truly I hope that God may bring my heart to rest!"
And hym in armes tok, and ofte keste.   feature IV
And she embraced him and kissed him often.

It is interesting to note that the two lovers remain on the "courtly lady – courtly lover" level for most of the time, as is indicated by the use of *ye*, the formal pronoun of address (l. 1499, l. 1504, l. 1506, l. 1507, ll. 1515-1517). The basic (formal) courtly tone of interaction is mitigated by the use of more intimate forms of address, namely *herte deere* (l. 1493), *herte myn* (l. 1510), and the incidental informal form of the pronoun of address, *thyn* (l. 1512), and, implicitly, in *beth* (i.e. 'be thou', l. 1511 and l. 1513), all used by Criseyde.

The dawn song sequence ends with renewed intimacy (l. 1519; embracing and kissing), a staggered increase in distance (Troilus gets up and puts on his clothes, l. 1521, referred to as feature VIIIa, then embraces her again and takes his leave), a last farewell by Troilus (l. 1525) in which he expresses his hope that they will meet again soon (l. 1526), and his vanishing from sight (l. 1529, feature VIIIb).

> *Agayns his wil, sith it mot nedes be,*   1520
> Against his will, since it had to be,
>
> *This Troilus up ros, and faste hym cledde,*   feature VIIIa
> Troilus rose and dressed quickly,
>
> *And in his armes took his lady free*   feature IV
> And in his arms he took his noble lady
>
> *An hondred tyme, and on his wey hym spedde;*
> A hundred times, and got ready to leave;
>
> *And with swich voys as though his herte bledde,*
> And in a voice as though his very heart were bleeding,
>
> *He seyde, "Farwel, dere herte swete;*   1525   feature VII
> He said, "Farewell, dear sweetheart;
>
> *Ther God us graunte sownde and soone to mete!"*   feature VI
> May God grant us to meet soon in good health!"
>
> *To which no word for sorwe she answerde,*
> To this she answered not a word for sorrow,
>
> *So soore gan his partyng hire distreyne;*
> So bitterly his parting anguished her;
>
> *And Troilus unto his paleys ferde,*   feature VIIIb
> And Troilus went homeward to his palace,
>
> *As wo-bygon as she was, soth to seyne.*   1530
> As woebegone as she, to tell the truth.

The passage discussed more or less conforms to the pattern of a model dawn song, though there are differences which can be ascribed to the fact that the sequence analysed is not a self-contained dawn song poem, but part of a longer work. Criseyde successfully invokes the dawn song conventions, yet it will not escape the notice of the critical reader that the basic constellation is not that of the model setting. The conventional dawn song motive for the knightly lover's departure at daybreak is the danger of being found out by a jealous husband. Yet, since Criseyde is a widow, and Troilus one of the most powerful men in Troy, they could just as well stay together and not care whether their relationship is discovered or not.[18] Furthermore, Troilus, who is a prince of royal blood, stands higher in the social hierarchy of Troy than Criseyde, who is the daughter of a priest-turned-traitor. Thus, the courtly love relationship with the lady in the superior position is, in fact, an inversion of the actual social structure.

From what I have said before about the function of the dawn song as a routine of parting within the context of courtly love, it becomes clear why Criseyde initiates the last stage of the nightly interaction by means of a dawn song. First, it "help[s] to maintain 'orderliness' of communication by (1) regulating emotional situations [the dawn song allows them to lament their separation, yet, by 'ritualizing' the expression of sorrow, takes off some of the edge]; (2) reducing the complexity of social interaction [they can follow a given pattern];" (characteristics which Coulmas 1979: 254 listed for routine formulae). Second, it re-establishes the courtly love frame and thus the lady's superiority – which has been jeopardized by the intimacy of the night and which would be equally threatened by the social reality of Troy.

In conclusion, we can say that, in this instance, the dawn song has been employed as a routine of parting, enabling the participants to successfully handle a delicate and precarious phase of an interaction, and setting the stage for their future interactions.

5. The Dawn Song Passage in Shakespeare's *Romeo and Juliet* (III, v, 1-59)

The second example is taken from Shakespeare's *Romeo and Juliet* (all references are to the Arden Shakespeare edition). Shakespeare has the scene begin *in medias res*, with Juliet's reaction to Romeo's attempt to leave (only implied in the text) by mentioning the song of the lark. The two lovers are, for practical reasons, not shown in the lady's bed, which makes their meeting less intimate than in the usual dawn song setting. It is also unclear whether they have spent the night together, or have met only shortly before the scene opens. Thus, Shakespeare dramatically condenses the night visit (the arrival of the lover, the time spent together, the leave-taking) into one scene and drastically reduces the erotic component. Moreover, there is no unambiguous "wake-up call" by the cock or by a watchman. All we have is the song of a bird which

Juliet identifies as *the nightingale and not the lark* (v, 2) – thus challenging Romeo's former (implied) statement.

        Enter Romeo *and* Juliet *aloft at the window*
Juliet. Wilt thou be gone? It is not yet near day.
        It was the nightingale and not the lark   feature II challenged
        That pierc'd the fearful hollow of thine ear.
        Nightly she sings on yond pomegranate tree.
        Believe me, love, it was the nightingale.   5

The two lovers are not able to agree immediately on a common activity type, since Juliet deliberately (?) misinterprets the song of the lark as that of the nightingale. This "ornithological mistake" has, of course, far-reaching implications. The lark is the traditional herald of morning and would thus indeed announce the imminent separation of the two lovers.[19] The nightingale, however, is not only a bird that sings at night, but it is at the same time the "singer of love" par excellence. Thus, we could translate Juliet's re- or misinterpretation as follows: 'I do not want you to leave, because I love you. I want you to remain with me and I do not accept the dawn song as the activity type for our interaction.'

Romeo, however, at first perceives only the referential and not the affective dimension of Juliet's utterance: he seems not to realize that Juliet may very well know that it is the lark and not the nightingale. Instead of responding to the affective message ('I love you and do not want you to leave me'), he pedantically points out that the bird is a lark, and thus the herald of dawn, and tries to persuade Juliet to agree to the dawn song activity type by listing additional signs of the coming of day.

Romeo. It was the lark, the herald of the morn,
        No nightingale. Look, love, what envious streaks   feature II reasserted
        Do lace the severing clouds in yonder east.
        Night's candles are burnt out, and jocund day
        Stands tiptoe on the misty mountain tops.   10
        I must be gone and live, or stay and die.   feature V

Furthermore, he stresses the fact that his life is in danger (v, 11) and continues in his efforts to persuade Juliet to accept the dawn song activity type as the model for their interaction. This would have them go on with mutual expressions of sorrow, cursing the daylight, lamenting their imminent separation, embracing for one last time, and so on. Unfortunately, Juliet persists in her way of seeing things and turns down Romeo's proposal of the dawn song pattern. She tries to maintain her own point of view for as long as possible and reinterprets the signs of daybreak as *some meteor that the sun exhales* (v, 13) – thus once more challenging Romeo's attempt to introduce typical dawn song features. At the same time, she turns the signs that herald danger to her beloved into something that will actually help him on his flight to Mantua (v, 14f.), and she concludes: *Therefore stay yet: thou need'st not to be gone* (v, 16).

Juliet. Yond light is not daylight, I know it, I.		feature II challenged
It is some meteor that the sun exhales		
To be to thee this night a torchbearer		feature V challenged
And light thee on thy way to Mantua.	15	
Therefore stay yet: thou need'st not be gone.		

The interaction so far could be summarized as follows:

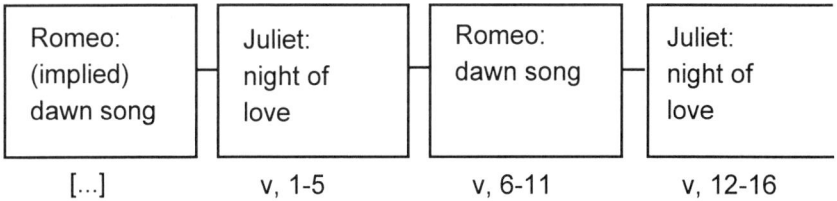

| [...] | v, 1-5 | v, 6-11 | v, 12-16 |

Romeo, exasperated, finally gives up his repeated attempts to establish the dawn song activity type as the blueprint for their interaction. Juliet's refusal to accept the proposed activity type forces him to render explicit what could have been left implicit within the dawn song convention: his wish to stay alive. He resignedly (?) places himself in her power and, against his better knowledge, accepts her misinterpretation of the signs of imminent daybreak.

Romeo. Let me be ta'en, let me be put to death,		feature V reasserted
I am content, so thou wilt have it so.		
'Tis but the pale reflex of Cynthia's brow.	20	
Nor that is not the lark whose notes do beat		feature II
The vaulty heaven so high above our heads.		'reinterpreted'
I have more care to stay than will to go.		
Come death, and welcome. Juliet wills it so.		feature V reasserted
How is't, my soul? Let's talk. It is not day.	25	

The way in which he does this, however, makes it clear that Juliet has not convinced him on the referential level. Rather, he points out that he gives in so as to stop quarrelling with his beloved, thus trying to be polite by minimising disagreement (cf. Holmes 1995: 62). He realizes that it is pointless to be simultaneously the amorous knightly lover and a watchman – or, to quote Wolfram von Eschenbach («Von der zinnen», verse 2, lines 7-10): "Ez wære unwæge, / swer minne pflæge, / daz ûf im læge / meldes last" (Backes 1992: 96; this could be translated as: 'It would not be commendable if the one who dedicates himself to love also had to take care of announcing dawn.'). In this way, Romeo is able to escape from the vicious circle of "more of the same" (i.e. here presenting even more arguments on the referential level). He recognizes the communicative deadlock and manages to switch from the referential level to the affective one.

Furthermore, in line 24, Romeo changes from directly addressing Juliet to talking to her in the third person: *Juliet wills it so*. He forces her to distance herself for a moment and to consider the situation from a somewhat more detached point of view. This change in perspective startles Juliet and she immediately relents and, at last, acts out her part of the dawn song script. In the following lines (v, 26ff.) we find all the elements of a dawn song parting: Juliet refers to the signs which herald the coming of day (feature II), recants her former (mis)interpretations, urges her lover to leave and simultaneously laments their imminent separation (feature III).

Juliet. It is, it is. Hie hence, begone, away.   feature II asserted
It is the lark that sings so out of tune,
Straining harsh discords and unpleasing sharps.
Some say the lark makes sweet division.   feature III
This doth not so, for she divideth us.   30
Some say the lark and loathed toad change eyes.
O, now I would they had chang'd voices too,
Since arm from arm that voice doth us affray,
Hunting thee hence with hunt's-up to the day.   feature V asserted
O now be gone, more light and light it grows.   35

Romeo dutifully adds his line of lament and is saved from further complications by the entrance of the nurse (v, 37).

Romeo. More light and light: more dark and dark our woes.   feature III
       Enter Nurse *hastily*

Nurse. Madam.   'watchman' motif
Juliet.   Nurse?
Nurse. Your lady mother is coming to your chamber.
       The day is broke, be wary, look about.   [*Exit*]   40

The appearance of a third person heightens the urgency of Romeo's departure, and the nurse takes the place of the "watchman" figure in the dawn songs, while Juliet's mother functions as the substitute for the "jealous husband". Juliet once more bemoans their imminent separation (v, 41, feature III). They kiss for the last time (feature IV), and farewells are exchanged several times (feature VII; yet only Romeo explicitly uses formulas of parting like *farewell*, v, 42 & 48; and *adieu*, v, 59). Furthermore, reference is made to future meetings (v, 44ff., feature VI), or at least to keeping in contact, and finally Romeo leaves (feature VIII).

Juliet.	Then, window, let day in and let life out.	feature III
Romeo.	Farewell, farewell, one kiss and I'll descend.	features VII and IV
	He goes down.	
Juliet.	Art thou gone so? Love, lord, ay husband, friend,	feature IV
	I must hear from thee every day in the hour,	feature VI
	For in a minute there are many days. 45	
	O, by this count I shall be much in years	
	Ere I again behold my Romeo.	
Romeo.	Farewell.	feature VII
	I will omit no opportunity	feature VI
	That may convey my greetings, love, to thee. 50	
Juliet.	O think'st thou we shall ever meet again?	feature VI
Romeo.	I doubt it not, and all these woes shall serve	feature VI
	For sweet discourses in our times to come.	
Juliet.	O God, I have an ill-divining soul!	
	Methinks I see thee, now thou art so low,	
	As one dead in the bottom of a tomb.	
	Either my eyesight fails, or thou look'st pale.	
Romeo.	And trust me, love, in my eye so do you.	
	Dry sorrow drinks our blood. Adieu, adieu.	feature VII
	Exit	feature VIII

This scene from *Romeo and Juliet* illustrates the communicative capacity of dawn songs, first *ex negativo*, then, in the second part of the scene (v, 26ff.), by means of the model interaction between the two lovers. It shows that the dawn song activity type pattern is "formulaic" and yet flexible enough to be invoked even without the preceding erotic elements and in a context that is quite different from the original one, since, strictly speaking, Romeo and Juliet are no courtly lady and knightly lover, but husband and wife. Because of this, there is no necessity for the dawn song to ensure the transition to a hierarchical courtly love level. Its sole purpose here consists in ensuring a mutually acceptable form of parting by assuaging possible feelings of rejection and announcing a continuing provisional consensus for future interactions.

6. Conclusion

This discussion of the genre of the dawn song and a close analysis of its two earliest extant English examples have shown the following:

First, the dawn song, as an originally lyrical form, has been modified and introduced as a literary representation of a routine of parting in the courtly epic by Chaucer, and in the drama by Shakespeare. Like other (non-literary) routines encountered in the closing phase of interactions, it aims at assuaging possible feelings of rejection and at consolidating the relationship between the interactors, and it helps to prepare the way for future interactions. It can therefore be ranked with other "routines of parting" in a wider sense of the term.

Second, on a more specific level, dawn songs are, in the context of the literary works analysed, employed to smooth the painful process of separating by gradually replacing the intimacy of physical interaction by language. In this way, they help to re-establish the mode of courtly love interaction, which is characterised by its "linguistic quality"; i.e., it is initiated by language, it is kept up by language, and it actually *is* language. In this context, dawn songs may be regarded as a kind of inverted "rites of passage", since they facilitate the return to a former mode of interaction (courtly love).

Third, in *Troilus and Criseyde*, we find that, along with the return to the mode of courtly love, there comes the re-establishment of the hierarchical structures between the two lovers, which were suspended in favour of equality for the time of nocturnal intimacy and which stand in contradiction to the social reality of Troy. This re-establishment of a courtly love hierarchy is no longer of any importance in *Romeo and Juliet*, which takes place in a more bourgeois setting and whose main protagonists are no longer courtly lovers, but actually husband and wife. The stress in the dawn song passage is laid on its function as what is, in the end, a mutually acceptable form of parting.

Fourth, the ritualization, or at least formalization, of the closing phase of the "night of love" interaction can be seen as being intended to reduce the risk of FTAs and to take the weight of responsibility off the interactors' shoulders. A pre-structured interactional pattern facilitates the successful handling of such a delicate interaction as the parting of two lovers in the morning.

Notes

1 Backes (1992) provides an excellent selection from the Middle High German tradition. Woledge (in Hatto 1965: 344-389) edited the Old Provençal and Old French dawn songs.
2 Spencer (1965, in Hatto 1965) provides an in-depth discussion of the English tradition.
3 E.g. in *Troilus and Criseyde* (III. 1415-1533) or the parodistic dawn song sequence in *The Reeve's Tale* (I, 4234-4249).
4 The adaptation and variation of the basic dawn song theme is most prominent in the Middle High German tradition, as the collection of dawn songs by Backes (1992) shows.
5 Coulmas (1979: 252) once observed: "Whether or not sneezing, yawning, or operating an elevator [and here we may add: leaving after a night of love] is accompanied by some kind of routinized speech behavior depends on the respective historical idiosyncrasies of the respective cultures."
6 It must not be forgotten that the conversational samples are literary products. I want to forego any conclusions that may be drawn as to the historical situation. On the influence of literary models on real-world love-behaviour, and vice versa, see Leisi (1993: 9 and 74).
7 Since, to my knowledge, no medieval English examples are extant and since the French tradition is also very limited, I am obliged to refer to examples of the Middle High German "tageliet" tradition: "Ez gienc ein juncfrou minneclîch" by Burggraf von Lienz and "Got willekomen, herre" by Ulrich von Lichtenstein (nos. XV and XIX in Backes 1992: 126-130 and 150-154).
8 In English, traces of this "serena"-type may be found in the tradition of "Songs on the Night Visit", as presented by Baskervill (1921).
9 I use Levinson's term, which he (1979: 368) defines as follows: "In particular I take the notion of activity type to refer to a fuzzy category whose focal members are goal-defined, socially constituted, bounded, events with *constraints* on participants, setting, and so on, but above all on the kinds of allowable contributions. Paradigm examples would be teaching, a job interview, a jural interrogation, a football game, a task in a workshop, a dinner party and so on."
10 Cf. the list of features typical of Old Provençal and Old French dawn songs by Woledge (in Hatto 1965: 354).
11 Cf. Watzlawick (1983: 99; letter by Rousseau to Madame d'Houdetot): "»Wenn Sie mein werden, so verliere ich, eben dadurch, dass ich Sie dann besitze, Sie, die ich ehre.« Zweimaliges Lesen hilft. Was Rousseau nämlich sagen zu wollen scheint, ist: Wer sich mir hingibt, ist *deshalb* nicht mehr geeignet, Inbegriff meiner Liebe zu sein."
12 On "form-centered" and "function-centered" categories, see Coulmas (1981: 10).
13 In this context, see also the formalized model-dialogues provided by Andreas Capellanus.
14 The translation of the Middle English text is based on Morrison (1977).
15 See Leisi (1993: 18ff.) on the importance of intimate (nominal) forms of address.

16 A very close verbal parallel can be found in the Middle High German "tageliet" "Wie hôhes muotes ist ein man" by Ulrich von Singenberg (no. XII in Brackes 1992: 120): "Der tac wil scheiden, [...] ez muoz eht sin".
17 "Negative politeness" aims at avoiding or at least redressing any restriction of the addressee's freedom of action or attention; cf. Brown and Levinson (1987: 131).
18 Sigal (1996: 90) sees "Chaucer's literary motive of seizing the opportunity to write a dawn-song [...] far more credible than the widowed Criseyde's motive for singing it."
19 The lark, French "alouette", is also mentioned in Old French dawn song poetry as the herald of dawn. Cf. No. 10 in Woledge (in Hatto 1965: 370).

References

Andreas Capellanus
    c. 1186   *The Art of Courtly Love [De amore et amoris remedio]* (Edited and translated by John Jay Parry 1960). New York: Columbia Unversity Press.
Backes, Martina (ed. and trans.)
    1992   *Tagelieder des deutschen Mittelalters. Mittelhochdeutsch/Neuhochdeutsch.* (Introduction by Alois Wolf). Stuttgart: Philipp Reclam jun.
Baskervill, Charles Read
    1921   English Songs on the Night Visit. *Publications of the Modern Language Association of America* 36, 565-614.
Benson, Larry D. (ed.)
    1987   *The Riverside Chaucer* (3rd edition, based on *The Works of Geoffrey Chaucer*, ed. F.N. Robinson). Boston: Houghton Mifflin; repr. Oxford: Oxford University Press, 1988.
Bloch, R. Howard
    1991   *Medieval Misogyny and the Invention of Western Romantic Love.* Chicago and London: The University of Chicago Press.
Brown, Penelope, and Stephen C. Levinson
    1987   *Politeness: Some Universals in Language Usage* (Studies in Interactional Linguistics 4). Cambridge: Cambridge University Press.
Coulmas, Florian
    1979   On the sociolinguistic relevance of routine formulae. *Journal of Pragmatics* 3, 239-266.
    1981   Introduction: Conversational Routine. In: Florian Coulmas (ed.). *Conversational Routine. Explorations in Standardized Communication Situations and Prepatterned Speech* (Rasmus Rask Studies in Pragmatic Linguistics 2). The Hague, Paris, New York: Mouton Publishers, 1-17.

Coulmas, Florian (ed.)
    1981   *Conversational Routine. Explorations in Standardized Communication Situations and Prepatterned Speech* (Rasmus Rask Studies in Pragmatic Linguistics 2). The Hague, Paris, New York: Mouton Publishers.

Dodd, William George
    1913   The System of Courtly Love. (Originally published in *Courtly Love in Chaucer and Gower*. Boston: Ginn & Co.) Reprinted in Richard J. Schoeck and Jerome Taylor (eds.), 1961. *Chaucer Criticism Volume II: Troilus and Criseyde and the Minor Poems*. Notre Dame: University of Notre Dame Press, 1-15.

Gibbons, Brian (ed.)
    1980   *Romeo and Juliet* (The Arden Shakespeare). London and New York: Methuen.

Hatto, Arthur T. (ed.)
    1965   *Eos: An Inquiry into the Theme of Lovers' Meetings and Partings at Dawn in Poetry*. The Hague: Mouton & Co.

Holmes, Janet
    1995   *Women, Men and Politeness*. London and New York: Longman.

Laver, John
    1975   Communicative Functions of Phatic Communion. In: Adam Kendon, Richard M. Harris and Mary Ritchie Key (eds.). *Organization of Behaviour in Face-to-Face Interaction*. The Hague and Paris: Mouton, 215-238.
    1981   Linguistic Routines and Politeness in Greeting and Parting. In: Florian Coulmas (ed.). *Conversational Routine. Explorations in Standardized Communication Situations and Prepatterned Speech* (Rasmus Rask Studies in Pragmatic Linguistics 2). The Hague, Paris, New York: Mouton Publishers, 289-230.

Leisi, Ernst
    1993   *Paar und Sprache: linguistische Aspekte der Zweierbeziehung*. (4th revised edition. First edition 1978. UTB 824). Heidelberg and Wiesbaden: Quelle und Meyer.

Leisi, Ernst, and Ilse Leisi
    1992   *Sprach-Knigge oder Wie und was soll ich reden?* Tübingen: Gunter Narr.

Levinson, Stephen C.
    1979   Activity types and language. *Linguistics* 17 (5/6), 365-399.

Morrison, Theodore (ed. and trans.)
    1977   *The Portable Chaucer*. (First edition 1949). New York and London: Penguin Books.

Sigal, Gale
    1996   *Erotic Dawn-Songs of the Middle Ages.* Gainesville: University Press of Florida.

Smith, A.J. (ed.)
    1973   *John Donne: The Complete English Poems.* (First edition 1971). Harmondsworth: Penguin.

Sucher, C. Bernd
    1996   *Hummer, Handkuss, Höflichkeit: Das Handbuch des guten Benehmens.* Munich: Deutscher Taschenbuch Verlag.

Tannen, Deborah
    1990   *You Just Don't Understand. Women and Men in Conversation.* New York: Ballantine Books.

Watzlawick, Paul
    1983   *Anleitung zum Unglücklichsein.* (Paperback edition 1988, reprinted 1996). Munich and Zurich: Piper.

Refugiate in a strange countrey
Learning English through Dialogues in the 16th Century

Richard J. Watts
University of Berne

1. Introduction

Imagine an English-language coursebook in which dialogues are used as linguistic input to the structural and lexical points being introduced and/or practised in each teaching unit. Imagine also that the coursebook is centred around a fictional family, mother, father and three sons, Peter and Stephen and James, and that one of the dialogues simulates the mother waking her children up in the morning to get them off to school. In that coursebook we might find a dialogue something like the following:

(1) Mother: Come on kids, don't you want to get up today?
    Peter: What time is it?
    Mother: It's seven o'clock.
    Stephen: I don't believe you.
    Mother: Why don't you believe me?
    Stephen: Because I still feel sleepy and I'm used to waking up at five o'clock.
    James: Listen to him! He's hardly awake at eight o'clock. How could he be awake at five?
    Mother: Quite right.
    Stephen: You're joking.

The dialogue is perhaps a little stilted and also a little unrealistic, but if we know that it is, after all, input to the teaching of certain grammatical structures and lexical items in English, we might want to overlook these aspects. For example, in the mother's third turn, we would expect her to say *Why not?* rather than to repeat the verb *believe*. On the other hand, if one of the structures being introduced or practised is the use of the auxiliary verb *do* in negative statements and questions, teachers and coursebook writers might even insist on it appearing in the mother's question.

What other structures look as though they are being focused on here? For a start, great play is made on the activity of asking and telling the time, e.g. *What time is it?*, *It's seven o'clock, at five o'clock, at eight o'clock, at five.* The auxiliary verb *do* with the negative operator *not* occurs three times, *Don't you want to get up today?*, *I don't believe you*, *Why don't you believe me?* There are a number of lexical items which might be presented to the learners for the first time, e.g. *get up, believe, sleepy, wake up, awake*, possibly also *joke*. So in addition to the pragmatic function of telling the time we also have a lexical field revolving around the notion of sleep.

I admit that it is not quite the sort of situation that would appeal to contemporary coursebook writers, teachers and learners of English as a foreign language, but let us ignore this aspect of the dialogue for the moment. Instead, let us ask ourselves why these structures and lexemes are presented in the form of an imaginary dialogue. One reason is obviously the modern insistence on oral forms of language, or at least the simulation of oral situations, at the beginning of an English language course rather than on written text types. On the assumption that oral discourse is prior to written discourse – an assumption that is open to challenge anyway – coursebook writers and teachers will generally focus on commonly occurring situations demanding an ability to communicate orally. A second reason is that introducing a new language in this way focuses on communicative goals even if the goals of grammatical correctness and lexical appropriateness are just as important *qua* learning goals as the development of communicative competence. A third reason might be that dialogues can be acted out with groups of learners, the language can be varied, the situation can be changed and/or extended, etc. In other words, dialogues are one way of moving away from a teacher-centred to a learner-centred form of foreign language teaching.

In point of fact the dialogue given above did occur in an English-language teaching book, but not in the latter half of the 20th century and not in the form that I have presented it. Here is the text as it appeared in James Bellot's *Familiar Dialogues/Dialogues familiers* (1586):

(2) Barbara: How now children, will you not rise to day?
    Peter: What ist a clock?
    Barbara: It is seuen a clock.
    Stephen: I beleue you not.
    Barbara: Why do you not beleue me?

Stephen: Because I am yet all sleepye and that I am accustomed to awake alwayes at fiue of the clock.
James: Beleue this bearer: he is scant well awake at eight of the clocke, how then could he be awake at fiue?
Barbara: You say true.
Stephen: You will iest.

In Bellot's text Barbara is the maid, and the only reason I have represented her as the boys' mother in (1) is to make the text compatible with the composition of families in the 20th century, although, of course, in modern terms Barbara could be the au pair. Obviously, changes in the language to adapt the form of early modern English of the late 16th century to the English of the latter part of the 20th century have also distorted the text a little – but not much. The auxiliary verb *do* loses the prominence I gave it in (1). But the pragmatic function of telling the time remains, e.g. *What ist a clock?*, *It is seuen a clock*, *at fiue of the clock*, *at eight of the clocke*, *at fiue*, as does the lexical field of sleep, e.g. *rise*, *sleepye*, *to awake*, *awake*, and the introduction of the lexeme *beleue* as a new item, all the more so as it occurs three times rather than just twice in (1).

Bellot's text was written for the benefit of French-speaking learners "refugiate in a strange countrey", i.e. for refugees living in England or more specifically in London, and my comparison between the fictive modernised version of the dialogue in (1) and the original dialogue in (2) raises the following interesting empirical and theoretical questions which I will address in this paper:

1. Who was the Bellot text written for, children, adults, or both?
2. What was the "refugiate" community for whom there was a need to learn English as a foreign language in London and how many learners might there have been in that community?
3. How was the text to be used in the teaching/learning of English?
4. What were the learning goals aimed at through the dialogues?
5. Was there a tradition of using dialogic teaching/learning materials in the 16th century?
6. Where in London was the text to be used, i.e. in what institutional setting, and in what physical location?
7. What socio-historical connections can be posited between the community for whom the text was written and other immigrant communities living in London in the 16th century?

8. How can these hypothesised connections enrich our knowledge of the importance of language as a factor in the assimilation, integration or exclusion of immigrant ethnic groups?

I shall focus on two texts to tackle these questions, Bellot's text and another text from earlier in the 16th century, the anonymous *A very profitable boke to lerne the maner of redyng, writyng, and speakyng english and Spanish/Libro muy prouechoso para saber la manera de leer, y screuir, y hablar Angleis, y Español* (which I will henceforth refer to as *A very profitable boke*). *A very profitable boke* appeared in 1554 with a second text attached to it entitled *The boke of Englyshhe and Spanysshe*. Both Bellot's text and *A very profitable boke* do not lie within the canonical frame of language learning texts printed for use in the grammar schools, since they make considerable use of dialogues to instruct the learner in English, in the former case, and in English and Spanish in the latter case. In addition, although *The boke of Englyshhe and Spanysshe* is structured rather like a modern foreign language phrasebook, some of the sentences it contains can be interpreted as embryonic dialogues. Despite the similarities between *Familiar Dialogues* and *A very profitable boke*, however, they present us with two different sets of learners and learning goals reflecting different relationships between the immigrant group and what that group of learners needed to know in dealing with life in London.

In the following section, I shall present *Familiar Dialogues* and *A very profitable boke* to the reader, dealing with the first two questions. Question 5 will be answered in the affirmative as we compare the two texts. In section 3, I shall focus more closely on questions 3 and 4 dealing with the ways in which the text might have been used and what the learning goals might have been. Section 4 will present a grossly simplified outline of certain historical facts from within which I shall attempt to answer questions 6 and 7. Question 8 will then be answered speculatively in the final section.

2. *A very profitable boke* and *Familiar Dialogues*

A very profitable boke was printed anonymously in 1554, although its author might have been one John Wyght if we interpret the final paragraph of the text – "Imprinted at London by John Kyngston and Henry Sutton dwellinge in Poules churchyarde for John Wyght" – as giving us the names of the printers and the "author" for whom they printed it. On the other hand, it is known to be a version of Noël van Barlement's *Vocabulare*, an edition of which was printed in Louvain in 1551 (cf. Alston 1967–1972: *English Linguistics* 292). There are a number of clues in the text that the English was simply transferred from

Barlement's Flemish version of the French. For example, the name *Barlamon* or *Barlemon*, in Spanish *Barlemont*, is mentioned a number of times in the fourth chapter "Of the waie to write epistles, obligacions, and quittaunces" in connection with houses in Antwerp and Bruges. In "The Preface to the seconde Booke" we also read the following, in which the tell-tale word is "Frenche":

> Wheras in the booke afore, thou haste heard diuerse maners and fashions, as certain examples of speakyng Frenche, in this seconde Booke, thou shalt here many vsual wordes, set in order of the Alphabete. A.b.c.d. whiche be as it wer a matter loquutious ar ioyned.

The boke of Englyshhe and Spanysshe was discovered without a title page bound together with *A very profitable boke*, thus predating by 32 years the first recorded book on Spanish printed in England. Both books are printed in two columns per page. In *A very profitable boke* the lefthand column is English and the righthand column Spanish, and a different font is used for each. In *The boke of Englyshhe and Spanysshe* each column consists of a series of phrases and sentences of English with the Spanish translations underneath, the English being in a larger print size than the Spanish.

A very profitable boke consists of three parts, the first a series of dialogues concerning the following topics:

- "a feast of x. interloquutours, in which be contained many dayly facions of speakyng, whiche we vse whan we sytte at meate"
- "the maner of byenge and sellyng"
- "the ways of callynge vpon your debtors"
- "the maner of writing epistles and letters of obligations, solutions, and of bargayns,"

the second a selected vocabulary in alphabetical order giving lexical items in English and Spanish, and the third and shortest part giving the Lord's Prayer, 'the salutation of the angel', 'the articles of the faithe' and 'the ten commaundements' in English and Spanish. *The boke of Englyshhe and Spanysshe* is divided into 16 thematic sections, which are called "chapters", although these are not always clearly signalled in the text. The quality of the printing in both texts is rather poor and the spelling of "English" as *Englysshe* and "Spanish" as *Spanysshe* in *The boke of Englyshhe and Spanysshe* indicates an earlier date than 1554.

Sets of dialogues as a method of presenting the learner with useful everyday structures in a rudimentary context had been produced prior to *A very profitable boke* (cf. the reference above to Barlement's text for speakers of Flemish learning French) and were a popular way of presenting language teaching materials. *Familiar Dialogues* clearly uses it as a model. It is therefore safe to talk of a tradition of dialogic texts in the learning of foreign languages. Bellot's text, however, departs from the tradition in a number of interesting ways, as we shall see later.

Texts like *The boke of Englyshhe and Spanysshe* also abounded in the Renaissance period and its precursors can be found for "learners" of French and Italian. In fact, many of the phrases/sentences were simply taken over wholesale and translated into the target language. *The boke of Englyshhe and Spanysshe* has been extracted from *Septem linguarum Latinæ Teutonicæ Gallicæ Hispanicæ Italicæ Anglicæ Almanicæ dilucidissimus dictionarius* since it contains many of the errors in the edition published at Venice in 1548 (Alston 1967–1972: *English Linguistics* 291). Taking these points into consideration *The boke of Englyshhe and Spanysshe* would appear to be just another foreigner's phrasebook like so many of its kind before and after. But there are two interesting facts which require more explanation. The first of these concerns the audience for whom it and *A very profitable boke* were printed. Since there is no explicit reference in the preface of *A very profitable boke* to the community of learners for whom it was written and no preface at all in *The boke of Englyshhe and Spanysshe*, we are forced back onto other interpretative leads.

The target English text in *Familiar Dialogues* is in the lefthand column and the native language translation in French and a quasi phonetic transcription for the learner are in the middle column and the righthand column respectively. So, if we are dealing with a tradition of dialogic learning texts in which *A very profitable boke* served as a model for *Familiar Dialogues*, we might hypothesise that the target language is in the lefthand column. In *A very profitable boke*, therefore, we could argue that the target language is English rather than Spanish. On the other hand, the book opens with a statement, also contained in its title, that "this booke is verye profitable to learn the maner of reding, writyng, and speakyng Englishe and Spanishe". Moreover, the second chapter begins with an indication of its subject "Of fashions of buiyng and sellyng in the Spanishe tongue". Ungerer (1965) discusses those books published in Spanish in England during the Elizabethan period and argues convincingly that there was a surprisingly widespread utilitarian interest in learning Spanish despite the negative experiences of the religious oppression of the Protestant religion in England during the reign of Mary. Much of this interest derived from the increasing interest in colonisation in the late Elizabethan era and the consequent rivalry with Spain.

However, to return to *A very profitable boke*, the reference to French which I quoted above indicates that, despite the comments on learning Spanish at the beginning of the second chapter, it was the lefthand column in Barlement's text in which the target language, French for Flemish-speaking learners, was presented. In addition, in *The boke of Englyshhe and Spanysshe* both the larger print size for the English and the fact that the Spanish always follows the English phrase/sentence indicates that the book was intended for use by Spanish speakers learning English.

The second interesting fact about *The boke of Englyshhe and Spanysshe* is that, although there is no explicit indication of the dialogic nature of some parts of the overall text, various series of sentences can easily be interpreted as dialogic. The following examples illustrate this:

(3) He wyll not
Wylt thou come
I wyll come now
Abyde a lytell
Comest thou

(4) Thou lettest noo man sleepe
Why?
For thou doest no thynge all nyght but snorke
Go sleepe
Not yet
Go, for thou must ryse to morow be tymes
What to do
Thou must beare letters to Mylan
My Legge greueth me so that I cannot go on fote
Take a horse
Chose me one

(5) I wyll go from hence
I maye remayne no longer
Thou byndeste to great a ferdell, and shalte not be able to bere it
I shall beare it well
Thou shalte se
Let me care for that
Gyue it me

I will leave it to the reader to decide how these "parts" should be allotted to different speakers, but the thematic links from sentence to sentence and the fact that we have two "speakers", as indicated by the use of the pronouns *I* and *thou*, provide clear evidence that what appear to be disconnected units of language are in fact meant to be taken together as embryonic dialogues and that

The boke of Englyshhe and Spanysshe is, marginally at least, also within the tradition of dialogic learning texts.

Alston's note on *The boke of Englyshhe and Spanysshe* (Alston 1967–1972: *English Linguistics* 291) suggests that "the book ... seems to have been published to meet, or anticipate, the increased interest shown by Englishmen in Spain and the Spanish language". His argument is based on the fact that Queen Mary married King Philip of Spain on July 25, 1554. However, Ungerer (1965) also mentions the significant numbers of Spanish courtiers, diplomats and merchants who came to London during the reign of Queen Mary, some of whom stayed well into the reign of Elizabeth I. There was also a small emigrant community of Spanish Protestants residing in London before Mary's accession to the throne (cf. Kinder 1975) and since that community was still in evidence in the reign of Queen Elizabeth I, we can assume that they somehow survived the attempted expulsion of all foreigners from England during the Marian persecution (cf. Pettegree 1986). The demand for Spaniards already living in London or coming to the English court during the reign of Queen Mary to know some English must therefore have been greater than for English travellers going to Spain and needing to know Spanish, although, paradoxically, the interest in learning Spanish did increase in the Elizabethan era.

The second dialogic text which I shall focus on, *Familiar Dialogues*, presents us with a slightly different situation. The book was published in 1586, six years after the printing of Bellot's *Le Maistre d'Escole Anglois*. The frontispiece or title-page of the text states unequivocally that it is "for the Instruction of them, that be desirous to learne to speake English, and perfectlye to pronounce the same". The author James Bellot styles himself a "Gentleman of Caen" and dedicates his preface to "the most vertuous Sir, Mark de Buffy Esquier L., of Beruille". The fact that the intended audience is French-speaking emerges from the French sonnet which precedes the text, the preface, the address to the reader and, above all, the layout of the text in three columns, the lefthand column containing the dialogues in English, the middle column a French translation in italics, and the righthand column a transcript of the English text written so that French speakers can pronounce it. The following is the first full sentence of the preface:

(6) The experi-   *L'Experien-*   Dé experience
    ence hauing   *ce m'aiant*   hàuing in
    in the olde tyme *iadis appris quel*   dé aùld teìm lèr-
    learned vnto me *ennuy apporte à*   ned ontou my
    what sorow is for *ceux qui sont*   houat soro is for

them that be refu-	reffugiez en pais	dem dat by refu-
giate in a strange	estranger, quand	giat in a strange
countrey, when	ilz ne peuuent	contré, houen
they can not vn-	entendre le lan-	dè can not on-
derstand the lan-	guage du lieu	sterstand dé lan-
guage of that	auquel ilz sont	gage of dat plàs
place in whiche	exilez & quand	in houitch dè
they be exiled:	ilz ne peuuent	by exeiled: and
and when they	se faire entendre	houen dè can
can not make	aux habitans de	not mék dem
them to be vnder-	la contrée en la-	tou by onder-
stood by speach	quelle ilz se sont	stoud by spìtch
to the inhabiters	retirez: i'ay esté	tou dé inhabi-
of that contrey,	(à ceste cause)	ters of dat con-
wherein they be	esmeu à com-	tré houèrin dè
retired: I haue	passion, ???	by reteired: ey
bene (therefore)	que pour tirer	hàf (dèrfòr) bin
moued to com-	de peine, une	mouued tou com-
passion, so that for	infinité de per-	passion, so dat for
to drawe out of	sonnes, que noz	tou dràà aut of
paine, an infinite	persecutions der-	paìn, en infinit
number of persons,	nieres ont fait	nomber of persons,
the whiche our	venir à ce pais,	dé houitch auor
last persecutions	I'ay trouvé bon	làst persecutions
have caused to	de leur mettre	hàf càsed tou
come into this con-	en main quel-	com in dis con-
trey, I thought	ques petits dia-	tré, ey taùt goud
good to put into	logues en Fran-	tou pout intou
their hands cer-	çois, & An-	dêr hands cer-
teine short Dia-	Anglois, ésquelz (	tain chart Deila-
logues in French,	pour leur plus	logs in Franch,
and Englishe in	ample instruc-	and Inglich, in
which (for their	tion) I'ay es-	houitch (for dêr
fuller Instructi-	crit l'Anglois,	fuller instructi-
on) I haue writ-	non seulement	on) ey hàf rouit-
ten the English,	selon que les	tin dé Inglish
not onely so as	habitans du	not ònelé so as
the inhabiters of	pais l'écriveent:	dé inhabiters of
the countrey do	Mais aussi ain-	dé contré dou
write it: But also,	sy qu'il est, &	rouit it: Bout al-

| so as it is, and must be pronoun- ced. | doit estre pro- noncé. | so, so às it is, and must by pronoun- ced. |

The French exiles mentioned by Bellot in his preface, of whom he was also one in the aftermath of the St. Bartholomew's Day massacre of Protestants in France in 1572, are the Huguenot refugees who had lately settled in various places in England, but primarily in London. There had been a well-established French-speaking immigrant community in London consisting not only of French Protestants but also of French-speaking Walloons from the Low Countries (or from what is now the French-speaking part of Belgium) for a number of decades prior to the 1580s. In 1551, during the Edwardian era, a reformed French church was established in Threadneedle Street to minister to the French-speaking community in London (Pettegree 1986) and the recent refugees from religious persecution would have found a supportive and close-knit social network to help them adapt to their new environment. One of their needs would obviously have been to learn the language of that environment.

In all there are 5 different dialogues in *Familiar Dialogues*, "The rising in the morning", encompassing 100 lines (which I shall henceforth refer to as Dialogue A), "To the market" which comprises 250 lines (henceforth Dialogue B), "At the table" with 121 lines (henceforth Dialogue C), "At playing" which covers 67 lines (henceforth Dialogue D) and "Vpon the way" covering 160 lines (henceforth Dialogue E). The central figures in Dialogues A and D are children; in Dialogues B, C and E they are adults, although children do occur in Dialogue C and adults also occur in Dialogues A and D. If the themes of the dialogues and the principal characters in them are any indication of the composition of the learners, a point for which I shall argue in the following section, then the intended learners are not only schoolchildren but also adults.

On the fairly safe assumption that this mixed group of learners is to be found amongst the French-speaking immigrant community in London in the last twenty years of the 16th century, we can now consider how many learners there might have been, whether we can extrapolate from this figure to gain a rough idea of the numbers of French-speaking emigrants in London in the 1580s, and whether this figure corresponds to other reliable assessments such as the periodic censuses during Elizabeth's reign of the numbers of foreigners resident in London (cf. Finlay 1981: 67-69, who cites the alien population as being 5,315 out of a total population of roughly 100,000 in 1573 and 5,450 out of a population of roughly 150,000 in 1594).

We know from a grammar written for the benefit of charity schoolchildren by Samuel Saxon in 1731, which appeared in only one edition, that he relied on 200 subscribers in order to cover his printing costs. It is not unreasonable to assume that roughly this number of purchasers of *Familiar Dialogues* would also have been necessary in 1586 for Bellot to break even financially. Let us now assume that one copy of the book, which is of rather poor quality printing with several printer's errors, would have served the members of a whole family. In Dialogue A Bellot presents us with a family of mother, father, maid and three children, from which we can speculate that the average size of a family was probably four to five. Taking the lower figure and multiplying it with the number of copies we assume that Bellot needed to sell to break even we reach the figure of 800. So we can assume that the number of learners in the 1580s would have been somewhere between 200 and 800. Since the book appeared in a second edition in 1622 and was the second book that Bellot had produced, it is probably safe to aim at the higher figure here.

We can assume that not every French-speaking family in London wanted or needed to use Bellot's book to learn English. If 50 per cent did, then we can estimate the number of French-speaking immigrants in London in the 1580s at c. 1,500–1,600. If, on the other hand, only 30 per cent of the families bought the book, the overall figure could have been as high as c. 2,500–2,700. Given that the total number of aliens resident in London during the 1580s lay between 5,300 and 5,400 (cf. Finlay 1981), this would constitute a reasonable estimate. Since we know that the French-speaking community had already been established since at least the early 1550s, we must conclude from this figure that there must have been a great deal of fluctuation in terms of movement back and forth from the continent to England during the years between 1550 to 1580. Every renewed persecution of French Protestants created a fresh wave of refugees, many of whom probably returned to France and the Low Countries as soon as it was safe to do so. The figures for the French-speaking community are still considerably higher than any which might be estimated for the Protestant Spanish community that was led by Casiodoro de Reina in the early 1560s and Antonio del Corro in the 1570s (cf. Hauben 1967) even if we add to them the relatively small number of courtiers and merchants who remained in London after Mary's death. The estimated number of Spaniards in and around London at that time was certainly no more than 400–500.

While almost half of *A very profitable boke* consists of an English–Spanish vocabulary, Bellot's book is explicitly set out as a series of dialogues with the French translation and a transcription of the English to help the French-speaking learners with their pronunciation. *The boke of Englyshhe and Spanysshe* contains no indication as to how the book is to be used by the learners, nor does it seem to have any specific addressees. Why, then, are there so many incipient dialogues in it? It is certainly not unusual to "dialogise" the presentation of certain phrases and sentences as a form of contextualisation in modern phrasebooks. However, *A very profitable boke* provides clear evidence that the presentation of language materials in a foreign language learning situation involved the use of dialogues in the 16th century. Hence the dialogues in *Familar Dialogues* do not constitute a new teaching method but simply the continuation of a foreign language teaching tradition. In addition there is also evidence that the model for *Familiar Dialogues* was *A very profitable boke*, which in its turn is a direct translation of Barlement's *Vocabulare*. The problem that we are confronted with, however, is to know how these dialogic texts were put to use in the teaching situation.

In the following section I shall consider the differences between *A very profitable boke* and *Familiar Dialogues* and consider how the texts might have been used in the teaching and learning of English as a non-native language. This will lead me into a discussion of how the learning goals reflected the degree of linguistic and non-linguistic integration of the immigrant community into the London of the late 16th century.

3. How might the dialogues have been used? Learning and teaching goals

The dialogues in *A very profitable boke* appear to be addressed to adult learners of English (or Spanish?) rather than to children, whereas at least two of the dialogues in *Familiar Dialogues* have children as their central characters and deal more directly with themes involving children, e.g. the need to get up in the morning in order to go to school, the question of what clothes they should put on and what books they should take to school, deciding on what games they want to play in the break between lessons at school, etc. *A very profitable boke*, on the other hand, is concerned more with the payment of debts, the settling of contracts, etc., i.e. with situations oriented toward trade and business. Both sets of dialogues contain scenes in which characters buy and sell various kinds of ware, but whereas in *A very profitable boke* the perspective is that of the seller, in *Familiar Dialogues* it is that of the buyer. In both texts the characters make great play of haggling over prices and quality.

There are few explicit indications of how the dialogues were meant to be used in language teaching/learning, but one difference does stand out. In *A very profitable boke* we read that "this booke is verye profitable to lern the maner of reding, writyng, and speakyng Englishe and Spanishe", i.e. that reading and writing take precedence over speaking. In *Familiar Dialogues* we read that they are "for the Instruction of them, that be desirous to learne to speake

English, and prefectlye to pronounce the same", i.e. speaking English is the primary goal for Bellot.

Two other indications of how Bellot conceived of the text being used are included in the dedication to Mark de Bussy and in the preface to the reader. In the dedication Bellot explains that the sorrowful experience of exile in a foreign country, in which emigrants cannot understand the language and cannot make themselves understood, has led him to "put into their hands certeine short Dialogues in French, and Englishe in which (for their fuller Instruction) I haue written the English, not onely as the inhabiters of the countrey do write it: But also, so as it is, and must be pronounced." On the one hand, therefore, Bellot is concerned to help them understand English and make themselves understood using English, and on the other hand, he seems to lay stress on the way in which native speakers write and pronounce the language. The dialogues thus seem to have been made for the learners to read, and this is made clear in the short preface to the reader, in which he gives them clear indications on how to pronounce the written text:

> Gentle Reader, To the ende that you stumble not about the reading, and vnderstanding of these little Dialogues whiche I made for your instruction: you shall marke that those letters must be pronounced long ...

Were the dialogues therefore meant for private study and/or for possible dramatisation within the family circle, or were they used in groups as the basis for oral practice in simulated everyday situations with a teacher directing and monitoring the learners' progress?

If we take a closer look at the dialogues in *Familiar Dialogues* and compare them to those in *A very profitable boke*, two significant differences between the two texts emerge, although it is clear that the former is modelled on the latter. The first difference relates to the degree of naturalness and vitality in the dialogues themselves. In *A very profitable boke* the second chapter is devoted to "fashions of buiyng and sellyng in the Spanishe (sic!) tongue", and it involves two women, Katerine and Margarete, selling their wares in the market-place and Daniel, a potential customer. In an effort to present the learner with a range of linguistic structures with which s/he can carry out the same communicative intent in different ways, the dialogue becomes somewhat stilted, repetitive and unnatural. In the following sequence Daniel is asking Katerine the price of a length of cloth and of a tankard of wine:

(7) D: Good wife, what is the price of an elle of this clothe.
    K: The price is thirty stuphers.
    D: What shall I paie for an elle of this clothe?
    K: It shall cost you twentie stuphers.

D: How holde you a tankard of this wine.
K: At three stuphers.
D: How holde you a pece of this clothe?
K: Shall I tell at oone word? At fiue Gelderns.

Familiar Dialogues uses the same setting of the market-place, but dramatises the action in a more realistic and humorous manner. In this case Ralph is sent to the market by his wife Ayles, and on the way he meets Androw, who is also off to the market. They decide to adjourn to the "Byshops head", or the "Cardinals hat" – it is not made clear to which inn they go – for a 'pynte of wine well drawen', where they are served by the innkeeper Simon. After downing their first pint and eating rolls and butter, Androw points out to Ralph that "the pot is emptie: There is no more" and asks him, "Shall we haue an other pynte?", whereupon Ralph reminds him that they should really be getting on to the market. At the market, Ralph, Androw, Simon and Ayles are all displayed bargaining at different stalls, Ralph at the poulterer's and the fishmonger's, Ayles at the draper's, Androw at the costermonger's and Simon at the butcher's. Each of these mini-scenes contains sequences of vigorous bargaining and haggling over the prices and quality of goods. The following sequence shows Ralph bargaining over goods at the fishmonger's:

(8) Ra: What shall I pay for a quarteron of waisters, for this side of salt fish. For this Thurnbacke, and for halfe a hundreth of smelts.
The Fishm: Will you haue but one word.
Ra: No.
The Fishm: You shall pay eight grotes for.
Ra: I shall not: I will pay, but fiue grotes for.
The Fishm: You come not to buy.
Ra: But I doe: But you will sell your waeres to deare.
The Fishm: Yea, with other: A word wye Syr. I will buy custume. Take all for two shillinges.
Ra: I will pay no more for.
The Fishm: I should be a looser by: Cast th'other two pence.
Ra: I can not.
The Fishm: Take it in Gods name.
Ra: Hold here is your monney. Fare you well.

In both (7) and (8) the linguistic focus is clearly on certain lexical items associated with the activity of buying and selling wares, e.g. "pay", "sell", "buy", terms denoting coins such as *stuphers*, *gelderns*, *grotes*, *shillings*, *pence*, etc., and with formulaic structures to be used in this type of situation. Whereas in (7) we do not have much more than question and answer pairs, in (8) the salesman asks Ralph whether he will be contented with one quotation and receives a blunt denial. When the salesman tells Ralph that he "shall pay eight grotes", Ralph flatly contradicts him and makes his own offer, whereupon the fishmonger accuses him of not having come to the market to buy anything. Ralph counters this with a further contradiction and accuses the fishmonger of trying to sell too dearly. The fishmonger tells Ralph confidentially that he needs customers and that he should take the wares at two shillings. Ralph agrees but says he will not pay any more than this, whereupon the fishmonger does another about-turn and tries to get Ralph to add two more pence to the price, otherwise he will be losing out on the deal. The whole interaction certainly contains the necessary lexical items and structures to be learnt, but it is also a realistic impression of what bargaining interactions may have sounded like in the late Elizabethan age.

This brings me to the second difference between the two dialogues. Both give the learner alternative structures and lexemes to carry out the same interaction, but in *Familiar Dialogues* the pace of the dialogues themselves is interrupted and held up from time to time by long lists of alternative words that a learner might want to insert in the relevant situation. In Dialogue A we have the following lexical sets:

(9) *Articles of clothing*:
hosen, shyrt, dwblet, handkercher, ierkin, garters
Colours:
redd, black, whit, graye, greene
Days of the week:
Sooneday, Monneday, Twesday, Weddnesday, Thursday, Friday, Sathurday
Objects from the schoolroom
booke, paper booke, paper, inkehorne, pennes, ink, penneknife, quilles

in Dialogue B the following:

(10) *Types of wine*
whitte wine, clairet wine, red wine, Frenche wine, Gaskyne wine, new Renishe wine, good sakke, good Mamesie, good Muscadene, new wine, old wine
A poulterer's wares
rabettes, a capon, a henne, a goose, a goseling, larkes, a stoke doue, a hayre, a mallart, a ducke, a drake, a crane, a sparow, a woodcoke, a swanne, a blackbirde, a parret.

A costermonger's wares
apples, pepines
Numbers
One, Two, Three, Foure, Fiue, Sixe, Seuen, Eight, Nyne, Ten, Eleuen, Twelfe, Thirteen, Foureten, Fiften, Sixten, Seuenten, Eighten, Ninten, Twenty. One and twenty, Two and twenty, Three and twenty, Foure and twenty, Fiue and twenty, fiue score and foure.
Types of cloth
broade cloth, caresie, caresie Flanders deye, cottun, Fryse, rugette, stamell, frisadoe, sardge, skarlatte, veluet, granadoe silke, satten, damaske, teffettey, sarsenet, grosgrayne, chamelet, worstede, mokadoe, braunched veluet, tuffte taffetey, Welshe plaine, fustiane, buckeren, sacke cloth, holland, trype veluet, tuffte veluet
Colours
fayre whitte, blacke, gray, fayre French taney, violet, greene, mingled collour, sheepes collour, yallow, blue, orenge, fayre straw collour, purple, darke greene
Types of fish on sale at the fishmonger's
salt fish, sole, plaise, viuers, rotches, gornettes, whittinges, waisters, thurnebacke, smeltes, redde hering, whitte hering, shrimpes, loupster, crabbes, picke, pickerell, millers shumbe, saumond, lamproye, elles, dotey, makerell, trouette, small lamproyes, moskels, cockelles, tenche, carpe, kempes, whale
Types of meat on sale at the butcher's
shippes flesh, side of porke, breast of beefe, vealle, nettes toung, roumpe of beefe, calfes plucke, calfes feete, sheepes feete, sheepes head, sheeps gather, calfes leagge, shoulder of motton, loygne of veale, lambe

in Dialogue C the following:

(11) *Things to buy at the market*
eggan, a pigge, nuttes, peasen, beanes, oatmeale, pudinges, saucerlings, apples, peares, pease cottes, cherises, raisins, figges, butter, rice, milke, plummes, prunes, almondes, turneps, pye, pasty, caeke, custarde, oringes, lymones, cabuche, a henne
Things to eat at table
whitte bread, mancher, the second course, fruit, a tarte, a custarde, a cake

in Dialogue D:

Learning English through Dialogues 231

(12) *Games to play*
dyce, tables, boules, tanyse, cartes
Playing cards
trompe, the Kyng, the Queene, the Knaue, the asse
Card terminology
deale, cut, trumpe, clubbes, hartes, speades, dyamondes, shufle

and in Dialogue E:

(13) *Riding terminology*
bootes, spurres also, bridle, pommell, sadle, styruppes, gyrtes, gyrdle
Craftsmen and trades
a saddler, a spurrier, a tayler, a shoomaker, a cabeller, a hattemaker, a capper, a seamester, a habredasher, a mercer, a grosser, an armourer, a cutteler, a chandeler, a grinder, a carier, a vintener, a brewer, a cooke, a cooper, a fishmonger, a butcher, a baker, a draper, a pewterer, a peinter, a smith, a locksmith, an yronmonger, a broker, a poulterer, a goldsmith, a carpendore, a loygner, a fruiterer, a woodmonger, a gyrdler, a clockmaker, a coalier, a tinker, a glouer, a jeweller
'Working' animals
horse, mowile, asse, oxe, hogge, dogge, grayhunde

These sets of lexical items pose a number of problems. Why is the overall natural impression that the dialogues make on the reader suddenly interrupted by such lists? Were the learners supposed to learn the script of the dialogues by heart and then to insert just one of the lexemes at the appropriate point? How many of the items in each list was the learner expected to know and be able to use? Were the dialogues simply read out by each learner and only one item in a list of items inserted at each reading?

Let us tackle this final question first. If only one of the items were meant to be inserted by a reader of the dialogues, this would contradict the tendency of a salesperson in Dialogue B, on being asked what goods s/he is offering for sale, to run through at least a few of those goods, or the head of a household in Dialogue C to run through a whole list of things the servant is required to go out and buy. Surely what we have here is a list of alternatives from which the learner, in simulating the role, may choose one or several.

If the learners were asked to learn the dialogues by heart, they must have been required to perform them orally and to make a choice of lexical item (or items) at the 'open' slots in which a list occurs, since only then could the natural impression of the dialogue be preserved. If the dialogues were meant for private study without a teacher, the learner might indeed try to learn as many of the items in a list as possible. The French translation and the rudimentary attempt to represent a quasi-phonetic transcription for French-speaking learners would certainly point towards the use of these dialogues in self-study rather than in teacher-monitored groups. On the other hand, the term "familiar" in the title would seem to refer to the everyday nature of the interactions. They would have been familiar to the learners in going about their daily lives. So, from this point of view one can certainly imagine them being performed in a group learning environment. Following on from this, if a choice of lexemes is made at the open slot, the overall effect of the dialogue will remain "natural" or "familiar".

We cannot of course know precisely how learners and teachers were supposed to use the dialogues in either of the two texts, but one fact at least is clear: in both texts learners are presented with structural alternatives with which to express the same communicative content. In the same dialogue from *A very profitable boke* between Katerine and Daniel, Katerine responds to Daniel's offer as follows:

(14) K: I cannot geue it for that price.
         You offer me losse.
         You offer to litle money.

The text sets up the frame "You offer –" into which the learner can either insert "losse" or "to litle money". The problem is that in the first alternative the indirect object "me" also has to be inserted and could be inserted into the second alternative, although it does not appear in this case. The syntactic frame provided for the options is thus somewhat inconsistent. In *Familiar Dialogues* the frames provided are both more consistent and more persistent. For example, in Dialogue A we see the following structures within about 34 lines of text:

(15) a. Stephen: Geue me my hosen.
     b. James: Bring me my whit hoses, and a clean shyrt ... bring me my graye hoses, my greene dwblet and a handkercher.
     c. Peter: Geue me my doublesoulshoes.
     d. Stephen: Geue me my pantables, and my pompes.
     e. Peter: Geue vs our breakefast.

The two frames are the imperative structures "geue me –" and "bring me –" followed by a noun phrase specified by the possessive determiner "my". This is then changed to the first person plural "giue us –" followed by a noun phrase specified by the possessive determiner "our". This latter structure is then repeated a few lines later when the children are reciting the Lord's Prayer: "Geue vs this day our dayly bread". There is no indication of how these highly regular syntactic patterns were to be practised, nor whether they were analysed into their component categories, but the sheer persistence of presentation here and elsewhere and the systematic variation in the structures point towards an explicit teaching strategy in which structure was both emphasised and also contextualised. To return to example (15) above, for example, we also see the following structure within those same 34 lines:

(16) Peter: You *brought* me a smock, in stead of my shirt.

focusing on the past tense form of the verb "bring" together with the indirect object "me" and a complex direct object. Throughout the *Familiar Dialogues*, Bellot not only offers alternative ways of expressing the same communicative intent, as in *A very profitable boke*, but also goes to great lengths to provide clusters of sentences in which one or two structural variations are offered to the learner. This may be an indication that the dialogues were meant to provide a blueprint of structure and lexis which could only be transformed into learning goals by a teacher, and less satisfactorily by the learners themselves. If this conjecture is true, it raises some intriguing questions about where the teaching took place, thus touching on central aspects of the lives of the refugee French speakers in London in the latter half of the sixteenth century, which I will go into in the following section.

4. The socio-historical framework of English language teaching in 16th century London

In the previous section I argued that *Familiar Dialogues* was used, in all probability, as teaching material in relatively institutionalised teaching/learning environments involving groups of learners under the supervision of teachers. But I also argued that the learners appear to have been both children and adults. The question now arises as to what that institutional framework might have been and where English language classes were held. In the final section we shall also consider whether *A very profitable boke* would have been used in similar locations.

The foreigner communities in the City of London in the latter half of the 15th century tended to cluster in the east of the city and in those wards bordering on the River Thames. Pettegree (1986: 21) estimates that in the two wards outside the city walls to the east (East Smithfield and St. Katherine's), the ward of Southwark on the south bank of the river and consequently outside the city, and (surprisingly) in St. Martin's ward inside the city walls and in the north-west of the city, the concentration of foreign residents had reached more than 20 per cent of the total population by the year 1550. Aldgate and

Langborne wards in the north east and Tower, Billingsgate and Dowgate bordering on the river show a population density of over 10 per cent of foreigners by 1550. By far the two most populous immigrant communities were Dutch-speaking (from the Low Countries) and French-speaking (from the Low Countries and France), but there was a fairly sizeable Italian community with its own church and a small Spanish community.

The two most important "stranger" churches, the old priory of Austin Friars serving the Dutch community and St. Anthony's chapel in Threadneedle Street serving the French community, were situated in Broad Street ward in the north of the city and inside the city walls. For a majority of the French-speaking population therefore a visit to the French church would have meant a lengthy walk from the river or from outside the walls of the city to the east. Pettegree (1986) maintains that the centre of cultural activities for the immigrant communities was their church, which would lead us to assume that English language courses for groups of both adults and children would have been held there. The distance from the church to the learners' homes, however, provides an argument against this hypothesis. In this case, where were such courses held? At the homes of some of the residents, in schoolhouses or perhaps in a cultural centre closer to the river? Who might the teachers have been? Other exiled French speakers who, like Bellot, had already acquired a good command of English, or native speakers of the language, schoolmasters perhaps? How were the lessons structured? By rote learning and recitation of the texts or by active participation in the form of the simulation of everyday communicative interactions?

We will, in all probability, never derive a satisfactory answer to any of these questions, but the text of *Familiar Dialogues* does offer some interesting hints, some of which have already been mentioned in passing, and there are, in addition, some other interesting historical facts which might also throw a certain amount of light on the matter.

The first fact to bear in mind is that the book was written in both English and French, i.e. it was bilingual. Hence the readers (or users) of it did not need to have any knowledge of English, and we are safe in assuming that whatever English they had was fairly rudimentary. Secondly, the user needed to be literate, an obvious fact but one that is underscored by the effort Bellot makes to provide a transliteration for French speakers to enable them to read the English text with an approximation to the native pronunciation.

Thirdly, Dialogue A makes direct reference to the fact that the children in the dialogue should prepare themselves to go to school and mentions the textbooks, exercise books, inkhorns and quills that they should remember to take with them, and Dialogue D deals with how a group of pupils amuse themselves playing cards at school during breaktime. If this was a "familiar" situation to the readers, then we must assume that the children of the refugee community did go to school. What we do not know is whether they attended a French-speaking school organised by the community or an elementary school for English children. Since the book was expressly written for the purposes of learning English, however, the former hypothesis is more likely. In addition, Pettegree (1986: 62) points to evidence that the Dutch community ran small schools throughout London and that the church had established its own school with a schoolmaster employed to teach on the premises. There is every reason to believe that the French community had established equivalent educational institutions within their own community.

Fourthly, the texts are meant for both adults and children, which indicates either that individual classes were arranged for the adults and the children in two different groups dealing with the appropriate dialogues in the book, or, more probably, that the classes were of mixed ages. In this case the teaching might indeed have been carried out at the church in Threadneedle Street or wherever the French-speaking schools were held.

My fifth point can be taken as an argument in favour of the church as a venue for English language teaching. In Dialogue A the children recite the Lord's Prayer and ask their parents to bless them. In Dialogue C the hosts and their guests comment on the wrongs done to their church in France and say an elaborate grace which also involves a blessing for "our Queene and the Realme" which we can only take to be a reference to Queen Elizabeth and England. Dialogue E also contains a number of lengthy prayer sequences. Indeed, however "familiar" the dialogues might be – and those which simulate situations in the market-place provide a rich set of insights into what was for sale on market stalls and how stallholders and customers must have bargained for the best prices – they are set very firmly within the framework of orthodox Calvinism. At the end of his dedication to the reader Bellot writes:

> ... the whiche Dialogues, I pray the Christian Reader, to receaue euen so acceptable, as though they did come out of a more sufficient hand than myne is, for a token of that good will which I bare to all them which do liue in the feare of God: Whom I pray to geue vs his peace. So be it.

The sixth point is tied up with the fifth in that it relates to the immigrants' concern about events in France and to the expression of a desire to return to the homeland as soon as circumstances will permit. In Dialogue C we have the following exchange between the "master" and his "neighbour":

(17) The maister: What newes?
     The neighb.: There is no other newes, but of the sickenesse and the

	dearth, which be now a dayes almost thoroughout all Fraunce.
The maister:	It is Gods hand which reuengeth the iniurie done to his Church.
The neighb.:	you say true.
The maister:	I beleue, that there scappes al wayes some of them.
The neighb.:	Few, or none at all.
The maister:	Is the number of them great, that they are come ouer into this countrey?
The neighb.:	Very great: and there be many of them whiche doe liue very hard, so great is their pouertie.
The maister:	Truely, I take great pitie of their miserable estate: But I hope that God will remember them, for he neuer forsaketh them which doe thrust in him.

In Dialogue E a gentleman is on his way to the Kentish coast with his servant when he sees a merchant in front of him who seems to be going in the same direction. He catches him up and asks him where he is bound, whereupon the merchant tells him that he wants to cross over to France. This is how Bellot presents the scene:

(18)	The Gentel.:	Neadd bring hether my horse, It is great tyme to be goyng.
	The seruing.:	When you please: sir here is your horse.
	The Gentel.:	Let vs ride a good passe to ouertake that man, which doth ride there afore vs: God saue you sir.
	The march.:	God blesse you Syr.
	The gentel.:	Whether go you sir.
	The march.:	I would fayne be in Fraunce.
	The gentl.:	And I also. But where about do you mynde to take shipping?
	The march.:	At Rye, God willing.
	The gentel.:	I would we were there.
	The march.:	I hope we shalbe there to morow betymes.

Like (17) this extract expresses not only concern for what is happening in France, but also a clear sense of homesickness. Hence, whether or not our learners managed to acquire enough English to deal with the everyday situations in which they found themselves, what they learned was meant to be purely utilitarian, enough to get them through life in London until such time as they might be able to return to France.

It is at this point that we encounter a set of contradictions. We know that a number of socially significant trades in London during the latter half of the sixteenth century were dominated by foreign residents, in particular the printing, weaving and coopering trades. In many cases the immigrants had become denizens, i.e. the 16th century equivalent to naturalised citizens, and were second or even third generation residents. Many of them had also taken English wives. Others, like Bellot himself, had come to London in the 1560s or 1570s and, although they might have always intended to return, in fact stayed and made their homes in England. These "foreigners" certainly acquired a more than adequate knowledge of English, and it is highly likely that their children grew up bilingual with a preference for English. They would not, therefore, have needed to use Bellot's text.

The only people who would have had occasion to learn English were freshly arrived immigrants, mostly refugees from the religious persecution of Protestantism in France and the Low Countries, for many of whom London was a temporary refuge before they were once again able to return to the continent. The census figures for the foreign community in London in the latter half of the sixteenth century show a great discrepancy between the large numbers of refugees entering England and the slow overall growth rate of the immigrant community. The only plausible explanation – bar the periodic recurrence of epidemics such as the plague – lies in the rapid turnover of newly arrived and returning refugees. In such a situation Bellot's text had to be easy to use (cf. the translation into French and the quasi phonetic representation of the pronunciation) and applicable to everyday situations.

5. The Spanish immigrant community in London and their need to learn English

From the later stages of Henry VIII's reign right through to the Elizabethan age and beyond, with a brief five-year interruption from 1553 to 1558 during the reign of Queen Mary, London served as a haven of refuge for those Protestants who suffered religious persecution in France and the Low Countries. In fact since the 16th century, playing host to refugee communities has become one of the city's traditional roles, the last significant occasion being the Second World War. It was of course significant that refugees in northern France and what is now Belgium and the Netherlands took the safe and relatively easy route across the English Channel and the North Sea rather than risk an overland journey into Germany and Switzerland. As long as the Anglican form of Protestantism was the official religion in England, it was after all safer to be on an island.

There was, however, another reason for their flight to London which has more to do with economic geography than with considerations of safety. The vast majority of the refugees were from urban centres throughout the Low Countries and northern France, e.g. Antwerp, Amsterdam, Bruges, Brussels, Lille, Rouen, Caen, etc., or from their immediate hinterlands. They practised trades which depended on those centres. In the 16th century the most significant urban area was the port of Antwerp, which was a member of the Hanseatic League and a nerve centre for international trade and shipping. So important was Antwerp that Spain, whose jurisdiction extended over the whole of the Low Countries, was more than hesitant about suppressing the movements of the reformed church in the city, even though their adherents clearly outnumbered members of the Roman Catholic church. London was also a Hanseatic port, probably the most important on the periphery of the Hanseatic trading routes, since it was the centre of a very large and protected hinterland, an important market in which foreign merchants had been operating for at least 300 years prior to Elizabeth's reign. Not only could tradesmen hope for freedom from religious persecution in London; they could also hope to be able to set up in business and capitalise on that hinterland. In addition, they knew that the more advanced continental technology in trades such as printing and weaving was in demand in London.

Refugees from religious persecution from outside the economic spheres of influence of the urban centres of the Low Countries and northern France, e.g. from the south of France, from Spain or from Italy, generally arrived in London by way of other centres of Protestantism, in particular by way of Geneva and Zurich. The principal reason for them moving on to London was often disagreement with the strict orthodoxy of the religious authorities in those two cities, or even, as in the case of the Spanish Protestants who had fled to Geneva from the Inquisition, the fear of further persecution by rigorous Calvinists. Most of the monks who fled from the Hieronymite monastery of San Isidro del Campo near Seville in 1557 made for Geneva following in the wake of a handful of Spanish Calvinists including Juan Pérez and Cipriano de Valera who escaped from Seville in 1555. Amongst those who fled in 1557 are Casiodoro de Reina and Antonio del Corro. After the death of Queen Mary, Reina and Valera made their way to London, whereas Corro first went to Antwerp, then later to Bordeaux, Toulouse and Antwerp again before moving on to London in 1567.

The small Spanish community in London at the beginning of Elizabeth's reign were not permitted to worship in public, and it was not until Reina's petition to Lord Cecil and the Bishop of London, Edmund Grindal, that they acquired their own church, St. Mary Axe, in 1560. Reina, however, was continually harrassed by the French church for his alleged lack of Calvinist orthodoxy, culminating in charges of adultery and sodomy, which forced him to leave England in 1564. At his departure the short-lived Spanish church fell apart, its members joining the French and Italian churches. Valera studied and taught in Oxford from 1559 till 1563, when his marriage forced him to give up a Fellowship of Magdalen College and move to London. After the collapse of the Spanish church, Valera worshipped at the Italian church in contradistinction to Corro, who joined the French church on his arrival in London in 1567. However, his close association with Reina and his disagreements with orthodox church policy in Geneva led to a quarrel with the officials of that church and his joining the Italian church. He finally ended up becoming Anglican.

This brief history of the most well-known Spanish Protestants in London in the first half of Elizabeth's reign indicates the low prestige in which Spanish immigrants to London were held both by the English Protestant authorities and by the Calvinist authorities of the French church. The charges against Reina were, in all probability, trumped up, not only in order to discredit him, but also to destroy him completely. Corro's difficulties with the Calvinist French church were a direct consequence of his friendship with Reina, and Valera's association with the Italian church is also an indication of the same type of problem that he must have experienced.

Let us now return to *A very profitable boke* and assess firstly whether, under these circumstances, it would have been in use at all amongst the Spanish community in London, and secondly what its significance might nevertheless have been. The Spanish community in London remained relatively small throughout Elizabeth's reign and was constantly suffering from the effects of the Marian persecution, on the one hand, and from a more subtle form of religious persecution from orthodox Calvinists in the French church on the other. Return to Spain for most Spanish nationals would have meant almost certain violent death and even a move to the Spanish ruled Low Countries, apart from Antwerp, would have been hazardous. Residence in England was therefore a long-term proposition, and the histories of Corro and Valera indicate the high degree to which they integrated into English society. There would therefore have been little or no use for English-language teaching materials amongst the Spanish community.

It is also important to note that *A very profitable boke* and *The boke of Englyshhe and Spanysshe* were published in 1554 at the beginning of Mary's reign and that they were directly translated from other books in use throughout continental Europe. They may well have been printed in anticipation of an increased demand on the part of Spanish speakers for acquiring English, or, as I have argued in this paper, vice versa. It is highly dubious that they were ever used after Elizabeth's accession to the throne in 1558. Neverthless, *A very profitable boke* served as the model for Bellot's *Familiar Dialogues*, indicating very strongly that there was a tradition in printing dialogic material for foreign language teaching which Bellot was able to capitalise on.

In this paper I have only considered the French-speaking and Spanish-speaking communities in London in the 16th century and their different needs in acquiring the English language. However, it would be interesting to extend this enquiry to cover other immigrant groups, in particular the Italians. I claim that the more peripheral a community is to the trading centres of the Hansa area in the 15th and 16th centuries, the longer its members will stay in the host country and the less movement there will be to and from the continent. As a result the members of that community will feel compelled to assimilate more readily, a major part of the assimilation process being the natural acquisition of the language. As a consequence, the need to learn the language through dialogic texts will decrease. Clarifying this, however, requires a lot more empirical research involving interdisciplinary cooperation between historical linguists, historians, geographers and sociologists.

References

Alston, R. A.
    1967–1972   *English Linguistics 1500–1800. A Collection of Facsimile Reprints.* Menston: The Scolar Press. Reissued in microfiche form by U.M.I., Ann Arbor, Michigan.

anonymous
    1554   *A very profitable boke to lerne the maner of redyng, writyng, and speakyng english and Spanish.* London.
    1554   *The boke of Englysshe, and Spanysshe.* London.

Bellot, James
    1580   Le maistre d'escole Anglois/The Englishe Scholemaister. London.
    1586   *Familiar Dialogues/Dialogues familiers.* London.

Finlay, Roger
    1981   *Population and Metropolis: The Demography of London 1580–1650.* Cambridge: Cambridge University Press.

Hauben, Paul J.
    1965   A Spanish Calvinist church in Elizabethan London, 1559–65. *Church History* XXXIV (1), 50–56.
    1967   *Three Spanish Heretics and the Reformation.* Genève: Librairie Droz.

Kinder, A. Gordon
    1975   *Casiodoro de Reina: Spanish Reformer of the Sixteenth Century.* London: Thamesis Books.
Pettegree, Andrew
    1986   *Foreign Protestant Communities in Sixteenth-Century London.* Oxford: Clarendon Press.
Rappaport, Steve
    1989   *Worlds within Worlds: Structures of Life in 16th-Century London.* Cambridge: Cambridge University Press.
Roberts, R. J.
    1970   Two early English–Spanish vocabularies. *The British Museum Quarterly* XXXIV (3–4), 86–91.
Saxon, Samuel
    1737   *The English Scholar's Assistant.* London.
Ungerer, Gustav
    1965   *The Printing of Spanish Books in Elizabethan England.* London: The Bibliographical Society.
van Barlement, Noël
    1551   *Vocabulare.* Louvain.

Dialogues in Late Medieval and Early Modern English Medical Writing

Irma Taavitsainen
University of Helsinki

1. Introduction

This paper assesses medical dialogues in Late Middle and Early Modern English and gives an overview of the evolution of medical dialogues in English between 1375 and 1750. The text forms of early English medical writing have not been assessed before, and there is no previous knowledge of the extent or type of dialogue used in this register. This information is not readily available and several sources have been used for compiling the data.[1] The material is puzzling and raises several questions. On the one hand, late medieval scientific writing is scholastic and dialectic. On the other hand, mimetic dialogues emerge in handbooks of the sixteenth century, and instruction was given in fictional conversations, reflecting natural speech to various extents. The underlying motivation for writing in the dialogue form is expressed by Thomas Gale, the author of a mimetic dialogue, in 1563. He thought it good to apply this form for *that it is moste apte to teche and instructe by* (f. 1v).

2. Dialogues and dialogic elements in written discourse

The monologue-versus-dialogue distinction is an important aspect of participant relations cutting across the medium and mode of communication; the evidence of the sender adjusting the text according to the addressee or the target group is important here, so that audience response is explicitly taken into account. Texts form a continuum in this respect: at the one end are texts that show no evidence of the receiver, and at the opposite end are texts which depend on overt receiver response and explicitly include such elements

(McCarthy and Carter 1994: 16-17). As regards written texts, maximally monologic texts can be found in expository scientific writing, for instance, and dialogues that imitate spoken conversation would be maximally dialogic. The material of historical studies is necessarily written, but in previous studies dialogues have been singled out as the most speech-based text form though there is a great deal of variation in them (see Culpeper and Kytö, forthcoming and this volume). Interaction is the key to the dialogic facet of language use, and features connected with reciprocity of communication can be used to measure this element. Such features can be found among those established as typical of spoken language (Chafe 1985; Halliday 1989) and attributed to the dimension of variation called "involved versus informational production" (Biber 1988: 104-108). Exclamations and other personal affect features are relevant here (Biber and Finegan 1989; Caffi and Janney 1994; Taavitsainen 1997), including pragmatic particles (for the bibliography, see Jucker 1997). But dialogic elements may have another source in this material, as they can be associated with the learned tradition of the early period, and the linguistic features connected with this influence have to be sought in scholastic style.[2]

The present material consists of written dialogues that vary in degrees of orality according to the underlying traditions. The hypothesis is that scholastic features are predominant in the early dialogues, but features of spoken language increase, and it may be possible to discern a line of evolution. The break-through of the new science took place gradually from the latter half of the sixteenth century onwards, and the new thought-style, with the new idea of how science should be shaped, is reflected in the language use (Taavitsainen 1994; Taavitsainen and Pahta 1995). Written dialogues are a special way of communicating knowledge in handbooks, and their relation to other subgenres of medical writing raises interesting questions. Do these dialogues reflect natural spoken language to any degree? Are there features that link them with modern institutional dialogues? And finally, are the various types distinct, or are the categories overlapping?

3. Traditions of medieval and early modern medical dialogues

Early English medical dialogues fall into two main types: scholastic formulae and mimetic dialogues. In the following survey, the specification of participant roles is taken as the basis of classification: the first group consists of texts that do not state them; in the second group the roles are explicit and participants named. Both types may ultimately be descendants of philosophical texts, and

Dialogues in English Medical Writing 245

the underlying traditions may intertwine and merge in actual texts. The main outlines help to discern these underlying influences.

3.1. Philosophical dialogues

The dialogue form in philosophy dates from the Greek philosophers; it was cultivated by Socrates in real dialogue, reported by Plato in writing, and pursued by Aristotle rather more abstractly, but with a residual aspect for dialogue (Ong 1958: 152). The traditions continued in the Middle Ages, and debates belonged to the teaching methods of universities, in medicine as in other fields closely allied to scholastic philosophy. Some changes started to be felt in the sixteenth century with Ramus' (1515-1572) concern for methodology. His ideas spread from Paris to other European universities, Cambridge and Oxford, and prepared the way for the philosophy of the new science by shifting the emphasis from traditional Aristotelian logic to the dialectic method (Gilbert 1960: 211-212). Philosophical language has its own conventions of sophisticated prose which may have served as a model for vernacular scientific writing.[3]

3.2. Scientific writing in question-answer form: the scholastic formula

The more contrived dialogue form had a classical model based on Aristotelian physical treatises, which embedded theological, medical, and scientific problems. The issues were dealt with in the form of *questiones.* In the thirteenth and fourteenth century the typical pattern had the question first, then the author suggested an affirmative or a negative answer according to a pattern. Central arguments are given first; they are followed by a description, definitions and explanations; conclusions sum up the opinions and viewpoints; finally the "principal arguments" are returned to and the problem is answered. The questions consisted of a standard stock valid for centuries (Grant 1974: 199, 610). The vernacularisation of scientific writings in the late medieval period involved an attempt to transfer features of the source language to the target language, and it can be assumed that this applies to text formats as well as stylistic features. Thus it is relevant to see whether this text structure can be found in the present material.

3.3. Mimetic dialogues in handbooks: conversational structure

Handbooks were a new genre in the fifteenth century. Their increasing popularity is connected with the rise of the middle class, increasing literacy, and the desire for improvement and edification. There was a demand for literature of this kind. Medical handbooks in dialogue form are extant from the middle of the sixteenth century, but they are built on earlier monologic texts to a large extent. Handbooks give advice on maintaining health, keeping fit, and making medicine, but some of them also include fictional characters, comical scenes and social satire. They are often addressed to a general and "unlearned" audience, but this may just be a rhetorical formula (see below). One of the main questions connected with this material is whether such mimetic dialogues replicate natural conversational structures to any degree, and how source materials were transformed into this form.

4. A survey of early English medical dialogues

The vernacularisation of scientific writings started with the nationalistic strivings of late fourteenth century England, with medical writing leading the way. The developments were parallel in several European vernaculars, and the topic has attracted a great deal of scholarly interest recently (Crossgrove, Schleissner and Voigts 1998). Yet the predominance of Latin in medicine in England continued till the middle of the seventeenth century (Webster 1975: 267).

4.1. The late medieval period

A major problem with medical material of this period is that much of it remains unavailable in modern editions, and much of it is unknown to scholars. The situation is improving with modern bibliographical tools. According to my knowledge there are no edited texts in question form or dialogue form from the medieval period, although such texts exist. The *Index of Middle English Prose, Handlists I-XI*, recorded one entry. The database of scientific incipits has ten entries for interrogatory texts, six alchemical and four medical texts.[4] The incipits point to expert-novice dialogues; an apprentice/learner is asking for advice and information. In one text the title states *how a disciple asketh questions* (1), and in the others the incipit includes a direct address, with a request to profit from the addressee's expertise, e.g. *Master I pray thee for saint charity the* [sic] *ye shew me a few medicines that I might help poor men* (2). In one alchemical text the teacher addresses the learner: *Right trusty and well beloved child I shall inform ye of this gracious science* (3). Although such beginnings would presuppose an interactive discourse form, the text may unfold as a monologue or a recipe collection like any other. I found no fictional dialogues from this period.

Next I wanted to check whether there are dialogic elements in any of the texts included in the first part of the *Corpus of Early English Medical Writing* (1375-1750; see Note 1). For this purpose I made lexical searches of *question, answer, ask, tell*, and I also checked personal pronouns of the first and second person, as their frequent occurrence would indicate texts worth looking at. The result was lean, as few dialogic elements could be found and the pronouns cluster in metatextual passages. The most interesting text in this respect was the *"Canutus" Plague Treatise*, one of the first incunabula that also circulated in manuscript copies. Some passages contain expert-novice dialogue as the author gives answers to questions posed by "some", and features typical of scholastic questions-literature and the scholastic thought-style are present, e.g. in references to authorities and the modality of knowing.[5]

(1) But *ij^{en} questions ys meued in this case*: what ys the cause that on dye & the tother not, and in summe tovne the[r] deyd men and in another not? *The secunde question* beth wheter this morbes pestilencial be contagius? *Atte furste* Y do say that this may fortune of ij^{en} maner of causes ... And to *the ijde question*, that suche morbes pestilencial be contagius (Pickett 1994: 272-3).

[But two questions are posed in this case: what is the cause of one dying and another not, and in one town and in another not. The second question is whether this epidemic disease is contagious?
To the first I say that this may happen in two ways ... And to the second that an epidemic disease is contagious.]

(2) And *summe wil aske the question* why that he shal not slepe yf yt hade a natural slepe, and in thys case *Y wyl answer* shorttely that in þe pestilence sesson, anon after met, yf he haue luste to slepe, then that luste moste be reuoked for a sesson ... and then the slepe natural may cumme, the space of an hore after dyner (Pickett 1994: 278).

[And someone will ask why he will not sleep in a natural way. In this case I will answer shortly that in the time of plague, if he wishes to sleep right after eating, then that desire must be postponed for an appropriate time ... and then he may fall asleep in a natural way, within an hour after dinner.]

Dialogic passages in some other texts seem to be of a different kind. *Lanfrank's Chirurgia Parva* contains questions and answers as part of a case report embedded in the discourse. It reports the events as first-person narrative and the story unfolds in direct speech quotations at this point. Thus the dialogue passage does not reflect any of the three underlying traditions, but it is a narrative that serves to illustrate medical practice.

(3) And I sawe in hym tokens of dethe and bad the spicer lede hym home to his house þat he myght dy in his bed. *And he answerd, maister is þer noon othir helpe with the? And I be þought me and said*, for sothe if þou haue eny nobill triacle to ȝeue hym a good quayntyte percase he myght lyffe. The spycer had hym home and yafe hym a noble triacle ... (Asplund 1970: 84-85).

[And I saw in him the tokens of death and asked the apothecary to lead him home to his house so that he could die in his bed. And he answered, "Master, is there no other help?" And I thought about it and said, "Truly, if you have any excellent antidote to give him a good quantity, perhaps he may live." The apothecary took him home and gave him some excellent antidote ... .]

4.2. Early modern period

Dialogue materials increase from the middle of the sixteenth century onwards. Both scholastic questions-literature and instructive dialogues with fictional characters are found. The mimetic mode seems to contain a wide range of texts, from strictly professional medical treatises to social satire and religious texts with a medical plot (see below).

4.2.1. The scholastic question-answer formula

The participants are not explicitly stated in these texts, but questions and answers alternate under respective headings. It is obvious that these are teaching texts in the scholastic tradition in the abstract dialogue form. There are no traces of natural conversation or interaction; no follow-up questions or reactions to the previous turns occur. The scholastic thought-style is predominant (see Taavitsainen and Pahta 1997 and 1998). First-person pronouns are used in metatextual phrases like *As I sayd before, First I say* (Taavitsainen forthcoming), but otherwise the tone is impersonal. This trend emerges in the middle of the sixteenth century and continues all through the period in focus.

Guido's Questions (1579). These questions and answers were first printed in 1542 under the title *Questyonary of cyrurygens*, and reissued as *Guido's Questions* in 1579; the name refers to the medieval surgery by Guy de Chauliac, which, however, is not written in this format. The book begins with a general part about what surgery is and what qualities are needed of a good surgeon; then it moves on to anatomical questions and the parts of the body.

The tone is neutral and matter-of fact. The questions are short, but the answers vary in length. The scholastic text format is explicit, though the pattern is much simpler than the Latin model described above. The logical form of the argument is important and close attention is paid to it, e.g. with an enumerative text strategy, marking the stages of argumentation. This is in accordance with the scholastic technique which employs common logical terms to organize discourse and build up the arguments.

(4) Question: How many considerations *ought the Chirurgion to haue* touching his forme and general manner to worke manually?
    Aunswere: *After Arnold de villa noua*, he *ought to* haue *iiij. The .j.* is, he *ought to* consider what operation it is that he *ought to* doe to mans body. And *it is knowen* by the diuision of the operations of Chyrurgerie *aforesayd, that is to knit* the thing deuided. *The second* consideration is, that he *ought to* consider ... *The thirde* consideration is, that he *ought to* consider ... And *the fourth* consideration is, that the Chyrurgion *ought to knowe* ... the *Chyrurgion ought to take heede* in dooing all things that he *ought to* doe, as touching this operation ... (ff. 2v-3r).

[How many points should a surgeon consider with regard to the form and manner of working manually?
According to Arnold of Villa Nova he should consider four points. The first is that he should consider what operation he should perform. The above-mentioned surgery makes known the divisions of the operations, to put together what is divided. The second point is that he should consider ... The third point is that he should consider ... And the fourth point is that the surgeon should know ... the surgeon should take heed of all things that he should do in connection with this operation ...]

References to authorities are frequent, and they are usually placed in a prominent position at the opening of a turn. The statements are given as absolute truths, and prescriptive phrases dominate. In some other passages guidance is more personal with second person pronouns. This is a typical feature of didactic texts, and the basic text type of instruction (Werlich 1983: 124). Deontic modality is predominant here, and the tone is extremely didactic:

(5) The which *iiij.* considerations *thou mayst* haue and perceiue by such an example. If *thou wilt* draw water from the bellyes ... *First thou oughtest to* consider that the operation which *thou wilt* do is to draw out *the sayd* water. *Secondly, thou oughtest to* consider *wherfore thou dost* it, for it is

for to heale ... *Thirdly*, whether such operation be necessary, needfull, or possible. And *thou oughtest to wit* that it is necessary ... (f. 3r).

[Which four points you may perceive by such an example. If you will let out water from the abdomen ... First you should consider that the operation that you will perform is to let out the said water. Secondly, you ought to consider why you do it, because the purpose is to heal ... Thirdly, whether such an operation is necessary, needful, or possible. And you should be convinced that it is necessary ...]

Approved Directions for Health (1612). This book represents a different layer of medical writing as it is a general guide for a wider audience *teaching how every Man should keepe his body and mind in health: and sicke, how hee may safely restore it himselfe* (p. 1). The text form follows the scholastic question-answer pattern, with passive voice and distanced phrases at the beginning:

(6) What be the causes of the preseruation of Mans health?
The causes of the preseruation of mans health be foure; the first, Aire, Fire and Water. The second, meate and drinke, and such as we vse for nourishment. The third, mirth, exercise, and tranquillity of the body. The fourth, auoydance of excrements ... .
What is Ayre? Aire naturally by it selfe, is an element (pp. 1-2).

[What are the factors contributing to man's health? The factors contributing to man's health are four: (1) air, fire, and water; (2) food and drink, such as we use for nourishment; (3) joy, exercise and tranquillity of the body; (4) avoidance of excrements ... .
What is air? Air naturally by itself is an element.]

In the course of the book the tone changes. It becomes more involved and personal. The questions start increasingly with *shew me* and the instructions are more personal with hedges and intensifiers, e.g. *I might here commend* (p. 86), *I cannot but commend* (p. 128), *I meane* (p. 130), *I verily beleeue* (p. 138) and *I praise aboue all others* (p. 186). This altered tone is evident in the last chapter. Instead of an impersonal question, the heading is in the form of a plea: *Declare vnto me a daily Diet, whereby I may liue in health, and not trouble my selfe in Physicke* (p. 143). The text begins as a direct response to it: *I will: first of all in the morning when you are about to rise up, stretch your selfe strongly ...* (p. 143), and the conversational instructive tone continues in passages like *But least (perhaps) your teeth become loose and filthy, I will shew you ...* (p. 144).

A Treatise upon the Small-pox (1723). A further development of the earlier tradition without explicit participants can be seen in texts in which the author conveys an imaginary discussion, raises imaginative objections and then dismisses them, thus carrying on his own argument leading to conclusions. The dialogic form emphasizes the argumentative interaction with the target audience, but at the same time this text form relies heavily on the dialectic conventions of medieval scientific texts in Latin.[6]

(7) If it be demanded, whether in such Cases purging Medicines ought to be administred to carry off the Putrefaction, and so bring the Contest to a happy Conclusion; I answer, I can by no means approve of that Practice: I have formerly made Tryal of it, but I must acknowledge, I never once saw any good Event (p. 75).

[If it is asked whether in such cases purging medicines ought to be administered to complete decomposition and so bring the struggle to a happy conclusion, I answer that I can by no means approve of that practice. I have tried it earlier, but I must acknowledge that I never saw any good result, not even once.]

The Rudiments of Physick (1753). This text shows that the question-answer formula continues throughout and beyond the period in focus. The contents are taken from an earlier work, following the practice of copying old materials without indicating the source. The same, or approximately the same, materials were printed under various names, e.g. *The Grounds of Physick* from 1715 is given here as *The Rudiments of Physick*. It is a teaching text according to the old scholastic formula, without changes in the deontic modality:

(8) Question: What is Physick?
    Answer: Physick is the Art of preserving Health, and restoring it, when lost; or it is that Science (as you will see in the following Treatise) by the Knowledge of whiche Life and Health are preserved, or lost Health restored.
    Question: From whence does Physick derive its Origin?
    Answer: From the Diseases which have happened to Men, from the Nature of our Food, from the Actions of Life and from the Construction itself of the human Frame (p. 17).

Similar tracts are found even later, e.g. *A Compendious System of the Theory and Practice of Modern Surgery In the Form of a Dialogue* by Hugh Munro, from 1792, shows this format.

4.2.2. Mimetic dialogues

The other main type of Early Modern English medical dialogues relies on fictional characters. These texts have explicit participants and unfold as interactive dialogues in direct speech quotations with overt responses to the previous turns. The first known author of medical books in this dialogue form is William Bullein (c. 1515-1576), and others soon followed him. At least five books from the sixteenth century have this form, and at least three medical and two alchemical dialogues date from the seventeenth century. The number increases in the following century.

Participant roles in mimetic dialogues are varied, though the doctor-student or expert-novice talk predominates. In some books several experts discuss, or there may be a mixture of experts and laymen, surgeons and students, etc. A broad range of characters is introduced in Bullein's *Dialogue against the Fever Pestilence* (1578): medicus and apothecary represent medical institutions. More abstract roles that echo medieval allegorical figures, such as Sickness and Health, are found in other books (*Bullein's Bulwarke of Defence againste Sicknes, Sornes, and Woundes* 1562). The seventeenth-century tracts are more directly connected with medical institutions, while the eighteenth century shows a greater variety, ranging from doctor-patient talk to a more philosophical vein, and conversations between gentlemen in polite society.

William Bullein's ***The Gouernement of Health*** (1558).[7] The interlocutors of the earliest mimetic dialogue are Iohn and Humphrey. The tract turns out to be a dialogue in which an old and wise man gives advice to a light-hearted youth, and thus it is linked with wisdom literature and parental instructions. The beginning contains Iohn's description of his own indulgent lifestyle, and Humphrey's answer with a learned allusion to Heliogubalus' court where Iohn *might haue claimed a great office* (f. 1v). Iohn takes this as an insult and his reaction shows surprise and anger, imitating natural conversation. The opposition is clear, and Humphrey resorts to folk wisdom, which is common in colloquial speech:

(9) Iohn: *What? Good sir, I require not your counsell, I pray you bee your owne caruer* [do it at your own discretion] *and giue mee leaue to serue my* fantasie. *I will not charge you, you* are verie auncient and graue, and *I* am but young, *wee be no matches*.

Hum.: *Good counsell is a treasure to wise men, but a verie trifle* [of little importance] *to a foole*, if *thou* haddest seene those things which *I* haue seene, I knowe *thou* wouldest not be such a man, nor thus spend *thy* time.

Iohn: What hast *thou* seene, that *I* haue not seene? (f. 1v; the reprint of 1595 is used in this study)

Iohn is thus characterized as arrogant and proud. He dismisses the old man's advice first, but becomes curious, and the dialogue proceeds to medical matters; the shift from the polite second person plural to singular could at this time be a sociolinguistic marker (see e.g. Calvo 1992), but here the use vacillates.

(10) Ioh.: Mee thinke *thou canst giue good counsell ... I pray thee*, is it so great hurt to delight in plentie of banquets?
Hum.: *Sir, if it will please you* to bee somewhat attentiue, *I will tell you...* .
Iohn.: Is it true that *you* haue said to mee? (f. 2)

The discussion is polite and considerate, as the phrases and forms of address indicate. Iohn uses interpersonal pleas frequently, and he even apologizes for his previous behaviour:

(11) *I pray thee friend* Humfrey, what is phisicke? I would bee glad to learne some of thy knowledge, for thou hast a good order in talking, and seeme to be grounded of authority [because you talk in an orderly way and seem to be well established in authority]. *Therefore I am sory that I haue contended* [argued] *with thee: I pray thee be not angry with my former talke* (ff. 4r-4v).

Iohn poses the questions and summarises Humphrey's answers in follow-up turns, which enhances the interactivity of the dialogue, e.g. *Seeing thou hast spoken of sundrie partes of Phisitions, I pray thee what partes be there of phisicke?* (f. 5v), or *... for they be good for mans nature.* Iohn. *For mans nature? that is maruell: For how can those bee good for mans nature ...* (f. 61v) Reactions may have the tone of spontaneity, e.g. *What, might not men ... I pray you tell me* (f. 8). The questions vary in their degrees of politeness from simple *What is Vinegar?* (f. 71), *What is Sorrell, might I know of thee, and the property thereof?* (f. 41) or *What thinkest thou of ...* (f. 40v) to more polite *I would bee glad to learne the vertue of...* (f. 81) or *Wilt thou be so good as to tel me the properties of water?* (f. 70v). Some pleas occur as well: *I pray thee tel me some good regiment for me & my family, if it please God ...* (f. 84) or *I would faine see the true forme ...* (f. 19) and *I would verie faine know the natures of...* (f. 38).

Humphrey's speeches are long didactic monologues with frequent references to authorities in the scholastic vein, e.g. *Hippocrates in his booke of windes or blastes saith ...* (f. 4v) *Herodotus sayeth: they greatly erre ... of this writeth Galen ...* (f. 4v). Prescriptive phrases are also frequent, e.g. *these things may not bee forgotten: you must note also ...* (f.. 10), *Thou oughtest also most chiefly to lerne ...* (f. 16v). Occasionally he addresses Iohn *my friend Iohn*, and some speechlike features occur in the use of discourse particles, such as *Well, ...* and *Oh Iohn, ...*.

The book also contains medical verse, inserted in the middle of the tract, and presented as Humfrey's compositions: *wilt thou heare it? take that chaire and sit downe, and I will teach thee my song.* Iohn: *I thanke thee* (f. 6v), or even more politely: *I Hartely thanke thee, gentle maister Humphrey: for thy paines taking ...* (f. 68v). Iohn's comment is positive: *This is a good song, and I will learne it: for though it seeme not verie pleasant, yet I perceiue it is profitable ...* (f. 2v), or *In good faith, me thinks thou sayest well, ...* (f. 10). Occasionally Humphrey responds: *I shall be glad for as much as thou hast taken paines to heare me all this while, to teach thee ...* (f. 84).

Thomas Gale's *Chirurgerie* (1563). The underlying vein of this book is in accordance with the classical question-answer formula, but it is presented in dialogue with named participants. One of the interlocutors is the author of the book, the others are also eminent surgeons. The style of most passages is in accordance with scholastic writing. The attitude to knowledge varies from obedient adherence to ancient authorities to more critical views, e.g.

(12) Tho. Gale: Then seyng our talke shal wholly be the institution of a Chirurgian, it ware mete, and conuenient first to vnderstande what Chirurgery is. Wherfore answere me I pray you, what call you Chirurgirie?

Iohn Yates: Guido de Cauliaco (in his boke which he calleth his Collectorie) defineth it in this sorte. Chirurgerie is a parte of therapeutike helinge ... (f. 2v).

[Then as I see that our talk shall cover the whole system of surgery, it is appropriate and convenient first to understand what surgery is. Therefore answer me, please, what do you call surgery?

Guy de Chauliac in his book called Collectory defines it in this way. Surgery is a part of therapeutic healing ...]

Iohn Feilde: In this definition *is to be notyd*, that Chirurgery doth not cure al greifes which require helpe of the hande: but onlye suche as are curable. Also *it is to be vnderstande*, though in the definition ... .

Tho. Gale: Truth it is ... (f. 3v).

[In this definition it is to be noticed that surgery does not cure all grievances that require the help of the hand, but only such that are curable. Also it is to be understood, though in the definition ...]

Yet the new style of writing is present as well, and the influence of revived rhetorical doctrines is obvious at places in which the old way of writing is abandoned in favour of a more imaginative mode. The tone in these passages is

Dialogues in English Medical Writing 255

eloquent, with classical references, e.g. the book begins with a long monologue by Iohn Yates: *Phoebus who chasith awaye the darke and vnconfortable night: castinge his goldyne beames on my face, woulde not sofer me to take anye longer slepe* ... (f. 1). He goes for a walk and meets two fellow surgeons by accident: *Yf the one be not my frende maister Gale, and the other maister Feilde. It is so indeade.* ... (f. 1v). Polite salutations are exchanged, and some colloquial phrases are used to flavour the conversation:

(13) Tho. Gale: Brother Yates the same we wishe vnto you, & you are welcome into our company.
Iohn Feilde: This faire and plesant mornynge, will not soffer [let] maister Yates to kepe his bed [stay in bed]: but leuynge the citye, he rometh the feildes (sic) [wanders around in the fields], to espie oute some strange herbes [to detect some rare plants] vnto hym yet vnknowen.
Iohn Yates: I muste of force confesse, that *you doe hitte the nayle on the heade*: but sence my happe is so fortunate, as to mete wyth you both ... (f. 1v).

The dialogue is carried on in a very polite tone, showing consideration to the other participants. Responses to preceding turns are given by tokens of agreement and discourse markers (see Brinton 1996), e.g. *right gladly, truth it is, it is surely so, well, well then, yet,* and *but yet* occur frequently. Once the previous speaker is interrupted, and an insertion sequence follows, which shows an attempt to follow the course of natural conversation to some extent:

(14) Iohn Yates: *Be not offended I praye you, though I seame to breake of your talke*, and or [before] you procede further, let me vnderstande what you call the hyer [higher] parte of a membre.
Iohn Field: I call wyth Galen the hyer parte of a menber (sic) that which is most neare the lyuer or hearte.
Iohn Yates: *Then I pray you retourne* to youre former talke (ff. 52v-53).

Bullein's *The Fever Pestilence* (1564). This book represents the extreme fictional end of the scale as in this dialogue several episodes are combined in a loose frame and two distinct storylines intertwine. About a third of the book is medical and consists of expert-novice talk, with an apothecary asking the doctor to reveal his superb medicines against pestilence.

(15) Antonius: What Pilles doo you vse againste the Plague?
    Medicus: The beste Pilles generallie vnder heauen, and is thus made. Take the beste Yellowe Aloes, twoo vnces, Myrrhe and Saffron, of eche one vnce, beate them together in a Morter a good while, putte in a little sweete vine, then rolle it vp, and of this make fiue Pilles, or seuen of one dragme; whereof take eurie daie next your harte [heart] a Scruple or more, it will expulse the Pestilence that daie, & c. (p. 41).

This part is like any other standard recipe collection or plague tract, with a grid of questions imposed upon a monologic text. In some parts a more satirical tone has been added, e.g. as in the answer by the doctor in which the scholastic method of logical argumentation is ridiculed:

(16) Antonius: What is the cause of the same, good maister doctour?
    Medicus: *That which we do see we do testifie, and that which we do testifie is true. Therefore no man ought* in maters whiche *appertaineth* [belongs] to the estate of life to write fables or lyes, *but that whiche is of great aucthoritie* and of good experience. The pestilent feuer, *saieth Hypocrates*, is in twoo partes considered; *the first* ... (p. 35).

Yet there is another, more indirect link with medical literature, as the short satirical episodes, *pills to purge melancholy*, were intended to be therapeutic; mirth could ward off melancholy and thus have a beneficial effect at a time of plague (Olson 1982: chapter 2; Taavitsainen and Nevanlinna forthcoming). This part includes a parody of doctor-patient talk in which professional medical consultation is twisted to serve an entertaining function. The doctor's speech has an emotive impact as he comments on the miserable look of the patient with affective expressions: *Lorde God, howe are you chaunged ! How chaunceth this? What is the matter that you looke so pale?* (p. 9).After this satirical opening, the discussion proceeds in a more professional tone. The end of the book is religious, and the aim seems to be that the readers should feel spiritually uplifted.

Thomas Becon's *The Sicke Mans Salue* (1587). Pestilence is used as a frame story in *Dialogue against the Fever Pestilence* (Bullein 1578), and here the plot is similar: sudden illness interferes and changes the course of life. The author was a theologian, and the purpose of the book is moral. The speakers have classical names, according to the literary fashion of the time (*Philemon*,

Eusebius, Theophilus, Christopher) and the sick man is called Epaphroditus. The beginning is a monologue on the transitory nature of human life, full of personal affect features, biblical allusions, appeals to Christ and direct questions to the reader. The style is eloquent and ornamented, and it resembles a sermon rather than the instructive texts of handbooks:

(17) Philemon: *Oh*, full trulie it is said of that *holie man Job*, that noble *mirror of* perfect patience: *Man that is borne of a woman, hath but a short time to liue*, and yet in the time that he liueth, he is replenished [burdened] with manie miseries. *He commeth vp and withereth awaie againe like a flower*. He *flieth as it were a shadow*, and neuer continueth in one state. It is not yet two daies since I saw my neighbour Epaphroditus (as we thought) well and lustie [joyful], yea and in perfect health: *and behold* he sent vnto me euen now his seruant Quesimus, that I would come vnto him with all expedition, all other businesse set apart, if I euer intended to see him aliue. *O good God what a world is this! Ah most louing Christ! What a sudden change is this? Our life is not without a cause compared of the holie apostle saint James to a vapour* ... (pp. 1-2).

The dialogue itself tries to imitate natural speech to some extent by giving reactions to previous turns, repeating parts of them, as if they were hard to believe, etc. In some passages the tone is extremely emotional, with invocations, interjections, rhetorical questions and exclamatory sentences:

(18) Epaph: *O mother, alas that euer thou didst beare me! Alas whie died not I in the birth? Whie did not I perish as soone as I came out of my mothers wombe?* ... *Welcome, welcome* neighbours all. *Oh how sicke am I! O that the end of my life were at hand!*
(p. 9)

Though the book deals with a man falling sick, it is not really medical. The influence of biblical style is evident in metaphors and allusions, and the book could perhaps be characterized as a theological pamphlet with the aim of enforcing religious thinking and converting people to a more pious life.

Enchiridion Medicum (1612)**.** This medical dialogue aims at explaining the basic conceptions and theories of medicine, and comes close to the question-answer formula; yet the participant roles are overt, and some conversational elements are present. This is not an expert-novice discussion in the usual form, but the doctor is examining the student, posing the questions, and he also comments on the student's answers with occasional approbations like *That is very true*. The beginning deals with the qualities of a good surgeon, and then it proceeds to basic issues:

(19) Doct.:   .... But to *let that passe*; *let mee heare your definition* of Physicke: *tell mee*, what is Physicke?
Stud.:   Physicke is an Arte that doth preserue the body of man in health; and being sicke, cureth the diseases of the same. Or Physicke, according to Hyppocrates, is adiection, and substraction: or according to Galen in his *Arte Parua*; It is the knowledge of things healthfull, of things vnhealthfull; and of neither.
Doct.:   *Shew me* how that may be?
Stud.:   It may bee three waies, as the body, the cause, and the signe: as that is a healthfull body which enioyeth health; a healthful cause which worketh or conserueth health: that is an healthfull signe which doth demonstrate health to be present: ... Or Physicke is the study of things naturall, of things not naturall, and of things against nature.
Doct.:   Into how many parts is Physicke diuided?
Stud.:   There are in generall fiue parts of Physicke: the first ... (pp. 2-3).

The style of the dialogue is scholastic, with frequent references to authorities; the statements are given with absolute certainty, in accordance with the thought-style. The last part of the volume contains another treatise called *A particvlar practise of Phisicke, teaching the trve cvre of all those inward diseases that doe affect the bodie of Man*. It begins as a dialogue in the above-quoted style, but abandons that form in the middle, reverting to a monologic text.

Kitchin-Physick: or, Advice to the poor (1676). This medical dialogue is a doctor-patient discussion based on questions and answers. The patient states his business politely: *I am glad, Sir, to find you within: I have brought you a water, and desire your opinion* ... (p. 17). The doctor's answers are didactic and condescending. Some discourse particles, direct addresses, and imperative forms have been added to make the discussion more speechlike, e.g. *Well, Lazarus, take it for an undoubted truth, that they are all but impudent lyes* . . . (p. 18). The patient goes on to ask questions, and the text proceeds as dialogue in the old scholastic style. Yet occasionally the doctor bursts into long monologues in the form of instructions from above about the right behaviour when consulting a doctor; these passages have a monologic form, with no traces of conversation, the second person pronouns are employed in giving orders and instructions:

(20) I shall conclude this Section, with these few directions.
 I. That *whenever you visit* the Physician, *you ever bring with you* the sick persons water: only that it may be in a readiness, if the Physician sees occasion to require it, but not with any expectation of being resolv'd any thing that is certain and material by it.
 II. Though the Physician should omit to ask, *yet do not you forget to tell him all you know* of the sick: tell him his age, sex, calling, complexion, habit of body and constitution: his customs in eating and drinking, and what course of life he has led: what time he was first taken: . . .
 III. *Let your visits be* ... (pp. 21-23).

The book ends with social matters about the health-care of the poor. The participants are doctors, who discuss the matter and mention the patient as an example. The genre seems to overlap and merge with pamphlets here.

(21) Phil.: But to come a little nigher the business I aim at: pray tell me Eugenius, what sick people have lately been with you? and *how mannage* [sic] *you that affair of Paupers?*
 Eugen.: There was with me just now a Lazar, so afflicted ... (pp. 34-35).

***Canterbury Wells* (1702).** The interlocutors of this dialogue are two gentlemen, one from London, the other from Canterbury. The tract is included in medical literature as it deals with the healthful effects of the mineral waters of the spa in Canterbury. It has the air of a more general conversation as it includes accounts of past events and thoughts in the narrative mode, and the text seems to continue the tradition of polite discussion in handbooks set by Isaac Walton's *The Compleat Angler* (1653), rather than previous medical dialogues:

(22) Cant.: Dear Sir, I'm glad to meet you: Your good Company will make the Waters pass well. I knew nothing of your being in Kent, till this minute, that I saw you on the Walks.
 Lon.: I came, Sir, to Town last Night, late and weary: So I took a small Supper and went to Bed: This morning I was to wait upon you ... (p. 1).

A dialogue Relating to the Practice of Physick (1735). The underlying tradition of *A dialogue (Betwixt Hygiea, Mercury and Pluto,) Relating to the Practice of Physick, As it is managed by a certain Illustrious Society* proved more difficult to identify, and it may be closer to the philosopical trend with classical allusions; it is a satirical work which, again, borders on pamphlets and contains social satire. The tone imitates natural conversation, but only sporadically:

(23) Hygeia: *Well, Mercury, now* that we are arrived at Pluto's Palace, *pray tell me what's my Business here?* You came to me with a distracted hurry in your looks, and desired me to follow you with all speed, which I did implicitly enough, expecting to learn from you on the road upon what strange emergency my presence was necessary in Hell ... (pp. 26-27).

5. Evolution and Intertextuality

Questions literature belongs to the core of scholasticism, and an attempt to transfer the text formula as well as individual linguistic features into the vernacular is evident. The English pattern is somewhat simplified from its Latin model, but the core is obviously the same. Scholastic language use, with frequent references to authorities as the source of knowledge, prescriptive phrases, and argumentation based on the classical model, is prominent even in the vernacular. The scholastic way of thinking prevailed in medical writing till the end of the sixteenth century and beyond. The vein continues all through the period discussed here; the influence of the new science can be seen in the latter part of the seventeenth century in texts for the most advanced scientists. The influence of the new thought-style with knowledge based on observations can be detected in texts that represent the forefront of scientific thought: the texts unfold as debates with pros and cons in an imaginary dialogue with the readers.

Dialogues that state the participant roles explicitly show variation in their adherence to the interactive pattern. Some mimetic dialogues achieve a conversational tone with features of spoken language such as responses to previous turns, follow-up questions, pragmatic particles, etc. In some parts the questions are added bluntly with the formula "What is X?", or they may be posed more indirectly with various degrees of politeness. Yet older texts with their conventions of plague tracts or recipe writing show no such variation. Intertextuality is obvious. These passages illustrate the transmission of medical materials: old tracts were repeated, adapted, and embedded into new frames, without changing their stylistic features. Old materials could be used freely whenever needed, and perhaps it was the attested popularity of the *"Canutus" Plague Tract* that inspired Bullein in his choice of materials, so that he used parts of it or other similar tracts in his new text. Some texts abandon the dialogue form in the middle, and insert long monologic passages of instruction; this may be interpreted as an indication of how superficially the dialogue form was imposed on traditional medical material.

In the eighteenth century, medical dialogues merge with pamphlets on social matters, such as the health-care of the poor, or social satire, or more general tracts with polite conversation. The changes reflect the general line of evolution of English prose style. Some of the dialogues discussed above and initially included in medical literature prove to be only superficially linked with medicine.

6. Audience

The contents help to place these books in their sociocultural context. It is obvious that texts like *Guido's Questions* (1579) could interest only practising surgeons or those learning the trade. The target group must have been professional, and it is only the most mimetic, satirical or otherwise marginal texts that could attract the attention of a wider readership (see below).

The prefaces of early medical dialogues name two different target groups: professional medical practitioners and lay people. Medical audience is specified in some, e.g. *Students in Physicke, Chyrurgians, and Apothecaries* are explicitly mentioned in *Enchiridion Medicum* (Valentinus 1612). Thomas Gale's *Chirurgerie* (1563) defines its professional teaching purpose overtly:

(24) ... require you to enter into some talke of Chirurgerye ... you shoulde meruaylouslye pleasure me, and profit other, for so may it come to passe, that it myghte be in the place of an Institution vnto those that shall here after desire the knowledge of Chirurgerye [that it could be a textbook for those who hereafter desire the knowledge of surgery] (ff. 1v-2).

A wider audience is implied in several books, especially those with mimetic dialogues, that follow the medieval modesty formula, with claims that they have been *reduced into the forme of a dialogue for better understanding of the unlearned* (Bullein, *The Gournement of Healthe* (1595), the long title). This statement seems to be a decoration, like many others that mention *the unlearned* as the target group of medical works in this period; likewise *the benefit of the poor* is given as the aim of some medieval manuscript copies. According to ownership studies and library catalogues, even these books were used by the social elite, including medical practitioners of the highest classes. It is certain that these books cannot have reached *the unlearned*, who were illiterate and did not read or own books (Slack 1979: 237, 273). Further evidence of a highly educated audience can be found in the language use, e.g. *Dialogue against the Fever Pestilence* (Bullein 1578) includes large parts in technical and theoretical language, even in Latin, which indicates a learned target group. Yet parts of it appealed to a wider readership, and the audience of the more general tracts must have been more heterogeneous. The title of *The Sicke Mans Salue* (Becon 1587) addresses the book to *all faithful Christians* with the aim of teaching them how to behave *patientlie and thankefullie in the time of sicknesse, and also vertuouslie to dispose their temporall goods, and finallie to prepare themselues gladlie and godelie to die*. The audience here is not restricted to medical professionals, but is extended to the general reading public of the period.

7. Conclusion

I set out to assess the underlying sources and models in early English medical dialogues, and how conversation is conveyed in them. According to the evidence of this material, there are two main traditions, the scholastic and the mimetic, different from one another in their origin, but co-occurring and merging in some tracts. It seems that these two forms were not distinguished by the original readership, but both served the same purpose of making texts more appealing to the audience. This form was considered ideal for instruction (see above).

It is somewhat surprising that the scholastic vein of writing is so strong in the mimetic dialogues. The new fictional frame is employed in various ways, and the range is wide, from direct borrowing of material from medieval medical tracts, doubtless for their instructive contents, to dialogue that imitates colloquial spoken language. In some, the new dialogue frame is only loosely incorporated into the texts in the form of questions. The discourse of these texts is in accordance with the medieval question-answer format; the underlying monologue text has remained unchanged and interaction is minimal. The traditional scholastic formula survives in an unaltered form at least to the end of the eighteenth century.

The mimetic end of the scale is found in texts that, in addition to the instructive purpose, have assumed an entertaining function: some may include parodies of old treatises and learned ways of argumentation, as well as social satire of the medical profession. Features of natural conversation are present in some dialogues that incorporate speech acts of normal everyday interaction, like apologies, insults, greetings and leave-takings, and other exchanges that

Dialogues in English Medical Writing 263

belong to personal communication, but this seems to be rare and achieved only in texts by the most skilful writers. The scale is wide; early medical writing shows a rich intertextual patchwork, overlapping and merging with the adjoining genres. Yet the main trend seems to follow established text conventions derived from classical antiquity and modified in different ways in different layers of writing.

Notes

[1] I did the search for this material as part of the background work for text selection for the *Corpus of Early English Medical Writing* (1375-1750). The present size of this computer-readable database is some 800,000 words; the target size is about 1.2 million words. For more information, see Taavitsainen and Pahta (1997a,b). For this survey, I searched the Wellcome Medical Library online database with keyword searches, and checked a list of early printed books on medicine given to me by Dr Chris Whitty; I would like to thank him for his generosity. For this article, I selected representative examples of the trends that I noticed; this is not intended to be a comprehensive list, but a pilot study on the text form.

[2] The relation of the oral mode of communication to written texts has varied in medicine; e.g. early issues of *The Lancet* and *The British Medical Journal* from the middle of last century contain a great deal of oral material in written form, and printed lectures are still found in scientific literature. Modern LSP studies have concentrated on doctor-patient dialogues. The interactional pattern has been found to be highly asymmetric, with heavy reliance on the question-answer (and possible follow-up) sequence. The doctor's professional role demands a neutral and objective attitude; he has the power and controls the situation (Linell and Luckmann 1991: 12). Institutional conversation is thus detached and the interactional turn-taking patterns are different from normal discourse. The second basic mode of oral communication is expert-novice, or doctor-student dialogue, with the purpose of transmitting knowledge to those learning the trade.

[3] Imaginary conversations are common in intellectual history; e.g. Boethius' *De consolatione philosophiae* was written in the dialogue form with the allegorical figure of Lady Philosophy as a participant. The influence of this book on Western thought has been deep. In the present material it can be seen in *The Young Gentleman and Lady's Philosophy, in a Continued Survey of the Works of Nature and Art By Way of Dialogue* (1759) by Benjamin Martin. It has also been noted that the whole history of philosophy can be seen as a conversation, so that the concept of dialogue becomes an extended metaphor for the interacting ideas (Myerson 1995: 1).

[4] The IMEP text is in MS. Ashmole 1481. *The Index of Scientific Incipits* (forthcoming) listed the following texts as dialogic: ALCHEMY: Bodl. Ashmole 1490, ff. 81-84, (sixteenth c.); BL, Harley 2407, f. 68v, prol; ff. 68v-69; BL, Harley 6453, ff. 25-29

(sixteenth c.); BL Sloane 3580B, ff. 120-130 (excerpt, sixteenth c.; quotation 3 above); BL Sloane 3580B, ff. 131-134v (sixteenth c.). In addition, an alchemical dialogue is found in the Royal Library, Copenhagen, MS, 6KS 1784, f. 6v (sixteenth c.). An edition by Peter Grund (Uppsala University) is in preparation. MEDICINE: Bodl. Bodley 591, ff. 1-12v; Longleat House, Wilt. 176, ff. 25-38 (quotation 2 above); 3) Cambr., St. John's College G.25, f. 1 prol. (quotation 1 above); ff. 1-16 ; BL Sloane 3489, ff. 29-42. I am grateful to Prof. Linda Voigts for this information.

[5] Italics have been added to the examples to point out the linguistic features under discussion, and modern English translations are provided for difficult passages.

[6] An extreme example of this trend can be seen in Henry Power's *Experiments* from 1664, in which he reports on experiments in physics and observations by microscope. This book was written for fellow-scientists, an elite group of pioneers in the forefront of development. The new way of doing science is reflected in the way of writing. One of the underlying conceptions of scientific thought in this period was the idea of "the matters of fact" that were supposed to generate consensus: everyone could agree on what happened in nature, even if there might be disagreement about the causal explanations (Dear 1991: 161; see also Taavitsainen and Pahta 1995).

[7] Bullein wrote three medical dialogues; his second work in chronological order is *Bullein's Bulwarke or defence against Sicknes, Sornes, and Woundes. The Book of Compounds: a dialogue between Sicknes and health* (1562).

Texts

Anonymous
    1735   *A Dialogue Relating to the Practice of Physick, As It Is Managed by a Certain Illustrious Society.* London: J. Wilford.
Approved Directions for Health
    1612   (not in STC). London: T.S. for Roger Iackson.
Asplund, Annika (ed.)
    1970   *A Middle English Version of Lanfrank's Chirurgia Parva: The Surgical Part.* (Stockholm Theses in English 2). Stockholm University.
Becon, Thomas
    [1560   STC 1756.5]
    1587   STC 1764.5. *The Sicke Mans Salue.* London: Richard Daie.
Blackmore, Richard
    1723   *A Treatise Upon the Small-pox.* London: John Clark.
Bullein, William
    [1558   STC 4039]
    1595   STC 4042. *The Gournement of Healthe.* London: Richard Day.

1562 STC 4033. *Bulleins Bulwarke of Defence againste Sicknes, Sornes, and Woundes.* London: John Kyngston.
[1564] 1578 STC 4038. A Dialogue against the Feuer Pestilence. In: Mark W. Bullen and A. H. Bullen (eds.). *William Bullein's Dialogue against the Feuer Pestilence. EETS, Extra Series* 52. 1888, rpt. 1931.

Canterbury-Wells: Or, a Discourse By way of Dialogue
1702 London: A. Baldwin.

"Canutus" Plague Treatise
see Pickett.

Gale, Thomas
1563 STC 11529. *Certaine Works of Chirurgerie.* London: Rouland Hall.

Groenvelt, John
1753 *The Rudiments of Physick.* Sherborne: R. Goaby/ London: W. Owen.

Guido's Questions
1579 STC 12469. London: Thomas East. Facsimile by Theatrum Orbis Terrarum. Amsterdam: Da Capo Press, 1968.

Kitchin-Physick: or, Advice to the Poor
1676 London: Norman Newman.

Lanfrank's Chirurgia Parva
see Asplund.

Martin, Benjamin
1759 *The Young Gentleman and Lady's Philosophy, in a Continued Survey of the Works of Nature and Art By Way of Dialogue.* London: W. Owen.

Munro, Hugh
1792 *A Compendious System of the Theory and Practice of Modern Surgery In the Form of a Dialogue.* London: E. Hodson.

Pickett, Joseph P.
1994 A Translation of the "Canutus" Plague Treatise. In: Lister M. Matheson (ed.). *Popular and Practical Science of Medieval England.* East Lansing: Colleagues Press, 263-282.

Power, Henry
1664 *Experimental Philosophy, In Three Books: Containing new Experiments Microscopical, Mercurial, Magnetical.* London: T. Roycroft.

Valentinus, Petrus Pomarius
1612 STC 24578. *Enchiridion Medicum: Containing an Epitome of the Whole Course of Pysicke.* London: N.O.

References

Biber, Douglas
    1988   *Variation Across Speech and Writing*. Cambridge: Cambridge University Press.

Biber, Douglas, and Edward Finegan
    1989   Styles of stance in English: Lexical and grammatical marking of evidentiality and affect. *Text* 9-1, 93-124.

Brinton, Laurel J.
    1996   *Pragmatic Markers in English: Grammaticalization and Discourse Functions*. Berlin/ New York: Mouton de Gruyter.

Caffi, Claudia, and Richard W. Janney
    1994   Toward a pragmatics of emotive communication. *Journal of Pragmatics* Vol. 22 (3-4), 325-373.

Calvo, Clara
    1992   Pronouns of address and social negotiation in *As You Like It*. *Language and Literature* 1, 5-27.

Chafe, Wallace L.
    1985   Linguistic differences produced by differences between speaking and writing. In: David R. Olson, Nancy Torrance, and Angela Hildyard (eds.). *Literacy, Language and Learning: The Nature and Consequences of Reading and Writing*. Cambridge: Cambridge University Press, 105-123.

Crossgrove, William, Margaret Schleissner, and Linda Ehrsam Voigts (eds.)
    1998   *Early Science and Medicine: A Journal for the Study of Science, Technology and Medicine in the Pre-modern Period*. Vol. III, No. 2. Special Issue on Vernacularisation.

Culpeper, Jonathan, and Merja Kytö
    Forthc.   Investigating non-standard language in a corpus of Early Modern English dialogues: Methodological considerations and problems. In: Irma Taavitsainen, Gunnel Melchers, and Päivi Pahta (eds.). *Writing in Nonstandard English*. Amsterdam: Benjamins.

Dear, Peter
    1991   Narratives, anecdotes, and experiments: Turning experience into science in the seventeenth century. In: Peter Dear (ed.). *The Literary Structure of Scientific Argument: Historical Studies*. Philadelphia: University of Pennsylvania Press, 135-163.

Gilbert, Neal W.
    1960   *Renaissance Concepts of Method*. New York: Columbia University Press.

Grant, Edward (ed.)
    1974   *A Source Book in Medieval Science.* Cambridge, Mass. Harvard University Press.
Halliday, Michael A. K.
    1989   *Spoken and Written Language.* Oxford: Oxford University Press.
Index of Middle English Prose, Handlists I-XI
    1984-95   Cambridge: Boydell and Brewer.
Index of Incipits of Scientific Writings
    Forthc.   CD-ROM, Comp. by Linda Ehrsam Voigts and Patricia Kurtz.
Jucker, Andreas H.
    1997   The discourse marker *well* in the history of English. *English Language and Linguistics* 1 (1), 91-110.
Linell, Per, and Thomas Luckmann
    1991   Asymmetries in dialogue: Some conceptual preliminaries. In: Ivana Marková and Klaus Foppa (eds.). *Asymmetries in Dialogue.* Hemel Hempstead: Harvester Wheatsheaf, 1-20.
McCarthy, Michael, and Ronald Carter
    1994   *Language as Discourse: Perspectives for Language Teaching.* London: Longman.
Myerson, George
    1995   Hypothetical dialogue and intellectual history: Frege, Freud and the disarming of negation. *History of the Human Sciences* 8 (4), 1-17.
Olson, Glending
    1982   *Literature as Recreation in the Later Middle Ages.* Ithaca/London: Cornell University Press.
Ong, Walter J.
    1958   *Ramus: Method, and the Decay of Dialogue.* Cambridge, Mass. Harvard University Press.
Slack, Paul
    1979   Mirrors of health and treasures of poor men: The uses of the vernacular medical literature of Tudor England. In: Charles Webster (ed.). *Health, Medicine and Mortality in the Sixteenth Century.* Cambridge: Cambridge University Press, 237-273.
Taavitsainen, Irma
    1994   On the evolution of scientific writings between 1375 and 1675: Repertoire of emotive features. In: Francisco Fernández et al. (eds.). *Papers from the 7th International Conference of English Historical Linguistics, Valencia, Sept. 1992.* Amsterdam/ Philadelphia: John Benjamins, 329-342.

1997 Genre conventions: Personal affect in fiction and non-fiction in Early Modern English. In: Matti Rissanen, Merja Kytö, and Kirsi Heikkonen (eds.). *English in Transition: Corpus-based Studies in Linguistic Variation and Genre Styles*. Berlin/ New York: Mouton de Gruyter, 185-266.

Forthc. Metatextual comments and the evolution of early English medical writing 1375-1550. In: John Kirk (ed.). Papers from the ICAME-19 Conference in Belfast, May 1998. Amsterdam: Rodopi.

Taavitsainen, Irma, and Päivi Pahta

1995 Scientific thought-styles in discourse structure: Changing patterns in a historical perspective. In: Sanna Kaisa Tanskanen et al. *Organization in Discourse. Anglicana Turkuensia* 14, 519-529.

1997a The corpus of early medical writing: Linguistic variation and prescriptive collocations in scholastic style. In: Terttu Nevalainen and Leena Kahlas-Tarkka (eds.). *To Explain the Present: Studies in the Changing English Language in Honour of Matti Rissanen*, (Mémoires de la Société Néophilologique de Helsinki), Helsinki: Société Néophilologique, 209-225.

1997b The Corpus of Early English Medical Writing. *ICAME Journal* 21, 71-78.

1998 Vernacularisation of medical writing in English: A corpus-based study of scholasticism. In: Crossgrove et al. 157-185.

Taavitsainen, Irma, and Saara Nevanlinna

Forthc. Pills to purge melancholy – Nonstandard elements in *A Dialogue against Fever Pestilence*. In: Irma Taavitsainen, Gunnel Melchers and Päivi Pahta (eds.). *Writing in Nonstandard English*. Amsterdam: Benjamins.

Webster, Charles

1975 *The Great Instauration: Science, Medicine and Reform 1626-1660*. London: Duckworth.

Werlich, Egon

1983 *A Text Grammar of English*. Heidelberg: Quelle and Meyer.

A Late Medieval French Bargain Dialogue (*Pathelin* II) Or: Further Remarks on the History of Dialogue Forms

Franz Lebsanft
Ruhr University, Bochum

Convenance ne se puet fere sans parole[1]

1. Introduction

Since the mid-nineties, historical pragmatics has entered a new phase of development. Due mainly to the work of Anglicists and Germanists, serious efforts have been made to delimit the fields of the discipline and to develop its methodological tools in order to systematise further research (Jacobs and Jucker 1995). As regards the history of dialogue forms (or genres), Fritz (1997; cf. also 1994, 1995) has given a critical review of valuable studies in this domain, indicating at the same time the main directions which the study of change in the history of dialogue forms may take in the future. Rather than discuss in a purely abstract way the problems raised by Fritz, my contribution will treat some of his main points in a more concrete manner by analysing a famous late medieval bargain dialogue. Instead of looking for examples to support theoretical considerations, I will proceed inversely, looking for what the analysis of concrete material may contribute to the development of theory, so that the general aspects of diachronic dialogue analysis will be complemented by a concrete case study.

According to Fritz (1997: 47f., 1995: 469), historical research on dialogue forms may proceed in at least three directions, viz. (i) the analysis of individual historical texts, (ii) the comparison of texts from different periods, and (iii), the systematic study of the evolution of dialogue forms. It seems obvious to me, even without being a theorist of hermeneutics, that these directions are complementary to one another insofar as it is impossible to analyse individual texts of the past without confronting them at least implicitly with texts of their own period. The well-known concept of "alterity", introduced by Hans Robert Jauss (1977) in order to characterise the "strangeness" of medieval texts, presupposes an implicit confrontation of these texts with those of the time the modern critic is living in. Consequently, the exploration of a single text suggests also an implicit theory of the evolution of the phenomenon under discussion. Therefore, a discussion of the problems of historical dialogue analysis may take evidence from texts of one and the same period, although it goes without saying that we have to be very careful before drawing general conclusions from a particular case.

My focus will be on the opening scenes of one of the most famous French comic dramas, the late medieval *farce de Maistre Pierres Pathelin* (ca. 1456-1460).[2] Pathelin, a lawyer who has the reputation of being a master deceiver, promises his wife Guillemette to buy fine cloths at the market, though he has no money at all (scene I). In the following bargain scene (II), the lawyer gets the clothier Guillaume Joceaulme to sell him in the first contract of that day six yards of cloth on credit. In fact, the clothier agrees to deliver the merchandise immediately, but to be paid later, in the evening, when he comes to the lawyer's house. Guillaume thinks he can be satisfied with having sold goods at an excessive price, but he will never get his money. When he arrives at Pathelin's house, Guillemette convinces him that her husband, who plays incredibly well a delirious, sick man, has not left his bed for many weeks and is not the man to whom he sold cloth in the morning (scene V).[3]

Much attention has been paid to understanding the farce as a whole, as well as these extraordinary opening scenes. Since Holbrook's monograph (1917), the critics' main concern has been the reconstruction of *Pathelin's* "Sitz im Leben" and also its place in the aesthetic and literary history of French drama.[4] This latter approach cannot, however, be the focus of a paper on the history of dialogue forms. Such a paper relies, of course, heavily on the amazing erudition contained in the editor's (André Tissier) notes, indispensable for understanding every line, every word of the text. But it will use this information in order to ascertain more about the medieval everyday practice of bargaining as one moment in the evolution of this dialogue form. Therefore, I will take into consideration two text types which, with the only noteworthy exception of Collingwood (1993), do not play an important role in the philology of *Pathelin*, i.e. (i) Philippe de Beaumanoir's (1252/54-1296) *Coutumes de Beauvaisis*, the best known Old French custumal, which contains precious information about medieval bargaining and contracts, and (ii) the so-called Middle French *Livre des mestiers* (ed. Gessler 1931) and the *Manières*

A Late Medieval French Bargain Dialogue (*Pathelin* II)   271

de langage, foreign language teaching books, which show how to use French in typical, recurrent everyday situations.[5]

I will describe and explain the verbal interaction in the scene from *Pathelin* in the light of these two types of sources. The juridical text will help understand how the practice of bargaining is embedded in legal institutions (section 4) and which communication principles have to be respected in bargaining (section 5). The didactic texts, well known to historians of dialogue forms (especially Radtke 1994), will be useful to confront information provided by fictional and non-fictional texts and to discuss the value of both types of sources (sections 2, 3, 6). Although neither the juridical nor the didactic texts are contemporary with the farce, they were well-known at the time of *Pathelin*. The *Coutumes de Beauvaisis*, written at the end of the 13th century, belong to the tradition of the older custumals which is still alive in the second half of the 15th century (Foviaux 1992: 886f.). The *Manières de langage*, written after the middle of the 14th century, founded a tradition which runs at least until the 17th century.

Whoever has come across older texts, on the one hand perceives how difficult it is to understand them due to their "alterity"; on the other hand, the more one enters an apparently foreign universe, the more it resembles the world that surrounds us today. As regards the alterity of older dialogue forms, I think a closer look at what really changes in their evolution can help us to understand this paradox. So the exploration of the *Pathelin* case will lead us finally to formulate a more general hypothesis on the evolution of dialogue forms (section 7), which accounts for what seems to be a hermeneutic enigma.

2. The data problem: Representation of verbal interaction, not reproduction of everyday talk

Since the eighties, concern with the history of spoken language has been a privileged field of research in Romance studies (Stimm 1980; Ernst 1985; and the review article by Holtus and Schweickard 1991). Investigators were interested in knowing how the enormous gap between today's spoken and written French (Söll [3]1985; Koch and Oesterreicher 1990: 136f.; Lodge 1993: 163-204) had come into being. Undoubtedly, in earlier periods of the language the difference between *code écrit* and *code parlé* was much smaller than nowadays. This does not mean, however, that the written records of ancient French give us a realistic picture of spontaneous oral language use in the Middle Ages. Actually, verbal interactions in medieval literary texts are not the reproduction or imitation of real contemporary face-to-face communication, but their sophisticated "representation" (Cerquiglini 1981: 247). Growing awareness of this fundamental insight has led researchers to look for more reliable sources of data. Some of the most promising candidates for investigation turned out to be, at least temporarily, non-fictional texts, viz. foreign language teaching books, beginning with the famous late-medieval *Livre des mestiers* (ed. Gessler 1931) and the *Manières de langage* (ed. Kristol 1995), written for Flemish, German and English merchants. A recent reconstruction of Early Modern French (16th - 17th century) is entirely based on manuals of this type (Radtke 1994). Nevertheless, its author is fully aware of the fact that the authenticity of the data thus collected is only relative. In fact, the reconstruction of so-called "sales dialogues" (Radtke 1994: 151-174) discloses such a high degree of stereotype in the arrangement and organisation of discourse that our intuition hardly deems them acceptable as representing mimetical dialogues of everyday bargaining conversation.

Consequently, there are no grounds for excluding the evidence of fictional texts. They are neither better nor worse sources than non-fictional texts. If their characteristics are sophisticated, historical dialogue analysis has to be sophisticated, too. Rather than considering efforts to extract valuable data from this type of source as naive, we should try to explore as seriously as possible its potentials. If we are right in thinking of medieval literary dialogues as the "representation" of everyday talk, then we may consider such dialogues as idealised constructions of possible verbal interactions, just as we do in the case of those non-fictional sources. Obviously, medieval writers did not intend to imitate oral speech; so we may at best find (and indeed do find) isolated "elements" of spontaneous orality (Kristol 1992; Selig 1997, including a valuable older bibliography). What we find is a representation of how, in the opinion of the writers, medieval speakers tried to arrange and construct their discourse. Instead of obtaining a faithful picture of how people "really" *talked* to one another, we can get a description of how people *intended to interact* orally. In this sense, literary dialogues are a valuable source for our knowledge of the principles of everyday practice, and are every bit as relevant as the dialogues found in non-fictional texts. In the case of so-called sales dialogues, we will even find that there was (and is) much more to learn from *Maistre Pathelin* than from any language teaching book, for while these books only tell us how to play the game according to the rules, the farce shows us how to violate those rules.[6]

A Late Medieval French Bargain Dialogue (*Pathelin* II)   273

3. Common designations of dialogue forms: Verbs, not nouns

Fritz (1995) cogently shows that there cannot be any doubt that the concept of dialogue form corresponds to the experience of everyday practice. According to him, strong evidence is given by everyday expressions which refer to genres of dialogue, in the same way as do expressions for the so-called text genres. It seems quite evident to me, however, that a dialogue form may exist without having a name of its own. Therefore, historical analysis feels the need for two complementary and (incidentally) traditional approaches, the semasiological and the onomasiological, by taking off either from an expression or from a concept. The historical analysis of so-called sales dialogues starts with today's models of "how to sell better" (Henne and Rehbock ^{2}1982, Wiegand 1994) and goes back to (purportedly) similar models of earlier periods (Radtke 1994). A closer look at the oldest of these models shows, however, that the viewpoint of the interacting persons makes a difference. So, whereas in the *Manières de langage* (1396, in Kristol 1995), the English reader learns how to sell cloth, in the *Livre des mestiers* (ca. 1349, ed. Gessler 1931, I), the Flemish reader is taught how to buy it.

In both cases, the sources do not offer nouns, but verbs to refer to the type of dialogue (1396: *viendre, vendre*, ed. Kristol 1995: 19; 6, 28; ca. 1349: *bargignier*, ed. Gessler 1931, I, 15, Flemish *dinghen*; English [Caxton, ca. 1483] *bergayne*, ed. Gessler 1931, III, 17). Of course, selling and buying are two sides of the same coin, but in these texts no verb appears that covers the two complementary activities. In fact, in Old French (OF) the whole process of "giving/obtaining a determinate good in exchange of money" is predominantly designated by

(1) *bargignier* + *achater / vendre*
(2) *achater* or *bargignier / vendre*

In (1), *bargignier* refers only to the talks over the terms of purchase, previous to the agreement, and to its execution (*achater / vendre*); in (2), *bargignier* includes the result of the agreement, as in the *Livre des mestiers*. An OF "rival" for *bargignier* (1) is *marcheander*, which has become the common verb in Middle and Modern French (MidF, ModF) to designate the act at issue (*marchander*). It is worthwhile noting that whereas the OF verb *bargignier* clearly refers to the buyer's perspective, who tries to obtain advantageous terms from the seller, the MidF and ModF *marchander* does not privilege any point of view. This is the case in our Middle French farce, where the characters exclusively use the verb *marchander* in the sense of '[buyer] to bargain' (v.

58), 'to buy' (v. 245), whereas *marchander ensemble* means '[buyer/seller] to bargain' (v. 668).[7]

4. Dialogue forms and institutional contexts: The "force" (*vertu*) of words

According to a reasonable etymological hypothesis, the OF form *bargignier* (instead of *bargaignier*) may be due to the influence of OF *engignier* 'to deceive, to cheat, to trick'.[8] It seems, then, that in the Middle Ages – as in other times – economic activities are surrounded by suspicion and lack of confidence on both sides, on the part of the seller and the buyer. The jurist Philippe de Beaumanoir, for example, remembers the proverb *mercheans ou lerres* 'merchant or thief'.[9] Therefore, we are not surprised to find that these activities are embedded in legal institutions, which give guarantees to the persons involved. There are dispositions concerning all the aspects of medieval economic life, i.e. persons (seller, buyer), objects (merchandise), and (speech) acts (bargaining, contracting, execution of the contract: payment and delivery of the merchandise).[10]

These dispositions are mainly laid down in the custumals, the most famous and best known being the *Coutumes de Beauvaisis* (1283) of the just mentioned Philippe de Beaumanoir.[11] The two chapters 34 (§§ 998-1072) and 35 (§§ 1073-1104) of his treatise deal with oral and written contracts. The starting point of chapter 34 is what lawyers are accustomed to calling the "conflictive case", i.e. an agreement (*convenance*) whose existence or terms raise doubts and entail legal actions. Hence, Philippe's main concern regards the validity of an agreement (*convenance*) or deal (*marchié*) and the arguments put forward to prove that validity in court. For a historian of dialogue forms, Philippe's most important statement refers to the use of words in bargaining. As the jurist states, an agreement cannot be made without words (§ 1061). So it is important that the contracting parties are completely in possession of their mental, i.e. linguistic abilities. An agreement, says Philippe, cannot be made by a mute or deaf person, etc.

The *Coutumes de Beauvaisis* do not specify the linguistic form that the contracting parties should impose on their oral agreement; they only oblige, in general terms and with clear reference to Roman and Canon law (Hubrecht 1974: 144), the parties to promise to fulfill the deal (§ 999). This, however, is only one of three ways to confirm a contract, the two others being the symbolic, in part non-linguistic act of delivering "God's penny" (*denier Dieu*) or a deposit (*erres*; § 1066).[12] Although Philippe does not describe all the moves which seller and buyer may make, or have to make, in order to conclude a deal, he pays attention to some of them, putting emphasis on the juridical consequences which the linguistic form of the agreement will have. The words chosen have a certain "force" (*vertu*) which implies different obligations (§ 1060).[13] A contracting party, for example, is more strongly obliged by saying *je ferai tant vers Jehan que* ... 'I will arrange for Jehan to ...', than by saying *je vous dis que* ... or *je vous pramet que* ... 'I say' or 'I promise'. As to written agreements (Chap. 35), Philippe gives much more detailed linguistic information. The written word has a certain "force" too (§ 1073), and the author gives plenty of models for stronger or weaker forms of *soi obligier par letres* 'undertake obligations in writing'. The contrast between scarcity of information for the spoken word on the one hand, and its abundance in the case of the written word, on the other, is not surprising at all. Apparently, there has not been any institutionalised form of teaching how to bargain orally. On the contrary, the teaching of letter writing, the so called *ars dictaminis*, has a long (both Latin and vernacular) tradition at medieval universities.[14]

In case of conflict, the "force" of the words used in an agreement amounts to nothing if there are no reliable witnesses. Let me note that this holds equally for oral and written agreements. According to Philippe (§ 1073), writings have been established as a kind of proof, but they may be denied such status as well. In this case, he adds (§ 1075), witnesses or writing experts must give proof of the agreements' authenticity. Given that the role of witnesses is decisive for the correct interpretation of agreements, perhaps the most important and symbolic sign of economic activities being embedded in legal institutions is the existence of markets. Philippe tells us that markets are established "so that you can buy and sell in public", that is, in the presence of witnesses. Transactions in public, he says, are the best guarantee against frauds and trickery, although they may occur there as well as anywhere else (§ 1049). This is the case in our bargaining scene from *Pathelin*. It takes place at the market (*fayre*), but early in the morning, when there are still no other customers, and not "in front of the clothier's shop" as we are often told (Tissier 1993: 196, "devant l'étal du drapier"), but rather inside it. In fact, Pathelin opens the scene by saying *N'esse pas siens, j'en fay doubte, Qu'on se mesle de draperie?* (v. 90f., 'Isn't it in here that you are talking about cloths?'). Furthermore, the Middle French greeting formula *Dieux y soit* (v. 93, 'God be with you'), used by Pathelin when addressing the clothier, corresponds to the Old French formula *Dieus soit o vos / ceanz*, which is normally used when entering a house or shop (cf. Lebsanft 1988: 198). These details are of course important: Pathelin deliberately chooses the place and the moment of the encounter in such a way as to be alone with Guillaume. Thus the lawyer can deceive the merchant more easily, for he knows that there will be no human witness to prove any claims against him.

5. Communication principles: Bargaining and promising

We have seen that the dispositions of the custumals clearly show the preoccupation of medieval society with giving rules for economic activities. Making a deal amounts to coming to a mutual agreement. Philippe de Beaumanoir (§ 999) postulates as the basic principle that "all agreements must be kept" (*toutes convenances font a tenir*), except, of course, the ones made "for bad reasons" (*mauveses causes*). The verb used in the collocation *convenances + tenir* shows that an agreement can be assimilated to the act of sincere or insincere promising.[15] In fact, an agreement signifies essentially the intention to fulfill mutually its terms. Consequently, the statement implies that the contractors abide by what Searle (1969: 63) calls the "sincerity rule".

Unfortunately, the jurist reports too little about the social and juridical limits which the interacting persons must respect in order to come to a "good" agreement. We are not surprised to find that, for example, the use of force or intimidation invalidates an agreement, but almost nothing is said about common tricks and stratagems in everyday sales dialogues. Nevertheless, Philippe gives us an interesting hint that might indicate that medieval society is quite tolerant in this respect. In fact, he tells us that drunkenness can cancel agreements:

> *Mes nepourquant l'en doit mout regarder en tel cas a la maniere du fet ou de la convenance, car se l'en n'i trueve aperte tricherie ou trop grant decevance, les convenances font a tenir, pour ce que cil qui marchandent ne se puissent pas legierement escuser par ivrece quant il ont fet marchié ou convenance de quoi il se repentent* (§ 221).
>
> [But in such cases you should nevertheless look very closely into the act or the contract, for if there is found no clear trickery, nor too great a deception, the contracts should be enforced, so that those who bargain cannot easily use drunkenness as a defence when they have made a deal or a contract which they regret.]

On the other hand, Philippe obliges merchants to tell the truth about the goods they sell. In this case a liar, he says, "should be punished as a thief" (§ 946, *il doit estre justiciés comme lerres*).

In our farce, the buyer clearly does not intend to keep the promise of the agreement with the merchant. Before going to the market, Pathelin tells his wife that he will buy cloth by paying "on Judgment Day, because it won't be paid any sooner" (v. 77-79, *L'on les me prestera vroyement A randre au jour du jugement, Quar plustout ne sera-ce point.*). In a fine "close reading" analysis, Maddox (1984: 122-124) has shown how Pathelin is successfully performing the act of insincere promising, insofar as he takes the responsibility for intending to buy cloth on certain conditions. The art of the master deceiver consists of persuading his victim to wrongly place trust in him. The crucial moment is certainly Pathelin's offer of "God's penny" (v. 220-223). I am quite sure that this does not constitute "less a formal, binding agreement than a fiduciary contract between parties" (Maddox 1984: 120, following Lemercier 1952: 203f.), but on the contrary, according to custom, the valid confirmation (*consentement*, § 1066) of the deal. The handing over of "God's penny" commits the lawyer to making a purchase (Collingwood 1993: 143). Moreoever, Pathelin himself explains to his wife that it was "God's penny" which sealed the deal (v. 382, *Ce fust pour le denier à Dieu*).

If this interpretation is correct, then the moment selected by Pathelin to settle the contract seems rather odd. In fact, he pays "God's penny" after having chosen the desired quality of cloth (v. 218, *pers* 'vivid blue'),[16] but before discussing the price and indicating the quantity of cloth he needs. Under normal circumstances, this would be an eccentric strategy, but in this case, it leads to success. In the subsequent utterances, Pathelin simulates astonishment about the exaggerated price of the cloth, but then he confirms his previous engagement explicitly, insisting on the fact that he will not discuss the price anymore (v. 244-246, *Par mon serment, sans plus debatre, Et puis qu'ainxi va, je marchande Seix aulnes.*). In doing so, the lawyer weakens the position of the clothier, who will agree to give credit until the evening instead of being paid at that very moment. The agreement on the credit, however, compels Pathelin to tell the only overt lie in the whole dialogue, and in accordance with the custumals,[17] to do so in the strongest possible form. When asked if he would pay at the end of the merchant's visit to his home, he answers "I'll do that" (v. 310, *Feré*).

Without any doubt, the lawyer violates the juridically established bargain rules. So his behaviour is, in the context of the custumals, undeniably a case of *trop grant decevance*, deserving punishment if only it could be proved. On the other hand, we may speculate, from a medieval viewpoint, whether or not there are any extenuating circumstances which can be put forward in his favour. In their sarcastic comments on the bargain (scene III), Guillemette and Pathelin insist on the fatuous character of Guillaume, whose vigilance had been lulled by the lawyer's previous extravagant flattery. Being self-satisfied, however, does not constitute a violation of any rule of bargaining. What really matters is the fact that the merchant heavily underestimates the lawyer, whose failure to discuss the price could have warned him. In a self-commentary on the outcome of the bargain, the merchant admits that the price he had asked for was extravagant. But this is not the only commercial machination of the merchant. As Collingwood (1993) has cogently shown, he tries to cheat not only on the currency, "confusing", to his own advantage, *sous de parisis* and *sous de tournois*,[18] but also on the measurement of the cloth. Insofar as Guillaume, too, violates the rules, he prepares his own defeat, which, in the words of Pathelin, is a kind of appropriate punishment: "He [the clothier] wouldn't sell at my price, only at his. But he'll be paid at mine." (v. 324-326, *Ha, dea! il ne l'a pas vandu A mon mot: s'a esté au sien; Mais il sera poyé au mien.*).

It has been said that the dialogue form of bargaining may be understood as the "solution to the problem of finding an adequate price for goods for which there is no value fixed in advance" (Fritz 1995: 488). The point that Fritz wants to stress is the problem-solving character of dialogue forms. But if the adjective "adequate", in this context, means something like 'reasonable, conforming to the value of the merchandise', then Fritz's definition implies a high degree of "invisible-hand" cooperation. I am quite sure that neither the seller nor the buyer intends to find the "adequate price" of an object; they only want to gain an advantageous price from the other party. The pragmatic commercial morality of both seller and buyer is based on self-interest (Collingwood 1993: 11f.). "Adequate", then, refers to the perspective of a third person, who does not take part in the bargain; the "adequate" price agreed upon would effectively be "the result of human action but not of human design" (Ullmann-Margalit 1978: 263).

If we replace "adequate" by "just", we give the problem the name under which it has been seriously discussed in the Middle Ages (de Roover 1958). In fact, the theologians defined the "just price" as the one obtained "according to the estimation of the market" (*secundum aestimationem fori*), i.e. the current market price. It will be perceived that the adequate or just price will normally not be established simply in one deal, but in a series of economic exchanges. We thus have to distinguish between (i) the meaning a single bargain has for the persons involved, and (ii) the meaning it has for an economic community. According to (i), and this is the case of our example, seller and buyer will not evaluate the result of the bargain with respect to other persons, but only in relation to their own expectations. Hence, from their respective viewpoints, bargaining is not a matter of compliance, but rather a conflictive game which can be either won or lost, and this is why it is often played unfairly.

6. Thematic elements and dialogue patterns

Most of the attention paid by modern research to bargain dialogues has been dedicated to the thematic elements a bargain is made up of. On the basis of foreign language teaching books, first Collingwood (1993: 75-129) and then Radtke (1994: 151-174, especially 171) have uncovered a structure consisting of the following elements and their sequencing:

(1) greetings
(2) seller's inquiry into the buyer's need
(3) seller's presentation of the merchandise
(4) price bargaining
(5) buyer's act of paying
(6) seller's delivery of the merchandise
(7) farewells

Radtke puts emphasis on two points, namely (i) that the number of the thematic elements and their sequencing are fixed, but (ii) that the nature of the single elements, i.e. individual, creative elaboration vs. conventionality, are subject to historical change. For example, while dialogues from older periods would develop element (4), modern sales talk would refine element (3). Radtke accounts for this change with the socio-historical change of the formation of prices, i.e. the alleged fact that in the older periods prices had been freely contracted (cf. Fr. *prix débattu*), while they are fixed in modern times (cf. Fr. *prix fixe*).

We may make the general observation that the alleged structure (i) presupposes something like a practical, everyday "logic" of sales dialogues. At first sight, it indeed makes some sense to suppose that normal bargaining proceeds step by step as described by Radtke. As to (ii), I will also subscribe to the general idea that socio-historical changes in relation to prices, goods, persons involved in economic transactions can influence the evolution of bargaining, though it is not *a priori* clear what exactly is undergoing change.[19] Yet I cannot agree completely to (i) and (ii). As I see it, sales dialogues have a rather loose sequencing structure, and as regards the explanation given in (ii), I think we have to proceed a little more cautiously before making such wide-reaching generalizations about the history of this dialogue form.

Before dealing more explicitly with thematic and dialogue patterns, let me first remark on this latter point, the alleged historical evolution of sales dialogues. At first sight, we might indeed think of a change based on the different ways of establishing a price. But I am not sure that this is so. For modern Western societies, bargaining is apparently an activity with pejorative and/or exotic connotations. Consider the tourist who has bargained for a carpet in Turkey and tells you that "we" have unfortunately lost the skill of bargaining while "the Orientals" know how to do this. But the tourist obviously forgets that he has bought his house by bargaining as well as his second-hand (or even his new) car or an old engraving at the flea market, etc. Evidently, societies "only" differ regarding the products that have (or do not have) a fixed price. This observation holds for the Middle Ages as well. So it would be incorrect to look at medieval dialogues as completely dominated by discussions about the price of an object, while their modern counterparts are said to focus on other aspects of a transaction (Radtke 1994: 170). What holds for the purchase of a certain product may not be true for other goods. In fact, there were also goods with a fixed price which was established and controlled by public authorities. When, for example, in the *Jeu de saint Nicolas* (ca. 1191-1202, ed. Henry ³1981, v. 258-260), Auberon asks for the price of the glass of wine offered to him in a tavern at Arras, he is answered *au ban de la vile*, i.e. 'for the official price'. And the taverner adds that this will prevent him from paying fines (*fourfait*) for any infringement of the law.[20]

As regards the thematic structure of sales dialogues, although a medieval or early modern foreign language teacher may indeed propose the mentioned structure, real dialogues can (and do) proceed in a somewhat different manner. With respect to the number of elements, I hold that any topic derived from the objects and persons taking part in a bargain may constitute an element of the dialogue. So seller or buyer may constitute a topic in bargain dialogues. For example, in our scene from *Pathelin*, the lawyer flatters the merchant in order to win (fraudulently) his confidence. This part of the scene is absolutely not external to the bargain dialogue, since confidence between seller and buyer is fundamental for the transaction.

As regards the sequencing of the thematic elements, we may distinguish between two levels of organization. On a higher, more general level, I think we can postulate a normally fixed, tripartite basic structure, consisting of

I. preparatory discussion + II. agreement + III. execution of the agreement

While this general sequencing indeed depends on the everyday logic of transactions – sellers/buyers are *a priori* expected to discuss the object and the terms of a deal before agreeing upon it; they are expected to come to terms *before* carrying them out –, the sequencing of elements on a lower, more specific level, i.e. inside each part of this fixed tripartite structure, is rather free. In the preparatory discussion, the buyer may first ask for the goods a merchant offers and then explain his own needs, but he may also first ask for prices and go on talking about the possibility of credit, etc.

A Late Medieval French Bargain Dialogue (*Pathelin* II)   281

From the conception of bargaining as a conflictive game, it follows that its success, to a large degree, depends on controlling how the discussion of the terms is conducted. This is what Pathelin masters splendidly, as can be observed from the structure of the dialogue (scene II):

I. Preparatory discussion
   1. Mutual greetings (v. 90-93)
   2. P's flattery of G (v. 94-179)
   3. G's presentation of the cloth (v. 180-183)
   4. P's intention of buying cloth (v. 184-201)
   5. G's presentation of the cloth (v. 202-217)

II. Agreement
   6. Mutual agreement (v. 218-219)
   7. P's paying of "God's penny" (v. 220-225)

III. Pursuit of the discussion
   8. Price bargaining (v. 226-244)
   9. P's indication of the quantity to buy and G's measurement of the cloth (v. 245-267)
   10. G's calculation of the amount to pay (v. 268-271)
   11. Credit bargaining (v. 272-294)
   12. Discussion on the delivery of the cloth (v. 295-307)
   13. Confirmation of the agreement on the credit (v. 308-322)

IV. Execution of the agreement
   14. G's delivery of the cloth (before v. 323)
   15. P's payment: ∅

On the higher level, as we have already noted, Pathelin changes the normally fixed sequence in a rather innovative and unexpected manner. The discussion about the cloth and the terms of the purchase is split up into two parts, with the agreement inserted between them.[21] On the lower level, the lawyer merely freely takes advantage of the possibilities of the game. The most important thing to note, in my view, is the double function of Pathelin's long flattery at the beginning of the interaction. It serves the purpose of gaining the merchant's confidence; but it is also designed to put off the moment when the lawyer reveals that he is seriously interested in buying something. In fact, the positions of Guillaume and Pathelin are asymmetrical. While, from the beginning, the merchant is supposed to have an interest in selling his merchandise, Pathelin feigns indifference; this is then suddenly changed into eagerness to purchase an expensive high-quality product. By this deceit, Pathelin wants the clothier to believe that he is not well prepared for the bargaining to come.

So far, we have explored the bargain dialogue in terms of thematic "elements". We can strengthen the analysis by moving downwards to a third level, namely the basic speech acts and their sequencing. Bargain dialogues obviously contain a wide range of questions and answers, consultations and advice, arguments built up of pros and cons. Here too, the contractors of a bargain are *a priori* free to choose their linguistic tools. But, although there is a wide range of possibilities, we find certain ritualised strategies. In fact, the linguistic art of the participants in a bargain consists of combining fixed and free elements in the manner that best fits their purposes.

The price bargaining (element 8, v. 219-244) consists of 13 speech acts in 11 turns, which have the following structure:

(1) P's question about the price
219 [...] *Combien m'en coustera*
220 *La premiere aulne?*

[(6) G's answer]
[v. 227-228, s. below]

(2) P's demand for contract
220   *Dieu sera*
221 *Des premiers poié, c'est raison.*
222 *Je vous pri que nous ne fasson*
223 *Marché si Dieu on ne nomme.*

(3) G's acquiescence
224 *Et, par Dieu, c'est dit de prudomme,*
225 *Et m'en avez moult resjouy.*

(4) G's question about the price rule
226 *Voulez-vous à ung mot?*

(5) P's answer
226 *Ouy.*

[(1) P's question about the price]
[v. 219-220, s. above]

(6) G's answer
227 *Chascune aulne vous coustera*
228 *xxiiii solx.*

(7) P's first refusal
228   *Non fera.*
229 *xxiiii solx! Doubce Dame!*

(8) G's first argument
230 *Il les me cousta, par ceste ame!*
231 *Tant en poirez, si les avez.*

(9) P's second refusal
232 *Certes, c'est trop!*

(10) G's second argument
232   *Vous ne sçavez*
233 *Comme le drap est enchery!*
234 *Trestout le bestiail est peri*
235 *Cest yver pour la grant froidure.*

A Late Medieval French Bargain Dialogue (*Pathelin* II)   283

(11) P's counter-offer
    236 *Vingt solx! xx solx!*

(12) G's refusal /third argument
    236   *Et je vous jure*
    237 *Que j'en aroy ce que je di.*
    238 *Ou actendez à sabmedi.*
    239 *Vous verrés que vault [la]*
          toeson
    240 *Dont il souloit estre foeson!*
    241 [..
    243 ..]

(13) P's acquiescence
    244 *Par mon serment, sans plus*
        debatre,
    245 *Et puis qu'ainxi va, je*
        marchande
    246 *Seix aulnes.*

As can easily be seen from this tabulation, Pathelin confines himself to expressing astonishment about the price, but he does not put forward any argument to support his claim that Guillaume should lower his price. The clothier, for his part, justifies his demand, though only with topical arguments. The price, he says, is high not because of his profit, but in consideration of the expenses he has had. The lawyer does not propose any counter-argument and so feigns to be convinced that the merchant's price is fair. In this case, the passivity of Pathelin is an adequate strategy to prepare the ground for the bargaining for credit (element 11), which is the creative counterpart and complement:

(1) P's question about credit
    272 *Or cza, le voulez-vous croyre*

    273 *Jucq à tantost quant vous*
        viendrez?
    274 *Non pas croyre, quar vous*
        prandrez
    275 *A mon hus or ou monnoye.*

(2) G's refusal
    276 *Par sainct Martin, je me*
        teurdroye
    277 *De beaucop [à] aller par là!*

(3) P's blame for G's refusal of his "invitation"
    278 [..
    280 ..]

(4) G's argument to support his refusal
    286 *Et! par sainct Jacques, je ne fay*
    287 *Guere aultre mestier que boyre.*

281 *C'est bien dit: vous vous*
   tortryez!
282 *C'est cela! vous ne vouldriez*
283 *Jamais trouver nulle achoeson*
284 *Boyre du vin de ma maison.*
285 *Or y vendrez-vous ceste foiz!*

288 *Mais il me fait bien mal de*
   croyre,
289 *Si sçavez-vous, à l'estraine.*

(5) P's offer to combine invitation with payment

290 *Souffit-il si je vous estrainne*

291 *D'escuz d'or, non pas de*
   monnoye?
292 *Et si mangeron de mon oaye,*
293 *Par Dieu, que [ma] femme*
   routist.

(6) G's acquiescence

294 *Vroyement, cest homme*
   m'assotit.
295 *Allez vous en; et je yray*
   doncquez
296 [..].

To state it briefly, Pathelin convinces Guillaume of the paradox that a credit is not a credit. The lawyer puts forward two arguments, namely (i) a short-term credit is not a "real" (i.e. long-term) credit, and (ii) the refusal to give credit is the (impolite) refusal of an invitation. The argumentation is, of course, clearly fallacious, and, by the way, full of allusive ambiguities,[22] but this time it is the merchant who is simply incapable of marshalling any convincing arguments once he has agreed to give credit, though only reluctantly, in the first bargain of a day (*estraine*, v. 288-289).

7. Conclusion: What changes in the history of bargaining?

In conclusion, we may ask: what can we learn from a case study like this for the diachronic study of dialogue forms? The bargain scene in *Pathelin* shows what I feel to be characteristic for the evolution of many types of dialogue form, i.e. on the one hand, a remarkable panchronic stability of the basic elements; on the other, diachronic transformations of rather secondary traits. The kernel structure of bargaining is something like "A and B discuss and agree upon the conditions x under which an object y is handed over from A to B in exchange for another object z which counts as payment for y." Although this structure is, of course, not as old as humanity, it goes back far beyond the societies which are within the purview of Romance studies.[23] What really changes are the historical circumstances which determine who may take the role of A or B; which are the objects that may be handed over; and which objects may function as payment. We feel that the serious difficulties we have to overcome in order to understand what happens in *Pathelin*, scene II, do not concern so much the kernel structure of bargaining, but those historical circumstances. We have to learn, for example, about the characteristics of 15th century French lawyers and clothiers, why a cloth called *pers* was so appreciated, and what is the difference between currencies from Paris or Tours on the one side, and between actual coin and money of account on the other side.

The question that we inevitably have to ask, then, concerns the object of change: What is changing, the dialogue form or the things themselves the dialogue form lets us talk about? My answer is: first of all the things; but insofar as strategies and linguistic tools in dialogues depend on things and knowledge about things, the dialogue form as well. Knowledge about things determines the way these strategies can be executed. If you are a 15th century person who knows the difference between *parisis* and *tournois*, you can try to cheat on the price; if you know that in medieval society it is difficult to obtain credit in the first sale of a day (*estraine*), then you will need all your cleverness to persuade the seller, etc. Although the kernel structure of bargaining remains invariable, its historical realization changes massively.

It is slightly more difficult, at least in the case of oral bargaining, to show that special linguistic tools correspond to this particular dialogue form. The utterances a 15th century French bargain dialogue is made up of are formed according to the rules of Middle French, but you will not easily find fixed utterances that you have to make in bargaining "in this and no other way".[24] Even if we cannot detect a strictly ritualised form needed to inquire about the merchandise or to ask for the price or for credit, etc., there is, however, at least one relatively fixed element affecting the crucial moment of the dialogue, the sealing of the deal. In our case, it is a non-linguistic symbol, the handing over of "God's penny". But it could also have been an association of a gesture and a ritualised phrase, e.g. *la main sur le pot* (v. 384). Without any doubt, the symbols as well as the phrase are testimonies of a formal, medieval conception of law (Hubrecht 1974: 143f.). And in this respect, at least, the "alterity" of 15th century bargaining remains intact.

Notes

1 "An agreement cannot be made without words", cf. below, section 4.
2 Synoptical ed. Tissier 1993, on the basis of ms. La Vallière, BN Paris, fonds fr. 25 467 – text I –, and ed. Le Roy and Levet 1485/1489 – text II –; Engl. translation by Alan E.

Knight, based on the ed. of text II by Holbrook 21937, in Maddox (1984: 173-199). My quotations are from text I, ed. Tissier.

3   Later, Pathelin successfully defends in court a shepherd, who had killed the clothier's sheep, against the claims of the merchant by convincing the judge that his client is mentally ill and cannot stand trial. The shepherd continues to play the role of a sick person and does not pay the fees he owes to the attorney. On Pathelin as a deceived deceiver, cf. Maddox (1984). On this old folkloristic theme, cf. also the article "Betrüger" in *Enzyklopädie des Märchens* 2, col. 230-238 (Elfriede Moser-Rath 1997).

4   For a recent bibliography on *Pathelin*, cf. ed. Tissier 1993: 15-186; *Dictionnaire des lettres françaises* (1992: 1103-1105).

5   Chapter 3 of Collingwood's Canadian Ph.D. (1993: 130-187) gives an interesting, though not totally convincing interpretation of the bargain scene from *Pathelin* in confrontation with the Middle French manuals of French conversation (Chap. 2, 1993: 75-129). Collingwood's focus is on the often neglected role of the drapier. Unfortunately, Collingwood is not fully aware of the importance of the *Coutumes de Beauvaisis*, which she only mentions in passing (1993: 116s.). – Abbreviations: OF = Old French (ca. 600-1350; first written record 842), MidF = Middle French (ca. 1350-1500), ModF = Modern French (1500-).

6   It is not by chance that Erich Auerbach (1892-1957) based his history of "the representation of reality in western literature" also on the medieval French drama, see ch. V of *Mimesis*, "Adam and Eve" (Auerbach 51971). When he says that Adam approaches his wife as a medieval French peasant or citizen might have done, he surely does not want to say that the *Jeu d'Adam* is a one-to-one imitation of spoken French. It is the representation of everyday verbal interaction in the sense described above.

7   For fuller and more detailed information on *bargaignier*, see TL I, col 842s., AND I 63, FEW 15/1, 189 (*borganjan*); *marcheander* TL V, col 1126-1128, AND I 406, FEW 6/2, 1-14, especially 11 (*mercatus*).

8   Cf. above, note 7 (FEW).

9   Cf. also below, section 5.

10 For detailed information about medieval economic life, see the well-informed, relevant articles in LexMA, especially: "Fernhandel" (IV, 378-382, E. Pitz), "Handel" (A. Westlicher Bereich, IV, col. 1895-1897, J.A. van Houtte), "Kauf, -recht" (5, 1080-1082, K.O. Scherner), "Kaufmann, Kaufleute" (V, 1083-1086, H. Kellenbenz), "Markt" (I. Westlicher Bereich, VI, 308-311, R. Sprandel). A brief introduction is the famous book by Le Goff (61980). On the representation of medieval commerce in Old French literature, cf. the well-informed dissertation by Sallentien (1912).

11 The edition of Salmon (1899/1900) – the only one available to modern readers – unfortunately presents what the philology à la Gaston Paris called a "critical text", which does not correspond to our standards of text editing. Engl. translation Akehurst (1992), juridical and historical commentary Hubrecht (1974).

A Late Medieval French Bargain Dialogue (*Pathelin* II)   287

12 Cf. HRG (1971), articles "Arrha" (I, col. 230-232, W. Orgis) and "Gottespfennig, Gottesheller" (I, col. 1766-1769, W. Sellert). Cf. also LexMA, "Arra" (I, col. 1025, M.J. Peláez). Cf. below, section 6 and 7.
13 Cf. also TL XI, col 345 "par la vertu (juristisch)". The relation of OF *vertu* with the rhetorical concept of the *virtus elocutionis* is evident.
14 For a first orientation, cf. LexMA "Ars dictaminis, ars dictandi" (I, col. 1034-1039, H.M. Schaller); HWR "Ars dictandi, dictaminis" (I, col. 1040-1046, M. Camargo, W.M).
15 Cf. TL X, s.v. tenir, col. 209 "halten, beobachten, einhalten (Versprochenes, Auferlegtes)".
16 Cf. TL VII, col. 781-787, article "pers". For a recent bibliography on medieval cloth in France, cf. Roy (1995: 10, footn. 9).
17 Cf. above, section 4.
18 The *tournois* is worth less than the *parisis*: According to the "Libra-system" (Taeuber 1933), 1 *livre* (or: *franc*) *de tournois* = 20 *sous de tournois*, 1 livre (or: *franc*) *de parisis* = 20 *sous de parisis*, but 1 *livre de tournois* = 16 *sous de parisis*. When Guillaume stipulates a price of 24 *sous* for 1 *aune* (v. 228), he means *sous de parisis*, because later on he fixes the final price 24 x 6 (*aunes*) = 9 *francs* (v. 269s.), i.e. 144 *sous* = 9 *francs*, therefore 16 *sous (de parisis)* = 1 *franc (de tournois)*. If he calculated in *sous de tournois*, the debt contracted by Pathelin would be of only 7 *francs* 4 *sous (de tournois)*. Note that the *livre* is a money of account, while the *sou* is an actual coin. – On coins and currencies in Old French literature, cf. Belz (1914) and the pertinent articles in TL. – According to Collingwood (1993: 27), the money of account would be a "foreign concept" to us. I am not quite sure that this is so: What about, for example, the American dollar, which at the time of writing was fixed at 1.783 (or 1.8234 etc.) *deutschmark*?
19 Cf. below, section 7.
20 Cf. TL III, col. 2094, s.v. *forfait*, "auferlegte Buße".
21 Cf. above, section 5.
22 Cf. especially Tissier's comment on v. 292 concerning the expression *mangier de l'oie*.
23 Bargaining partakes of (not only economic) exchange as an anthropological constant of human behaviour, cf. Mauss' famous book on the gift (1950). A decisive change in the history of economic exchanges perhaps took place when the older form of bartering was replaced by the newer form of bargaining, cf. Coulmas (1992: 60). Bartering does not need the use of words. Let me note in passing that the invention of the great majority of basic dialogue forms as well as of basic speech acts does not belong to history, but to the realm of prehistory which some modern linguists explore by means of "conjectural history" in a way that is reminiscent of 18th century speculations on the origin of language. For an early discussion on the historicity of basic speech acts, cf. two pioneers of historical pragmatics, Schlieben-Lange and Weydt (1979); cf. also Schlieben-Lange (1983: 140-144). The Middle Ages developed a theory of exchange based upon Aristotelian philosophy, cf. Konrad von Megenberg (1309-1374), *Yconomica* I.4, Chap. 14, *De modo vivendi commutativo*, and also Chap. 16, *De commutacione rerum in peccuniam et econtra* (ed.

Krüger 1973: I, 343). Konrad defines bargaining as *commutacio etherogenea mercatoria*, which changes "things" into money or money into "things", the "things" being an object of trade. The *commutacio mercatoria* is threefold, the third (as in our example) being the *commutacio mercatoria assistiva*, (I, 343, l. 25-27) *que dicitur ab assistendo, quia fit per institores, qui stantes in cellis mercionariis vendunt merces particulatim, quas a mercatoribus summatim comparant.*

24 Of course, I do not want to say that there are no idioms used in bargaining, but they do not exclusively belong to this dialogue form.

Sources

Gessler, Jean (ed.)
 1931 *Le "Livre des Mestiers" de Bruges et ses Dérivés*. Quatre anciens manuels de conversation. 6 vols. Bruges: Consortium des Maîtres Imprimeurs Brugeois.
Holbrook, Richard T. (ed.)
 ²1937 *Maistre Pierre Pathelin, Farce du XVe Siècle*. Paris: Champion.
Jean Bodel d'Arras
 ³1981 *Le Jeu de Saint Nicolas de Jehan Bodel*. ed. par Albert Henry. Bruxelles: Palais des Académies.
Konrad von Megenberg
 1973/1984 *Werke. Ökonomik Buch I-III*. Sabine Krüger (ed.). 3 vols. Stuttgart: Hiersemann.
Kristol, Andres Max (ed.)
 1995 *Manières de Langage (1396, 1399, 1415)*, London: Anglo-Norman Text Society.
Philippe de Beaumanoir
 1899/1900 *Coutumes de Beauvaisis*. A. Salmon (ed.). 2 vols. Paris: Picard.
 1992 *The "Coutumes de Beauvaisis" of Philippe de Beaumanoir*. Translated by F.R.P. Akehurst. Philadelphia: University Press.
Tissier, André (ed.)
 1993 *Recueil de Farces* (1450-1550). Tome VII, Maître Pathelin. Genève: Droz.

French Dictionaries

AND – Stone, Louise W. and William Rothwell (eds.)
 1977-1992 *Anglo-Norman Dictionary*. 2 vols. London: Modern Humanities Research Association.

FEW – Wartburg, Walther von
  1928-   Französisches Etymologisches Wörterbuch. Eine Darstellung des galloromanischen Wortschatzes. 25 vols. Tübingen, Basel: Zbinden.
TL – Tobler, Adolf and Erhard Lommatzsch
  1925-   Altfranzösisches Wörterbuch. 11 vols. (A-V). Berlin, Wiesbaden, Stuttgart: Steiner.

Encyclopedic Dictionaries

Grente, Georges (ed.)
  ²1992   Dictionnaire des Lettres Françaises, Le Moyen Age. Nouv. éd. Geneviève Hasenohr et Michel Zink. Paris: Fayard.
HRG – Erler, Adalbert and Ekkehard Kaufmann (eds.)
  1971-   Handwörterbuch zur Deutschen Rechtsgeschichte. 4 vols. + fascicles (A-Zunft). Berlin: Erich Schmidt.
HWR – Ueding, Gert (ed.)
  1992-   Historisches Wörterbuch der Rhetorik. 3 vols. (A-Hör). Tübingen: Niemeyer.
LexMA – Angermann, Norbert (ed.)
  1980-   Lexikon des Mittelalters. 8 vols.+ fascicles (A-Veroneser Bund). München, Zürich: Artemis, Lexma.
Ranke, Kurt (ed.)
  1977-   Enzyklopädie des Märchens. Handwörterbuch zur historischen und vergleichenden Erzählforschung. 8 vols. (A-Maggio). Berlin, New York: de Gruyter.

References

Auerbach, Erich
  ⁵1971   Mimesis. Dargestellte Wirklichkeit in der abendländischen Literatur. Bern, München: Francke.
Belz, Gustav
  1914   Die Münzbezeichnungen in der Altfranzösischen Literatur. PhD. Straßburg i.E.: DuMont.
Cerquiglini, Bernard
  1981   La Parole médiévale. Discours, syntaxe, texte. Paris: Éditions de Minuit.

Collingwood, Sharon L.
1993   *Commercial Relations in French Farce, 1450-1550.* London (Ontario): Microfilm.
Coulmas, Florian
1992   *Die Wirtschaft mit der Sprache. Eine sprachsoziologische Studie.* Frankfurt am Main: Suhrkamp.
Ernst, Gerhard
1985   *Gesprochenes Französisch zu Beginn des 17. Jahrhunderts. Direkte Rede in Jean Héroards "Histoire Particulière de Louis XIII" (1605-1616).* Tübingen: Niemeyer.
Foviaux, Jacques
1992   Juridique (Littérature). In: G. Grente (ed.). *Dictionnaire des Lettres Françaises.* Nouv. éd. Geneviève Hasenohr et Michel Zink. Paris: Fayard, 875-904.
Fritz, Gerd
1994   Geschichte von Dialogformen. In: Gerd Fritz and Franz Hundsnurscher (eds.). *Handbuch der Dialoganalyse.* Tübingen: Niemeyer, 545-562.
1995   Topics in the history of dialogue forms. In: Andreas H. Jucker (ed.). *Historical Pragmatics. Pragmatic Developments in the History of English.* Amsterdam, Philadelphia: Benjamins, 469-498.
1997   Remarks on the history of dialogue forms. In: Etienne Petri (ed.). *Dialogue Analysis V. Proceedings of the 5th Conference Paris 1994.* Tübingen: Niemeyer, 47-55.
Henne, Helmut, and Helmut Rehbock
²1982   *Einführung in die Gesprächsanalyse.* Berlin, New York: de Gruyter.
Holbrook, Richard T.
1917   *Étude sur Pathelin, essai de bibliographie et d'interprétation.* Baltimore, Paris: Champion.
Holtus, Günter, and Wolfgang Schweickard
1991   Zum Stand der Erforschung der historischen Dimension gesprochener Sprache in der Romania. *Zeitschrift für Romanische Philologie* 107, 547-574.
Hubrecht, Georges
1974   *Philippe de Beaumanoir, Coutumes de Beauvaisis.....* Tome III Commentaire historique et juridique. Paris: Picard.
Jacobs, Andreas, and Andreas H. Jucker
1995   The historical perspective in pragmatics. In: Andreas H. Jucker (ed.). *Historical Pragmatics. Pragmatic Developments in the History of English.* Amsterdam, Philadelphia: Benjamins, 3-33.

Jauss, Hans Robert
1977   *Alterität und Modernität der mittelalterlichen Literatur. Gesammelte Aufsätze 1955-1976.* München: Fink.
Koch, Peter, and Wulf Oesterreicher
1990   *Gesprochene Sprache in der Romania: Französisch, Italienisch, Spanisch.* Tübingen: Niemeyer.
Kristol, Andres Max
1992   Que dea! Mettes le chapron, paillard, com tu parles a prodome! La représentation de l'oralité dans les Manières de langage du XIVe/XVe siècle. *Romanistisches Jahrbuch* 43, 35-64.
Lebsanft, Franz
1988   *Studien zu einer Linguistik des Grußes. Sprache und Funktion der altfranzösischen Grußformeln.* Tübingen: Niemeyer.
Le Goff, Jacques
^{6}1980   *Marchands et banquiers du moyen âge.* Paris: PUF.
Lemercier, P.
1952   Les éléments juridiques de *Pathelin* et la localisation de l'Œuvre. *Romania* 73, 200-226.
Lodge, R. Anthony
1997   *Le français. Histoire d'un dialecte devenu langue.* Paris: Fayard. [Engl. original 1993].
Maddox, Donald
1984   *Semiotics of Deceit. The Pathelin Era.* Lewisburg: Bucknell University Press / London, Toronto: Associated University Press.
Mauss, Marcel
1950   *Essai sur le don.* Paris: PUF.
Radtke, Edgar
1994   *Gesprochenes Französisch und Sprachgeschichte. Zur Rekonstruktion der Gesprächskonstitution in Dialogen französischer Sprachlehrbücher.* Tübingen: Niemeyer.
Roover, Raymond de
1958   The concept of the just price: Theory and economic policy. *Journal of Economic History* 18, 418-434.
Roy, Bruno
1995   Quand les Pathelin achètent du drap. *Médiévales* 29, 9-22.
Sallentien, Victor
1912   Handel und Verkehr in der altfranzösischen Literatur. *Romanische Forschungen* 31, 1-154.

Schlieben-Lange, Brigitte
1983   *Traditionen des Sprechens. Elemente einer pragmatischen Sprachgeschichtsschreibung.* Stuttgart etc.: Kohlhammer.

Schlieben-Lange, Brigitte, and Harald Weydt
1979   Streitgespräch zur Historizität von Sprechakten. *Linguistische Berichte* 60, 65-78.

Searle, John R.
1969   *Speech Acts. An Essay in the Philosophy of Language.* Cambridge: Cambridge University Press.

Selig, Maria
1997   'Mündlichkeit' in mittelalterlichen Texten. In: Martin-Dietrich Gleßgen and Franz Lebsanft (eds.). *Alte und neue Philologie.* Tübingen: Niemeyer, 201-225.

Söll, Ludwig
³1985   *Gesprochenes und Geschriebenes Französisch.* (Bearbeitet von Franz Josef Hausmann).[¹1974]. Berlin: Erich Schmidt.

Stimm, Helmut (ed.)
1980   *Zur Geschichte des Gesprochenen Französisch und zur Sprachlenkung des Gegenwartsfranzösischen.* Wiesbaden: Steiner.

Taeuber, Walter
1933   *Geld und Kredit im Mittelalter.* Berlin: Heymann. (Reprinted 1968. Frankfurt a.M.: Sauer & Auvermann).

Ullmann-Margalit, Edna
1978   Invisible-hand explanations. *Synthese* 39, 263-291.

Weigand, Edda
1994   Dialoganalyse und Gesprächstraining. In: Gerd Fritz and Franz Hundsnurscher (eds.). *Handbuch der Dialoganalyse.* Tübingen: Niemeyer, 451-469.

Modifying Pragmatic Force
Hedges in Early Modern English Dialogues

Jonathan Culpeper
Lancaster University

Merja Kytö
Uppsala University

1. Introduction

What was the spoken conversation of the past like? Broadly speaking, this is our over-arching research question. Of course, much has been written about the "speech" of the past – the spoken sounds – but relatively little has been written from a historical perspective about the words and grammar of speech, the interactional characteristics of spoken conversation, and so on. This may seem an odd state of affairs, given the importance of the spoken language in issues such as language change and standardisation. But it is not so odd if one remembers that it is only relatively recently that we have been able to record speech: the linguistic research of earlier periods is hampered by lack of evidence.

This paper represents one small step in the direction of trying to understand the spoken conversation of the past. Our aim is to explore the hedges (including phenomena which other commentators have labelled "discourse markers") in a corpus containing Early Modern English dialogues, which can all be claimed to reflect spoken conversation in some way. We intend to elaborate on the first question posed by Brinton for the study of discourse markers: "First, can discourse markers, which, synchronically, are a feature of oral discourse be found in the written texts of earlier periods?" (1996: 49). In particular, we shall consider:

1. the overall frequency of hedges in our data and how this compares with hedges generated from a data-set consisting of contemporary conversational English, and
2. the frequencies of particular types of hedges and how they correlate with the text types in our corpus.

A number of studies have considered individual hedges from a historical perspective. Our investigation – risking a number of dangers which will be described later – attempts to look at the more global picture.

Why investigate hedges in a corpus consisting of dialogic texts? Dialogue, by definition, involves interaction, and hedges play a central role in the interpersonal dynamics that are played out in any kind of person-to-person interaction. As Nikula puts it, "they help signal speakers' feelings and attitudes to their messages, their coparticipants and the situation as a whole" (1996: 11-12). For example, we might have started this paper in a very different way:

> "Well, we think that we would quite like to explore hedges, I mean, those kind of little words that, you know, get sort of sprinkled around in people's utterances."

Of course, that would be an inauspicious start to any academic paper. Why? Because we do not seem to be certain about what we want to do, we are vague about what hedges are, we seem to be pretending that you know what we are talking about, and, in addition, we seem to have adopted an oddly colloquial style. Note from this example that hedges clearly have a pragmatic function: they tell us about the relationship between a message and its context. Note also that the example referred to "utterances". Hedges are strongly associated with oral discourse, both in terms of frequency (Quirk *et al.* 1985: 444) and perceptual salience (Watts 1989: 208). Our corpus consists of dialogues which purport to be related to speech in some way, so the representation of hedges in our corpus is going to be of interest.

We will begin this paper with a description of our corpus and then briefly outline the notion of hedges. We then move on to introduce and discuss the frequencies of hedges in our corpus.

2. The corpus

Our ultimate aim is to construct a corpus of around 1.2 million words. Covering the period 1550-1750, we are taking 10,000 word extracts of dialogue from a diverse range of text-types, such as courtroom proceedings, witness depositions, "eye-witness" accounts, play texts and prose fiction. The provisional structure of our corpus is displayed below:

Dialogue	Recorded	Re-constructed	Constructed
Minimum of narratorial intervention	Trial proceedings Meeting records Parliamentary journals (debates)	(History, biographies)	Drama Handbooks in dialogue form
Narratorial intervention	Witness depositions Witness accounts	History, biographies	Prose fiction

Table 1: Structure of the Corpus of Dialogues, 1550-1750

We hope that the structure represented here is not a mere contrivance for the purpose of constructing a corpus, but a reflection of the key dimensions along which texts containing dialogues may be organised. In brief, the horizontal parameter of the table represents a scale of authenticity. Three broad categories are distinguished:

- *Recorded* – texts produced from notes taken down by an individual, such as a clerk, present during a particular speech event;
- *Re-constructed* – texts which purport to present dialogue which actually took place at some point in the past (invariably, the narrator was present at the speech event in question); and
- *Constructed* – texts which contain constructed imaginary dialogue.

The vertical parameter represents a scale of narratorial[1] intervention. Two broad categories are distinguished:

- *Minimum of Narratorial Intervention* – texts which present dialogue as it was supposedly spoken and which minimise the explicit presence of the narrator (typically, the narrator's role is limited to speaker identification and contextual comment, such as stage directions); and
- *Narratorial Intervention* – texts in which dialogue is embedded in first or third person narration and in which the narrator's presence is made explicit (typically, through reporting clauses).

The even representation of each part of the corpus across this entire period is unlikely, as preliminary work has shown. Thus, the aim is to have a number of clusters of material, representing subperiods determined by (a) the periodization of the Helsinki Corpus (and thus facilitating comparative work), (b) key periods of change (e.g. the Civil War), and (c) the availability of material.

Work began on the corpus in June 1996. As a first step we decided to aim at a pilot corpus of 360,000 words,[2] divided equally between four text types – trial proceedings, witness depositions, drama, and prose fiction – taken from the period 1590 to 1720, i.e. the middle three periods of our corpus. Thus, half of the corpus would contain naturally occurring speech (supposedly recorded verbatim or nearly so) and half constructed imaginary speech. Furthermore, half (trial proceedings and drama) would be recorded with minimal explicit narratorial interference and half (witness depositions and prose fiction) with considerable interference. At the time when this study was undertaken, the corpus consisted of 254,062 words distributed amongst the four text-types accordingly:

Text type	Words
Trials	71,660
Drama	91,028
Depositions	51,449
Prose Fiction	39,925
Grand Total	254,062

Table 2: Distribution of words in the pilot corpus

It is clear that the distribution of words across the four text-types is not even: drama is the only text-type where we have reached our target. In particular, finding depositions and prose fiction samples which contain reasonable quantities of speech has proved especially difficult.

3. Hedges, hedging and corpus searching

What are hedges? A starting point for any discussion of hedges is likely to be George Lakoff's (1972) seminal work on semantic criteria and fuzzy logic. For Lakoff, hedges are "words whose meaning implicitly involves fuzziness – words whose job is to make things fuzzier or less fuzzy" (1972: 195). Thus, in rather simple terms, the hedge *sort of* increases fuzziness, whereas the hedge *very* decreases it. Note immediately that the notion of a hedge covers both increasing and decreasing fuzziness. Some later researchers have associated the term hedges exclusively with increasing fuzziness, often for the purpose of reducing the pragmatic force with which something is said. Such hedges have been referred to as "downtoners". Conversely, hedges which decrease fuzziness have been referred to as "emphatics", and also "upgraders", "boosters".

Lakoff (1972) also very briefly raised the possibility of a further distinction. He noted that some hedges, like *I think, I suppose*, could add fuzziness to performatives. Thus, in an utterance such as *I think that it's good* the strength of the assertion is toned down – it is a hedged performative. Other researchers (e.g. Fraser 1975 and Holmes 1984) have gone on to develop hedges in relation to the notion of illocutionary force. Note here that we have moved away from fuzziness within a proposition to fuzziness – or certainty – between a speaker and a proposition. Prince *et al.* (1982) make this kind of distinction and suggest the labels "approximators" and "intensifiers" for hedges that signal more or less fuzziness within a proposition, and "shields" and "certainty markers" for hedges that signal more or less speaker certainty. This four-way distinction might be illustrated with the following examples:

Shield   Approximator
I guess   it's   sort of   good

Certainty marker   Intensifier
I'm sure   it's   really   good

A broad understanding of a hedge includes an additional group of linguistic items which do not easily fall into the groups above, but which do play a role in modifying pragmatic force. Other researchers have referred to them as "discourse markers", "pragmatic particles", "pragmatic markers" or "implicit modifiers". Examples which were used in the introduction to this paper, would include *Well, I mean* and *you know*. This additional group can be characterised as more "implicit" than other hedges. The explicit/implicit distinction was developed by Östman (1981, 1986, 1987) and is further discussed by Nikula (1996: 50-55). Broadly speaking, at the explicit end of the scale, we typically have attitudinal adverbs, adverbs of degree or parenthetical verbs which are fairly explicit in signalling the speaker's certainty about or vagueness in a particular message. At the implicit end of the scale, we typically have pragmatic markers which orientate primarily towards the speaker/hearer relationship, rather than the utterance, and they tend to be relatively empty in semantic terms and relatively ambivalent in context.

Given our global concerns in this paper, we adopted a relatively inclusive approach to hedging phenomena, including, for example, implicit modifiers. We have introduced the categorisation above in order to suggest how the notion of a hedge has developed. It is, of course, not possible to produce a hard and fast categorisation of hedges: hedges are fuzzy themselves. For example, the division between a shield and an approximator is not always clear. The key criterion (whether the fuzziness is between the speaker and the proposition or within proposition) is difficult to apply, because what constitutes the proposition is often problematic. Furthermore, if an approximator is interpreted as a sign of speaker uncertainty, should it then be a shield?[3] Similarly, the distinction between an "explicit" hedge and an "implicit" one can be difficult. Some tangential evidence of this is in the fact that there is only partial agreement in various studies about which hedges are implicit (Brinton 1996: 31). In sum, it is safer to view all the distinctions made so far as scalar. One might consider the categories mentioned from the perspective of prototype theory, whereby membership of a particular category is determined by the similarity to the category's best exemplar.[4] Thus, *really* might be a fairly prototypical intensifier, and the fact that it can be used to express doubt (e.g. *I like her, really*; said with the appropriate intonation and context) does not invalidate this.[5]

Turning more closely to the function of hedges, we could, as other researchers have done (e.g. Brinton 1996), produce a long list of detailed functions. Instead, we shall suggest that hedges are generally used for the strategic management of one or more of four areas:

- *Information* – A speaker may simply lack necessary information for exact statements or may deliberately withhold information, perhaps to mislead or bias the hearer towards a particular interpretation.
- *Face* – Here one should mention the work of Brown and Levinson (1987). However, unlike Brown and Levinson (1987), who concentrate on the mitigating function of hedges in relation to the hearer (hedges as a negative politeness strategy), we would argue that hedges – understood broadly – can also be used in relation to positive face, can be used to protect the speaker's face and can be used to attack face.
- *Discourse* – Hedges can be used to facilitate the production and reception of discourse. For example, they can be used as devices to signal the relationship between one segment of discourse and another, or as devices to hold the conversational floor.
- *Style* – Hedges can be used to create a certain style. For example, they can be used to reduce formality, perhaps to put an interactant at ease and create a sense of involvement or solidarity.

Hedges in Early Modern English Dialogues   299

Of course, these areas are not mutually exclusive. On the contrary, an area such as style is involved whenever a hedge is used. Nevertheless, there are many occasions when a hedge is used primarily to manipulate one area. We shall illustrate some of these functions a little later in our paper.

Before turning to the data in our corpus, we need to consider the issue of form and function. This is particularly pertinent for us, since the corpus methodology has an in-built bias towards form. Put simply, if you want to look for a particular form in a corpus, you call it or type it in and the examples appear on your screen. With automated grammatical tagging, we can also look for parts of speech. More recently, semantic tagging has been developed (see, for example, Schmidt 1991). However, despite advances in computational pragmatics, pragmatic tagging – if it is possible at all – would seem to be some way off.[6] What linguistic forms can perform the function of hedging? Brown and Levinson (1987: 146) argue that an "indefinite number of forms" can be used. From a corpus point of view, this is not very helpful! We made a decision, like many other studies, to concentrate on words and expressions. An exhaustive approach would involve us going through the corpus picking out hedging words and expressions. With the corpus currently at around 250,000 words (and with plans to expand to 1.2 million words) this would be very time-consuming. Therefore, we decided to generate a list of forms to search for from three sources:

- Nikula (1996), who draws up a list of contemporary hedges taken from 20,480 words of tape recorded informal impromptu conversation.
- Stoffel (1901), who conducts a historical survey of what he calls "intensives" and "down-toners".
- Our own readings of data in the corpus.

In total we searched for approximately 80 forms.

Armed with our list of forms, could we now simply go ahead and generate frequencies? The problem is that one cannot guarantee that any particular form will always be acting as a hedge, or indeed, if it acts as a hedge at all.[7] For example, *why* is not always used as a hedge in the example below (the emphasis in all examples is ours):

(1)   WAS. Numps? S'blood, you are fine and familiar ! how
      long ha' wee bin acquainted, I pray you ?
      QVAR. I thinke it may be remembred, Numps , that ?[8]
      'twas since morning sure.
      WAS. *Why*, I hope I know't well enough, Sir, I did not
      ask to be told.
      QVAR. No ? *why* then ?

WAS. It's no matter *why*, you see with your eyes, now, what I said to you to day ? you'll beleeue me another time ? (1600-1640/Drama/Jonson/*Bartholomew Fair*)

In the first instance it is a hedge. Waspe uses it to signal his objection to what Qvarlous has just said. *Why* has a discoursal function (relating Waspe's discourse to Qvarlous's) and a face function (acting as a challenge). The second and third instances are more propositional than pragmatic: in the second instance *why* is an interrogative adverb and in the third a simple relative adverb. Thus our main task was to go through our concordances, study the context and eliminate examples which did not involve hedging. In cases such as *I think* or *perhaps* this is relatively simple, because they are quite explicit hedges. But other cases required much more careful consideration of the context. Consider the hedge *a little* in the example below:

(2) *Dor.* And I hope you have made much of him?
Arch. O yes, Madam, but the Strength of your Ladyship's Liquor is *a little* too potent for the Constitution of your humble Servant.
Mrs. Sull. What, then you don't usually drink Ale?
Arch. No, Madam, my constant Drink is Tea, or *a little* Wine and Water ; 'tis prescrib'd me by the Physician for a Remedy against the Spleen.
(1680-1720/Drama/Farquhar/*The Beaux Stratagem*)

The first instance of *a little* seems to be used for the purpose of face management. Archer mitigates his criticism of the drink in a context of great power imbalance: he is a servant, she is a gentlewoman. At first, the second instance of *a little* seems to have the sense of 'a small quantity', and thus would not be a hedge. But is that right? One might see a case of strategic information management here: Archer may be being deliberately vague about the precise quantity of wine he consumes. Perhaps his explanation – that it is for medicinal purposes – is rather suspicious.

Clearly then, some of our frequency counts rely very heavily on the interpretative decisions we have made.

4. Frequencies

Table 3 below displays the distribution of the ten most frequent hedges in the corpus.[9] Given that the four text-types are unequal in size, it is important to focus on the frequencies per 1,000 words.

	Trials	Witness depositions	Drama	Fiction	Total
some	129	121	107	56	413
	1.8	2.4	1.2	1.4	1.6
very	90	65	170	72	397
	1.3	1.3	1.9	1.8	1.6
about	50	126	6	5	187
	0.7	2.4	0.1	0.1	0.7
though	34	17	83	41	175
	0.5	0.3	0.9	1.0	0.7
I think	48	2	84	7	141
	0.7	0.04	0.9	0.2	0.6
a little	20	30	67	32	149
	0.3	0.6	0.7	0.8	0.6
well	31	1	83	22	137
	0.4	0.02	0.9	0.6	0.5
why	10	0	94	19	123
	0.1	0	1.0	0.5	0.5
sure	27	9	71	17	124
	0.4	0.2	0.8	0.4	0.5
may	18	1	67	7	93
	0.3	0.02	0.7	0.2	0.4
	457	372	832	278	1939
	6.4	7.2	9.1	7.0	7.6

Table 3: The distribution of the ten most frequent hedges in the corpus (raw frequencies and the incidence counted per 1,000 words).

4.1. The grand total

If we consider the proportion of hedges relative to the total number of words in the corpus, they represent about one percent. Nikula's figure for her contemporary data was 12.1% (1996: 81). Of course, such a comparison is not really valid, since we are not comparing like with like. Nikula recorded informal, unstructured conversation. We have, on the one hand, formal, structured conversation converted into the written medium, and, on the other hand, constructed literary dialogue. Nevertheless, it is intriguing to speculate that hedges were generally less used in conversation. This would indeed be consistent with Biber and Finegan's work (e.g. 1989, 1992), which suggests that certain text-types – fiction, essays and letters – have drifted towards a more "oral" style.

4.2. Text-type totals

Turning to the text-type totals for the top ten hedges given in Table 3, note that the constructed data is much denser in hedges than the recorded data. (The figures displayed are relative to each text-type. Relative to the corpus as a whole, the constructed data still wins out; the figures being 8.5 for constructed data and 6.7 for recorded.) One might postulate a number of reasons for this:

- The recorded data takes place in a formal situation, the courtroom, whereas the constructed data tends to take place in relatively informal contexts, such as a room in a house, an inn or a street. (Note also that all our drama texts are from comedies and that our prose texts – written by, for example, Robert Armin, Thomas Deloney – tend to be comic.)
- The recorded data is relatively structured. It revolves around question-answer adjacency pairs. Thus there is less need for hedges in the management of discourse.
- The recorded data almost invariably involves asymmetric power relationships. The judges and prosecutors have the power to abuse the witnesses' faces with impunity. There is no need, one might think, for them to soften the force of what they say. Note here that in this period the English judicial system had a more adversarial basis, as opposed to inquisitorial (see, for example, Beattie 1986 and Sharpe 1984).
- For the recorded data, it is quite likely that many hedges, particularly implicit ones, have been lost in the transference from one medium to another. Indeed, remember that these courtroom note-takers were battling to

Hedges in Early Modern English Dialogues   303

jot down real time speech. It would be no surprise if they sacrificed those words which appeared to have less semantic content.
• Finally, there may also be reasons for the high density of hedges in the constructed data. For example, an author might employ hedges, such as *well* or *why*, to create rapidly and efficiently a particularly oral or emotionally involved kind of style. We will return to these particular hedges later.

4.3. Ranking hedges in terms of frequency

Let us compare – with all suitable caveats and hedges – our frequency ranking of hedges with that of Nikula (1996: 75):

Our data	Nikula (1996: 75)
1. some	I mean
2. very	you know
3. about	I think
4. though	well
5. I think	just
6. a little	like
7. well	really
8. why	sort of
9. sure	(tag question)
10. may	actually

Note that our ranking has some similarities with Nikula's (1996): *I think* and *well* are in fairly similar positions. However, there have been changes. The top two slots in Nikula's (1996) list are taken by implicit hedges, which is not the case in our list, where the first implicit hedges are *well* and *why* in seventh and eighth place respectively.[10] Some possible reasons as to why implicit hedges are not higher in our list include:
• Given the relative formality and the relatively structured nature of some of our data, one might expect implicit hedges not to occur in great quantity, because such hedges often have a colloquial flavour and often serve to manage the discourse. Implicit hedges would surely have suffered in the transference to the written medium.
• Not only is it likely that implicit hedges would have been perceived as carrying little semantic content, but they are easily detachable elements: implicit hedges usually form a separate tone group in speech and tend to

occur outside the syntactic structure of an utterance or are loosely attached to it.

- The particularly high ranking of some explicit hedges in our list, notably *about* and *some*, may relate to the information management which is crucial to some of our text-types. We will discuss this further in the next subsection.

4.4. Specific hedges

As can be seen from Table 3, *some* and *about* are the most densely occurring hedges in any one text-type, in this case witness depositions. Compared with the other text-types *about* occurs with striking frequency in witness depositions. Why? Witness depositions are statements made to a judge or magistrate about past events. An examination of examples of *about* reveals that in almost every case *about* refers to a period of time, and in many cases is followed by a number. Consider example (3):

(3) The sayd Examinate *Iames Deuice* sayth,
that *about* a month agoe, as this
Examinate was comming towards his Mothers
house, and at day-gate of the same night,
this Examinate mette a browne Dogge
comming from his Graund-mothers house, *about* tenne
Roodes distant from the same house : and *about* two or
three nights after, that this Examinate heard a voyce of a
great number of Children screiking and crying pittifully,
about day-light gate ; and likewise, *about* ten Roodes
distant of this Examinates sayd Graund-mothers house.
And *about* fiue nights then next following, presently after
daylight, within 20. Roodes of the sayd *Elizabeth
Sowtherns* house, he heard a foule yelling like vnto a great
number of Cattes : but what they were, this Examinate
cannot tell. And he further sayth, that *about* three nights
after that, *about* midnight of the same, there came a thing,
and lay vpon him very heauily *about* an houre, and went
then from him out of his Chamber window, coloured
blacke, and *about* the bignesse of a Hare or Catte. And
he further sayth, that *about* S. *Peters* day last, [...]
(1600-1640/Depositions/*Pendle Witches*)

Of the eleven instances of *about*, eight relate to a period of time and five are followed by a specific number.[11] *About* is often being used in the strategic management of information, to add fuzziness to a claim about the specific span of time that has elapsed between the witness' 'now' and some past event. Given the failings of human memory and the specificity of the claim, it is not surprising that a hedge is used. Also, remember the situation: this is a formal hearing before a magistrate or judge; the witness is formally committed to saying the truth. Thus, there are powerful social reasons why a witness may not wish to be overly exact.[12] Of course, there is always the possibility that the high density of this particular hedge may also be due to the court recorder treating it as a kind of all-purpose hedge employed to capture any kind of vagueness expressed by the witness, including perhaps paralinguistic hedging (e.g. hesitations).

Why are the hedges *well* and *why* so frequent in drama and to a lesser extent fiction? We would suggest a couple of possible reasons. The discourse in drama and fiction is not subject to the same kind of rigid turn-taking structure, such as you find in the courtroom. These play a role in managing that discourse. *Why* has been rather less studied than *well*, so we shall focus briefly on *why*, though it is worth bearing in mind that *well* does share a number of functional similarities.[13] *Why*, as in example (1), often expresses surprise at or challenges something the previous speaker has said. Moreover, the vast majority of our examples of *why* signal a change of speaker (as in examples (4) and (5)) or a change from narrator to character (as in example (6)).

(4) DORILANT. What a Divel are these?
HORNER. *Why*, these are pretenders to honour, as criticks
to wit, only by censuring others; and as every raw
peevish, out-of-humour'd, affected, dull, Tea-drinking,
Arithmetical Fop sets up for a wit, by railing at men
of sence, so these for honour, by railing at the Court,
and Ladies of as great honour, as quality.
(1640-1680/Drama/Wycherley/*Country-Wife*)

(5) [...] Will tels
the king how Terrils Frith was inclosed. Tirrels Frith! sayes
the king; what is that? *Why*, the heath where I was borne,
called by the name of Tirrels Frith: now a gentleman of that
name takes it all in, and makes people beleeue it is all his, for
it took the name from him; so that, Harry, the poore pine, and
their cattle are all undone without thy help.
(1600-1640/Fiction/Armin/*Nest of Ninnies*)

(6) Would the boots were in your belly, quoth the cobler; once
againe, they are gone home. By and by comes the gentleman

in his white linen boot hose, ready to the purpose. A poxe of lazy coblers! sayes hee; my boots! shall I forfeit a bond for your pleasure? The cobler puts off his condisering cap. *Why*, sir, sayes hee, I sent them home but now. By whom? sayes he. By John, blew John, sayes the cobler.
(1600-1640/Fiction/Armin/*Nest of Ninnies*)

This is an easy way for an author to flag up the fact that there has been a change in speaking voice, before it is confirmed by a reporting clause. *Well* exhibits this kind of pattern even more strongly in our data.

When *why* is used in trial proceedings, it often occurs at points of particular acrimony and also when there is a break-down in question-answer sequences. This is illustrated in examples (7) and (8):

(7) *Raleigh.* Here is a Book supposed to be
treasonable; I never read it, commended it, or deliver'd
it, nor urged it.
Attorn. Why this is cunning.
Raleigh. Every thing that doth make for me is
cunning, and every thing that maketh against me
is probable.
(1600-1640/Trial/Raleigh)

(8) *Mr. Just. Dolben.* Nay, now, Mistris, you
have spoil'd all; for in *October* this business was
done.
Mr. Justice Jones. You have undone the Man,
instead of saving him.
Mary Tilden. Why, my Lord, I only mistook
the Month.
(1640-1680/Trial/Green, Berry and Hill)

Within question-answer sequences, *why* is invariably used by the judges to express disbelief in a witness's evidence (see example (9)), and by witnesses to present an answer as if it were a self-evident truth (see example (10)).

(9) *Mr. Att. G.* My Lord, in that we were
mistaken, I understand now, it was only Berry
denied that he did know *Gerald.*
L. C. J. Why, did you never know Mr.
Girald?

Berry, Never in my Life.
(1640-1680/Trial/Green, Berry and Hill)

(10) *Mr. Justice Wild.* By what means did you get
into his Acquaintance?
Mr. Bedlow. Why, I pretended to get Warrants
for the Good Behaviour against Persons, that
there were none such.
(1640-1680/Trial/Green, Berry and Hill)

A positive reason for the frequency of *why* and *well* in drama and fiction might be that this is one way in which an author can swiftly and easily create a particular style, a highly "oral" style.[14] For instance, in example (11) three instances of *well* and one of *why* cluster amongst the oral disfluencies of Lady Touchwood's speech:

(11) Ld. *T.* Sorry, for what ? 'Death you rack me with delay.
Ldy *T.* Nay, no great matter, only – *well* I have your
promise – Pho, *why* nothing, only your Nephew had a
mind to amuse himself, sometimes with a little Gallantry
towards me. Nay, I can't think he meant any thing seriously,
but methought it look'd odly.
Ld. *T.* Confusion and Hell, what do I hear !
Ldy *T.* Or, may be, he thought he was not enough a-kin
to me, upon your account, and had a mind to create a
nearer relation on his own ; a Lover you know, my Lord – Ha,
ha, ha. *Well* but that's all – now you have it ; *well*
remember your promise, my Lord, and don't take any notice of
it to him.
(1680-1720/Drama/Congreve/*The Double-Dealer*)

This example also illustrates another reason for the high occurrence of *well* and *why* in literary texts, namely, the high degree of involvement of the participants.

The use of *well* and *why* in or in creating highly oral language could also explain why they are so infrequent in witness depositions. The witness depositions in our corpus contain witness reports of dialogue noted down by somebody, sometimes a clerk, present in the courtroom.[15] Indirect speech is by far the most dominant mode of speech presentation. In other words, we are relatively distant from the original speech, and thus it is no surprise that *well* and *why* hardly appear.

5. Conclusion

Let us return to our over-arching research question: what was the spoken conversation of the past like? The evidence we have presented would corroborate with the notion that English was becoming more "oral" in style over time, but our evidence must be treated with caution, since our comparison with Nikula (1996) involves two different media, speech and writing. There are, however, ways in which our work might be improved. In theory, there is a scale of "orality" varying from written texts through speech-based texts to spoken conversation. We may never be able to construct a definitive linguistic picture of spoken conversation, since the features that are most indicative of spoken conversation are often the ones that are least likely to survive the transference into the written medium, as we have suggested with regard to implicit modifiers. However, we can reconstruct the other end of the scale, namely, a picture of written texts, and measure the distance between written texts and speech-based written texts. If our corpus were expanded we could: 1) see if there is a style shift over time within the corpus, and 2) see if the distance between written texts proper and speech-based texts remains constant over time. Biber and Finegan (see 1992 in particular) have already made significant advances along these lines. Using factor analysis,[16] they have shown the gap between written texts proper and speech-based texts, and also shown that, in general, there is a diachronic shift in speech-based texts towards a more "oral" style. However, Biber and Finegan's work is limited, as they point out (1992: 701-2), by the fact that their speech-based texts are all literary. In this pilot study, we have provided evidence that different hedges correlate with different text-types, and we have suggested reasons why this might be the case. In so doing we hope to have cast some light on both the text-types of Early Modern English and also the functionings of hedges.

We have given some glimpses of what one can do with this kind of corpus and how it can help us explore issues of interest. Of course, this is only the beginning. For example, we have yet to do close-up studies of particular hedges and how they have developed over time, and we have yet to consider other variables such as author or the gender of the speaker. Moreover, we need to widen our perspectives by including other speech-based text-types in the corpus. This would place us in a much better position to make generalisations about global shifts of hedges in the English language.

Notes

1 There are circumstances where the terms "author" or "reporter" may seem more appropriate than "narrator", or circumstances where more than one term applies. For the sake of simplicity, we have adopted "narrator" as the general term for the mediator of the dialogue, and make further distinctions only when necessary. The term "narrator" facilitates the use of the term "narrative" to describe "non-dialogue" parts of texts – such as descriptions of people, places and events – or in other words, parts of the text for which the narrator is responsible, rather than a reported speaker.
2 The construction of the pilot corpus was made possible through the support of British Academy research grant SG-AN2887/APN3846.
3 See Skelton (1988) for other criticisms of the shield/approximator distinction.
4 For the application of prototype theory to various areas of linguistics see, for example, Taylor (1995).
5 An alternative approach might be to relate hedges to an underlying cognitive mechanism. Some studies have used Sperber and Wilson's (1986/1995) Relevance Theory in relation to hedges (e.g. Jucker 1993; Watts 1988).
6 However, see Stiles (1992) for a relatively convincing attempt to tag a corpus for speech acts. Also, Leech *et al.* (1997) provide an interesting discussion of attempts to tag discoursal/pragmatic phenomena (Stiles 1992 is also summarised here).
7 Surprisingly, some studies of hedges (e.g. McMillan *et al.* 1977) have done simple frequency counts of linguistic forms and paid little attention to function or context.
8 This oddly positioned question mark appears in the original.
9 The form *so* occurs with great frequency in our corpus (some 1180 times). However, we had great difficulty devising operable criteria for the inclusion or exclusion of instances from our hedge count. In the collocation *or so*, *so* is clearly acting as a hedge, but instances of *or so* are relatively few. For the remaining cases, if *so* (as either a conjunction or adverb) had the sense of *thus* or *in this way*, then we thought it should be excluded. However, in some instances it seemed possible that *so* also had an intensifying effect, in which case we should count it as a hedge. For example: "Adams. This is the thing: if you please to help my memory; for there are *so* many particulars in this correspondency, that I cannot tell whereabout it is I am to speak to [...]". The problem here is one of ambiguity: *so* is interpretable as meaning 'thus' and/or as an intensifier. We decided that for cases such as these if the 'thus' interpretation were possible, we would exclude the example. As a result, *so* does not appear in our top-ten table. If we had not applied this criterion, *so* would have been in the top-ten. Clearly, *so* could benefit from the attention of an individual study.
10 Our ranking list continues as follows (no attempt has been made here to indicate the hedges grouping under one and the same frequency): *something, I believe, rather, others, I know not/I don't know, what, might, almost, I suppose, even, at all, I find, like, certainly, verily, perhaps, you know, pretty, surely, altogether, it seems, absolutely, quite, I have heard,*

really, must, maybe, somewhat, right, full, fully, possibly, I expect, exactly, extremely, I guess, or something, I presume, clean, consumedly, totally, you see, and everything, far, I feel, I trowe, merely, of course, purely, and/or whatever, probably, actually, apparently, could not, nearly, pure and *without doubt*. We also searched for the following words or expressions but found no clear instances of hedges: *basically, cannot, damnable, damnably, definitely, fairly, just, kind of, a lot, I mean, obvious, obviously, presumably, slightly, sort of, supposedly, tend, terribly, tolerably, virtually*, and tag questions.

11 *Some* follows a similar pattern, though to a lesser degree.
12 The situation is more complex. Witnesses must perform a rather tricky balancing act: on the one hand, they need to appropriately hedge what they are not sure about, but on the other hand, too much hedging and they will not be seen as reliable witnesses. So, along with hedges like *about, some, I think* and *I believe* (approximately 90% of instances are used by witnesses), we find that witnesses account for all of our examples of the emphatics *certainly* and *verily*, hedges which can make them sound more certain about information.
13 This is not to say that *well* has received a lot of attention from a historical perspective, but there are at least some illuminating studies (e.g. Blake 1992-3; Finell 1989; Jucker 1997).
14 However, Jucker (1997) points out that it is towards the end of the Early Modern period that the first examples of *well* were occurring in fictional texts without being closely connected to spoken language.
15 A criterion for the selection of witness depositions for our corpus was that they should contain reports of speech. Thus, for example, shipping depositions, which tend to include reports of tonnage, customs and excise duties, and so on, were excluded, whereas the depositions of "witches", which tend to have reports of past conversations, were included.
16 It might be noted that hedges were one diagnostic feature in their analysis.

References

Beattie, John M.
    1986   *Crime and the Courts in England, 1660-1800*. Oxford: Clarendon Press.
Biber, Douglas, and Edward Finegan
    1989   Drift and evolution of English style: a history of three genres. *Language* 65(3), 487-517.
    1992   The linguistic evolution of five written and speech-based English genres from the 17th to the 20th centuries. In: Matti Rissanen, Ossi Ihalainen, Terttu Nevalainen and Irma Taavitsainen (eds.). *History of Englishes: New Methods in Interpretations and Historical Linguistics*. Berlin: Mouton de Gruyter, 688-704.
Blake, N.F.
    1992-3   Shakespeare and discourse. *Stylistica* 2(3), 81-90.

Brinton, Laurel J.
  1996   *Pragmatic Markers in English: Grammaticalization and Discourse Functions*. Berlin: Mouton de Gruyter.
Brown, Penelope, and Stephen C. Levinson
  1987   *Politeness*. Cambridge: Cambridge University Press.
Finell, Anne
  1989   Well now and then. *Journal of Pragmatics* 13, 653-56.
Fraser, Bruce
  1975   Hedged performatives. In: Peter Cole and J.L. Morgan (eds.). *Syntax and Semantics, Vol. 3: Speech Acts*. New York: Academic Press, 187-210.
Holmes, Janet
  1984   Modifying illocutionary force. *Journal of Pragmatics* 8(3), 345-65.
Jucker, Andreas H.
  1993   The discourse marker *well*: a relevance-theoretical account. *Journal of Pragmatics* 19, 435-52.
  1997   The discourse marker *well* in the history of English. *English Language and Linguistics* 1(1), 91-110.
Lakoff, George
  1972   Hedges: a study in meaning criteria and the logic of fuzzy concepts. In: P.M. Peranteau, J.N. Levi and G.C Phares (eds.). *Papers from the Eighth Regional Meeting, Chicago Linguistic Society*. Chicago: Chicago Linguistic Society, 183-228.
Leech, Geoffrey N., Tony McEnery and Martin Wynne
  1997   Further levels of annotation. In: Roger Garside, Geoffrey N. Leech and Tony McEnery (eds.). *Corpus Annotation: Linguistic Information from Computer Corpora*. London: Longman, 85-101.
McMillan, Julie R., Kay A. Clifton, Diane McGrath and Wanda S. Gale
  1977   Woman's language: uncertainty or interpersonal sensitivity and emotionality? *Sex Roles* 3(6), 545-59.
Nikula, Tarja
  1996   *Pragmatic Force Modifiers: A Study in Interlanguage Pragmatics*. Jyväskylä: University of Jyväskylä.
Östman, Jan-Ola
  1981   *You know: a discourse-functional view*. Pragmatics and Beyond II:7. Amsterdam: John Benjamins.
  1986   *Pragmatics as Implicitness: An Analysis of Question Particles in Solf Swedish, with Implications for the Study of Passive Clauses and the Language of Persuasion*. Unpublished Ph.D. thesis, University of California, Berkeley.

1987 Implicit involvement in interactive writing. In: Jef Verschueren and Marcella Bertucelli-Papi (eds.). *The Pragmatic Perspective. Selected Papers from the 1985 International Pragmatics Conference.* Amsterdam: John Benjamins, 203-21.

Prince, Ellen F., Joel Frader and Charles Bosk
  1982 On hedging in physician-physician discourse. In: R.J. Di Pietro (ed.). *Linguistics and the Professions.* N.J. Norwood, Ablex, 83-97.

Quirk, Randolph, Sidney Greenbaum, Geoffrey Leech and Jan Svartvik
  1985 *A Comprehensive Grammar of the English Language.* London: Longman.

Schmidt, Klaus M.
  1991 Ein Datenbanksystem für das Begriffswörterbuch mittelhochdeutscher Epik und Fortschritte bei der automatischen Disambiguierung. In: K. Gärtner, P. Sappler and M. Trauth (eds.). *Maschinelle Verarbeitung altdeutscher Texte IV.* Tübingen: Max Niemeyer, 192-204.

Sharpe, James
  1984 *Crime in Early Modern England, 1550-1750.* London: Longman.

Skelton, John
  1988 The care and maintenance of hedges. *ELT Journal* 42(1), 37-43.

Sperber, Dan, and Deirdre Wilson
  1986/95 *Relevance: Communication and Cognition.* Oxford: Blackwell.

Stiles, William B.
  1992 *Describing Talk: A Taxonomy of Verbal Response Modes.* Beverly Hills: Sage.

Stoffel, C.
  1901 *Intensives and Down-toners: A Study in English Adverbs.* Heidelberg: Carl Winter.

Taylor, John R.
  1995 *Linguistic Categorization: Prototypes in Linguistic Theory.* 2nd edition. Oxford: Clarendon.

Watts, Richard J.
  1988 A relevance-theoretic approach to commentary pragmatic markers: the case of *actually, really* and *basically. Acta Linguistica Hungarica* 38, 235-60.

  1989 Taking the pitcher to the *well*: native speakers' perception of their use of discourse markers in conversation. *Journal of Pragmatics* 13, 203-37.

So he says to her, he says, "Well," he says ...:
Multiple Dialogue Introducers from a Historical Perspective

Anne Herlyn
Albert Ludwigs University, Freiburg

1. Introduction

In this study, I will be discussing a phenomenon which I call "multiple dialogue introducers". The title of this article features a typical example of this type of structure, taken from the transcription of a spontaneously told narrative in Present-Day English. While structures of this sort occur in unplanned oral storytelling in English, they are not normally used in Present-Day English written or literary language. It is striking, however, that in Middle English narratives, similar constructions are quite frequent. Here, they occur mostly in the form of the well-known pattern *He/she answered and said.*

The most striking feature that the structures in both contexts have in common is the seeming redundancy of the second verb of saying. I will be pursuing the question of what possible function this second verb of saying might have, and if the structures observed in present-day English oral stories and those in Middle English narratives serve similar purposes.

To my knowledge, there exists no study that specifically targets multiple dialogue introducers in English. Discussions of this feature occur rarely and in diverse sources. One goal of the present study is to collect and evaluate these different explanations; another is to add my own interpretation, claiming a common function for the feature both in Middle English and in Present-Day English.

2. Examples of multiple dialogue introducers

What I consider as multiple dialogue introducers are instances of quotation in which one turn is attributed to its speaker by more than one verb of saying, without this being accompanied by the introduction of new information, such as a change of addressee, a change in the mode of speaking, etc. (Such "motivated" repetitions of dialogue introducers are frequent in Present-Day English literary usage, while the structures I am concerned with in the following do not occur there.)

The Middle English examples which will be analyzed in the following are taken from the romances *Guy of Warwick, Floris and Blauncheflour* and *Amys and Amylion.* The Present-Day English examples were collected from transcripts of spontaneous oral narrative in British and American English in various publications on oral storytelling (Euler 1991; Fludernik 1991; Johnstone 1990, 1993; Polanyi 1989; Schiffrin 1981; Wolfson 1982).[1]

I will exclude from my analysis cases in which the dialogue introducer is repeated after embedded orientation material, as in example (1):

(1) he says
  he stopped
  and looked back,
  he was nae used to it,
  he says, "..." (Fludernik 1991: 383).

In these cases, I interpret the repetition of the verb of saying as the multiple filling of a syntactic slot, which typically occurs after embeddings in spoken English (cf. Halford 1996: 76f, 89).

In general, I distinguish between two major types of multiple dialogue introducer. Both are combined in the title quote, so I will refer to the title for a description of both types:

(2) So he says to her, he says, "Well," he says, "The person at thirty-four backed out" (Wolfson 1982: 26).

The first type of multiple dialogue introducer always precedes the quotation. A second verb of saying is inserted between the inquit phrase and the quotation.

In the second type of multiple dialogue introducer, the repeated verb of saying is embedded in the quotation.

2.1. Examples of the first type of multiple dialogue introducer

In Middle English romances, the second verb of saying typically occurs in the form of a coordinated verb, as in examples (3) and (4).

(3) The mery maide asked anon   'The merry young woman asked
      Of here maydens everychon,   each of her maids
      and seide: "..." (*Amys*, 37.4-6)   and said: "..."'
(4) þerl answerd & seyd þo: "..."   'Then the earl answered and said:
      (*Guy*, 695)   "..."'[2]

In the Present-Day English examples, the second verb of saying is usually part of a verb phrase which is asyndetically joined to the preceding syntagm:

(5) He finally told me he said: "..." (Johnstone 1993: 63)
(6) the guy says to me, says, "..." (Wolfson 1982: 26)

Note that the repetition of the verb of saying can occur in the shape of a complete syntagm, as in example (5), or in a reduced form which contains only the verb (example (6)).

There are rare instances of the asyndetic form, which is typical of the Present-Day English texts, in the Middle English romances:

(7) þer cam an angel fram heven liȝt   'Then an angel came from the
          bright heavens
      and seyd to þe king ful riȝt   and said to the king
      þurȝ grace of godes sond.   through the mercy of God's
          providence
      He seyd: "..."   he said: "..."'
      (*Guy*, 234.1-4)

Thus, even in this small corpus there are numerous examples of the first type of multiple dialogue introducer, which occur in different forms. Not only do they differ in their syntactic forms (coordinated vs. asyndetic), but also in the combination of lexemes. The typical form in Middle English is the occurrence of two different verbs (*answer*, *ask*, *tell* etc. as the first, and *say* as the second verb of saying), while in Present-Day English there can be two different verbs (cf. example (5)), but it is more common for the verb *say* to be repeated.[3] In Middle English, a repetition of the same verb only seems to occur in the rare cases where the asyndetic form is used (cf. example (7)). Thus, the coordinated form seems to be correlated with a combination of two different verbs of saying, the asyndetic form also allows for a repetition of the same verb.

2.2. Examples of the second type of multiple dialogue introducer

A typical example of the second type of multiple dialogue introducer in Middle English is example (8), in which one dialogue introducer precedes the quotation, and another is inserted after an initial address:

(8) Al wepyng seide þenne schee,   'Crying, she then said:
    "Sir," schee seide, "deede." (...)   "Sir," she said, "dead." (...)'
    (*Floris*, 238-239)

There can also be variation between the initial and the inserted verb, as in example (9):

(9) Sir Gij answerd to the king   'Sir Guy answered the king
    "Youn," he said, "withouten lesing,   "Youn," he said, "truly,
    Men clepeþ me in mi cuntre."   is what they call me in my
    (*Guy* 81.10-11)   country."'

While in the above examples the second dialogue introducer is inserted shortly after the beginning of the quotation, it is also quite common for this to occur towards the end of the quotation, or, in the case of stanzaic narrative, for an additional dialogue introducer to occur at the beginning of a new stanza in quotations which extend over more than one stanza.

In general, while there is variation in the verb preceding the quotation, the verb inserted into the quotation in Middle English is almost exclusively *quoþ/quaþ* or a form of "seien".

In Present-Day English, there is a similar limitation of the inserted verb of saying to a form of "say". Typical positions are after a term of address, a discourse marker, or between sentences or clauses. As in the first type of multiple dialogue introducer, the inserted verb of saying can appear in the form of a complete inquit phrase (example (10), or be reduced to just the verb (example (11)):

(10) So I says, "Ah, don't be silly," I says, "Look, you just take it to her."
     (Wolfson 1982: 26)
(11) I said "Oooh"
     said "Unless it's the starter it should jump,"
     said "Got lights and everything?"
     (Johnstone 1990: 98)[4]

The common denominator of all the examples I quoted above is an additional verb of saying, usually the least marked verb "say" (in Middle English alternatively *quoþ*) used in the attribution of an utterance to a speaker. Since one verb of saying is usually sufficient to fulfill the function of speech attribution, I will now turn to the question of which other function(s) this seemingly redundant additional verb of saying may have.

3. The discourse functions of multiple dialogue introducers

Dialogue introducers in oral narratives have received increasing attention in recent publications (cf. Johnstone 1987, 1990; Romaine and Lange 1991; Blyth, Recktenwald and Wang 1990; Ferrera and Bell 1995). For Middle English, there are sporadic discussions of dialogue introducers in different studies, focusing on specific aspects (e.g. the formulaic character of dialogue introducers; Wittig 1978: 19-24). The multiple occurrence of verbs of saying in one quotation, however, has so far only rarely been discussed.

The few comments on multiple dialogue introducers explain the phenomenon as a means either to meet the requirements of a situation of oral communication or to attribute a specific textual function to the repeated verb of saying. In the latter case, one can roughly differentiate between attempts to classify the additional verb(s) of saying as discourse markers or mere signals of quotation, and those that interpret the second verb of saying (in the first type of multiple dialogue introducer) as a syntactic subordinator.

After discussing these approaches, I will present my own interpretation of the phenomenon.

3.1. The function of multiple dialogue introducers in oral communication

Discussing the function of dialogue introducers ("projecting clauses" in his terminology), Halliday compares the repeated use of quotation marks at the beginning of a new paragraph in a longer quotation in written English with the repetition of the dialogue introducer in spoken English, claiming that "(w)ithout this kind of repetition, the fact that a passage of discourse is projected [i.e. quoted; A.H.] may easily be lost sight of" (Halliday 1985: 228-9). This explanation accounts for the second type of multiple dialogue introducer. However, Halliday's example (example (12) below) also contains an instance of the first type, which cannot be explained as having the same reminder function:

(12) My brother, he used to show dogs, and he said to me, he said, "Look," he said, "I really think you've got something here," he said, "Why don't you take it to a show?" (...) (Halliday 1985: 228).

Studies by Halford and Chafe provide theoretical frameworks on the basis of which the first type of multiple dialogue introducer can be explained as a linguistic feature which meets the requirements of oral communication.

The basic unit of spoken English in Halford's model is the "talk unit", which roughly corresponds to the sentence in written English, but allows for a greater variety of ways in which syntagms are tied together.

Since Halford does not discuss the specific structures in question, I propose that a separate category for this particular structure be set up. I claim that there are non-syntactic ties between the repetitive instances of verbs of saying, and also between the introducer(s) and the quotation proper. The whole structure can then be interpreted as one complex "talk unit".

Halford's general remarks on the communicative functions of some structures particular to spoken English prove very useful in the analysis of the structures I am dealing with here. Halford (e.g. 1996: 136-7) repeatedly points out the relevance – in spoken discourse – of presenting information in small steps in order to facilitate planning and decoding processes.

By adding a second verb of saying, a complex piece of information – somebody says something to somebody – is presented in two steps: "X speaks to Y" and "X utters 'Z'". The repetition of the verb of saying in the second step serves two purposes: it separates the utterance into two entities, but at the same time it ensures the cohesion between the two parts. Including now the second type of multiple dialogue introducers into the analysis, it can be claimed that each new inquit phrase plus the ensuing quotation forms a new subunit "X utters 'Z'" (cf. Halliday's reminder function).

The presentation of an utterance in several smaller steps can also be interpreted as a result of "planning in progress". Each one of the "steps" might well correspond to what Chafe calls an "intonation unit", which "verbalizes the information active in the speaker's mind at its onset" (Chafe 1994: 63).[5]

In the analysis of the Middle English examples, this interpretation obviously cannot be applied without reservation. While it is feasible to assume that many of the romances were actually performed orally, it is most unlikely that they were also composed "orally" (see e.g. Spahn 1991: 196-200). We certainly are not dealing with the production of spontaneous, unplanned discourse. In the medieval context, the question of a possible communicative function of the structures in question has to be seen in a different light.

Wherever (as in the case of the second type of multiple dialogue introducer) a longer stretch of direct speech is interrupted by a repetition of the dialogue introducer, or where inquit phrases occur at the beginning of a new stanza, one can assume a reminder function for this phenomenon, as well, if a situation of oral delivery is presupposed.

As for the first type of multiple dialogue introducer, one can assume that in cases such as example (7) a longer stretch of narrative has to be bridged between the first verb of saying and the quotation proper, and that this bridging is facilitated by the insertion of a second verb of saying immediately before the quotation. However, this explanation fails to explain the majority of the cases, in which the second verb of saying follows the first immediately, separated only by the conjunction *and*, as in example (4).

An alternative suggestion has been made by Gabriele Klewitz for Present-Day English.[6] Among the examples of multiple dialogue introducers (type one) in her corpus, the most frequent collocation is that of "tell", followed by "say". She assumes that the form of "say" has been added to make it possible for a direct quotation to follow "tell", which does not usually introduce direct speech. Interestingly, Leisi offers the same interpretation for the respective structure in Middle English (Leisi 1947: 74), adding that "say" is the usual verb in the introduction of direct speech in Caxton's works and that it is therefore used even if another verb of saying is there.

In the context of research on oral narrative, these suggestions may have some validity. Nessa Wolfson (1982: 25) lists as one of the main features of performed narrative the occurrence of direct speech. The collocation of "tell" and "say" could be interpreted as a form of self-correction: a structure which would normally entail an indirect quotation is changed into one which enables the narrator to use the preferred form of speech representation, direct speech. While this may be plausible for some cases of multiple dialogue introducers in oral communication, I hesitate to accept instances of self-correction as "oral residue" in Middle English literature, especially since the phenomenon is still common in Caxton's prose works, which are much further removed from an oral tradition than are the romances which make up my corpus.

Moreover, the suggestions discussed above do not explain the cases in which "say" is repeated (cf. examples (2), (6), (7), (12), (14)), nor those in which the first verb of saying is one which could by itself introduce direct speech (examples (3), (4), (13)).

However, I would like to take up both Klewitz' and Leisi's suggestions and propose, conversely, that since the option exists of using a structure which involves a combination of a verb of saying, plus "say", to introduce a quotation, there is greater freedom in the lexical choice of the first verb, since the second verb already functions as an introducer of direct speech.

3.2. Textual functions of multiple dialogue introducers

As we have seen, an analysis restricted to the communicative function of multiple dialogue introducers in an oral context (reminder function, facilitating planning and decoding in progress, self-correction) only explains some aspects of the phenomenon. In the following, I will take up the argument that the second verb of saying in multiple dialogue introducers of the first type creates cohesion between the dialogue introducer and the quotation. (I proposed this above in connection with the function of this verb as a decoding aid). In order to achieve a more encompassing explanation of the phenomenon, which accounts for all the forms of multiple dialogue introducers I have discussed, it is necessary to include into the discussion the notion of textual functions in a wider sense than just that of unplanned oral communication.

The notion of textual function used here is based on Elizabeth Traugott's model of grammaticalization as presented in her 1982 article "From propositional to textual and expressive meanings: Some semantic-pragmatic aspects of grammaticalization." Following Halliday and Hasan, Traugott distinguishes between three functional-semantic components of language (Traugott 1982: 247-8): the propositional component, which "involves the resources of the language for making it possible to talk about something," the textual component, which "has to do with the resources available for creating cohesive discourse," and the expressive component, which "bears on the resources a language has for expressing personal attitudes to what is being talked about, to the text itself, and to others in the speech situation."

Traugott claims that if in a grammaticalization process shifts occur from one of these components to the other, the direction is typically from propositional to textual to expressive (cf. her hypothesis B, p.256).

Halliday and Hasan (1976: 267) include in their discussion of cohesive elements in the textual component of language items which they call "continuatives", and which are treated by others as "discourse markers" (cf. Schiffrin 1987).

Some studies which discuss multiple dialogue introducers classify them as semantically empty entities whose function is comparable to that of punctuation marks. Thus, Johnstone (1990: 78) observes that "one reported turn may include several discourse attributors, (...)." She discusses the difference in function of the verbs "say" and "go" (in their function as dialogue introducers) from other verbs of speaking, claiming that they have the status of "semantically neutral 'discourse markers' (Schiffrin 1987), indicating only that what follows is supposed to be taken as someone else's words"

(Johnstone 1990: 81). As an illustration, she quotes the following example, which contains an instance of the first type of multiple dialogue introducer:

(13) He asked me
he said ...
"Do you know why I stopped you?"
(Johnstone 1990: 82)

Johnstone remarks that "the verb *ask* does not seem to be enough to get the reported discourse going and has to be supplemented with the less specific *said* in the next line" (1990: 82). Similarly, Euler (1991: 129, 131) classifies the inserted inquit phrase in the second type of multiple dialogue introducers as a structure comparable to discourse markers.

For the first type of multiple dialogue introducer in Middle English, Leisi claims a purely grammatical function for the *and said*, which he compares to that of a colon (cf. Leisi 1947: 74).[7]

In most of these studies, the main function of the additional verb of saying in the first type of multiple dialogue introducer is assumed to be that of a signal of direct speech, with no further meaning than that of a colon. More positively, by fulfilling this signalling function, the added verbs of saying could be said to stress the "quotedness" of the respective quotation (a function which is also implied in the reminder function attributed to these structures by Halliday). However, the semantic reduction of the verb "say" which is presupposed here is, in my opinion, too radical in the case of a verb which, in its function as a speech attributor, is mostly used as a finite verb in a complete syntagm (as opposed to its use as a hypothetical marker, where it has undergone a much higher degree of semantic reduction, cf. Romaine and Lange 1991: 232). For the same reason I hesitate to endorse classifying the additional verb of saying as a discourse marker. In Schiffrin's definition of the term, discourse markers are "independent of sentential structure", while the second verb of saying in multiple dialogue introducers (at least those of the first type) is not.

In another, related approach, the second verb of saying in type one is analyzed as a complementizer, introducing direct speech complements. In his study of biblical Hebrew, Talmy Givón discusses the Hebrew equivalent of the Middle English *answered and said* pattern under the heading "Direct-quote complements". In his view, the second verb of saying serves as a subordinator with respect to verbs introducing direct speech (Givón 1995: 275).

The link between the Middle English collocation *answered and said* and the respective pattern in Hebrew, which is discussed by Givón, is established by Inna Koskenniemi in her study on *Repetitive Word Pairs in Old and Early*

Middle English Prose. She treats the pattern in question as just one, albeit very frequent, example of what she calls repetitive word pairs; a structure, which, as she points out, is typical of biblical style. Koskenniemi further suggests that, since word pairs of this type are frequent in classical Hebrew, their occurrence in the English language might be "a reflection of Hebrew patterns, transmitted through the Vulgate," often through interlinear glosses (1968: 41; see also 27, 115).

A suggestion similar to Givón's for Hebrew is made for various (non-European) languages by William Eilfort (1986) in his study on "Complementizers from introducers of direct speech". Eilfort discusses grammaticalization processes by which a second verb of saying is – often temporarily – employed in dialogue introducers to mark direct speech.[8] Without much further explanation, he suggests that "this type of innovation is also seen in English sentences like the following" (Eilfort 1986: 60):

(14) So I says to this guy, I says, "Charlie, bet on Glow Worm in the third."
(Eilfort 1986: 60)

Applying Givón's approach to the structure in Middle English (which may be a borrowing from Hebrew), and combining it with Eilfort's to the Present-Day English form of the first type of multiple dialogue introducers, one could claim a common function for the second verb of saying in the Middle English and Present-Day English structures, namely that of a complementizer introducing direct speech.

However, for the following reasons I hesitate to fully endorse this claim. First of all, as I mentioned above, the second verb of saying has not been emptied completely of its lexical meaning and thus cannot be said to have been reduced to a marker with purely grammatical function, even though a certain reduction in lexical meaning has taken place.

Secondly, the assumption that the second verb of saying serves as a subordinator implies that the direct quotation has the status of a subordinated clause. The syntactic status of direct quotations, however, has been discussed rather controversially and seems to call for a more subtle classification than just that of subordination.[9] Thus, the interpretation of the second verb of saying (in type one) as a syntactic subordinator does not appear to be well-founded.

Finally, I do not agree with Eilfort's assumption that a process of grammaticalization is taking place in the case of the second verb of saying (cf. his English example). It is my assumption that this feature serves a specific function both in the Middle English and Present-Day English examples, and that this function is essentially the same in both contexts. I therefore also disagree with Eilfort's claim that the instance of the first type of multiple dialogue introducer in his example represents an innovation. In fact, the – albeit rare – occurrence of this structure in Middle English (see my example (7)) proves the opposite.[10]

My own interpretation of the structure seeks to combine elements of some of the approaches discussed above.

By analyzing the second verb of saying in multiple dialogue introducers of the first type as a subordinator, I assign it the role of creating syntactic cohesion between the dialogue introducer and the quotation. Above, I have dismissed this solution as problematic. However, at the level of discourse, the inserted verb of saying can be said to have a cohesive function without necessarily presupposing syntactic subordination. My argument for taking the second verb of saying as a marker of discourse cohesion is based on the following observations:

The second verb of saying, in all my examples, is a reiteration of the first one. Reiteration, according to Halliday and Hasan, can mean repetition of the lexeme, the use of a synonym, of a superordinate, or of a general word (cf. Halliday and Hasan 1976: 278, 288), and is seen by them as one means of creating cohesive discourse. At the same time, by signalling the "quotedness" of the ensuing stretch of speech, the reiterated verb of saying creates cohesion between the dialogue introducer and the quotation proper. The inserted verb is, on the level of discourse, a pivotal element, creating cohesion both anaphorically and cataphorically.

The interpretation of the additional verb of saying as a means of creating discourse cohesion is independent of the question whether or not this verb can be interpreted as a discourse marker (in Schiffrin's sense), and of the problematic syntactic status of the quotation with respect to the dialogue introducer. As for the question of semantic reduction, which is relevant both in the approaches taking the additional verb as a discourse marker, and in those interpreting it as a subordinator, I have pointed out above that in my opinion, this second verb of saying cannot be said to have undergone total loss of lexical meaning. Yet, I agree that this verb does not carry the same semantic content as the initial verb of saying. Using Traugott's terms, this added verb of saying – both in the medieval and in the modern examples – does not carry the full propositional semantic function which is carried by the first verb of saying. In its function, it has shifted from the propositional to the textual component of language. This interpretation accounts for both the Middle English (co-ordinated) and the Present-Day English (asyndetic) structures.

In the second type of multiple dialogue introducers, the reiteration of the verb of saying within the quotation fulfills the same textual function as its reiteration immediately before the quoted speech.

4. Narrative functions of multiple dialogue introducers

I will now briefly discuss the implications of the results of the preceding section for the analysis of narrative texts.

The second verb of saying in the first type of multiple dialogue introducer was found to create cohesion between the phrase introducing the direct quotation and the quotation proper on the level of discourse. From the perspective of analyzing narrative structures, this second verb of saying may be said to serve to tie the quoted material more tightly to the narrative context. The term "subordinator" could here be applied in a non-grammatical way, insofar as the quotations seem to be subordinated to the narrative by this device.

The second type of multiple dialogue introducer serves the same function as type one: the permeation of quoted speech (which is meant to create the illusion of representing a character's words) by elements belonging to the surrounding narrative likewise intensifies the ties between the quotation and the narrative. To put it informally: By using either one of the structures, the narrator seems to have a "tighter grip" on the quoted dialogue and appears more foregrounded in his/her role as the organizer of the narrative and the passages of reported speech contained in it.

Furthermore, it is of interest that the two types of multiple dialogue introducers tend to occur together in the same romance or (longer) oral narrative. They also frequently occur in combination, as in the title quote. This tendency to co-occurence may be explained by the similar narrative functions of the two structures. They seem to reinforce each other in their quality of tying the quoted speech to the narrative context and of foregrounding the presence of the narrator in a text.

5. Conclusion

By way of conclusion, I would now like to integrate my results into a larger context of research on the development of narrative structures. I am referring to the model of episodic narrative structures which has recently been proposed by Monika Fludernik. This model, which has been developed in the analysis of conversational narratives in Present-Day English, has been found to be applicable to Middle English and Early Modern English narratives as well (Fludernik 1991, 1992, 1996: chapters 2 and 3).

It can be assumed that oral patterns of storytelling still shaped these early narratives, which, although they are most likely products of written composition, are closely related to institutionalized forms of oral storytelling. However, due to several factors – the greater length of the stories, the different subject matter, and the different status of the bard as compared with the narrator of a story of personal experience – a change in the organization of the story material occurred (cf. Fludernik 1996: 77, 129ff.). Individual episodes with the same setting or protagonist were linked together, episode boundaries slowly became obsolete. Gradually, a mode of narrative evolved in which narrative scenes were arranged to form a more teleologically oriented pattern (Fludernik 1996: 130). One decisive factor at the beginning of this development was the expansion of dialogic sequences within the episode, bringing the narrative closer to the structure of the dramatic (dialogue) scene.

Thus, Fludernik's model of the development of narrative structures (a) suggests a similarity in structure of medieval (written) and today's oral narratives, and (b) highlights the important role of the dialogue scene in the development of narrative structures. To explain the fact that multiple dialogue introducers occur both in Middle English and Present-Day English oral narratives, while they have disappeared in written Modern English, the following (rather speculative) suggestions are offered, based on the part that these introducers play in the organization of narrative dialogue in both types of text:

Multiple dialogue introducers have been found to allow conclusions about the way dialogue is dealt with by a narrator. Narrators in my Present-Day English oral and Middle English (written) texts seem to play a foregrounded role in the presentation of dialogue, one sign of which is the insertion of an additional verb of saying either before or within the quotation. In the development of a more "written" type of narrative, different ways of presenting dialogue could develop; in the evolution of the dialogue scene, the speech attributed to characters has gained increasing independence from the narrative context.[11] The reinforced statement of its "quotedness", one of the functions of multiple dialogue introducers, has become superfluous. Moreover, in forms of narrative which are rooted in a tradition of writing, there is no need for the corporeal narrator of oral narrative, the reflections of whom are found in Middle English narratives. (The occurrence of multiple dialogue introducers in Middle English narratives support the latter argument.)

Much research remains to be done on multiple dialogue introducers in the history of English literature after the Middle English period, and on their occurrence and distribution in Present-Day English oral narrative. What I hope to have achieved in this study is to throw light on a seemingly insignificant linguistic feature which could be seen as an indicator of significant changes in narrative modes.

Notes

1 Multiple dialogue introducers (MDI) are a frequent feature in the corpora which are cited in these studies, all of which deal with oral storytelling in general and not with speech representation exclusively. Thus, the occurrence of the structures in question was taken to be representative. A preliminary search for MDIs of the first type was conducted in a large corpus of spoken narrative in English compiled by a research group under Prof. Elizabeth Couper-Kuhlen and Dr. Susanne Günthner within the interdisciplinary research project (SFB 511) on 'Literature and Anthropology' at the University of Konstanz, Germany. The result was different from mine: the pattern was found to be unexpectedly rare.

   I wish to thank Gabriele Klewitz and Gurly Schmidt for their help in conducting the search and conveying the results to me. Further research is planned in collaboration with Gabriele Klewitz in order to clarify the questions of frequency and intonational patterns of MDIs in the Konstanz corpus and further corpora of spoken English narrative.

2 All translations are mine.
3 The instances of MDIs found in the Konstanz corpus, however, contained predominantly a combination of *tell* and *say*.
4 I wish to thank Peter Koch for pointing out to me a comparable feature in spoken Italian and for bringing to my attention a number of studies in which this feature is discussed (Spitzer 1922; Stammerjohann 1970; Koch 1985, 1988; Koch/Oesterreicher 1990).
5 The application of both Halford's and Chafe's models would require a thorough intonational analysis of a large number of examples in order to be substantiated and refined. The planned research mentioned in note 1 is to include intonational analyses and will hopefully answer some of the questions which had to remain open here.
6 Personal communication.
7 In his discussion of the feature in spoken Italian, Spitzer also compares the function of the repeated verb of saying with that of a colon (Spitzer 1922: 164).
8 For further instances of this phenomenon, see the literature quoted by Romaine and Lange (1991: 259). Givón (1992: 307, n16) points out that "(t)he use of 'say' as a subordinator for utterance verb complements, direct as well as indirect, is widespread cross-linguistically."
9 For reasons of space, a full discussion of the issue is not possible here. See Munro (1982) for a detailed analysis of the "transitivity of 'say' verbs", including reference to previous studies. Opinions vary between the assumption of no syntactic ties between quotation and introducer (Partee, as quoted by Munro 1982: 301; also Euler 1991: 129) and the classification of direct (along with indirect) quotes as subordinate clauses (cf. Romaine and Lange 1991: 233). See also Givón's scale of complements, in which direct quotes rank lowest in the syntactic dimension of clause integration (Givón 1995: 125).
10 There is, of course, the possibility of a development from the coordinated form as it mostly occurs in Middle English, to the asyndetic form which is already attested in Middle English

but is the norm in Present-Day English, to the reduced form, as in examples (6) and (14), and, for type two, (11). At this point, this has to remain pure speculation and requires much further research. In fact, the asyndetic structure occurs frequently in the late Middle English romances *The Grene Knight* and *The Turke and Gowin* (both from around 1500). (These results were obtained only recently and could therefore not be incorporated into the present paper.) In the respective structures in Italian (cf. note 3), the reiterated verb of saying often occurs in a form which does not agree (in tense and/or person) with the initial verb (cf. Koch 1985: 62; Stammerjohann 1970: 343). Koch suggests an interpretation of this phenomenon as the result of a lexicalization process (personal communication). In my experience, reiterated verbs of saying always agree in person and tense in English (the common form *I says* is used, when it occurs, consistently throughout a quotation). For this reason, I hesitate to apply the framework of lexicalization to my examples. Of course, a similar process could occur in English in the future, which would then make it necessary to discuss the issue of lexicalization.

11 For a discussion of the growing independence of literary dialogue from its narrative context in 19th and 20th century novels, see Głowiński (1974). An examination of the issue in earlier (English) narratives is being undertaken by the present author (Anne Herlyn, in progress).

References

Primary Texts

Amys and Amylion
    1993   Ed. Francoise leSaux. Exeter: University of Exeter Press.
Floris and Blauncheflur
    1901   Ed. J. Rawson Lumby, re-ed. George H. McKnight. London: Trübner (EETS.OS. 14).
The Romance of Guy of Warwick.
1883, 1887, 1891 Ed. Julius Zupitza. London: Trübner (EETS.ES. 42, 49, 59).

Criticism

Blyth, Carl, Sigrid Recktenwald, and Jenny Wang
    1990   I'm like, "Say what?!": A new quotative in American oral narrative. *American Speech* 65.3, 215-227.

Chafe, Wallace
1994 *Discourse, Consciousness, and Time: The Flow and Displacement of Conscious Experience in Speaking and Writing.* Chicago, London: The University of Chicago Press.

Eilfort, William
1986 Complementizers from introducers of direct speech. In: Soonja Choi, Dan Devitt, Janis Wynn, Terry McCoy and Zheng-sheng Zhang (eds.). *Proceedings of the Second Eastern States Conference on Linguistics.* Department of Linguistics, Ohio State University, 57-66.

Ermarth, Elizabeth Deeds
1981 Realism, perspective and the novel. *Critical Inquiry* 7, 499-520.

Euler, Bettina
1991 *Strukturen mündlichen Erzählens.* (ScriptOralia 31). Tübingen: Gunter Narr Verlag.

Ferrera, Kathleen, and Barbara Bell
1995 Sociolinguistic variation and discourse function of constructed dialogue introducers: The case of *be* + *like*. *American Speech* 70.3, 265-290.

Fludernik, Monika
1991 The historical present tense yet again: Tense switching and narrative dynamics in oral and quasi-oral storytelling. *Text* 11, 365-97.

1992 The historical present tense in English literature: An oral pattern and its literary adaptation. *Language and Literature* (Texas) 17, 77-107.

1996 *Towards a 'Natural' Narratology.* London, New York: Routledge.

Givón, Talmy
1992 The evolution of dependent clause morpho-syntax in Biblical Hebrew. In: Bernd Heine and Elizabeth Closs Traugott (eds.). *Approaches to Grammaticalization.* Vol. II. Amsterdam, Philadelphia: Benjamins, 257-310.

1995 *Functionalism and Grammar.* Amsterdam, Philadelphia: Benjamins.

Glowiński, Michal
1974 Der Dialog im Roman. *Poetica* 6, 1-16.

Halford, Brigitte
1996 *Talk Units: The Structure of Spoken Canadian English.* (ScriptOralia 87). Tübingen: Gunter Narr Verlag.

Halliday, M.A.K.
1985 *An Introduction to Functional Grammar.* London: Edward Arnold.

Halliday, M.A.K., and Ruqaiya Hasan
1976 *Cohesion in English.* London: Longman.

Herlyn, Anne
in prep. *Dialogue and Narrative Structure in Middle English Romances.*

Johnstone, Barbara
    1987   "He says ... so I said": Verb tense alternation and narrative depictions of authority in American English. *Linguistics* 25(1), 33-52.
    1990   *Stories, Community and Place*. Bloomington, Indianapolis: Indiana University Press.
    1993   Community and contest: Midwestern men and women creating their worlds in conversational storytelling. In: Deborah Tannen (ed.). *Gender and Conversational Interaction*. Oxford etc.: Oxford University Press, 62-80.

Koch, Peter
    1985   Gesprochenes Italienisch und sprechsprachliche Universalien. In: Günter Holtus and Edgar Radtke (eds.). *Gesprochenes Italienisch in Geschichte und Gegenwart*. (Tübinger Beiträge zur Linguistik, 252). Tübingen: Gunter Narr Verlag, 42-67.
    1988   Italienisch: Gesprochene und geschriebene Sprache. In: Günter Holtus, Michael Metzeltin and Christian Schmitt (eds.). *Lexikon der Romanistischen Linguistik*. Vol. IV. Tübingen: Niemeyer, 189-206.

Koch, Peter, and Wulf Oesterreicher
    1990   *Gesprochene Sprache in der Romania: Französisch, Italienisch, Spanisch*. (Romanistische Arbeitshefte, 31). Tübingen: Niemeyer.

Koskenniemi, Inna
    1968   *Repetitive Word Pairs in Old and Early Middle English Prose*. Turku: Turun Yliopisto.

Leisi, Ernst
    1947   *Die tautologischen Wortpaare in Caxton's "Eneydos". Zur synchronischen Bedeutungs- und Ursachenforschung*. New York: Hafner Publishing Company.

Munro, Pamela
    1982   On the transitivity of 'say' verbs. In: Paul J. Hopper and Sandra A. Thompson (eds.). *Syntax and Semantics*. Vol. 15: *Studies in Transitivity*. New York: Academic Press, 301-318.

Polanyi, Livia
    1989   *Telling the American Story*. Cambridge, MA: The MIT Press.

Romaine, Suzanne, and Deborah Lange
    1991   The use of *like* as a marker of reported speech and thought: A case of grammaticalization in progress. *American Speech* 66, 227-279.

Schiffrin, Deborah
    1981   Tense variation in narrative. *Language* 57, 45-62.
    1987   *Discourse Markers*. (Studies in International Sociolinguistics 5). Cambridge: Cambridge University Press.

Spahn, Renate
    1991   *Narrative Strukturen im* Guy of Warwick. (ScriptOralia 36). Tübingen: Gunter Narr Verlag.

Spitzer, Leo
    1922   *Italienische Umgangssprache.* Bonn, Leipzig: Schroeder.

Stammerjohann, Harro
    1970   Strukturen der Rede. Beobachtungen an der Umgangssprache von Florenz. *Studi di Filologia Italiana* 28, 295-397.

Traugott, Elizabeth Closs
    1982   From propositional to textual and expressive meanings: Some semantic-pragmatic aspects of grammaticalization. In: Winfried P. Lehmann and Yakov Malkiel (eds.). *Perspectives on Historical Linguistics.* Amsterdam, Philadelphia: Benjamins, 245-271.

Wittig, Susan
    1978   *Stylistic and Narrative Structures in the Middle English Romances.* Austin, London: University of Texas Press.

Wolfson, Nessa
    1982   *CHP: The Conversational Historical Present in American English Narrative.* Dordrecht: Foris.

Que fais, Adam?
Questions and Seduction in the *Jeu d'Adam*

Angela Schrott
Ruhr University, Bochum

1. Introduction

In order to apply the principles of dialogue analysis to questions and their linguistic realisations in Old French I have chosen as a textual basis the *Jeu d'Adam*, because this play views the well-known story of the Fall of Man also as a dialogic play with the seductive power of questions.[1] Thus, the *Jeu d'Adam* seems a good field of examination for a linguist who wants to ask some questions about the forms and functions of interrogatives. A study of questions implies on the one hand the specific formal type of interrogative sentences and on the other hand the interrogative act as the illocution of asking a question. The crucial point in a linguistic analysis is here to model the relations between interrogative sentences and interrogative acts, separating both levels methodically, then bringing them together again in a synthesis when describing the illocutionary potential of certain interrogative sentence types.

In the following analysis I will limit myself to certain types of interrogative acts which occur with a high frequency and which in my opinion express basic communicative needs. In a next step, I will illustrate the verbal realisations of these illocutionary acts with examples taken from the *Jeu d'Adam*, putting my emphasis on interrogative sentence types.

In the first paragraphs I will expose some special characteristics of the adjacency pair of question and answer and try to formulate a definition of the illocutionary act of asking a question. Then I shall turn to a presentation of various types of interrogative acts described as typical illocutions which I will try to illustrate with examples from the *Jeu d'Adam*, i. e., the method applied will be onomasiologic, focusing on the contextual function of the interrogative act. In a synoptic view I will then summarise and link the results to the dialogue types used in the play and concentrate on their possible roots in historical circumstances.

2. *Anrede und Erwiderung* – 'Question and answer'

According to the well-known dictum by Wilhelm von Humboldt, the dualism of language is expressed in the unity of *Anrede* and *Erwiderung*, 'address' and 'reply', which is inherent in any act of speaking:[2]

> Es liegt aber auch in der Sprache selbst ein unabänderlicher Dualismus, und alles Sprechen ist auf Anrede und Erwiederung gestellt. Das Wort ist kein Gegenstand, vielmehr den Gegenständen gegenüber etwas Subjectives, nun aber soll es im Geiste des Denkenden doch ein Object, von ihm erzeugt und auf ihn zurückwirkend seyn. Damit es sich nun von einem bloßen Scheinobjecte, einem Traumbilde, unterscheide, muß es Wesenheit in einem Hörenden und Erwiedernden gewinnen. (Wilhelm von Humboldt: "Natur der Sprache überhaupt", quoted after the edition by Christmann 1977: 26).

This general concept of 'address and reply' becomes especially obvious in the pair of question and answer.[3] This adjacency pair is not only a good illustration of Humboldt's philosophical approach to language, but is likewise able to serve as a pattern for the exchange of active and passive roles in dialogic interaction and thus, finally, represents a model of the dynamism of dialogue.[4] In both perspectives the adjacency pair of question and answer is regarded as a sequence which contains two directly succeeding expressions of different speakers and forms an integrated whole: the answer closes what the question opened and the question as first element draws the answer as second element after it.[5] Lack of an answer is always regarded as a violation of rules which requires a justification, because the functional unity is usually broken and a continuation of the dialogue will be more difficult.[6]

This typical character of dialogue secures question-answer sequences the increased attention of academics, since they enable us to analyse the several different organisational levels of dialogues (Bucher 1994: 239f.): the patterns of action, the propositional and thematic links, the control of the flow of information and the strategies used to govern the dialogue. Since question-answer sequences prototypically illustrate the functioning of dialogues, the viewpoint of dialogue analysis is almost ideal to give insights in the connections between interrogative acts and interrogative forms. This contextual method permits to capture the different pragmatic potential of interrogative sentences and work out their profiles as illocutionary acts. In order to point out

Que fais, Adam? – Questions and Seduction in the *Jeu d'Adam*   333

the close link of the interrogative act with its context, I will refer to this illocution not as a speech act but as a dialogue act to underline its reciprocity and interactional power (cf. also Franke 1990: 8f., 15; Oksaar 1981: 130f., 146).

As a textual basis for this pragmatic approach I refer to the *Jeu d'Adam* or *Ordo representacionis Ade*, a bilingual liturgic play which probably dates from the middle of the 12th century and combines liturgic Latin elements with dramatised parts written in the vernacular such as the story of Adam and Eve. The *Jeu d'Adam* as a drama grows out of liturgy and represents the Christian story of redemption in the frame of a figural interpretation of the world.[7] The examples quoted here are from the first part, which dramatises the Fall of Man in dialogues between the protagonists Adam, Eve, Diabolus and Figura, who is a personalisation of God as the *salvator mundi*.

When analysing the pragmatic potential of interrogative acts, it is crucial to distinguish between the organisation of turn-taking and the illocutionary level.[8] In the case of the adjacency pair of question and answer, the organisation of turns and that of illocutions are mostly homologous, i.e., question and answer can be identified with different turns (Fritz 1994a: 184). However, the turn-taking organisation need not necessarily coincide with the structure of the acts of asking and answering questions. This point is illustrated by the following text from the *Jeu d'Adam*, where Figura shows Adam the paradise:[9]

(1) V.188-198
     188 *Tunc Figura manu demonstret paradisum Ade, dicens:*
     189   *Adam!*
     190 *Adam*
     191   *Sire!*
     192 *Figura*
     193   *Dirrai toi mon avis.*
     194   *Veez cest jardin?*
     195 *Adam*
     196   *Cum ad num?*
     197 *Figura*
     198   *Paradis.*
           Figura Adam!
           Adam   Yes, my Lord!
           Figura I want to tell you what my intention is. Do you see this garden?
           Adam   How is it called?
           Figura Paradise.

In the sense of knowledge distribution the question *Cum ad num?* (V.196) is prototypical. Adam, who asks the question, does not have any knowledge about the garden. The questioned Figura, however, is very likely to possess this knowledge as he has called Adam's attention to it. On the level of the illocutionary acts, this interrogative sentence is a clear case of an interrogative act, but if we have a closer look on the level of turns, it occupies a marked position. The interrogative act *Cum ad num?* (V.196) follows directly after another question *Veez cest jardin?* (V.194), but is neither an evasive counter-question nor a comprehensive question. Instead, *Cum ad num?* contains the answer to *Veez cest jardin?* as a presupposition: asking for the name of the garden presupposes that Adam does see the garden. Including in its presupposition an answer to Figura's question, *Cum ad num?* closes the sequence V.194-196 and simultaneously opens another question-answer sequence V.196-198. The interrogative act thus forms the intersection of two adjacency pairs and creates a structure of elliptical coupling (cf. Conrad 1986: 430; Merritt 1976: 341ff.; Stenström 1988: 309). This overlay of function in *Cum ad num?* also proves that the illocutionary value of a question can only be determined contextually (cf. Bucher 1994: 244, 245).

After having sketched the interrogative act as the initiative part of the adjacency pair of question and answer in the light of the dialogic nature of language I will now concentrate on the illocutionary act of asking a question. This accentuation of the one part of the adjacency pair seems legitimate to me, as the interrogative act is the more narrowly determined part of the pair, whereas it appears harder to find a common pragmatic denominator for answers. Answers contain an extremely broad range of reactions – even no answer can be an answer.[10] Intuitively, it makes sense to say that everything that follows a question is in a certain way an answer, whereas this sequential definition does not work vice versa. This asymmetric relation indicates that the interrogative act is the more narrowly determined element of the adjacency pair of question and answer. Therefore, it seems more promising to start a characterisation of question/answer pairs, based on a description of the question as an illocutionary act, as I will do in the next section.

3. Questions as dialogue acts

The fact that the concept of questions is familiar to all speakers and forms part of our general knowledge does not make life easier for the linguist. In everyday life we subsume a large range of illocutionary acts under the label of question. It is therefore very difficult to find a common illocutionary denominator (cf.

Lang 1993: 44ff.). After a short review of the previous research in this area, I will try to put forward an outline of a solution to this "question about questions".

On the level of their propositional content, questions are analysed as propositions presenting a deficit of knowledge, a missing parameter in the set of information. In the wh-question *Where is the garden?* the propositional content presents a missing parameter, the location, which is represented by the interrogative adverb *where*, while the rest of the information set is presupposed to be known. In contrast, yes/no-questions like *Do you see the garden?* offer a complete proposition but put the truth value of the proposition as a whole into question (cf. Weydt 1985: 313).

In a tradition that goes back to Searle (1969: 66, 69, and 1979: 44-47, 48-51), this deficit of knowledge is mostly viewed as a motivation for the interrogative act so that the question functions as a request to fill the knowledge gap.[11] As the question calls for an answer that delivers the relevant information, the interrogative speech act is traced back to another speech act, namely the directive speech act.[12] That interpretation of the question act as a directive, however, excludes types of interrogative acts that for various reasons do not aim at an answer as a supplier of lacking information like for example the often discussed type of the rhetorical question. What is more, a comparison of forms of dialogue organisation shows that interrogative acts and directives, while they have a high degree of reciprocity and "interactive power" (Bucher 1994: 242) in common, open up different ranges of possible responses. Thus, the utterances *What are interrogative acts?* and *Define the interrogative act* dispose of different pragmatic potentials and will equally trigger different reactions of the interlocutor.[13]

Therefore, interrogative acts can only be understood to a limited extent via the common denominator of the directive as a means of adapting the world to the words. The basic semantic-pragmatic value of the interrogative act lies much more in indicating a gap in the correspondence between the words and the aimed-at world[14] – and that indication of a deficit does not necessarily have to involve a volitional nuance (cf. Lang 1993: 49f.). The gap in the correspondence of world and words now results in the fact that the speaker can only take a limited guarantee for his enunciation concerning a certain situation and therefore cannot perform an assertion. As the speaker's knowledge of the situation proves to be fragmentary, he expresses himself only with "limited liability". Therefore, the disclosing of a gap via an interrogative act does not only have impact on the propositional content, but in a pragmatic extension also has to be related to the speaker and his limited commitment. In order to describe the pragmatic phenomenon of the speaker commitment as a responsibility in conversation, Heger (^{2}1976: 276f.) has coined the term of *kommunikative Regreßpflicht*, i.e., the speaker is "liable to recourse" and so has to take on a "communicative liability". With the performance of an assertion, the speaker invests his enunciation with a truth value and must assume the responsibility for this assignment towards his interlocutors. This pragmatic extension not only includes the speaker but also the addressee and proves to have an impact on the attitude of both interlocutors. If the speaker points to a knowledge deficit, he can "point to" the relevance of this deficit and by doing so simultaneously perform a directive that aims at closing the gap.

The interrogative act understood as the act of pointing at a gap, coupled with limited communicative liability, seems to be a basic illocutionary act that is not to be localised on the same level as the directive. My hypothesis is that the interrogative act forms an illocutionary level of its own. The assumption of such a basic level is also backed by models of question theory that define the interrogative act in relation to the assertion and conceive question and assertion as poles that establish a pragmatic continuum.[15] This complementary way of interpreting questions and assertions, which may at first sight appear as a circular definition, is substantiated by the nature of questions and assertions, because both illocutionary acts can be described by using the same parameter, i.e., the degree of speaker commitment, of "communicative liability".

Based on these preliminaries, a definition of assertion and interrogative act can now be undertaken. With an assertion, the speaker takes total communicative liability and thus signals that the proposition is true and the propositional content complete: words and world are in full correspondence. By uttering an interrogative act, the speaker does not assume this communicative liability and indicates that he has to step back from that responsibility, because he does not know yet whether world and words are in correspondence, be it that the propositional content itself is marked by a gap or that a complete proposition has not yet been tested as to its correspondence with the world.

Viewing the interrogative act as a reference to an incongruity or a propositional gap in the correspondence of world and words is admittedly a wide pragmatic denominator. However, it seems that this "fuzziness" also forms a characteristic quality of the interrogative act as an act that leaves a large margin of interaction to the speaker and the interlocutor as well (cf. also Traverso 1991: 211, 213, 220). The fact that the interrogative act points in an almost deictic way to a gap may also explain the highly activating quality of questions that call up responses even if they, like rhetorical questions, don't aim at an answer.

In this context it is of vital importance to draw a sharp borderline between the level of sentence types and the illocutionary level of the acts that are performed by sentence types such as declarative and interrogative sentences (cf. Altmann 1987: 22, 25, 30; Meibauer 1987a: 3, 9; Padučeva 1986: 374; Bucher 1994: 240, 244). Thus, interrogative sentences may perform "pure" interrogative acts, and declarative sentences may realise prototypical assertions. In those cases, the utterances would be located at the poles of the continuum. But an illocution performed by an interrogative sentence may as well take an intermediate position on the continuum or even be closer to the pole of assertion than to the affinitive pole of the interrogative act (cf. Maury 1973: 309f.; Kerbrat-Orecchioni 1991b: 95-108 (*actes intermédiaires*); Gelas 1991: 364f.). The localisation on the continuum is the result of many heterogeneous factors. It is remarkable that syntactic and grammatical factors like the sentence type seem to have less impact on the pragmatic potential than the propositional content or the knowledge distribution between the interlocutors (cf. Kerbrat-Orecchioni 1991b: 91, 92f., 95).[16] Concerning the relation between interrogative sentences and interrogative acts, it can be said that interrogative sentences have elective affinities to interrogative acts, but may as well realise enunciations that are close to the pole of assertion.[17] Vice versa, interrogative acts are prototypically realised with interrogative sentence types, but can also be performed using other sentence types such as declarative sentences.

The continuum of question and assertion forms a basic layer of pragmatic values that concern the parameter of communicative liability, which is inherent in every kind of enunciation. Of course, there are more pragmatic values than question and assertion like those listed by the various classifications of illocutionary acts (cf. Searle 1979: 12-20; Schoenthal 1979: 47-52; Meibauer 1986: 9-18; Lang 1993: 44-47). If those acts cannot be hosted on that first level, this is because they belong to a secondary illocutionary level. On this secondary level, interrogative acts and assertions receive a second pragmatic "layer" of illocutionary values and can for example function as commissives or directives.[18] This illocution of a second order can determine an utterance in a different way – a phenomenon which may explain why interrogative acts are volitional to different extents.

Talking of question types, we must therefore methodically operate a strict separation between the *signifiant* of interrogative sentences and the *signifié*, i.e., the types of interrogative acts. Those interrogative acts are to be characterised via two pragmatic levels: a basic level formed by the continuum of communicative liability ranging from assertion to question, and a secondary level of illocutions of second order depending on the given context of conversational interaction.

After having sketched the outline of the interrogative act in general, I will now turn to a presentation of selected types of interrogative acts.

4. Types of interrogative acts

Recent research in the domain of questions shows a tendency to renounce mere stock-taking of intonational or syntactic characteristics of interrogative sentences and concentrates instead on a pragmatic approach to the formulation of functional identities. This semantic-pragmatic identity is supposed to be a basic pragmatic value of an interrogative sentence type and thus represents the *signifié* of the sentence type that forms the *signifiant*. The basic value is supposed to be present in all uses of that interrogative sentence type whose semantic-pragmatic profile may of course vary according to contextual determinants.

For my examination of interrogative acts in Old French texts I will use as a starting point the pragmatic profiles that have been elaborated in order to describe the interrogative sentence types of contemporary French. These illocutionary acts will be separated from the interrogative sentences that realise them in modern French and will instead be considered as types of illocutions that perform frequent communicative tasks.[19] Having formulated such a functional profile, I will try to extract the syntactic structures which fulfil that communicative task in the dialogues of the *Jeu d'Adam*. The selected method is onomasiologic, and thus the prototypes of interrogative acts are to be regarded as onomasiologically based prototypes. The functional identity, originally elaborated as *signifié* of an interrogative sentence type, is disconnected from the *signifiant* and considered as a concept of human interactions whose linguistic realisations are to be examined.[20] It is, evidently, of special interest to know whether there is a corresponding interrogative sentence type in Old French.[21]

Interrogative sentences in Old French show inversion (verb-subject-object) with such frequency that the inversion can be considered as the syntactic marker for interrogative sentences.[22] Only very rarely do we find interrogative sentences with the "canonical" word order subject-verb-object, which lack the syntactic marking of interrogatives and are characterised as interrogative sentences only by a rising intonation (cf. Brunot and Bruneau ³1949: 486, 528; Gamillscheg 1957: 614; Kaiser 1980: 105-106).[23] This sentence type corresponds to the intonation-marked interrogative sentence of the type *Pierre arrive demain?*, which is very frequent in spoken contemporary French. This rare usage of the intonation-marked interrogative sentence may be due to the fact that the intonation as a marker is restricted to the spoken language and therefore does not appear in the written documents which are our only source of information.[24] However, it seems to me equally possible that this type of interrogative sentence is rarely found in written texts because its pragmatic profile may have an affinity to spoken language in the sense of face-to-face interaction marked by spontaneity and a close relationship of the interlocutors. This language type, for which Koch and Oesterreicher (1985: 19-24 and 1990: 8-12) coined the term *Nähesprache*, is rarely granted access to the level of the written word; thus we cannot entirely exclude the possibility that the intonation-marked type may also have been used in Old French but did not fully succeed in entering the universe of written texts.[25]

4.1. Interrogative acts containing orientation

The functional type of interrogative acts containing orientation is confined to the so-called yes/no-questions. I take this type from Stempel and Fischer (1985), who described this functional identity in their analysis of the intonation-marked question type in contemporary French. An interrogative act contains orientation in the sense that a question of the type *p?* does not present an enunciation *p* to the interlocutor as an open yes/no-decision (*p* or *non-p*). In the case of orientation, the speaker presents a favoured hypothesis that functions as a pre-decision and introduces the speaker's preferences in the interaction.[26] Questions containing orientation function as projections of a favoured answer and are therefore asymmetric, as they insinuate a speaker-preference (cf. Stempel and Fischer 1985: 254f., 265).[27] Thus, the interrogative acts containing orientation have a functional identity defined by interactional qualities that permit the speaker to ask for relevant information while bringing forward a hypothesis of his own and building up a positive image (cf. Stempel and Fischer 1985: 262, 264; Stempel 1994b: 324f.).

The following example forms part of a dialogue between Adam and Diabolus that can be characterised as a competitive and antagonistic dialogue (cf. Franke 1990: 78, 81ff.; Haug 1984: 281). By provoking Adam skilfully into asking questions and then retarding his own answers in an even more skilful way, Diabolus has succeeded in arousing Adam's *curiositas*.[28] Adam is now ready for the revelation of the long announced secret of the tree of knowledge:

(2) V. 269-272; 294-301
    269   Diabolus
    270   Vols le tu saver?

271	Adam	
272		*Bien en iert mon talent.*
[...]		
294	Diabolus	
295		*Kar tu ne deiz nul bien aver.*
296		*Tu as le bien, ne seiez joïr.*
297	Adam	
298		*E jo coment?*
299	Diabolus	
300		*Voldras l'oïr?*
301		*Jol te dirrai priveement*
	Diabolus	Would you like to know?
	Adam	I'd like to very much.
	[...]	
	Diabolus	Because you are not supposed to have anything good. You have the good and you don't know how to use it.
	Adam	And why?
	Diabolus	Do you want to hear it? I will tell it to you secretly.

The interrogative sentence *Vols le tu saver?* (V.270) is marked by an inversion and presents the word order that is typical of interrogative sentences. The second interrogative sentence *Voldras l'oïr?* (V.300) is marked by the ellipsis of the subject pronoun so that it cannot be decided whether it has "canonical" word order (subject-verb-object) or inversion: the word order difference in this case is neutralised. This neutralisation of the syntactic question marker generates an interrogative sentence type of its own, characterised by the fronting of the verb and probably also by a rising interrogative intonation that differentiates the interrogative sentence from declarative sentences that frequently present the same word order (cf. Foulet 1921: 244; Lerch 1934: 314-316; Gamillscheg 1957: 558; Kaiser 1980: 244).

With both interrogative sentences Diabolus does not offer an open alternative to Adam but presents a hypothesis about Adam's wishes, which Adam is meant to confirm. From the context it seems that V.300 contains a stronger orientation than V.270, because at the beginning of the conversation Adam still shows stronger resistance, allowing only a weak hypothesis on the part of the devil. However, as the conversation continues, Adam becomes more tempted to ask questions so that Diabolus, anticipating the dispositions of his interlocutor, then only needs to ask for confirmation and can insinuate his own preference for reasons of persuasion. Here, the presentation of a hypothesis "I assume that you want to know about it" is meant to exercise influence on the interlocutor. The examples also show that the concept of the knowledge gap to be filled not only refers to the propositional content and validity but also to the attitude of the interlocutor, which Diabolus wants to find out about by asking for confirmation of his assumptions.

The argumentation here is rooted in the contextual colouring of the interrogative acts and in the organisation of the dialogue. But it seems possible that the different strengths of the hypotheses are also determined by the different syntactic structures. Thus, in *Vols le tu saver?* (V.270) we have the inversion as marker of the interrogative sentence that typically performs an interrogative act, and therefore the interrogative character may be stronger than in *Voldras l'oïr?* (V.300) where the difference of word order is neutralised.[29] In order to verify this hypothesis, similar sequences of both interrogative sentence types would have to be analysed. Yet with examples from Old French it is unfortunately not possible to elucidate the pragmatic profile of both types with commutations and speaker testing – an aspect that underlines the importance of the contextual approach of dialogue analysis.

Interrogative acts containing orientation are not necessarily always a means of persuasion but can also be used for the constitution of the text, especially for the establishment of topics – the strategy is centred on the message so that we could speak of a referential function. This function can be illustrated by the already quoted question (3) that Figura addresses to Adam:

(3) V. 194
    Figura
        Veez cest jardin?
        Do you see this garden?

The interrogative act of V.194 *Veez cest jardin?*, rather then disclosing a knowledge deficit, asks for confirmation of the very probable possibility that Adam sees the garden. Each time they talk of paradise the players are instructed to point at the garden, which is represented on the scene on an elevated place, and thus Figura, according to the stage direction, also points to the garden while asking the question. From these circumstances it follows that in spite of the still pending confirmation, Figura can enunciate a hypothesis which is so strongly validated that the speaker could almost assume the communicative liability: if Figura cannot presuppose the fact of Adam seeing the garden, Figura can at least presuppose the possibility of that fact. The progression of the dialogue further establishes the reason why Figura formulates this presupposition as a "weak" interrogative act. The question *Veez cest jardin?* emphasises the object *cest jardin* and establishes the garden as a new topic exactly by using an interrogative act which in itself has a focusing effect. Even weak interrogative acts that are quite close to the pole of assertion still have a momentum of openness that may be used in order to capture the attention of the interlocutor.

The following dialogue parts are meant to illustrate the finding that the degree of the contained orientation can be intensified by lexical elements, but also by the use of negation, which is the case in the next example, where the orientation is strengthened by a negation external to the proposition. In the text Diabolus tries to play down the power of Figura on the God-fearing Adam by emphasising the *gloire* Adam lives in:

(4) V. 332-338
    332   Diabolus
    333   Molt es entré en fol jornal.
    334   Quant creiez mal te poisse venir.
    335   N'es tu en gloire? Nen poez morir!
    336   Adam
    337   Deus le m'a dit que je murrai
    338   Quant son precept trespasserai.
    Diabolus   You are completely mistaken if you believe that anything bad could happen to you. Don't you live in glory? You can't die!
    Adam   God told me I have to die if I trespass his command.

The interrogative sentence *N'es tu en gloire?* (V.335) which is marked by an inversion contains a negation that is external to the proposition, i.e., the negation is not part of the proposition but is related to the act of enunciation and expresses a negating and refusing attitude of the speaker. Whereas internal negations, which form part of the logic of the proposition of a question, are to be paraphrased with "Is it the case that non-p?", an external negation amounts to "Is it not the case that p?" and thus refers to the illocutionary act (cf. Searle 1969: 32; Borillo 1979: 35, 38).[30] By uttering the assumption "Is it not the case that you live in glory?" Diabolus asks for a positive confirmation and "negates" a deviating opinion – the possible refusal of the assumed life in glory would reject the expectations of the speaker and would constitute a possible face-threatening act (cf. Brown and Levinson 1987: 59, 61-65).

The next dialogue part illustrates the way lexical elements can make the orientation more intensive. Diabolus has met with a rebuff in his effort to seduce Adam, and now makes a second attempt:

(5) V. 394-395
    Diabolus
            Adam, que fais? Changeras tun sens?
            Es tu encore en fol porpens?

Adam, what are you going to do? Will you change your mind? Do
you insist on your foolish resolution?

Trying to convince Adam Diabolus uses a whole volley of interrogative acts whose orientation gets stronger and stronger and results in a climax. Whereas the interrogative act in *Changeras tun sens?* (V. 394) contains a rather weak orientation and functions as a careful investigation of Adam's mind, the insinuated preference of Diabolus in *Es tu encore en fol porpens?* (V.395) comes out very clearly with the lexical semantics of *fol porpens* that denigrates Adam's formerly enunciated opinions as foolish resolutions – a reproach hard to swallow for Adam, who is characterised by his *ratio* as *imago Dei*.

4.2. Loaded interrogative acts

The concept of the "loaded" question concerns interrogative acts that contain presuppositions which have not yet been ratified by the interlocutors and thus have not already been covered by the conversation. The ammunition of a loaded question is a presupposition that does not form part of the mutual consensus of the interlocutors (cf. Walton 1988: 198, 200, 207f., 214ff.; Bucher 1993: 97, 100f., 102; Bucher 1994: 250f.). The loaded interrogative act as functional element is supposed to leave the interlocutor with his back to the wall: if he answers the question according to the principle of co-operation he has to accept a presupposition that can damage his image heavily, but if he refuses to answer he appears as an interlocutor who violates the co-operative principle.

Considering the "diabolic" mechanism of this pragmatic type, it is not surprising that this question-technique is one of Diabolus' favourites and appears with high frequency in the dialogues of Diabolus with Adam.[31] As loaded interrogative acts are exclusively used by Diabolus, they strongly characterise that figure. The following dialogue excerpt begins with Adam, who explains his convictions to Diabolus:[32]

(6) V. 319-326
319 Adam
320   *Jol te dirrai.*
321   *Mon creator pas ne offendrai.*
322 Diabolus
323   *Criens le tu tant?*
324 Adam
325   *Oïl, par veir.*
326   *Jo l'aim e criem.*

Adam   I will tell you: I will not offend my Creator.
Diabolus   Do you fear him so much?
Adam   Yes, indeed, I love him and I fear him.

As Adam is as a faithful liege man linked to God by the bonds of a vassal to his king – *Mon creator pas ne offendrai* (V.321) – this relation cannot be attacked bluntly and has to be eroded with the technique of the loaded question. With the interrogative act *Criens le tu tant?* (V.323) Diabolus presupposes that Adam's attitude is caused by mere fear so that Adam in the case of giving an affirmative answer risks a negative self-image, appearing as a coward trembling before his master. However, a negative answer would be even more compromising as it would imply giving in to Diabolus' argumentation. Here, Adam counters elegantly by extending the propositional content and naming not only fear but also love as the powers that guide him (V.326).

As the conversation goes on, the temperature rises and Diabolus loads a whole volley of interrogative acts with presuppositions that Adam cannot ratify without violating his duties as a vassal of God:

(7)   V. 403-408
        Diabolus
   403   *Ne munteras james plus halt?*
   404   *Molt te porras tenir por chier*
   405   *Quant Deus t'as fet sun jardenier!*
   406   *Deus t'a feit gardein de son ort,*
   407   *Ja ne querras altre deport?*
   408   *Forma il toi por ventre faire?*
            Don't you have any higher ambitions? You can consider
            yourself very happy that God has made you his gardener! God
            has called upon you to be the warden of his garden, won't you
            ever seek any higher fulfilment? Did he create you just to fill
            your belly?

Performing the interrogative acts *Ne munteras james plus halt?* (V. 403) and *Forma il toi por ventre faire?* (V. 408) Diabolus tries to impart presuppositions to Adam that have not been covered in the course of the conversation and that are impossible to accept.[33] Of course, God did not create Adam as a being that dedicates himself to a life in ease and to physical comforts. For that reason Adam cannot simply negate the first question *Ne munteras jamas plus halt?* (V.403), neither can he answer positively the second interrogative act *Forma il toi por ventre faire?* (V. 408) – both answers would imply that Adam accepts a presupposition that violates the Divine commands. On the other hand, however, a positive answer to the first and a negative answer to the second question would equally imply a trespassing of God's command – Diabolus indeed has set a diabolically skilful trap for Adam. Thus, with his back against the wall, Adam decides to cut the Gordian knot, he chases Diabolus away and thwarts the attempts of Diabolus to start a new conversation by asking more questions – the end of the conversation also puts an end to the attempted seduction.

4.3. Rhetorical questions

Rhetorical questions, which in rhetoric are treated under the term of *interrogatio* (cf. Lausberg 1990: §§ 766-779),[34] present themselves as a special case of interrogative acts for several reasons. On the level of propositional content the illocutionary act seems to signal a deficit of knowledge; however the speaker disposes of all the information necessary to fill the gap and presupposes that this is also the case on the side of the addressee. The interrogative act implies the answer that can be deduced from the question using the pattern of "reversed polarity".[35] For take the example of a yes/no-question, the interrogative act *Don't you see that I'm trying to concentrate on my work?* implies the statement *You see that I'm trying to concentrate on my work* and leads to the inference that the addressee is supposed to let the speaker work and should stop being a nuisance. Because of this implication of an assertion, rhetorical questions not only presuppose the answer – the notion of "presupposition" here in my opinion is too weak and should rather be reserved for interrogative acts containing orientation. It proves more adequate to say that rhetorical questions imply the answer as it can be deduced completely (see for example Rehbock 1984: 168 and 1987: 360). Thus, as the propositional content of the answer is evident in the context, the act of answering is not expected from the interlocutors.[36] The degree of obviousness of the deduced answer depends on the context and on the norms and convictions shared by the interlocutors (cf. Rehbock 1985: 182; Schwitalla 1984: 133, 139, 140).[37] Of course, the obviousness of the answer may also be reinforced by the fact that the speaker continues his turn directly after the question, thereby preventing any answer from someone else (cf. Rehbock 1984: 158, 161; Grésillon 1980: 276; Meibauer 1986: 160-164, 183). As the rhetorical question implies a statement that can be deduced from the interrogative sentence, the illocutionary value of the rhetorical question is close to the pole of assertion or can be the equivalent of an assertion (cf. Grésillon 1980: 275). Thus, rhetorical questions, being interrogative sentences that perform assertions via deduction, can be classified as "tropical" (Kerbrat-Orecchioni 1991b: 105)[38] uses of interrogative sentences, i.e., the contextual factors of usage change the illocutionary value completely. Rhetorical questions establish a consensus among the interlocutors by two means. Firstly, they recur to shared knowledge that can be described as static and given, and secondly, they create consensus in a dynamic process by the implied answer that can be deduced from the rhetorical question – a process the speaker and addressee perform together. In this case, the speaker does not ask for lacking information, he asks for a consensus with his interlocutor and wants his opinion to be accepted.[39]

This sketch of the rhetorical question makes clear that an interrogative act functions as a rhetorical question because of contextual factors – the functional profile of the rhetorical question is not correlated with a certain type of interrogative sentence (cf. Grésillon 1980: 273f.; Schwitalla 1984: 134; Rehbock 1984: 153f.; 176s).[40] This means that the rhetorical question as a concept is not linked to a *signifiant* and therefore forms an onomasiologically based prototype.

Rhetorical questions often assume a referential function in more monologic texts in that they structure the text and focus important parts of an argumentation. Rhetorical questions and the answers they imply also establish the line of argumentation and thereby prove to be closely related to the rhetorical figure of *subiectio*, i.e., a feigned dialogue in monologic speech supposed to render an argumentation more vivid.[41] Thus, the act of speaking is modelled as such in a *mise en scène de la parole* (Cerquiglini 1981: 86). This subtype of a rhetorical question is illustrated in the next text where Adam, after the Fall, mourns his offence in long monologic replies while Eve as interlocutor is eclipsed most of the time (cf. Plantin 1991: 75).

(8) V.665-674
    665 *Ai, mort! por quoi me laisses vivre?*
    666 *Que n'est li monde de moi delivre?*
    667 *Porquoi faz encombrer al mond?*
    668 *D'emfer m'estoet tempter le fond.*
    669 *En emfer serra ma demure*
    670 *Tant que vienge qui me sucure.*
    671 *En emfer si avrai ma vie;*
    672 *Dont me vendra iloc aïe?*
    673 *Dont me vendra iloec socors?*
    674 *Ki me trara d'itel dolors?*
    Oh Death, why do you let me live? Why is the world not freed from me? Why am I still a burden to this earth? I should feel the depths of hell with my own flesh. In hell I will dwell till comes the one that will redeem me. In hell I will spend my life. Wherefrom will help come to me? Wherefrom will I receive support? Who will free me from such pain?

Through the sequence of rhetorical questions in V.665-667 Adam implies that there is no reason why the earth should not be freed from him: he is, as the following verses further pronounce, destined for hell. The volley of interrogative sentences in V.672-674 in which Adam maintains that there is no possibility of salvation for him functions in an analogic way. The interrogative sentences *Dont me vendra iloec aïe?/ Dont me vendra iloec socors?/ Ki me trara d'itel dolors?* (V.672-674) function as rhetorical questions whose assertion can be deduced with the pattern of "reversed polarity": 'Wherefrom will I receive help?' – 'From nowhere'; 'Who will help me?' – 'No one'.

As the rhetorical questions convey not only rational argumentation – the reasons for Adam's damnation – but also the speaker attitude, i.e. Adam's despair, the rhetorical interrogative acts also show expressive value and this expressivity establishes a kind of "family resemblance" with exclamative acts.[42] According to Rosengren (1992: 264f., 296, 301f.),[43] exclamative acts signal the evaluation of a proposition by the speaker whereby the evaluation as such – surprise, indignation, joy etc. – is not expressed by the exclamative act, which is confined to signalling that an evaluation by the speaker does take place. As rhetorical questions and exclamative acts share the strong expressive component of speaker attitude in their functional profile, the transition between the two illocutions is often fluid.

One more striking detail of Adam's lamentations is that Adam already seems to know about the history of salvation when he says *En emfer serra ma demure/ Tant que vienge qui me sucure* (V.669-670)[44] – an insight that goes far beyond the knowledge of the dramatical figure at that moment of the play. This knowledge, however, though it cannot be justified in the drama context, is not due to the naivity of the poet or proof of the inexperience of the early days of medieval drama. On the contrary, the author here integrates into his play the concept of history of medieval man for whom the history of salvation is present at every moment (cf. Auerbach 1946: 146, 150, 152). Adam here represents this notion of medieval man and he thus bridges the gap to the audience. Looking at it from the dimension of the history of salvation, the audience as Christians embraces the wisdom of salvation that Adam professes as a representative of Christianity. Against this background the pragmatic function of the interrogative sentences can be constituted on the two levels of communication which characterise dialogue in drama:[45] the fictional situation of the dramatic figures and the external communicative situation of the representation of the play that includes the audience. Within the limited scope of knowledge of Adam as a dramatic figure, salvation seems out of reach, but if we look at the scene from the perspective of the omnipresent history of salvation which was then central to the audience, the interrogative sentences receive a second, perhaps more profound interpretation.[46] An audience of devout Christians can answer Adam's questions so that the interrogative sentences may be viewed as question acts. This two-fold interpretation also proves that the functional profile of rhetorical questions is context-dependent and cannot be correlated to a pre-determined *signifiant*.

Next to analysing rhetorical questions in monologic texts, it is important to point out that this function type equally abounds in more dialogic replies where it takes on a more appealing value (cf. Schwitalla 1984: 150, 153). In the next dialogue sequence the rhetorical question fills a whole turn. After Eve has sworn "fiance" as a vassal to Diabolus, she is about to learn the secret of the forbidden tree but she first has to renew her vow of keeping silent about the secret. This is where the following quotation starts:

(9) V. 499-506
499 Diabolus
500   Nen sache nuls!
501 Eva
502   Ki le deit saver?
503 Diabolus
504   Neïs Adam!
505 Eva
506   Nenil, par moi!

(9a)
Diabolus   Nobody must know about it.
Eva   (But) Who should know about it?
Diabolus   Not even Adam!
Eva   No, not through me!

Eve counters the repeated exhortations of Diabolus with the rhetorical question *Ki le deit saver?* (V. 502) '(But) Who should know about it?' which implies, according to the pattern of "reversed polarity", that nobody will ever know about it. Diabolus refers to that implied assertion with his precision *Neïs Adam!* (V.504) which would not be an adequate answer to an interrogative act. Diabolus' reaction thus confirms that a reply to a rhetorical question is not an answer to the question but a reaction to the assertion it implies. Eve reacts with a renewal of her vow to this more specified command.

Yet I think that a second interpretation of Diabolus' reaction V.504 is possible. Diabolus' reply could be interpreted as a counter-question to which Eve gives an affirmative answer. As punctuation in medieval manuscripts is not consistent, it seems justified to understand a reply in adequate contexts as an interrogative act even when there is no punctuation mark that may indicate an interrogative sentence:[47]

(9b)
	Diabolus	Nobody must know about it.
	Eve	(But) Who should know about it?
	Diabolus	Not even Adam?
	Eve	No, not through me!

This reading of the dialogue implies a pragmatic reversal of the sentence types. Thus, *Ki le deit saver?* introduced with the interrogative pronoun *ki* and overtly marked as an interrogative sentence contains an assertion and functions as answer whereas the elliptical *Neïs Adam* (V.504) that is not marked as an interrogative sentence could function as an interrogative act.

4.4. Echo-questions

Echo-questions form a functional type that repeats a preceding reply and combines it with rising intonation so that it builds up an interrogative sentence that functions as an interrogative act. In most cases, the echo-question signals an implicit speaker-comment that refers to the topic, the presuppositions or to the performed illocution of the previous enunciation.[48] Echo-questions, which are most closely linked to their context, reflect everyday spoken language and the dynamics of orality in general (cf. Stempel 1993: 290f. and 1995: 46). Echo-questions can repeat a reply word for word, but they may equally summarise its sense in their own words. An echo-question of the latter type is to be found in the following example that is taken from one of the monologic lamentations of Adam. After reaching the conclusion that God may still save him, Adam then doubts the possibility of salvation one more time:

(10) V. 714-718
   714 De grant haltesce sui mis a val:
   715 N'en serrai trait por home né,
   716 Si Deu nen est de majesté.
   717 Que di jo, las? Porquoi le nomai?
   718 Il me aidera? Corocé l'ai.
   From great heights I've been thrown down. No mortal man can pull me out, at most God the Lord of Glory can do that. What do I say, miserable man that I am? Why did I pronounce his name? He would help me? I have raised his anger.

In the interrogative act *Il me aidera?* (V.718) Adam doubts the hope of salvation expressed immediately before in V.715f. by questioning the presupposition that underlies V.716: God Almighty can help him, but Adam has forfeited the right to receive God's help.

The interrogative sentence *Il me aidera?* is the only record of an interrogative sentence in the whole play that has the "canonical" word order of subject-verb-object and consequently is not marked syntactically by an inversion.[49] This type of interrogative sentence corresponds to the intonation-marked question in contemporary French. Because of its exclusively intonational marking, this interrogative sentence type, which does not show the syntactic question marker, is often hard to trace. As in the quoted example the intonation is not expressed in punctuation, the readers – and the editors – are left with contextual interpretation.[50] Because this sentence type is extremely rare in the texts of earlier periods that have been passed on to our time, the use of an intonation-marked question that seems closely linked to orality calls for an explanation. In this example the intonation-marked question is used because the two functions of summarising and asking a question at the same time can only be achieved through the use of rising intonation. The intonation as question-marker refers to the act of enunciation, challenges this act and thus conveys the opinion that Adam has lost the right to profess such a "hopeful" reply. This line of argumentation is illustrated by the sequence of echo-question and answer forming a dialogue that approaches the rhetorical strategy of *subiectio* (cf. Lausberg 1990: § 771). Thus, the evolution of Adam's thoughts follows a dialogue structure in the pattern of address and reply and illustrates his introspection and purification – in this sense Adam's *subiectio* also proves a model of the "dialogic" process of thinking.

4.5. Focusing interrogative acts

The concept of focusing is based on Seelbach (1985: 278, 285ff., 290), who discusses this function of questions when analysing periphrastic questions with *est-ce que*. A focusing question works not only as an interrogative act, but it is also meant to emphasise this act within a dialogue sequence: here, the question itself is centred independent of the speaker-listener interaction.[51] It is a means of controlling the level of attention in a dialogue and can be used to focus certain conversational topics or interventions. With respect to modern French, this effect is derived from the *est-ce que* formula that presents the question act as a question act from the very first beginning.[52] Consequently, the focusing power that is part of the *signifié* is the result of the syntactic constitution of the sentence type, i.e., the *signifiant*. In Old French this effect is achieved with the help of a different syntactic tool on the part of the *signifiant*, the *dislocation à gauche*. In this syntactic construction the element that is to be emphasised, usually the subject or the object, is projected out of the sentence-frame and fronted as a conversational topic (cf. Foulet 1921: 247, 249f.; Kaiser 1980: 90f., 94f.; Stenström 1988: 318; Stempel 1993: 291).[53] The *dislocation à gauche* marks in a more general sense emotional speech and is a common phenomenon in interrogative sentences in Old French. The syntactic procedure is not completely grammaticalised and consequently still preserves an expressive value used to emphasise the topic. The next example from a monologic passage of the penitent Adam illustrates this effect:[54]

(11) V. 657-662
    657 Jo ai guerpi mun criator
    658 Par le conseil de mal uxor.
    659 Allas! pecchable! que frai?
    660 Mun criator cum atendrai?
    661 Cum atendrai mon criator
    662 Que jo ai guerpi por ma folor?
    I have turned myself away from my Creator through the advice of my evil wife. Woe! What shall I sinful man do? My Creator, how shall I expect him? How shall I expect my Creator from whom I dissented in my foolishness?

The self-accusations of Adam concentrate on the aspect of Creator and creature. The Fall of Man appears as an incomprehensible insurrection against the Creator: how shall Adam now face the Creator? This central question is focused in *Mun criator cum atendrai?* (V.660) by positioning the marked *mun criator* in front in the first sentence, while the focus is then switched to the breach of faith in the next phrase (V.661).[55] This central idea is emphasised not only by the dislocation but also by the *expolitio* of the question sequence V.659-662 as a whole (cf. Lausberg 1990: § 830-§ 842).

After the presentation of different interrogative types in their dramatic contexts of questioning and seducing, I will now turn to some aspects of the dialogue types in which the questions I looked at occurred. As this also implies situating the illocutionary types in a historical frame, the next section will treat the complex problem of the historicity of illocutions and dialogue forms.

5. Questions and the type of dialogue

An analysis of interrogative acts in an Old French text means that the linguist investigates a "fragment" of dialogue interaction of by-gone times. Thus, the last part of my study, apart from giving a brief outline of the presentation and evaluation of interrogative acts in the *Jeu d'Adam*, also has to look at some of the core subjects of historical dialogue analysis.

Historical dialogue analysis is essentially concerned with the evolution of dialogue forms; it attempts to distinguish between possible universals of dialogue and time-period specific strategies and norms of dialogues and it examines the evaluations given to these strategies and norms in their time.[56] As a discipline of historical pragmatics, historical dialogue analysis aims at explaining dialogue forms as social interactions regulated by language structures and historical contexts of acting and communicating (cf. Cherubim 1980: 8f., 13-15; Sitta 1980: 32f., 129-136; Henne 1980: 89; Bax 1991: 199-201; Schlieben-Lange and Weydt 1979: 69-71).

Furthermore, historical dialogue analysis often also aims at a reconstruction of the spoken language of former periods of language evolution – an attempt that has to be aware of the many filters of conservation and interpretation the "authentic" language use had to pass through.[57] However, medieval texts, in spite of their alterity and reduced authenticity, are still regarded as good material for the investigation of conversational types and spoken language, as literature in this period embraced *la rhétorique du conversationnel*.[58] This vitality of everyday-language is also present in the *Jeu d'Adam*, which is regarded as an early document of "realism" (cf. Auerbach 1946: 146f., 150; Schmeja 1974: 42) in the sense that it interweaves *sublimitas* and *humilitas*. Because of this integration of aspects of everyday life in the story of redemption, which also may have repercussions on the language of the vernacular parts, the analysed interrogative acts may be close to the spoken language of that era.

Historical dialogue analysis assumes that dialogues, being historically determined structures, undergo changes in their communicative principles and in their patterns of illocutionary sequencing – two domains that are closely interwoven and linked to the whole complex of human interaction (cf. Fritz 1994b: 547f.; 1995: 495; 1997: 47ff.).

On the illocutionary level, changes may manifest themselves in the patterns of speech act sequencing and in the evaluation of these sequences. As a fixed sequence such as the adjacency pair of question and answer can be considered as a solution of a vital communicative task, it seems evident that the modification of that task in history may equally lead to a modification of the characteristic form of utterance (cf. Fritz 1994b: 547f., 1995: 471f.). The illocutions and their combinations therefore do not form a static inventory of dialogue techniques, and the conversational presentation of questions as well as the combination of the interrogative act with other illocutions and the social and ethical evaluation are subject to change. These transformations are documented by the historical specifications that the adjacency pair has undergone – specifications that are in most of the cases coupled with a varying evaluation of the illocutionary sequence (cf. Fritz 1994b: 547f.).[59]

Up to now, it seems clear that processes of change can affect interrogative acts in two ways. Firstly, on the part of the *signifiant* as the verbal realisation, the type of interrogative sentence can alter, and new structures like the *est-ce que* sentence type may emerge. Secondly, in the presentation of the interrogative act, its embedding in the dialogue form and its evaluation as a form of interaction may change – here language change is considered to correspond to a change in human interaction (cf. Weigand 1988: 159). However, we have to consider a third, widely disputed, possibility: the interrogative act itself could be subject to change over time because of altered communicative needs. Speech acts, after having been considered as universals for a long time, are now seen in their historical dimension as verbal interaction.[60] As socially mediated and historically determined ways of interacting, dialogue acts are not characteristics of languages but of communities and therefore historical in the sense that they form part of the traditions of a community (Coseriu in Schlieben-Lange and Weydt 1979: 75ff.).

However, it seems that elementary dialogue acts such as interrogative acts are less exposed to historical change, whereas norms and patterns of action as well as topics of talks and communicative principles are more strongly rooted in historical circumstances (Fritz 1994b: 546f.; 1997: 49, 51f.; see also Schlieben-Lange 1979: 3f., 23, 26f.). The adjacency pair of question and answer corresponds to a basic communicative need, the pointing out of a knowledge deficit and searching for information. Therefore, it seems likely that the interrogative act in its basic value may constitute a prototype on the illocutionary level. Such an illocutionary prototype is an abstraction in the sense that it manifests itself in historical types determined by the evolution of the guiding principles of dialogue interaction (cf. Fritz 1997: 49, 51f.). Furthermore, these types are coined by the socially and ethically established communicative principles of a community. This last point is most obvious in the *Jeu d'Adam* where questions are regarded not only as a lack of etiquette (cf. Fritz 1997: 51), but are seen as a manifestation of sinful *curiositas* in the light of Christian ideology.[61]

In the *Jeu d'Adam* the seduction of Adam and Eve is therefore a seduction through questions leading to more questions. In order to corrupt the innocent and ignorant Adam, who lives in paradisiacal happiness, Diabolus first has to arouse Adam's *curiositas*, which is identical to the aim of seducing him to ask questions:

(12) V. 257-272

257	*Tunc veniat Diabolus ad Adam et dicet ei:*	
258		*Que fais, Adam?*
259	*Adam*	
260		*Ci vif en grant deduit.*
261	*Diabolus*	
262		*Estas tu bien?*
263	*Adam*	
264		*Ne sen rien qui m'enoit.*
265	*Diabolus*	
266		*Poet estre mielz.*
267	*Adam*	
268		*Ne puis saver coment.*
269	*Diabolus*	
270		*Vols le tu saver?*
271	*Adam*	
272		*Bien en iert mon talent.*
	Diabolus	What are you doing, Adam?
	Adam	I live here in great happiness.
	Diabolus	Are you fine?
	Adam	I feel nothing that worries me.
	Diabolus	But it could be better.
	Adam	I don't know how.
	Diabolus	Do you want to know it?
	Adam	I would like to.

Diabolus' opening question *Que fais, Adam?* (V.258) is answered by Adam in an evasive way by referring to his life in *grant deduit* (V. 260). Diabolus' insisting on his question by repeating it in another form, *Estas tu bien?* (V.262), indicates that his desire to close his knowledge gap is actually subordinated to another illocutionary strategy. Adam basically confirms his first answer, but his happiness is now formulated *ex negativo*: *Ne sen rien qui m'enoit* (V.264), so that the possibility of incomplete happiness arises. Diabolus uses this opportunity by giving the exposed statement *Poet estre mielz* (V.266) in order to arouse Adam's *curiositas* by the assertion. Adam is now in a dilemma: to ask what could be better would be the same as to doubt the word of God, as Figura has shown him the paradise as a place of perfect happiness. His *curiositas* results in an illocutionary hybrid *Ne puis saver coment* (V. 268). This assertion of ignorance can on the one hand function as an interrogative act, but on the other hand it can be interpreted as Adam's disbelief in Diabolus' statement. Adam thus secures himself a possible retreat. However, the success of Diabolus' seduction becomes clear in the next question-answer sequence: with *Bien en iert mon talent* (V.272) Adam explicitly acknowledges his *curiositas*. While Diabolus' strategy to provoke questions only succeeds after some detours with Adam and utterly fails in the end, he has a much easier game with Eve from the start:[62]

(13) V. 440-443
 440 Diabolus
 441 Eva, ça sui venuz a toi.
 442 Eva
 443 Di moi, Sathan, et tu pur quoi?
  Diabolus Eve, I have come to you.
  Eve Tell me, Satan, what for have you come?

As soon as Diabolus addresses her with a phatic phrase, Eve already asks for the purpose of his visit and thus reveals her *curiositas* from the beginning.

The quoted sequences V.257-272 and V.440-443 model the basic structure of "seducing" as a pattern of action in which questions play an important part. The goal of Diabolus' strategy is to induce Adam to take the initiative of acting (and asking questions). The Fall of Man does not start when Adam eats the apple, but already has begun when Adam gives in to his *curiositas* and allows himself to be seduced to ask questions. The scene thus illustrates the medieval view of *curiositas* as a search of knowledge that leads to *superbia* and detracts man from the *memoria* of his real destination (cf. Weddige [2]1992: 62f.). Since Augustine, *curiositas* has been considered a breach of faith towards God, because truth and knowledge are the privilege of God that man shall not desire. In the pursuit of knowledge man loses himself in the pleasure of his intellect and becomes addicted to *superbia*. The *cupiditas scientiae* is identified with the seduction of Adam and Eve in paradise.[63]

6. Some final remarks

This study of questions and seduction in the *Jeu d'Adam* proceeds from onomasiologically based pragmatic prototypes of interrogative acts. The analysis of the question types is not only pragmatic in its integration of the dialogue context but also in the chosen method which is, as a whole, based on pragmatic functional identities. For a study on Old French, this approach proves to be fruitful, as it is the only way to gain access to the usage of language as a historical form of social interaction in by-gone days.

Thus, the undertaken examination shows that only a pragmatic approach, backed by the results of historical dialogue analysis, may be able to shed light on the multiplicity of interrogative forms in Old French. Further research should concentrate on the question whether the polymorphism of interrogative sentences is the mere agglutination of contingent evolutions, or whether it forms a coherent system of complementary pragmatic profiles at the speaker's disposal – one of the many questions in this field that may arouse the nowadays less severely frowned-on *curiositas* of the linguist.

Notes

1 For constructive and insightful comments I thank Franz Lebsanft and Wolf-Dieter Stempel. Special thanks go to Verena Jung and Sönke Siemßen for the proof-reading of the English version.
2 I translate "Erwiderung" as 'reply' to use a more general term than 'answer'. For a definition of reply vs. answer see Walton (1988: 196).
3 For the dualism of conversation see also Sacks, Schegloff and Jefferson (1974: 699-701, 706, 725-727); Goffman (1976: 263); Wenz (1984: 80); Henne and Rehbock (31995: 13).
4 Bucher (1994: 239) regards the question/answer pair as a prototype of dialogue; cf. also Stenström (1988: 304, 307). For an opposed view consult Stierle (1984: 300f.), who sees questions and answers as an elementary sequence that fixes the dialogue and thus limits the openness of conversation.
5 For definitions of adjacency pair cf. Sacks, Schegloff and Jefferson (1974: 711, 716f., 728); Goffman (1976: 258, 260, 263, 270ff., 280, 309); Merrit (1976: 327f., 336); Stenström (1988: 304, 307); Franke (1990: 155f.); Kerbrat-Orecchioni (1991a: 9); Moeschler (1994: 81f.); Henne and Rehbock (31995: 24, 174f.).
6 Henne and Rehbock (31995: 204ff., 210f.) regard the question as an unconditional obligation, whose non-fulfilment is sanctioned in conversation; see also Franke (1990: 18f., 155f.).
7 Auerbach (1946: 141, 148-152); Noomen (1968: 148-154) and (1971: 6, Introduction); Hunt (1975: 374, 381f., 387); Schmeja (1974: 44); for a further thematic analysis consult Auerbach (1946) and Noomen (1968: 163-180).
8 Cf. Bucher (1994: 240); Kerbrat-Orecchioni (1991a: 34). Henne and Rehbock (31995: 180, 182ff., 184ff.) capture this problem in their distinction of two levels: the level of turns (*Gesprächsschrittebene*) and the level of illocutionary acts (*Handlungsebene*).

Que fais, Adam? – Questions and Seduction in the *Jeu d'Adam*   357

9   This and the following texts are quoted from Noomen's edition; I also take over his counting of the verses. The English translation is mine and partly follows the German version by Ebel.
10 Here I refer to pragmatic profiles of questions and answers, as the approach of formal semantics has proved to be of limited value to dialogic approaches. For formal semantics of questions and answers see Böttner (1979: 66, 68-70) and for a critical review on that method see Bucher (1994: 241f.) and Fritz (1994c: 132).
11 For the concept of the knowledge gap see Teyssier (1974: 8); Schlieben-Lange (1983: 96); Parret (1988: 281f., 298); Kerbrat-Orecchioni (1991a: 18 (*vide cognitif* vs. *plénitude cognitive*)); Rémi-Giraud (1991: 45f. (*complétude* vs. *incomplétude*)); Rehbock (1992: 189-191, 201-204, 207f.).
12 This view is widely represented: Grewendorf (1981: 95f.); Weydt (1985: 313); Kerbrat-Orecchioni (1991a: 14); Parret (1988: 281f., 298). This interpretation seems to be backed by the English performative verb *ask* which is polysemous and means the performance of a question (*I asked whether he would come tomorrow*) but also of a directive (*I asked him to come tomorrow*). See also Wunderlich's (1976: 75-86, especially 77f.) classification and the comment by Lang (1993: 44-47).
13 Cf. an analogic example in Searle, (1969: 69); for Searle, *Tell me the name of the first President of the United States* is the equivalent of *What's the name of the first President of the United States?*
14 Concerning the characterisation of acts with the relation of words and world consult Searle (1979: 3f., 12-20) and Lang (1993: 44f., 46, 49f., 51: "[...] daß der Fragende in dem, was er sagt, auf eine Lücke in der (zumindest ins Auge gefaßten) Übereinstimmung zwischen seinen Worten und der anvisierten Welt hinweist" (ibid. 49f.)); see also Schlieben-Lange (1983: 96) for the referentiality of language in general.
15 For the concept of a continuum see Fontaney (1991: 157); Kerbrat-Orecchioni (1991b: 88f.); Rémi-Giraud (1991: 56, 58f.); Traverso (1991: 203f.).
16 Most of the factors like intonation and knowledge distribution are of gradual nature – a fact that speaks in favour of a continuum.
17 Cf. also Berrendonner (1981: 51f.); Bucher (1994: 240f., 244); Kerbrat-Orecchioni (1991b: 105-108). Altmann (1987: 22) embraces this affinity in the term of *Satzmodus* as a regular combination of a formally defined sentence type and a pragmatic function.
18 Similar thoughts are expressed by Fontaney (1991: 157); Kerbrat-Orecchioni (1991a: 25f.); Lang (1993: 51).
19 For the concept of communicative task see Fritz (1994a: 186); Fritz (1994b: 547f.); Fritz (1995: 471f.); Meng (1994: 377ff.).
20 Cf. Koch (1996: 225, 230-237) for a critical review of semasiologically based prototypes and a plea in favour of onomasiologically based prototypes.
21 In this context I can of course not cover the field of investigation on interrogative sentences in Old French and I will limit myself to some remarks that are relevant for my approach.

For further research consult Schulze (1888), Foulet (1921), Lerch (1934), Gamillscheg (1957), Renchon (1967), Ménard (1976) and Kaiser (1980).

22 Schulze (1888: 184f.); Foulet (1921: 262, 346ff.); De Boer (1926: 311-317, 327); Lerch (1934: 399); Brunot and Bruneau (31949: 486-488); Renchon (1967: 37); Ménard (1976: 105); Kaiser (1980: 88f., 127). In Old French, interrogative as well as exclamative sentences are marked by inversion, but the inversion is also possible in declarative sentences and does therefore not qualify as an exclusive question-marker according to Lerch (1934: 396, 399).

23 A different view is found in Schulze (1888: 242f.), who maintains that intonation-marked questions are not that rare.

24 For this problem see Foulet (1921: 244); Kaiser (1980: 109); and Kotschi (1985: 10).

25 For this hypothesis see Schulze (1888: 242f.); Stempel and Fischer (1985: 266) and Stempel (1994b: 323-326). Cf. also Ernst (1984: 441f. n.3, 444) and (1985: 96) on the problem of the intonation-marked type. According to Ernst, the intonation-marked question is already found in the earliest French texts but seems to have acquired a dominant position in spoken language only in the course of the 17th century.

26 Stempel and Fischer (1985: 247f., 251, 254f.); cf. also Weydt (1985: 317ff.); Rehbock (1985: 178, 193f.) and (1987: 358-360) for further discussion of the term *Antwortpräferenz*.

27 They are moreover asymmetric in the sense that they do not always call upon an affirmative or negative answer but may equally express a certain concern and ask for an explanation or justification.

28 DuBruck (1979: 167) points out that seduction functions via the appeal to the *curiositas*.

29 For a similar idea of correlation between syntax and pragmatic potential see also Behnstedt (1973: 179); Callebaut (1987: 214ff.).

30 For the functioning of the negation see also Muller (1991: 8, 20f., 40ff.); Moeschler (1992: 11ff., 15ff.).

31 For the characterisation of figures through frequent illocutions consult Betten (1994: 529).

32 For a characterisation of Adam's *ratio* as *imago Dei* compared to the weakness of Eve see Schmeja (1974: 52, 59).

33 For a comment on these verses cf. also Lerch (1934: 316).

34 For a classification of question types in rhetoric consult also Schwitalla (1984: 131ff.).

35 Gamillscheg (1957: 616); Grésillon (1980: 279f.); Borillo (1981: 1-4); Stempel and Fischer (1985: 257-259); Rehbock (1987: 373ff., 378), who gives some exceptions; Meibauer (1986: 160-164, 183); Meibauer (1991: 227, 229-231, 238f.); Rosengren (1992: 296f.).

36 Cf. Lausberg (1990: § 767): "Die *interrogatio* ist der Ausdruck eines gemeinten Aussagesatzes als Frage, auf die keine Antwort erwartet wird, da die Antwort im Sinne der sprechenden Partei als evident angenommen wird." Rehbock (1984: 158, 161) indicates that this may also be the other way round: by not permitting an answer-reaction, the speaker suggests that the answer is evident even if that evidence is questionable.

Que fais, Adam? – Questions and Seduction in the *Jeu d'Adam*   359

37 The further conversation is based on the deduced answer cf. Rehbock (1984: 168, 170).
38 I.e., a speech act is tropically replaced (or 'turned around' in 'reversed polarity') by another speech act.
39 Stempel (1984: 162) describes this procedure as not only typical of rhetorical questions: "Es ist sogar vielfach unbeanstandete Praxis, gerade Äußerungsformen der Höflichkeit sozusagen als Alibi für die Inszenierung eines gewünschten Identitätsbildes auszunutzen, wie z.B. viele Frageformen zeigen, die weit über den Einzelfall der sog. rhetorischen Frage hinaus zu reinen Zustimmungs- oder Bestätigungsformen herabgesunken sind."
40 Of course, specific lexical or syntactic means can have affinities to the pragmatics of rhetorical questions, but are not to be regarded as proper markers; cf. Rehbock (1984: 160, 164f.); Meibauer (1986: 112ff., 127ff., 136ff., 154-157).
41 Lausberg (1990: § 771): "Die *subiectio* ist ein in die Rede hineingenommener fingierter (also monologischer) Dialog mit Frage und Antwort (meist mit mehreren Fragen und Antworten) zur Belebung der Gedankenfolge." Cf. Schwitalla (1984: 132); Rehbock (1984: 169f.).
42 Cf. Lerch (1934: 408), who points out that in Old French interrogatives and exclamatives are equally marked by inversion; cf. Gamillscheg (1957: 611).
43 Rosengren classifies the exclamative act as an illocution that can be traced back to interrogative and declarative acts. The consideration of exclamatives as special cases of interrogatives is also to be found in Gamillscheg (1957: 611).
44 For an interpretation of these verses see likewise Hunt (1975: 511).
45 On literary dialogue and the doubling of communicative levels see Betten (1994: 520); Kästner (1978: 21-25, 30-35).
46 Betten (1994: 529) points out that speech acts have to be interpreted against the background of the doubled communicative situation. Cf. also Rehbock (1985: 217).
47 The manuscript in the edition by Sletsjöe shows no "question mark", just a point that indicates the end of the reply; on the practice and variations of punctuation in interrogative sentences in medieval manuscripts see also Bischoff (21986: 225).
48 Lebsanft (1984: 283f., 286f.); Meibauer (1987b: 346, 349-352); Reis (1991: 50, 56f.); Bucher (1994: 245). See also Schulze (1888: 144-146, 150f., 154f.), who describes this type as *Wiederholungsfrage*.
49 It seems probable that there is an affinity between echo-questions and the intonation-marked question type, as in modern French echo-questions can only be realised by this interrogative sentence type; cf. Ashby (1977: 37f.); Stempel and Fischer (1985: 246.) Schulze (1888: 243f., 141, 147) brings forward material that proves that intonation-marked questions mostly function as echo-questions.
50 In this case Noomen (V.718) and Aebischer (V.380) both understand the reply as an interrogative act and put a question mark in their editions.
51 Consult equally Weydt (1985: 319f.) for the interaction of question type and context.

52 For the development of this interrogative sentence type see Foulet (1921: 253, 257) and Kaiser (1980: 129).
53 For the use of interrogative sentences with dislocation in modern French see Morel (1997: 289f.).
54 On Adam's conduct as a sinner see also Schmeja (1974: 59).
55 For an interpretation of this passage see also Gamillscheg (1957: 558).
56 For the questions related to the historicity of dialogue forms cf. Fritz (1994b: 545); Fritz (1995: 469, 470f.); Fritz (1997: 47f.). See also Henne and Rehbock (31995: 234, 236); Gloning (1993: 207); Luckmann (1984: 58f.) for historical communicative forms in general. For a more general view see also Weigand (1988: 159); Sitta (1980: 32f.); Bax (1991: 199-201). On the notion of historicity see also Coseriu in Schlieben-Lange and Weydt (1979: 75f.).
57 For the problems of this reconstruction cf. Kristol (1992: 39, 49ff.), Henne and Rehbock (31995: 234, 236). The problem of the literary stylisation is pointed out by Burger and von Matt (1974: 285f.); Henne (1980: 91); Sitta (1980: 129f.); Betten (1994: 520f., 533); Fritz (1997: 54). Besides, the attempt to trace back fragments of spoken language in written texts touches the problem of written and spoken language and the variations which texts undergo when changing the medium of tradition; cf. also Grosse (1985: 1187) and Selig (1997: 202-208, 212-218), for a general view on spoken and written language in the Middle Ages.
58 This term was coined by Stempel (1994a: 66f.); cf. also Stempel (1995: 43, 45). This positive view is shared by Grosse (1972: 657).
59 As the history of the question-answer adjacency pair is not yet written, I have to limit myself to some examples to illustrate at least the broad range of the spectrum. Jauß (1984:393) comments on questioning in Platonic discourse and in scholasticism. Felten (1972: 18f., 21, 25, 30f.) writes on questions motivated by *admiratio* in Dante's *Divina Commedia*; Kästner (1978: 159-164, 122) presents his ideas on the catechetic pattern of question and answer in didactic and liturgic texts in the Middle Ages. Fritz (1994b: 552, 557; 1995: 482, and 1997:51) cites as an example the evaluation of questioning as a lack of education and etiquette in the Middle Ages, which is illustrated by the instruction Gurnemanz gives to Parzival. The advice is as follows (I cite after the edition by Lachmann, 171, 17-21): "irn sult niht vil gevrâgen:/ ouch sol iuch niht betrâgen/ bedâhter gegenrede, diu gê/ reht als jenes vrâgen stê/ der iuch wil mit worten spehen."
60 See Schlieben-Lange (1976: 114); Schlieben-Lange and Weydt (1979: 67); Schlieben-Lange (1982: 104, 106ff.) and Stetter (1991: 68, 75-79) for a plea in favour of the historical dimension of speech acts. In Schlieben-Lange and Weydt (1979) note especially the dispute about the degree of historical fixation of speech acts.
61 The negative judgement on the question with all its dialogic dynamic may be a reflection of the fact that the Middle Ages are dominated by the "one-voiced" discourse on theology so that the "two-voiced" dialogue plays a minor role; cf. Stierle (1984: 306f.).

62 This crucial difference in behaviour is the illustration of the topos that the man as *imago Dei* has *ratio* himself whereas the woman can achieve *ratio* only by the guidance of man; see also Schmeja (1974: 52, 59).

63 For a history of the discrimination of *curiositas* see Blumenberg (1973: 71ff., 79, 84, 94, 96ff., 105ff. 108, 110f., 129f.): "Der Griff nach dem Baum der Erkenntnis hat die unregulierte Wißbegierde zur *vana cura* einer heillosen Weltverfallenheit ausarten lassen" (ibid. 110).

References

Primary sources

Le Jeu d'Adam (Ordo representacionis Ade). Publié par Willem Noomen. Paris: Champion, 1971.
Le Mystère d'Adam (Ordo representacionis Ade). Texte complet du manuscrit de Tours publié avec une introduction, des notes et un glossaire par Paul Aebischer. Genève: Droz, et Paris: Minard, 1964.
Le Mystère d'Adam. Edition diplomatique accompagnée d'une reproduction photographique du manuscrit de Tours et des leçons des éditions critiques. Publié par Leif Sletsjöe. Paris: Klincksieck, 1968.
Das Altfranzösische Adamsspiel. Übers. und eingeleitet von Uda Ebel. München: Fink, 1968.
Wolfram von Eschenbach. *Parzival*. Sechste Ausgabe von Karl Lachmann. Berlin und Leipzig 1926. (Nachdruck Berlin: de Gruyter, 1964).

Works cited

Altmann, Hans
    1987   Zur Problematik der Konstitution von Satzmodi als Formtypen. In: Meibauer (ed.): 22-56.
Ashby, William
    1977   Interrogative Forms in Parisian French. *Semasia* 4: 35-53.
Auerbach, Erich
    1946   Adam und Eva. In: Erich Auerbach. *Mimesis. Dargestellte Wirklichkeit in der abendländischen Literatur*. 7. Auflage 1982. Bern: Francke, 139-166.
Bax, Marcel M. H.
    1991   Historische Pragmatik: Eine Herausforderung für die Zukunft. In: Busse (ed.): 197-215.

Behnstedt, Peter
1973 *'Viens-tu? Est-ce que tu viens? Tu viens?' Formen und Strukturen des direkten Fragesatzes im Französischen.* Tübingen: Tübinger Beiträge zur Linguistik.

Berrendonner, Alain
1981 Zéro pour la question. Syntaxe et sémantique des interrogations directes. *Cahiers de linguistique française* 2: 41-69.

Betten, Anne
1994 Analyse literarischer Dialoge. In: Fritz and Hundsnurscher (eds.): 519-544.

Bischoff, Bernhard
²1986 *Paläographie des römischen Altertums und des abendländischen Mittelalters.* Zweite, überarbeitete Auflage. Berlin: Erich Schmidt.

Böttner, Michael
1979 Frage-Antwort-Dialoge. In: Wilfried Hendrichs and Gerhard Charles Rump (eds.). *Dialoge. Beiträge zur Interaktions- und Diskursanalyse.* Hildesheim: Gerstenberg, 66-85.

Blumenberg, Hans
1973 *Der Prozeß der theoretischen Neugierde.* Frankfurt: Suhrkamp.

Borillo, Andrée
1979 La négation et l'orientation de la demande de confirmation. *Langue française* 44: 27-41.
1981 Quelques aspects de la question rhétorique en français. *DRLAV Revue de linguistique* 25: 1-33.

Brown, Penelope, and Stephen C. Levinson
1987 *Politeness. Some Universals in Language Usage.* Cambridge: CUP.

Brunot, Ferdinand, and Charles Bruneau
³1949 *Précis de grammaire historique de la langue française.* Paris: Masson.

Bucher, Hans-Jürgen
1993 Geladene Fragen. Zur Dialogdynamik in politischen Fernsehinterviews. In: *Dialoganalyse IV. Referate der 4. Arbeitstagung Basel 1992.* Herausgegeben von Heinrich Löffler unter Mitarbeit von Christoph Grolimund und Mathilde Gyger. Teil II. Tübingen: Niemeyer, 97-107.
1994 Frage-Antwort-Dialoge. In: Fritz and Hundsnurscher (eds.): 239-258.

Burger, Harald, and Peter von Matt
1974 Dramatischer Dialog und restringiertes Sprechen. F. X. Kroetz in linguistischer und literaturwissenschaftlicher Sicht. *Zeitschrift für Germanistische Linguistik* 2: 269-298.

Busse, Dietrich
1991 Konventionalisierungsstufen des Zeichengebrauchs als Ausgangspunkt semantischen Wandels. In: Busse (ed.): 37-65.

Busse, Dietrich (ed.)
　1991　　*Diachrone Semantik und Pragmatik. Untersuchungen zur Erklärung und Beschreibung des Sprachwandels.* Tübingen: Niemeyer.
Callebaut, Bruno
　1987　　Pour une pragmatique de l'ordre des mots. La phrase interrogative française. *Travaux de linguistique* 14/15: 209-220.
Cerquiglini, Bernard
　1981　　*La parole médiévale: discours, syntaxe, texte.* Paris: Minuit.
Cherubim, Dieter
　1980　　Zum Programm einer historischen Sprachpragmatik. In: Sitta (ed.): 3-21.
Conrad, Rudi
　1986　　Bedeutung von Fragen und Gegenfragen im Dialog. In: Mey (ed.): 419-432.
De Boer, C.
　1926　　L'évolution des formes de l'interrogation en français. *Romania* 52: 307-327.
DuBruck, Edelgard
　1979　　The Devil and Hell in Medieval French Drama. *Romania* 100: 165-179.
Ernst, Gerhard
　1984　　Review of: Egbert Kaiser. 1980. *Romanische Forschungen* 96, 441-445.
　1985　　*Gesprochenes Französisch zu Beginn des 17. Jahrhunderts. Direkte Rede in Jean Héroards "Histoire particulière de Louis XIII" (1605-1610).* Tübingen: Niemeyer.
Felten, Hans
　1972　　*Wissen und Poesie. Die Begriffswelt der Divina Commedia im Vergleich mit theologischen Lateintexten.* München: Fink.
Fontaney, Louise
　1991　　A la lumière de l'intonation. In: Kerbrat-Orecchioni (ed.): 113-161.
Foulet, Lucien
　1921　　Comment ont évolué les formes de l'interrogation. *Romania* 47: 243-348.
Franke, Wilhelm
　1990　　*Elementare Dialogstrukturen. Darstellung, Analyse, Diskussion.* Tübingen: Niemeyer.
Fritz, Gerd
　1994a　　Grundlagen der Dialogorganisation. In: Fritz and Hundsnurscher (eds.): 177-201.
　1994b　　Geschichte von Dialogformen. In: Fritz and Hundsnurscher (eds.): 545-562.
　1994c　　Formale Dialogspieltheorien. In: Fritz and Hundsnurscher (eds.): 131-152.
　1995　　Topics in the History of Dialogue Forms. In: Andreas H. Jucker (ed.): *Historical Pragmatics. Pragmatic Developments in the History of English.* Amsterdam/Philadelphia: Benjamins, 469-498.

1997 Remarks on the History of Dialogue Forms. In: *Dialoganalyse V. Referate der 5. Arbeitstagung Paris 1994.* Herausg. von Etienne Petri unter Mitarbeit von Danielle Laroche-Bouvy und Sorin Stati. Tübingen: Niemeyer, 47-55.

Fritz, Gerd, and Franz Hundsnurscher (eds.)
1994 *Handbuch der Dialoganalyse.* Tübingen: Niemeyer.

Gamillscheg, Ernst
1957 *Historische französische Syntax.* Tübingen: Niemeyer.

Gelas, Nadine
1991 La question dans les romans de Marguerite Duras. In: Kerbrat-Orecchioni (ed.): 359-367.

Gloning, Thomas
1993 Sprachreflexive Textstellen als Quelle für die Geschichte von Kommunikationsformen. In: *Dialoganalyse IV. Referate der 4. Arbeitstagung Basel 1992.* Herausgegeben von Heinrich Löffler unter Mitarbeit von Christoph Grolimund und Mathilde Gyger. Tübingen: Niemeyer, 207-217.

Goffman, Erving
1976 Replies and responses. *Language in Society* 5: 257-313.

Grésillon, Almuth
1980 Zum linguistischen Status rhetorischer Fragen. *Zeitschrift für Germanistische Linguistik* 8: 273-289.

Grewendorf, Günther
1981 Pragmatisch sinnvolle Fragen. In: Dieter Krallmann and Ernst Stickel (eds.). *Zur Theorie der Frage. Vorträge des Bad Homburger Kolloquiums, 13.-15. November 1978.* Tübingen: Narr, 95-117.

Grosse, Siegfried
1972 Literarischer Dialog und gesprochene Sprache. In: Herbert Backes (ed.). *Festschrift für Hans Eggers zum 65. Geburtstag.* Tübingen: Niemeyer, 649-668.

1985 Reflexe gesprochener Sprache im Mittelhochdeutschen. In: Werner Besch, Oskar Reichmann and Stefan Sonderegger (eds.). *Sprachgeschichte. Ein Handbuch zur Geschichte der deutschen Sprache und ihrer Erforschung.* Zweiter Halbband. Berlin/New York: de Gruyter, 1186-1191.

Gülich, Elisabeth, and Thomas Kotschi (eds.)
1985 *Grammatik, Konversation, Interaktion. Beiträge zum Romanistentag 1983.* Tübingen: Niemeyer.

Haug, Walter
1984 Der Ackermann und der Tod. In: Stierle and Warning (eds.): 281-286.

Heger, Klaus
²1976 *Monem, Wort, Satz und Text.* Zweite, erw. Auflage. Tübingen: Niemeyer.

Henne, Helmut
1980   Probleme einer historischen Gesprächsanalyse. Zur Rekonstruktion gesprochener Sprache im 18. Jahrhundert. In: Sitta (ed.): 89-102.
Henne, Helmut, and Helmut Rehbock
³1995   *Einführung in die Gesprächsanalyse.* Berlin/New York: de Gruyter.
Humboldt, Wilhelm von
1824-26   Natur der Sprache überhaupt. (Auszug aus: Grundzüge des allgemeinen Sprachtypus). In: Hans Helmut Christmann (ed.). 1977. *Sprachwissenschaft des 19. Jahrhunderts.* Darmstadt: Wissensch. Buchgesellschaft, 19-46.
Hunt, Tony
1975   The Unity of 'The Play of Adam' (Ordo representacionis Ade). *Romania* 96: 368-388, 497-527.
Jauß, Hans Robert
1984   Der dialogische und der dialektische 'Neveu de Rameau' oder: Wie Diderot Sokrates und Hegel Diderot rezipierte. In: Stierle and Warning (eds.): 393-419.
Kaiser, Egbert
1980   *Strukturen der Frage im Französischen. Synchronische und diachronische Untersuchungen zur direkten Frage im Französischen des 15. Jahrhunderts (1450-1500).* Tübingen: Narr.
Kästner, Hannes
1978   *Mittelalterliche Lehrgespräche. Textlinguistische Analysen, Studien zur poetischen Funktion und pädagogischen Intention.* Berlin: Erich Schmidt Verlag.
Kerbrat-Orecchioni, Catherine
1991a   Introduction. In: Kerbrat-Orecchioni (ed.): 5-37.
1991b   L'acte de question et l'acte d'assertion: opposition discrète ou continuum? In: Kerbrat-Orecchioni (ed.): 87-111.
Kerbrat-Orecchioni, Catherine (ed.)
1991   *La question.* Lyon: Presses universitaires de Lyon.
Koch, Peter
1996   La sémantique du prototype: sémasiologie ou onomasiologie? *Zeitschrift für französische Sprache und Literatur* 106: 223-240.
Koch, Peter, and Wulf Oesterreicher
1985   Sprache der Nähe – Sprache der Distanz. Mündlichkeit und Schriftlichkeit im Spannungsfeld von Sprachtheorie und Sprachgeschichte. *Romanistisches Jahrbuch* 36: 15-43.
1990   *Gesprochene Sprache in der Romania: Französisch, Italienisch, Spanisch.* Tübingen: Niemeyer.

Kotschi, Thomas
　　1985　　　Einleitung. In: Gülich and Kotschi (eds.): 1-18.
Kristol, Andres Max
　　1992　　　'Que dea! Mettes le chapron, paillard, comme tu parles a prodome!' La représentation de l'oralité dans les Manières de langage du XIVe/XVe siècle. *Romanistisches Jahrbuch* 43: 35-64.
Lang, Jürgen
　　1993　　　Frage und Fragehandlung. *Romanistisches Jahrbuch* 44: 43-56.
Lausberg, Heinrich
　　^{3}1990　　　*Handbuch der literarischen Rhetorik: Eine Grundlegung der Literaturwissenschaft.* Dritte Auflage. Stuttgart: Steiner.
Lebsanft, Franz
　　1984　　　'¿Quien te mostro esto? – ¿*Quien*? Ellas.' Untersuchungen zur Echofrage und zu ihrem Gebrauch in der 'Celestina'. In: Francisco J. Oroz Arizcuren (ed.). *Navicula Tubingensis. Studia in honorem Antonii Tovar.* Tübingen: Narr, 277-289.
Lerch, Eugen
　　1934　　　*Historische französische Syntax. Bd. III: Modalität.* Leipzig: O.R. Reisland.
Luckmann, Thomas
　　1984　　　Das Gespräch. In: Stierle and Warning (eds.): 49-63.
Maury, Nicole
　　1973　　　Observations sur les formes syntaxiques et mélodiques de l'interrogation dite totale. *The French Review* 47: 302-311.
Meibauer, Jörg
　　1986　　　*Rhetorische Fragen.* Tübingen: Niemeyer.
　　1987a　　　Probleme einer Theorie des Satzmodus. In: Meibauer (ed.): 1-21.
　　1987b　　　Zur Form und Funktion von Echofragen. In: Rosengren (ed.): 335-356.
　　1991　　　Existenzimplikaturen bei rhetorischen w-Fragen. In: Reis and Rosengren (eds.): 223-242.
Meibauer, Jörg (ed.)
　　1987　　　*Satzmodus zwischen Grammatik und Pragmatik. Referate anläßlich der 8. Jahrestagung der Deutschen Gesellschaft für Sprachwissenschaft. Heidelberg. 1986.* Tübingen: Niemeyer.
Ménard, Philippe
　　1976　　　*Manuel du français du moyen âge: Syntaxe de l'ancien français.* Nouvelle édition entièrement refondue. Bordeaux: Sobodi.
Meng, Katharina
　　1994　　　Die Entwicklung der Dialogfähigkeit bei Kindern. In: Fritz and Hundsnurscher (eds.): 377-392.

Merritt, Marilyn
    1976   On questions following questions in service encounters. *Language in Society* 5: 315-357.
Mey, Jacob L. (ed.)
    1986   *Language and Discourse: Test and Protest. A Festschrift for Petr Sgall.* Amsterdam/Philadelphia: Benjamins.
Meyer, Michel (ed.)
    1988   *Questions and Questioning.* Berlin/New York: de Gruyter.
Moeschler, Jacques
    1992   Une, deux ou trois négations? *Langue française* 94: 8-25.
    1994   Das Genfer Modell der Gesprächsanalyse. In: Fritz and Hundsnurscher (eds.): 69-94.
Morel, Mary-Annick
    1997   Corrélation entre forme syntaxique et intonative de la question et forme de la réponse. In: *Dialoganalyse V. Referate der 5. Arbeitstagung Paris 1994.* Herausgegeben von Etienne Petri unter Mitarbeit von Danielle Laroche-Bouvy und Sorin Stati. Tübingen: Niemeyer, 285-296.
Muller, Claude
    1991   *La négation en français. Syntaxe, sémantique et éléments de comparaison avec les autres langues romanes.* Genève: Droz.
Noomen, Willem
    1968   Le 'Jeu d'Adam'. Etude descriptive et analytique. *Romania* 89: 145-193.
Oksaar, Els
    1981   Kommunikative Akte und Textanalyse am Beispiel von dialogischen Erzähltexten. *Zeitschrift für Germanistische Mediävistik* 9: 129-151.
Padučeva, Elena V.
    1986   Question-Answer Correspondence and the Semantics of Questions. In: Mey (ed.): 373-382.
Parret, Herman
    1988   The epistemics of the question-answer sequence and its psycho-pragmatic limitations. In: Meyer (ed.): 280-303.
Plantin, Christian
    1991   Question → argumentions → réponses. In: Kerbrat-Orecchioni (ed.): 63-85.
Rehbock, Helmut
    1984   Rhetorische Fragen im Gespräch. In: Dieter Cherubim, Helmut Henne and Helmut Rehbock (eds.). *Gespräche zwischen Alltag und Literatur. Beiträge zur germanistischen Gesprächsforschung.* Tübingen: Niemeyer, 151-179.
    1985   Herausfordernde Fragen. Zur Dialogrhetorik von Entscheidungsfragen. In: Helmut Sucharowski (ed.). *Gesprächsforschung im Vergleich. Analysen zur Bonner Runde nach der Hessenwahl 1982.* Tübingen: Niemeyer, 177-227.

1987 Arten der Antworterwartung in Ergänzungsfragen. In: Rosengren (ed.): 357-384.

1992 Fragen stellen – Zur Interpretation des Interrogativsatzmodus. In: Rosengren (ed.): 173-211.

Reis, Marga, and Inger Rosengren (eds.)

1991 *Fragesätze und Fragen.* Tübingen: Niemeyer.

Reis, Marga

1991 Echo w-Sätze und Echo w-Fragen. In: Reis and Rosengren (eds.): 49-76.

Rémi-Giraud, Sylvianne

1991 Question et assertion. De la morpho-syntaxe à la pragmatique. In: Kerbrat-Orecchioni (ed.): 39-62.

Renchon, Hector

1967 *Etudes de syntaxe descriptive. Vol. II. La syntaxe de l'interrogation.* Bruxelles: Palais des Académies.

Rosengren, Inger

1992 Zur Grammatik und Pragmatik der Exklamation. In: Rosengren (ed.): 263-306.

Rosengren, Inger (ed.)

1987 *Sprache und Pragmatik. Lunder Symposium 1986.* Lund: Almqvist & Wiksell.

1992 *Satz und Illokution. Bd. I.* Tübingen: Niemeyer.

Sacks, Harvey, Emanuel A. Schegloff, and Gail Jefferson

1974 A simplest systematics for the organization of turn-taking for conversation. *Language* 50: 696-735.

Schlieben-Lange, Brigitte

1976 Für eine historische Analyse von Sprechakten. In: Heinrich Weber and Harald Weydt (eds.). *Sprachtheorie und Pragmatik. Akten des 10. Linguistischen Kolloquiums. Tübingen 1975.* Tübingen: Niemeyer, 113-119.

1979 Ai las – Que planhs? Ein Versuch der historischen Gesprächsanalyse am Flamenca-Roman. *Romanistische Zeitschrift für Literaturgeschichte* 3: 1-30.

1982 Für eine Geschichte von Schriftlichkeit und Mündlichkeit. *Zeitschrift für Literaturwissenschaft und Linguistik* 12: 104-118.

1983 *Traditionen des Sprechens. Elemente einer pragmatischen Sprachgeschichtsschreibung.* Stuttgart: Kohlhammer.

1985 Fragen über Fragen. Koreferat zum Beitrag von Wolf-Dieter Stempel und Renate Fischer. In: Gülich and Kotschi (eds.): 269-276.

Schlieben-Lange, Brigitte, and Harald Weydt (mit Beiträgen von E. Coseriu und H.-U. Gumbrecht)

1979 Streitgespräch zur Historizität von Sprechakten. *Linguistische Berichte* 60: 65-78.

Schmeja, Wendelin
1974 Der 'Sensus Moralis' im Adamsspiel. *Zeitschrift für romanische Philologie* 90: 41-72.
Schoenthal, Gisela
1979 Sprechakttheorie und Konversationsalanyse. In: Jürgen Dittmann (ed.): *Arbeiten zur Konversationsanalyse*. Tübingen: Niemeyer, 44-72.
Schulze, Alfred
1888 *Der altfranzösische direkte Fragesatz*. Leipzig: Hirzel.
Schwitalla, Johannes
1984 Textliche und kommunikative Funktionen rhetorischer Fragen. *Zeitschrift für Germanistische Linguistik* 12: 131-155.
Searle, John R.
1969 *Speech Acts. An Essay in the Philosophy of Language*. Cambridge: Cambridge University Press.
1979 *Expression and Meaning. Studies in the Theory of Speech Acts*. Cambridge: Cambridge University Press.
Seelbach, Dieter
1985 Fokussierung mit der *est-ce que*-Frage. In: Gülich and Kotschi (eds.): 277-312.
Selig, Maria
1997 'Mündlichkeit' in mittelalterlichen Texten. In: Martin-Dietrich Gleßgen and Franz Lebsanft (eds.): *Alte und neue Philologie*. Tübingen: Niemeyer, 201-225.
Sitta, Horst
1980 Pragmatisches Sprachverstehen und pragmatikorientierte Sprachgeschichte. In: Sitta (ed.): 23-34.
Sitta, Horst (ed.)
1980 *Ansätze zu einer pragmatischen Sprachgeschichte. Zürcher Kolloquium 1978*. Tübingen: Niemeyer.
Stempel, Wolf-Dieter
1984 Bemerkungen zur Kommunikation im Alltagsgespräch. In: Stierle and Warning (eds.): 151-169.
1993 La 'modernité' des débuts: la rhétorique de l'oralité chez Chrétien de Troyes. In: Maria Selig, Barbara Frank and Jörg Hartmann (eds.). *Le passage à l'écrit des langues romanes*. Tübingen: Narr, 275-298.
1994a Ceci n'est pas un conte, la rhétorique du conversationnel. *Littérature* 93: 66-79.
1994b Stylistique et interaction verbale. In: Georges Molinié and Pierre Cahné (eds.): *Qu'est-ce que le style?* Paris: PUF, 313-330.

1995   Bewegung nach innen. Neue Ansätze poetischer Sprache bei Rutebeuf. In: Wolf-Dieter Stempel (ed.): *Musique naturele. Interpretationen zur französischen Lyrik des Spätmittelalters*. München: Fink, 41-73.

Stempel, Wolf-Dieter, and Renate Fischer
1985   Die französische Intonationsfrage in alltagsrhetorischer Perspektive. In: Gülich and Kotschi (eds.): 239-268.

Stenström, Anna-Brita
1988   Questioning in Conversation. In: Meyer (ed.): 304-325.

Stetter, Christian
1991   Text und Textur. Hat die Sprechakttheorie eine historische Dimension? In: Busse (ed.): 67-81.

Stierle, Karlheinz
1984   Gespräch und Diskurs. Ein Versuch im Blick auf Montaigne, Descartes und Pascal. In: Stierle and Warning (eds.): 297-334.

Stierle, Karlheinz, and Rainer Warning (eds.)
1984   *Das Gespräch*. München: Fink.

Traverso, Véronique
1991   Question et commentaire dans la conversation familière. In: Kerbrat-Orecchioni (ed.): 201-223.

Walton, Douglas N.
1988   Question-asking fallacies. In: Meyer (ed.): 195-221.

Wandruszka, Mario
1970   Réflexions sur la polymorphie de l'interrogation française. In: *Phonétique et linguistique romanes. Mélanges offerts à Georges Straka. Vol. II*. Lyon/ Strasbourg: Société de Linguistique Romane Lyon/Strasbourg, 65-77.

Weddige, Hilkert
[2]1992   *Einführung in die germanistische Mediävistik*. Zweite, durchgesehene Auflage. München: Beck.

Weigand, Edda
1988   Historische Sprachpragmatik am Beispiel: Gesprächsstrukturen im Nibelungenlied. *Zeitschrift für deutsches Altertum und deutsche Literatur* 117: 159-173.

Wenz, Gunther
1984   Sprechen und Handeln. In: Stierle and Warning (eds.): 77-84.

Weydt, Harald
1985   Zu den Fragetypen im Französischen. Koreferat zum Beitrag von Dieter Seelbach. In: Gülich and Kotschi (eds.): 313-322.

Wunderlich, Dieter
1976   *Studien zur Sprechakttheorie*. Frankfurt: Suhrkamp.

Dialoge im Rechtsprotokoll
Ein Wetzlarer Erbstreit a. 1309 und die Entstehung einer neuen Textsorte

Hans Ramge
Justus Liebig University, Giessen

Abstract

In an undated parchment document that can nevertheless be traced to the year 1309, the jurors of the free city of Wetzlar testify their knowledge of an inheritance argument among members of an influential urban family and of the development of initiated, amicable arbitration proceedings. As these finally failed, the text was obviously written to be presented at the royal court of justice that was ultimately to pass judgement. In this sense, this text is a kind of record of proceedings and probably the oldest one in German to contain dialogue sequences on a large scale. Here, the opponents present their legal positions in the form of argument and counter-argument.

Fortunately, two precursory records still exist alongside the document, in which the legal case is presented from the point of view of both parties. By comparing the two versions it is possible to reconstruct reasonably accurately how the authors solve the new communicative task of writing a record that is part of increasingly complex legal proceedings in the late Middle Ages. This is reflected in the transition from orality to literacy. In the present case, the formal adaptation to the pattern of medieval private documents is striking.

A comparison of the versions shows that the final text is not only intended to maintain the balance between the statements of either party, but to achieve as high a level of referential unambiguity, legal clarity, optimal comprehensibility of the text as possible, by means of numerous, albeit mostly minor, rephrasings of the earlier versions. An interesting point is that the earlier versions already pay special attention to the correct representation of direct speech. The seven dialogues follow the same scheme: appeal – reaction – consequences. But they situate each conversation in its personal, local and temporal situation. The apparent authenticity of a (presumed) reality of the conversational situation is mainly reduced to a linguistic construction of the exact legal position. At the same time, and to a greater extent, the relevant sociocommunicative structures of each dialogue situation are modelled in a sharp and nuanced way. The communicative function of the dialogues is presumably to guarantee the correctness and objectivity of the recorded events in relation to the totality of the incident as far as they are legally relevant to the judgement. In this respect, the dialogues mirror only partially real orality and are already modelled to fulfil the legal purpose of the record. The source material mirrors an important aspect of the genesis of the new text type. Oral legal proceedings, common up to that time, continue to have enough influence for the dialogues to be recorded in direct speech. In later records, indirect speech prevails.

1. Mittelalterliche Dialoge in nicht-fiktionalen Texten

Wenn als eine der Hauptaufgaben der historischen Pragmatik gefordert ist, Formen und Modi dialogischen Handelns der Vergangenheit in Gleichartigkeit und Differenz zu heutigen Dialogstrukturen zu rekonstruieren (Fritz 1994), so stellt sich, soweit damit auch die mündliche Gesprächswirklichkeit gemeint ist, zunächst die Frage nach den empirischen Daten. Die alte Streitfrage, inwieweit sich in schriftlichen historischen Quellen Reflexe (regionalen oder lokalen) mündlichen Sprachgebrauchs aufspüren lassen, pflegt für ältere literate Dialogformen unter dem Gesichtspunkt des Grades der Authentizität behandelt zu werden. Soweit damit gewissermaßen die Abbildung von real Gesprochenem gemeint ist, ist natürlich kein schriftlicher Text (jenseits von Transkriptionen) im strengen Sinn authentisch, weisen auch moderne Texte, die sich bewusst um Nähe zur gesprochenen Sprache bemühen, bekanntlich nur sehr vage Annäherungswerte auf (Betten 1985, 1995). Direkte Rede wird nicht einmal in gesprochener Sprache wirklich als wörtliches Zitat wiedergegeben (von Roncador 1988), sondern regelhaft der Sprecherperspektive angepasst. Die Frage nach der Authentizität lässt sich daher eher aus der Perspektive des schriftlichen Textes angehen: Inwieweit formuliert der Autor Dialoge mit dem (erkennbaren) Anspruch, damit dialogische Ereignisse der realen Welt textlich zu repräsentieren? Insofern hängt die Frage der Authentizität zunächst von der Textsorte ab, in der die Dialoge auftreten.

Dialoge im Rechtsprotokoll 373

Die an mittelalterlichen Dialogstrukturen interessierte Dialogforschung steht vor dem Problem, dass es erst seit der frühen Neuzeit dialoghaltige Quellen nichtfiktionalen Charakters in größerem Umfang gibt. Für die Zeit davor hat man, von wenigen Sondertexten wie z. B. dem ahd. Gesprächsbüchlein abgesehen, hauptsächlich auf literarische Dialoge, wie sie im *Hildebrandslied* und im *Nibelungenlied* wiedergegeben sind, zurückgegriffen und musste sozusagen hoffen, jedenfalls plausibel machen, dass diese Dialoge in bestimmten Aspekten der kommunikativen Realität der Zeit entsprechen (Bax 1991, v. Polenz 1981, Weigand 1988), was ja schon aus Gründen der Verständlichkeit und der Akzeptierbarkeit durch zeitgenössische Rezipienten ziemlich wahrscheinlich ist.

Darüber hinaus gibt es aber zumindest für das späte Mittelalter mehrere Quellengruppen mit dem Anspruch, reale Sachverhalte wiederzugeben, die nicht nur vereinzelt dialogische Sequenzen enthalten: Rechtstexte wie Gerichtsurteile und Weistümer, Realität Erzählendes wie Chroniken. Sie sind, soweit ich sehe, bisher als Quellen für die historische Pragmatik und Dialogforschung erst ansatzweise wahrgenommen worden (Sonderegger 1990 für Chroniken; vgl. Werkmüller 1972 für Weistümer). Neuerdings hat Arend Mihm (1995) auf „die Textsorte Gerichtsprotokoll im Spätmittelalter und ihr(en) Zeugniswert für die Geschichte der gesprochenen Sprache" aufmerksam gemacht und dabei die überlieferten direkten Reden in Gerichtsprotokollen untersucht.

Es ist nun allerdings sehr die Frage, welche Art von Authentizität man Dialogwiedergaben auch in diesen durchaus realiengebundenen Quellengruppen zubilligen darf, besonders wenn es um die (angebliche) Wiedergabe in direkter Rede geht. Die Vorannahme scheint plausibel, dass die Modi der Wiedergabe mündlicher Rede funktional bedingt und gebunden sind an der generellen Funktion und der kommunikativen Intention des Gesamttextes, also der Textsorte. Die Wiedergabe spiegelt dann als real wahrgenommene gesprochene Dialoge in zu bestimmender Weise auf der Grundlage globaler Zwecke der Textsorte.

Im Folgenden befasse ich mich mit einem Rechtstext, nämlich einem Schöffenprotokoll, aus dem Anfang des 14. Jahrhunderts, das sieben Sequenzen mit direkten Reden enthält, die in die Darstellung eines Erbstreits eingebettet sind. Wie noch zu zeigen ist, ist dieser Text ein Rechtsprotokoll und damit m. W. das älteste Gerichtsprotokoll in deutscher Sprache, das als eine Art Verlaufsprotokoll direkte Reden in mehr als marginalem Umfang enthält. Unter dieser Voraussetzung sind wir damit in der glücklichen Lage, die Genese einer Textsorte (des Gerichtsprotokolls) mit der Genese der Wiedergabe direkter Reden in nicht-fiktionalen Zusammenhängen untersuchen zu können. Wir können damit aus genetischer Perspektive die Frage reflektieren, wozu und warum man für Rechtsprotokolle Dialoge und direkte Reden zu brauchen glaubt.

2. Der Rechtsfall

Das *Protokoll der Wetzlarer schöffen über den rechtsstreit zwischen Konrad Waldschmidt und seiner schwägerin Demudis* (Wiese 1911: Nr. 489) ist ein schwieriges, aber in mehrfacher Hinsicht einzigartiges Dokument. Da der Text in seinen verschiedenen Fassungen genau dokumentiert und in seinen historischen und juristischen Zusammenhängen rekonstruiert ist (Ramge 1997), beschränke ich mich hier auf eine zusammenfassende Darstellung:

Mittels einer gesiegelten Pergamenturkunde beglaubigen die Schöffen von Wetzlar, dass sie in Bezug auf den Streit zwischen Conrad Waldschmidt und seiner Schwägerin Demud und deren Sohn Hencle über die Teilung eines Gutes, das ihr Vater bzw. Schwiegervater Heinrich Waldschmidt, früherer Vogt von Wetzlar, hinterlassen hat, von beiden Seiten rechtsgültige Auskunft erfahren haben (*kuntschaft irvarin von bedin sithin in dose wiȝ*).

Nach dem Tode der Witwe Heinrich Waldschmidts setzt sich Conrad in den Besitz des Landguts, auf das auch Demud für sich und ihren Sohn Hencle Anspruch erhebt. Conrad verweigert die Herausgabe und wird deshalb von Demud vor das städtische Schöffengericht geladen. Vor Gericht erklärt sich Conrad mit einer schiedsgerichtlichen oder rechtsprozessualen Entscheidung (*mit minnen odir mit reitte*) einverstanden, verschwindet dann aber für elf Wochen und schickt auch seinen Neffen Hencle gegen den Willen Demuds nach Speyer.

Das Schöffengericht erhält nun *kuntschaft* über eine Reihe von Treffen zwischen den verfeindeten Parteien, in denen ein gütlicher Ausgleich angestrebt wird. Die Treffen finden in Anwesenheit ehrbarer Zeugen, Bürger und z. T. Schöffen in Wetzlar, statt und werden von diesen vor Gericht berichtet und bezeugt: In einem ersten Treffen zwischen Conrad und Hencle vor engen Verwandten als Zeugen erklärt sich Conrad zur Teilung bereit, und Hencle erklärt daraufhin, dass er sich den Beschlüssen seines Onkels unterwerfen wolle. In einem weiteren Treffen mit neutralen Zeugen an einem neutralen öffentlichen Ort wird das sinngemäß wiederholt. Danach kommt es an dem zentralen Rechtsort der Stadt, zwischen Dom und Gerichtsplatz, zu einem Streitgespräch zwischen Demud und Conrad, in dem sie ihn um Teilung mit ihr, ihrem Sohn Hencle und ihren anderen Kindern bittet. Conrad weist das scharf zurück und erklärt sich zur Teilung nur bereit, wenn er rechtlich dazu verpflichtet werde (*von reitte*) und wenn er von dem Miterben dazu aufgefordert werde. Ein zweiter Versuch einer gütlichen Einigung, den Demuds Schwager und andere Verwandte (wieder in der Nähe des Domes) unternehmen, scheitert daran, dass Conrad seine Rechtsauffassung wiederholt. Schließlich wird von gemeinsamen Verwandten Conrads und Hencles bezeugt, dass ein Einigungsversuch vor Conrads Haus stattgefunden hat, in dem Hencle um die Teilung des Guts bittet. Conrad erklärt sich damit unter dem Hinweis einverstanden, dass Hencle zuvor *zu Rome* gewesen sein müsse.

Abschließend beglaubigen die Schöffen, dass die vorgenannten Zeugen ihre Aussage beschworen haben.

Die Schöffen dokumentieren also einen Erbstreit und das darüber veranlasste gütliche Schiedsverfahren, wobei sich die Dialogsequenzen vor allem in den Phasen der verschiedenen Treffen finden. Der Erbstreit findet in einer der führenden Wetzlarer Familien statt mit vielfachen und engen verwandtschaftlichen Versippungen, auch mit den Schöffen und Ratsherren der Zeit. Der wichtigste Schöffe der Zeit, Ernst von Nauborn, der bei dem Schiedsverfahren eine wichtige Rolle spielt, ist zugleich Schwiegervater Conrad Waldschmidts und Demuds (über deren verstorbenen zweiten Ehemann Heinrich). Es ist aber nach den Rechtsnormen der Zeit völlig klar, dass Conrad als der älteste (und überlebende) Sohn der verstorbenen Waldschmidts der einzige Erbe ist und dass streng rechtlich weder Demud noch Hencle (über seinen verstorbenen Vater) einen Erbanspruch haben.

Der undatierte Text ist mit sehr hoher Wahrscheinlichkeit Anfang 1309 geschrieben worden und diente als Beweismittel für eine Entscheidung des königlichen Hofgerichts (Ramge 1997: 307-309), das erwartungsgemäß zugunsten Conrads entschied. Vermutlich hatte sich eine der Streitparteien an das Hofgericht gewandt und die Schöffen zu einer Bestandsaufnahme veranlasst. Insofern kann man davon sprechen, dass hier eine Vorgeschichte und ein Verfahrensablauf protokolliert werden. Dieses beglaubigte Protokoll repräsentiert ein bestimmtes Stadium im Verlaufe des Prozesses: Das bis dahin mündlich geführte Rechtsverfahren wird in eine schriftliche Form überführt. Die Schrift dient Zwecken einer räumlich, zeitlich und institutionell entfernten Instanz, dem Hofgericht.

Für die Beteiligten ist dies offenbar eine neue kommunikative Aufgabe, die zu lösen Problemlösungsstrategien fordert. Ungewöhnlich, aber für unsere Zwecke überaus hilfreich ist, dass zwei konzeptartige Vorfassungen des Textes erhalten sind, die Aussagen jeweils aus der Sicht einer Streitpartei enthalten. So lässt sich die Genese der Endfassung über den Textvergleich sehr genau rekonstruieren: Wir können beobachten,

– wie das Protokoll zusammengestellt wurde,

– wie Textverfasser und Schreiber[1] mit dem ‚Protokollieren' der direkten Reden umgegangen sind,

und gewinnen so einen Einblick in die kommunikativen Prinzipien und Maximen, die eine funktionale Bestimmung der Dialogsequenzen im Rahmen der Textorganisation erlauben.

3. Konfigurierung des Textes

Die historischen und rechtshistorischen Zusammenhänge rechtfertigen die Annahme, dass der Text als Beweismittel für das Hofgerichtsurteil verfertigt wurde. Der generelle Zweck des Textes muss deshalb in einer neutral-‚objektiven' Darstellung dessen liegen, was sich bis dahin ereignet hat: Die Schöffen müssen in ihrem Text ‚unparteiisch' sein in dem Sinne, dass Konsens über den Gang der Ereignisse und zentralen Intentionen und Rechtspositionen der Streitparteien besteht – als Grundlage für das Hofgerichtsurteil. Wie lösen die Schöffen und ihr Schreiber diese neue kommunikative Aufgabe? Betrachtet man Vor- und Endfassungen zusammen, so sieht man, dass drei Prozeduren angewendet werden: Anpassung an das Urkunden-Modell, Protokollierung der Parteipositionen, umstrukturierende Neukonfiguration in der Endfassung.

3.1 Anpassung an das Urkunden-Modell

Der Text ist auf Pergament geschrieben, sehr sorgfältig in gotischer Kursive, war mit Siegeln versehen und entspricht nicht nur mit dieser äußeren Form, sondern auch im Aufbau den Privaturkunden des mittelhessischen Raumes im 14. Jh.: Zwischen Eingangsprotokoll und Eschatokoll finden sich die *narratio* und als formales Substitut der *dispositio* die Bezeugung der Schiedsgerichtsszenen. Insofern kann man sagen, dass Textverfasser und Schreiber in extremer Weise bemüht waren, die kommunikative Aufgabe durch innere und äußere Anpassung an den Modus, wie Privaturkunden verfasst wurden, zu lösen. In formaler Hinsicht gibt es zwei charakteristische Abweichungen: Im Eingangsprotokoll fehlt die *publicatio*, im Schlussprotokoll die Datumzeile. Das Fehlen dieser Informationen erschwert die historische Verortung des Textes, ist aber andererseits auch Beweis dafür, dass es sich nicht um eine echte Urkunde handelt, sondern um ein Protokoll. Das wird inhaltlich dadurch bestätigt, dass anstelle der verfügenden *dispositio* die Wiedergabe der Zeugenaussagen erfolgt: Das Protokoll tritt formal als Quasi-Urkunde auf.

3.2 Protokollierung der Parteipositionen

Von den beiden konzeptartigen Vorfassungen, flüchtig auf grob beschnittenem Pergament geschrieben, gibt die eine die Position Demuds (und Hencles) wieder, die andere die Conrads. Obwohl in der ersten, längeren auch eingangs behauptet wird, die Schöffen hätten die Kundschaft *von bedin sitthen* erfahren, wird das Schlussprotokoll mit der Formulierung eröffnet: *Dese geʒcuichnusse vnd kundschaft sint geleydit von vir Demude wegen*, d.h. die Gesamtheit der Bezeugungen und verbindlichen Aussagen wurden auf Veranlassung Frau Demuds getroffen. Hier werden nach der *narratio* nur zwei Schiedsgerichtsszenen bezeugt: die Szene zwischen Conrad und Hencle, in der Conrad zu teilen einwilligt, wenn Hencle zuvor *zu Rome* gewesen wäre, und das Streitgespräch zwischen Conrad und Demud vor dem Wetzlarer Dom.

Der zweite Vorentwurf stellt – mit gleichem Eingangsprotokoll, aber ohne *narratio* – die Dinge aus der Sicht Conrads dar, indem die beiden Gesprächssequenzen wiedergegeben werden, die auf die Unterwerfung Hencles vor seinem Onkel hinauslaufen. Dieser Text endet mit *Dose vrkunde hait geseit Conradis geʒcuich gen vrkunde vir Demude*, d.h. die Gesamtheit der Zeugen Conrads sagt das gegen die Aussage Frau Demuds aus.

Auch diese höchst unterschiedlichen Aussagen der Parteien wurden vor dem Schöffengericht gemacht und von diesem durch Siegel beglaubigt, so dass es sich keineswegs um eine informelle Vorbefragung handelt. Andererseits wird durch die konzeptartige Form der beiden Texte deutlich, dass von Anfang an eine Vereinigung der beiden Parteiaussagen intendiert war, d.h. die Endfassung ist als ein für einen besonderen Zweck überarbeitetes Protokoll zu rekonstruieren.

3.3 Umstrukturierung und Konfiguration der Endfassung

Beide Protokoll-Versionen werden in der Endfassung addiert und zugleich verändert. Dabei bedient sich der Textautor dreierlei Verfahren:

– *Addition:* Indem die jeweils von einer Partei (im Konzept) vorgetragenen Szenen einfach addiert werden, wird ein logischer Widerspruch in Kauf genommen: Es ist – in der Endfassung – durchaus unklar, warum nach der eingangs erklärten Teilungsbereitschaft Conrads und der Unterwerfung Hencles unter die Beschlüsse seines Onkels dann noch die Teilungsszenen mit Demud und die letzte mit der *Rom*-Formel notwendig sind. Da kein Hinweis auf die parteiliche Herkunft gegeben wird, stehen die einzelnen schiedsgerichtlichen Szenen zunächst jeweils einzeln für sich als scheinbar neutrale Berichte.

– *Hinzufügung:* Die zweite Teilungsverweigerung Conrads gegenüber den Verwandten Demuds wird neu eingeführt. Damit stehen zwei Szenen mit Einigungskonzept (Teilung und Unterwerfung Hencles) und zwei Szenen mit Dissenserklärung (Conrad gegen Demud) einander gegenüber: Die durch die doppelte Hencle-Unterwerfung vorstellbare Idee, die Einigung sei gesicherter als der Dissens zwischen Demud und Conrad, wird dadurch formal neutralisiert.

– *Umordnung:* Die Szenenfolge wird umgeordnet, indem die in Demuds Protokoll als erste genannte Szene zwischen Conrad und Hencle mit der *Rom*-Formel ans Ende der Gesamtsequenz gerückt wird. Indem sie inhaltlich einerseits die grundsätzliche Teilungsbereitschaft Conrads (mit Hencle) signalisiert, sie andererseits an eine bestimmte Voraussetzung knüpft (s. Abb. 1), können beide Parteien ihren Standpunkt in dieser Sequenz vertreten finden: Sie nimmt also als letzte nicht nur eine hervorgehobene, sondern auch eine vermittelnde Stellung ein. Zugleich wird damit aber die durch die Partei-Protokolle suggerierte zeitliche Abfolge der Szenen zugunsten dieser Pointierung aufgehoben.

Die Endfassung ist also offensichtlich mit großem Bedacht zusammengestellt, strukturell auf Gleichgewichtigkeit hin komponiert. Weder die Argumentationskohärenz noch die realen Zeitabfolgen bestimmen dabei die Darstellungsstruktur, sondern formale Symmetrie- und Steigerungsprinzipien, die einerseits die neutrale Position der Textverantwortlichen (der Schöffen), andererseits die strukturelle Konfiguration des Geschehenskomplexes textsymbolisch herauszustellen bemüht sind. Das deutet darauf hin, dass der mutmaßliche Zweck des Textes, nämlich Grundlage für die Hofgerichtsentscheidung zu sein, die Gestaltungsintention der Textautoren bestimmt hat: Die Struktur des Rechtsproblems, nicht dessen (zufällige) Ablaufdetails definieren den Text als rechtsrelevanten Text.

Wenn dies das Organisationsprinzip des Textes ist, dann steht von vornherein außer Frage, dass die wiedergegebenen Dialoge und die direkten Reden unter der Vorgabe der Rechtsrelevanz zu analysieren sind. Wir brauchen keinesfalls zu bezweifeln, dass die reportierten Reden in realen Gesprächssituationen stattgefunden haben; aber es steht auch hier von vornherein zu vermuten, dass sie bewusst und mit Blick auf bestimmte Funktionen gestaltet sind.

4. Struktur der Dialogsequenzen

Die folgende Zusammenstellung präsentiert die direkten Reden des Textes mit ihren vorangehenden Kontexten[2] in der Endfassung A (s. Abb. 3); entsprechend

werden parallel die Formen der Sequenzen in den Vorfassungen B und C
(s. Abb. 4) geboten.
  Die formale Struktur der Dialogsequenzen ist zunächst dadurch gekennzeichnet, dass in den Sequenzen (3) bis (7) Rede und Gegenrede tatsächlich in Form direkter Reden wiedergegeben werden, wobei jede mit *sprach/spreche(n)* angekündigt ist, während in den Sequenzen (1) und (2) die Dialogeröffnung durch ein handlungsbezeichnendes Verb (*hiʒ, badin*) charakterisiert wird und nur die Antwort in direkter Form angegeben wird. Hierin spiegelt sich zunächst die Differenz der Einbettung von Dialogen in die *narratio* ((1) und (2)) und den Kern des Textes, der Wiedergabe der Befriedungsversuche.
  Das insoweit erkennbare Muster eines in Zweierschritten modellierten Dialogs wird allerdings in Sequenz (3) durchbrochen, indem hier ein dreigliedriges Muster (Aufforderung: Hencle *hiʒe vnd muthe,* d.h. ,forderte und begehrte' – Akzeptieren der Aufforderung durch Conrad – Entschuldigung Hencles) realisiert wird. Legt man ein solches Muster zugrunde, das die Schritte Aufforderung (AUFF), Reagieren (REAG) und die Folgen (FOLG) der Reaktion umfasst, lassen sich die Sequenzen wie in Abb. 2 analysieren.
  Es zeigt sich, dass im Rahmen dieser allgemeinen Dialogstruktur eine Fülle von verschiedenen Sprechhandlungen und Sequenzmustern möglich sind: Bitten/Auffordern, Akzeptieren/Ablehnen, Versprechen, Vorwerfen, Entschuldigen.
  Für unseren Zusammenhang ebenso wichtig sind aber zwei andere Beobachtungen:

– Conrad ist in allen Fällen (mit Ausnahme der 1. Sequenz) nicht nur an den Dialogen beteiligt, sondern darüber hinaus jeweils in der (formal) reagierenden Rolle. Sein Sprachhandlungsspektrum ist das umfangreichste. Indem jeder seiner Züge in direkter Rede wiedergegeben wird, tritt er in seinem Sprachhandeln besonders hervor und ist der scheinbar Initiativ-Aktive, obwohl er von der Grundstruktur her stets in der Reaktionsposition ist. Seine Position wird dadurch gesprächsstrukturell hervorgehoben – mit der Wirkung, dass damit auch der Rechtsanspruch erkennbar verteidigt wird.

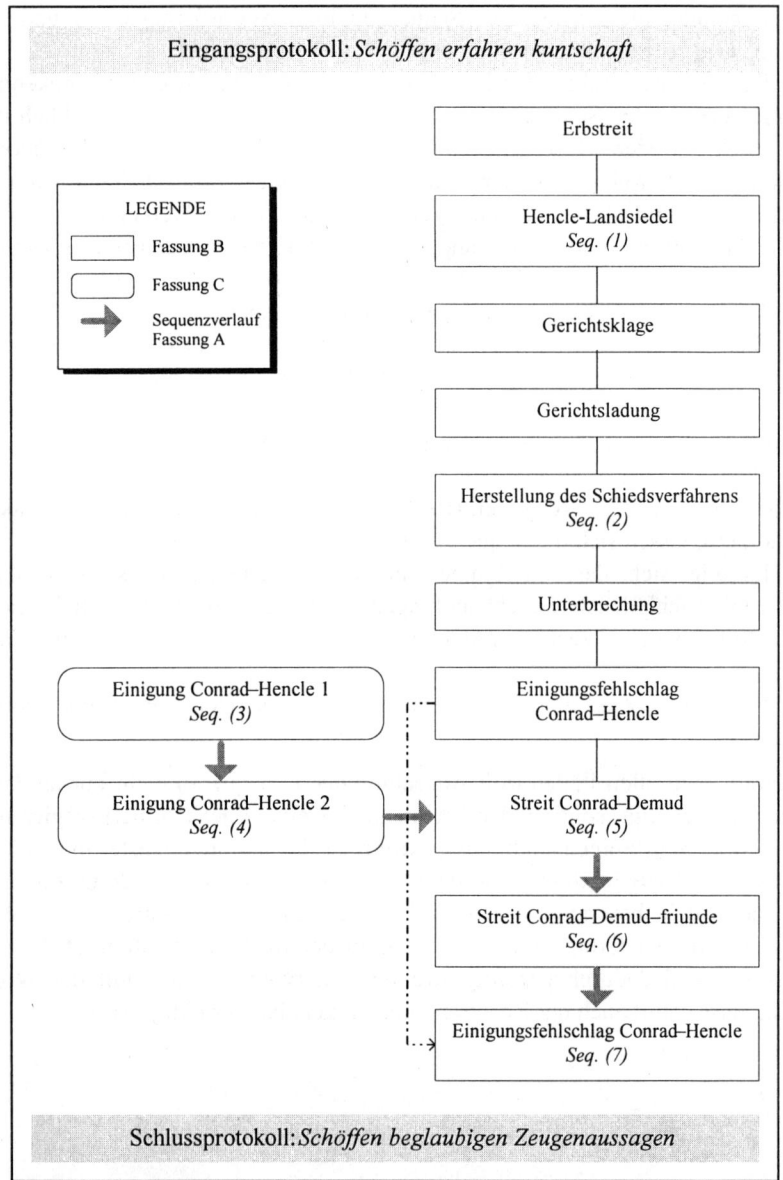

Abb. 1: Vorfassungen und Textkonfiguration

– Bei aller Variabilität im Einzelnen führt die rekonstruierbare Dialogbasis in Dreierschritten zu relativ statisch charakterisierten Handlungsabläufen. Indem meist zwei Positionen durch direkte Rede hervorgehoben werden, werden die antagonistischen Positionen klar und unzweideutig herausgearbeitet.

Mit Blick auf die zur Globalorganisation des Textes gewonnenen Einsichten kann man wohl unterstellen, dass mit der Präsentation in klar modellierten Dialogstrukturen besonders durch die direkten Reden die Positionen präzisiert und die allseitige Beteiligung Conrads herausgearbeitet werden soll. Auch unter diesem Gesichtspunkt kommt den direkten Reden also Anspruch auf eine erhöhte Aufmerksamkeit zu.

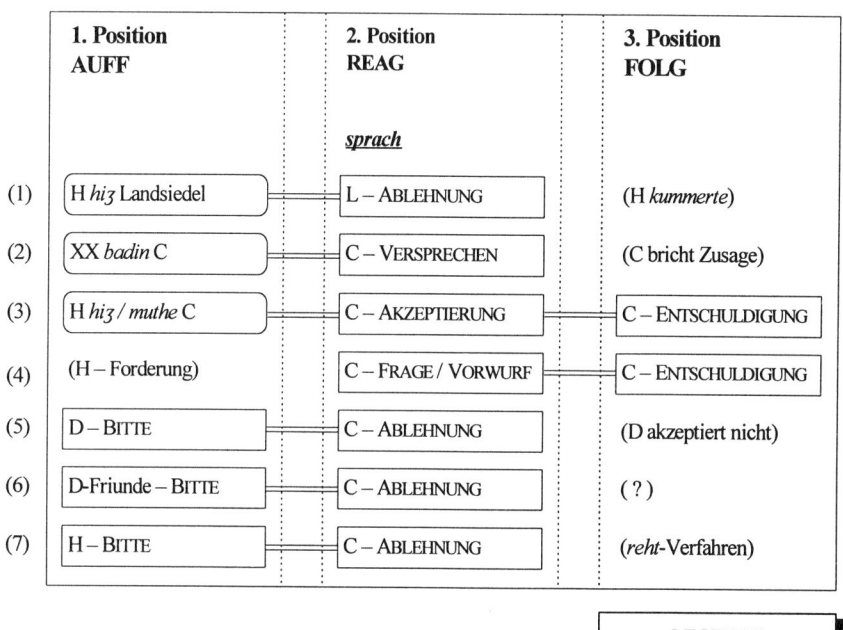

Abb. 2: Sequenzmuster

(1) A Z. 7-9
dů <u>quam</u> Hencle .
vn*d* <u>hiʒ</u> von dem lantsidelin des patis sin deil
dů <u>sprach</u> . der lantsidele .
ich entworthin desen pait . **dar ich ein geenwortthit han / vn*d* andirs neren** (dů ...)
(2) A Z. 14-18
dů <u>nam</u> in Her . Ernist / von Nuu*e*ren / sin sweihir / ...
vn*d* <u>badin</u> Conradin / daʒ
her sich liʒce / rittin mit . Henclen sines bruder sůne . vn*d* mit sin*er* muder/
dů <u>sprach</u> . Conrad .
Daʒ welich dun . tussen hy*e* . vn*d* fridage / mit minnen / odir mit reitte. (In ...)
(3) A Z. 26-29
Her Ernist von Nuu*e*ren ein scheffene / vn*d* . mauche / sin sůn . <u>sprechint</u> daz .
Hencle delunge <u>hiʒe</u> / von Conrade sime federin / vn*d* <u>muthe</u>
dů <u>sprach</u> . Conrad .
druwen / gerne deylich mit dir wanne daʒ du wilt
dů <u>sprach</u> . Henclo
federe mir ist leit daʒ ich dich irʒcornit han / ich inwil mit mime gude nith důn also dů wilt /
(4) A Z. 30-35
Nu <u>sprechint</u> andirwerbe . der ersam / man / Her Henrich . ʒoliner von / marbu*r*g ... daʒ
Conrad . waltsmeit . <u>spreche</u> . wider . Henclen . sines bruder sun . vor Her Heyneman*n*is huse. her Gerbratis / sůn.
sage neve . wy ist din wille nů . bist dů noch in dem můde . so dů leist were
dů <u>sprach</u> . Henclo /
Federe / Han ich dich irʒcornith / daʒ ist mir leith . ich inwil nit důn mit mime gude / vn*d* inwil vʒ dime rade nit gein . sunder ich wil důn na dime rade .
(5) A Z. 36-42
Nů andirwerbe <u>sprechit</u> . Her . Conrad . c*r*awe ... daʒ
vir Demud . Henclen . mudir . <u>spreche</u> . zů . Conrade . eris sůnes federin / vn*d* ereme / svagere / tussen / dem geritte / vn*d* dem windilsteynne / zů / wetflar /
Conrad . ich bedin dich . daʒ dů vollis deylin solich gůith / so dů deylin salt . mit mir vn*d* mit mime sů ne Henclin . vn*d* mit mine*n* kindin .
Dů <u>sprach</u> / Conrad
ich in/han mit dir nit zů deylinne . sundir ich wil deylin . mit deyme . ich von reitte deylen sal . wanne her mir zů /sprichit so ein reit ist /
(6) A Z. 43-48
Nů <u>sprichit</u> abir Her Conrad c*r*awe ... daz
Theoderich ... <u>quemen</u> ... vn*d* <u>sp*r*echin</u> von vir demude wegin /
Conrad . deyle . mit . Demude .
dů . <u>sprach</u> . Conrad .
Ich inbin ir nit deylunge schul/dich . sundir ich weiʒ wol daʒ ich deylin . sal . wanne mir der deylunge mudit mit dem ich deylin sal also reit ist . so deylen ich gerne mit eme /
(7) A Z. 49-57
Na desen redin . <u>sprichit</u> her . Ernist von . Nuu*e*ren . ... eymutliche . daʒ
Hencle . Conradis brudir sůn . <u>quam</u> vʒ siner mudir hůiz <u>gegangen</u> vor Conradis huis .vn*d* <u>sprach</u>
federe / ich bedin dich . daʒ dů mit mir deylis solich gůuit . so dů mit mir deylen . salt von reitte .
Dů <u>sprach</u> . Conraid
neve dů bist nů in eynnen andirn wech gevallen . ich sal gerne mit dir deylen . also dů mostis aber liber zů Rome dar vore sin .

Abb. 3: Sequenzen der Fassung A

Dialoge im Rechtsprotokoll 383

(1) B Z. 7-10
dů quam Henclin /
vnd hi3 von dem lantside / lin des patistis / sy deyl
dů sprach der lantsidele /
ich entworthen desen pait / aldar / dar ich ein bi3her geben vnd geentwortte han vnd andirs neren /
(Dů …)
(2) B Z. 15-18
dů nam in her Ernist sin sveir / vnd …
vnd badin in da3
her sich li3ce / ritthen mit sime (Neven) bruders sune / vnd siner muder
dů sprach / Conrad .
da3 wil ich dů thussen hye vnd fridage / mit minnen / odir mit reitthe / (in …)
(3) C Z. 6-9
Her Ernist (scheffininn) vnd mauche sin sůn sprechint da3 da3
henclo / deylunge hi3he / von Conrade sime federen / vnd muthe /
dů sprach Conrad
druwen . Gerne deylin ich mit dir wanne da3 du wilt /
dů sprach hencle
federe mir ist leit da3 ich dich ir3cornit hain / ich in wil mit mime Gude nit důn / dan also dů wilt /
(4) C Z. 10-14
Anderwerbe / sprechet / der esamer mann her henrich 3coler von / marburg … / da3
Conrad / der waltsmeit / spreche wider Henclo / sinen neven vor her Heynemanns hůis . her Gerbratis sůnis
sage neve / wy ist din wille nů / bist dů noch in dem můde / so dů leist were
dů sprach / henclo
federe / hain ich dich ir3cornit da3 ist mir leit ich inwil nit důn mit mime gude / vnd inwil v3 dime rade nit gein /
(5) B Z. 32-38
Andir werbe / sprichet her Conrad / crawe … da3
vir Demud / Henclin mudir / spreche wider Conraden / eris sůns federin vnd erin / svagir / tussen / dem gerittin / vnd dem windilsteyne / zů / wetflar /
Conrad . ich bedin dich / da3 dů wollis deylin / solich guit so dů deylin salt mit mir vnd mit mime sůne henclin vnd mit minen / kinden /
dů sprach / Conrad
ich in hain mit dir nit 3ů deylen / sundir ich wil deylen / mit deyme / ich von reitte deylin sal wanne her mir zů sprechit / so ein reit ist /
(6) B Z. 26-31
Na desen / reden / sprechet her Ernist / … eindreitliche / da3
Hencle . Conrads (neve) brudir sůn quam v3 siner muder hůis gegangen / vor Conradis / hůis /
vnd sprach
federe / ich bedin dich da3 dů mit mir delis solich gut so dů mit mir deylen salt von reitthe
dů sprach Conrad /
neve dů bist nů in einen andirn / wech gewallen / ich sal gerne mit dir deylen / also dů moinsthis abir liber zů Rome / dar vore sin .

Abb. 4: Sequenzen der Vorfassungen

5. Veränderungen im Fassungsvergleich

Einen Einblick in mögliche Intentionen von Textautor und Schreiber gewinnen wir, wenn wir die Endfassung mit den Vorfassungen vergleichen und dabei unser Augenmerk vor allem auf die Frage lenken, welche Rolle die Konzentration auf die Redewiedergabe spielt. Unmittelbar vergleichbar sind Veränderungen in den direkten Reden selbst und dem vorangehenden referierenden Kontext. Dabei sind drei Veränderungstypen zu unterscheiden: Schreibvarianten, Schreibfehlerkorrekturen, Umformulierungen.

5.1 Schreibvarianten

Mit Schreibvarianten sind die zeit- und ortsüblichen graphemischen Repräsentationsformen gemeint, die bekanntlich von Schreibern meist ohne erkennbare Regelhaftigkeit verwendet werden: z.B. Dehnungs-<i> (z.B. <han> vs. <hain> ‚habe(n)' (Seq. 4, 5)), <h> nach Konsonant (z.B. <mit/von reitthe> vs. <reitte> ‚Recht' (Seq. 2, 5, 6), <hizhe> vs. <hize> ‚heischte' (Seq. 3)), <e>/<i>-Varianz im Nebenton, Groß- vs. Kleinschreibung (z.B. <Gude> vs. <gude> ‚Gut' (Seq. 3)) u.v.a. Was diese Art von Schreibvarianz angeht, so lässt sich keine klare Tendenz herausarbeiten.

5.2 Korrektur von Schreibfehlern

Anders steht es mit der Korrektur von erkennbaren Schreibfehlern, die nicht als Schreibvarianz zu identifizieren sind (s. Abb. 5). (Grenzfälle sind dabei natürlich nicht auszuschließen.)

Die Fehlschreibungen beziehen sich auf einfache Verschreibungen (1, 14, 15), Wortwiederholung (7), Buchstabenauslassung (2, 4, 9, 10?), aber auch grammatische Korrekturen wie Flexion und Rektion (3, 4, 8, 11, 12, 13). In zwei Fällen wird der Schreibfehler erst in der Endfassung erzeugt:

dů wollis → dů vollis ‚du wollest' (Seq. 5)
hůis → hůiʒ ‚Haus' (Seq. 7)

Der Schreiber bemüht sich also erkennbar in der Endfassung um eine ordentliche Recht-Schreibung. Umso bemerkenswerter ist, dass von den 15 korrigierten Fehlern nur vier in den direkten Reden vorkommen, während bei etwa gleicher Wortzahl immerhin 11 Fehler im berichtenden Text korrigiert werden. Das zeigt zumindest, dass der Schreiber offensichtlich schon bei der Konzeptfassung bemüht war, die direkten Reden korrekt und richtig aufzuschreiben.

(1)	des patistes	→ des patis	‚der Pacht' (Gen.Sg.)	(Seq. 1)
(2)	sy	→ sin	‚sein'	(Seq. 1)
(3)	geentwortthe	→ geenwortthit	‚überantwortet'	(Seq. 1)
(4)	mit sime bruders sůne	→ sines bruder sůne	‚Brudersohn'	(Seq. 2)
(5)	dů	→ důn	‚tun'	(Seq. 2)
(6)	scheffininn	→ ein scheffene	‚Schöffe' (Sg.)	(Seq. 3)
(7)	daʒ daʒ	→ daʒ	‚dass'	(Seq. 3)
(8)	sprechet	→ sprechint	‚sprechen' (3.Pl.)	(Seq. 4)
(9)	esamer	→ ersam	‚ehrsam'	(Seq. 4)
(10)	zcoler	→ zoliner	‚Zöllner' (FamN)	(Seq. 4)
(11)	wider Henclo	→ wider Henclen	‚zu Hencle' (Akk.)	(Seq. 4)
(12)	her Gerbratis sůnis	→ her Gerbratis sůn	‚Herrn G.s Sohn'	(Seq. 4)
(13)	tussen dem gerittin	→ tussen dem geritte	‚zwischen dem Gericht'	(Seq. 5)
(14)	gewallen	→ gevallen	‚gefallen'	(Seq. 7)
(15)	dů moinsthis	→ dů mostis	‚du müsstest'	(Seq. 7)

Abb. 5: Liste der Fehlerkorrekturen

5.3 Reformulierungen

Bei der Analyse der zahlreichen Umformulierungen im gesamten Text lassen sich drei Reformulierungsmaximen erkennen (Ramge 1997: 314-318):

– Personen und ihre Rollen werden eindeutig formuliert; z.B. wird *neve* schon im Konzept zu *bruder sun* verbessert (Seq. 2 u. ö.).
– Es wird auf präzise Rechtssprachlichkeit hin formuliert; z.B. wird *eindreitliche* ‚einträchtig' in der Endfassung durch *eymutliche* (zu mhd. *einmuotlich* ‚einmütig') ersetzt (Seq. 7) und damit durch den üblicheren urkundlichen Ausdruck, der stärker auf das gemeinsame Handlungswissen abhebt.
– Es wird auf Verständlichkeitsoptimierung hin formuliert, z.B. durch syntaktisch-stilistische Umstellungen oder erläuternde Zusätze wie *man sal wiʒin daʒ ...* ‚man muss wissen, dass ...'.

Aus dieser Perspektive sind auch die beiden textlichen Veränderungen in den direkten Reden zu betrachten:

(1) *aldar dar ich ein biȝher geben vn(d) geen(t)wortte han* → *dar ich ein geentwortthit han*
    ‚wo ich ihn (= die Pacht) /bisher übergeben/ und überantwortet habe' (Seq. 1)
(2) (Zusatz zur Rede Hencles:) *sunder ich wil důn na dime rade*
    ‚sondern ich will mich nach deinen Beschlüssen richten' (Seq. 4)

Im ersten Fall weist der Landsiedel, d. h. der nach dem hessischen Landsiedelrecht das strittige Landgut bewirtschaftende Pächter, den Anspruch Hencles auf einen Teil der Pacht mit Hinweis auf die Tradition zurück und verwendet dabei die rechtliche Paarformel ‚übergeben und überantworten'. In der Endfassung wird diese rituelle Formulierung so verkürzt, dass die Aussage allgemeiner, aber auch deutlich schwerer verständlich wird. Diese Veränderung passt nicht recht zu den sonst zu beobachtenden Reformulierungsmaximen.

Im zweiten Fall endet die Szene zunächst mit der Unterwerfungsformel Hencles *(ich) inwil vȝ dime rade nit gein* ‚Ich will mich deinem Ratschluss nicht widersetzen'. Durch den Zusatz in der Endfassung wird die Unterwerfungsgeste verschärft: Hencle verpflichtet sich nicht nur zum Stillhalten, sondern weiter gehend dazu, die Beschlüsse seines Onkels freiwillig zu befolgen.

Dass unter den zahlreichen Reformulierungen des Textes nur zwei Stellen in direkter Rede betroffen sind, belegt wiederum, dass der Textautor schon beim Konzeptschreiben großen Wert auf die exakte Wiedergabe der Aussagen gelegt hat. Zumindest im zweiten Fall ist offenkundig, dass der Zusatz im Interesse Conrads liegt und deshalb wohl auch als Korrektur von diesem veranlasst wurde. In jedem Fall wird erkennbar, dass ganz großer Wert auf die rechtliche Eindeutigkeit und Präzision der Formulierungen in direkter Rede gelegt wird.

In Bezug auf die Frage, wie Textautor und Schreiber mit der kommunikativen Aufgabe der Protokollierung fertig geworden sind, ist zusammenfassend festzuhalten, dass auf die ‚richtige' Form der direkten Reden in formaler und inhaltlicher Hinsicht schon bei den Konzeptfassungen erhöhter Wert gelegt wurde, so dass hier nur noch wenige Änderungen notwendig waren.

5.4   Markierung der direkten Reden im Text

Allerdings hat sich diese erkennbar erhöhte Aufmerksamkeit für die wörtlichen Reden nicht in einer besonderen Behandlung auf der graphischen Ebene niedergeschlagen. Zitierzeichen können nicht verwendet werden: Sie kommen erst im Humanismus auf (Saenger 1982: 410). In der Regel wird die direkte Rede durch Punkt oder Virgel begrenzt; aber wo Veränderungen in den Schreibfassungen vorgenommen wurden, ist keine Regel, nicht einmal eine Tendenz festzustellen. Es gibt eine schwache Tendenz zur Großschreibung des Redeanfangs (Seq. 2, 4, 6). Die Binnengliederung mittels Punkten und Virgeln tendiert zur Markierung von Sinneinheiten, Sprechrhythmen und Hervorhebungen; aber auch hier gibt es keine klaren Bearbeitungsprinzipien.

Die Markierung der wörtlichen Reden wird vielmehr mit Hilfe sprachlicher Indikatoren vorgenommen (vgl. Betten 1985: 30, 35):

– Eröffnungselemente sind: Anrede (*Conrad, federe, neve*), Partikel (*druwen* Seq. 3), Redeaufforderung (*sage neve* Seq. 4). Schlusssignale hingegen fehlen.
– Die Redeeinleitung erfolgt in der Regel durch einen expliziten Akt von der Form *du sprach X*, der meist in einen doppelten Kontext eingebettet ist.

Einerseits sind die direkten Reden von Zeugen wiedergegebene Reden (XX *sprechent daz* ...), andererseits ist die *sprach*-Redeeinleitung für die Dialogeröffnung meist zweiter Teil einer formulierten zweigliedrigen Handlungsfolge:

(3) quam vn(d) hiʒ: dů sprach (Seq. 1)
(4) quam, nam vn(d) badin: dů sprach (Seq. 2)
(5) hiʒe vn(d) muthe: dů sprach (Seq. 3)
(6) quemen vn(d) sp(re)chin (Seq. 6)
(7) quam gegangen vn(d) sprach (Seq. 7).

Nimmt man die ausführliche Ortscharakterisierung in den Seqq. 4 und 5 hinzu, wird deutlich, dass die Mehrgliedrigkeit der Handlungsbeschreibung in ihrer Differenzierung (und Dehnung) funktional zugleich die dialogische Rede vorbereitet, auf sie aufmerksam macht und sie zugleich breit einbettet (Weigand 1988: 162ff.).

Auch hier ist bemerkenswert, dass wohl bei der Interpunktion (entsprechend der graphemischen Varianz) eine relative Zufälligkeit waltet, nicht aber bei der sprachlich-textuellen Organisation der Redemarkierung, bei der gar keine Änderungen in den Fassungen vorgenommen wurden, so dass man auch hier auf die von Anfang an bestehende erhöhte Aufmerksamkeit als Erklärung zurückgreifen kann.

6. Textfunktionen der direkten Rede bei der Protokollherstellung

Wir haben bislang herauszuarbeiten versucht, dass die neue kommunikative Aufgabe der schriftlichen Protokollerstellung in Anlehnung an das Urkunden-modell durch Herstellung einer strukturellen Ereigniskonfiguration einerseits und starke Fokussierung auf die richtige Formulierung dialogischer Einheiten andererseits gelöst wurde. Wir können uns nun deshalb der Frage zuwenden, welche Funktionen den Reden (vermutlich) zugeschrieben wurden, warum – modern gesprochen – die Textsorte Rechtsprotokoll historisch mit direkten Reden beginnt.

Es ist nahe liegend, dass die im schriftlichen Text repräsentierte Mündlichkeit der Dialoge genetisch Reflex des bis dahin ausschließlich mündlich geführten Rechtsverfahrens ist, sei es des ordentlichen Rechtsverfahrens oder des (gleichberechtigten) gütlichen Schiedsverfahrens. Hier galt es, wenn es zum urteilsrelevanten Kern des Verfahrens kam, sehr genau auf Form und Wortwahl zu achten, sollte der Prozess nicht wegen eines (scheinbar belanglosen) Formfehlers unwiderruflich verloren gehen. Dies (bei in Prozessdingen unerfahrenen Beteiligten) zu verhindern, war der Fürsprech da.[3] Insofern besteht zwischen der rechtsrelevanten Präzision der wörtlichen Reden im Text und den im Ergebnis in den realen mündlichen Dialogen der Streitparteien erfolgten letztendlichen Formulierungen vermutlich keine allzu große Differenz.

Dass unsere Dialoge dennoch nur eine sehr rudimentäre Kurzfassung der realen Dialoge bieten, liegt auf der Hand. Die Frage ist, warum und in welcher Weise (unterstellbar) reduziert oder kondensiert (Mihm 1995: 42) wurde.

Die Dialoge selbst liefern zur Beantwortung der Frage einige Anhaltspunkte. Zunächst ist festzuhalten: So intensiv die szenische Beschreibung das Ambiente der Gespräche imaginiert und sprachlich eine Gesprächssituation inszeniert, so wenig wird strukturell ein Gespräch wiedergegeben: Hauptelemente von (Alltags-) Gesprächen wie Gesprächseröffnung und Gesprächsschluss fehlen ebenso wie gesprächsstrukturierende Elemente wie z.B. verständnissichernde Prozeduren. Der Dialog reduziert sich, wie bereits oben beschrieben, auf den harten Kern von Sequenzen in Zweier- oder Dreierschritten, die den Antagonismus der Streitsituation hervorheben und markieren. Aber vergleichbar der Variationsbreite der Sprechhandlungen beobachten wir auch eine erhebliche Streubreite in der Konstitution der einzelnen Äußerungseinheiten der Züge durch einzelne sprachliche Elemente. Auf die gesprächsstrukturell nicht obligatorischen Eröffnungselemente Anrede, Partikel und Redeaufforderung wurde bereits hingewiesen, da sie formal als Indikatoren zur Markierung der wörtlichen Rede im Schreibtext dienen. Ihre Funktion kann sich darin aber nicht erschöpfen, wenn wir unterstellen, dass diese Eröffnungselemente Bestandteil des realen Gesprächs waren.

Betrachten wir unter diesem Gesichtspunkt Sequenz 5, die zentrale Streitsequenz vor dem Wetzlarer Dom, so muss unter textorganisatorischen Gesichtspunkten zunächst offen bleiben, ob die *Conrad*-Anrede Demuds

Textmarkierer (zur Markierung der direkten Rede) ist, so dass das Fehlen einer komplementären Anrede in der Antwort Conrads zufällig-belanglos wäre, oder ob sich darin nicht auch etwas vom Gesprächsduktus des realen Gesprächs widerspiegelt. Dass eben dieses wahrscheinlich ist, ergibt sich daraus, dass Demud ihre Erbforderung als *Bitte* formuliert: *Conrad . ich bedin dich . daʒ dű vollis deylin* ... Konventionell werden damit Höflichkeitsformen indiziert, unabhängig vom Inhalt der Äußerung: neben der expliziten Formulierung als Bitte auch noch durch den Verweis auf die Handlungsfreiheit Conrads mittels der Modalform *vollis* ‚mögest'. Schroff hingegen ist die Ablehnung Conrads formuliert: *ich inhan mit dir nit ʒu deylinne.* Kein Indikator mildert die Äußerung. Im Gegenteil: Der Vergleich mit der entsprechenden Formulierung in Seq. 6 (*ich inbin ir nit deylunge schuldich*) macht deutlich, dass die Entschiedenheit und Schärfe der modalen *haben*-Formulierung, damit die die Unhöflichkeit streifende Attitüde Conrads, durchaus bewusst gesetzt ist.[4]

Der Vergleich der parallel strukturierten Sequenzen 5 und 6 verdeutlicht damit, dass die Kommunikation zwischen den Verwandten Demuds und Conrad unter Höflichkeitsmaximen in etwa gleichgewichtig-verbindlich ist, während die zwischen Demud und Conrad in dieser Hinsicht ausgesprochen komplementär formuliert ist. Bei der Präzision, mit der erwiesenermaßen Textautor und Schreiber vorgehen, scheint es schwer vorstellbar, dass diese rekonstruierbaren sprachlichen Abstufungen unbeabsichtigt entstanden sein sollten. Wenn dies richtig ist, folgt daraus, dass die direkte Rede intendiertermaßen mehr bindet als die ‚reine' Proposition. Sie spiegelt zugleich etwas von den sozialen Verhaltensweisen der Kontrahenten, von der individuellen Weise des Umgangs miteinander, von emotional-affektiven Attitüden, von der Art der Sozialbeziehungen, kurz: Sie spiegelt etwas von der (wahrscheinlichen) Wirklichkeit der Streitgespräche als individuell situierten Ereignissen. Der Text reportiert auch auf der Ebene der Kommunikation etwas von dem Wirklichen, wie es gewesen ist und wie es die Beteiligten wahrgenommen haben.

Da dies wohl so ist, haben wir einen ersten guten Grund gefunden, warum direkte Rede verwendet wird. Denn beim Einsatz der indirekten Rede, der natürlich auch möglich gewesen wäre und in späteren Gerichtsprotokollen auch weit vorherrschender Usus wird, wären nicht alle Nuancen formulierbar gewesen. In Seq. 5 wäre Demud auch beim Gebrauch der indirekten Rede auf die Rolle der höflich Bittenden festlegbar gewesen: * ... *dass Demud sagte, sie bitte / bäte Conrad, er möge teilen* ... Aber es bleibt als unaufhebbare Differenz, dass sich die namentliche Anrede Conrads durch Demud in diesem Fall nicht wiedergeben lässt. Wenn diese aber, aus welchen Gründen auch immer, Bestandteil der reportierten Wirklichkeit sein soll, muss deshalb direkte Rede eingesetzt werden.

Auch die Antwort Conrads verändert sich in ihrem rhetorischen Habitus, wenn sie (versuchsweise) in indirekter Rede formuliert wird: * ... *dass Conrad sagte, er habe mit ihr nicht zu teilen, sondern er wolle / werde* ...: Die unversöhnliche Schärfe der Wiedergabe in direkter Rede geht unwiederbringlich verloren.

Da sich Ähnliches für die Widerspiegelung von Attitüden und Sozialbeziehungen in den anderen Sequenzen leicht entsprechend zeigen ließe, scheint als Begründung für die Verwendung der wörtlichen Rede in unserem Text generell plausibel, dass der Textverfasser damit die Spezifika der dialogischen Ereignisse präziser in den Griff bekommen konnte als beim Gebrauch der indirekten Redeformen. Die Frage ist dann natürlich, warum ihm die präzise Wiedergabe bei allen Einkürzungen und Kondensierungen so wichtig war.

Dies hängt m. E. aufs Engste mit dem zweiten Grund zusammen, der für diese Art der Gesprächskonstitution verantwortlich ist, nämlich der Rechtsrelevanz der direkten Reden (so auch Mihm 1995: 38). Nehmen wir dafür als Analysebeispiel Seq. 2, in der Conrad der Bitte seines Schwiegervaters Ernst von Nauborn und anderer Bürger und Schöffen, sich einem Verfahren zu unterziehen, folgt: *daȝ welich důn . ţussen hye . vnd fridage / mit minnen / odir mit reitte*. Diese Äußerung enthält drei Teilaussagen:

– Die explizite Zusage mittels des den Handlungsentschluss bezeichnenden Modalverbs *wil* gilt konventionell als Akt des Versprechens.
– Die deiktisch gebundene, aber auf die nähere Zukunft gelegte Ausführung des Beschlusses (später als *heute*) fixiert das Versprechen chronologisch-situativ.
– Die Paarformel *mit minnen odir mit reitte* ist juristisch relevant, weil er sich damit einem freiwilligen Schiedsverfahren (*minne*) sowie einem etwa notwendig werdenden förmlichen Prozessverfahren (*reht*) unterwirft.

Damit sind genau die Faktoren benannt, die das folgende Schiedsverfahren konstituieren. Conrad legt sich prozedural unwiderruflich fest, und genau diese Bindung wird in der wörtlichen Rede gefasst: Sie lässt kein Hintertürchen offen, und es kann, wo denn dieser Wortlaut von Conrad anerkannt wird, keine Missverständnisse und denkbare Interpretationen geben, die eine Wiedergabe in indirekter Rede möglicherweise zuließe. Von all dem, was bei der Festlegung des Güteverfahrens sonst noch verhandelt und besprochen wurde, wird nichts berichtet. Da er nach der *narratio* daraufhin *uȝ der gegene* ritt, hat er das Versprechen eindeutig gebrochen.[5]

Nur der juristisch relevante Punkt wird formuliert. Damit wird die generelle kommunikative Leistung der wörtlichen Rede genutzt, nämlich den Textautor von der Verantwortung für die Richtigkeit des Gesagten zu dispensieren. Diese Verantwortung übernimmt er immer dann, wenn er etwas in indirekter

Rede wiedergibt. Die direkte Rede reduziert die Gespräche auf das, was für den Zweck des Textes maßgebend ist, die Protokollierung der Aussagen zur Herbeiführung eines übergeordneten Gerichtsbeschlusses durch das königliche Hofgericht.

Betrachten wir unter diesem Gesichtspunkt die Dialogsequenzen, so erkennen wir unschwer, dass die Formulierungen durchweg rechtserheblich sind: Die Wörtlichkeit reduziert oder kondensiert das wirklich Gesprochene auf das für die Rechtsfindung Maßgebliche und kodifiziert sich in seiner Sprachlichkeit genau an diesen juristischen Normen. Von daher erklärt sich m.E. die Breite, ja Weitschweifigkeit vieler Formulierungen.[6] Es kommt – intentional – auf Präzision und Wiedergabe des rechtserheblichen Gesichtspunkts an. Und so muss man – entgegen dem ersten Anschein – jedes Wort fast auf die berühmte Goldwaage legen.

Nehmen wir als (abschließendes) Beispiel die letzte Seq. 7, die in Ausdruck und Intention einigermaßen dunkel ist. Wenn Conrad feststellt, dass sein Neffe jetzt ‚einen anderen Weg eingeschlagen habe', so liegt der Schlüssel für diese Qualifizierung in der vorangegangenen Bitte Hencles um Teilung *so dů mit mir deylen . salt von reitte*. ‚das du auf rechtlicher Grundlage mit mir teilen sollst'. Der Unterschied zum früheren Verhalten Hencles besteht darin, dass dieser vorher die Teilung *hiʒe ... vnd muthe* ‚heischte und verlangte' (Seq. 3), d.h. ohne Verweis auf eine Rechtsgrundlage. Wenn sich Hencle jetzt in Seq. 7 an den Rechtsweg bindet, hat Conrad gut frohlocken: *also dů mostis aber lieber zu Rome dar vore sin* heißt dann wohl soviel wie ‚da musst du dir erst ein oberstes Urteil zu deinen Gunsten besorgen.'[7] Denn Conrad wusste ja, dass er nach den geltenden Erbrechtsnormen der Zeit der Erbe war.

Zusammenfassend kann deshalb festgehalten werden: Die Analyse der sprachlichen Formen der direkten Reden zeigt, dass in überaus präziser Weise die (unterstellbare) Gesprächswirklichkeit mit Blick auf zwei Prinzipien reduziert wird: Es wird ‚eingedampft' auf die minutiöse und nuancierte Konstruktion der Rechtspositionen in den einzelnen Verfahrensschritten des Schiedsverfahrens, und es wird so formuliert, dass die relevanten sozialkommunikativen Strukturen und Attitüden scharf und ebenfalls nuanciert wiedergegeben werden. Auch dies ist rechtsrelevant, damit sich Andere, mit der Entscheidung Befasste eine Vorstellung machen können von den strukturellen Eigenschaften des individuellen Rechtsstreits.

Dies passt ins Bild der gesamten Textkonstitution: Die Sachverhalte werden über globale Konfigurationen und Kondensate der Gesprächs-handlungen so strukturiert, dass alles Überflüssige im Hinblick auf den Textzweck ausgeschieden wird.

Die Bevorzugung der wörtlichen Rede bewirkt nicht nur die Dispension der Textverfasser von der Verantwortung für die Richtigkeit der Formulierungen und Standpunkte, sondern bewirkt darüber hinaus vor allem einen sonst nicht erreichbaren Nuancierungsgrad als *memoria* des Geschehenen für einen zukünftigen Zweck.

7. Textualisierte Mündlichkeit und Rechtsprotokoll

Aufgrund der Analyse der Textgenese und dialogischer Mikrostrukturen kann man m. E. ziemlich präzise sagen,

– was die verschriftete Fassung der Dialoge mit der reportierten Gesprächswirklichkeit gemein hat und was sie davon unterscheidet,
– und was Funktionen und Zwecke der direkten Reden in diesem Text sind.

Die zentrale Funktion der *memoria* des schriftlichen Textes für den Zweck des Textes, Beweismittel und Entscheidungsgrundlage für das Urteil des königlichen Hofgerichts zu sein, beherrscht offensichtlich die Intentionen der Textverfasser, die damit vor einer für sie neuen Aufgabe stehen: Schöffengerichte verhandeln und urteilen mündlich; die Verfahrensverläufe werden nirgends schriftlich festgehalten, äußerstenfalls das Ergebnis von Verhandlungen und Urteilen, wobei auch diese Protokolleinträge das Grundschema von *narratio* und *dispositio* reflektieren (Mihm 1995: 29). Diese inhaltlichen Hauptteile der Urkunde bilden also das Vorbild. Deutschsprachige Urkunden treten in Hessen erst seit dem Ende des 13. Jahrhunderts vereinzelt auf; auch im Wetzlar des beginnenden 14. Jahrhunderts ist die deutschsprachige Urkunde erst ansatzweise etabliert. Kurz: Die volkssprachliche Literalisierung der Manifestationen öffentlichen städtischen Lebens hat gerade erst begonnen, auch und gerade in der Literalisierung des Gerichtsverfahrens und seines zentralen neuen Verfahrens, des auf individueller Beobachtung und Bezeugung beruhenden Beweisrechts. „Das Verfahrens- und Beweisrecht bildet damit die wichtigste Einbruchstelle der neuen Rationalität" (Dilcher 1992: 18). Damit verbunden ist die weitere Elaborierung und Formalisierung der Rechtssprache (Schmidt-Wiegand 1990).

In dieser medienhistorischen Situation orientiert sich die Lösung des kommunikativen Problems, einen Ereignis- und Verfahrensgang protokollartig festzuhalten, notwendig an etablierten Textmustern einerseits und tradierten Modi der Relevanzen von Mündlichkeit andererseits. Aus der mündlichen Rechtstradition stammt die Fixierung auf den Wortlaut (im ‚buchstäblichen' Sinne), d. h. das worauf die Person/Partei sich unstrittig festlegt oder was ihr als rechtlich zu Beurteilendes zugeschrieben/vorgeworfen wird. Insofern dominiert hier notwendig der Aspekt der Rechtsrelevanz mit der Folge, dass die Formulierungen sich konsequent an den rechtssprachlichen Normen und Konventionen orientieren.

Aus der Textmustertradition stammt die Einbindung in die Prinzipien urkundlicher Rechtssetzung (Steinbauer 1989), damit im Prinzip die Anpassung der realen Abläufe an die formalen Bedingungen des Textmusters Urkunde.

In den Dialogstrukturen und den direkten Reden spiegelt sich die Leistung von Textautor und Schreiber, die realen Abläufe unter rechtsrelevanten Gesichtspunkten zu reformulieren. Die Dialogizität und auch die Direktheit der Reden selbst ist schon unmittelbarer Reflex davon, denn die Tatsache, dass und die Weise, wie die Streitparteien versucht haben, den Streit zu schlichten, ist eminent rechtserheblich. Die (kommunikative) *Funktion* der Dialoge und der darin eingebetteten direkten Reden besteht deshalb darin, die Richtigkeit und Objektivität der protokollierten Ereignisse in Bezug auf ihre rechtsrelevanten Handlungszüge zu garantieren.

Insofern spiegeln insbesondere die direkten Reden Elemente der Gesprächsrealität, allerdings nicht in dem Sinne, dass sie die reale Mündlichkeit nachzeichnen oder simulieren wollen, schon gar nicht, indem sie Formen gesprochener Sprache oder Dialektismen reproduzieren: Die direkten Reden weisen die gleichen Erscheinungen der mittelhessischen Urkundensprache des späten Mittelalters auf, die für Raum und Zeit üblich sind (Ramge 1997: 295). M. E. kann man auch nicht davon ausgehen, dass die Grundstruktur des Wortlautes erhalten bleibt oder dass die Äußerungen auf das damals Typische „übercharakterisiert" werden (Mihm 1995: 53 f.).

Sie kondensieren vielmehr die Gesprächsrealität mit Perspektive auf den Verwendungszweck des schriftlichen Textes und interpretieren natürlich insoweit auch die realen Aussagen. Sowohl die rechtsrelevanten Äußerungselemente wie diejenigen, die sozialkommunikative Attitüden repräsentieren, erscheinen entsprechend dem Textzweck kondensiert. Insofern spiegeln sie nur noch resthaft die tatsächliche Mündlichkeit. Die Leistung der direkten Reden besteht dann vor allem darin, dass sie diese Rechts- und Sozialaspekte trotz Konventionalisierung und Standardisierung nuancierter (und damit protokollarisch präziser und dem Textzweck angemessener) formulierbar macht, als dies mittels indirekter Rede oder in Form handlungsbezeichnender Verben und Sprachgesten möglich wäre. Für unseren Text jedenfalls kann man m. E. ausschließen, dass damit die „Aussagen realistischer und wahrscheinlicher" gestaltet werden (Mihm 1994: 24), speziell die „Eigenwahrnehmung der Zeugen ... verdeutlichen und damit ihre Glaubwürdigkeit ... demonstrieren" (Mihm 1995: 50).

Damit ist eine zentrale Aufgabe bewältigt, die für die Textsorte ‚Protokoll' konstitutiv ist (Rolf 1993: 185), die der sinngemäß richtigen Wiedergabe der Gesprächsverläufe (allerdings nicht der Sequenzfolge, weil hier das Konfigurationsprinzip interferiert). Insofern spiegeln die Dialoge und direkten Reden bei aller Zweckorientiertheit und Kondensierung der Gesprächswirklichkeit noch manches von (spät)mittelalterlicher Gesprächswirklichkeit und deren Einbindung in gerichts-institutionelle Abläufe, was später im Zuge weitergehender Literalisierung untergegangen oder zumindest marginalisiert worden ist. Nach der Blütezeit der Verwendung direkter Reden in Rechtsprotokollen im 14. Jahrhundert „verebbt" sie Ende des 16. Jahrhunderts (Mihm 1995: 37) und taucht nur noch sporadisch etwa in Verhörprotokollen auf, „weil ihre Form für das Gericht erkenntnis- und urteilsrelevant sein kann" (Macha 1991: 42). Aber schon im 14. Jahrhundert herrschen indirekte Reden weit vor, wie z.B. die Protokolle des Ingelheimer Oberhofs zeigen (Erler 1952-1963). Das hängt vielleicht mit Tendenzen zur Linearisierung zusammen, sicher aber mit der Neigung zur stilistischen Homogenisierung von Texten.

Gerade deshalb lohnt trotz aller Einschränkungen, die mit der Textualisierung der Mündlichkeit verbunden ist, die Beschäftigung mit Quellengruppen wie Gerichtsprotokollen, Chroniken, Weistümern als Quellen mit nichtfiktionalem Sprachgebrauch, weil hier die Realitätshaltigkeit auch der kommunikativen Strukturen, Momente der Gesprächswirklichkeit zumindest resthaft erhalten und rekonstruierbar sind.

Die direkten Reden in unserer Quelle sind nicht mit dem Konzept der Semi-Oralität (Schlieben-Lange 1983: bes. 48f.) in Verbindung zu bringen: Dazu ist die Überformung durch den Rechtszweck zu stark ausgeprägt. Nicht einmal „semi-literal" (Biere 1985: 350, Anm. 11) wird man unsere Textstrukturen mit Fug und Recht nennen dürfen, wenngleich in diesem Ausdruck die angemessene Perspektive verdeutlicht wird. Auf der Skala Nähe und Distanz nähern sich die direkten Reden sehr dem ‚Distanz'-Pol und entsprechen eher dem, was Koch und Oesterreicher (1985: 30) als ‚elaborierte Mündlichkeit' bezeichnet haben.

Insgesamt wird wohl deutlich, dass es kein Zufall ist, dass die Literalisierung realitätshaltiger Dialogstrukturen mit direkten Reden in deutscher Sprache zuerst in Rechtsprotokollen begegnet. Diese neue Textsorte entsteht durch das im Zuge der Verschriftlichung immer differenzierter und komplexer werdende Rechtswesen des späten Mittelalters, das zu seiner Bewältigung neuer Formen der *memoria* bedarf. Aus genetischer Sicht spiegelt unsere Quelle vielleicht die reale Entstehungszeit der neuen Textsorte, in der die Reflexe der juristischen Mündlichkeit des Verfahrens noch so stark sind, dass sie als direkte Rede in den Dialogen erscheinen.

Dialoge im Rechtsprotokoll 395

Danksagung

Für viele hilfreiche Anregungen und Diskussionen danke ich J. Riecke, H. Schmidt und B.-M. Schuster, für die sorgfältige Textbearbeitung G. Richter.

Anmerkungen

1 Beide sind unbekannt; es ist auch nur spekulativ einzuschätzen, welchen Anteil der Schreiber an der Konzeption und den Formulierungen des Textes hat; vermutlich einen ziemlich hohen. Zum Verhältnis Autor-Schreiber vgl. zuletzt Ludwig 1996.
2 Die Wiedergabe ist textgenau, der besseren Verständlichkeit wegen aber leicht bearbeitet:
   - Abkürzungen sind aufgelöst und kursiv wiedergegeben.
   - Auslassungen im Kontext (...) beziehen sich ausschließlich auf die Kürzung von aufgezählten Namen.
   - Die direkten Reden sind in Fettdruck wiedergegeben.
   - Es wird eine optische Gliederung nach den einzelnen Handlungsschritten vorgenommen.
   - Unterstreichungen der handlungsbezeichnenden Verben sind hinzugefügt.
3 Dessen Versagen in diesem Punkt einklagbar war; vgl. für ein schönes Beispiel a. 1427 aus den Ingelheimer Oberhof-Urteilen Erler: 1952–1963: Nr. 2402.
4 Im übrigen sind die Sequenzen 5 und 6 in dieser Hinsicht formal gleich aufgebaut: Der *Conrad*-Anrede Dietrichs folgt ein Imperativ; der Ablehnung durch Conrad folgt seine Rechtsposition, die in Seq. 6 deutlich versöhnlicher-freundlicher formuliert ist (*so deylen ich gerne mit eme*) als in der Streitsequenz mit Demud.
5 Es ist nicht ganz klar, warum diese Tatsache nicht zum Scheitern des Schiedsverfahrens führte. Vermutlich hatten die vielfach miteinander versippten und verwandten Streitparteien ein starkes Interesse, den Streit friedlich beizulegen (Ramge 1997: 298).
6 Die aber auch allgemeines stilistisches Merkmal waren; vgl. z. B. das *Melusine*-Beispiel in Betten (1995: 265 f).
7 Vgl. für eine genauere Diskussion der Verhältnisse Ramge (1997: 299, 308 f).

Literatur

Bax, Marcel M. H.
   1991   Historische Pragmatik: Eine Herausforderung für die Zukunft. In: Dietrich Busse (Hg.). *Diachrone Semantik und Pragmatik.* Tübingen: Niemeyer, 197–215.

Betten, Anne
1985 Direkte Rede und epischer Bericht in der deutschen Romanprosa. *Sprache und Literatur in Wissenschaft und Unterricht* 16 (H. 55), 25–41.
1990 Zur Problematik der Abgrenzung von Mündlichkeit und Schriftlichkeit bei mittelalterlichen Texten. In: Anne Betten (Hg.) und Mitarbeit Claudia Riehl. *Neuere Forschungen zur historischen Syntax des Deutschen.* Tübingen: Niemeyer, 324–335.
1995 Stilphänomene der Mündlichkeit und Schriftlichkeit im Wandel. In: Gerhard Stickel (Hg.). *Stilfragen* (Jahrbuch des Instituts für deutsche Sprache). Berlin, New York: de Gruyter, 257–279.

Biere, Bernd Ulrich
1985 Schriftlichkeit und Mündlichkeit – Vereinheitlichung und Verständlichkeit. In: Georg Stötzel (Hg.). *Germanistik – Forschungsstand und Perspektiven. Vorträge des Deutschen Germanistentages 1984, 1. Teil: Germanistische Sprachwissenschaft, Didaktik der Deutschen Sprache und Literatur.* Berlin, New York: de Gruyter, 346–365.

Dilcher, Gerhard
1992 Oralität, Verschriftlichung und Wandlungen der Normstruktur in den Stadtrechten des 12. und 13. Jahrhunderts. In: Hagen Keller (Hg.). *Pragmatische Schriftlichkeit im Mittelalter.* München: Fink, 9–19.

Erler, Adalbert (Hg.)
1952–63 *Die älteren Urteile des Ingelheimer Oberhofes.* 4 Bde. Frankfurt: Klostermann.

Fritz, Gerd
1994 Geschichte von Dialogformen. In: Gerd Fritz und Franz Hundsnurscher (Hg.). *Handbuch der Dialoganalyse.* Tübingen: Niemeyer, 545–562.

Koch, Peter, und Wulf Oesterreicher
1985 Sprache der Nähe – Sprache der Distanz. *Romanistisches Jahrbuch* 36, 15–43.

Ludwig, Otto
1996 Vom diktierenden zum schreibenden Autor. In: Helmuth Feilke und Paul R. Portmann (Hg.). *Schreiben im Umbruch.* Stuttgart: Klett, 16–28.

Macha, Jürgen
1991 Kölner Turmbücher – Schreibsprachwandel in einer seriellen Quelle der Frühen Neuzeit. *Zeitschrift für deutsche Philologie* 110, 36–61.

Mihm, Arend
1994 Zur Konvergenz von Sprachvariation und sozialen Kategorien in der stadtsprachlichen Überlieferung des Spätmittelalters. In: Gisela Brandt (Hg.).

Historische Soziolinguistik des Deutschen. Stuttgart: Akademischer Verlag, 17–25.

1995   Die Textsorte Gerichtsprotokoll im Spätmittelalter und ihr Zeugniswert für die Geschichte der gesprochenen Sprache. In: Gisela Brandt (Hg.). *Historische Soziolinguistik des Deutschen II.* Stuttgart: Akademischer Verlag, 21–57.

Ramge, Hans

1997   Heinrich Waldschmidts Erbe. Ein Erbstreit in Wetzlar zu Beginn des 14. Jahrhunderts und die Anfänge des gerichtlichen Protokollierens. In: Walter Heinemeyer (Hg.). *Hundert Jahre Historische Kommission für Hessen 1897–1997. Erster Teil.* Marburg: Elwert, 293–321.

Rolf, Eckard

1993   *Die Funktionen der Gebrauchstextsorten.* Berlin, New York: de Gruyter.

Saenger, Paul

1982   Silent Reading: Its Impact on Late Medieval Script and Society. *Viator* 13, 367–414.

Schlieben-Lange, Brigitte

1983   *Traditionen des Sprechens.* Stuttgart: Kohlhammer.

Schlosser, Hans

1971   *Spätmittelalterlicher Zivilprozeß nach bayerischen Quellen.* Köln, Wien: Böhlau.

Schmidt-Wiegand, Ruth

1990   Rechtssprache. In: Adalbert Erler und Ekkehard Kaufmann (Hg.). *Handwörterbuch zur deutschen Rechtsgeschichte* Bd.4. Sp. 344–360.

Sonderegger, Stefan

1990   Syntaktische Strukturen gesprochener Sprache im älteren Deutschen. In: Anne Betten (Hg.) und Mitarbeit Claudia Riehl. *Neuere Forschungen zur historischen Syntax des Deutschen.* Tübingen: Niemeyer, 310–323.

Steinbauer, Bernd

1989   *Rechtsakt und Sprechakt.* (Innsbrucker Beiträge zur Kulturwissenschaft. Germanistische Reihe Bd. 36). Innsbruck: Institut für Germanistik.

von Polenz, Peter

1981   Der Ausdruck von Sprachhandlungen in poetischen Dialogen des deutschen Mittelalters. *Zeitschrift für germanistische Linguistik* 9.3, 249–273.

von Roncador, Manfred

1988   *Zwischen direkter und indirekter Rede.* Tübingen: Niemeyer.

Weigand, Edda
    1988   Historische Sprachpragmatik am Beispiel: Gesprächsstrukturen im Nibelungenlied. *Zeitschrift für deutsches Altertum und deutsche Literatur* 117: 161–173.

Werkmüller, Dieter
    1972   *Über Aufkommen und Verbreitung der Weistümer*. Berlin: Erich Schmidt.

Wiese, Ernst (Hg.)
    1911   *Urkundenbuch der Stadt Wetzlar*, Bd. 1: 1141–1350. Marburg: Elwert.

Court Records and Cartoons
Reflections of Spontaneous Dialogue
in Early Romance Texts

Peter Koch
Eberhard Karls University, Tübingen

1. Introduction

Philology need not be divorced from life. For people with historical interests even written texts from past times are occasionally a window to a wonderful vista of colourful and even earthy forms of communication. It is my intention to demonstrate this with recourse to two text types from the early period of Romance languages, in which "dialogicity" – the meaning of which is to be defined – plays an important role.

2. Orality, literacy, and historical dialogue research

The title of this volume points to two seemingly conflicting domains of language. We generally think of dialogue as a sequence of oral utterances, whereas an historical investigation of the language of past centuries can be based only on written sources. This apparent contradiction becomes resolved, however, in the framework of a more complex conceptualisation of orality and literacy as developed in particular by Ludwig Söll (1985: 17-25). He distinguishes between the phonic and the graphic medium on the one hand and spoken and written conception on the other. If two, in medial terms, totally neutral expressions like "communicative immediacy" vs. "communicative distance" are allocated to the latter contrast, the following combinations of conceptualisation and medium arise (cf. Koch and Oesterreicher 1985: 17-19; 1990: 5-12; 1994: 587f.):

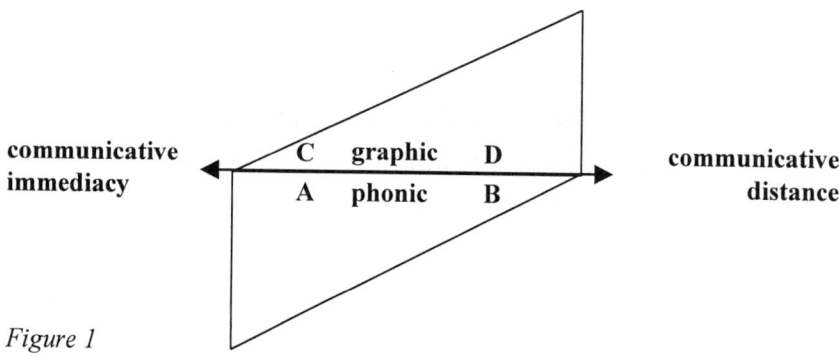

Figure 1

Figure 1 illustrates the medial dichotomy and by comparison the conceptional continuum of linguistic utterances, and it also shows the – indisputable – affinities between medium and conception which, however, are only of a prototypical nature (cf. Koch 1997: 152). The phonic realisation of communicative immediacy, for instance in spontaneous everyday conversation (area A), seems to us just as obvious as communicative distance is in the graphic medium, for example in a legal text (area D). But we also know that communicative immediacy does exist in the graphic medium (area C: e.g. spontaneous private correspondence) and likewise communicative distance in the phonic medium (area B: e.g. funeral oration).[1]

The terms "immediacy"/"distance" may be factorised as they comprise a number of different communicative parameters. Extreme communicative immediacy may be characterised as follows (see Table 1):

Table 1: Parameters of "communicative immediacy"

(i)	physical (spatial, temporal) immediacy
(ii)	privacy
(iii)	familiarity of the partners
(iv)	high emotionality
(v)	context embeddedness
(vi)	deictic immediacy (*ego-hic-nunc*, immediate situation)
(vii)	dialogue
(viii)	communicative cooperation of the partners
(ix)	free topic development
(x)	spontaneity

For communicative distance the opposite values of these parameters will be true, namely: (i) physical distance, (ii) publicness, (iii) lack of familiarity of the partners etc. The values of parameters (i) to (x) may well vary in ratio, thereby contributing decisively to the continual character of the conception of linguistic utterances.[2] On this basis it is easy to see what combination of parameter values and what position in the conceptional continuum may be allotted, for example, to a panel discussion, a newspaper interview, a sermon etc.

Within the framework of the subject under discussion, it is, of course, parameter (vii), "dialogue", which particularly attracts our attention (cf. Table 1 above). To be accurate, it is exclusively the aspect of turn-taking that is meant here: the dialogue as a communication form with completely free turn-taking between the conversation partners, as opposed to the monologue as a communication form in which, without any turn-taking, only one of the communication partners speaks (of course with continual transitions between both extremes: think of discussions, correspondence etc.).

This understanding of the term "dialogue" must not mask the fact that different academic fields (such as linguistics, sociology and philosophy) and specialised areas within these fields sometimes use the terms "dialogue" and "dialogicity" to mean quite different (groups of) communication forms.[3] If the parameters listed in Table 1 are applied, we may arrive at a relatively precise definition of the salient points of the variety in terminology observed here. From the conceptual point of view, we may distinguish between three prototypical concepts of dialogue:

Table 2: Dialogicity

		Dialogue$_1$	Dialogue$_2$	Dialogue$_3$
(i)	physical (spatial, temporal) immediacy	0	0	+
(ii)	privacy	0	0	+
(iii)	familiarity of the partners	0	+	+
(iv)	high emotionality	0	+	+
(v)	context embeddedness	0	+	+
(vi)	deictic immediacy (*ego-hic-nunc*, immediate situation)	0	(*thou*)	+
(vii)	**dialogue**	**+**	**±**	**+**
(viii)	communicative cooperation of the partners	0	0	+
(ix)	free topic development	0	0	+
(x)	spontaneity	0	0	+

"Dialogue$_1$" means a whole family of communication forms which have one parameter, i.e. (vii) "dialogue", in common (hence +), whereas all the other parameters are specified at random (hence '0'). This family of communication forms ranges from dialogues characterised by full communicative immediacy, such as spontaneous everyday conversation, to dialogue forms which are essentially distant, such as courtly conversation or official correspondence. (As can be seen here, the medium is evidently indifferent.)

The term "dialogue$_2$" also appears to be quite widespread. Here "dialogicity" first and foremost means addressee orientation. It thus implies a certain familiarity (iii), a certain emotionality (iv), a certain context embeddedness (v), and a predominant address orientation (vi. Dialogicity in the sense of parameter (vii), on the other hand, does not necessarily have to be realised (hence ±); the remaining parameters are likewise conceptionally indifferent here (hence '0').

Finally, there is the concept of "dialogue$_3$" mentioned at the beginning, which implies spontaneous everyday dialogue; here all the parameters (i) to (x) – of course including (vii) – are specified in the sense of communicative immediacy.

As far as the medium is concerned, dialogue$_2$ and dialogue$_3$ undoubtedly have an affinity to phonic realisation (area A in Figure 1). Given the bounds of historical linguistics, however, it goes without saying that we may gain access to these dialogue forms only through written records, in other words via area C in Figure 1. The data I treat below therefore oscillate, within the graphic medium, between the dialogue$_2$ and dialogue$_3$ types. In the case of type C data, two questions must necessarily be asked. First, to what happy circumstances do we owe the fact that these written testimonies emerged with a conceptional character which was not totally prototypical? and second, to what degree do these written testimonies reflect features of the communication forms of area A?

Cultural history and linguistic history teach us – more and more over the last few decades – that the communication forms of area C in Figure 1 are definitely widespread. They form one facet of what is labelled "orality in literate cultures", usually without any differentiation (cf. Koch 1997: 152f., 161ff.). Nevertheless, as their specific combination of conceptional and medial aspects is rather ambivalent, it is definitely worth examining how they came into being and how they should be typified. In various publications, Wulf Oesterreicher (e.g. 1995, 1997: 200-206) has designed a typology of "writing characterised by linguistic immediacy" (*nähesprachlich geprägtes Schreiben*) comprising the following eight types:

Court Records and Cartoons 403

Table 3: Typology of "writing characterised by linguistic immediacy" (according to Oesterreicher)

(1)	Writing by semiliterate persons
(2)	Writings by (semiliterate) bilingual persons in a di-/triglossic situation
(3)	Sloppy writing (also by educated writers)
(4)	"Documentation" of informal speech
(5)	Writing adapted to the language competence of less educated recipients
(6)	Writing subjected to "simple" discourse traditions or genres (as a pragmatic option)
(7)	Writing in the *stilus humilis* (as a rhetorical-poetic option)
(8)	Mimetic or simulated orality in literature, parody and similar contexts

These types of writing characterised by linguistic immediacy are encountered, for instance, in the Romance languages at widely varying times in the history of the respective languages: we find them in sources relevant for the investigation of the so-called "Vulgar Latin", in the most ancient Romance writings, in Spanish colonial historiography of the early modern period, in sources relevant for the investigation of the history of spoken French, in the French Revolution, in letters from prisoners of war in our own century etc.[4] My data are at the crossroads between the two perspectives "writing characterised by linguistic immediacy" and "earliest Romance writings".[5] As we shall see, Oesterreicher's types (4) and (8) play a particular role here.

Before proceeding I briefly want to add the following basic consideration. Sources characterised by linguistic immediacy – especially dialogue$_{2/3}$ sources – from earlier periods and realised in the graphic medium may be examined for a variety of linguistic reasons. Here it is important to distinguish between the following levels and areas of human language taking up and specifying some of Coseriu's basic ideas:[6]

Table 4: Levels and domains of human language

Level	Domain
universal	language activity
historical	specific language
historical	discourse tradition
individual/actual utterance	discourse

Since linguists use discourse realised in the form of individual and actual utterances merely as data and must not see it as an end in itself, their focal interest can only remain in the universal and the two historical domains. The analysis of the relevant sources for research into the history of oral varieties, which corresponds to the domain of specific languages, is very widespread.[7] The sources may, however, also be regarded as samples of certain discourse traditions and serve for the study of the history of dialogue traditions ("dialogue forms" in the sense of Fritz 1994 and 1995). Finally – and this is the decisive aspect for what follows – the relevant sources may, of course, also be analysed with regard to the level of language activity, in other words the level of the basic variables of human communication. The problem then arises of the authenticity or the filtering processes to which the texts in area C in Figure 1 compared to area A have been subjected. How much dialogicity$_{2/3}$, how much immediacy is contained in the relevant written testimonies and in what configuration? What are the motives for the conceptional form of these texts? Within the latter perspective, the relation to the discourse-traditional area of the historical level becomes obvious.

I should like to illustrate this point briefly by means of two sample texts which date from outside the period of my research. In example (1), l. 3-4, angry exclamations are quoted which the Romans shouted out when Pope Vigilius, who had made himself extremely unpopular, set sail. In (2) we find an excerpt from eye-witness accounts, in which direct speech is again quoted.

(1) Rome, 545 (Liber Ponitificalis, cit. Herman 1990: 147)
   1 *Videntes Romani quod movisset navis, in qua sedebat Vigilius,*
      'When the Romans saw the ship moving on which Vigilius was sitting,
   2 *tunc populus coepit post eum iactare lapides fustes cacabos et dicere:*
      the people began to throw stones, sticks and metal pots at him and to say:
   3 *"famis tua tecum! mortalitas tua tecum! male fecisti cum Romanis,*
      "Hunger to you! Death to you! You did wrong to the Romans,
   4 *male invenias ubi vadis."*
      may evil accompany you wherever you go."'

(2) Siena, 715 (*Breve de inquisitione,* cit. Roncaglia 1965: 146)
   1 *Ego respondi ei: "Cave ut non interroget; nam si interrogatus fuero,*
      'I replied to him: "Prevent him from asking [me], for if I am asked,
   2 *veritatem dicere habeo." Sic respondit mihi: "Ergo tace tu viro*
      I will tell the truth." He replied to me: "So, you be silent to a man
   3 *qui est missus domni regi."*
      who is the ambassador of the king!"'

(1) is in principle a purely "Latin" text. As it contains a quotation of the dialogue$_2$ type, its authenticity with regard to the Latin spoken at that time ("Vulgar Latin") has been discussed.[8] Text (2) is likewise basically a Latin

text, but it reveals clear signs of vernacular elements which can, of course, be pin-pointed.[9] All this, however, purely concerns the domain of a specific language as described above, in which there is comparatively little to be seen on the surface. By contrast, the matter looks completely different if – on the level of language activity – the interest lies in the characteristic style of dialogue$_2$ or dialogue$_3$ in the instances of speech quoted here, and from this point of view both texts are relevant to my questions.[10]

3. Court records

3.1. The data

Following example (2), let us remain in the law courts and look at excerpts from court records.

My first example comes from the *Atti dei podestà* of Lio Mazor, an island in the Lagoon of Venice destroyed by the Genoese in 1380. They are records relating to trials on disputes. Our text is written in a vernacular variety which is not identical to Venetian, but which is certainly very similar to it. It originated in the year 1312 and thus belongs to the early texts of the region.[11]

(3) Lio Mazor (near Venice), 1312 (*Atti dei podestà di Lio Mazor*, cit. Levi 1904: 17f.; my quotation marks)
 1 *Die martis X mense otubrj Felip Musolin de S.to Nicolò çurà*
    'On 10th October F.M. of S.N. swore
 2 *li comandamenti de miser la potestà et de dir la uerità dela briga*
    obedience to the Podestà and <he swore> to tell the truth about the dispute
 3 *ch'el aue cum Pero Seren et colo Saracho da Maçorbo.*
    which he had with P.S. and S.d.M.
 4 *Lo qual dis ch'el mançà et beuè cum li diti Pero et Saracho*
    He said that he ate and drank with the said P. and S.
 5 *in casa d'Andrea Dalmatin, creçando ch'eli fos sui amisi;*
    at A.D.'s house believing them to be his friends;
 6 *et cusì ne partisem dela dita casa e çesem ensenbra uia.*
    and then we left the said house and went away together.
 7 *Et cum nu fosem a Sto Antolin, et eli s'aurì cum entranbe le barche*
    And when we got to S.A., they moved their boats apart
 8 *et mis-me denter sì, et en questa Pero Seren me dis:*
    and put me between them, and then P.S. said to me:
 9 *"Felipo, el è ça II anni che t'ò uardà d'auerte a sto parti;*
    "F., two years ago I warned you not to show up in these parts;

10 *che se t'aues entes en canal Corno quando tu me dies*
   for if I had heard you say to me in the Corno canal
11 *ch'el me nases lo uermo can, e' t'auraui pur morto!"*
   that you wish a mangy dog on me, I would have killed you!"
12 *et e'dis: "Fra', qua non è grande fato,*
   And I said to him: "Brother, that is no great matter,
13 *se te lo dis per cerchar la uia de uerità*
   I said it to you for the sake of truth,
14 *ch'el me cunpagnun no pares laro!"*
   so that my companion wouldn't appear to be a thief!"
15 *et el dis: "Tu menti per la gula!"*
   and he said: "You are lying through your back teeth!"
16 *et e' li dis: "tu menti per lo cul!"*
   and I said: "You are lying through your arse!"
17 *et en questa el fo a ladi dela mia barcha per uolerme sair en barcha,*
   and then he got alongside my boat in order to get into my boat
18 *et he' me-lo spensi da dos per no uoler briga;*
   and I pushed him off my back because I didn't want an argument;
19 *et en questa el leuà lo rem et uos-me dar ço per la testa; [...]*
   and then he raised the oar and wanted to hit me on the head with it; [...]'

Our interest focuses on dialogue$_3$ quoted in lines 9-16 (in particular l. 16). Note the textual layers in which this dialogue is embedded (cf. also Figure 2 below):

Level I: Legal framework of questioning with mention of the cause (l. 2: *briga*) and of the swearing of the oath (l. 1: *çurà*).
Level II: Report of the statement by Felip Musolin (from l. 4: *Lo qual dis ch(e)* ...). A noteworthy feature is the abrupt jump in l. 5 from indirect speech in the 3rd person singular (l. 4/5: *el mançà et beuè ... creçando ch'eli fos sui amisi*) to direct speech in the 1st person (l. 6: *ne partisem*).
Level III: Embedded in Level II, a dialogue is rendered as a quotation (l. 9-16).

This threefold layering may serve as a model case for the text organisation of the following documents, too, even if not all the levels are reported, depending on the respective editions (which concentrate on the vernacular passages in the text).

Our next group of examples comes from court records of statements in slander suits. These records are the *Libri criminali* of Lucca in the period 1330 to 1384. In the context of the emergence of the vernacular in Tuscany, this is actually no longer particularly early (by way of comparison, Dante died in 1321);[12] but even at this point in time in Tuscany numerous discourse traditions were still practised in Latin. As opposed to the case of Lio Mazor, this was apparently also true of court records, so that the fragments of the dialogue$_3$ type which are of interest to us occur as vernacular quotations within a Latin text (or as in case (4b), even appear partly in Latin). This in itself is particularly pertinent to our purposes: the vernacular brings us closer to the reality of dialogue$_3$ within texts which are basically still Latin.

(4) Lucca: 1335, 1330 (*Libri criminali*, cit. Marcheschi 1983: 22, 19)
 (a) *Sosso cane, ascino fastiggioso.*
  'Dirty dog, puffed up donkey.'
 (b) *Tu fecisti me predari: oportet q(uod) te int(er)ficiam, soçço ladrone*
  'You wanted to have me robbed; I must kill you, dirty thief,
  che me venisti a robbare, che maledecta scia la pocta che ti cachò.
  who wanted to rob me, damn the whore who crapped you.'

The examples quoted belong to level III of the system defined under (3). (The Latin texts from the other levels are not quoted in the edition available to me.)

Our third group of examples comes from court registers (*Registres audienciers*) belonging to various administrative districts in the Forez ((5a) Malleval, (5b) Saint-Maurice-sur-Loire, (5c) La Tour-en-Jarez; all in today's Département Loire). Linguistically this is the Franco-Provençal area. According to the documents which have survived, written vernacular in the Forez did not emerge until the 1280s, so documentation in particular from the 14th century may be reasonably considered as "early".[13]

(5) Forez: 1358, 1385, 1433 (*Registres audienciers de la châtellenie comtale*, cit. Gonon 1974: 391, 372, 384f.)
 (a) [angry culprit to the bailiff wanting to take his sword off him:]
  Ven la me otiar, quar eo la te balirey par la pointa.
  'Come and take it off me; I'll give it to you with the point.'
 (b) *tu murras de malveysi mort, comme tes pares.*
  'You will die a nasty death, like your father.'
 (c) *Johannes Jaquerii Olerii, de Strata, ... quia eidem imponebatur:*
  'J.J.O. of St., ... since he is accused of
  vocasse J. Boniti filius de la tres orra vil puta merdosa, que moz pares
  calling J.B.:. Son of the very dirtiest vilest bloody whore; my father
  a fotu ta mare mais de .c. veis en ung an,
  has fucked your mother more than a hundred times in one year.'

As particularly exemplified by (5c), levels I and II are rendered in Latin (level I: *Johannes ... imponebatur*; level II: *vocasse J. Boniti*). Only level III is again quoted in the vernacular (and the edition restricts itself mainly to these quotations).

3.2. Analysis of conceptional aspects

The texts or passages under scrutiny here contain clear reflexes of the dialogue₃ type. The philologists who have examined these texts unanimously stress the proximity to actual speech.[14] Even if the supposed authenticity of the quotations can only be of a relative nature (see also below 3.3.), salient signs of communicative immediacy may be detected in the quotations or from the respective context in which they are embedded. I should like to define this more precisely using parameters (i)-(x) of Table 1 above:

(i) Level II of the text reveals that the quoted utterances go back to the physical immediacy of a face-to-face situation – if, that is, this level is visible in the edition. On level II the *I-thou* speech situation can be reconstructed metacommunicatively as in: (3) l. 6 *çesem ensenbra uia* etc.; (5c) *(Johanni Jaquerii Olerii imponebatur) vocasse J. Boniti.*

(ii) It may be deduced mostly from the content of the insults that these scenes are very private; in (3) this becomes directly visible in the edition through the inclusion of text level II (account of the events).

(iii) The intimacy between the interlocutors is particularly apparent in (3): after a meal in company – where the wine probably flowed freely – three people, evidently long acquainted with each other, leave the house together. The narrator erroneously considers the others to be his friends: l. 5 *creçando ch'eli fos sui amisi*; anyway, they have had some common – and also unpleasant – experience which is partially referred to quite implicitly in l. 9-14. In other texts, intimacy is also revealed indirectly, such as in the allusion to (supposed) knowledge about the insulted party or his relatives: (5b) how the father of the insulted party died; (5c) alleged sexual intercourse between the speaker's father and the mother of the insulted party.

(iv) The high degree of emotionality is no doubt the most significant parameter in these texts on slander suits. The purpose of the quotations in the legal context is indeed to reveal that a basic rule of politeness in spoken language has been infringed by the accused: his emotionality has caused him to threaten the plaintiff's negative and positive face and he has brutally invaded the latter's personal territory.[15] Linguistically, this effect arises through certain semantic and pragmatic options.[16]

The choice of words is of prime importance. The expressions are derogatory (in the framework of a characteristic syntactic type of the appellation of the interlocutor: (4a) *sosso cane, ascino fastiggioso*; (4b) *soçço ladrone*; (5c) *filius de la ... puta*). Here and elsewhere, the use of swear words of a faecal and sexual nature flouts language taboos: (3) l. 16 *cul*, (4b)/(5c) *pocta/puta*, (5c) *merdosa, fotre*, (4b) *cachare* (the last example is an extreme dysphemism for 'to give birth'). In (5a) *balir par la pointa* for 'to stab' there is a scurrilous challenge within the linguistic representation of the situation.

Emotional expressiveness is heightened by intensifications which outdo each other, such as in (3) l. 15/16 *mentir per la gula* and *mentir per lo cul*. But this kind of hyperbole concerns not only linguistic expression but often also the content, the immoderacy of which gives rise to a lawsuit as in (5c), particularly in the second part, possibly also in (4b) (where apart from the possibly unfounded accusation of theft, there is the indirect insinuation of descent from a whore).

The speech acts in the individual utterances are also extremely emotional: derogatory address ((4a) and (5c) *filius ... merdosa*); reproach ((3) l. 15/16: *tu menti per la gula/per lo cul*); accusation ((4b) *tu fecisti me predari ... soçço ladrone que me vinisti a robbare*); threat ((4b) *oportet quod te interficiam*; (5a)); curse ((5b)). The speech act of cursing (4b) *maledecta scia ...* is a downright flouting of a taboo.

(v) The context embeddedness is generally only indirect: as a rule, we are dealing with insults resulting from a conflict of action. By contrast, (5a) is set very directly in an extremely violent conflict, where a speech act of challenge is followed by a speech act that can only through the given situation be interpreted as threat.

(vi) In the personal deixis, there are unmistakable elements of referential immediacy. The first and second person are well represented in the utterances. A pronounced dialogic$_2$ reference to the addressee is, of course, implicitly contained in the abusive appellation (see above under (iv)). There is a marked referential immediacy, too, in (5a) where reference to the sword in the form of an exophoric[17] pronoun in the third person (*la*) may only be understood in the context of the situation. On the other hand, however, a certain degree of referential distance must be conceded if one considers the numerous references to factors extraneous to the situation, i.e. mothers, fathers and (alleged) earlier actions such as robbery, sexual intercourse etc. and even prior communication ((3), l. 9-14).

(vii) All the relevant passages are dialogical in the sense of this parameter. In (3) this is quite explicit in the threefold layering (I – II – III). But even where the edition does not reveal this fact, we may safely assume that such accusations, insults, challenges etc. always occurred only in real, lively dialogue.

(x) When we consider the parameter of spontaneity, it is necessary to distinguish between the marked deliberation of quoting and of record-taking during the trial on the one hand, and on the other the spontaneity of the utterance quoted – a spontaneity which is preserved (or must be preserved; I shall come back to this point in 3.3.) as far as the quoter's memory will allow. From the purely linguistic point of view, certain elements of authenticity cannot be overlooked: for example, the syntax of (5c) reveals the uncomplicated, polyvalent *que* situated between hypotaxis and parataxis, which keeps the logical link implicit;[18] moreover, the wording generally tends towards accumulation or even climax ((4a), (4b), (5c)).

3.3.   Motivation for writing characterised by linguistic immediacy

The records just examined belong to type (4) in Oesterreicher's model for writing characterised by linguistic immediacy (see Table 3): "documentation" of informal speech. Besides the act of reading aloud, Lüdtke (1964) already highlighted records as a communication type in earlier Romance texts. By contrast, Wunderli (1965) gave prominence to reading aloud and assigned a more marginal role to records. Obviously, our texts (3) and (5) do not belong to the central documents of early Romance, but they are at least relatively early in the history of the language in question. Records therefore play an interesting role here, at any rate in certain regions (cf. Koch 1993: 46).

The motivation for the style of immediacy in these court records is of a legal nature. Their starting point is to be found in spontaneous, immediate, dialogue$_3$-type utterances in the phonic medium, which are addressed to a hearer H by a speaker S. Depending on the circumstances, they are experienced by a witness W: S → H (W). Once such utterances have been heard, they would normally "die out", but for the fact that they belong to a context which, thanks to H's reaction, later becomes justiciable. Thus, the primary communication act S → H (W) triggers off a chain of further communication acts, the textual end-product being a mirror reflection of the layers III – II – I. A perfect model of this is to be found in example (3).

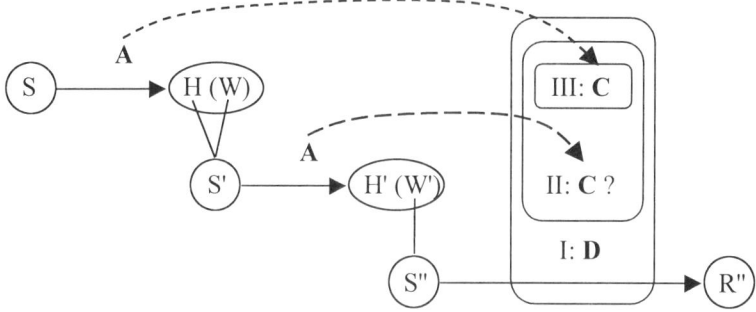

Figure 2 (letters A, C and D refer to the areas in Figure 1)

In the framework of the courtroom, there is a secondary communication S' → H' (W') in which S' = H or W makes a statement as the plaintiff or witness. Within the statement by S', the relevant utterance made by S is quoted as literally as possible. Statement (II) and quotation (III) together with the communicative-legal modalities of statement (I) are then recorded in writing by a court clerk S" = W' in a tertiary communication act S" → R" for a later reader R".

In a conceptional-medial respect (i.e. with reference to Figure (1)), the tertiary communication act S" → R" on textual level I should lean towards communicative distance and thus in the main belong to area D. The secondary communication act of the statement S' → H' (W') presumably tends towards communicative immediacy (area A), which under certain circumstances is even perceptible to a certain degree in the graphic medium on textual level II (area C?).[19]

The primary communication act S → H (W) was most definitely characterised by a very pronounced communicative immediacy (area A). As it is on account of their emotionality and spontaneity that the utterances themselves become justiciable, the use of Latin on textual level III poses a great problem. By this level at the latest a "translation" into Latin is therefore dispensed with (in Lio Mazor also on all upper levels) and there is an attempt to reproduce the utterances as authentically as possible with regard to the specific language and the conceptional aspects. The lexical level is of particular relevance here. It is therefore the legal context which provides the root for a later written conservation of immediate language, which, as we saw in 3.2., may definitely be allocated to area C in Figure 1.

As it is the spoken facts themselves that are justiciable, philologists generally assume that the texts are highly authentic – authentic, it should be observed, with regard to the writer, S'', who records the linguistic part of the secondary communication act S' → H' (W') on textual levels II and III. However, even a record of this kind must be expected to contain a certain degree of mediation and filtering. Indeed, part of a quotation is even translated into Latin at the beginning of (4b).[20] More complex still is the relationship between text passages on level III and the primary (!) "original utterances" S → H (W), because the power of memory and honesty of S' = H or W come into play here, but above all because the communication form used for quoting is different from the quoted communication form itself. We must not forget that a quotation is not the same as a tape-recording.

As confirmed by the analysis in 3.2., the institutional framework, strictly speaking, only guarantees that the wording on level III is sufficiently expressive in its immediacy to become legally relevant at all – no more and no less.

4. Cartoons

4.1. The data

The second group of data I would like to treat here is of a completely different nature. We now turn our attention to inscriptions from the 11th to the 12th century in northern and central Italy.

Our first example is the famous *Iscrizione di San Clemente* (Rome, late 11th century), which belongs to a fresco – sadly now fading – in the lower basilica of the church of San Clemente. It is one of the ten oldest vernacular documents in Italy altogether (excluding Sardinia) and the third oldest in Rome.[21] The reproduction of the inscription here is the more readily legible watercolour painted by Carlo Tabanelli at the beginning of the 20th century after a negative by Pompeo Sansaini (text (6a)); there then follows a reconstruction by Marazzini of the dialogue, to which I have supplied an English translation (text (6b)).

Court Records and Cartoons 413

(6) Rome: End of the 11th century (*Iscrizione di San Clemente*)
 a. Facsimile of the Tabanelli watercolour from Rafaelli (1987: Table VI)

b. Analytical scheme after Marazzini (1994: 158)

A: "FALITE DERETO/CO LO A: "Go at him from behind with the
   PALO/CARVON/CELLE"   stick, Carboncello!"
B: "D/U/R/I/TIAM COR/DIS/V(EST)/RIS" B: "Owing to your hard heartedness ...
C: "S/A/X/A/TRAERE/MERUI/S/TIS" C: ... you deserve to haul stones."
D: "ALBERTEL/TRAI<TE>"   D: "Albertello, pull!"
E: "GOS/MARI"   E: (Name label)
F: "SISIN/IUM"   F: (Name label)
G: "FILI/DELE/P/U/T/E/TRA/I/TE"   G: "Sons of a bitch, pull!"

The background to this little scene is a legend about Saint Clement (the fourth Pope at the end of the 1st century). Theodora, a Christian convert married to the heathen Sisinnius (a friend of the Caesar, Domitian), goes to Mass, which Clement is celebrating. Sisinnius suspects she has become unfaithful to him and follows her, whereupon he is struck with blindness and deafness. Although

Clement heals him, Sisinnius assumes that it is Clement who visited this evil on him. He orders his vassals to overpower Clement and take him away. Then the miracle depicted in the fresco takes place. While held by the vassals, Clement is transformed into a stone column which they now attempt to carry away.

What we have here is basically a precursor of present-day cartoons,[22] even if the notation conventions are rather different. As the distribution of linguistic elements on the fresco is not easy to follow, they have become a bone of contention. I opt for the interpretation which now appears to be the most likely (cf. Rafaelli 1987: 40ff., 51-53). The mosaic contains two pure name labels, namely *Sisinium* (F) for the person standing on the far right and *Gosmari* (E) for the vassal standing next to him on the left. Sisinnius first cries to the vassals: *Fili dele pute traite!* (G). Then it is either Gosmari or Sisinnius who shouts the following command to the vassal Albertello (the third person from the right): *Albertel trai(te)!* (D). Albertello or Gosmari then calls out to Carboncello (the vassal on the far left): *Falite dereto colo palo Carvoncelle!* (A). Finally, Saint Clement, "offstage" as it were, speaks the, grammatically not totally correct, Latin words: *Duritiam cordis vestris saxa traere meruistis* (B and C).

The next two examples are the oldest vernacular texts from Piemont. Within Italy as a whole, their chronological ranking is just, or at least almost, as high as text (6).[23] The first is a mosaic from the church of S. Maria Maggiore in Vercelli (about 1040):

(7) Vercelli (Piemont); about 1040 *(Mosaic from the church of S. Maria Maggiore*, illustration from Coppo 1965/66: 245)

This portrays two fighters duelling with shields and swords. The utterances they shout at each other are reproduced in written form: *fol!* 'idiot' on the lefthand edge of the picture and *fel!* 'villain' on the righthand.

The other Piemontese mosaic (mid 11th/early 12th century) used to be in the cathedral of S. Evasio in Casale Monferrato. As the current photograph (8a) reveals, restoration work on the cathedral rendered the inscription illegible; however, it has been passed down to us in the form of a sketch by Mella, (8b):

(8) Casale Monferrato (Piemont): mid 11th/early 12th century *(Mosaic in the cathedral of S. Evasio*; illustration (a) and reconstruction (b) from Coppo 1965/66: 254)

a.

b.

Here again we are presented with two fighters armed with shields and swords. The lefthand edge of the picture bears the inscription TOSCANA, which presumably should be read as a cartoon-style caption shouted out by one of the fighters. From the purely linguistic point of view, there are two interpretations compatible with the northern Italian character of the vernacular used here: 1. *tö scanna!* (corresponding to present-day standard Italian *to' scanna!*) 'Hey, go on, kill (me)!'; 2. *t'ò scanà!* (in line with present-day standard Italian *ti scannerò!*) 'I'm going to kill you!' (cf. Coppo 1965/66: 258f.; Stella 1994: 78).

4.2.   Analysis of conceptional aspects

Communicative immediacy is clearly apparent in these cartoon-style inscriptions, too. Their immediacy predominantly stems from the iconic component. Let us now run through all the conceptional parameters:[24]

(i) The physical immediacy of a face-to-face situation is produced by iconic means in all these cases: in (6) between the four protagonists, in (7) and (8) between the two respectively.

(ii) (7) and (8) are unequivocally private scenes. In (6) this is also the case for the violent part of the story, but the saint's words in Latin *ex cathedra* produce a higher degree of publicness.

(iii) No conclusions may be drawn about the degree of intimacy in (7) and (8). In (6) the intimacy between the master and his vassals is relatively strong, but the intimacy between the four perpetrators and the saint is not. This links up well with (ii).

(iv) As is the case with the court records, the high degree of emotionality is poignant here. The choice of words is derogatory (in the frame of the syntactic type of the appellation of the interlocutor): (7) *fol, fel*; (6) *fili dele pute* (the latter case blatantly flouting a taboo). The implementation of *scanà* in (8) is particularly expressive. The negative and positive face of the opposite partner is constantly threatened. In (6) the master can afford to goad on his vassals in this way; in (7) and (8) this verbal violation of territory reinforces the challenge in a fight.

(v) Context embeddedness, too, is a prominent parameter of the most startling kind. (7) and (8) contain but mere traces of language; everything else concerning the action is expressed in the physical images into which these "speech bubbles" are firmly integrated. Of particular note are the verb forms and the speech acts they express, all of which are distinguished by a strong, direct action reference. Whereas (7) contains no verb form at all, elsewhere it is the imperative which is the most dominant. In (6), *traite, trai(te)* and *falite dereto* stand for directive speech acts with the additional support of the vocative, which goads into action: *fili dele pute, Albertello, Carboncello*. According to one of the interpretations, *scana* in (8) is an imperative expressing a speech act of challenge, intensified by the discourse particle *tö*.[25] The other interpretation defines this as a future form, with which a speech act of threat (and in the final analysis an overpoweringly directive speech act) is performed.

(vi) A large proportion of referential immediacy is evident here. Where verbs actually do exist, the only grammatical person is the second person of the imperative: (6) *traite, trai(te), fa(lite)*; (8) *scana* (however, the latter may be understood as a component of the first person singular, *t'ò scanà*, depending on the interpretation).

In the vernacular parts of the inscriptions, the referential expressions all relate explicitly or implicitly only to people or things which are located in the *hic-nunc* area; no reference is made to people or things extraneous to the situation. In (6), for instance, the exophoric reference plays an important role: in *-li-* (in *falite*) in the pronominal form, in *-lo palo* with a definite article + description. The object of *trai* or *traite* remains purely implicit, but of course Saint Clement/the column is meant here on the grounds of his/its presence in the situation. The vocatives *fili dele pute, Albertello* and *Carboncello* refer *eo ipso* to an addressee within the speaking situation (likewise *fel* and *fol* in (7)). A special role has, of course, to be assigned to the saint's dictum in (6) as it is distinguished from the vernacular utterances not only on account of the choice of language, but also owing to its conceptional style. The use here of the abstract *duritia* and the generic plural *saxa* (instead of a singular *saxum*) is an indirect reference to elements of the situation (and the form of the second person plural is, of course, a direct reference to the addressees in the situation), but nevertheless it transcends this situation referentially, simply on account of the generic style. – If we are to adopt the interpretation *t'ò scanà* in (7), we find here a clear exophoric reference to the addressee.

(vii) It is not easy to speak of "dialogicity" in our three inscriptions in the sense of this conceptional parameter. (6) does not present real turn-taking in the vernacular, but rather shouts fired in all directions. The saint's voice offstage, of course, stands quite apart in its own right. (7) and (8) may well illustrate a constellation of two (in a duel!), but the written text in (7) sketches the bare minimum of an exchange and may be classified as an absolute border case of dialogicity$_1$; in (8) there is only one rudimentary utterance without any real exchange of words. However, these mosaics are indeed examples of dialogue$_2$, characterised by immediacy in many parameters, not least of all thanks to the frequent reference to *thou/ye*.

(x) As we saw in the court records (3.3.), we must again distinguish between two levels when considering the parameter of spontaneity. On the one hand, there are the iconic and graphic elements of the cartoon, due to an artistic act which certainly involves deliberation, and on the other the spontaneity of the communication processes invented by the artist. On the latter level, a high degree of spontaneity is most definitely indicated by the choice of words, the references to the situation and the use of the vocative.

4.3. Motivation for writing characterised by linguistic immediacy

The final parameter considered in 4.2., parameter (x), makes clear the essential difference between the texts examined in sections 2 and 3. Whereas the focus of section 2 was the quoting and recording of dialogues$_3$ in a three-step process (Figure 2), the inscriptions of section 3 do not pretend to be a written record of the occurrence of communication acts; on the contrary, these dialogues$_2$ are a fictional and staged creation in word and illustration. According to Oesterreicher's typology of writing characterised by linguistic immediacy (Table 3), the inscriptions may be categorised as type (8): mimetic or simulated orality in literature, parody and similar contexts.

Cartoons may be considered a form of literature in the broadest sense of the term. Indeed, it is in this form of literature, thanks to the omnipresence of illustration, that the problem of immediacy and distance is posed most drastically. (This does not, however, mean that all cartoons embody the same high level of immediacy.) Both the *Iscrizione di San Clemente* and the mosaic inscriptions are most definitely precursors of cartoons characterised by immediacy of language, and their role in early writing in certain regions of Italy is not to be neglected (cf. Koch 1993: 46).

It is, of course, legitimate to ask why the authors of these texts chose the form of the cartoon to reproduce dialogic$_2$, emotional oral language. The reason in the case of the *Iscrizione di San Clemente* (6) possibly lies in social and ecclesiastical tensions in Rome under Pope Paschalis II (1099-1118). While Paschalis II stood for the traditional power of the Church, at the same time there was a revolting laiety supporting the counter-popes (Theodoricus, Albertus, Silvester IV). It was presumably at this "incorrigible" laiety that the Church propaganda was levelled.[26] The cartoon may well have been implemented as a propaganda device, depicting the contrasts in the Church and society by means of contrasts in language and conception. St. Clement's Latin dictum implying reserve and distance symbolises the traditional power of the Church whereas the spontaneity and immediacy of the vernacular is used to represent the coarse, incorrigible laiety.

The inscriptions of Casale and Vercelli are also Church propaganda, this time as part of a attested moral campaign against the iniquities of *ira*. In those days duels frequently took place as a trademark of *ira*. The Church took up the issue and campaigned for the Christian ideal of *temperantia*. The particularly effective medium of comic-like cartoons was chosen as a persuasive means, the component of caricature applying both to the language and to the illustrations.[27]

If these interpretations are right, it must be assumed that in all three inscriptions, the produced communicative immediacy, supported by vivid illustration, had an ideological-persuasive function. In this framework, Latin would not have been able to reproduce adequately the depravity of the emotionality depicted – particularly as read out to a lay person – and this may well explain the choice of the vernacular, as well as the contrast between the vernacular and Latin in (6).

5. Conclusion

The paths along which spontaneous dialogical$_{2/3}$ immediacy in early Romance texts reaches the graphic medium belong, as we have seen, first and foremost to types (4) and (8) according to the typology in Table 3.[28] Writing characterised by linguistic immediacy of types (4) and (8) apparently requires a kind of staging, a specific frame, but one which is completely different in both cases.

Where immediacy of type (4) is documented, the setting is institutional, the stage being a courtroom providing a record of the justiciability of the facts treated. In the case of examples (4) and (5), this institutional frame makes its mark on the specific language itself right down to level II (defined in 3.1.), where Latin is used (for the main part not reproduced in the editions used here), whereas the vernacular does not emerge until on level III in quotations within the Latin framework. The pattern in example (3) is different, since the vernacular is already in use on levels II and I. The choice of the specific language apart, the conceptional style of the text is narrative as far down as level II; it is only within this narrative framework that the high degree of dialogicity$_3$ can be implemented on level III.

The mimetic type (8) is set in a frame of persuasive propaganda, which in turn implements the special medium of illustration in order to stage in a comic-strip-like form spontaneous dialogue$_2$ with linguistic immediacy.

Types (4) and (8) both require a motive for a permanent written record of dialogue$_{2/3}$ of the immediate kind, a motive which lies in the nature of the reproduced (type 4) or fictional (type 8) communication itself. In line with parameter (iv), this communication is in both cases highly emotional-expressive since its basis is conflict. The dialogues in the court records and the cartoon-type scenes both revolve around arguments. In example (6), we are assisting at a conflict between Sisinnius in his anger and blindness and the wisdom of Saint Clement, a conflict which is staged by the specific language and conceptional contrast as outlined above.

One point strikes me as being worthy of note. In all the examples analysed here, the writing characterised by dialogic$_{2/3}$ immediacy projects – either implicitly or even explicitly – a negative image of the protagonists. Quarrels and conflicts are the order of the day, whether they are set within the framework of a lawsuit or of persuasive fiction.

Notes

1 In a historical perspective, the affinities between medium and conception can, however, in part be differently represented. Thus, thanks to the omnipresent medial transcoding process of reading aloud/reciting and dictating, communicative distance in the phonic medium (area B) is particularly typical of the European Middle Ages (cf. Koch 1997a: 150, 157-160).
2 Add to this the fact that all communicative parameters bar (i) are of a continual nature.
3 For the situation in current linguistics cf. for example Fritz and Hundsnurscher (1994: XIIIf.); for the accentuation on the connection between dialogue and spoken language cf. Schwitalla (1994). For concepts of "dialogue" with different focusses, cf. for example Mukarovský (1967: 115); Weinrich et al. (1967: 117); Luckmann (1984: 53). Concerning the role of "dialogue" in philosophy, one might think of the Socratic "dialogue" or the Humboldtian view (1979: 137-139, 195f., 200-202 et passim); cf. also Habermas (1971); Bubner (1982: 52 ss, 227-237).
4 Cf. for example Tagliavini (1972: 212-220); Durante (1981: 53ff., 109ff.); Oesterreicher (1994); Schmidt-Riese (1997); Stimm (1980); Balibar (1985: 132-142); Schlieben-Lange (1996: 48-51, 55-59); Spitzer (1921/1976); Bruni (1984: 174-236, 479-517); cf. also note 5.
5 Cf. with special reference to Italian Radtke (1984); on the Romance languages in general: Koch (1993: 43-54).
6 Cf. Coseriu (1973: 6, 1981: 7, 35-47); Schlieben-Lange (1983, 1990); Koch (1988: 343f., 1997b: 43-54).

Court Records and Cartoons 421

7   Cf. for example for this viewpoint: Stimm (1980); Radtke (1984); Ernst (1985); D'Achille (1990); Holtus and Schweickard (1991); Schmidt-Riese (1997: 56f.).
8   Cf. the considerations in Herman (1990) and Ineichen (1993: 84f.) – This Latin text is, of course, not included in the *Inventaire* by Frank and Hartmann (1997).
9   Cf. Muller and Taylor (1932: 212 notes 14 and 15); Roncaglia (1965: 146f.); for another excerpt from the same text see also Renzi (1985: 237f.) – Frank and Hartmann (1997: I, 20, 37) exclude this document from their documentation on the grounds of its being too Latin.
10 With regard to text (2), Roncaglia refers quite explicitly to the "vivacità analitica e persino dialogica del fraseggio" (1965: 147).
11 In Lio Mazor itself, these *Atti dei podestà* are the oldest texts of all. In relation to the Venetian area (including the Lagoon), they are not quite at the beginning of the written vernacular, but definitely belong to its early phase. The following vernacular documents are chronologically earlier in this area: *Recordacione di Piero Corner* (3rd-4th quarter of the 12th century; still bears strong Latin elements); *Proverbi de femene* (mid 12th century or after 1216?); 50-60 documents and wills (from 1253); a version of the *Disticha Catonis* and the *Panfilo* (both mid 13th century); a Venetian sonnet (1308 or later). The tract *De regimine rectoris* by Paolino Minorita is from about the same period (1313-15). Cf. Stussi (1965: 1-86, 1980, 1995: 125); Tomasoni (1994: 212-221). None of these texts is included in the *Inventaire* by Frank and Hartmann (1997): in one case (the *Recordacione*) the editors consider the proportion of Latin to be too great (I, 37); in the other cases the date of the surviving manuscript is outside the documented period (up to 1250).
12 Only after having finished the manuscript of this article had I access to Zaccagnini (1909: 124f.), who quotes similar passages in vernacular from the (still not edited) Latin *Condanne di Manetto degli Scali, podestà di Pistoia* going back as far as 1295.
13 Cf. Gonon (1974: particularly XIII-XXV, XXXIII; moreover XIVf. for the sidelined texts No. 1-3 of an earlier date and which belong to Occitan-speaking Midi); Vurpas (1995: 390-398). The documentation in Frank and Hartmann (1997) does not include any text from the Forez before 1250 (No. 9028 belongs to the Lyonnais: Durdilly 1975: No. 1; cf. Vurpas 1995: 394).
14 With respect to Lio Mazor, Tomasoni speaks of a "tipo di scrittura [...] piuttosto immediata", in which "minacce, insulti, imprecazioni realisticamente oscene denunciano l'immediatezza delle registrazioni" (1994: 217 f; cf. also below note 20). D'Achille also categorises these documents "tra i testi più vicini al parlato" (1990: 39). Bongi (1890) calls the subtitle of his edition of insults of Lucca *Saggio di lingua parlata del Trecento* and Marcheschi, too, stresses: "si avvicinano al parlato presumibilmente più di altri testi" (1983: 7; this, however, does not prevent a differentiation in their views: see below 3.3.).
15 For the concepts of "negative" and "positive" face cf. Brown and Levinson (1987: 61ff.); for the concept of "territory": Goffman (1967).
16 In general on communication and emotion: Fiehler (1990). For expressive semantic procedures of communicative immediacy: Koch and Oesterreicher (1990: 114-120; 1996:

68-74); for the 'everyday rhetoric' effective in the latter and especially on hyperbolics: Stempel (1983). For linguistic taboos and dysphemisms (euphemisms are not relevant here!): Ullmann (1962: 204-209); Allan and Burridge (1991).

17 For the difference between exophoric and endophoric relations cf. Heger (1963: 19f.); Brown and Yule (1983: 192f.).

18 Cf. Koch and Oesterreicher (1990: 99f.).

19 Here differences between the individual groups of examples must be expected. (As already observed, the editions of texts (4) and (5) either do not print at all or include only fragments of level II, here in Latin.) As far as the texts from Lio Mazor are concerned, where all three levels are written in the vernacular, Stussi expressly ascribes immediacy also to level II when he speaks of "narrazioni vivacissime [i.e. level II] costellate di energico turpiloquio popolare [i.e. level III]" (1965: LXXIII). An interesting point in this respect is to be found in text (3), l. 4, namely indirect speech "slipping" into direct speech, which itself is responsible for producing level II in its textual and conceptual independence.

20 Gonon remarks on the *Registres audienciers*: "ils [sc. les clercs] préfèrent le latin jusqu'au XVIe s., mais reproduisirent scrupuleusement les dépositions des plaignants et des témoins, lesquels ne parlaient que le dialecte de leurs villages. [...] Le dialecte, vocabulaire surtout, apparaît pour transcrire les 'realia' et les paroles de gens du cru, dont la justice devait apprécier l'exact témoignage" (1974: XXIV). Benincà is a little more cautious in her judgment of the language form of the texts from Lio Mazor: "se non è la trascrizione stenografica del parlato, certamente riflette la lingua usata dal testimone. Le uniche oscillazioni verso una forma leggermente più colta sono di ordine fonetico e talvolta morfologico [...]" (1983: 187f.; these facts concerning the specific language are not, however, relevant to the aspects we are considering here). – Bongi still made a very definite statement on the texts from Lucca: "ne' processi e nelle sentenze per delitti commessi mediante la parola [...] dove una qualsiasi alterazione al corpo del delitto sarebbe stata falsità ed offesa alla giustizia" (1890: 75). Marcheschi (1983: 8) observes on the other hand that we are here dealing with more complex processes of selection, processing and copying.

21 Cf. Castellani (21976: 111-121); Renzi (1985: 298-304); Raffaelli (1987); Marazzini (1994: 156-159); Petrucci (1994: 47, 67-69); Frank and Hartmann (1997: No. 1003).

22 This inscription has indeed frequently been compared with today's *fumetti*: Roncaglia (1965: 219); Renzi (1985: 302); Petrucci (1994: 67); Marazzini (1994: 159). A standard work on comic strips expressly categorises the inscription as a precursor of this modern art form (Strazzulla 21980: 19).

23 Cf. Coppo (1965/66: 244-266); Stella (1994: 77f.); Gasca Queirazza (1995: 100f.); Frank and Hartmann (1997: No. 1002; inscription (8) is missing from the *Inventaire* because the original no longer exists).

24 Cf. the theoretical foundations laid down in notes 15-17 for the following analysis.

25 On the role of discourse markers in communicative immediacy cf. for example Gülich (1970); Schiffrin (1988); Koch and Oesterreicher (1990: 51-72).
26 Cf. Raffaelli (1987: 57f.). – Many points here remain hypothetical and indefinite. The arrest of Paschalis II by Emperor Henry V in 1111 cannot be connected to the fresco as it was created prior to this year. On the other hand, if Paschalis II, who was a cardinal-priest at the church of St. Clemente before being elected pope, really did commission the frescoes in the lower basilica (Frank and Hartmann 1997: II, 13), the inscription would have been too early for the dispute over his papacy.
27 Cf. Coppo (1965/66: 247-253, 257). Apart from the brutality of the fighting, the cartoon style comes to the fore in the fact, for example, that both mosaics depict one of the opponents with black skin. This does not mean that a black man is involved, but rather black is a symbol here of the power of darkness.
28 These early documents – especially in Italy – do also bear testimony to other forms of communicative immediacy (area C in Figure 1), but these cannot be classified as dialogical2/3 to the same extent. Here we should bear in mind the *Graffito della catacomba di Commodilla* (Rome, end of the first half of the 9th century) or the record-like *Testimonianze di Travale* (Tuscany, 1158); cf. Koch (1993: 45f.); Frank and Hartmann (1997: No. 1001 and 73.005).

References

Allan, Keith, and Kate Burridge
    1991   *Euphemism and Dysphemism. Language Used as Shield and Weapon*. New York/Oxford: Oxford University Press.
Balibar, Renée
    1985   *L'institution du français. Essai sur le colinguisme des Carolingiens à la République*. Paris: PUF.
Benincà, Paola
    1983   Osservazioni sulla sintassi dei testi di Lio Mazor. In: Christian Angelet, Ludo Melis, Frans Josef Mertens and Franco Musarra (eds.). *Langue, dialecte, littérature. Etudes romanes à la mémoire de H. Plomteux*. (Symbolae Facultatis Litterarum et Philosophiae Lovaniensis A 12). Leuven: Leuven University Press, 187-197.
Bongi, Salvatore (ed.)
    1890   Ingiurie, improperi, contumelie, ecc. Saggio di lingua parlata del Trecento cavato dai libri criminali di Lucca. *Il Propugnatore* N.S. 3/1, 75-134.
Brown, Gillian, and George Yule
    1983   *Discourse Analysis*. Cambridge: Cambridge University Press.

Brown, Penelope, and Stephen C. Levinson
  1987   *Politeness. Some Universals in Language Use.* (Studies in International Sociolinguistics 4). Cambridge: Cambridge University Press.
Bruni, Francesco
  1984   *L'italiano. Elementi di storia della lingua e della cultura.* Torino: UTET.
Bubner, Rüdiger
  ²1982   *Handlung, Sprache und Vernunft. Grundbegriffe praktischer Philosophie.* (stw 382). Frankfurt: Suhrkamp.
Castellani, Arrigo
  ²1976   *I più antichi testi italiani. Edizione e commento.* (Storia della lingua italiana e dialettologia 9). Bologna: Pàtron.
Coppo, Angelo
  1965/66   Tre antiche iscrizioni volgari su frammenti musivi pavimentali di Casale e di Vercelli. *Rendiconti della Pontificia Accademia Romana di Archeologia* 38, 237-266.
Coseriu, Eugenio
  1973   *Die Lage in der Linguistik.* (Innsbrucker Beiträge zur Sprachwissenschaft, Vorträge 9). Innsbruck: Institut für Sprachwissenschaft.
  ²1981   *Textlinguistik. Eine Einführung.* Ed. Jörn Albrecht. (TBL 109). Tübingen: Narr.
D'Achille, Paolo
  1990   *Sintassi del parlato e tradizione scritta della lingua italiana. Analisi di testi dalle orgini al secolo XVIII.* (I volgari d'Italia 4). Roma: Bonacci.
Durante, Marcello
  1981   *Dal latino all'italiano moderno. Saggio di storia linguistica e culturale.* (Fenomeni linguistici 1). Bologna: Zanichelli.
Durdilly, Paulette (ed.)
  1975   *Documents Linguistiques du Lyonnais (1225-1425)* (Documents linguistiques de la France, Série francoprovençale 2). Paris: Editions du CNRS.
Ernst, Gerhard
  1985   *Gesprochenes Französisch zu Beginn des 17. Jahrhunderts. Direkte Rede in Jean Héroards "Histoire particulière de Louis XIII" (1605-1610)* (Beihefte zur Zeitschrift für Romanische Philologie 204). Tübingen: Niemeyer.
Fiehler, Reinhard
  1990   *Kommunikation und Emotion. Theoretische und empirische Untersuchungen zur Rolle von Emotionen in der verbalen Interaktion.* Berlin/New York: de Gruyter.
Frank, Barbara, and Jörg Hartmann
  1997   *Inventaire systématique des premiers documents des langues romanes.* 5 vol. (ScriptOralia 100). Tübingen: Narr.

Fritz, Gerd
1994   Geschichte von Dialogformen. In: Fritz and Hundnurscher 1994, 545-562.
1995   Topics in the history of dialogue forms. In: Andreas H. Jucker (ed.). *Historical Pragmatics. Pragmatic Developments in the History of English.* (Pragmatics & Beyond. New Series 35). Amsterdam/Philadelphia: Benjamins, 469-498.
Fritz, Gerd, and Franz Hundsnurscher (eds.)
1994   *Handbuch der Dialoganalyse.* Tübingen: Niemeyer.
Gasca Queirazza, Giulano
1995   Veneto. In: Holtus *et al.* 1988 ff.: II,2, 98-111.
Goffman, Erving
1967   *Interaction Ritual. Essays on Face-to-Face Behaviour.* (Anchor Books A 596). Garden City: Doubleday.
Gonon, Marguerite (ed.)
1974   *Documents Linguistiques du Forez (1260-1498).* (Documents linguistiques de la France, Série francoprovençale 18). Paris: Editions du CNRS.
Gülich, Elisabeth
1970   *Makrosyntax der Gliederungssignale im gesprochenen Französisch.* (Structura 2). München: Fink.
Habermas, Jürgen
1971   Vorbereitende Bemerkungen zu einer Theorie der kommunikativen Kompetenz. In: Jürgen Habermas and Niklas Luhmann (eds.). *Theorie der Gesellschaft oder Sozialtechnologie – Was leistet die Systemforschung?* Frankfurt/M.: Suhrkamp, 101-141.
Heger, Klaus
1963   *Die Bezeichnung temporal-deiktischer Begriffskategorien im französischen und spanischen Konjugationssystem.* (Beihefte zur Zeitschrift für Romanische Philologie 104). Tübingen: Niemeyer.
Herman, Joseph
1990   Sur un exemple de la langue parlée à Rome au VIe siècle. In: Gualtiero Calboli (ed). *Latin vulgaire – latin tardif II.* Tübingen: Niemeyer, 145-157.
Holtus, Günter, Michael Metzeltin and Christian Schmitt (eds.)
1988ff. *Lexikon der Romanistischen Linguistik.* Tübingen: Niemeyer.
Holtus, Günter, and Wolfgang Schweickard
1991   Zum Stand der Erforschung der historischen Dimension gesprochener Sprache in der Romania. *Zeitschrift für Romanische Philologie* 107, 547-574.
Humboldt, Wilhelm von
1979   *Werke in fünf Bänden.* Eds. Andreas Flitner and Klaus Giel. Vol. 3: *Schriften zur Sprachphilosophie.* Darmstadt: Wissenschaftliche Buchgesellschaft.

Ineichen, Gustav
- 1993 L'apparition du roman dans des contextes latins. In: Selig *et al.* 1993, 83-90.

Koch, Peter
- 1988 Italienisch: Externe Sprachgeschichte I. In: Holtus *et al.* 1988ff.: IV, 343-360.
- 1993 Pour une typologie conceptionnelle et médiale des plus anciens documents/monuments des langues romanes. In: Selig *et al.* 1993, 39-81.
- 1997a Orality in literate cultures. In: Clotilde Pontecorvo (ed.). *Writing Development. An Interdisciplinary View.* (Studies in Written Language and Literacy 6). Amsterdam/Philadelphia: Benjamins, 149-171.
- 1997b Diskurstraditionen: zu ihrem sprachtheoretischen Status und ihrer Dynamik. In: Barbara Frank, Thomas Haye and Doris Tophinke (eds.). *Gattungen mittelalterlicher Schriftlichkeit.* (ScriptOralia 99). Tübingen: Narr, 43-79.

Koch, Peter, and Wulf Oesterreicher
- 1985 Sprache der Nähe – Sprache der Distanz. Mündlichkeit und Schriftlichkeit im Spannungsfeld von Sprachtheorie und Sprachgeschichte. *Romanistisches Jahrbuch* 36, 5-43.
- 1990 *Gesprochene Sprache in der Romania: Französisch, Italienisch, Spanisch.* (Romanistische Arbeitshefte 31). Tübingen: Niemeyer.
- 1994 Schriftlichkeit und Sprache. In: Hartmut Günther and Otto Ludwig (eds.). *Schrift und Schriftlichkeit/Writing and Its Use. Ein interdisziplinäres Handbuch internationaler Forschung/An Interdisciplinary Handbook of International Research.* Vol. 1 (Handbücher zur Sprach- und Kommunikationswissenschaft 10.1). Berlin/New York: de Gruyter, 587-604.
- 1996 Sprachwandel und expressive Mündlichkeit. *Zeitschrift für Literaturwissenschaft und Linguistk* 102, 64-96.

Levi, Ugo
- 1904 *I monumenti del dialetto di Lio Mazor.* Venezia: Federico.

Luckmann, Thomas
- 1984 Das Gespräch. In: Karlheinz Stierle and Rainer Warning (eds.). *Das Gespräch.* (Poetik und Hermeneutik 11). München: Fink, 49-63.

Lüdtke, Helmut
- 1964 Die Entstehung romanischer Schriftsprachen. *Vox Romanica* 23, 3-21.

Marazzini, Claudio
- 1994 *La lingua italiana. Profilo storico.* Bologna: il Mulino.

Marcheschi, Daniela
- 1983 *Ingiurie improperi contumelie ecc. Saggio di lingua parlata del Trecento cavato dai libri criminali di Lucca per opera di Salvatore Bongi. Nuova edizione rivista e corretta con introduzione, lessico e indici onomastici.* Lucca: Maria Pacini Fazzi.

Mukarovský, Jan
    1967   *Kapitel aus der Poetik.* (edition suhrkamp 230). Frankfurt: Suhrkamp.

Muller, Henri François, and Pauline Taylor (eds.)
    1932   *A Chrestomathy of Vulgar Latin.* Boston/New York: Heath [reprint Hildesheim etc.: Olms 1990].

Oesterreicher, Wulf
    1994   El español en textos historiográficos escritos por semicultos. Competencia escrita de impronta oral en la historiografia indiana. In: Jens Lüdtke (ed.). *El español de América en el siglo XVI.* Frankfurt/M.: Vervuert, 155-190.

    1995   L'oral dans l'écrit. Essai d'une typologie à partir des sources du latin vulgaire. In: Louis Callebat (ed). *Latin vulgaire – latin tardif IV.* Hildesheim etc.: Olms-Weidmann, 145-157.

    1997   Types of orality in text. In: Egbert J. Bakker and Ahuvia Kahane (eds.). *Written Voices, Spoken Signs. Tradition, Performance, and the Epic Text.* Cambridge, Mass., 190-214.

Petrucci, Livio
    1994   Il problema delle Origini e i più antichi testi italiani. In: Serianni and Trifone, 1994, 5-73.

Radtke, Edgar
    1984   Zur Quellenlage für die Erforschung des gesprochenen Italienisch in der Sprachgeschichte vor 1860. *Italienisch* 12, 20-28.

Raffaelli, Sergio
    1987   Sull'iscrizione di San Clemente. Un consuntivo con integrazioni. In: Francesco Sabatini, Sergio Raffaelli and Paolo D'Achille. *Il volgare nelle chiese di Roma. Messaggi graffiti, dipinti e incisi dal IX al XVI secolo.* (I volgari d'Italia 1). Roma: Bonacci, 35-66.

Renzi, Lorenzo
    1985   *Nuova introduzione alla filologia romanza.* Bologna: il Mulino.

Roncaglia, Aaurelio
    1965   Le Origini. In: Emilio Cecchi and Natalino Sapegno (eds.). *Storia della letteratura italiana,* Vol. I: *Le origini e il Duecento.* Milano: Garzanti, 1-269.

Schiffrin, Deborah
    1987   *Discourse Markers.* Cambridge: Cambridge University Press.

Schlieben-Lange, Brigitte
    1983   *Traditionen des Sprechens. Elemente einer pragmatischen Sprachgeschichtsschreibung.* Stuttgart: Kohlhammer.

    1990   Normen des Sprechens, der Sprache und der Texte. In: Werner Bahner, Joachim Schildt and Dieter Viehweger (eds.). *Proceedings of the Fourteenth*

International Congress of Linguists, 3 vols. Berlin: Akademie-Verlag, I, 114-124.
1996 *Idéologie, révolution et uniformité de la langue*. Sprimont: Mardaga.

Schmidt-Riese, Roland
1997 Schreibkompetenz, Diskurstradition und Varietätenwahl in der frühen Kolonialhistoriographie Hispanoamerikas. *Zeitschrift für Literaturwissenschaft und Linguistik* 108, 45-86.

Schwitalla, Johannes
1994 Gesprochene Sprache – dialogisch gesehen. In: Fritz and Hundsnurscher 1994, 17-36.

Selig, Maria, Barbara Frank and Jörg Hartmann (eds.)
1993 *Le passage à l'écrit des langues romanes*. (ScriptOralia 46). Tübingen: Narr.

Serianni, Luca, and Pietro Trifone (eds.)
1994 *Storia della lingua italiana*. Vol. 3: *Le altre lingue*. Torino: Einaudi.

Söll, Ludwig
1985 *Gesprochenes und geschriebenes Französisch*. (Grundlagen der Romanistik 6). Berlin: Schmidt.

Spitzer, Leo
1921 *Italienische Kriegsgefangenenbriefe. Materialien zu einer Charakteristik der volkstümlichen italienischen Korrespondenz*. Bonn: Hanstein [new Italian edition: *Lettere di prigionieri di guerra italiani 1915-1918*. Torino: Boringhieri].

Stella, Angelo
1994 Piemonte. In: Serianni and Trifone 1994, 75-105.

Stempel, Wolf-Dieter
1983 "Ich vergesse alles". Bemerkungen zur Hyperbolik in der Alltagsrhetorik. In: Manfred Faust, Roland Harweg, Werner Lehfeldt and Götz Wienold (eds.). *Allgemeine Sprachwissenschaft, Sprachtypologie und Textlinguistik. Festschrift für Peter Hartmann*. (TBL 215). Tübingen: Narr, 87-98.

Stimm, Helmut (ed.)
1980 *Zur Geschichte des gesprochenen Französisch und zur Sprachlenkung im Gegenwartsfranzösischen*. (Beihefte zur Zeitschrift für französische Sprache und Literatur, N.F. 6). Wiesbaden: Steiner.

Strazzulla, Gaetano
²1980 *I fumetti*. 2 vols. Firenze: Sansoni.

Stussi, Alfredo (ed.)
1965 *Testi veneziani del Duecento e dei primi del Trecento*. (Studi di lettere, storia e filosofia 27). Pisa: Nistri-Lischi.
1980 Antichi testi dialettali veneti. In: M. Cortelazzo (ed.). *Guida ai dialetti veneti II*. Padova: CLEUP, 85-100.

Stussi, Alfredo
    1995   Veneto. In: Holtus *et al.* 1988ff.: II,2, 124-134.
Tagliavini, Carlo
    ⁶1972   *Le orgini delle lingue neolatine.* Bologna: Pàtron.
Tomasoni, Piera
    1994   Veneto. In: Serianni and Trifone 1994, 212-240.
Ullmann, Stephen
    1962   *Semantics. An Introduction to the Science of Meaning.* Oxford: Blackwell.
Vurpas, Anne-Marie
    1995   Les scriptae francoprovençales. In: Holtus *et al.* 1988ff.: II,2, 389-405.
Weinrich, Harald *et al.*
    1967   Syntax als Dialektik (Bochumer Diskussion). *Poetica* 1, 109-126.
Wunderli, Peter
    1965   Die ältesten romanischen Texte unter dem Gesichtswinkel von Protokoll und Vorlesen. *Vox Romanica* 24, 44-63.
Zaccagnini, Guido
    1909   Studi e ricerche di antica storia letteraria pistoiese. I. Il volgare pisotiese dall' VIII al XIV secolo. *Bullettino storico pistoiese* 11, 111-143.

Dialogue and Violence
The Inca Atahualpa meets Fray Vicente de Valverde
(Cajamarca, Peru, 16th November 1532)[1]

Wulf Oesterreicher
Ludwig Maximilians University, Munich

Las agonías

En Cajamarca empezó la agonía.
El joven Atahualpa, estambre azul,
árbol insigne, escuchó al viento
traer rumor de acero.
Era un confuso
brillo y temblor desde la costa,
un galope increíble
– piafar y poderío –
de hierro y hierro entre la hierba.
Llegaron los adelantados.
El Inca salió de la música
rodeado por los señores.

Las visitas
de otro planeta, sudadas y barbudas,
iban a hacer la reverencia.
El capellán
Valverde, corazón traidor, chacal potrido,
adelanta un extraño objeto, un trozo
de cesto, un fruto
tal vez de aquel planeta
de donde vienen los caballos.
Atahualpa lo toma. No conoce
de qué se trata: no brilla, no suena,
y lo deja caer sonriendo.
"Muerte,
venganza, matad, que os absuelvo",
grita el chacal de la cruz asesina [...]

(Pablo Neruda, *Canto general*, III, XV)

1. Introduction

The importance of the written word in the conquest and colonisation of the New World may not always be immediately obvious, but its role cannot be overestimated. As a Spanish priest rightly put it in the 17th century: *Sin la pluma no corta la espada* 'Without the quill the sword will not cut.' The Spanish successively enveloped the continent in a tight net of written and printed texts, thereby introducing European literacy.[2]

The 'representative' texts on the discovery and conquest of America are well known.[3] They have long been the subject of analysis for historians, theologians, anthropologists and ethnologists, sociologists, literary theorists and linguists. It is particularly striking that in the first half of the 16th century in America a remarkable number of simple soldiers, who had experienced the discovery, conquest and colonisation at first hand, wrote down or dictated their experiences of their own accord. These conquistadors without any real literary training were partly encouraged by various, even official, parties to put their oral reports and accounts into writing.[4]

The texts produced by these *soldados cronistas* are of interest to linguistics, in particular to studies of linguistic variation, in that they display verbalisation processes and language forms which so-called experts in writing who adhere to the prescriptive norm do not use.[5] These texts by inexperienced authors are of interest for our purposes because unfiltered evaluations, interpretations and details appear which are completely absent from, or are embellished or censored in the representative historiographic writings of the upper echelons.[6]

American written communication is characterised by a number of fundamental communicative asymmetries. At the beginning of the 16th century, the indigenous people – including the advanced civilizations of Mesoamerica and the Andes – were in principle excluded from written communication. Communication with the Indios existed only in the phonetic form, i.e. conversation, reports and the reading out of written texts, whereby a change in media was introduced. Genuine written communication with reception of the written, in other words reading, was initially non-existent. However, a switching between languages was always required in the form of translation and interpreting. This switching was involved in all language communication between speakers of Spanish and Indian languages and explains the utmost importance placed on translators, *lenguas*, by Spanish conquistadors in the early days.[7] We should always bear in mind this distortion and systematic medial and linguistic asymmetry of communication when we treat the following subject matter.[8]

2. Sources

The subject of our discussion is a certain historical event, namely a conversation which has often been described in literature as a significant encounter between two worlds which was to change the course of history, not only in the eyes of Spanish authors of the period.[9]

The talks were held in the north Peruvian town of Cajamarca on 16th November 1532 about two hours before sunset in the central town square overlooked by buildings. It is this exchange between the Inca ruler, Atahualpa, and the Dominican priest sent by Francisco Pizarro, Fray Vicente de Valverde, which immediately preceded the massacre of the Indios and the capture of Atahualpa by the Spanish, that we wish to examine here.[10]

From the plethora of accounts of this historic event I have chosen ten reports and taken care that the following variables are included (these are exclusively reports by Spaniards – there is no inclusion of the so-called *visión de los vencidos*):[11]

a. the texts, in an extended meaning of the word historiographic, correspond to different discourse traditions (letters, reports, chronicles, etc.);
b. eye-witness accounts of the conversation stand alongside texts written by mere onlookers of the events at Cajamarca and by authors with information received at second-hand;
c. the differences in the textual competence of the writers lead to considerable differences in the description and the conceptional profile of the texts; there are also different appreciations of the event;
d. the chronological diversity in the dates of the texts, from 1533 – just a few months after the event – to 1571, the year in which two eye witnesses recorded the event, is also significant;
e. in the case of a number of reports a particular type of intertextuality is important which specialists in American studies like to call *los otros piratas de América* and which may be considered as specific to American written communication. The use of other people's texts by certain authors is what we would nowadays refer to as plagiarism.[12]

These ten historiographic texts, in which the contradictory reports and interpretations of the conversation between Atahualpa and Valverde are likely to baffle the attentive reader, are to be confronted with a legal text which brings the problems to a surprising solution. This solution is, to my mind, of significance to a number of questions concerning the analysis of non-fictional historical discourse in general and historical dialogue analysis in particular.[13]

3. Historical background

In this paper, I do not wish to elaborate on the details of the historical background to the event under discussion[14]; a brief synopsis may suffice. After Hernán Cortés conquered Mexico in 1519, the Spanish began to explore the west and south Pacific coast, starting from Panama. Francisco Pizarro, Diego de Almagro and the cleric Hernando de Luque, who represented the main financial backer of the enterprise, the privy counsellor Espinosa, attempted to reach Peru in 1530 in their third expedition, after two failures. For this third attempt they were in possession of a crown contract, a *capitulación*, which Pizarro received in 1529 after an audience with Charles V – no doubt partly owing to the strong impression Cortés had made at the Court with his Indios and valuable gifts from Mexico. On 26th July 1529 the queen signed the contract with Pizarro. His assignment was to discover, conquer and populate the area of Túmbez. He was made governor of the region in order that he might rule and preside over justice there (*para que descubra, conquiste y pueble las tierras e provincias de Túmbez de la Mar del Sur [...] e le habemos proveido de la gobernación de la dicha tierra para que él la gobierne e tenga en justicia*).[15] Pizarro therefore received the title of Governor and General Captain, Almagro was knighted and was to command the town and fortress of Túmbez, while Luque was to become bishop of the town. Captain Bartolomé Ruíz was appointed *piloto mayor de la Mar del Sur*.

In January 1530, the Spanish set sail from Panama on three ships. It was not until September 1532, after Hernando de Soto and Sebastián Benalcázar had brought reinforcements from Nicaragua, that Pizarro was able to found the first Spanish town in the north of Peru. 60 Spaniards remained as *vecinos fundadores* in the town of San Miguel de Piura, which Pizarro left with 168 soldiers, 62 of them cavalry, on 24th September 1532.

The important constellations and results of the civil war between the two sons of the Inka Huayno-Capac, which in the long run turned out to be favourable to the Spanish, do not need further discussion here. The conflict which broke out after Huayno-Capac's death in 1525 ended in a victory for Atahualpa over his half-brother Huáscar. In 1532, Atahualpa was on the move with his victorious army from the northern provinces, with Quito as the capital, to the actual capital of the Inca kingdom, Cuzco. Before this march began, he had already heard his people complain about the Spanish, who had threatened villagers, stolen gold and even killed a *cacique* on their way southwards. This had prompted Atahualpa to send an ambassador to the coast to the Spanish in order to lodge the complaint and to invite them to Cajamarca to elucidate the accusations. The Spanish took the audacious step of responding to the 'summons'. They encountered no hazards on their journey through the barely accessible valleys in the Andes and finally reached Cajamarca. It was there that they met with the shock of finding that Atahualpa and his army had set up camp near the town. There was no way back.

After due deliberation, Pizarro sent a squadron of cavalrymen to Atahualpa who was partaking in a ritual fast about six Spanish miles away from Cajamarca. The encounter between Captain Hernando de Soto and his cavalry and Atahualpa was the first contact between the Spanish and the Inca. The account of this meeting by Francisco López de Gómara in his *Historia general de las Indias* (Text No. I) of 1552 clearly expresses the Spaniards' awe. Atahualpa's majesty and authority were impressive and the number, discipline and arms of the soldiers at the camp were frightening (*Fernando Pizarro volvió espantado de la grandeza y autoridad de Atabalipa, y de la mucha gente, armas y tiendas que había en su campamiento*, I, 6-8). Atahualpa provided quarters for the Spanish in Cajamarca and left them, announcing his arrival in the town for the following day.

The Spanish spent an anxious night in fear of attack in a building in the central square of Cajamarca. It was not only the simple soldiers who panicked. The young Pedro Pizarro remembered that "*yo vi a muchos españoles que sin sentirlo se orinaban de puro terror.*"[16] The fear of being outnumbered and the unknown methods of combat and fighting morale of the Indios led Pizarro and his men to decide to attempt an ambush and try to capture Atahualpa. The location seemed suitable since streets leading off the square could be easily blocked off. The Spanish placed their hopes in the effect of the surprise attack, in the impression made on their opponents by unfamiliar horses, firearms, steel swords and armour – and above all in the successful outcome of taking Atahualpa hostage.

The next day Atahualpa took his time over coming to Cajamarca. The Spanish, needing daylight for their plan to work, were obviously getting rather agitated. Not until the late afternoon did Atahualpa arrive at the main square of Cajamarca, borne on a litter and accompanied by high dignitaries and an unarmed crowd of his people. Once the procession had stopped, Pizarro sent the Dominican priest, Vicente de Valverde, to Atahualpa. We have now arrived at the episode we wish to examine and the ambiguous and contradictory accounts supplied by our authors.

4. Presentations of the event

I would now like to discuss a selection of texts, namely Nos. II-XI, printed in Spanish in the appendix, in chronological order.

In his *Carta a los oidores de Santo Domingo* (1533) (Text No. II), Franzisco Pizarro's brother, Hernando, has the Dominican Valverde announce to Atahualpa that the *gobernador*, Pizarro, wishes to speak to him at his lodgings and that he, Valverde, has been sent by the emperor to teach Atahualpa and his people the Christian faith if they want to become Christians (*si quisiesen ser cristianos*, II, 5). Atahualpa requests the book, which according to Valverde contains the *cosas de Dios*, then throws it to the ground, threatening the Spaniards with his people if they do not return their stolen possessions (*Yo no pasaré de aquí hasta que me deis todo lo que habéis tomado en mi tierra*, II, 8-9). Atahualpa's threat is the only passage in direct speech. Thereupon Valverde returns to Francisco Pizarro, who orders his brother to have the cannon fired as the signal to start the attack (*Yo tenía concertado con el capitán de la artillería que, haciéndole una seña, disparase dos tiros, e con la gente que, oyéndolos, saliesen todos a un tiempo. E así se hizo*, II, 14-16). This text is surprisingly clear in its account of the planned attack.

The soldier Cristóbal de Mena (Text No. III) also reports that Valverde offers talks with Pizarro. But Atahualpa demands that the stolen property be returned. He remains visibly unimpressed by the speech made by Valverde, who held a cross in his hand and spoke of the Christian faith (*con un libro que traya en las manos le empeçó a dezir las cosas de Dios que le convenían: pero el no las quiso tomar*, III, 8-9). Atahualpa does, however, wish to see the book – a breviary or the Bible – and Valverde hands it to him. Curiously, Mena remarks that Valverde believes Atahualpa wants to kiss the book (*pidiendo el libro, el padre se lo dio, pensando que lo quería besar*, III, 9-10), but Atahualpa throws it into the crowd. The translator returns it into Valverde's hands. This profanation of Holy Writ causes Valverde to curse the Indios as 'dogs' and exhort his men to attack. This is the only passage in direct speech (*salid, salid, cristianos, y venid a estos enemigos perros, que no quieren las cosas de Dios: que me ha hechado aquel cacique en el suelo el libro de nuestra santa ley*, III, 14-16). The command is given for the cannon to be fired into the crowd *(Y en esto hizieron señas al artillero que soltasse los tiros por medio dellos*, III, 16-17). The cannon fire is the signal to attack. It is important to note here that to Mena the opening of hostilities was the inevitable consequence of the desecration of Holy Writ.

The soldier and secretary to Pizarro, Francisco de Xerez, is the first author (Text No. IV) to explicitly mention the participation of a translator. Holding the cross in one hand and the Bible in the other, Valverde has the translator say that he, as a priest, wishes to preach the holy faith, that God's Word is in the book and that Atahualpa should meet the *gobernador*, Pizarro, who is willing to hold talks. When Atahualpa is handed the book, he is not able to open the clasp. When Valverde tries to come to his aid, he arrogantly hits Valverde's outstretched arm (*y no acertando Atabaliba a abrirle, el religioso estendió el brazo para lo abrir, y Atabaliba con gran desdén le dio un golpe en el brazo, no queriendo que lo abriese*, IV, 15-18). Surprisingly, Xerez finds it curious that Atahualpa does not marvel at the script or the paper (*no maravillándose de las letras ni del papel como los otros indios*, IV, 18-20). He, on the contrary, tosses the book away and says – *con mucha soberbia* – that he will not leave the square until he has reclaimed the possessions stolen by the Spanish. Valverde reports back to Pizarro, upon which the latter takes up his arms (*El religioso dijo al Gobernador todo lo que había pasado con Atabaliba, y que había echado en tierra la sagrada Escriptura. Luego el Gobernador se armó*, IV, 29-31). In Xerez's text the basic structure is clearly dialogue form, in which Valverde and Atahualpa's words are frequently recorded in direct speech. Xerez introduces the new element of humiliation when Atahualpa strikes a servant of the Christian faith. He emphasizes the arrogance with which Atahualpa desecrates the Bible and treats the Spanish like thieves and robbers.

In Text No. V, Miguel de Estete, an ordinary soldier, also makes specific mention in his *Noticia del Perú* of 1535 of the interpreter who accompanies Valverde and translates his words (*salió [...] con la Biblia en la mano y con él Martín Lengua; y así juntos, llegaron por entre la gente a poder hablar con Atabalica; al cual le comenzó a decir cosas de la Sagrada Escritura y que Nuestro Señor Jesucristo mandaba que entre los suyos no hubiese guerra ni discordia sino toda paz*, V, 4-11). Atahualpa listens to Valverde's speech for a long time without replying. Again the book is handed to Atahualpa, who opens it and turns the pages, apparently more fascinated by the script than by the content, as Estete points out (*admirándose, a mi parecer, más de la escritura que de lo escrito en ella*, V, 17-18). Red with anger, he then throws the book into the crowd and demands reparations for the damage perpetrated by the Spanish. This passage is in direct speech. Valverde thereupon hurriedly returns to Pizarro and urges him to attack, since negotiations with such an arrogant dog (*con este perro lleno de soberbia*, V, 27) appear to be impossible and since more and more Indios were streaming into the square. He grants the Spanish an absolution in advance (*¡Salid a él, que yo os absuelvo!*, V, 28) and with the cry of *¡Santiago a ellos!* the Spanish rush upon their opponents (V, 31).

Juan Ruiz de Arce, a soldier and eyewitness, provides a great deal of dialogue in his account (Text No. VI). He quite openly states that Valverde's first order was to invite Atahualpa to supper with Pizarro in order to encourage him to advance and to entice him to step forward (*porque se saliese mas de la jente*, VI, 4). Atahualpa, however, strictly demands the return of the stolen gold, silver, slaves and clothing, and threatens the Spanish with death if they do not respond to these demands (*no e De pasar de aqui si no me traeis todo el oro y plata y esclavos y rropa que me traeis y teneis y no lo trayendo tengoos de matar a todos*, VI, 8-10). Valverde replies that this is not God's will and speaks of the Maker of all and his commandment of love (*no manda Dios eso, sino que nos amemos a nosotros*, VI, 12), saying that all this is written in the Holy Bible. Atahualpa demands the book and, making fun of Valverde, throws it far away from himself (*arrojolo por ay burlando del flaire*, VI, 16-17). Valverde retrieves it and, weeping and beseeching God, returns to Pizarro, who gives the pre-arranged signal for attack (*toma su libro y vuelve donde el governador estava llorando y llamando a Dios*, VI, 17-18).

The Spaniards' massacre of the unarmed Indios lasts two hours. Fleeing Indios trample each other to death. Atahualpa, when captured, relates that 7000 Indios have been killed (*mataronse muchos yndios confesado por boca de atabalica que le aviamos muerto En aq^a batalla siete mill yndios Avia dos oras de sol duro la batalla dos oras*, VI, 26-28).

The detailed account, consisting to a great extent of dialogue, by the historian Gonzalo Fernández de Oviedo (Text No. VII) – incidentally not an eyewitness – is similar to the *Relación* by Francisco de Xerez on most scores. Valverde tells of his duty to preach the Christian faith and he invites Atahualpa to speak to Pizarro. Atahualpa asks for the Bible and throws it into the crowd, demanding reparations from the thieving Spaniards. A new element introduced by Oviedo is the passage in which Atahualpa, from his litter, incites his men against the Spanish (*E Atabalipa se puso de pie en sus andas, volviéndose a una parta e a otra hacia los suyos, e los habló con soberbia, que paresció que los apercebía y esforzaba*, VII, 33-36). Numerous instances in his *Historia* of 1547 show that Fernández de Oviedo very often copied passages word for word from Xerez's text. By way of example, compare these two passages: Atahualpa strikes Valverde (VII, 17-19) and Atahualpa's lack of astonishment when he opens the Book (VII, 20-22).

Pedro Cieza de León, who was not an eyewitness, chooses indirect speech for his entire report of the meeting written in 1553 (*Llevó el fraile a Felipillo para que su razón fuese entendida por Atabalipa*, IX, 1-2). Holding his breviary, Valverde speaks of his duty as a priest to preach the Christian faith and peace among men. Atahualpa is amused by Valverde's speech and asks for the book. Turning the many pages, he finds their content useless. Unaware of what he has in his hands, he throws the book away. Cieza de León makes the perspicacious comment that had Atahualpa received an adequate explanation, he would have had a clearer understanding of the matter (*para que lo entendiera, habíanselo de decir de otra manera, y de esta manera no tenía lugar*, IX, 11-13). He then strongly criticises those priests who only preach properly when there is no threat of danger (*mas los frailes por acá nunca predican sino donde no hay peligro ni lanza enhiesta*, IX, 13-14). When Atahualpa says that he will wait until Pizarro has returned the stolen gold, silver, jewels, clothes and Indios along with everything else, Valverde hurries back to Pizarro and exhorts him to attack Atahualpa (*con mucha prisa volvió a Pizarro, diciéndole que el tirano Atabalipa venía, como dañado perro, ¡que diesen en él!*, IX, 19-21).

In 1571 the simple soldier Diego de Trujillo, records his own memories of his experiences. His account (Text No. X) is based on a narrative frequently and very cleverly related as is evident from its microstructure, which consists of fast-moving dialogue (X, 3-4, 4, 10, 11, 12, 14-15, 15, 18). (This is why Trujillo, as we know, was ordered directly by the fifth viceroy of Peru, Francisco de Toledo, to write down his *Relación*[17]). Trujillo reports that Valverde explains to Atahualpa the mission commanded by the emperor and the Pope, shows him the breviary and tells him of the Gospel (*[Valverde] procuró dalle a entender al efecto que veniamos, y que por mandado del Papa un hijo que tenía capitán de la cristiandad que era el Emperador Nro Sor, y que hablando con él palabras del Sto. Evangelio*, X, 6-10). Atahualpa peruses the book, asks Valverde questions and finally throws the book into the crowd with a threatening gesture (*le arrojó [...] como un tiro de herrón de allí diciendo, ea, ea, no escape ninguno*, X, 13-15). Valverde returns in haste to the *gobernador*, calling Atahualpa a devil (*que hace vmd. que Atabalipa está hecho un Lucifer*, X, 18). The massacre then ensues and Atahualpa is pulled from his litter and captured.

He is promised his freedom on condition that he fill a room with golden treasure for the Spanish (*le hicieron entender que él se iría a Quito a la tierra que su padre le dejó, y por esto mandó un buhío lleno de oro*, X, 33-35). A year later, on 29 August 1533, Atahualpa will nonetheless be murdered by the Spanish.[18]

In retrospect it would be tempting to agree with the following interpretation of the 'conversation'. In these texts the Spanish intended their planned attack on Atahualpa and his unarmed retinue to be interpreted by a number of different reporters as the inevitable consequence of Atahualpa's hostility, pride and refusal to co-operate which had been manifested in the course of the talks. Indeed, in these texts Atahualpa's attitude, i.e. his spurning of the Christian faith and its servants, his scorn of the Spanish, is step by step functionalised as a justification of the attack by the Spaniards and the capture of Atahualpa. Atahualpa had to be punished as his unseemly behaviour had provoked the Spanish attack. However, such an interpretation of the testimony in these texts is not acceptable for the reasons stated in the next section.

5. Reanalysis of the communication situation

I believe the key to an adequate understanding of the passages in the texts lies in the analysis of the concrete communication situation. I am convinced that the meeting between Atahualpa and Valverde was not a 'conversation' at all. The character of the dialogue and conversation visible in all the texts results from factors which have lower priority than the Spaniards' real intention. It is these factors which systematically lead readers, and modern readers in particular, to the wrong conclusions.

If we take as our starting point the systematically distorted communication type which is asymmetrical both medially and in the use of language, the following characteristics emerge:

a. the necessary inclusion of a translator leads to three speakers being involved;
b. during translation Valverde's utterances are of necessity fragmented;
c. the translator – responsible for the change of language – addresses Atahualpa himself when translating;
d. this obviously gives Atahualpa the opportunity to get involved in the communcication process and take an active part.

In this way, a formal impression of a "conversation" is created, which functions to a certain extent as a "dialogic basic structure" in all the reports treated here.

An important key to the correct interpretation of the events is provided by a text by the eyewitness Pedro Pizarro, which was not put into writing until 1571 (Text No. XI). He makes mention of an extremely important detail which Cieza de León also refers to: when speaking to Atahualpa, Valverde holds a breviary in his hand (*Llevaba en las manos un breviario cuanto esto decía*, IX, 5-6). Pizarro, 17 years of age at the time, remembers it in more detail. Valverde's "sermon" which the interpreter translates is in the breviary – in other words, Valverde "reads what he preaches" (*predicó cosas de nuestra*

Dialogue and Violence 441

Sancta Fee, declarándoselas la lengua. Lleuaba un breuiario el Padre en las manos, donde leya lo que predicaua, XI, 2-4). But what did Valverde read out?

6. Towards a solution

At this point, the *Historia general de las Indias* by Francisco López de Gómara written in 1552 gives key information, so to speak as a convergence point for all the accounts named so far. Gómara may not have been an eyewitness at Cajamarca, but he is to be considered altogether as an extremely well-informed historian (Text No. VIII). After Atahualpa's polite address, Gómara has Valverde say in direct speech (and I paraphrase):

"The Holy Trinity created the world from nothing and He created Adam from whom all men are descended. Yet Adam sinned against his Creator and since then all have been and will be born in original sin, excepting Jesus Christ, who was born of the Virgin Mary as the true God to redeem us from our sins. He died on the Cross, was resurrected on the third day and ascended into Heaven after forty days. As His representative on Earth He left Saint Peter and his successors, the Popes, who conferred on the mighty king of Spain the conquest and conversion of these lands. Therefore Francisco Pizarro has now been sent to ask you to become friends and subjects of the King of Spain, the Roman Emperor, the ruler of the world. You shall obey the Pope and assume the Christian faith, which is holy, for your own faith is false. And know that if you act to the contrary, we shall wage war against you and take away your false idols from you that you might spurn your false religion and gods." (VIII, 4-22)

Gómara continues (in indirect speech): Atahualpa replied in a rage that he as a free man would pay tribute to no one and that he had never heard of a lord greater than himself. Nevertheless, he would gladly become a friend of the Emperor who sent so many armies into the world. Yet he would not obey the Pope since the latter gave away lands that were not his own and would not let someone he had never seen keep the kingdom which he had inherited from his father. As to religion, he had always held his own in high esteem and would never question such an ancient and venerable thing. Christ had died, but the sun and the moon would live forever. And how did Valverde know that the God of the Christians had created the world? Valverde answered Atahualpa by saying that the answer was contained in the book, and handed him his breviary. Atahualpa took the book, turned the pages, said it told him nothing of all this and threw it to the ground. We know the rest...

This comparatively detailed text, which does not introduce dialogue until close to the end and in which, significantly enough, no translator is mentioned, is often considered to be an embellishment and as a learned compilation of the original drafts and reports provided by informants on the Atahualpa-Valverde talks, rendered in indirect speech. In a certain respect, then, this text has not been taken seriously. It is therefore not surprising that as late as 1994, in his book *Escribir en el aire. Ensayo sobre la heterogeneidad socio-cultural en las literaturas andinas* the Peruvian author, Antonio Cornejo Polar, as so many before him, should support the view that Gómara's text was written later and made considerable use of Catholic dogma and certain legal texts:

> Es imposible ofrecer ahora una recopilación exhaustiva de todas las versiones posteriores, pero es claro que son en su mayor parte *ampliaciones y/o estilizaciones de la materia de los primeros relatos*, aunque no se pueda omitir el hecho de que sus fuentes no siempre residen sólo en la tradición escrita sino también en otra – la oral – que a trechos parece discurrir de manera paralela, según acabo de insinuar. De ampliación se trata en casos como los de Zárate o Gómara que *'transcriben' (obviamente lo imaginan)* el largo parlamento del padre Valverde: *un más o menos prolijo recuento de los dogmas de la fe católica y de las ordenanzas del Rey en una versión que deriva de manera harto directa del texto del 'requerimiento' redactado por Palacios Rubios en 1512.* (Cornejo Polar 1994: 32-33; my italics)

7. Conclusions

Why the decisive step towards a correct understanding has not been taken here is hard to comprehend. Interpretations of the kind referred to above are simply no longer possible once we recognise in Valverde's conduct and speech a concept which has its own name in Castilian legal history: Valverde is in fact proclaiming the *requerimiento* which had been in use at the end of the 15th century in a preliminary form at the time of the conquest of the Canary Islands and which became compulsory in America from 1514 onwards.[19]

This formal legal act comprises the reading out of a text – originally written by the lawyer Juan López de Palacios Rubios – which calls for submission and conversion and simultaneously serves to justify the presence of the Spanish and their military actions in foreign parts. Apart from the common practice of taking land as *res nullius*, in other words *non per bellum sed per acquisitionem*, legalistic-thinking Spain developed this specific alternative form for a declaration of war based on the 1494 Treaty of Tordesillas under Ferdinand of Aragon in the discussion over the legal title regarding the conquest and colonisation of America.

The *requerimiento* used by Pedrarias Dávila is to be found in the appendix as Text No. XII,[20] which Pizarro is likely to have known and used. It contains exactly the same points as those mentioned by Gómara, the final passage culminating in a formal threat of violence:

> Sy no lo hizierdes, o en ello dilaçion maliçiosamente pusierdes, çertificos que con la ayuda de Dios yo entraré poderosamente contra vosotros y vos haré guerra por todas las partes y maneras que yo pudiere, y vos subjetaré al yugo y obediençia de la Yglesia y de Sus Altezas, y tomaré vuestras personas y de vuestras mugeres e hijos y los haré esclavos, y como tales los venderé y disporné dellos como Su Alteza mandare, y vos tomaré vuestros bienes, y vos haré todos los males e daños que pudiere, como a vassallos que no obedeçen ni quieren reçibir a su señor y la (sic) resisten y contradizen; y protesto que las muertes y daños que dello se recrecieren, sean a vuestra culpa, y no de Su Alteza, ni mia, ni destos cavalleros que conmigo vinieron; y de cómo los digo y requiro pido al presente escriuano que me lo dé por testimonio sinado, y a los presentes ruego dello sean testigos. (Morales Padrón 1979: 340)

If we interpret the events at Cajamarca as the fulfilment of the *requerimiento*, a comparison of the complete text of the *requerimiento* with the account by Francisco López de Gómara, combined with a re-reading and reanalysis of the other reports suddenly sheds new light on the texts presented, no matter how much they lack in unity, are inconsistent and fragmentary. All the information contained in those texts now becomes coherent in that it in some way refers to the *requerimiento*. Figure 1 elucidates this point.

As we do not share any common ground with the people living in that period, we have to bear in mind that some of our authors and their readers were possibly well acquainted with events in America, knew exactly what Valverde was doing and immediately recognised the procedure in the different accounts. Nevertheless, it is surprising that the term *requerimiento* only appears in the texts by López de Gómara and the soldier Miguel de Estete, and even here it is used in the plural and in combination with another term: *enviaban embajadores y requerimientos* (López de Gómara, I, 5-6) and *estáis en comedimientos y requerimientos* (Estete, V, 26). Perhaps the other authors did not consider the exact definition of terms necessary; perhaps they were trying to make the blame placed on Atahualpa as plausible as possible; or perhaps their pride and sense of shame prevented them from making explicit reference to the procedure. No matter what the underlying reason for this omission may be, our assessment is corroborated not only by the legal practice which demanded the *requerimiento*, but also by the fact that the different texts do not present a coherent whole until this assumption has been made.

(1) communication acts, which are no longer directly accessible to us, between Atahualpa, Valverde and the translator in Cajamarca

(2) reconstructable communication situation which is medially and linguistically asymmetrical

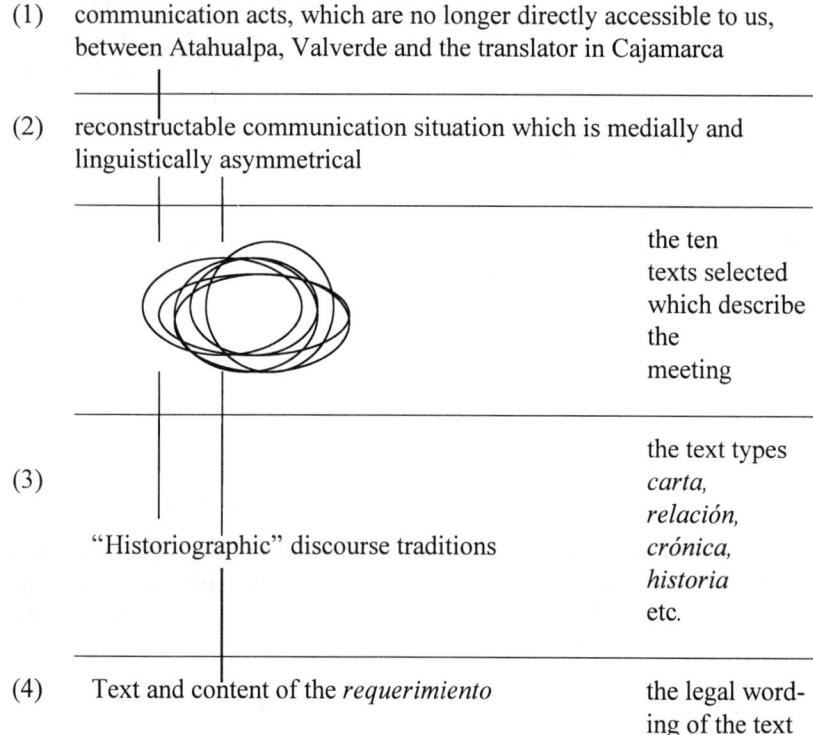

the ten texts selected which describe the meeting

(3) "Historiographic" discourse traditions

the text types
carta,
relación,
crónica,
historia
etc.

(4) Text and content of the *requerimiento*   the legal wording of the text

Figure 1: Levels of understanding of the Spanish *relatos*

What has been said so far demonstrates quite clearly how important it is to historical dialogue analysis, and historical text interpretation altogether, to undertake a concrete analysis of communicative contexts and to adopt a discourse-traditional perspective, i.e. to adopt a perspective which takes seriously the dynamics and scope of contemporary legal, theological, historiographic and literary text genres and which spells out their specific pragmatics.

Quite apart from the tragic events of Cajamarca, it is true that the reading of the *requerimiento* generally culminated in 'weird' scenarios. Even lawyers of the time had to admit this fact. Fighting frequently took place before the *requerimiento* was even read out. The distance from the Indio groups was often so great that they could not even hear the recitation. And even if they were able to hear it, they could not understand a single word, anyway. It was not until 1526[21] – in other words, six years before the 'declaration of war' against

Atahualpa in Cajamarca – that a simultaneous translation of the *requerimiento* was stipulated by law.

Apart from these communication-practical aspects, it is important to emphasize another decisive point, which a Eurocentric view of these American events tends to neglect. The theological, legal and political concepts proclaimed in the *requerimiento*, with terminology such as 'trinity', 'creation', 'fall from grace', 'virgin birth', 'crucifixion', 'resurrection', 'papacy', 'emperor', 'mission', 'idolatry', cannot have been translated so as to produce any meaning to the Indio way of thinking. It is therefore understandable that the Dominican friar Bartolomé de las Casas, the famous *protector de los indios*, together with other monks and a number of jurists, considered the *requerimiento* to be an inexecusable form of cynicism.[22] Las Casas once remarked that he did not know whether to laugh or cry: the *requerimiento* was *injusto, impío, escandaloso, irracional y absurdo, infamante para la fe y para la religión cristiana* 'unjust, impious, scandalous, irrational and absurd, a disgrace to the Faith and the Christian religion'.[23]

Notes

1 This paper, here revised, enlarged and adapted, is based on my article entitled "Das Gespräch als Kriegserklärung. Atahualpa, Pizarro und das Gold von Peru" (Oesterreicher 1997).
2 Cf. Scharlau (1982); Mignolo (1982); Goic (1988); Janik and Lustig (1989): 9-11; Mignolo (1991); Oesterreicher (1994b): 379-381. Above all, cf. the documents in Porras Barrenechea (1944); Konetzke (1953); Otte (1993).
3 Cf. for example Griffin (1971); Wilgus (1975); Esteve Barba (1992); also Schmitt (1986). Cf. also Kohl (1982); Jara and Spadacini (1989).
4 Cf. Oesterreicher (1994b): 383 note 16 and 411-412.
5 Cf. Oesterreicher (1992), (1994a) and (1994b).
6 This also sheds a somewhat different light on the rather sweeping statements made by Gumbrecht (1987); cf. also Oesterreicher (1994b): 385 and 412-413. Cf. above all Stoll (1997).
7 Cf. Oesterreicher (1995): 105 and (1996): 162-163.
8 Cf. above all Martinell Gifre (1988) and (1996); also Scharlau/Münzel (1986).
9 Here may I refer by way of example to Michel de Montaigne's famous text 'Des coches' in the *Essais* (Montaigne 1967: 876-894).
10 For the traumatic effects of this event on the Indio sense of identity cf. the impressive account in Huhle (1992). For the complete event cf. above all Hemming (1982): 13-74;

Lockhart (1986/87); also Prescott (1986): 234-310; Porras Barrenechea *et al.* (1988): 120-131; Carrillo Espejo (1987); Morales Padrón (1988), (1990).
11 The texts are by the following authors which appear here with the date of the publications: Cieza de León (1985); Miguel de Estete (1938); Fernández de Oviedo (1959); Francisco López de Gómara (1954); Cristóbal de Mena (1937); Hernando Pizarro (1953); Pedro Pizarro (1986); Juan Ruiz de Arce (1933); Diego de Trujillo (1948); Francisco López de Xerez (1988). For linguistic and textual aspects of a number of the texts listed cf. Stoll (1997).
12 Cf. Oesterreicher (1994a): 171.
13 Note that the problem outline developed below, though based on a concrete example, unfortunately plays no role in the discussion on the theoretical and methodological basis of current discourse and dialogue analysis; compare various papers presented at conferences on dialogue research since (1986), which in other respects are extremely rich and valuable (cf. Hundsnurscher and Weigand 1986; Weigand and Hundsnurscher 1989; Stati, Weigand and Hundsnurscher 1991; Löffler 1993; also Fritz and Hundsnurscher 1994). What is required is an orientation guided by problem awareness, such as already achieved in the field of 'Poetics and Hermeneutics' (cf. above all Koselleck and Stempel 1973). It is therefore all the more pleasing that a number of papers in our colloquium on historical dialogue analysis treat more or less directly the problematic constellation of 'dialogue'/'discourse tradition'/'author interest' and the so-called 'authentic communicative event'.
14 Cf. here, and with regard to the following events, the accounts in Hemming (1982): 13-74; Prescott (1986): 234-319; Porras Barrenechea *et al.* (1988): 120-131.
15 Cited in Hemming (1982): 17 note 3.
16 Cited in Hemming (1982): 33.
17 Cf. Oesterreicher (1994b): 383 note 16 and 411-412.
18 Cf. Porras Barrenechea *et al.* (1988): 128-131. – Cf. also the impressive poem N° XV 'La línea colorada' from the *Canto general* by Pablo Neruda (1976).
19 Rainer Huhle also believes that Valverde is reading out the *requerimiento*. Although he is arguing differently – namely, using the 'logic of events' – and does not consider the communication situation itself (which he still refers to as a 'conversation'), his conclusion is unequivocal: "La lógica de los hechos y las múltiples referencias en las crónicas nos convencen de que el texto del requerimiento fue leído por Valverde, lo que no excluye que la conversación haya tocado otros temas o que Valverde haya usado sus propias palabras para adornar el mensaje chantatista" (Huhle 1992: 389); cf. also the picture subtitle in König (1992): 186, which complies with Estete's account (but see also my argument below). – Regarding the *requerimiento* cf. above all Morales Padrón (1979): 329-347; also Hanke (1988), ch. 4: 48-56.
20 Printed in Morales Padrón (1979): 338-340.
21 Cf. Huhle (1992): 389.

22 Cf. in this connection the general discussion on the entitlement to conquer and colonise Hispano-America in Morales Padrón (1979); Ramos *et al.* (1984); Hanke (1988); cf. also the papers in Kohut (1991).
23 Cited in Morales Padrón (1979): 336.

Appendix

(I) Francisco López de Gómara (1552)
1   "[...] y para concluir dijo que sería buen amigo del Emperador y del capitán si devolviese todo el oro, plata y otras cosas que había tomado a sus vasallos y amigos, y se fuese luego de su tierra, y que uno de los días siguientes estaría con él en Cajamarca para dar orden en la vuelta, y para saber quiénes
5   eran el Papa y el Emperador, que de tan lejanas tierras le enviaban embajadores y requerimientos. Fernando Pizarro volvió espantado de la grandeza y autoridad de Ataballba, y de la mucha gente, armas y tiendas que había en su campamiento [...]"
(Francisco López de Gómara: Historia general de las Indias, 198)

(II) Hernando Pizarro (1533)
1   "Entrado hasta la mitad de la plaza, reparó allí e salió un fraile dominico que estaba con el Gobernador a hablarle de su parte, que el Gobernador le estaba esperando en su aposento, que le fuése a hablar. E díjole cómo era sacerdote e que era enviado por el Emperador para que les enseñase
5   las cosas de la fe, si quisiesen ser cristianos. E díjole que aquel libro era de las cosas de Dios. Y el Ataballba pidió el libro e arrojóle en el suelo e dijo:
    – 'Yo no pasaré de aquí hasta que deis todo lo que habéis tomado en mi tierra; que yo bien sé quién sois vosotros y en lo que andáis'.
10 E levantóse en las andas e habló a su gente e hubo murmullo entre ellos, llamando a la gente que tenían las armas.
    El fraile fué al Gobernador e díjole que qué hacía, ya que no estaba la cosa en tiempo de esperar más. El Gobernador me lo envió decir.
    Yo tenía concertado con el capitán de la artillería que, haciéndole una
15 seña, disparase los tiros, e con la gente que, oyéndolos, saliesen todos a un tiempo. E así se hizo."
(Hernando Pizarro: Carta a los oidores, 57)

(III) Cristóbal de Mena (1534)
1   "Y un frayle de la Orden de santo Domingo con una cruz en la mano queriendole dezir las cosas de Dios, le fue a hablar: y le dixo, que los christianos eran sus amigos: y que el señor governador le queria

mucho y que entrasse en su posada a ver le. El cacique respondio que
5   el no passaria mas adelante hasta que le bolviessen los christianos
todo lo que le havian tomado en toda la tierra y que despues el haria
todo lo que le viniesse en voluntad. Dexando el frayle aquellas
platicas, con un libro que traya en las manos le empeço a dezir las
cosas de Dios que le convenian: pero el no las quiso tomar: y pidiendo
10 el libro, el padre se lo dio, pensando que lo queria besar: y el lo tomo,
y lo echo encima de su gente. y el mochacho que era la lengua, que
alli estava diziendo aquellas cosas, fue corriendo luego: y tomo
el libro, y diolo al padre: y el padre se bolvio luego dando bozes,
diziendo, salid salid cristianos, y venid a estos enemigos perros,
15 que no quieren las cosas de Dios: que me ha hechado aquel cacique
en el suelo el libro de nuestra santa ley. Y en esto hizieron señas
al artillero que soltasse los tiros por medio dellos [...]"
(Cristóbal de Mena: La conquista del Perú llamada la Nueva Castilla, 85-6)

(IV) Francisco de Xerez (1534)
1   "En llegando Ataballa en medio de la plaza, hizo que todos estuviesen
quedos, y la litera en que él venía y las otras en alto: no cesaba de entrar
gente en la plaza. De la delantera salió un capitán, y subió en la fuerza
de la plaza, donde estaba el artillería, y alzó dos veces una lanza
5   a manera de seña. El Gobernador, que esto vio, dijo al frey Vicente que
si quería ir a hablar a Ataballa con un faraute; él dijo que sí, y fue con
una cruz en la mano y con la Biblia en la otra, y entró por entre
la gente hasta donde Ataballa estaba, y le dijo por el faraute:
'Yo soy sacerdote de Dios, y enseño a los christianos las cosas de
10 Dios, y asimesmo vengo a enseñar a vosotros. Lo que yo enseño es
lo que Dios nos habló, que está en este libro. Y por tanto, de parte
de Dios y de los christianos te ruego que seas su amigo, porque
así lo quiere Dios; y venirte ha bien dello; y ve a hablar al
Gobernador, que te está esperando'. Ataballa dijo que le diese
15 el libro para verle y él se lo dio cerrado; y no acertando Ataballa
a abrirle, el religioso estendió el brazo para lo abrir, y Ataballa
con gran desdén le dio un golpe en el brazo, no queriendo que lo
abriese; y porfiando él mesmo a abrirlo, lo abrió; y no
maravillándose de las letras ni del papel como los otros indios,
20 lo arrojó cinco o seis pasos de sí. E a las palabras que el religioso
había dicho por el faraute respondió con mucha soberbia diciendo:
'Bien sé lo que habéis hecho por ese camino, cómo habéis tratado
a mis caciques y tomado la ropa de los bohíos'. El religioso

respondió: 'Los christianos no han hecho esto; que unos indios
25 trujeron ropa sin que él lo supiese; y él la mandó volver'.
Atabaliba dijo: 'No partiré de aquí hasta que toda me la traigan'.
El religioso volvió con la respuesta al Gobernador. Atabaliba
se puso en pie encima de las andas, hablando a los suyos que
estuviesen apercebidos. El religioso dijo al Gobernador todo
30 lo que había pasado con Atabaliba, y que había echado en tierra
la sagrada Escriptura. Luego el Gobernador se armó [...]"
(Francisco de Xerez: Verdadera relación de la conquista del Perú, 111-2)

(V) Miguel de Estete (1535)
1   "[...] comó él vió que ninguna persona salía a él ni parecía, tuvo
creído y así lo confesó él después de preso, que nos habíamos
escondido de miedo de ver su poder y dió una voz y dijo:
'¿Dónde están éstos?', a la cual salió del aposento del dicho
5   gobernador Pizarro, el Padre Fray Vicente de Valverde, de la
Orden de los Predicadores, que después fué Obispo de aquella
tierra, con la Biblia en la mano y con él Martín lengua; y así
juntos, llegaron por entre la gente a poder hablar con Atabalica;
al cual le comenzó a decir cosas de la Sagrada Escritura y que
10 Nuestro Señor Jesucristo mandaba que entre los suyos no hubiese
guerra ni discordia sino toda paz; y que él en su nombre así se lo
pedía y requería; pues había quedado de tratar de ella el día antes,
y de venir solo, sin gente de guerra; a las cuales palabras y otras
muchas que el Fraile le dijo, él estuvo callando sin volver
15 respuesta; y tornándole a decir que mirase lo que Dios mandaba,
lo cual estaba en aquel libro que llevaba en la mano escrito,
admirándose, a mi parecer, más de la escritura que de lo escrito
en ella, le pidió el libro, y le abrió y le ojeó, mirando el molde
y la orden de él y después de visto le arrojó por entre la gente,
20 con mucha ira y el rostro muy encarnizado, diciendo: 'Decidles
a ésos que vengan acá, que no pasaré de aqui hasta que me den
cuenta y satisfagan y paguen lo que han hecho en la tierra'.
Visto esto por el fraile y lo poco que aprovechaban sus
palabras, tomó su libro y abajó su cabeza y fuese para donde
25 estaba el dicho Pizarro casi corriendo y díjole: '¡No veis lo
que pasa!, ¿para qué estáis en comedimientos y requerimientos
con este perro lleno de soberbia, que vienen los campos llenos
de indios? ¡Salid a él, que yo os absuelvo!'; y así acabadas
de decir estas palabras que todo fué un instante, tocan las

30 trompetas, y parte de su posada con toda la gente de pie que
    con él estaba,diciendo: '¡Santiago a ellos!' Y así salimos todos
    a aquella voz a una [...]"
    (Miguel de Estete: Noticia del Perú, 223-4)

(VI) Juan Ruiz de Arce (ca. 1545)
1   "Entra Atabalica en la plaça con tanto poderio que era cosa
    de ver En medio de la plaça se paro. como el governador vido
    aquello Enviole un flaire para que llegase m^s adelante a hablar
    con el governador porque se saliese mas de la jente. El flaire fue
5   y le dixo estas palabras Atabalica el governador te esta
    esperando para çenar y te ruega que vayas porque no çenara sin
    ti. El rrespondio aveisme rrobado la tierra por Donde aveis venido
    y agora estame esperando para çenar no e De pasar de aqui si
    no me traeis todo el oro y plata y esclavos y rropa que me
10 traeis y teneis y no lo trayendo tengoos de matar a todos
    Entonces le rrespondio el flaire y le Dixo mira Atabalica que
    no manda Dios eso, sino que nos amemos a nosotros Entonçes le
    pregunto Atabalica quien es ese dios El flaire le Dixo el que te hizo
    a ti y a todos nosotros, y Esto que te digo lo Dexo aqui escripto
15 En este libro Entonces le pidio Atabalica el libro y el flaire se lo
    dio y como Atabalica vido El libro arrojolo por ay burlando del
    flaire, toma su libro y vuelve donde el governador estava llorando
    y llamando a Dios, y luego el governador hizo la seña que estava
    conçertada y como vimos la seña salimos De tropel con muy gran
20 grito y dimos en ellos y fue tanto el temor que huvieron que se
    subieron unos encima de otros en tanta manera que hicieron sierras
    que se ahogaban unos a otros y en la muralla que cercava la plaça
    cargo tanta gente de yndios sobre ella que la derrivaron y hizieron
    un portillo de hasta treinte pasos por alli salio mucha jente huyendo
25 y todos los demas de a cavallo salimos al campo tras ellos Estava
    un campo llano De unas vegas mataronse muchos yndios confesado
    por boca de atabalica que le aviamos muerto En aq^a batalla
    siete mill yndios Avia dos oras de sol duro la batalla dos oras"
    (Juan Ruiz de Arce: Relación de los servicios, 362-3)

(VII) Gonzalo Fernández de Oviedo (1547)
1   "El gobernador vía todo esto desde su aposento. Visto que
    Atabaliba había reparado, dijo a un reverendo padre de la
    Orden de los Predicadores, llamado fray Vicente de Valverde,
    que con él estaba, e Sus Majestades le habían mandado ir a

5   aquella tierra, para la conversión de los indios, que si quería
    ir a hablarle con una lengua, y él dijo que sí, e fué con una cruz
    en la mano y en la otra una Biblia de la Sagrada Escriptura,
    y entró por entre la gente de Atabaliba hasta llegar a la litera
    donde estaba, e díjole por la lengua: 'Yo soy siervo de Dios
10 y enseño a los cristianos las cosas de Dios, e asimesmo vengo
    a enseñar a vosotros; y lo que les enseño es lo que Dios
    nos habló, que está en este libro. Y por tanto, de parte de Dios
    e los cristianos, te ruego que seas su amigo, porque así lo
    quiere Dios, e venirte ha bien dellos, e vete a asentar con
15 el gobernador, porque te está esperando.' Dijo Atabaliba
    al religioso que le diese el libro para velle: el religioso se lo dió
    cerrado; e queriéndolo abrir el Atabaliba e no acertando, el
    religioso extendió el brazo para se lo abrir, y el Atabaliba,
    con gran desdén, le dió un golpe en el brazo, apartándosele,
20 que no quería que le abriese; e porfiando a abrille, le abrió,
    e no maravillándose de la letras ni del papel, como otros indios
    suelen hacer, le arrojó luego cinco o seis pasos de sí; y
    entendidas por Atabaliba las palabras del religioso, respondió:
    'Bien sé todo lo que habéis hecho por ese camino; que habéis
25 rancheado mis pueblos e tomado la ropa a mis caciques, e cómo
    los habéis tractado, e aquí habéis saqueado mis buhíos e tomado
    la ropa que en ellos tenía.' El religioso le dijo: 'Los cristianos
    no han hecho nada: que unos indios suyos ayer fueron a unos
    buhíos e trujeron ropa, sin que el gobernador lo supiese,
30 e toda la mandó volver esta mañana a un principal tuyo.'
    Atabaliba replicó: 'No partiré de aquí hasta que todo me lo traigan
    delante'. Y el religioso se volvió al gobernador a le dar la
    respuesta e decir lo que es dicho. E Atabaliba se puso de pie
    en sus andas, volviéndose a una parta e a otra hacia los suyos,
35 e los habló con soberbia, que paresció que los apercebía y
    esforzaba.
    El religioso dijo al gobernador lo que con Atabaliba había
    pasado, e la mucha soberbia con que había echado la Sagrada
    Escriptura por el suelo, e que le parescía que venía de mal
40 arte. El gobernador se armó luego [...]"
    (Gonzalo Fernández de Oviedo: *Historia general y natural de las Indias*, 55-6)

(VIII) Francisco López de Gómara (1552)
1   "Llegóse entonces a él fray Vicente de Valverde, dominico, que

llevaba una cruz en la mano y su breviario, o la Biblia como
algunos dicen. Hizo reverencia, le santiguó con la cruz, y le dijo:
'Muy excelente señor, cumple que sepáis cómo Dios trino y uno
5   hizo de la nada el mundo y formó al hombre de la tierra, que
llamó Adán, del cual traemos origen y carne todos. Pecó Adán
contra su Criador por desobediencia, y en él cuantos después
han nacido y nacerán, excepto Jesucristo, que siendo verdadero
Dios, bajó del cielo a nacer de María virgen, para redimir
10 el linaje humano del pecado. Murió en cruz semejante a ésta,
y por eso la adoramos. Resuscitó el tercer día, al cabo de
cuarenta subió al cielo, dejando como vicario suyo en la tierra
a San Pedro y a sus sucesores, que llaman papas, los cuales
habían dado al potentísimo rey de España la conquista y
15 conversión de aquellas tierras; y por eso, viene ahora Francisco
Pizarro a rogaros seáis amigos y tributarios del rey de España,
emperador de romanos, monarca del mundo; y obedezcáis al
Papa, y recibáis la fe de Cristo, si la creyereis, que es
santísima, y la que vos tenéis es falsísima. Y sabed que si
20 hacéis lo contrario os daremos guerra y os quitaremos los
ídolos, para que dejéis la engañosa religión de vuestros
muchos y falsos dioses." Respondió Atabaliba muy enojado que
no quería tributar siendo libre, ni oír que hubiese otro mayor
señor que él, sin embargo, que se alegraría de ser amigo del
25 Emperador y de conocerle, pues debía de ser gran príncipe,
cuando enviaba tantos ejércitos como decían, por el mundo;
que no obedecería al Papa, porque daba lo ajeno, y por no
dejar a quien nunca vió, el reino de su padre. Y en cuanto a la
religión, dijo que muy buena era la suya y que se hallaba bien
30 con ella, y que no quería ni mucho menos debía poner en disputa
cosa tan antigua y aprobada; y que Cristo murió, y el sol y la luna
nunca morían, y que ¿cómo sabía el fraile que el Dios de los
cristianos creara el mundo? Fray Vicente respondió que lo decía
aquel libro, y le dió su breviario. Atabaliba lo abrió, miró, hojeó,
35 y diciendo que a él no le decía nada de aquello, lo arrojó al
suelo. Tomó el fraile su breviario, y se fué a Pizarro gritando:
'Los evangelios en tierra; venganza, cristianos; a ellos, a ellos,
que no quieren nuestra amistad ni nuestra ley'. Pizarro, entonces
mandó sacar el pendón y jugar la artillería [...]"
(Francisco López de Gómara: Historia general de las Indias, 199)

(IX) Cieza de León (1553)
1   "[Valverde] Llevó el fraile a Felipillo para que su razón fuese
    entendida por Atabalipa, a quien contó, como a él llegó, lo que
    se ha dicho: y que él era sacerdote de Dios que predicaba su ley
    y procuraba cuanto en sí era, que no hubiese guerra sin paz,
5   porque de ello se serviría Dios mucho. Llevaba en las manos
    un breviario cuanto esto decía. Atabalipa, oíalo como cosa de
    burla; entendió bien con el intérprete todo ello; pidió a fray
    Vicente el breviario; púsoselo en las manos, con algún recelo
    que cobró de verse entre tal gente. Atabalipa lo miró y remiró,
10 hojeólo una vez y otra; pareciéndole mal tantas hojas, lo arrojó
    en alto sin saber lo que era; porque para que lo entendiera,
    habíanselo de decir de otra manera, y de esta manera no tenía
    lugar; mas los frailes por acá nunca predican sino donde no hay
    peligro ni lanza enhiesta; y mirando contra fray Vicente y
15 Felipillo, les dijo que dijesen a Pizarro que no pasaría de
    aquel lugar donde estaba hasta que le volviesen y restituyesen
    todo el oro, plata, piedras, ropa, indios e indias con todo lo demás
    que le habían robado. Con esta respuesta, cobrado el breviario,
    alzadas las faldas del manto, con mucha prisa volvió a Pizarro,
20 diciéndole que le tirano Atabalipa venía, como dañado perro,
    ¡que diesen en él!"
    (Cieza de León: La Crónica del Perú, 156-7)

(X) Diego de Trujillo (1571)
1   "Entrado que fué Atabalipa en la plaza de Caxamalca, como no
    vido christianos ningunos preguntó al Inga que avía venido
    con nosotros de Maxicavilca, y Carran, que es de estos de
    las barvas y respondió estarán escondidos, y hablando el que
5   se bajase de las andas en que venía no lo quiso hacer, y entonces
    con la lengua salió a hablalle fr. Vicente de Valverde, y procuró
    dalle a entender al efecto que veniamos, y que por mandado
    del Papa un hijo que tenía capitán de la cristiandad que era
    el Emperador Nro Sor, y hablando con él palabras del Sto.
10 Evangelio, le dixo Atabalipa, quien dice eso, y él repondió
    Dios lo dice, y Atabalipa dixo como lo dice Dios, y fr. Vicente
    le dijo veslas aquí escritas, y entonces le mostró un Breviario
    abierto y Atabalipa se lo demandó, y le arrojó despues que lo
    vió como un tiro de herrón de allí diciendo, ea, ea, no escape
15 ninguno, y los Indios dieron un grande alarido diciendo ho, Inga,

que quiere decir hágase así, y el alarido puso gran temor;
y entonces se volvió fr. Vicente y subió a donde estava el
Governador, que hace vmd. que Atabalipa está hecho un Lucifer;
y entonces el Governador se desnudó, y tomó un sayo de armas
20 y una espada, y una adarga, y una zelada, y con los 24 que
estávamos con él, salimos a la plaza, y fuimos derechos a las
andas de Atabalipa, haciendo calle por la gente y estandole
sacando de las andas, salieron los de a caballo, con pretales
de cascaveles, y dieron en ellos; y como los indios huyeron, y
25 en las calles les defendían la salida, apechugaron con un lienzo
de unas parés, y lo hallanaron por el suelo, y allí, y en la plaza
cayó tanta gente una sobre otra que se ahogaron muchos, que
de ocho mil indios que allí murieron, más de las dos partes
fueron muertos de esta manera, siguióse el alcance de los
30 Indios aquella tarde, mas de media legua, metiose a Atabalipa
en la fortaleza, y preguntava si a el sile avían de matar, y le
dijeron que no, porque los christianos con aquel impetu
matavan, mas que después no, y le hicieron entender que él
se iría a Quito a la tierra que su padre le dejó, y por esto
35 mandó un buhío lleno de oro."
(Diego de Trujillo: Relación del descubrimiento del reyno del Perú, 58-9)

(XI) Pedro Pizarro (1571)
1 "Llegado que fué el Padre a las andas en donde Ataualpa benía,
le habló y dixo a lo que yua y predicó cosas de nuestra Sancta
Fee, declarándoselas la lengua. Lleuaba un breuiario el Padre
en las manos, donde leya lo que predicaua. El Ataualpa se lo
5 pidió, y él se lo dió çerrado, y como lo tubo en las manos no
supo abrille, arroxólo en el suelo. Llamó al Aldana que se
llegase a él y le diese el espada, y el Aldana la sacó y se la
mostró, pero no quiso darsela. Pues pasado lo dicho,
el Ataualpa les dixo que se fuesen para bellacos ladrones,
10 y que los auía de matar a todos.
Pues oydo esto, el Padre se uoluió y contó al Marqués lo que
auía pasado; el Ataualpa entró en la plaça con todo su trono
que traya, y el señor de Chincha tras él, y desque ubieron
entrado vió que no paresçía español ninguno, preguntó a sus
15 capitanes: '¿Dónde están estos christianos, que no parescen?';
ellos le dixeron: 'Señor; están escondidos de miedo'."
(Pedro Pizarro: Relación del descubrimiento y conquista de los reinos del Perú, 38)

(XII) El requerimiento
El requerimiento que se ha de hazer a los indios de Tierra Firme

Notificaçion y requerimiento que se ha de hazer a los moradores de las yslas e tierra firme del mar Oçeano que aun no estan subjetos al rey nuestro señor. De parte del muy alto e muy poderoso y muy catolico defensor de la Yglesia, siempre vençedor y nunca vençido, el gran rey don Hernando el quinto de las Españas, de las Dos Çiçilias, de Iherusalem y de las yslas e Tierra Firme del Mar Oçeano, etc., domador de las gentes barbaras, y de la muy alta e muy poderosa señora la Reyna doña Juana, su muy cara e muy amada hija, nuestros señores. Yo, Pedrarias Davila, su criado, mensajero y capitan, vos notifico y hago saber como mejor puedo, que Dios Nuestra Señor, Uno y Eterno, crió el çielo y la tierra y un honbre y una muger, de quien nosotros y vosotros y todos los honbres del mundo fueron y son desçendientes y procreados, y todos los que despues de nosotros vinieren mas por la muchedunbre de la generaçion que destos ha subçedido desde çinco mill y mas años qu el mundo fue criado, fue nesçesario que los unos onbres fuesen por una parte, y otros por otra, y se dividiesen por muchos reynos y provinçias, que en una sola no se podrian sostener ni conservar.

De todas estas gentes Dios nuestro Señor dio cargo a uno que fue llamado Sant Pedro, para que de todos los honbres del mundo fuese señor e superior, a quien todos ovedesçiesen e fuesen cabeça de todo el linaje umano donde quier que los honbres biviesen y estubiesen, y en qualquier ley, seta o creençia y diole a todo el mundo por su reyno, señorio y juridiçion.

Y como quier que le mandó que pusiese su silla en Roma, como en lugar mas aparejado para regir el mundo, mas tambien le permitio que pudiese estar y poner su sylla en qualquier otra parte del mundo, y juzgar y governar a todas las gentes, Christianos, moros, judios, gentiles y de qualquier otra seta o creençia que fuesen.

A este llamaron Papa, que quiere dezir admirable, mayor, padre y goardador, porque es padre y governador de todos los honbres.

A este San Pedro obedesçieron y tomaron por señor, rey y superior del universo los que en aquel tiempo vivian, y ansymismo an tenido todos los otros que después del fueron al pontificado heligidos; ansy se a continuado hasta agora y se continuará hasta que el mundo se acabe.

Uno de los Pontifiçes passados que en lugar deste suçedio en aquella silla e dignidad que he dicho, como señor del mundo, hizo donaçion destas yslas y tierra firme del mar Oçeano a los dichos Rey y Reyna y a sus subçessores en estos reynos, nuestros señores, con todo lo que en ellas ay, segund se contiene en ciertas escripturas que sobre ello pasaron, segund dicho es, que podeys ver sy quisieredes; ansy que Sus Altezas son reyes y señores destas yslas e tierra firme, por virtud de la dicha donaçion, y como a tales reyes y señores, algunas yslas mas y casy todas a quien esto ha seydo notificado han reçibido a Sus Altezas y les an obedesçido y servido y sirven como subditos lo deven hazer, y con buena voluntad y sin ninguna resistençia, luego sin dilaçión, como fueron ynformados de lo suso dicho, obedeçieron y reçibieron los varones religiosos que Sus Altezas les enbiavan para que les predicasen y enseñasen nuestra santa fee, y todos ellos de su libre agradable voluntad, sin premia ni condiçion alguna, se tornaron Christianos, y lo son, y Sus Altezas los reçibieron alegre y benignamente, y ansy los mandó tratar como a los otros sus subditos y bassallos, y vosotro[s] soys tenidos y obligados a hazer lo mismo.

Por ende, como mejor puedo vos ruego y requiero que entendays bien esto que os he dicho, y tomeys para entenderlo y deliberar sobre ello el tiempo que fuero (sic, por fuere) justo, y reconoscays a la Yglesia por señora y superiora del universo mundo, y al Sumo Pontifiçe, llamado Papa, en su nonbre, y al Rey y a la Reyna nuestros señores en su lugar, como a superiores e señores y reyes desas yslas y tierra firme, por virtud de la dicha donaçion, y consintays y deys lugar que estos padres religiosos vos declaren y prediquen lo susodicho.

Sy ansy lo hizierdes, hareys bien, y aquello a que soys tenidos y obligados, y Sus Altezas, y yo en su nonbre, vos reçibiran con todo amor y caridad, y vos dexaran vuestras mugeres, hijos y haziendas libres sin servidunbre, para que dellas y de vosotros hagays libremente todo lo que quisierdes e por bien tubierdes, y no vos conpeleran a que vos torneys christianos, salvo sy vosotros, ynformados de la verdad, os quisierdes convertir a nuestra santa fee catolica, como lo han hecho casy todos los veçinos de las otras yslas, y allende desto, Su Alteza vos dara muchos privilejios y esençiones, y vos hara muchas mercedes.

Sy no lo hizierdes, o en ello dilaçion maliçiosamente pusierdes, çertificos que con el ayuda de Dios yo entraré poderosamente contra vosotros y vos haré guerra por todas las partes y maneras que yo pudiere, y vos subjetaré al yugo y obediençia de la Yglesia y de Sus Altezas, y tomaré vuestras personas y de vuestras mugeres e hijos y los haré esclavos, y como tales los venderé y disporné dellos como Su Alteza mandare, y vos tomaré vuestros bienes, y vos haré todos los males e daños que pudiere, como a vassallos que no obedeçen ni quieren reçibir a su señor y la (sic) resisten y contradizen; y protesto que las muertes y daños que dello se recrecieren, sean a vuestra culpa, y no de Su Alteza, ni mia, ni destos cavalleros que conmigo vinieron; y de cómo los digo y requiero pido al presente escriuano que me lo dé por testimonio sinado, y a los presentes ruego que dello sean testigos.

Firmada del Obispo de Palençia y del Obispo fray Bernardo e de los del Consejo e frailes dominicos.   (Morales Padrón 1979, 338-40)

(XIII)   Las agonías

En Cajamarca empezó la agonía.

El joven Atahualpa, estambre azul,
árbol insigne, escuchó al viento
traer rumor de acero.
Era un confuso
brillo y temblor desde la costa,
un galope increíble
– piafar y poderío –
de hierro y hierro entre la hierba.
Llegaron los adelantados.
El Inca salió de la música
rodeado por los señores.

Las visitas
de otro planeta, sudadas y barbudas,
iban a hacer la reverencia.
El capellán
Valverde, corazón traidor, chacal podrido,
adelanta un extraño objeto, un trozo
de cesto, un fruto
tal vez de aquel planeta
de donde vienen los caballos.
Atahualpa lo toma. No conoce
de qué se trata: no brilla, no suena,
y lo deja caer sonriendo.

"Muerte,
venganza, matad, que os absuelvo",
grita el chacal de la cruz asesina.
El trueno acude hacia los bandoleros.
Nuestra sangre en su cuna es derramada.
Los príncipes rodean como un coro
al Inca, en la hora agonizante.

Diez mil peruanos caen
bajo cruces y espadas, la sangre
moja las vestiduras de Atahualpa.
Pizarro, el cerdo de Extremadura,
hace amarrar los delicados brazos
del Inca. La noche ha descendido
sobre el Perú como una brasa negra.

(Pablo Neruda, *Canto general*, III, Los conquistadores, N° XIV)

References

Adorno, Rolena
    1986   Literary Production and Suppression: Reading and Writing about Amerindians in Colonial Spanish America. *Revista de Crítica Literaria Latinoamericana* (Lima) 11/2, 109-135.

Bachorski, Hans-Jürgen
    1994   Das Erzählen neuer Welten. Medienwandel und Wahrheitsbeglaubigung. In: Horst Wenzel (ed.). *Gutenberg und die Neue Welt*. München: Fink, 135-157.

Carrillo Espejo, Francisco (ed.)
    1987   *Cartas y cronistas del descubrimiento y la conquista*. (Enciclopedia histórica de la literatura peruana 2). Lima: Horizonte.
    1989   *Cronistas de las guerras civiles, así como del levantamiento de Manco Inca y el de don Lope de Aguirre llamado 'la ira de Dios'*. (Enciclopedia histórica de la literatura peruana 3). Lima: Horizonte.

Cieza de León, Pedro de
    ³1985   *La crónica del Perú*. Edición, introducción y notas de Manuel Ballesteros Gaibrois. (Crónicas de América 4). Madrid: Historia 16.

Cornejo Polar, Antonio
    1994   *Escribir en el aire. Ensayo sobre la heterogeneidad sociocultural en las literaturas andinas*. Lima: Horizonte.

Estete, Miguel de
    1938   Noticia del Perú. In: Horacio H. Urteaga (ed.). *Los cronistas de la conquista. Selección, prólogo, notas y concordancias de H.H.U.* Paris: Desclée, 195-251.

Esteve Barba, Francisco
    ²1992   *Historiografía indiana*. Madrid: Gredos.

Fernández de Oviedo y Valdés, Gonzalo
    1959   *Historia general y natural de las Indias*. Ed. Juan Pérez de Tudela Bueso, Vol. 5. Madrid: Atlas.

Fritz, Gerd, and Franz Hundsnurscher (eds.)
    1994   *Handbuch der Dialoganalyse*. Tübingen: Niemeyer.

Goic, Cedomil (ed.)
    1988   *Historia y crítica de la literatura hispanoamericana*, Vol. I: *Epoca colonial*. Barcelona: Crítica.

Griffin, Charles C. (ed.)
    1971   *Latin America. A Guide to the Historical Literature*. Austin/London: University of Texas Press.

Gumbrecht, Hans Ulrich
    1987   Wenig Neues in der Neuen Welt. Über Typen der Erfahrungsbildung in spanischen Kolonialchroniken des XVI. Jahrhunderts. In: Wolf-Dieter Stempel and Karl-Heinz Stierle (eds.). *Pluralität der Welten. Aspekte der Renaissance in der Romania*. München: Fink, 227-249.

Hanke, Lewis
    1988   *La Lucha por la Justicia en la Conquista de América*. Madrid: Aguilar.

Hemming, John
    1982   *La Conquista de los Incas*. México: FCE (Engl. original 1970).

Huhle, Rainer
    1992   El terremoto de Cajamarca. La derrota del Inca en la memoria colectiva: Elementos para un análisis de la resistencia cultural de los pueblos andinos. *Ibero-Amerikanisches Archiv* 18, 387-426.

Hundsnurscher, Franz, and Edda Weigand (eds.)
    1986   *Dialoganalyse. Referate der 1. Arbeitstagung*, Münster 1986. (Linguistische Arbeiten 176). Tübingen: Niemeyer.

Janik, Dieter, and Wolf Lustig (eds.)
    1989   *Die spanische Eroberung Amerikas. Akteure, Autoren, Texte*. Frankfurt a.M.: Vervuert.

Jara, René, and Nicolas Spadacini (eds.)
    1989   *1492-1992: Re/Discovering Colonial Writing*. (Hispanic Issues 4). Minneapolis: Prisma Institute.

König, Hans-Joachim
    1992   *Die Entdeckung und Eroberung Amerikas, 1492-1550*. Freiburg/Würzburg: Ploetz.

Kohl, Karl-Heinz (ed.)
    1982   *Mythen der Neuen Welt. Zur Entdeckungsgeschichte Lateinamerikas*. Berlin: Fröhlich & Kaufmann.

Kohut, Karl (ed.)
    1991   *Der eroberte Kontinent. Historische Realität, Rechtfertigung und literarische Darstellung der Kolonisation Amerikas*. Frankfurt a.M.: Vervuert.

Konetzke, Richard (ed.)
    1953   *Colección de documentos para la historia de la formación social de Hispanoamérica, 1493-1810*, Vol. 1: *1493-1592*. Madrid: CSIC.

Koselleck, Reinhart, and Wolf-Dieter Stempel (eds.)
    1973   *Geschichte – Ereignis und Erzählung*. München: Fink.

Lockhart, James
    1986/1987 *Los de Cajamarca. Un estudio social y biográfico de los primeros conquistadores del Perú*, 2 Vols. Lima: Milla Batres.

Löffler, Heinrich (ed.)
    1993   *Dialoganalyse IV. Referate der 4. Arbeitstagung, Basel 1992*, 2 Vols. (Beiträge zur Dialogforschung 4). Tübingen: Niemeyer.

López de Gómara, Francisco
    1954   *Historia general de las Indias 'Hispania Victrix' cuya segunda parte corresponde a la conquista de Méjico*. Ed. Pilar Guibelalde, Vol. 1. Barcelona: Iberia.

Martinell Gifre, Emma
    1988   *Aspectos lingüísticos del descubrimiento y de la conquista*. Madrid: CSIC.

Martinell Gifre, Emma, and Mar Cruz Piñol (eds.)
    1996   *La conciencia lingüística en Europa. Testimonios de situaciones de convivencia de lenguas* (ss. XII-XVIII). Barcelona: PPU.

Mena, Cristóbal de
    1937   La conquista del Perú. In: Raúl Porras Barrenechea (ed.). *Las relaciones primitivas de la conquista del Perú*. Paris: Les Presses Modernes, 79-101.

Mignolo, Walter D.
    1982   Cartas, crónicas y relaciones del descubrimiento y la conquista. In: Luis Iñigo Madrigal (ed.). *Historia de la literatura hispanoamericana*, Vol. 1, *Epoca colonial*. Madrid: Cátedra, 57-116.
    1991   Zur Frage der Schriftlichkeit in der Legitimation der conquista. In: Karl Kohut (ed.). *Der eroberte Kontinent. Historische Realität, Rechtfertigung und literarische Darstellung der Kolonisation Amerikas*. Frankfurt a.M.: Vervuert, 86-102.
    1995   *The Darker Side of the Renaissance: Literacy, Territoriality, and Colonization*. Ann Arbor: The University of Michigan Press.

Montaigne, Michel de
    1967   *Œuvres complètes*. (Pléiade). Paris: Gallimard.

Morales Padrón, Francisco (ed.)
    1979   *Teoría y Leyes de la Conquista*. Madrid: Ediciones Cultura Hispánica del Centro Iberoamericano de Cooperación.
    1988   *Atlas Histórico Cultural de América*, Vol. 1. Las Palmas de Gran Canaria: Gobierno de Canarias, V Centenario.
    ^{5}1990   *Historia del Descubrimiento y Conquista de América*. Madrid: Gredos.

Neruda, Pablo
    1976   *Canto general*. Prólogo y cronología Fernando Alegría. Caracas: Biblioteca Ayacucho.

Oesterreicher, Wulf
- 1992 Nähesprachlich geprägtes Schreiben in der Kolonialhistoriographie Hispanoamerikas (1500-1615). In: Wolfgang Raible (ed.). *Sieben Jahre Sonderforschungsbereich 321. Eine Bilanz.* Freiburg i.Br.: Albert-Ludwigs-Universität, 76-78.
- 1994a El español en textos escritos por semicultos. Competencia escrita de impronta oral en la historiografía indiana. In: Jens Lüdtke (ed.). *Normas del español americano en el siglo XVI.* Frankfurt a.M.: Vervuert, S. 155-190.
- 1994b Kein sprachlicher Alltag – der Konquistador Alonso Borregán schreibt eine Chronik. In: Annette Sabban and Christian Schmitt (eds.). *Sprachlicher Alltag. Linguistik – Rhetorik – Literaturwissenschaft, Festschrift für Wolf-Dieter Stempel, 7. Juli 1994.* Tübingen: Niemeyer, 379-418.
- 1995 Ein Ereignis – unterschiedliche Sichtweisen: Das Massaker von Cholula, Mexiko, 1519. In: Wolfgang Raible (ed.). *Kulturelle Perspektiven auf Schrift und Schreibprozesse.* Tübingen: Narr, 98-120.
- 1996 Zwei Spanier als Indios: Deutungsmuster von Kulturkontakt und Kulturkonflikt in Augenzeugenberichten und frühen Chroniken Hispanoamerikas. In: Werner Röcke and Ursula Schaefer (eds.). *Mündlichkeit – Schriftlichkeit – Weltbildwandel. Literarische Kommunikation und Deutungsschemata von Wirklichkeit in der Literatur des Mittelalters und der frühen Neuzeit.* Tübingen: Narr, 147-183.
- 1997 Das Gespräch als Kriegserklärung. Pizarro, Atahualpa und das Gold von Peru. In: Horst Wenzel (ed.). *Gespräche – Boten – Briefe. Körpergedächtnis und Schriftgedächtnis im Mittelalter.* (Philologische Studien und Quellen 143). Berlin: Erich Schmidt, 296-319.

Otte, Enrique (ed.)
- 1993 *Cartas Privadas de Emigrantes a Indias, 1510-1616.* Mexiko: FCE.

Pizarro, Hernando
- 1953 Carta relación. In: Horacio U. Urtega (ed.). *Los cronistas de la conquista.* Paris: Desclée, 253-264.

Pizarro, Pedro
- ²1986 *Relación del Descubrimiento y Conquista de los Reinos del Perú.* Guillermo Lohmann Villena (ed.). Lima: Pontificia Universidad Católica del Perú.

Porras Barrenechea, Raúl (ed.)
- 1944 *Cedulario del Perú, siglo XVI, XVII y XVIII,* 2 Vols. Lima: Sociedad de Bibliófilos Peruanos.
- 1962 *Los Cronistas del Perú* (1524-1543). Lima: Sanmartí y Cía.

Porras Barrenechea, Raúl, *et al.*
- ¹¹1988 *Historia General de los Peruanos,* Vol. 2: *El Perú virreinal.* Lima: Peisa.

Prescott, William H.
    1986   *Historia de la Conquista del Perú*. Madrid: Ariel (Engl. original 1847).
Ramos, Demetrio, *et al.*
    1984   *Francisco de Vitoria. La Escuela de Salamanca*. Madrid: CSIC.
Ruiz de Arce, Juan
    1933   Relación de los servicios en Indias de don Juan Ruiz de Arce, conquistador del Perú. *Boletín de la Academia de la Historia* 102, 327-384.
Scharlau, Birgit
    1982   Beschreiben und Beherrschen. Die Informationspolitik der spanischen Krone im 15. und 16. Jahrhundert. In: Karl-Heinz Kohl (ed.). *Mythen der Neuen Welt. Zur Entdeckungsgeschichte Lateinamerikas*. Berlin: Fröhlich and Kaufmann, 92-100.
Scharlau, Birgit, and Mark Münzel
    1986   *Qellqay. Mündliche Kultur und Schrifttradition bei den Indianern Lateinamerikas*. Frankfurt a.M.: Campus.
Schmitt, Eberhard (ed.)
    1986   *Dokumente zur Geschichte der europäischen Expansion*, Vol. 3: *Der Aufbau der Kolonialreiche*. München: Beck.
Stati, Sorin, Edda Weigand and Franz Hundsnurscher (eds.)
    1991   *Dialoganalyse III. Referate der 3. Arbeitstagung, Bologna 1990*, 2 Vols. (Beiträge zur Dialogforschung 1). Tübingen: Niemeyer.
Stoll, Eva
    1996   Ethnographie in spanischen Soldatenchroniken (Peru, XVI. Jahrhundert). In: Christian Foltys and Brigitta Rohdewold (eds.). *Expansion der Romania ab dem 15. Jahrhundert. Beiträge zum Romanistentag 1995*. (Neue Romania 17). Berlin: Freie Universität, 109-127.
    1997   *Konquistadoren als Historiographen – Diskurstraditionelle und textpragmatische Aspekte in den Chroniken von Francisco de Jerez, Diego de Trujillo, Pedro Pizarro und Alonso Borregán (Peru XVI. Jahrhundert)*. (ScriptOralia 91). Tübingen: Narr.
Todorov, Tzvetan
    1982   *La conquête de l'amérique. La question de l'autre*. Paris: Seuil.
Trujillo, Diego de
    1948   *Relación del descubrimiento del reyno del Perú*. Ed. Raúl Porras Barrenechea. Sevilla: CSIC.
Wenzel, Horst (ed.)
    1994   *Gutenberg und die Neue Welt*. München: Beck.
Weigand, Edda, and Franz Hundsnurscher (eds.)
    1989   *Dialoganalyse II. Referate der 2. Arbeitstagung, Bochum 1988*, 2 Vols. (Linguistische Arbeiten 229/230). Tübingen: Niemeyer.

Wilgus, Alva Curtis
    1975   *The Historiography of Latin America: A Guide to Historical Writing (1500-1800)*. Metuchen NJ: The Scarecrow Press.

Xerez, Francisco López de
    1985   *Verdadera relación de la conquista del Perú*. (Crónicas de América 14). Edición de Concepción Bravo Guerreira. Madrid: Historia 16.

Index

- A -

A Compendious System of the Theory and Practice of Modern Surgery In the Form of a Dialogue 251
A dialogue Relating to the Practice of Physick 259
a little 299-301, 303, 307
A Treatise upon the Small-pox 250
Abercrombie, D. 4, 21
Abfertigung der vermeindten Replic Christophori Rosenbusches 83
about 293-4, 297-304, 310
achater 273
actes intermédiaires 337
actuality 4
Adegbija, E. 139, 140, 161
adjacency pair 331-4, 352-3, 356, 360, 371
Adorno, R. 458
Adorno, T. W. 142, 161
Advice to the poor 258
alba 189, 193-4
Allan, K. 421, 423
Alston, R. A. 218-22, 240
alterity 270, 271, 285
Althusius, J. 149, 161
Altmann, H. 336, 357, 361
Amthor, C. H. 140, 161
Amys and Amylion 314, 327
AND See *Anglo-Norman Dictionary*
Andreae, J. 94, 95
Anglo-Norman Dictionary 286, 288, 293
Anrede 332
Antwort vnd Ehrerrettung auff die verbottne Schmachschrifft Lucae Osiandri 82

apology 146, 147, 152, 153, 156, 157
Approved Directions for Health 250
approximators 297
Arndt, H. 141, 164
Arnovick, L. K. 15, 21
ars dictaminis 275
Ashby, W. 359, 361
Asplund, A. 248
Atahualpa 431-63
Atti dei podestá 405, 421, 430
aubade 189
Auerbach, E. 76, 286, 289, 293, 347, 352, 356, 361, 371
Augenspiegel 115-7, 120, 124-6, 129-36
Austin, J. L. 40, 76
Ayres-Bennett, W. 3, 21

- B -

Bachorski, H.-J. 458
Backes, M. 208, 210, 211, 212
Balibar, R. 420, 423, 430
bargain dialogue 269-70, 273-81, 284-6, 293
bargignier 273, 274
Barker, J. R. V. 53, 54, 76
Barth, J. C. 149, 161
Bary, R. 144, 162
Baskervill, C. R. 211, 212
Bauche, H. 3, 21
Bax, M. M. H. 11-2, 20-1, 35-49, 58, 64, 75-7, 352, 360, 361, 377, 399
Beattie, J. M. 302, 310
Beaumanoir, P. de 274, 276, 288, 290
Becker, C. L. 59, 77
Becon, T. 262
Beetz, M. 11, 13, 20, 22, 139-45, 150, 156-62, 167, 178, 186

Behnstedt, P. 358, 361
Beinhauer, W. 4, 22
Bell, B. 317, 328
Bellegarde, J.-B. Morvan de 158, 162
Bellot, J. 217, 222-7, 233-7, 240
Belz, G. 287, 289
Benincà, P. 422, 423
Benson, L. D. 212
Benveniste, E. 7, 22
Beowulf 48
Bergner, H. 16, 22
Berrendonner, A. 357, 361
Beschirmung 114-5, 132, 133, 136
Betten, A. 10, 22, 32, 358, 359, 360, 361, 376, 391, 399
Biber, D. 244, 302, 308, 310
Biere, B. U. 398
Bischoff, B. 359, 361
Blake, N. F. 15, 22, 310, 311
Bloch, R. H. 58, 77, 195, 212
Blumenberg, H. 360, 362
Blumenthal, P. 8, 22
Blyth, C. 317, 327
Bodel d'Arras, J. 288
Bogner, R. G. 184, 186
Bogoch, B. 15, 24
Bohse, A. 148-57, 160-2, 167
Börner, A. 158, 162
Bongi, S. 421-3, 426, 430
boosters 297
Borillo, A. 342, 358, 362
Bosk, C. 312
Böttner, M. 356, 362, 371
bracketing 44
Brandspiegel 115, 120, 135
Braungart, G. 11, 22
Break of Day 190
Breuer, H. 14, 22
Brinton, L. J. 15, 22, 255, 293, 298, 311
Brod, M. 127, 136

Brown, G. 422, 423
Brown, P. 14, 16, 23, 139, 151, 160-2, 165-7, 186, 211-2, 298-9, 311, 342, 362, 421, 423
Brown, R. 14, 23
Bruneau, C. 338, 357, 362
Bruni, F. 420, 424, 430
Brunot, F. 338, 357, 362
Bubner, R. 420, 424, 430
Bucher, H.-J. 332-6, 343, 356-9, 362, 37
Bullein, W. 252, 256, 260-2
Bullein's Bulwarke of Defence againste Sicknes, Sornes, and Woundes 252
Burger, H. 10, 23, 360, 362
Burkhardt, A. 10, 23
Burridge, K. 421, 423
Busse, D. 361-2, 370

- C -

Caffi, C. 244
Callebaut, B. 358, 362
calumniations 96, 98
Calvo, C. 252
Canterbury Wells 259
Canutus' Plague Treatise 247
Capellanus, A. 170, 177, 183, 185, 189, 211-2
Carillo Espejo, F. 446, 458, 463
Carter, R. 243
cartoon 415-8, 420, 423
Castellani, A. 422, 424
Castiglione, B. 159, 162
Cerquiglini, B. 8, 23, 29, 271, 289, 346, 362
certainty markers 297
Chafe, W. L. 244, 318, 328
challenging 35, 38-44, 47-50, 53-5, 58, 61, 64, 74-5

Charlemagne and Elegast See *Karel ende Elegast*
Cherubim, D. 352, 362, 367
chevalier errant 54
Chirurgerie 254
chivalric romances 36, 55
Christmann, H. H. 3, 8, 23
Cieza de León, P. de 438-40, 453, 458
Clifton, K. A. 311
Clover, C. J. 48, 77
code écrit 4, 271
code graphique 4
code parlé 4, 271
code phonique 4
Collingwood, S. L. 270, 277-8, 286-7, 290, 293
Collins, R. 43, 77
colloquial language 3
communicative budget 83, 84, 104
communicative distance 399-401
communicative immediacy 399, 400, 402, 408, 411, 419, 421-3
communicative liability 335-7, 341
communicative stratagems 101
compliment 142-5, 148, 150, 153, 154
conceptualization of language 4
Conrad, R. 334, 362
consentement 277
context embeddedness 400-1
contractual motive 35
controversies 81, 83-8, 93-4, 102-4
convenance 274, 276
copiosa sermonis facundia 177
Coppo, A. 414-6, 422-4
Cornejo Polar, A. 442, 458
Corpus of Early English Correspondence 18, 30
Corpus of Early English Dialogue 19
Corpus of Early English Medical Writing 247, 263

cortezia 170
Coseriu, E. 353, 360, 368, 420, 424, 430
Cosnier, J. 7, 24
Coulmas, F. 147, 152, 160-4, 167, 205, 211-3, 287, 290
court records 405-6, 410, 416-7, 420
courtoisie 170, 172
Coutumes de Beauvaisis 270-1, 274, 288-90
Crossgrove, W. 246
cue 47, 49, 67
Culpeper, J. 244, 293–309

- D -

D'Achille, P. 420, 421, 424, 427, 430
Danet, B. 15, 24
Dausendschön-Gay, U. 7, 24
dawn song 189–214
De Boer, C. 357, 363
De Spiegel der Minnen 65, 68, 70, 72-3, 75
De Wellustige Mensch 67, 70, 71, 73, 75
Dear, P. 259
decorum 140, 145, 158, 159
Defensio 126, 127, 132, 136
deictic immediacy 400, 401
denier Dieu 274, 277, 281, 285
Der Deutsche Cato 173, 175, 183-5, 189
Der heimliche Bote 170, 184-5, 189
Der welsche Gast 175, 186
Deutsch Missive, warum die Juden solange im Elend sind 116, 122, 130, 136
Deutsche Liederdichter des 13. Jahrhunderts 185
Dialogicity 401
Dialoglied 170-1, 179, 182-3, 187, 189
Dialogue against the Fever Pestilence 252, 256, 262
didactic texts 249

Die Wrake van Ragisel 40, 75
Diez, F. 3, 24
diglossia 3
Dilcher, G. 396
directness 4
direct-quote complements 321
discourse markers 4, 6, 8, 15, 18, 22, 25, 293, 297, 312
dislocation à gauche 350
dispositio 380, 396
distance 411, 418, 420, 430
Distanzsprache 6
Dodd, W. G. 193, 213
Donald, M. 61, 77
downtoners 297
DuBruck, E. 363
Ducrot, O. 7, 24
Dundes, A. 48, 77
Durante, M. 420, 424, 430
Durdilly, P. 421, 424, 430

- **E** -

Early Modern English 293, 308
echo-question 349, 350
Eck, J. 130, 131
Edwards, M. U. 133, 136
EGO-HIC-NUNC See deictic immediacy
Ehlich, K. 140, 141, 162, 164, 166, 188
Ehre und Glimpf 123
Ehrismann, G. 10, 24
Eikelmann, M. 172, 186
Eilfort, W. 322, 328
Eisbrenner, A. 168, 172, 186
elaborierte Mündlichkeit 398
Elias, N. 40, 77, 184, 187
elliptical coupling 334
emotionality 400-2, 408, 411, 416, 419
emphatics 297, 310
Enchiridion Medicum 257, 261

Endtliche Abfertigung Der beider Jesuiter/ Christoffen Rosenbuschen/ vnd Georgen Scherers 83, 88
engignier 274
énonciation 7, 23, 30
Ensenhamen 170
Erasmus, D. 156, 163
ererede 54
eristic motive 35, 74
Erler, A. 398, 399
Ermarth, E. D. 328
Ernst, G.
Ernst, G. 5, 8, 24, 271, 290, 358, 363-4, 420, 424, 430
Erwiderung 332, 356, 371
Estete, M. de 437, 443, 446, 449-50, 458, 463
Esteve Barba, F. 445, 458, 463
estraine 284, 285
ethnography of communication 7
ethnomethodology 7
Ethophilus 161, 167
Euler, B. 314, 321, 326-8, 331
Eyb, A. von 158, 163

- **F** -

face 139, 141, 149, 298, 300, 416
threat 139, 143, 147, 151-3, 156-7, 160
-work 141
familiarity 400, 401
Fanshel, D. 66, 78
farce 270-3, 276
Fauser, M. 11, 24
Fein, E. 184, 187
Felten, H. 360, 363
Ferguson, C. 3, 24, 147, 163
Fernández de Oviedo y Valdés, G. 458
Fernández, M. 3, 25, 32
Ferrera, K. 317, 328

FEW See *Französisches Etymologisches Wörterbuch*
Feyerabend, G. H. 160, 163, 167
Fiehler, R. 421, 424
Finegan, E. 244, 308, 310
Finell, A. 310, 311
Finkenstaedt, T. 14, 25
Finlay, R. 224, 225, 240
Fischer, A. 15, 18, 25
Fischer, R. 339, 358-9, 368-9
Flamenca 8
Fleischman, S. 5, 25
Flood, J. F. 133, 136
Floris and Blaunchefflour 314, 327
Fludernik, M. 15, 25, 314, 324, 325, 328
focusing interrogative acts 331, 341, 350
Foley, W. A. 43, 45, 59, 77
Fontaney, L. 357, 363
foreign language learning 216-8, 226, 240
Fortsetzung Deß Triumphs der Warheit/ wider Lucam Osiandrum 83
Foulet, L. 340, 350, 357, 359, 363
Foviaux, J. 271, 290
Frader, J. 312
frame 43-4
    analysis 43-4
    primary 44-9
Franck, D. 66, 77, 173, 187
François, D. 7, 25
Frank, B. 420-30
Franke, W. 333, 339, 356, 363, 371
Französisches Etymologisches Wörterbuch 286, 289, 293
Fraser, B. 160-1, 163, 167, 297, 311
Frauenpreis 172, 177, 187
Frei, H. 3, 25
French 269–85
frequency 294, 300, 303-4, 307, 309, 313
Fridankes Bescheidenheit 176, 185
Friedrich von Sonnenburg 178, 185

Fries, C. C. 4, 25
Fries, U. 25
Fritz, G. 1, 9-12, 22, 25-6, 29, 105, 269, 272, 278, 290-2, 333, 352-3, 356-66, 371, 376, 404, 420, 424-30, 446, 458, 463
fuzziness 296-8, 305

- **G** -

Glowinski, M. 328
Gale, T. 243, 254, 255
Gale, W. S. 311
Gamillscheg, E. 338, 340, 357-9, 363
Garner, T. 48, 77
Gasca Queirazza, G. 422, 425
Geertz, C. 44, 77
Geiger, L. 127, 136
Gelas, N. 337, 363
gen parlar 170
Gerichtsprotokoll 377
Gessler, J. 272, 273, 288
Gevallen en weer opstaande Mensch 63, 67, 72, 74, 75
Gibbons, B. 213
Gilbert, N. W. 245
Gilman, A. 14, 23
Givón, T. 321, 326, 328, 331
Gliederungssignale 4, 26
Gloning, T. 81, 359, 363
God's penny See *denier Dieu*
Goethe, J. W. 160, 163
Goffman, E. 7, 43-7, 77, 141, 163, 356, 364, 371, 421, 425
Goic, C. 445, 458, 463
Gonon, M. 407, 421, 422, 425, 430
Grant, E. 245
Greflinger, G. 143, 163
Grente, G. 289, 290
Grésillon, A. 345, 346, 358, 364

Gretser, J. 103
Grewendorf, G. 357, 364, 371
Grice, H. P. 69, 77
Griffin, C. C. 445, 458, 463
Grimm, J. 3
Grosse, S. 10, 26, 360, 364
Guevara, A. de 155, 163
Guido's Questions 248, 261
Gülich, E. 4, 6, 7, 26, 364-70, 422, 425
Gumbrecht, H. U. 368, 445, 459, 463
Gumperz, J. J. 77, 78, 79
Guy of Warwick 314, 327, 330

- H -

Habermas, J. 420, 425, 430
Halford, B. 314, 318, 328
Hallbauer, F. A. 146, 160, 163, 167
Halliday, M. A. K. 244, 317, 320-3, 328
handbook 243-6, 257, 259
Handspiegel 114-35
Handwörterbuch zur Deutschen Rechtsgeschichte 287, 289
Hanke, L. 446-7, 459, 463
Harsdörffer, G. P. 159-3, 167
Hartmann, J. 420-4, 428, 430
Hasan, R. 320, 323, 328
Hatto, A. T. 210-3
Hauben, P. 225, 240
Haug, W. 339, 364
Hausmann, F. J. 3, 4, 5, 26, 27, 32
He/she answered and said 313
Hebenstreit-Wilfert, H. 135
hedges 293–311
Heger, K. 335, 364, 422, 425
Heidloff, G. 135, 136
Heikkonen, K. 31, 33
Heilbrunner, P. 87, 96, 105
Held, G. 4, 26, 160, 161, 163, 167
Helsinki Corpus of English Texts 17, 29

Hemming, J. 445, 446, 459, 463
Henne, H. 10, 11, 27, 273, 290, 352, 356, 359-60, 364, 367, 371
Hentschel, E. 10, 27
Herman, J. 3, 27, 404, 420, 425, 430
Heusler, A. 10, 27
Hilty, G. 7, 27
Historisches Wörterbuch der Rhetorik 287, 289
Hofmann, J. B. 4, 27
Holbrook, Richard T. 286, 288, 290, 293
Holmes, J. 207, 213, 297, 311
Holtus, G. 4, 8, 27, 271, 290, 420, 425-6, 429-30
honestum 140
Hope, J. 14, 27
Hosch, S. 6, 27
hövesch 171, 174
hövescheit 172
HRG See *Handwörterbuch zur Deutschen Rechtsgeschichte*
Huber, S. 86, 87, 90, 97
Hübner, G. 172, 187
Hubrecht, G. 274, 285, 286, 290
Huhle, R. 445, 446, 459, 463
Huizinga, J. 40, 78
Humboldt, W. von 332, 364, 420, 425, 430
Hummelen, W. M. H. 62-4, 69-70, 75, 78
Hundsnurscher, F. 105, 178, 187, 361-3, 366, 420, 425, 428-30, 446, 458-9, 462-3
Hunold, C. F. 143, 146, 151, 164
Hunt, T. 356, 359, 364, 371
Hutten, U. von 132, 135
HWR See *Historisches Wörterbuch der Rhetorik*
Hymes, D. 43, 77, 78, 79

- I -

I mean 294, 297, 303, 310
I suppose 297, 309, 313
I think 297, 300-3, 310
Ide, S. 162-6, 188
Ihalainen, O. 31
Il Filostrato 190
immediacy 4, 6, 9
implicit modifiers 297, 308
impoliteness 140, 149, 155
Ineichen, G. 420, 426, 430
intensifiers 297
interaction rituals 142-5, 155
interrogative 331-62
intimacy 408, 416
intonation 338-40, 349, 357-9
intonation unit 318

- J -

Jackson, S. 43, 78
Jacobs, A. 269, 290
Jacobs, S. 43, 78
Jakob von Hochstraten 134
Janik, D. 445, 459, 463
Janney, R. W. 141, 164, 244
Jara, R. 445, 459, 463
Jauss, H. R. *See* Jauß, H. R.
Jauß, H. R. 270, 291, 360, 365
Jefferson, G. 356, 368, 371
Jespersen, O. 78
Jesuiter Latein 92, 105
Jeu d'Adam 331-3, 338, 351-5, 361
Jhering, R. von 140-2, 164
Johnstone, B. 314-7, 320-1, 329
Joseph, een historiaalspel van Jeronimus van der Voort 75
Journal d'Héroard 5
Jrrgeist 98

Jucker, A. H. 1, 4, 15, 18, 22-33, 36, 78, 244, 269, 290, 309-13
justum 140

- K -

Kaiser, E. 338-40, 350, 357-65
Karel ende Elegast 36, 42, 59, 75
Kasper, G. 160, 164, 167
Kasten, I. 187
Kästner, H. 10, 13, 20, 28, 133, 136, 359-60, 365
Kastner, R. 88
Kemmerich, D. H. 144, 149, 164
Kerbrat-Orecchioni, C. 7, 24, 28, 337, 345, 356-67, 370-1
keying 43
Kinder, A. G. 222, 240
Klag über alle Klag 113, 130-6
Klein, L. 15, 28
Klewitz, G. 319, 326, 331
Knowles, G. 14, 28
Koch, P. vi, 5-11, 21, 28, 271, 291, 326-31, 339, 357, 365, 398-402, 410, 418, 420-6, 430
Kochman, T. 48, 78
Kohl, K.-H. 445, 459, 462, 463
Köhler, H.-J. 112, 135, 136, 137
Kohut, K. 447, 459-60, 463
kommunikative Regreßpflicht See *communicative liability*
Konetzke, R. 445, 459, 463
König, H.-J. 446, 459, 463
König, J. U. von 160, 164
Kopytko, R. 14, 28
Koselleck, R. 459
Koskenniemi, I. 321-2, 329
Kotschi, T. 7, 26, 357, 364-70
Kraus, C. von 169, 185-7
Krebs, R. 85

Kristol, A. M. 8, 28, 272-3, 288, 291, 360, 365
Kryk-Kastovsky, B. 15, 28
Kytö, M. 11, 17-21, 29-33, 244, 293-309

- L -

Labov, W. 40, 48, 66, 78
Lakoff, G. 296, 297, 311
Lanfrank's Chirurgia Parva 247
Lang, J. 334-7, 357, 365
Lange, D. 317, 321, 326, 329, 331
language teaching 216, 220, 226, 235, 239
language-games 40, 42, 43, 62
Lausberg, H. 345, 350, 351, 358, 359, 365
Laver, J. 153, 164, 191, 194, 213
Le Goff, J. 286, 291
Leach, J. W. 77
leaflet 111, 112
Lebhaffte Abbildungen und Grundrisse Der Thorheit und Klugheit 161
Lebsanft, F. 1, 7-9, 21, 29, 32, 269, 275, 291-2, 356, 359, 366-71
Leech, G. N. 309-13
Leisi, E. 191, 211-3, 319-21, 329
Leisi, I. 191, 213
Lemercier, P. 277, 291
Lepp, F. 10, 29
Lerch, E. 340, 357, 358, 359, 366
Leube, H. 85
Levi, U. 405, 426
Levinson, S. C. 14, 16, 23, 42, 78, 186, 211-3, 298-9, 311, 342, 362, 421-3
Lexikon des Mittelalters 286-9
LexMA See *Lexikon des Mittelalters*
Linell, P. 263
Locher, J. 134, 136
Lochner, J. H. 145, 148-52, 164
Locke, J. 141, 164

Lockhart, J. 446, 459, 463
Lodge, R. A. 3, 29, 271, 291
Löffler, H. 446, 460, 463
Loomis, R. S. 61, 78
Loos, E. 159, 164
López de Gómara, F. 435, 441-7, 451-2, 460, 463
Loredano, G. F. 156, 164
Lötscher, A. 10, 29
Luckmann, T. 105, 263, 359, 366, 420, 426, 430
Lüdtke, H. 3, 29, 30, 410, 426, 427
Ludwig, O. 399
Lustig, W. 445, 459, 463

- M -

Maas, H. 10, 29
Macha, J. 398
Machwirth, E. 140, 164
Maddox, D. 276-7, 286, 291-3
Magendie, M. 161, 165, 167
Manier zu Reden bey Gebuhrt, Hochzeiten und Absterben 147, 161
mannjafnaðr 48, 76
marcheander 273, 286, 293
Marchello-Nizia, C. 8, 29
Marcheschi, D. 407, 421-2, 426, 430
marchié 274-6
Marrazini, C. 426
Martens, W. 157, 165
Martin, B. 263
Martin, E. 113-5, 132-3, 137
Martinell Gifre, E. 445, 460, 463
Maury, N. 337, 366
Mauss, M. 287, 291
McCarthy, M. 243
McEnery, T. 311
McGrath, D. 311
McMillan, J. R. 309, 311, 313

medical writing 243-6, 250, 260-2
Megenberg, K. von 287, 288
Meibauer, J. 336-7, 345, 358-61, 366
Meier, A. J. 139-40, 160-1, 165, 167
memoria 396, 398
Mena, C. de 436, 446-8, 460, 463
Menantes *See* Hunold, C. F.
Ménard, P. 357, 366
Meng, K. 357, 366
Merritt, M. 334, 366
Metcalf, G. F. 10, 29
Metzeltin, M. 425
Mey, J. L. 362, 366-7
Meyer, M. 366-70
Middle Dutch 35, 36, 40, 51, 54
Middle English 313-30
Mignolo, W. D. 445, 460, 463
Mihm, A. 377, 392, 394, 396-8
mimetic dialogues 243-6, 252, 260-2
Minne 167-70, 175, 179, 186
Minnegespräche 167, 183
Minnesang 167-75, 178, 182-4, 188
Minnesangs Frühling 171, 182-5, 189
Mittelhochdeutsche Minnelyrik 185
Modern English 313-25
Moeschler, J. 7, 29-30, 356-8, 366, 371
Montaigne, M. de 445, 460, 463
Montandon, A. 187
Morales Padrón, F. 443-7, 456, 460, 463
Morel, M.-A. 359, 367
Moriaen 45-7, 53, 75
Morrison, T. 211, 213
Moscherosch, J. M. 159, 165
Muckenhaupt, M. 11, 26
Mukarovsky, J. 420, 427, 430
Muller, C. 358, 367
Muller, H. F. 421, 427, 430
Müller, M. 183, 187
multiple dialogue introducers 313–25
Munro, H. 251

Munro, P. 326, 329, 331
Münzel, M. 445, 462, 463
Myerson, G. 263

- N -

Nähesprache 6, 402
narratio 380-3, 394, 396
Neruda, P. 431, 446, 457, 460, 463
Neu A la modisch Nach itziger gebräuchlichen Arth eingerichtetes Complementir–, Frisier– Trenchier– und Kunst–Buch 161
Neukirch, B. 146, 160, 165
Nevalainen, T. 15-9, 30, 31
Nevanlinna, S. 256
Niedner, F. 53, 78
Nietzsche, F. 143, 165
Nikula, T. 294, 297-9, 302-3, 308, 311
Nølke, H. 7, 30
Noomen, W. 356, 359, 361, 367, 371

- O -

Oesterreicher, W. 5-9, 21, 28, 30, 271, 291, 326, 329-31, 398-403, 420-7, 430-1, 445-6, 461, 463
Oksaar, E. 333, 367
Old French 331–56
Olson, G. 256
Ong, W. J. 245
Ordo representacionis Ade See *Jeu d'Adam*
Osiander, L. 81-105
Östman, J.-O. 297, 311
Otte, E. 445, 461, 463
Owen, D. D. R. 58, 79
Oxford English Dictionary 17
Özkök, B. 77

- P -

Padmos, T. 48, 76
Paduceva, E. V. 336, 367
Pahta, P. 244, 248, 263
Palander-Collin, M. 29, 31, 32
pamphlet 82-9, 92-9, 102-4, 111-5, 124-6, 130-4
Panegyrik 172
Papist 98
Parks, W. 48, 49, 74, 79
Parret, H. 356-7, 367, 371
Pathelin 269-93
perceptual salience 294
perhaps 298, 300, 310, 313
Peristiany, J. G. 40, 79
Petrucci, L. 422, 427
Pettegree, A. 222-4, 233-5, 241
Pfeffer, M. 58, 79
Pfefferkorn, J. 111-37
phatic communion 143, 144
philosophical dialogues 245
physical immediacy 400
Pickett, J. P. 247
Pietri, E. 25, 30
Piñol, M. C. 460
Pizarro, H. 434-5, 445-9, 452-3, 457, 461-3
Pizarro, P. 440, 454, 461
Plummer, J. F. 169, 187
Plutarch 149, 165
Polanyi, L. 314, 329
polemics 98
Polenz, P. von 11, 30, 377
polite answer 139
politeness strategies 139, 143
Pomerantz, A. 161, 165, 167
Porras Barrenechea, R. 445-6, 460-3
pragmatic markers 297, 312
pragmatic particles 297

Prescott, W. H. 446, 462-3
Prince, E. F. 297, 312
principle of brevity 91, 99, 102-3
principle of comprehensive reply 102, 104
principle of immediate answer 102-3
principle of thematic restriction *See* principle of thematic rigour
principle of thematic rigour 102-4
privacy 400-1
prohibition 148
projecting clauses 317
proto-romance 3
proximity 4

- Q -

questiones 245
Questyonary of cyrurygens See *Guido's Questions*
Quirk et al. 294, 312
quop 316

- R -

Radtke, E. 8, 30, 271-3, 279-80, 291, 420, 427, 430
Raffaelli, S. 422, 423, 427
Ramge, H. 375, 378-9, 389, 397-9
Ramos, D. 447, 462-3
Ranke, K. 289
Rappaport, S. 241
Raumolin-Brunberg, H. 15, 18-9, 30
really 297-8, 303, 310, 312
Reboul, A. 7, 30
reciprocity 4
Recktenwald, S. 317, 327
referential distance 409
referential immediacy 409, 417
Rehbock, H. 273, 290, 345, 346, 356-60, 364, 367, 371

Reinmar 170-2, 176, 183-5, 188-9
Reis, M. 359, 366-7
Relevance Theory 309, 313
Religionsgespräche 89
Rémi-Giraud, S. 356-7, 367, 371
Renchon, H. 357, 368
Renzi, L. 421-2, 427, 430
repertoire of linguistic acts 96, 104
requerimiento 442-6, 455, 463
Rettung der Jesuiter Unschuld wider die Giftspinnen Lucam Osiander 83
Reuchlin, J. 111-36
rhetorical question 335, 345-8
rhétorique du conversationnel 352, 369
Riches, D. 55, 79
Richter, D. 148, 165
Rigney, A. 59, 79
Rissanen, M. 17-8, 29-33
ritual levelling 35
Roberts, R. J. 241
Rohr, B. von 142-5, 165
Rolf, E. 397
Romaine, S. 317, 321, 326, 329, 331
Roman van den Riddere metter Mouwen 50, 56, 76
Romeo and Juliet 189-90, 205-6, 209-13
Roncador, M. von 376
Roncaglia, A. 404, 421, 422, 427, 430
Roover, R. de 278, 291
Rosenbusch, C. 81-3, 85-8, 93, 100
Rosengren, I. 347, 358-9, 366-8
routine formulae 205, 212
Roy, B. 285, 287, 291, 293
Rudanko, J. 16, 31
Ruhmer, W. 158, 165
Ruiz de Arce, J. 438, 446, 450, 462-3

- S -

Sacks, H. 54, 67, 79, 356, 368, 371

Saenger, P. 390
Sallentien, V. 286, 291
Sandig, B. 10, 31
Saville-Troike, M. 43, 79
Saxon, S. 224, 241
Scharlau, B. 445, 462-3
Schegloff, E. A. 66-7, 79, 356, 368, 371
Scherer, G. 81-105
Schiffrin, D. 4, 31, 314, 320, 329, 422, 427
Schilling, M. 111, 137
Schlieben-Lange, B. 7, 8, 31, 287, 292, 352-3, 356-60, 368, 371, 398, 420, 427, 430
Schmeja, W. 352, 356-60, 368, 371
Schmidt, K. M. 299, 312
Schmidt-Riese, R. 420, 428, 430
Schmidt-Wiegand, R. 396
Schmitt, C. 5, 8, 27, 31, 425
Schmitt, E. 445, 461-3
Schneider, S. 184, 187
Schnell, R. 168, 187
Schoenthal, G. 337, 368
Scholz, M. G. 183, 188, 189
Schultz, A. 53, 79, 357-9, 368
Schulze, R. 161, 165, 167
Schütz, E. 133, 136
Schwarz, A. 11, 31
Schweickard, W. 4, 8, 27, 271, 290
Schweizer Minnesänger 186
Schwitalla, J. 11, 13, 20, 31, 111, 115, 137, 345-8, 358-9, 369, 420, 428, 430
Scultetus, A. 105
Searle, J. R. 39-40, 59, 79, 276, 292, 335, 337, 342, 357, 369
Seelbach, D. 350, 369, 370
Segal, C. P. 56, 79
Selig, M. 5, 32, 272, 292, 360, 369, 426, 428
Sell, R. D. 15, 32

Seneca 149, 151, 166
senna 48, 76
sequence-signals 4
Serianni, L. 427-9
Sharpe, J. 302, 312
shields 297
Sigal, G. 193-5, 212-3
sinneken 62, 65, 70-3, 75
　Begheerte van Hoocheden 65
　Jalours Ghepeyns 62
　Nijdigh Herte 73
　Ontrouwen Dienst 63
　Quaet Ingheven 73
　Tversteent Hertte 74
　Vleyschelijcke Sin 62, 71
　Vreese voor Schanden 63, 65
Sitta, H. 352, 360-4, 369
Skelton, J. 309, 312-3
Slack, P. 261
Smith, A. J. 190, 213
solatz 170
soldados cronistas 432
Söll, L. V, 271, 292, 399, 428
Sommer, A. 160, 166, 167
Sommervogel, C. 85
Sonderegger, S. 10, 26, 32, 377
Spadacini, N. 445, 459, 463
spaehe rede 177, 184
Spahn, R. 318, 330
speech events 43
Sperber, D. 309, 312-3
Spitzer, L. 4, 32, 326, 330-1, 420, 428, 430
spontaneity 400-2, 410-1, 417-9
Städtler, K. 188
Stammerjohann, H. 326, 327, 330, 331
Stati, S. 446, 462-3
status quaestionis 104
Steinbauer, B. 397
Stella, A. 416, 422, 428

Stempel, W.-D. 339, 349-50, 356-60, 368-71, 421, 428, 446, 459, 461, 463
Stenström, A.-B. 334, 350, 356, 369, 371
Stetter, C. 360, 370
Stevens, A. 172, 188
Stieler, K. 152, 155, 161, 166-7
Stierle, K. 356, 360, 364-71
Stiles, W. B. 309, 312, 313
Stimm, H. 5, 24, 26, 31-2, 271, 292, 420, 428, 430
Stoffel, C. 299, 312
Stoll, E. 445-6, 462-3
Strazzulla, G. 422, 428
Streitbüchlein 115-6, 126-36
Strosetzki, C. 161, 166-7
Stussi, A. 421, 422, 429-30
style 294, 298, 302-3, 307-8, 310
subiectio 346, 350, 359
Sucher, C. B. 191, 214
swear words 409

- T -

Taavitsainen, I. v, 15-21, 31-2, 243-4, 248, 256, 263
tact 141, 164
Taeuber, W. 287, 292
Tagelied 170, 177, 183-4, 189
Tagelieder des deutschen Mittelalters 186
tageliet 189, 211
Tagliavini, C. 420, 429-30
Talander 162
talk unit 318
Tannen, D. 43, 79, 191, 214
Taylor, J. R. 309, 312-3
Taylor, P. 421, 427, 430
text-retrieval programs 17
The Avenging of Ragisel See *Die Wrake van Ragisel*

The boke of Englysshe, and Spanysshe 240
The Complete Angler 259
The Decent Man See *De Wellustige Mensch*
The Fever Pestilence 255
The Gouernement of Health 252
The Grounds of Physick See *The Rudiments of Physick*
The Man Who Fell but was Again Resurrected See *Gevallen en weer opstaande Mensch*
The Mirror of Love See *De Spiegel der Minnen*
The Play of the Unjust Steward See *Tspel van den Ontrouwen Rentmeester*
The Romance of Blackamoor See *Moriaen*
The Romance of the Knight with the Sleeve See *Roman van den Riddere metter Mouwen*
The Rudiments of Physick 251
The Sicke Mans Salue 256, 262
Thomasin von Zerklaere See *Der welsche Gast*
Tilmans, K. 59, 79
Tissier, A. 270, 275, 285-6, 288, 293
TL See *Tobler-Lommatzsch*
Tobler/Lommatzsch 286-7, 289, 293
Todorov, T. 462
Tomasoni, P. 421, 429-30
Toulmin, S. 12, 33
Traugott, E. C. 320, 328, 330
Traverso, V. 336, 357, 370
Trifone, P. 427-9
Triumph Der Warheit/ wider Lucam Osiandrum 81, 83
Troilus and Criseyde 189, 195, 202, 210-3
tropical use 345
Trujillo, D. de 439, 446, 453-4, 462-3

Tspel van den Ontrouwen Rentmeester 63, 74, 76

- **U** -

Ullmann, S. 421, 429
Ullmann-Margalit, E. 278, 292
Ungerer, G. 220, 222, 241
upgraders 297

- **V** -

vagueness 297, 305
Valentinus, P. P. 261
Valverde, Fray Vicente de 431-63
van Anrooij, W. 54, 80
van Caenegem, R. C. 58, 80
van Gennep, A. 153, 166
van Winter, J. M. 54-5, 80
vendre 273
Verantwortung wider die zwo Gifftspinnen Georgen Scherern vnd Christophorum Rosenbusch 83
verbal interactions 7, 19
Verbruggen, J. F. 40, 55, 80
vertu 274, 287
Very Profitable Boke 218-20, 225-7, 232-3, 239-40
Vetter, C. 87, 95, 102-3
Vives, J. L. 158, 166
Voigts, L. E. 246
Vom Faßnacht Triumph/ Georgij Scherers 83
Von des todes gehugde 176, 185
von Matt, P. 360, 362
Vuijk, W. 64, 77
Vurpas, A.-M. 421, 429-30

- **W** -

Wächtler, J. C. 142-3, 166
Walther von der Vogelweide 171-2, 176, 179, 183-9
Walton, D. N. 343, 356, 370-1
Wandruszka, M. 370
Wang, J. 317, 327
Warning, R. 364-6, 369-70
Warnung Vor der Jesuiter blutdurstigen Anschlägen vnnd bösen Practicken 82
Watts, R. v, 16, 19-20, 33, 140, 160-7, 188, 294, 309, 312-3
Watzlawick, P. 211, 214
Webster, C. 246
Weddige, H. 355, 370
Weigand, E. 11, 33, 273, 292, 353, 360, 370, 377, 391, 446, 459, 462-3
Weinrich, H. 420, 429-30
Weise, C. 141, 151-2, 161, 166-7
Weismann, C. 135
well 294, 297-307, 310-2
Wenz, G. 356, 370, 371
Wenzel, H. 458, 461-3
Werbungslied 169
Werkhofer, K. T. 143, 160, 166-7
Werkmüller, D. 377
Werlich, E. 249
Wertheim, H. Volck von 144, 166
Weydt, H. 7, 10, 31, 33, 287, 292, 335, 352-60, 368-71
White, H. 59, 80
why 299-307
Wichtig vnd hochnötig Bedencken 95
Wiese, E. 378
Wilgus, A. C. 445, 463
Willms, E. 168-9, 172, 176, 181, 184-9
Wilson, D. 312
Wimpfeling, J. 134
Winsbeckische Gedichte nebst Tirol und Fridebrant 186
Wirbelgeist 98

Wittgenstein, L. 11-2, 33, 42, 80
Wittig, S. 317, 330
Wolf, N. R. 135, 137
Wolfram von Eschenbach 208
Wolfson, N. 314-9, 330
world of significance 45, 59
Wunderli, P. 410, 429
Wunderlich, D. 357, 370
Wynne, M. 311

- X -

Xerez, F. L. de 437-8, 446-9, 463

- Y -

you know 294, 297, 303, 307, 310, 313
Yule, G. 422, 423

- Z -

Zeyen, S. 188
Ziv, Y. 4, 28

In the PRAGMATICS AND BEYOND NEW SERIES the following titles have been published thus far or are scheduled for publication:

1. WALTER, Bettyruth: *The Jury Summation as Speech Genre: An Ethnographic Study of What it Means to Those who Use it*. Amsterdam/Philadelphia, 1988.
2. BARTON, Ellen: *Nonsentential Constituents: A Theory of Grammatical Structure and Pragmatic Interpretation*. Amsterdam/Philadelphia, 1990.
3. OLEKSY, Wieslaw (ed.): *Contrastive Pragmatics*. Amsterdam/Philadelphia, 1989.
4. RAFFLER-ENGEL, Walburga von (ed.): *Doctor-Patient Interaction*. Amsterdam/Philadelphia, 1989.
5. THELIN, Nils B. (ed.): *Verbal Aspect in Discourse*. Amsterdam/Philadelphia, 1990.
6. VERSCHUEREN, Jef (ed.): *Selected Papers from the 1987 International Pragmatics Conference. Vol. I: Pragmatics at Issue. Vol. II: Levels of Linguistic Adaptation. Vol. III: The Pragmatics of Intercultural and International Communication* (ed. with Jan Blommaert). Amsterdam/Philadelphia, 1991.
7. LINDENFELD, Jacqueline: *Speech and Sociability at French Urban Market Places*. Amsterdam/Philadelphia, 1990.
8. YOUNG, Lynne: *Language as Behaviour, Language as Code: A Study of Academic English*. Amsterdam/Philadelphia, 1990.
9. LUKE, Kang-Kwong: *Utterance Particles in Cantonese Conversation*. Amsterdam/Philadelphia, 1990.
10. MURRAY, Denise E.: *Conversation for Action. The computer terminal as medium of communication*. Amsterdam/Philadelphia, 1991.
11. LUONG, Hy V.: *Discursive Practices and Linguistic Meanings. The Vietnamese system of person reference*. Amsterdam/Philadelphia, 1990.
12. ABRAHAM, Werner (ed.): *Discourse Particles. Descriptive and theoretical investigations on the logical, syntactic and pragmatic properties of discourse particles in German*. Amsterdam/Philadelphia, 1991.
13. NUYTS, Jan, A. Machtelt BOLKESTEIN and Co VET (eds): *Layers and Levels of Representation in Language Theory: a functional view*. Amsterdam/Philadelphia, 1990.
14. SCHWARTZ, Ursula: *Young Children's Dyadic Pretend Play*. Amsterdam/Philadelphia, 1991.
15. KOMTER, Martha: *Conflict and Cooperation in Job Interviews*. Amsterdam/Philadelphia, 1991.
16. MANN, William C. and Sandra A. THOMPSON (eds): *Discourse Description: Diverse Linguistic Analyses of a Fund-Raising Text*. Amsterdam/Philadelphia, 1992.
17. PIÉRAUT-LE BONNIEC, Gilberte and Marlene DOLITSKY (eds): *Language Bases ... Discourse Bases*. Amsterdam/Philadelphia, 1991.
18. JOHNSTONE, Barbara: *Repetition in Arabic Discourse. Paradigms, syntagms and the ecology of language*. Amsterdam/Philadelphia, 1991.
19. BAKER, Carolyn D. and Allan LUKE (eds): *Towards a Critical Sociology of Reading Pedagogy. Papers of the XII World Congress on Reading*. Amsterdam/Philadelphia, 1991.
20. NUYTS, Jan: *Aspects of a Cognitive-Pragmatic Theory of Language. On cognition, functionalism, and grammar*. Amsterdam/Philadelphia, 1992.

21. SEARLE, John R. et al.: *(On) Searle on Conversation*. Compiled and introduced by Herman Parret and Jef Verschueren. Amsterdam/Philadelphia, 1992.
22. AUER, Peter and Aldo Di LUZIO (eds): *The Contextualization of Language*. Amsterdam/Philadelphia, 1992.
23. FORTESCUE, Michael, Peter HARDER and Lars KRISTOFFERSEN (eds): *Layered Structure and Reference in a Functional Perspective. Papers from the Functional Grammar Conference, Copenhagen, 1990*. Amsterdam/Philadelphia, 1992.
24. MAYNARD, Senko K.: *Discourse Modality: Subjectivity, Emotion and Voice in the Japanese Language*. Amsterdam/Philadelphia, 1993.
25. COUPER-KUHLEN, Elizabeth: *English Speech Rhythm. Form and function in everyday verbal interaction*. Amsterdam/Philadelphia, 1993.
26. STYGALL, Gail: Trial Language. *A study in differential discourse processing*. Amsterdam/Philadelphia, 1994.
27. SUTER, Hans Jürg: *The Wedding Report: A Prototypical Approach to the Study of Traditional Text Types*. Amsterdam/Philadelphia, 1993.
28. VAN DE WALLE, Lieve: *Pragmatics and Classical Sanskrit*. Amsterdam/Philadelphia, 1993.
29. BARSKY, Robert F.: *Constructing a Productive Other: Discourse theory and the convention refugee hearing*. Amsterdam/Philadelphia, 1994.
30. WORTHAM, Stanton E.F.: *Acting Out Participant Examples in the Classroom*. Amsterdam/Philadelphia, 1994.
31. WILDGEN, Wolfgang: *Process, Image and Meaning. A realistic model of the meanings of sentences and narrative texts*. Amsterdam/Philadelphia, 1994.
32. SHIBATANI, Masayoshi and Sandra A. THOMPSON (eds): *Essays in Semantics and Pragmatics*. Amsterdam/Philadelphia, 1995.
33. GOOSSENS, Louis, Paul PAUWELS, Brygida RUDZKA-OSTYN, Anne-Marie SIMON-VANDENBERGEN and Johan VANPARYS: *By Word of Mouth. Metaphor, metonymy and linguistic action in a cognitive perspective*. Amsterdam/Philadelphia, 1995.
34. BARBE, Katharina: Irony in Context. Amsterdam/Philadelphia, 1995.
35. JUCKER, Andreas H. (ed.): *Historical Pragmatics. Pragmatic developments in the history of English*. Amsterdam/Philadelphia, 1995.
36. CHILTON, Paul, Mikhail V. ILYIN and Jacob MEY: *Political Discourse in Transition in Eastern and Western Europe (1989-1991)*. Amsterdam/Philadelphia, 1998.
37. CARSTON, Robyn and Seiji UCHIDA (eds): *Relevance Theory. Applications and implications*. Amsterdam/Philadelphia, 1998.
38. FRETHEIM, Thorstein and Jeanette K. GUNDEL (eds): *Reference and Referent Accessibility*. Amsterdam/Philadelphia, 1996.
39. HERRING, Susan (ed.): *Computer-Mediated Communication. Linguistic, social, and cross-cultural perspectives*. Amsterdam/Philadelphia, 1996.
40. DIAMOND, Julie: *Status and Power in Verbal Interaction. A study of discourse in a close-knit social network*. Amsterdam/Philadelphia, 1996.
41. VENTOLA, Eija and Anna MAURANEN, (eds): *Academic Writing. Intercultural and textual issues*. Amsterdam/Philadelphia, 1996.
42. WODAK, Ruth and Helga KOTTHOFF (eds): *Communicating Gender in Context*. Amsterdam/Philadelphia, 1997.

43. JANSSEN, Theo A.J.M. and Wim van der WURFF (eds): *Reported Speech. Forms and functions of the verb.* Amsterdam/Philadelphia, 1996.
44. BARGIELA-CHIAPPINI, Francesca and Sandra J. HARRIS: *Managing Language. The discourse of corporate meetings.* Amsterdam/Philadelphia, 1997.
45. PALTRIDGE, Brian: *Genre, Frames and Writing in Research Settings.* Amsterdam/Philadelphia, 1997.
46. GEORGAKOPOULOU, Alexandra: *Narrative Performances. A study of Modern Greek storytelling.* Amsterdam/Philadelphia, 1997.
47. CHESTERMAN, Andrew: *Contrastive Functional Analysis.* Amsterdam/Philadelphia, 1998.
48. KAMIO, Akio: *Territory of Information.* Amsterdam/Philadelphia, 1997.
49. KURZON, Dennis: *Discourse of Silence.* Amsterdam/Philadelphia, 1998.
50. GRENOBLE, Lenore: *Deixis and Information Packaging in Russian Discourse.* Amsterdam/Philadelphia, 1998.
51. BOULIMA, Jamila: *Negotiated Interaction in Target Language Classroom Discourse.* Amsterdam/Philadelphia, 1999.
52. GILLIS, Steven and Annick DE HOUWER (eds): *The Acquisition of Dutch.* Amsterdam/Philadelphia, 1998.
53. MOSEGAARD HANSEN, Maj-Britt: *The Function of Discourse Particles. A study with special reference to spoken standard French.* Amsterdam/Philadelphia, 1998.
54. HYLAND, Ken: *Hedging in Scientific Research Articles.* Amsterdam/Philadelphia, 1998.
55. ALLWOOD, Jens and Peter Gärdenfors (eds): *Cognitive Semantics. Meaning and cognition.* Amsterdam/Philadelphia, 1999.
56. TANAKA, Hiroko: *Language, Culture and Social Interaction. Turn-taking in Japanese and Anglo-American English.* Amsterdam/Philadelphia, n.y.p.
57 JUCKER, Andreas H. and Yael ZIV (eds): *Discourse Markers. Descriptions and theory.* Amsterdam/Philadelphia, 1998.
58. ROUCHOTA, Villy and Andreas H. JUCKER (eds): *Current Issues in Relevance Theory.* Amsterdam/Philadelphia, 1998.
59. KAMIO, Akio and Ken-ichi TAKAMI (eds): *Function and Structure. In honor of Susumu Kuno.* 1999.
60. JACOBS, Geert: *Preformulating the News. An analysis of the metapragmatics of press releases.* 1999.
61. MILLS, Margaret H. (ed.): *Slavic Gender Linguistics.* 1999.
62. TZANNE, Angeliki: *Talking at Cross-Purposes. The dynamics of miscommunication.* n.y.p.
63. BUBLITZ, Wolfram, Uta LENK and Eija VENTOLA (eds.): *Coherence in Spoken and Written Discourse. How to create it and how to describe it. Selected papers from the International Workshop on Coherence, Augsburg, 24-27 April 1997.* 1999.
64. SVENNEVIG, Jan: *Getting Acquainted in Conversation. A study of initial interactions.* n.y.p.
65. COOREN, François: *The Organizing Dimension of Communication.* n.y.p.
66. JUCKER, Andreas H., Gerd FRITZ and Franz LEBSANFT (eds.): *Historical Dialogue Analysis.* 1999.

67. TAAVITSAINEN, Irma, Gunnel MELCHERS and Paivi PAHTA (eds.): *Dimensions of Writing in Nonstandard English.* n.y.p.
68. ARNOVICK, Leslie: *Diachronic Pragmatics. Seven case studies in English illocutionary development.* n.y.p.
69. NOH, Eun-Ju: *The Semantics and Pragmatics of Metarepresentation in English. A relevance-theoretic account.* n.y.p.
70. SORJONEN, Marja-Leena: *Recipient Activities Particles nii(n) and joo as Responses in Finnish Conversation.* n.y.p.